**16th Edition**

# UNDERSTANDING COMPUTERS:
## TODAY AND TOMORROW

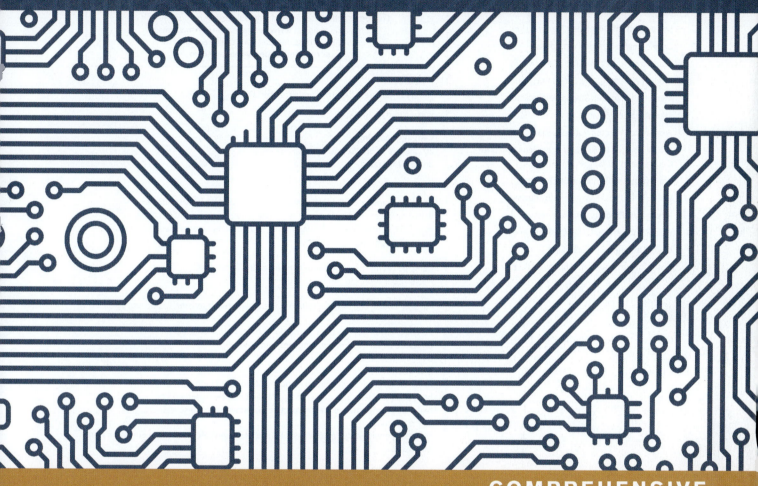

## COMPREHENSIVE

**DEBORAH MORLEY**

**CHARLES S. PARKER**

CENGAGE
Learning·

Australia • Brazil • Mexico • Singapore • United Kingdom • United States

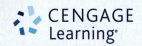
CENGAGE
Learning®

**Understanding Computers: Today and Tomorrow, Comprehensive, 16th Edition**
Deborah Morley and Charles S. Parker

Product Director: Kathleen McMahon

Senior Director of Development: Marah Bellegarde

Product Team Manager: Amanda Lyons

Product Development Manager: Leigh Hefferon

Senior Content Developer: Marjorie Hunt

Developmental Editor: Pam Conrad

Associate Product Manager: Sarah Marks

Product Assistant: Cara Suriyamongkol

Marketing Manager: Stephanie Albracht

Marketing Coordinator: Cassie Cloutier

Production Director: Patty Stephan

Senior Content Project Managers: Jennifer Feltri-George, Jennifer Goguen McGrail

Manufacturing Planner: Fola Orekoya

Senior IP Project Manager: Kathy Kucharek

Intellectual Property Analyst : Amber Hill

Production Service: GEX Publishing Services

Cover Designer: Diana Graham

Cover Image: moosa art/Shutterstock.com

For product information and technology assistance, contact us at **Cengage Learning Customer & Sales Support, 1-800-354-9706**

For permission to use material from this text or product, submit all requests online at **www.cengage.com/permissions.**
Further permissions questions can be e-mailed to **permissionrequest@cengage.com**

Library of Congress Control Number: 2015959301

ISBN: 978-1-305-65631-4

**Cengage Learning**
20 Channel Center Street
Boston, MA 02210
USA

Cengage Learning is a leading provider of customized learning solutions with employees residing in nearly 40 different countries and sales in more than 125 countries around the world. Find your local representative at **www.cengage.com**

Cengage Learning products are represented in Canada by Nelson Education, Ltd.

For your course and learning solutions, visit **www.cengage.com**

Purchase any of our products at your local college store or at our preferred online store **www.cengagebrain.com**

Trademarks:
Some of the product names and company names used in this book have been used for identification purposes only and may be trademarks or registered trademarks of their respective manufacturers and sellers.

Unless otherwise noted all screenshots (and or images) are Used with permission from Microsoft.

Printed in the United States of America
4 5 6 7 20 19 18 17 16

# PREFACE

**In today's technology-oriented society, computers and technology impact virtually everyone's life.** *Understanding Computers: Today and Tomorrow, 16th Edition* is designed to ensure that students are current and informed in order to thrive in our technology-oriented, global society. With this new edition, students not only learn about relevant cutting-edge technology trends, but they also gain a better understanding of technology in general and the important issues surrounding technology today. This information gives students the knowledge they need to succeed in today's world.

This nontechnical, introductory text explains in straightforward terms the importance of learning about computers and other computing devices, the various types of devices and their components, the principles by which computers work, the practical applications of computers and related technologies, the ways in which the world is being changed by these technologies, and the associated risks and other potential implications of computers and related technologies. The goal of this text is to provide readers with a solid knowledge of computing fundamentals, an understanding of the impact of our technology-oriented society, and a framework for using this knowledge effectively in their lives.

## WHAT'S NEW IN THIS EDITION?

Accommodating a wide range of teaching styles, *Understanding Computers: Today and Tomorrow, 16th Edition* provides comprehensive coverage of traditional topics while also covering relevant, up-to-the-minute new technologies and important societal issues. This edition has an increased emphasis on mobile computing, cloud applications, social media, and smart devices, and includes the following new topics:

➤ New hardware developments, including flexible smartphones, modular smartphones, self-driving cars, Apple Watch and other wearables, USB 3.0 and 3.1, USB-C, smart clothing, HAMR (heat-assisted magnetic recording) hard drives, neuromorphic chips, graphene chips, Intel Compute Stick and other thumb drive PCs, Surface Hub, portable 3D scanners, Ultra HD (4K) displays, Microsoft HoloLens, silk ink and protein ink, Amazon Echo, drones, and robot butlers and orderlies.

➤ New software developments, including Windows Edge, Windows 10, OS X El Capitan and OS X Yosemite, Android Marshmallow, iOS 9, Firefox OS, Tizen, Cortana, crapware, Office 2016, Web site builders, social commerce, mobile UX (user experience), NoSQL databases, and new programming languages such as F# and B#.

➤ New mobile applications, including smartphone drivers licenses, digital watermark icons, Bitcoins and other mobile payment options, biometric authentication, and Apple Pay and other digital wallets.

➤ New networking technologies, including personal clouds, Google Fiber, 802.11ax, 802.11af (White-Fi), 802.11ah (Low Power Wi-Fi), LTE-Advanced, LTE-Unlicensed (LTE-U), 5G, and point-to-multipoint (PMP) and point-to-point (PP) networks.

➤ New security and privacy risks and precautions, including waterproof smartphones, Transport Layer Security (TLS), tracking cookies, skimming and EMV credit cards, digital IDs, and privacy issues surrounding wearable devices.

In addition, the textbook has been streamlined for more efficient coverage and is now a total of 13 chapters instead of 16 chapters to make it easier to teach this course in a single semester. Key changes include:

> The security and privacy topics from Chapter 15 in previous editions are now combined with the network and Internet security topics in Chapter 9 so that all of the computer, network, and Internet security and privacy topics are included in a single chapter (Chapter 9).

> Key multimedia and e-commerce concepts from Chapters 10 and 11 in previous editions have been moved into appropriate chapters in this edition.

## KEY FEATURES

Just like its previous editions, *Understanding Computers: Today and Tomorrow, 16th Edition* provides current and comprehensive coverage of important topics. Flexible organization and an engaging presentation, combined with a variety of learning tools associated with each chapter, help students master the important computing concepts they will encounter in school, on the job, and in their personal lives.

### Currency and Accuracy

The state-of-the-art content of this book reflects the latest technologies, trends, and classroom needs. To reflect the importance of mobile computing today, the entire text has an increased emphasis on smartphones, tablets, mobile apps, wearables, and the issues that surround them, such as security and privacy. All topics and figures have been updated for currency and, to ensure the content is as accurate and up to date as possible, numerous **Industry Expert Reviewers** provided feedback and suggestions for improvements to the content in their areas of expertise. Throughout the writing and production stages, enhancements were continually made to ensure that the final product is as current and accurate as possible.

### Readability

We remember more about a subject if it is made interesting and exciting, as well as presented in a straightforward manner. This book is written in a conversational, down-to-earth style—one designed to be accurate without being intimidating. Concepts are explained clearly and simply, without the use of overly technical terminology. More complex concepts are explained in an understandable manner and with realistic examples from everyday life.

### Chapter Learning Tools

1. **Outline**, **Learning Objectives, and Overview**: For each chapter, an **Outline** of the major topics covered, a list of student **Learning Objectives**, and a **Chapter Overview** help instructors put the subject matter of the chapter in perspective and let students know what they will be reading about.

2. **Boldfaced Key Terms and Running Glossary**: Important terms appear in boldface type as they are introduced in the chapter. These terms are defined at the bottom of the page on which they appear and in the end-of-text glossary.

3. **Chapter Boxes**: In each chapter, a **Trend** box provides students with a look at current and upcoming technology trends; an **Inside the Industry** box provides insight into some of the practices and issues related to the computer industry; a **How It Works** box explains in detail how a technology or product works; and a **Technology and You** box takes a look at how computers and technology are used in everyday life.

4. **Ask the Expert Boxes**: In each chapter, three **Ask the Expert** boxes feature a question about a computing concept, a trend, or how technology

is used on the job or otherwise in the real world along with the response from an expert. Experts for this edition include a former Navy pilot, a guitarist from a rock band, an iOS software engineer from WillowTree Inc., a professional animator, and executives from notable companies like McDonald's, Microsoft, SONIC, Reddit, Dice, iRobot, Western Digital, Coursera, Logitech, SanDisk, Kingston, Seagate, The Linux Foundation, ACM, Rhapsody, The Computer Ethics Institute, Sony Animations, D-Link, GreenDisk, The Unicode Consortium, ARM, Arubixs, Infodatix, Trustwave, and Symantec.

5. **Marginal Tips and Caution Elements**: **Tip** marginal elements feature time-saving tips or ways to avoid a common problem or terminology mistake, or present students with interesting additional information related to the chapter content. **Caution** elements warn of a possible problem students should avoid.

6. **Illustrations and Photographs**: Instructive, current, full-color illustrations and photographs are used to illustrate important concepts. Figures and screenshots show the latest hardware and software and are annotated to convey important information.

7. **Summary and Key Terms**: The end-of-chapter material includes a concise, section-by-section **Summary** of the main points in the chapter. The chapter's Learning Objectives appear in the margin next to the relevant section of the summary so that students are better able to relate the Learning Objectives to the chapter material. Every boldfaced key term in the chapter also appears in boldface type in the summary.

8. **Review Activities**: End-of-chapter **Review Activities** allow students to test themselves on what they have just read. A matching exercise of selected **Key Terms** helps students test their retention of the chapter material. A **Self-Quiz** (with the answers listed at the end of the book) consists of ten true-false and completion questions. Five additional easily graded matching and short-answer **Exercises** are included for instructors who would like to assign graded homework. Two short **Discussion Questions** for each chapter provide a springboard to jump-start classroom discussions.

9. **Projects**: End-of-chapter **Projects** require students to extend their knowledge by doing research and activities beyond merely reading the book. Organized into six types of projects (**Hot Topics**, **Short Answer/Research**, **Hands On**, **Ethics in Action**, **Presentation/Demonstration**, and **Balancing Act**), the projects feature explicit instructions so that students can work through them without additional directions from instructors. A special marginal icon denotes projects that require Internet access.

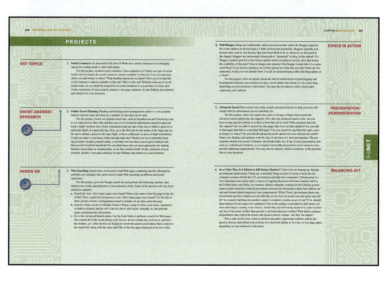

## References and Resources Guide

A **References and Resources Guide** at the end of the book brings together in one convenient location a collection of computer-related references and resources, including a **Computer History Timeline**, a **Guide to Buying a PC**, **A Look at Numbering Systems** feature, and a **Coding Charts** feature.

---

**TIP**

To add a tile for a folder to the Start menu, right-click the folder and select *Pin to Start*.

---

**CAUTION    CAUTION    CAUTI**

Be careful which smartphone apps you allow to use location services. While popular with many individuals for checking in and other

## NEW and Updated Expert Insight Features

In the exciting **Expert Insight** feature located at the end of each module, industry experts provide students with personal insights on topics presented in the book, including their personal experiences with technology, key points to remember, and advice for students. The experts, professionals from these major companies—**D-Link**, **Logitech**, **Microsoft**, **Intel Security**, **ACM/Google**, and **eBay**—provide a unique perspective on the module content and how the topics discussed in the module impact their lives and their industry, what it means for the future, and more!

## MindTap

The digital version of *Understanding Computers 16th Edition* is available in **MindTap**, a personalized online learning platform. In addition to the digital version of the book, MindTap includes flashcards, quizzing, online videos, activities, and more based on an instructor-designed learning path that guides students through the course. MindTap is a cost-effective alternative to a printed textbook. Students can purchase access to MindTap from www.cengagebrain.com. The MindTap for this book includes:

> **Interactive digital book**—gives students the full content of the book with additional links to online videos embedded throughout, as well as searching, note taking, and highlighting capabilities.

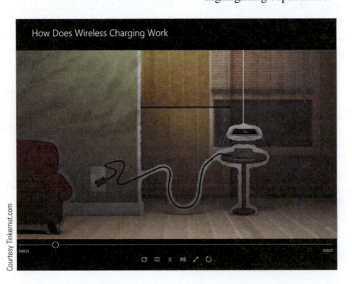

> **Flashcards**—allow students to test their knowledge of selected chapter key terms.

> **Quizzing**—allows students to test their retention of chapter concepts.

> **SAM Concepts**—provides training videos and hands-on reinforcement activities and assessments on hundreds of computer tasks and topics.

> **Chapter Study Guides**—consist of downloadable study guides for each chapter that can help students prepare for exams.

> **Online Videos**—include several videos per chapter related to the topics in that chapter, as well as practical "How To" information related to chapter topics.

## Instructor Companion Site

Everything you need for your course in one place! This collection of book-specific lecture and class tools is available online via **www.cengage.com/login**. Access and download PowerPoint presentations, images, Instructor's Manual, videos, and more.

## Instructor's Manual

The **Instructor's Manual** is written to provide instructors with practical suggestions for enhancing classroom presentations. The Instructor's Manual provides: **Lecture Notes**, **Teacher Tips**, **Quick Quizzes**, **Classroom Activities**, **Discussion Questions**, **Key Terms**, a **Chapter Quiz**, and more!

## Cengage Learning Testing Powered by Cognero®

**Cengage Learning Testing Powered by Cognero is a flexible, online system that allows you to:**

- ➤ Author, edit, and manage test bank content from multiple Cengage Learning solutions
- ➤ Create multiple test versions in an instant
- ➤ Deliver tests from your LMS, your classroom, or wherever you want

## PowerPoint Presentations

This book has **Microsoft PowerPoint presentations** available for each chapter. These are included as a teaching aid for classroom presentation, to make available to students on a network for chapter review, or to be printed for classroom distribution. Instructors can customize these presentations to cover any additional topics they introduce to the class. **Figure Files** for all figures in the textbook are also available online.

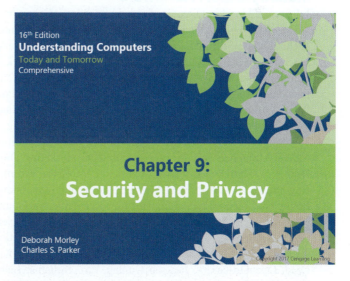

16th Edition
**Understanding Computers**
Today and Tomorrow
Comprehensive

## Chapter 9:
## Security and Privacy

Deborah Morley
Charles S. Parker

Copyright 2017 Cengage Learning

## SAM: Skills Assessment Manager

Get workplace-ready with **SAM**, the market-leading proficiency-based assessment and training solution for Microsoft Office! SAM's active, hands-on environment helps students master Microsoft Office skills and computer concepts that are essential to academic and career success, delivering the most comprehensive online learning solution for your course. Through skill-based assessments, interactive trainings, business-centric projects, and comprehensive remediation, SAM engages students in mastering the latest Microsoft Office programs on their own, giving instructors more time to focus on teaching. Computer concepts labs supplement instruction of important technology-related topics and issues through engaging simulations and interactive, auto-graded assessments. The MindTap Reader version of *Understanding Computers 16th Edition* works within the SAM environment for courses that combine concepts and Office skills. Let SAM be an integral part of your students' learning experience! Please visit *www.cengage.com/sam*.

# ACKNOWLEDGMENTS

We would like to extend a special thank you to all of the industry professionals who provided their expertise for the **Expert Insight** features:

**Introduction Module**: Daniel Kelley, Vice President, Marketing, D-Link Systems, Inc.
**Hardware Module**: Ali Moayer, Senior Director of Engineering, Logitech
**Software Module**: Stephen Rose, Senior Product Marketing Manager and Industry Vertical Lead for U.S. Windows and Devices, Microsoft
**Networks and the Internet Module**: Shishir Singh, Vice President and General Manager, Network Security Business Unit, Intel Security Group
**Systems Module**: Stuart Feldman, Former President of ACM and Vice President, Engineering, Google
**Computers and Society Module**: Jim Griffith, Dean of eBay Education, eBay

In addition, we are very grateful to the numerous Industry Expert Reviewers that perform technical reviews and provide helpful suggestions each edition to ensure this book is as accurate and current as possible. We would also like to thank the Educational Reviewers who have helped to define and improve the quality of this text over the years. In particular, we would like to thank the following individuals:

## Industry Expert Reviewers

Julie Anne Mossler, Director of Communications, Groupon; Alan Tringham, Senior Marketing Communications Manager, ARM; The Wi-Fi Alliance; Mike Hall, Corporate Communications, Seagate Technology; Kevin Curtis, CTO, InPhase Technologies; Sriram K. Peruvemba, Vice President, Marketing, E Ink Corporation; Jim Sherhart, Senior Director of Marketing, Data Robotics; Jack Dollard, Marketing, Mitek Systems; Joe Melfi, Director of Product Marketing for Cloud Solutions, D-Link Systems; Dave Gelvin, President, Tranzeo Wireless USA; Kevin Raineri, Director, Sales and Marketing, Innovative Card Technologies; Bill Shribman, Executive Producer, WGBH Interactive; Mike Markham, Vice President of Sales, Cadre Technologies; Renee Cassata, Marketing Manager, iDashboards; Russell T. Cross, Vice President of AAC Products, Prentke Romich Company; Dr. Kimberly Young, Director, The Center for Internet Addiction Recovery; Jason Taylor, Worldwide Director of Corporate Communications, MobiTV; Nicole Rodrigues, Public Relations Manager, MobiTV; Stephen Yeo, Worldwide Strategic Marketing Director, IGEL Technology; Bob Hirschfeld, Public Information Officer, Lawrence Livermore National Lab; Bryan Crum, Vice President of Communication, Omnilert, LLC; David Bondurant, MRAM Product Manager, Freescale Semiconductor, Inc.; Rick McGowan, Vice President & Senior Software Engineer, Unicode, Inc.; Margaret Lewis, Director of Commercial Solutions, AMD; Mark Tekunoff, Senior Technology Manager, Kingston Technology; Billy Rudock, Customer Service Staff Engineer, Seagate Technology; James M. DePuydt, Ph.D., Technology Director, Imation Corporation; Dan Bloom, Sr. PR Manager, SanDisk; Kevin Curtis, CTO, InPhase Technologies; Gail Levy, Director of Marketing, TabletKiosk; Novell Marketing; John McCreesh, Marketing Project Lead, OpenOffice.org; Jackson Dunlap, ESP Systems; Laura Abram, Director of Corporate Marketing, Dust Networks; Kevin Schader, Communications Director, ZigBee Alliance; Mauro Dresti, Linksys Product Marketing Manager; Lianne Caetano, Executive Director, WirelessHD, LLC; Brad Booth; Howard Frazier; Bob Grow; Michael McCormack; George Cravens, Technical Marketing, D-Link Systems; Christiaan Stoudt, Founder, HomeNetworkHelp.Info; Douglas M. Winneg, President, Software Secure, Inc.; Frank Archambeault, Director of Network Services, Dartmouth College; Adam Goldstein, IT Security Engineer, Dartmouth College; Ellen Young, Manager of Consulting Services, Dartmouth College; Becky Waring, Executive Editor, JiWire.com; Ellen Craw, General Manager, Ilium Software; Michael Behr, Senior Architect, TIBCO; Joe McGlynn, Director of Product Management, CodeGear; John Nash, Vice President of Marketing, Visible Systems; Josh Shaul, Director of Technology Strategy, Application Security, Inc.; Jodi Florence, Marketing Director, IDology, Inc.; Dr. Maressa Hecht Orzack, Director, Computer Addiction Services; Janice K. Mahon, Vice President of Technology Commercialization, Universal Display Corporation; Dr. Nhon Quach, Next Generation Processor Architect, AMD; Jos van Haaren, Department Head Storage Physics, Philips Research Laboratories; Terry O'Kelly, Technical Communications Manager, Memorex; Randy Culpepper, Texas Instruments RFID Systems; Aaron Newman, CTO and Co-Founder, Application Security Inc.; Alan Charlesworth, Staff Engineer, Sun Microsystems; Khaled A. Elamrawi, Senior Marketing Engineer, Intel Corporation; Timothy D. O'Brien, Senior Systems Engineer, Fujitsu Software; John Paulson, Manager, Product Communications, Seagate Technology; Omid Rahmat, Editor in Chief, Tom's Hardware Guide; Jeremy Bates, Multimedia Developer, R & L Multimedia Developers; Charles Hayes, Product Marketing Manager, SimpleTech, Inc.; Rick McGowan, Vice President & Senior Software Engineer, Unicode, Inc.; Russell Reynolds, Chief Operating Officer & Web Designer, R & L Multimedia Developers; Rob Stephens, Director, Technology Strategies, SAS; Dave Stow, Database Specialist, OSE Systems, Inc.

## Educational Reviewers

Marc Forestiere, Fresno City College; Beverly Amer, Northern Arizona University; James Ambroise Jr., Southern University, Louisiana; Virginia Anderson, University of North Dakota; Robert Andree, Indiana University Northwest; Linda Armbruster, Rancho Santiago College; Michael Atherton, Mankato State University; Gary E. Baker, Marshalltown Community College; Richard Batt, Saint Louis Community College at Meremec; Luverne Bierle, Iowa Central Community College; Fariba Bolandhemat, Santa Monica College; Jerry Booher, Scottsdale Community College; Frederick W. Bounds, Georgia Perimeter College; James Bradley, University of Calgary; Curtis Bring, Moorhead State University; Brenda K. Britt, Fayetteville Technical Community College; Cathy Brotherton, Riverside Community College; Chris Brown, Bemidji State University; Janice Burke, South Suburban College; James Buxton, Tidewater Community College, Virginia; Gena Casas, Florida Community College, Jacksonville; Thomas Case, Georgia Southern University; John E. Castek, University of Wisconsin-La Crosse; Mario E. Cecchetti, Westmoreland County Community College; Jack W. Chandler, San Joaquin Delta College; Alan Charlesworth, Staff Engineer, Sun Microsystems; Jerry M. Chin, Southwest Missouri State University; Edward W. Christensen, Monmouth University; Carl Clavadetscher, California State Polytechnic University; Vernon Clodfelter, Rowan Technical College, North Carolina; Joann C. Cook, College of DuPage; Laura Cooper, College of the Mainland, Texas; Cynthia Corritore, University of Nebraska at Omaha; Sandra Cunningham, Ranger College; Marvin Daugherty, Indiana Vocational Technical College; Donald L. Davis, University of Mississippi; Garrace De Groot, University of Wyoming; Jackie Dennis, Prairie State College; Donald Dershem, Mountain View College; John DiElsi, Marcy College, New York; Mark Dishaw, Boston University; Eugene T. Dolan, University of the District of Columbia; Bennie Allen Dooley, Pasadena City College; Robert H. Dependahl Jr.; Santa Barbara City College; William Dorin, Indiana University Northwest; Mike Doroshow, Eastfield College; Jackie O. Duncan, Hopkinsville Community College; John Dunn, Palo Alto College; John W. Durham, Fort Hays State University; Hyun B. Eom, Middle Tennessee State University; Michael Feiler, Merritt College; Terry Felke, WR Harper College; J. Patrick Fenton, West Valley Community College; James H. Finger, University of South Carolina at Columbia; William C. Fink, Lewis and Clark Community College, Illinois; Ronald W. Fordonski, College of Du Page; Connie Morris Fox, West Virginia Institute of Technology; Paula S. Funkhouser, Truckee Meadows Community College; Janos T. Fustos, Metropolitan State; Gene Garza, University of Montevallo; Timothy Gottleber, North Lake College; Dwight Graham, Prairie State College; Wade Graves, Grayson County College; Kay H. Gray, Jacksonville State University; David W. Green, Nashville State Technical Institute, Tennessee; George P. Grill, University of North Carolina, Greensboro; John Groh, San Joaquin Delta College; Rosemary C. Gross, Creighton University; Dennis Guster, Saint Louis Community College at Meremec; Joe Hagarty, Raritan Valley Community College; Donald Hall, Manatee Community College; Jim Hanson, Austin Community College; Sallyann Z. Hanson, Mercer County Community College; L. D. Harber, Volunteer State Community College, Tennessee; Hank Hartman, Iowa State University; Richard Hatch, San Diego State University; Mary Lou Hawkins, Del Mar College; Ricci L. Heishman, Northern Virginia Community College; William Hightower, Elon College, North Carolina; Sharon A. Hill, Prince George's Community College, Maryland; Alyse Hollingsworth, Brevard College; Fred C. Homeyer, Angelo State University; Stanley P. Honacki, Moraine Valley Community College; L. Wayne Horn, Pensacola Junior College; J. William Howorth, Seneca College, Ontario, Canada; Mark W. Huber, East Carolina University; Peter L. Irwin, Richland College, Texas; John Jasma, Palo Alto College; Elizabeth Swoope Johnson, Louisiana State University; Jim Johnson, Valencia Community College; Mary T. Johnson, Mt. San Antonio College; Susan M. Jones, Southwest State University; Amardeep K. Kahlon, Austin Community College; Robert T. Keim, Arizona State University; Mary Louise Kelly, Palm Beach Community College; William R. Kenney, San Diego Mesa College; Richard Kerns, East Carolina University, North Carolina; Glenn Kersnick, Sinclair Community College, Ohio; Richard Kiger, Dallas Baptist University; Gordon C. Kimbell, Everett Community College, Washington; Robert Kirklin, Los Angeles Harbor Community College; Judith A. Knapp, Indiana University Northwest; Mary Veronica Kolesar, Utah State University; James G. Kriz, Cuyahoga Community College, Ohio; Joan Krone, Denison University; Fran Kubicek, Kalamazoo Valley Community College; Rose M. Laird, Northern Virginia Community College; Robert Landrum, Jones Junior College; Shelly Langman, Bellevue Community College; James F. LaSalle, The University of Arizona; Chang-Yang Lin, Eastern Kentucky University; Linda J. Lindaman, Black Hawk College; Alden Lorents, Northern Arizona University; Paul M. Lou, Diablo Valley College; Deborah R. Ludford, Glendale Community College; Kent Lundin, Brigham Young University-Idaho; Barbara J. Maccarone, North Shore Community College; Wayne Madison, Clemson University, South Carolina; Donna L. Madsen, Kirkwood Community College; Randy Marak, Hill College; Gary Marks, Austin Community College, Texas; Kathryn A. Marold, Ph.D., Metropolitan State College of Denver; Cesar Marron, University of Wyoming; Ed Martin, Kingsborough Community College; Vickie McCullough, Palomar College; James W. McGuffee, Austin Community College; James McMahon, Community College of Rhode Island; William A. McMillan, Madonna University; Don B. Medley, California State Polytechnic University; John Melrose, University of Wisconsin—Eau Claire; Dixie Mercer, Kirkwood Community College; Mary Meredith, University of Southwestern Louisiana; Marilyn Meyer, Fresno City College; Carolyn H. Monroe, Baylor University; William J. Moon, Palm Beach Community College; Marilyn Moore,

Purdue University; Marty Murray, Portland Community College; Don Nielsen, Golden West College; George Novotny, Ferris State University; Richard Okezie, Mesa Community College; Joseph D. Oldham, University of Kentucky; Dennis J. Olsen, Pikes Peak Community College; Bob Palank, Florissant Community College; James Payne, Kellogg Community College; Lisa B. Perez, San Joaquin Delta College; Savitha Pinnepalli, Louisiana State University; Delores Pusins, Hillsborough CC; Mike Rabaut, Hillsborough CC; Robert Ralph, Fayetteville Technical Institute, North Carolina; Herbert F. Rebhun, University of Houston-Downtown; Nicholas John Robak, Saint Joseph's University; Arthur E. Rowland, Shasta College; Kenneth R. Ruhrup, St. Petersburg Junior College; John F. Sanford, Philadelphia College of Textiles and Science; Kammy Sanghera, George Mason University; Carol A. Schwab, Webster University; Larry Schwartzman, Trident Technical College; Benito R. Serenil, South Seattle Community College; Allanagh Sewell, Southeastern Louisiana University; Tom Seymour, Minot State University; John J. Shuler, San Antonio College, Texas; Gayla Jo Slauson, Mesa State College; Harold Smith, Brigham Young University; Willard A. Smith, Tennessee State University; David Spaisman, Katherine Gibbs; Elizabeth Spooner, Holmes Community College; Timothy M. Stanford, City University; Alfred C. St. Onge, Springfield Technical Community College, Massachusetts; Michael L. Stratford, Charles County Community College, Maryland; Karen Studniarz, Kishwaukee College; Sandra Swanson, Lewis & Clark Community College; Tim Sylvester, Glendale Community College; Semih Tahaoglu, Southeastern Louisiana University; Jane J. Thompson, Solano Community College; Sue Traynor, Clarion University of Pennsylvania; William H. Trueheart, New Hampshire College; James D. Van Tassel, Mission College; James R. Walters, Pikes Peak Community College; Joyce V. Walton, Seneca College, Ontario, Canada; Diane B. Walz, University of Texas at San Antonio; Joseph Waters, Santa Rosa Junior College, California; Liang Chee Wee, University of Arizona; Merrill Wells, Red Rocks Community College; Fred J. Wilke, Saint Louis Community College; Charles M. Williams, Georgia State University; Roseanne Witkowski, Orange County Community College; David Womack, University of Texas, San Antonio; George Woodbury, College of the Sequoias; Nan Woodsome, Araphoe Community College; James D. Woolever, Cerritos College; Patricia Joann Wykoff, Western Michigan University; A. James Wynne, Virginia Commonwealth University; Robert D. Yearout, University of North Carolina at Asheville; Israel Yost, University of New Hampshire; and Vic Zamora, Mt. San Antonio College.

We would also like to thank the people on the Cengage team—their professionalism, attention to detail, and enormous enthusiasm make working with them a pleasure. In particular, we'd like to thank Amanda Lyons, Marjorie Hunt, Jennifer Feltri-George, Jennifer Goguen McGrail, Kathryn Kucharek, Amber Hill, and Pam Conrad for all their ideas, support, and tireless efforts during the design, writing, rewriting, and production of this book. We would also like to thank Marissa Falco for the interior design, Cheryl Du Bois and her team at Lumina Datamatics, Inc., and Marisa Taylor and the team at GEX Publishing Services for all their help managing the production of the book. Thanks also to Kathleen McMahon.

We are also very appreciative of the numerous individuals and organizations that were kind enough to supply information and photographs for this text and the many organizations, as well as Daniel Davis of Tinkernut.com, that generously allowed us to use their content for the Online Videos, which can be found on MindTap.

We sincerely hope you find this book interesting, informative, and enjoyable to read.

**Deborah Morley**
**Charles S. Parker**

# BRIEF CONTENTS

# CONTENTS

**TECHNOLOGY AND YOU** Modular Phones 60
**HOW IT WORKS** USB-C 72
**INSIDE THE INDUSTRY** Moore's Law 74
**TREND** Smart Clothing 82

# Chapter 3 Storage 92

**HOW IT WORKS** More Storage for Your Tablet 98
**INSIDE THE INDUSTRY** Data Recovery Experts 101
**TREND** Ultra HD (4K) 110
**TECHNOLOGY AND YOU** Tiny PCs 113

**MODULE Networks and the Internet 254**

16th Edition

# UNDERSTANDING COMPUTERS:

## TODAY AND TOMORROW

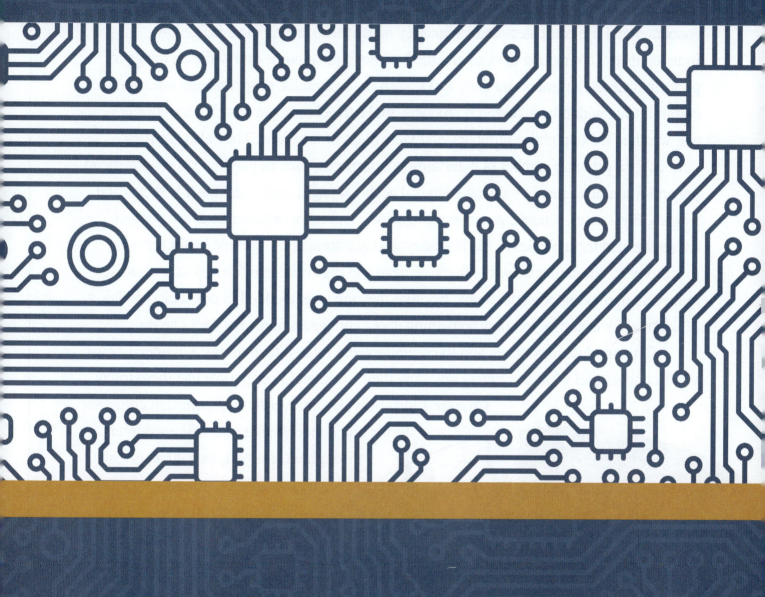

# module

# Introduction

Today, computers and other technology are virtually everywhere in our society. People encounter and use computers and technology many times during the average day. Individuals use computing devices and the Internet both at home and while on the go to perform a variety of important daily tasks, such as to pay bills, shop, manage investments, communicate with others, research products, make travel arrangements, check current news and weather, look up phone numbers, and view maps of locations. They also use these devices for a growing number of entertainment purposes, such as playing games, downloading and listening to music, viewing friends' Facebook pages, and watching TV shows and movies. Businesses, schools, government agencies, and other organizations use computers and related technologies to facilitate day-to-day transactions, provide better services to customers, communicate with others, retrieve and disseminate information, and assist managers in making good decisions. Because they are so embedded in our society today, it is essential for everyone to know something about computers and what they can do.

This module introduces you to computers and related technology. Chapter 1 helps you to understand what computers are, how they work, and how people use them today. Chapter 1 also provides an overview of common computer terms and concepts that you will encounter throughout this text, as well as gives you a brief look at how to perform basic computing tasks and to access resources on the Internet and the World Wide Web.

*"The evolution from the first massively sized computers to today's small devices, such as the iPhone, has created a major shift in the industry."*

For more comments from Guest Expert **Daniel Kelley** of D-Link Systems, see the **Expert Insight on . . . Computers and Technology** feature at the end of the module.

# chapter 1

# Introduction to the World of Technology

**After completing this chapter, you will be able to do the following:**

1. Explain why it is essential to learn about technology today and discuss several ways computing devices are integrated into our business and personal lives.

2. Define a computer and describe its primary operations.

3. List some important milestones in computer evolution.

4. Identify the major parts of a personal computer, including input, processing, output, storage, and communications hardware.

5. Define software and understand how it is used to instruct the computer what to do.

6. List the six basic types of computers, giving at least one example of each type of computing device and stating what that type of device might be used for.

7. Explain what a network, the Internet, and the World Wide Web are, as well as how computers, people, and Web pages are identified on the Internet.

8. Describe how to access a Web page and navigate through a Web site.

9. Discuss the societal impact of computers and technology, including some benefits and risks related to their prominence in our society.

# OVERVIEW

Computers and other forms of technology impact our daily lives in a multitude of ways. We encounter computers in stores, restaurants, and other retail establishments. We use computers or smartphones and the Internet regularly to obtain information, experience online entertainment, buy products and services, and communicate with others. Many of us carry a smartphone or other mobile device with us at all times so we can remain in touch with others on a continual basis and can access Internet information as we need it. We also use these devices to pay for purchases, play online games with others, watch TV and movies, access real-time traffic conditions, and much, much more.

Businesses also use computers extensively, such as to maintain employee and customer records, manage inventories, maintain online stores and other Web sites, process sales, control robots and other machines in factories, and provide business executives with the up-to-date information they need to make decisions. The government uses computers to support our nation's defense systems, for space exploration, for storing and organizing vital information about citizens, for law enforcement and military purposes, and other important tasks. In short, computers and technology are used in an endless number of ways.

*Understanding Computers: Today and Tomorrow* is a guide to computers and related technology and how they are being used in the world today. It will provide you with a comprehensive introduction to computer concepts and terminology and give you a solid foundation for any future courses you may take that are related to technology or its use in the world today. It will also provide you with the basic knowledge you need to understand and use computing devices in school, on the job, and in your personal life, as well as give you an overview of the societal issues related to technology, such as security and privacy issues, ethical considerations, and environmental concerns.

Chapter 1 is designed to help you understand what computers are, how they work, and how people use technology today. It introduces the important terms and concepts that you will encounter throughout this text and in discussions about technology with others, as well as includes an overview of the history of computers. It also takes a brief look at how to use a computer to perform basic tasks and to access online resources in order to provide you with the knowledge, skills, and tools you need to complete the projects and online activities that accompany this textbook. The chapter closes with an overview of the societal impact of computers. ■

> **TIP**
>
> Most of the concepts introduced in this chapter are discussed in more detail in subsequent chapters of this text.

## TECHNOLOGY IN YOUR LIFE

Computers and other technologies are integrated into virtually every aspect of most individuals' lives—at home, at school, at work, and while on the go. The next few sections provide an overview of the importance of computers and some of the most common computer-related activities that individuals may encounter every day.

## Why Learn About Computers and Technology?

Fifty years ago, computers were used primarily by researchers and scientists. Today, computers and technology are an integral part of our lives. Experts call this trend *pervasive computing*, in which few aspects of daily life remain untouched by computers and computing technology. With pervasive computing—also referred to as *ubiquitous computing*—computers are found virtually everywhere and computing technology is integrated into an ever-increasing number of devices to give those devices additional functionality, such as enabling them to retrieve *Internet* information or to communicate with other devices on an ongoing basis. Because of the prominence of computers in our society, it is important to understand what a computer is, a little about how a computer works, and the implications of living in a technology-oriented society.

Prior to about 1980, computers were large and expensive, and few people had access to them. Most computers in organizations were used for high-volume processing tasks, such as issuing bills and keeping track of inventories. The average person did not need to know how to use a computer for his or her job, and it was uncommon to have a computer at home. Furthermore, the use of computers generally required a lot of technical knowledge and the use of the Internet was reserved primarily for researchers and educational institutions. Because there were few good reasons or opportunities for learning how to use computers, the average person was unfamiliar with them.

Beginning in the early 1980s, things began to change. *Microcomputers*—inexpensive *personal computers* that you will read about later in this chapter—were invented and computer use increased dramatically. The creation of the *World Wide Web* (*WWW*) in the late 1980s and the graphical *Web browser* in the early 1990s started the trend of individuals buying and using computers for personal use. Today, the vast majority of U.S. households have a computer or smartphone, and most individuals use some type of computing device on the job. Whether you become a teacher, attorney, doctor, engineer, restaurant manager, salesperson, professional athlete, musician, executive, or skilled tradesperson, you will likely use a computer to obtain and evaluate information, to facilitate necessary on-the-job tasks, and to communicate with others.

In addition to being very useful tools, today's computers are taking on new roles in our society, such as delivering entertainment on demand. In fact, computers and the traditional communications and entertainment devices that we use every day—such as telephones, televisions, and gaming devices—are *converging* into single units with multiple capabilities. For instance, you can check your *e-mail* and view other Internet content on your living room TV, you can make telephone calls via your personal computer, and you can view Internet content and watch TV on your *smartphone* (see Figure 1-1). As a result of this *convergence* trend, the computer is no longer an isolated productivity tool; instead, it is an integral part of our daily lives.

Just as you can learn to drive a car without knowing much about car engines, you can learn to use a computer without understanding the technical details of how a computer works. However, a little knowledge gives you a big advantage. Knowing something about cars can help you make wise purchasing decisions and save money on repairs. Likewise, knowing something about computers can help you buy the right one for your needs, get the most efficient use out of it, be able to properly *upgrade* it as your needs change, and have a much higher level of comfort and confidence along the way. Therefore,

> ✔ **TIP**
>
> About two-thirds of all U.S. mobile phone users today are smartphone users; that is, their mobile phones include Internet capabilities and the ability to run mobile programs or apps.

⌄ **FIGURE 1-1**

**Convergence.**

Many devices today include computing or Internet capabilities.

**TELEVISIONS**

Can be used to access Web pages, e-mail, streaming movies, and other Internet content, in addition to viewing TV content.

Source: Amazon.com, Inc.

**SMARTPHONES**

Can be used to access Web pages, e-mail, movies, and other Internet content; play music; run apps and games; and take photos, in addition to making phone calls.

Georgejmclittle/Shutterstock.com

basic **computer literacy**—knowing about and understanding computers and their uses—is an essential skill today for everyone.

## Computing Devices in the Home

Home computing has increased dramatically over the last few years as computers, smartphones, and the Internet have become mainstream, and as a vast array of online consumer activities have become available. Use of the Internet at home to look up information, exchange e-mail, shop, watch TV and videos, download music and movies, research products, pay bills and manage bank accounts, check news and weather, store and organize *digital photos*, play games, make vacation plans, and so forth is now the norm for many individuals (see Figure 1-2). Many individuals also use a computer at home for work-related tasks, such as to review work-related documents or check work e-mail from home.

As the Internet, wireless technology, and devices such as computers, televisions, smartphones, and *gaming consoles* continue to converge, the computer is also becoming a central part of home entertainment. *Wireless networking* allows the use of computers in virtually any location and both online and offline content to be sent wirelessly from one device to another.

Computing technologies also make it possible to have *smart appliances*—traditional appliances (such as refrigerators, thermostats, or ovens) with some type of built-in computer or communications technology that allows them to be controlled by the user via a smartphone or the Internet, to access and display Internet information, or to perform other smart functions. *Smart homes*—homes in which household tasks (such as watering the lawn, turning the air conditioning on or off, making coffee, monitoring the security of the home and grounds, and managing home entertainment content) are controlled by a main computer in the home or by the homeowner remotely via a smartphone—have arrived, and they are expected to be the norm in less than a decade.

## Computing Devices in Education

Today's youth can definitely be called the *computing generation*. From *handheld gaming devices* to *mobile phones* to computers at school and home, most children and teens today have been exposed to computers and related technology all their lives. Although the amount of computer use varies from school to school and from grade level to grade level, most students today have access to computers at school—and some schools have completely integrated computers into the curriculum, such as by adopting *e-book* (electronic) textbooks that run on school-owned portable computers, or allowing students to bring in computers or smartphones to use in class (referred to as *BYOD* or *Bring Your Own Device*). Many schools (particularly college campuses) today also have *wireless hotspots* that allow students to connect their devices wirelessly to the Internet and to campus resources from anywhere on campus. Today, students at all levels are typically required to use a computer to some extent as part of their normal coursework—such as for preparing papers, practicing skills, doing Internet research, accessing Internet content (such as class *Web pages*), or delivering presentations—and some colleges require a computer for enrollment.

Computers are also used to facilitate *distance learning*—an alternative to traditional classroom learning in which students participate, typically at their own pace, from their

**REFERENCE**
Retrieving information, obtaining news, viewing recipes, shopping online, and exchanging e-mail are popular reference activities.

**PRODUCTIVITY**
Online banking and shopping, editing and managing digital photos and home videos, creating and editing work-related documents, and paying bills are common productivity tasks.

**ENTERTAINMENT**
Watching online TV and movies, viewing photos and videos, playing games, and viewing Web content are popular entertainment activities.

**FIGURE 1-2**
**Technology use at home.**

---

> **Computer literacy.** The knowledge and understanding of basic computer fundamentals.

**COMPUTER LABS AND CLASSROOMS**
Computers and Internet access are often available in the classroom and/or a computer lab for student use.

**CAMPUS WIRELESS HOTSPOTS**
Students can often access the Internet from anywhere on campus to do research, check e-mail, and more, via a campus hotspot.

**DISTANCE LEARNING**
With distance learning, students—such as these U.S. Army soldiers—can take classes from home or wherever they happen to be at the moment.

 **FIGURE 1-3**
Technology use in education.

current location (via their computers and Internet connections) instead of physically going to class. Consequently, distance learning gives students greater flexibility to schedule class time around their personal, family, and work commitments, as well as allows individuals located in very rural areas or stationed at military posts overseas to take courses when they are not able to attend classes physically. Some examples of technology in education are shown in Figure 1-3.

## Computing Devices on the Job

Although computers have been used on the job for years, their role is continually evolving. Computers were originally used as research tools for computer experts and scientists, and then as productivity tools for office workers. Today, computers are used by all types of employees in all types of businesses—including corporate executives, retail store clerks, traveling sales professionals, artists and musicians, engineers, police officers, insurance adjusters, delivery workers, doctors and nurses, auto mechanics and repair personnel, and professional athletes. In essence, the computer has become a universal tool for on-the-job decision making, productivity, and communications (see Figure 1-4). Computers are also used extensively for access control at many businesses and organizations, such as *authentication systems* that allow only authorized individuals to enter an office building, punch in or out of work, or access the company network via an access card or a fingerprint or hand scan. In addition to jobs that require the use of computers by employees, many new jobs have been created simply because computers exist, such as jobs in electronics manufacturing, online retailing, Internet applications, and technology-related computer support.

 **FIGURE 1-4**
Technology use on the job.

**DECISION MAKING**
Computers are used to help make on-the-job decisions.

**PRODUCTIVITY**
Computers are used to perform on-the-job tasks efficiently and accurately.

**OFF-SITE COMMUNICATIONS**
Portable devices are used to record data, access data, or communicate with others.

## TECHNOLOGY AND YOU

### Restaurant iPad Ordering Systems

You may have used your iPad or other device to place a pickup order at your local eatery; you may also have had a server use an iPad to take your order at a restaurant. Nice innovations, but guess what's next? Placing your order yourself at a restaurant using an iPad.

This new trend of using iPads and *e-menus* to have customers place their orders in restaurants is growing rapidly. In addition to enabling customers to place their orders at their convenience without waiting for a server, it also allows the restaurant to provide more resources to customers (such as photographs of menu items, pairing suggestions for appetizers and drinks, and so forth). The overall goal is to allow customers to control their dining experience from the time they are seated until they choose to pay the check. And, yes, they pay via the iPad as well (see the credit card reader at the top right of the iPad shown in the accompanying photo).

iPad ordering systems work especially well for restaurants that offer customized menu items. For example, Stacked, one of the first large-scale adopters of restaurant iPad ordering systems, offers typical American food (such as pizza, burgers, and salads) at its Southern California restaurants but everything on the menu is customizable—customers choose from a wide variety of ingredients, toppings, and sauces. The iPad systems enable customers to build their selections, adding or removing ingredients, until they are satisfied with the order (the price adjusts as they change their selections). This allows customers to build their orders at a comfortable pace without having to remember them until a server arrives, or having to make that many decisions with a server waiting.

E-menu-enabled iPads are also used at some airport restaurants for other purposes. In addition to being used for placing orders, they provide travelers with free access to Facebook, Twitter, e-mail, games, news, and flight updates while they wait (for security purposes, all personal information is wiped from the device as soon as the home button is pressed).

The two biggest risks for restaurants introducing iPad ordering systems is customer acceptance (most offer assistance from servers if the customer desires to help alleviate any customer concerns about using the devices) and technology issues. To avoid network or Internet outage issues, some restaurants are implementing redundant systems, such as multiple routers that can be used if the main router goes down or a 4G Internet connection that the system can use to access the Internet via a cellular connection if the main Internet source goes down.

Source: Square, Inc.

Computers are also used extensively by military personnel for communications and navigational purposes, as well as to control missiles and other weapons, identify terrorists and other potential enemies, and perform other necessary national security tasks. To update their computer skills, many employees in all lines of work periodically take computer training classes or enroll in computer certification programs.

## Computing Devices on the Go

In addition to using computers in the home, at school, and on the job, most people encounter and use all types of computing devices in other aspects of day-to-day life. For example, it is common for consumers to use *consumer kiosks* (small self-service computer-based stations that provide information or other services to the public, including those used for ATM transactions and bridal registries), *point-of-sale (POS) systems* (such as those found at most retail stores to check customers out—see the Technology and You box for a look at how iPads are being used to place orders at restaurants), and *self-checkout systems* (which allow retail store customers to scan their purchases and pay for them without a salesclerk) in retail stores and other public locations.

Source: Sony Electronics

**MOBILE DEVICES**
Enable individuals to remain in touch with others and to access Internet resources while on the go.

Source: Redbox Automated Retail, LLC

**CONSUMER KIOSKS**
Are widely available to view conference or gift registry information, print photographs, order products or services, and more.

Source: Verifone

**MOBILE PAYMENT SYSTEMS**
Allow individuals to pay for purchases using a smartphone or other device.

Source: Sony Electronics

**WEARABLE DEVICES**
Enable individuals to easily view smartphone messages or their fitness activities while on the go.

**FIGURE 1-5**
Technology use while on the go.

Individuals may also need to use a computer-based consumer authentication system to gain access to a local health club or other membership-based facility. Some examples of technology use on the go are shown in Figure 1-5.

In addition, many individuals carry a smartphone or other portable device with them on a regular basis to remain electronically in touch with others and to access information (such as driving directions, airline flight updates, movie times, and more) as needed while on the go. These devices are also commonly used to watch TV, download and listen to music, access *Facebook* pages and other *social media*, and perform other mobile entertainment options. Smartphones can also be used to pay for products and services (as shown in Figure 1-5), as well as to remotely deposit checks, transfer money to others, pay bills electronicially, and perform other *mobile banking* applications. A growing trend is wearing a *smart watch* or fitness band to add additional capabilities to your smartphone or to monitor your fitness and activity levels (refer again to Figure 1-5). *GPS* (*global positioning system*) capabilities are frequently built into smartphones, cars, and other devices to provide individuals with driving directions and other navigational aids while traveling or hiking.

## WHAT IS A COMPUTER AND WHAT DOES IT DO?

A **computer** is a programmable, electronic device that accepts data, performs operations on that data, presents the results, and stores the data or results as needed. The four operations described in this definition are considered the four primary operations of a computer. They can be defined as follows:

> ➤ **Input**—entering data into the computer.

> ➤ **Processing**—performing operations on the data.

> ➤ **Output**—presenting the results.

> ➤ **Storage**—saving data, programs, or output for future use.

>**Computer.** A programmable, electronic device that accepts data input, performs processing operations on that data, and outputs and stores the results. >**Input.** The process of entering data into a computer; can also refer to the data itself. >**Processing.** Performing operations on data that has been input into a computer to convert that input to output. >**Output.** The process of presenting the results of processing; can also refer to the results themselves. >**Storage.** The operation of saving data, programs, or output for future use.

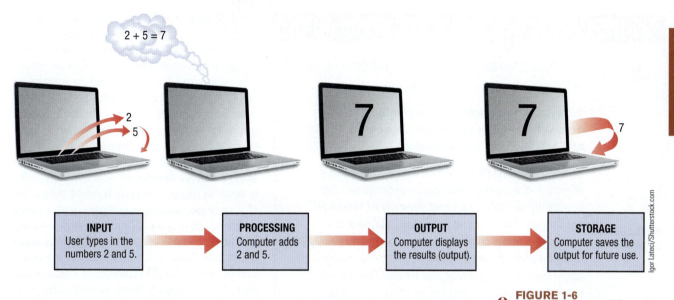

Igor Latecj/Shutterstock.com

**FIGURE 1-6**

The information processing cycle.

Because a computer is *programmable*, it will do whatever the instructions—called the *program*—tell it to do. The programs used with a computer determine the tasks the computer is able to perform.

For example, assume that you have a computer that has been programmed to add two numbers. As shown in Figure 1-6, input occurs when data (in this example, the numbers 2 and 5) is entered into the computer, processing takes place when the computer program adds those two numbers, and output happens when the sum of 7 is displayed on the computer screen. The storage operation occurs any time the data, a change to a program, or the output is saved for future use.

For an additional example, look at a supermarket *barcode reader* to see how it fits this definition of a computer. First, the grocery item being purchased is passed over the barcode reader—input. Next, the description and price of the item are looked up—processing. Then, the item description and price are displayed on the cash register and printed on the receipt—output. Finally, the inventory, ordering, and sales records are updated—storage.

This progression of input, processing, output, and storage is sometimes referred to as the *IPOS cycle* or the *information processing cycle*. In addition to these four primary computer operations, today's computers almost always perform **communications** functions, such as sending or retrieving data via the Internet, accessing information located in a shared company database, or exchanging data or e-mail messages with others. Therefore, communications—technically an input or output operation, depending on which direction the information is going—is often considered the fifth primary computer operation.

## Data vs. Information

As just discussed, a user inputs **data** into a computer, and then the computer processes it. Almost any kind of fact or set of facts can become computer data, such as the words in a letter to a friend, the numbers in a monthly budget, the images in a photograph, the notes in a song, or the facts stored in an employee record. When data is processed into a meaningful form, it becomes **information**.

---

>**Communications.** The transmission of data from one device to another. >**Data.** Raw, unorganized facts. >**Information.** Data that has been processed into a meaningful form.

# ASK THE EXPERT

**Francois Chardavoine,** Executive Director, Head of Pipeline, Sony Pictures Imageworks

**What position might a college student graduating with a computer degree qualify for at Sony Pictures Imageworks?**

At Sony Pictures Imageworks, and in the visual effects and animation industry in general, we are constantly faced with a great diversity of technical challenges. For a recent graduate, this means that regardless of his or her specialization, there's likely to be an appropriate position in one of our many departments. In particular, our Production Services team is a great place to start as it's responsible for all aspects of resource management, which involves writing robust workflows for handling and tracking enormous amounts of data. Entry-level experience is also valuable in R&D when writing shading and light propagation algorithms, image processing for noise reduction, real-time visualization, simulation solvers, or general tools to automate tasks for the artists. A pragmatic attitude and a willingness to compromise in order to find the most efficient development path that meets production deadlines are critical to being successful in the industry.

Information is frequently generated to answer some type of question, such as how many of a restaurant's employees work less than 20 hours per week, how many seats are available on a particular flight from Los Angeles to San Francisco, or what is Hank Aaron's lifetime home run total. Of course, you don't need a computer to process data into information; for example, anyone can go through time cards or employee files and make a list of people who work a certain number of hours. If this work is done by hand, however, it could take a lot of time, especially for a company with a large number of employees. Computers, however, can perform such tasks almost instantly, with accurate results. *Information processing* (the conversion of data into information) is a vital activity today for all computer users, as well as for businesses and other organizations.

## Computers Then and Now

The basic ideas of computing and calculating are very old, going back thousands of years. However, the computer in the form in which it is recognized today is a fairly recent invention. In fact, personal computers have only been around since the late 1970s. The history of computers is often referred to in terms of *generations*, with each new generation characterized by a major technological development. The next sections summarize some early calculating devices and the different computer generations.

### Precomputers and Early Computers (before approximately 1946)

Based on archeological finds, such as notched bones, knotted twine, and hieroglyphics, experts have concluded that ancient civilizations had the ability to count and compute. The *abacus* is considered by many to be the earliest recorded calculating device; it was used primarily as an aid for basic arithmetic calculations. Other early computing devices include the *slide rule*, the *mechanical calculator*, and Dr. Herman Hollerith's *Punch Card Tabulating Machine and Sorter*. This latter device (see Figure 1-7) was the first electromechanical machine that could read *punch cards*—special cards with holes punched in them to represent data. Hollerith's machine was used to process the 1890 U.S. Census data and it was able to complete the task in two and one-half years, instead of the decade it usually took to process the data manually. Consequently, this is considered to be the first successful case of an information processing system replacing a paper-and-pen-based system. Hollerith's company eventually became *International Business Machines (IBM)*.

### First-Generation Computers (approximately 1946–1957)

The first computers were enormous, often taking up entire rooms. They were powered by thousands of *vacuum tubes*—glass tubes that look similar to large light bulbs—which needed replacing constantly, required a great deal of electricity, and generated a lot of heat. *First-generation computers* could solve only one problem at a time because they needed to be physically rewired with cables in order to be reprogrammed (see Figure 1-7), which typically took several days or weeks to complete and several more days to check before the computer could be used. Usually paper punch cards and paper tape were used for input, and output was printed on paper.

Two of the most significant examples of first-generation computers were *ENIAC* and *UNIVAC*. ENIAC, shown in Figure 1-7, was the world's first large-scale, general-purpose computer. Although it was not completed until 1946, ENIAC was developed during World War II to compute artillery-firing tables for the U.S. Army. Instead of the 40 hours required for a person to compute the optimal settings for a single weapon under a single set of conditions using manual calculations, ENIAC could complete the same calculations in less than two minutes. UNIVAC, released in 1951, was initially built for the U.S. Census Bureau and was used to analyze votes in the 1952 U.S. presidential election. Interestingly, its correct prediction of an Eisenhower victory only 45 minutes after the polls closed was not publicly aired because the results were not trusted. However, UNIVAC became the first computer to be mass produced for general commercial use.

## Second-Generation Computers (approximately 1958–1963)

The second generation of computers began when the *transistor*—a small device made of *semiconductor* material that acts like a switch to open or close *electronic circuits*—started to replace the vacuum tube. Transistors allowed *second-generation computers* to be smaller, less expensive, more powerful, more energy-efficient, and more reliable than first-generation computers. Typically, programs and data were input on punch cards and *magnetic tape*, output was on punch cards and paper printouts, and magnetic tape (see Figure 1-7) was used for storage. *Hard drives* and *programming languages* (such as *FORTRAN* and *COBOL*) were developed and implemented during this generation.

**PRECOMPUTERS AND EARLY COMPUTERS**
Dr. Herman Hollerith's Punch Card Tabulating Machine and Sorter is an example of an early computing device. It was used to process the 1890 U.S. Census data.

**FIRST-GENERATION COMPUTERS**
First-generation computers, such as ENIAC shown here, were large and bulky, used vacuum tubes, and had to be physically wired and reset in order to run programs.

**SECOND-GENERATION COMPUTERS**
Second-generation computers, such as the IBM 1401 mainframe shown here, used transistors instead of vacuum tubes so they were smaller, faster, and more reliable than first-generation computers.

**THIRD-GENERATION COMPUTERS**
Third-generation computers used integrated circuits, which allowed the introduction of smaller computers such as the IBM System/360 mainframe shown here.

**FOURTH-GENERATION COMPUTERS**
Fourth-generation computers, such as the original IBM PC shown here, are based on microprocessors. Most of today's computers fall into this category.

**FIFTH-GENERATION COMPUTERS**
Some aspects of fifth-generation computers, such as the natural language input and artificial intelligence used by the IBM Watson computer shown competing on *Jeopardy!* here, already exist.

Source: IBM Corporate Archives; U.S. Army; IBM Corporation

## Third-Generation Computers (approximately 1964–1970)

The replacement of the transistor with *integrated circuits* (*ICs*) marked the beginning of the third generation of computers. Integrated circuits incorporate many transistors and electronic circuits on a single tiny silicon *chip*, allowing *third-generation computers* to be even smaller and more reliable than computers in the earlier computer generations. Instead of punch cards and paper printouts, *keyboards* and *monitors* were introduced for input and output; hard drives were typically used for storage. An example of a widely used third-generation computer is shown in Figure 1-7.

**FIGURE 1-7**
**A brief look at computer generations.**

INT

**TIP**

For a more detailed timeline regarding the development of computers, see the "Computer History Timeline" located in the References and Resources Guide at the end of this book.

## Fourth-Generation Computers (approximately 1971–present)

A technological breakthrough in the early 1970s made it possible to place an increasing number of transistors on a single chip. This led to the invention of the *microprocessor* in 1971, which ushered in the fourth generation of computers. In essence, a microprocessor contains the core processing capabilities of an entire computer on one single chip. The original *IBM PC* (see Figure 1-7) and *Apple Macintosh* computers, and most of today's traditional computers, fall into this category. *Fourth-generation computers* typically use a keyboard and *mouse* for input, a monitor and *printer* for output, and *hard drives*, *flash memory media*, and *optical discs* for storage. This generation also witnessed the development of *computer networks*, *wireless technologies*, and the Internet.

## Fifth-Generation Computers (now and the future)

*Fifth-generation computers* are most commonly defined as those that are based on *artificial intelligence*, allowing them to think, reason, and learn (see one example in Figure 1-7). Some aspects of fifth-generation computers—such as voice and touch input and *speech recognition*—are in use today. In the future, fifth-generation computers are expected to be constructed differently than they are today, such as in the form of *optical computers* that process data using light instead of electrons, tiny computers that utilize *nanotechnology*, or as entire general-purpose computers built into desks, home appliances, and other everyday devices.

**FIGURE 1-8**

Common hardware listed by operation.

| INPUT | PROCESSING |
|---|---|
| Keyboard | CPU |
| Mouse | GPU |
| Microphone | **STORAGE** |
| Scanner | Hard drive |
| Digital camera | CD/DVD/Blu-ray disc |
| Digital pen/stylus | CD/DVD/Blu-ray drive |
| Touch pad/touch screen | Flash memory card |
| Gaming controller | Flash memory card reader |
| Fingerprint reader | USB flash drive |
| **OUTPUT** | **COMMUNICATIONS** |
| Monitor/display screen | Modem |
| Printer | Network adapter |
| Speakers | Router |
| Headphones/headsets | |
| Data projector | |

## Hardware

The physical parts of a computer (the parts you can touch and discussed next) are called **hardware**. The instructions or programs used with a computer—called *software*—are discussed shortly. Hardware components can be *internal* (located inside the main box or *system unit* of the computer) or *external* (located outside the system unit and connected to the system unit via a wired or wireless connection). There are hardware devices associated with each of the five computer operations previously discussed (input, processing, output, storage, and communications), as summarized in Figure 1-8 and illustrated in Figure 1-9.

### Input Devices

An *input device* is any piece of equipment that is used to input data into the computer. The input devices shown in Figure 1-9 are a *keyboard* and *mouse* and an integrated *video camera*. Other common input devices include *microphones*, *scanners*, *digital pens* and *styluses*, *touch pads* and *touch screens*, *fingerprint readers*, and *gaming controllers*. Input devices are discussed in more detail in Chapter 4.

### Processing Devices

The main *processing device* for a computer is the *central processing unit* (*CPU*). The CPU is located inside the system unit and performs the calculations and comparisons needed for

> **Hardware.** The physical parts of a computer system, such as the keyboard, monitor, printer, and so forth.

INTEGRATED VIDEO CAMERA
(input)

MONITOR WITH INTEGRATED SPEAKERS
(output)

MODEM/ROUTER
(communications)

PRINTER
(output)

KEYBOARD AND MOUSE
(input)

SYSTEM UNIT
(houses processing and storage hardware; contains ports to connect external hardware)

USB FLASH DRIVE
(storage)

iStockphoto.com/Sergiy1975; LG; National Park Service; Ubee Interactive; SanDisk Corporation

**FIGURE 1-9**
Typical computer hardware.

processing; it also controls the computer's operations. For these reasons, the CPU is often considered the "brain" of the computer. Also involved in processing are various types of *memory* that are located inside the system unit and used to store data and instructions while the CPU is working with them, as well as additional processors such as the *graphics process-ing unit* (*GPU*). The CPU, GPU, memory, and processing are discussed in detail in Chapter 2.

## Output Devices

An *output device* accepts processed data from the computer and presents the results to the user, most of the time on the display screen (*monitor*), on paper (via a *printer*), or through a *speaker*. Other common output devices include *headphones* and *headsets* (used to deliver audio output to a single user) and *data projectors* (used to project computer images onto a projection screen). Output devices are covered in more detail in Chapter 4.

## Storage Devices

*Storage devices* (such as *DVD drives* and *flash memory card readers*) are used to store data on or access data from *storage media* (such as *DVD discs* and *flash memory cards*). Some storage hardware (such as a *hard drive* or a *USB flash drive*) includes both a storage device and storage medium in a single piece of hardware. Storage devices are used to save data, program settings, or output for future use; they can be installed inside the computer, attached to the computer as an external device, or accessed remotely through a network or wireless connection. Storage is discussed in more detail in Chapter 3.

## Communications Devices

*Communications devices* allow users to communicate electronically with others and to access remote information via the Internet or a home, school, or company computer network. Communications hardware includes *modems* (used to connect a computer to the Internet), *network adapters* (used to connect a computer to a computer network), and *routers* (used to create a small network so a variety of devices can share an Internet connection and data). A variety of modems and network adapters are available because there are different types of Internet and network connections—a modem used to connect to the Internet via a wireless connection and that also contains a built-in wireless router is shown in Figure 1-9. Communications hardware and computer networks are discussed in more detail in Chapter 7; connecting to the Internet is covered in Chapter 8.

## Software

The term **software** refers to the programs or instructions used to tell the computer hardware what to do. Software is traditionally purchased on a CD or DVD or is downloaded from the Internet; in either case, the software typically needs to be *installed* on a computer before it can be used. Software can also be run directly from the Internet (via Web pages) without being installed on your computer; this is referred to as *cloud software, Web-based software, Software as a Service* (*SaaS*), and *cloud computing* and is discussed in more detail in Chapter 6.

Computers use two basic types of software: system software and application software. The differences between these types of software are discussed next.

### System Software

The programs that allow a computer to operate are collectively referred to as *system software*. The main system software is the **operating system**, which starts up the computer and controls its operation. Common operating system tasks include setting up new hardware, allowing users to run other software, and allowing users to manage the documents stored on their computers. Without an operating system, a computer cannot function. Common *desktop operating systems* designed for personal computers are *Windows, OS X,* and *Linux*; these and other operating systems (such as *Android, iOS,* and other *mobile operating systems* used with smartphones and other mobile devices) are discussed in detail in Chapter 5.

When a computer or other computing device is powered up, it begins to **boot**. During the *boot process*, part of the computer's operating system is loaded into memory, the computer does a quick diagnostic of itself, and then it launches any programs—such as *security software*—designated to run each time the computer starts up. A username and password may be required to *log on* to the computer in order to finish the boot process.

Once a computer has booted, it is ready to be used and waits for input from the user. Most software today uses a variety of graphical objects (such as *icons, buttons,* and *tiles*) that are selected with the mouse (or with a finger or stylus for a computer that supports touch or pen input) to tell the computer what to do. For instance, the **Windows desktop** (the basic workspace for computers running the Windows operating system; that is, the place where documents, folders, programs, and other objects are displayed when they are being used), along with some common graphical objects used in Windows and many other software programs, is shown in Figure 1-10.

---

> **Software.** The instructions, also called computer programs, that are used to tell a computer what it should do. > **Operating system.** The main component of system software that enables a computer to operate, manage its activities and the resources under its control, run application programs, and interface with the user. > **Boot.** To start up a computer. > **Windows desktop.** The background work area displayed on the screen for computers running Microsoft Windows.

**ICONS**
Represent folders, documents, or other items that can be opened.

**TOOLBAR**
Contains buttons or icons that can be used to issue commands.

**WINDOWS**
Contain programs, documents, or other data.

**SIZING BUTTONS**
Resize or close a window.

**START BUTTON**
Opens the Start menu that is used to launch programs.

**TASKBAR BUTTONS**
Represent programs that can be launched, as well as open windows.

**TASKBAR**
Usually located at the bottom of the desktop.

**NOTIFICATION AREA**
Shows the clock and other indicators.

**FIGURE 1-10**
The Windows desktop.

## Application Software (Apps)

Programs (like the ones shown in Figure 1-11) designed to allow people to perform specific tasks using a computer, such as creating letters, preparing budgets, managing inventory and customer databases, playing games, watching videos, listening to music, scheduling appointments, editing digital photographs, designing homes, viewing Web pages, burning DVDs, and exchanging e-mail are called **application software (apps)**. Apps are launched via the operating system, such as by using the *Windows Start menu* on Windows computers, and are discussed in greater detail in Chapter 6.

There are also application programs that help users write their own programs in a form the computer can understand using a *programming language* like *Visual Basic*, *COBOL*, *C++*, *Java*, or *Python*. Some languages are traditional programming languages for developing applications; others, such as *markup* and *scripting languages* like *HTML*, *XHTML*, and *JavaScript*, are designed to be used to create Web pages. Programming, markup, and scripting languages are discussed in detail in Chapter 11.

## Computer Users and Professionals

In addition to hardware, software, data, and *procedures* (the predetermined steps to be carried out in particular situations), a computer system includes people. *Computer users* are the people who use computers to perform tasks or obtain information. Anyone who uses

---

> **Application software (apps).** Programs that enable users to perform specific tasks on a computer, such as writing letters or playing games.

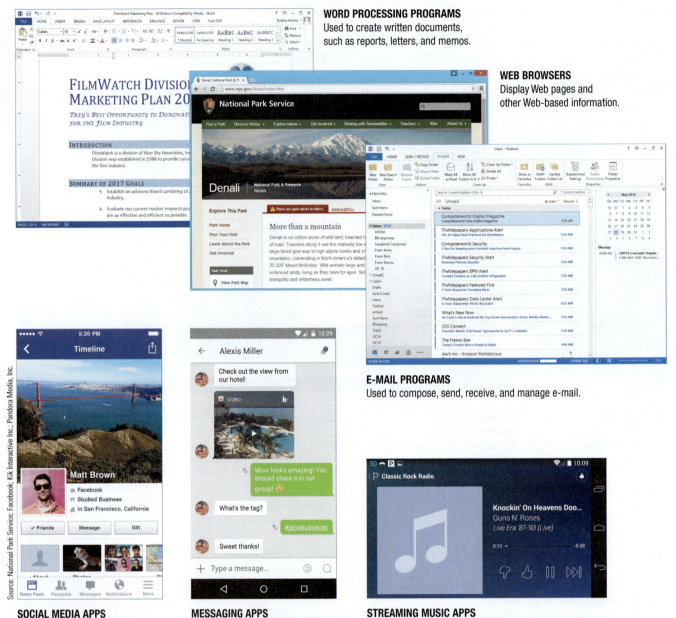

**WORD PROCESSING PROGRAMS**
Used to create written documents, such as reports, letters, and memos.

**WEB BROWSERS**
Display Web pages and other Web-based information.

**E-MAIL PROGRAMS**
Used to compose, send, receive, and manage e-mail.

**SOCIAL MEDIA APPS**
Display social media content.

**MESSAGING APPS**
Used to exchange real-time messages.

**STREAMING MUSIC APPS**
Deliver customized Internet music.

Source: National Park Service; Facebook; Kik Interactive Inc.; Pandora Media, Inc.

⚠ **FIGURE 1-11**
**Examples of application software (apps).**

a computer is a computer user, including an accountant electronically preparing a client's taxes, an office worker using a word processing program to create a letter, a supervisor using a computer to check and see whether or not manufacturing workers have met the day's quotas, a parent e-mailing his or her child's teacher, a college student researching a topic online, a doctor updating a patient's electronic medical record, a child playing a computer game, and a person shopping online.

*Programmers*, on the other hand, are computer professionals who write the programs that computers use. Other *computer professionals* include *systems analysts* (who design computer systems to be used within their companies as discussed in Chapter 10), *computer operations personnel* (who are responsible for the day-to-day computer operations at a company, such as maintaining systems or troubleshooting user-related problems), and *security specialists* (who are responsible for securing the company computers and networks against *hackers* and other intruders as discussed in detail in Chapter 9). Computer professionals are discussed in more detail in Chapter 10.

## COMPUTERS TO FIT EVERY NEED

The types of computing devices available today vary from the tiny computers embedded in consumer products, to the pocket-sized mobile devices that do a limited number of computing tasks, to the powerful and versatile desktop and portable computers found in homes and businesses, to the superpowerful computers used for scientific research and to control critical government systems. Computers are generally classified by the following categories, based on size, capability, and price.

- ➤ *Embedded computers*—tiny computers embedded into products to perform specific functions or tasks for that product.
- ➤ *Mobile devices*—smartphones, small tablets, and other small personal devices that contain built-in computing or Internet capabilities.
- ➤ *Personal computers*—fully functioning portable or desktop computers that are designed to be used by a single individual at a time.
- ➤ *Servers*—computers that host data and programs available to a small group of users.
- ➤ *Mainframe computers*—powerful computers used to host a large amount of data and programs available to a wide group of users.
- ➤ *Supercomputers*—extremely powerful computers used for complex computations and processing.

In practice, classifying a computer into one of these six categories is not always easy or straightforward. For example, some high-end personal computers today are as powerful as servers, and some personal computers today are the size of a smartphone or smaller. In addition, new trends impact these categories. For example, small tablet devices (sometimes called *media tablets*) are considered mobile devices because they are only slightly larger than a smartphone, are typically used primarily for viewing Web content and displaying multimedia content instead of general-purpose computing, and usually run a mobile operating system. However, larger, more powerful tablet computers running a desktop operating system are typically considered personal computers. So even though the distinction between some of the categories (particularly mobile devices and personal computers) is blurring, these six categories are commonly used today to refer to groups of computers designed for similar purposes.

### Embedded Computers

An **embedded computer** is a tiny computer embedded into a product designed to perform specific tasks or functions for that product. For example, computers are often embedded into household appliances (such as dishwashers, microwaves, ovens, coffeemakers, and so forth), as well as into other everyday objects (such as thermostats, treadmills, sewing machines, DVD players, and televisions), to help those appliances and objects perform their designated tasks. Cars (see Figure 1-12) also use many embedded computers to assist with diagnostics, to notify the user of important conditions (such as an under-inflated tire or an oil filter that needs changing), to facilitate the car's navigational and entertainment systems, and to control the use of the airbag and other safety devices (such as cameras that alert a driver

**V** **FIGURE 1-12**
**Google's self-driving car prototype.**

Source: Google Inc.

---

>**Embedded computer.** A tiny computer embedded in a product and designed to perform specific tasks or functions for that product.

## TREND

### Apple Watch

Smart watches and other *wearables* are one of the hottest trends today. One example of a smart watch is *Apple Watch* shown in the accompanying photo. While it does contain a computer on a chip and has some built-in features (such as timekeeping, Maps, Music, Photos, a heart rate sensor, and Activity and Workout apps), Apple Watch is designed to work in conjunction with your iPhone for much of its functionality. For example, you can answer phone calls via your Watch and then transfer them to your iPhone for longer conversations. You can also get real-time notifications for incoming mail or messages, as well as reminders of upcoming calendar items.

For input, Apple Watch uses a unique Digital Crown button as a pointing device to zoom and scroll; pressing the button returns to the Home screen. From the Home screen, you can launch apps and select options via touch; a light touch on the screen issues different commands than pressing on the screen. Apple Watch also supports voice input, such as for voice searches and for dictating outgoing messages. For output, Apple Watch has the display screen on the face of the watch, the ability to tap you on your wrist to indicate an alert or notification, and audio output.

One popular new feature of Apple Watch is *Apple Pay*, which enables you to make payments via a store's contactless payment terminal. After entering your credit card information into the *Apple Passbook* digital wallet, Apple Watch can be used to make payments even if you don't have your iPhone with you. For security, your credit card information is assigned a unique number that is encrypted and stored in a dedicated chip in your Apple Watch so your actual credit card number is not transmitted when you make purchases.

Source: Apple, Inc.

that a vehicle is in his or her blind spot or that assist with parking). *Self-driving cars* (such as the one shown in Figure 1-12), which are currently being road tested, contain a large number of embedded computers (as well as lasers, sensors, cameras, and other technology) to enable the car to safely operate without a driver. Embedded computers are designed for specific tasks and specific products and so cannot be used as general-purpose computers.

### Mobile Devices

A **mobile device** is loosely defined as a small (typically pocket-sized) device that has built-in computing or Internet capability. Mobile devices are commonly used to make voice and video calls, send text messages, view Web pages and other documents, take digital photos, play games, download and play music, watch TV shows, and access calendars, social media, and other tools. Mobile devices today include conventional mobile phones, **smartphones** (mobile phones that can access the Internet and run apps), and small **tablet** devices (such as iPads and Android tablets)—see Figure 1-13. Handheld gaming devices, *portable digital media players* (such as the *iPod Touch*), smart watches, and other personal devices that include Internet capabilities can also be referred to as mobile devices. For

---

> **Mobile device.** A very small device that has built-in computing or Internet capability. > **Smartphone.** A mobile phone that has Internet capabilities and can run mobile apps. > **Tablet.** A mobile device, usually larger than a smartphone, that is typically used to access the Internet and display multimedia content.

a closer look at one wearable mobile device—Apple Watch—see the Trend box. Mobile devices are powered by rechargeable batteries and typically include wireless connectivity to enable the device to connect to the Internet.

Today's mobile devices tend to have small screens and keyboards. Because of this, mobile devices are most appropriate for individuals wanting continual access to e-mail and the ability to look up information online when needed, rather than for those individuals wanting general Web browsing or more extensive computing capabilities. This is beginning to change, however, as mobile devices continue to grow in capabilities, as wireless communications continue to become faster, and as mobile input options (such as voice and touch input) continue to improve. For instance, many mobile devices can perform Internet searches and other tasks via voice commands, some can be used to pay for purchases while you are on the go, and many can view virtually any Web content as well as view and edit documents stored in a common format, such as *Microsoft Office* documents. For a look at how your smartphone may one day function as your driver license, see the Inside the Industry box.

TABLETS

SMART WATCHES

SMARTPHONES

Source: HTC

Source: RealNetworks

Source: Sony Electronics

**FIGURE 1-13**
**Mobile devices.**

**CAUTION CAUTION CAUTION CAUTION CAUTION CAUTION CAUT**

Because many mobile devices and personal computers today are continually connected to the Internet, securing those devices against computer viruses and hackers—as introduced later in this chapter and discussed in detail in Chapter 9—is essential for both individuals and businesses.

## Personal Computers (PCs)

A **personal computer** or **PC** (originally called a **microcomputer**) is a small computer designed to be used by one person at a time. Personal computers are widely used by individuals and businesses today and are available in a variety of shapes and sizes, as discussed next.

**TIP**

For tips on buying a personal computer, see the "Guide to Buying a PC" in the References and Resources Guide located at the end of this book.

### Desktop Computers

Conventional personal computers that are designed to fit on or next to a desk (see Figure 1-14) are often referred to as **desktop computers**. Desktop computers can use different types of cases. For example, a *tower case* is designed to sit vertically, typically on the floor; a regular- or mini-sized *desktop case* is designed to be placed horizontally on a desk's surface; and an *all-in-one case* (which was shown in Figure 1-9) is designed to incorporate the monitor and system unit into a single piece of hardware.

**FIGURE 1-14**
**Desktop computers.**

TOWER COMPUTERS

MINI DESKTOP COMPUTERS

Source: Hewlett-Packard Development Company, L.P.; Apple, Inc.

> **Personal computer (PC).** A type of computer based on a microprocessor and designed to be used by one person at a time; also called a **microcomputer**. > **Desktop computer.** A personal computer designed to fit on or next to a desk.

# INSIDE THE INDUSTRY

## Smartphone Driver Licenses

Your smartphone digital wallet can hold your credit cards, airline boarding passes, digital coupons, gift cards, and more. Next up? Your driver license.

Several U.S. states (including Delaware, Iowa, and California) are currently in the process of testing, and likely implementing, *digital driver licenses* (*DDLs*). DDLs (see the accompanying photo) resemble your paper driver license, and contain the same information (your name, address, birthdate, photo, and so forth). In some states, they will also include a barcode to be compatible with law enforcement systems. It is expected that, initially, DDLs will be considered secondary driver licenses so drivers will receive a traditional paper license as well as a DDL.

Instead of being a static copy of your driver license, however, DDLs are mobile apps that are capable of including other features, such as being able to get real-time updates as your information (your address or the license expiration date, for instance) changes. For security purposes, DDLs are expected to be protected by a biometric ID feature (such as a fingerprint image) or a PIN. To prevent fraud, one DDL app currently being tested includes a moving photo, similar to the moving photos in the Harry Potter movies.

One privacy concern is what might happen if you have to hand over your smartphone to a police officer when you are pulled over. For example, can the officer look at other items on your phone if you willingly hand it over? What if the officer inadvertently sees something (such as a pop-up text or e-mail message) of a questionable nature—will he or she be able to use that information against you? Currently cell phones are protected from warrantless searches (according to a recent U.S. Supreme Court ruling), but regulations and protocols may need to be adjusted before DDLs become a widespread reality. One possible solution under development is making the DDL app lock the phone as soon as the DDL is displayed, which would prevent other content from being accessed.

Courtesy MorphoTrust

Desktop computer systems usually conform to one of two standards or *platforms*: *PC-compatible* or *Mac*. PC-compatible computers (sometimes referred to as *Windows PCs* or *IBM-compatible PCs*) evolved from the original IBM PC—the first personal computer widely accepted for business use. They are made by companies such as Dell, Hewlett-Packard, Acer, Lenovo, and Gateway and typically run the Microsoft Windows operating system, although some may run an alternative operating system (such as Linux) instead. Mac computers are made by Apple and use the OS X operating system. Windows, Linux, and Mac computers typically use different software. Although PC-compatible computers are by far the most widely used in the United States, the Mac is traditionally the computer of choice for artists, designers, and others who require advanced graphics capabilities. Extra powerful desktop computers designed for computer users running graphics, music, film, architecture, science, and other powerful applications are sometimes referred to as *workstations*.

## ASK THE EXPERT

Courtesy SONIC

**Sarah Beddoe,** Vice President of Marketing, Sonic, America's Drive-In

**How long will it be until paying for fast-food purchases by smartphone is the norm?**

Consumers are adopting mobile technology faster because it is at the center of many solutions that make life easier. The reality is people now depend more on their mobile devices than ever before, and mobile payments could be the norm within a few short years. For this to happen, a mobile payment not only needs to be a trusted transaction but also a consistent experience widely adopted by the majority of retailers.

**NOTEBOOKS**

**TABLETS**

**HYBRID NOTEBOOK-TABLETS**

**FIGURE 1-15**
Portable computers.

## Portable Computers

**Portable computers** are small personal computers designed to be carried around easily. This portability makes them very flexible and enables individuals to use the same personal computer at home and at school, or same work computer in the office, while on vacation, at off-site meetings, and other locations. Like mobile devices, portable computers are designed to be powered by rechargeable batteries so they can be used while on the go. Portable computers are essential for many workers, such as salespeople who need to make presentations or take orders from clients off-site, agents who need to collect data at remote locations, and managers who need computing and communications resources as they travel. In addition, they are typically the computer of choice today for students and for individuals buying a new personal computer. In fact, portable computers now outsell desktop computers in the United States. Portable computers are available in a variety of configurations, as discussed next and shown in Figure 1-15.

➤ **Notebook computers** (also called **laptop computers**) are about the size of a paper notebook and open to reveal a screen on the top half of the computer and a keyboard on the bottom. They are typically comparable to desktop computers in features and capabilities. Very thin and very light notebooks are often referred to as *subnotebooks* or *ultraportables*; ultraportables conforming to Intel's standards can be marketed as *Ultrabooks*.

➤ **Tablet computers** are typically about the size of a notebook computer and are designed to be used with a digital pen/stylus or touch input. Unlike notebooks, they don't have a physical keyboard but they typically can use an on-screen or attached keyboard as needed.

➤ **Hybrid notebook-tablet computers** (also called *convertible tablets* and *2-in-1 computers*) can function as either a notebook or a tablet computer because they have a display screen that folds shut to resemble a tablet. Some are detachable—that is, designed to separate the display part from the keyboard part when a tablet is needed.

➤ **Netbooks** are similar to notebook computers but are smaller and are designed primarily for accessing Internet-based applications and resources.

It is important to realize that while a portable computer offers the convenience of mobility, it typically isn't as comfortable to use for a primary home or work computer as a desktop computer is, without additional hardware. For instance, many individuals find it more convenient to connect and use a conventional monitor, keyboard, and mouse when using a notebook computer at a desk for a long computer session. This hardware can be connected individually to many portable computers via a wired or wireless connection; there are also

**TIP**

Computers that allow pen or touch input—such as tablet computers— are convenient in crowded situations, as well as in places where the clicking of a keyboard would be annoying to others.

**TIP**

Portable computers (typically netbooks) that run the Chrome operating system are often referred to as *Chromebooks*.

> **Portable computer.** A small personal computer, such as a notebook or tablet computer, that is designed to be carried around easily.
> **Notebook computer.** A fully functioning portable computer that opens to reveal a screen and keyboard; also called a **laptop computer**.
> **Tablet computer.** A portable computer about the size of a notebook computer that is designed to be used with a digital pen or touch input.
> **Hybrid notebook-tablet computer.** A portable computer designed to function as both a notebook and a tablet computer. > **Netbook.** A small notebook computer that is designed primarily to access Internet applications and resources.

## ASK THE EXPERT

**ARUBIXS**

Brandon Mairs, CEO, President, Arubixs

**How will emerging hardware technologies impact computing in the future?**

Wearable smart devices will replace smartphones, tablets will replace PCs and TVs, and 3D printers will replace the process of ordering basic products online. Let's face it–you can't forget your phone, or drop it and break it, when it's worn on your arm. Why have a TV that is only a TV when you could use a large tablet as both a TV and a portable computer? Why drive to the store to buy a pair of tennis shoes when you could just buy the source code online and print name brand shoes in your desired size and color within seconds without ever leaving your home? These are the changes I expect to see in the near future.

docking stations and USB hubs that can be used to connect a portable computer easily to the hardware devices that are attached to the docking station or USB hub. Docking stations and other ergonomic-related topics are discussed in more detail in Chapter 13.

## Thin Clients and Internet Appliances

Most personal computers today are sold as stand-alone, self-sufficient units that are equipped with all the necessary hardware and software needed to operate independently. In other words, they can perform input, processing, output, and storage without being connected to a network, although they are often connected to the Internet or another network. In contrast, a device that must be connected to a network to function is referred to as a *dumb terminal*. Two types of personal computers that may be able to perform a limited amount of independent processing but are designed to be used with a network are thin clients and Internet appliances.

A **thin client** (see Figure 1-16) is designed to be used in conjunction with a network, such as a company network, a school network, or the Internet. Instead of using local hard drives for storage, programs are typically accessed from and data is stored on a *network server.* One advantage of thin clients over desktop computers is lower cost because hardware needs to be replaced less frequently, and costs are lower for computer maintenance, power, and air conditioning. Additional benefits include increased security (because data is not stored on the computer) and easier maintenance (because all software is located on a central server). Disadvantages include having limited or no local storage (although this is an advantage for companies with highly secure data that need to prevent data from leaving the facility) and not being able to function as a stand-alone computer when the network is not working. Thin clients are often used in businesses, school computer labs, retail stores, and medical offices. *Mobile thin clients* (such as Chromebooks) are designed to be used with online apps and storage.

Ordinary devices that can be used for accessing the Internet can be called **Internet appliances** (sometimes referred to as *Internet-enabled devices* or *smart appliances*). Some Internet appliances (such as *smart TVs* and the *smart refrigerator* shown in Figure 1-16) use apps to deliver news, sports scores, weather, music, and other Web-based information. Gaming consoles (such as the *Nintendo Wii*, *Xbox*, and *Sony PlayStation*) that can be used to view Internet content, in addition to their gaming abilities, can also be classified as Internet appliances.

## Servers

A **server**—also sometimes called a *midrange server, minicomputer,* or *midrange computer*—is a computer used to host programs and data for a network. Typically larger, more powerful, and more expensive than a desktop computer, a server is usually located in an

### TIP

Virtually any device (such as a smartphone) being used to access a company network or cloud resource can also be referred to as a "thin client" while it is being used for that purpose.

---

> **Thin client.** A personal computer designed to access a network for processing and data storage, instead of performing those tasks locally.
> **Internet appliance.** A device that can be used to access the Internet. > **Server.** A computer used to host programs and data for a small network.

**THIN CLIENTS**

**CHROMEBOOK MOBILE THIN CLIENTS**

**SMART FRIDGES**

**INT**

**FIGURE 1-16**
**Thin clients and
Internet appliances.**

out-of-the-way place and can serve many users at one time. Users connect to the server through a network, using a computer, thin client, or dumb terminal consisting of just a monitor and keyboard (see Figure 1-17). Servers are often used in small- to medium-sized businesses (such as medical or dental offices), as well as in school computer labs. There are also special *home servers*, which are used to *back up* (make duplicate copies of) the content located on all the computers in a home, as well as to host music, photos, movies, and other media to be shared via a *home network*. Some home servers also allow you to securely access your stored content remotely via the Internet—this is called creating a *personal cloud*.

One trend involving servers (as well as mainframe computers discussed next) is **virtualization**—creating *virtual* (rather than actual) versions of a computing resource. *Server virtualization* uses separate server environments that, although physically located on the same computer, function as separate servers and do not interact with each other. For instance, all applications for an organization can be installed in virtual environments on one or more physical servers instead of using a separate server for each application. Using a separate server for each application often wastes resources because the servers are typically not used to full capacity—one estimate is that often only about 10% of server capability is utilized. With virtualization, a company can fulfill its computing needs with fewer servers, which results in lower costs for hardware and server management, as well as lower power and cooling costs. Consequently, one of the most significant appeals of server virtualization today is increased efficiency.

With the wide use of portable computers and mobile devices in the workplace, *desktop virtualization* is a growing trend. Desktop virtualization separates the user's desktop environment from his or her physical computer so that each user's desktop (stored on a central server) can be delivered to that individual via any authorized device; the user interacts with the virtual desktop in the same way he or she would interact with a physical desktop. Desktop virtualization adds flexibility to where and how each worker performs daily tasks. Virtualization is also used in other computing areas, such as networking and storage.

**FIGURE 1-17**
**Servers.** Are used to host data and programs, such as for a school computer lab or medical office network.

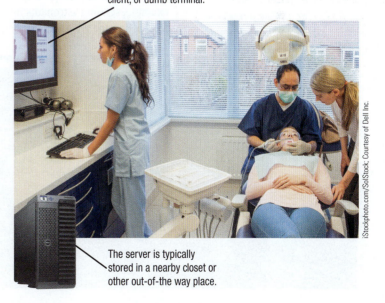

The user connects to the server using a computer, thin client, or dumb terminal.

The server is typically stored in a nearby closet or other out-of-the-way place.

---

> **Virtualization.** Creating virtual (rather than actual) versions of a computing resource.

## Mainframe Computers

A **mainframe computer** is a powerful computer used in many large organizations—such as hospitals, universities, large businesses, banks, and government offices—that need to manage large amounts of centralized data. Larger, more expensive, and more powerful than servers, mainframes can serve thousands of users connected to the mainframe via personal computers, thin clients, or dumb terminals. Mainframe computers are typically located in climate-controlled *data centers* and are connected to the rest of the company computers via a computer network. During regular business hours, a mainframe typically runs the programs needed to meet the different needs of its wide variety of users. At night, it commonly performs large processing tasks, such as payroll and billing. Today's mainframes are sometimes referred to as *high-end servers* or *enterprise-class servers* and they usually cost at least several hundred thousand dollars each.

One issue facing businesses today is the high cost of electricity to power and cool the mainframes, servers, and personal computers used in an organization. Consequently, making the computers located in a business—particularly mainframes and servers—more energy efficient is a high priority. Virtualization is often used today to utilize a company's mainframes more efficiently. Another recent focus for mainframes is ensuring they can handle new and emerging needs (such as having the computational power to process data from *smart meters* and other new technology and having the ability to run mobile and social networking applications). For example, the mainframe shown in Figure 1-18 is designed to process mobile data—it supports 8,000 virtual servers and can process 2.5 billion transactions per day.

**⌐ FIGURE 1-18**

**Mainframes.** Perform large processing tasks.

**⌐ FIGURE 1-19**

**Supercomputers.** Have immense processing speed and capabilities.

## Supercomputers

Some applications require extraordinary speed, accuracy, and processing capabilities—for example, sending astronauts into space, controlling missile guidance systems and satellites, forecasting the weather, exploring for oil, breaking codes, and designing and testing new products. **Supercomputers** (see Figure 1-19)—the most powerful and most expensive type of computer available—were developed to fill this need. Some relatively new supercomputing applications include hosting extremely complex Web sites (such as search sites and social networking sites) and *three-dimensional applications* (such as 3D medical imaging, 3D image projections, and 3D architectural modeling). Unlike mainframe computers, which typically run multiple applications simultaneously to serve a wide variety of users, supercomputers generally run one program at a time, as fast as possible.

Conventional supercomputers can cost several million dollars each. They tend to be very large and contain a large number of processors. For example, the *Titan* supercomputer shown in Figure 1-19

> **Mainframe computer.** A computer used in large organizations that need to manage large amounts of centralized data and run multiple programs simultaneously. > **Supercomputer.** The fastest, most expensive, and most powerful type of computer.

occupies 4,352 square feet of floor space and contains more than 300,000 processors. This supercomputer is installed at the U.S. Department of Energy Oak Ridge National Laboratory and is used for scientific research, including climate change and astrophysics; its speed is expected to give researchers unparalleled accuracy in their simulations and facilitate faster research breakthroughs. With a peak speed of 27,000 trillion calculations per second, Titan is one of the fastest computers in the world.

## COMPUTER NETWORKS AND THE INTERNET

A **computer network** (see Figure 1-20) is a collection of computers and other devices that are connected in order to enable users to share hardware, software, and data, as well as to communicate electronically with each other. Computer networks exist in many sizes and types. For instance, home networks are commonly used to allow home computers to

**FIGURE 1-20**

Example of a computer network.

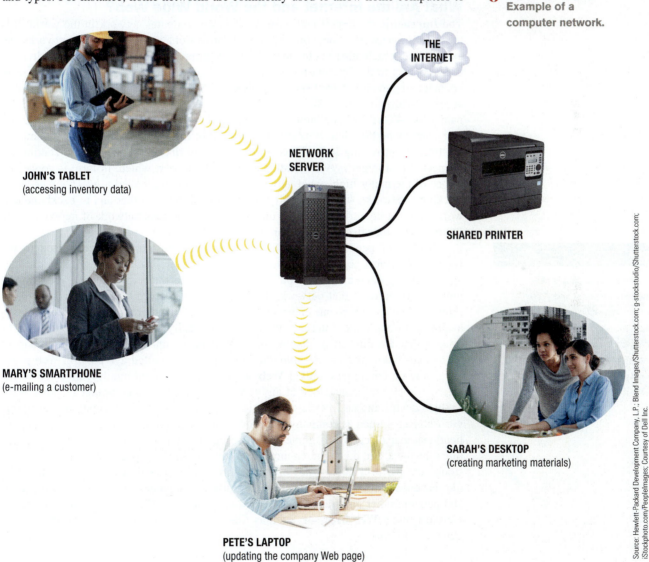

THE INTERNET

NETWORK SERVER

SHARED PRINTER

**JOHN'S TABLET**
(accessing inventory data)

**MARY'S SMARTPHONE**
(e-mailing a customer)

**PETE'S LAPTOP**
(updating the company Web page)

**SARAH'S DESKTOP**
(creating marketing materials)

Source: Hewlett-Packard Development Company, L.P.; Blend Images/Shutterstock.com; g-stockstudio/Shutterstock.com; iStockphoto.com/PeopleImages; Courtesy of Dell Inc.

> **Computer network.** A collection of computers and other devices that are connected in order to share hardware, software, and data, as well as to communicate electronically with one another.

share a single printer and Internet connection, as well as to exchange files. Small office networks enable workers to access company records stored on a network server, communicate with other employees, share a high-speed printer, and access the Internet. School networks allow students and teachers to access the Internet and school resources, and large corporate networks often connect all of the offices or retail stores in the corporation, creating a network that spans several cities or states. Public wireless networks—such as those available at some coffeehouses, restaurants, public libraries, and parks—provide Internet access to individuals via their portable computers and mobile devices. Mobile telephone networks provide Internet access and communications capabilities to smartphone users. Most computers and mobile devices today are used with computer networks. Chapter 7 discusses networks in greater detail.

## What Are the Internet and the World Wide Web?

The **Internet** is the largest and most well-known computer network in the world. It is technically a network of networks because it consists of a vast collection of networks that can all access each other via the main *backbone* infrastructure of the Internet. Individual users connect to the Internet by connecting their computers or mobile devices to servers belonging to an **Internet service provider** (**ISP**)—a company that provides Internet access, usually for a fee. ISPs (which include conventional and mobile telephone companies like AT&T, Verizon, and Sprint; cable providers like Comcast and Time Warner; and stand-alone ISPs like NetZero and EarthLink) function as gateways or onramps to the Internet, providing Internet access to their subscribers. ISP servers are continually connected to a larger network, called a *regional network*, which, in turn, is connected to one of the major high-speed networks within a country, called a *backbone network*. Backbone networks within a country are connected to each other and to backbone networks in other countries. Together they form one enormous network of networks—the Internet. Tips for selecting an ISP are included in Chapter 8.

Billions of people and organizations all over the world are connected to the Internet. The most common Internet activities today are exchanging e-mail messages and accessing content located on Web pages. While the term *Internet* refers to the physical structure of that network, the **World Wide Web** (often just called the **Web**) refers to one resource—an enormous collection of documents called **Web pages**—available through the Internet. Web pages typically contain **hyperlinks**—text or images that are clicked to display other Web pages or Web resources. A group of Web pages belonging to one individual or company is called a **Web site**. Web pages are stored on computers (called **Web servers**) that are continually connected to the Internet; they can be accessed at any time by anyone with a computer or other Web-enabled device and an Internet connection. A wide variety of information is available via Web pages, such as company and product information, government forms and publications, maps, school assignments and resources, news, weather, sports results, airline schedules, and much, much more. You can also use Web pages to shop, bank, trade stock, and perform other types of online financial transactions; access social media like Facebook and *Twitter*; and listen to music, play games, watch television shows, and perform other entertainment-oriented activities (see Figure 1-21). Web pages are viewed using a **Web browser**, such as *Edge*, *Internet Explorer* (*IE*), *Chrome*, *Safari*, *Opera*, or *Firefox*.

>**Internet.** The largest and most well-known computer network, linking billions of devices all over the world. >**Internet service provider (ISP).** A business or other organization that provides Internet access to others, typically for a fee. >**World Wide Web (Web).** The collection of Web pages available through the Internet. >**Web page.** A document, typically containing hyperlinks to other documents, located on a Web server and available through the World Wide Web. >**Hyperlink.** Text or an image on a Web page that is clicked to access additional Web resources. >**Web site.** A collection of related Web pages usually belonging to an organization or individual. >**Web server.** A computer that is continually connected to the Internet and hosts Web pages that are accessible through the Internet. >**Web browser.** A program used to view Web pages.

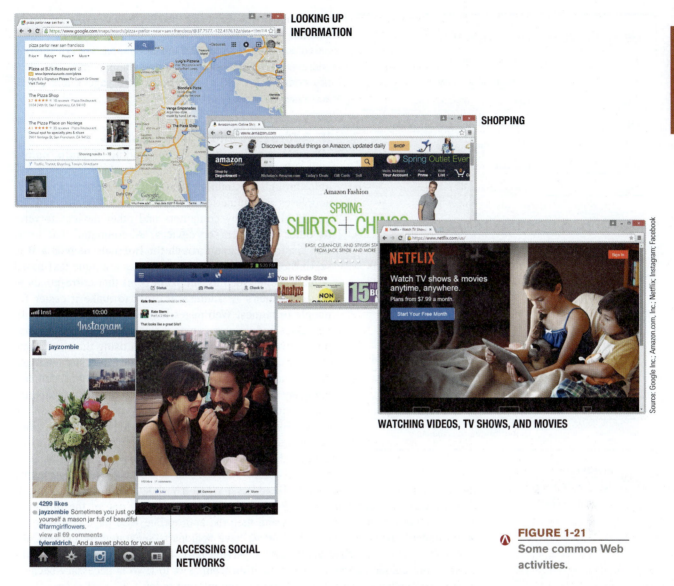

**LOOKING UP INFORMATION**

**SHOPPING**

**WATCHING VIDEOS, TV SHOWS, AND MOVIES**

**ACCESSING SOCIAL NETWORKS**

Source: Google Inc.; Amazon.com, Inc.; Netflix; Instagram; Facebook

**FIGURE 1-21**
Some common Web activities.

## Accessing a Network or the Internet

To access a network (such as a home network, a school or company network, or a public wireless hotspot), you need to use a network adapter (typically built into your computer or other device being used) to connect your device to that network. With many networks you need to supply logon information (such as a username and a password) to connect to the network. Once connected, you can access network resources, including the network's Internet connection. If you are connecting to the Internet without going through a computer network, your computer needs to use a modem to connect to the communications media (such as a telephone line, cable connection, or wireless signal) used by your ISP to deliver Internet content. Network adapters and modems are discussed in more detail in Chapter 7.

Most Internet connections today are *direct* (or *always-on*) *connections*, which means the computer or other device being used to access the Internet is continually connected to the ISP's computer. With a direct connection, you only need to open your Web browser to begin using the Internet. With a *dial-up connection*, however, you must start the program that instructs your computer to dial and connect to the ISP's server via a telephone line, and then open a Web browser, each time you want to access the Internet. The different types of connections you can use to access the Internet are discussed in more detail in Chapter 8.

| ORIGINAL TLDS | INTENDED USE |
|---|---|
| .com | Commercial businesses |
| .edu | Educational institutions |
| .gov | Government organizations |
| .int | International treaty organizations |
| .mil | Military organizations |
| .net | Network providers and ISPs |
| .org | Noncommercial organizations |

| NEWER TLDS | INTENDED USE |
|---|---|
| .aero | Aviation industry |
| .biz | Entrepreneurs and growing businesses |
| .expert | Individuals branding themselves as an expert |
| .fr | French businesses |
| .info | Resource sites |
| .jobs | Employment sites |
| .name | Individuals (personal branding) |
| .nyc | New York City businesses |
| .us | United States businesses |

**FIGURE 1-22**

Sample top-level domains (TLDs).

**TIP**

Only the legitimate holder of a trademarked name (such as Microsoft) can use that trademarked name as a domain name (such as microsoft.com); trademarks are discussed in detail in Chapter 13.

To request a Web page or other resource located on the Internet, its **Internet address**—a unique numeric or text-based address—is used. The most common types of Internet addresses are IP addresses and domain names (to identify computers), URLs (to identify Web pages), and e-mail addresses (to identify people).

## IP Addresses and Domain Names

**IP addresses** and their corresponding **domain names** are used to identify computers and other devices available through the Internet. IP (short for *Internet Protocol*) addresses are numeric, such as *134.170.185.46*, and are commonly used by computers and other devices to refer to other computers or devices. A computer that hosts information available through the Internet (such as a Web server hosting Web pages) usually has a unique text-based domain name (such as *microsoft.com*) that corresponds to that computer's IP address in order to make it easier for people to request Web pages located on that computer. IP addresses and domain names are unique; that is, there cannot be two computers on the Internet using the exact same IP address or exact same domain name. To ensure this, specific IP addresses are allocated to each network (such as a company network or an ISP) to be used with the computers on that network, and there is a worldwide registration system for domain name registration. When a domain name is registered, the IP address of the computer that will be hosting the Web site associated with that domain name is also registered; the Web site can be accessed using either its domain name or corresponding IP address. When a Web site is requested using its domain name, the corresponding IP address is looked up using one of the Internet's *domain name system* (*DNS*) *servers* and then the appropriate Web page is displayed. While today's IP addresses (called *IPv4*) have four parts separated by periods, the newer *IPv6* addresses have eight parts separated by colons in order to have significantly more unique addresses. The transition from IPv4 to IPv6 is necessary because of the vast number of devices connecting to the Internet today.

Domain names typically reflect the name of the individual or organization associated with that Web site and the different parts of a domain name are separated by a period. The far right part of the domain name (which begins with the rightmost period) is called the *top-level domain* (*TLD*) and traditionally identifies the type of organization or its location (such as *.com* for businesses, *.edu* for educational institutions, *.jp* for Web sites located in Japan, or *.fr* for Web sites located in France). The part of the domain name that precedes the TLD is called the *second-level domain name* and typically reflects the name of a company or an organization, a product, or an individual. There were seven original TLDs used in the United States; since then, numerous additional TLDs and two-letter *country code TLDs* have been created (see some examples in Figure 1-22) and more are in the works. Nearly 300 million domain names are registered worldwide.

---

>**Internet address.** A unique address that identifies a computer, person, or Web page on the Internet, such as an IP address, a domain name, a URL, or an e-mail address. >**IP address.** A numeric Internet address used to uniquely identify a computer or other device on the Internet. >**Domain name.** A text-based Internet address used to uniquely identify a computer on the Internet.

Web page URLs usually begin with http:// (for nonsecure Web pages) or https:// (for secure Web pages).

This part of the URL identifies the Web server hosting the Web page.

Next comes the folder(s) in which the Web page is stored, if necessary.

This is the Web page document that is to be retrieved and displayed.

(http://)(google.com)(about/careers)(index.html)

**FIGURE 1-23**
A Web page URL.

## Uniform Resource Locators (URLs)

Similar to the way an IP address or a domain name uniquely identifies a computer on the Internet, a **Uniform Resource Locator** (**URL**) uniquely identifies a specific Web page (including the *protocol* or standard being used to display the Web page, the Web server hosting the Web page, the name of any folders on the Web server in which the Web page file is stored, and the Web page's filename, if needed).

The most common Web page protocols are *Hypertext Transfer Protocol* (*http://*) for regular Web pages or *Secure Hypertext Transfer Protocol* (*https://*) for *secure Web pages* that can be used to transmit sensitive information, such as credit card numbers, safely. *File Transfer Protocol* (*ftp://*) is sometimes used to upload and download files. The *file extension* used in the Web page filename indicates the type of Web page that will be displayed (such as *.html* and *.htm* for standard Web pages). For example, looking at the URL for the Web page shown in Figure 1-23 from right to left, we can see that the Web page is called *index.html*, is stored in a folder called *careers* inside another folder called *about* on the Web server associated with the *google.com* domain, and is a regular (nonsecure) Web page because the *http://* protocol is being used.

## E-Mail Addresses

To contact people using the Internet, you often use their **e-mail addresses**. An e-mail address consists of a **username** (an identifying name), followed by the @ symbol, followed by the domain name for the computer that will be handling that person's e-mail (called a *mail server*). For example,

jsmith@cengage.com
maria_s@cengage.com
sam.peterson@cengage.com

are the e-mail addresses assigned respectively to jsmith (John Smith), maria_s (Maria Sanchez), and sam.peterson (Sam Peterson), three hypothetical employees at Cengage Learning, the publisher of this textbook. Usernames are typically a combination of the person's first and last names and sometimes include periods, underscores, and numbers, but cannot include blank spaces. To ensure a unique e-mail address for everyone in the world, usernames must be unique within each domain name. So, even though there could be a *jsmith* at Cengage Learning using the e-mail address *jsmith@cengage.com* and a *jsmith* at Stanford University

>**Uniform Resource Locator (URL).** An Internet address (usually beginning with http:// or https://) that uniquely identifies a Web page. >**E-mail address.** An Internet address consisting of a username and domain name that uniquely identifies a person on the Internet. >**Username.** A name that uniquely identifies a user on a specific computer network.

# HOW IT WORKS

## Cloud Computing

In general, *cloud computing* refers to accessing data, applications, and other resources stored on computers available via the Internet—in a "cloud" of computers—rather than on users' computers. With cloud computing, you can access Web-based software and apps, store and retrieve data via a cloud storage provider, and print documents to a cloud printer located anywhere in the world. Cloud computing resources are available on demand, whenever the user needs them. These resources can be accessed by any Web-enabled device, and users typically pay only for the resources that they use.

One advantage of cloud computing is the ability to access data from anywhere the user has an active Internet connection. Another advantage is that, because data is stored online instead of on the user's device, the data is safe if that device is lost, stolen, or damaged. Disadvantages of cloud computing include no or reduced functionality without an Internet connection and the potentially high expense related to data transfer for companies and individuals using high-bandwidth applications.

While most individuals use cloud computing to some extent, users of Chromebooks are full-time cloud users. Chromebooks are designed to be used with online Google Apps (such as Google Docs, Gmail, and Google Play Music), and all documents, mail, photos, music, and more are stored in the cloud. An example of using Google Docs and Google Drive is shown in the accompanying illustration.

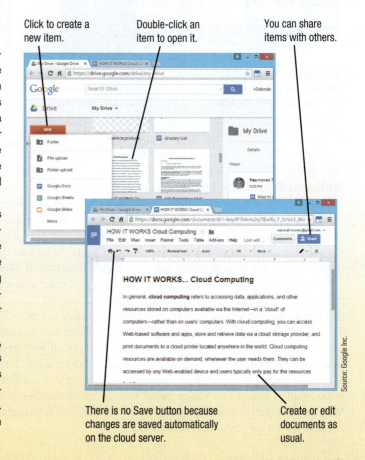

Click to create a new item.

Double-click an item to open it.

You can share items with others.

There is no Save button because changes are saved automatically on the cloud server.

Create or edit documents as usual.

Source: Google Inc.

---

using the e-mail address *jsmith@stanford.edu*, the two e-mail addresses are unique. It is up to each organization with a registered domain name to ensure that one—and only one—exact same username is assigned to its domain. Using e-mail addresses to send e-mail messages is discussed later in this chapter; other forms of online communications—such as text messaging and chat—are covered in Chapter 8.

## Pronouncing Internet Addresses

Because Internet addresses are frequently given verbally, it is important to know how to pronounce them. Figure 1-24 shows some examples of Internet addresses and their proper pronunciations, and a few guidelines are listed next.

> **FIGURE 1-24**
> Pronouncing Internet addresses.

| TYPE OF ADDRESS | SAMPLE ADDRESS | PRONUNCIATION |
|---|---|---|
| Domain name | berkeley.edu | berkeley dot e d u |
| URL | irs.gov/freefile | i r s dot gov slash free file |
| E-mail address | president@whitehouse.gov | president at white house dot gov |

➤ If a portion of the address forms a recognizable word or name, it is spoken; otherwise, it is spelled out.

➤ The @ sign is pronounced *at.*

➤ The period (.) is pronounced *dot.*

➤ The forward slash (/) is pronounced *slash.*

## Surfing the Web

Once you have an Internet connection, you are ready to begin *surfing the Web*—that is, using a Web browser to view Web pages. The first page that your Web browser displays when it is opened is your browser's starting page or *home page.* Often this is the home page for the Web site belonging to your browser, school, or ISP. However, you can use your browser's customization options to change the current home page to any page that you plan to visit regularly. From your browser's home page, you can move to any Web page you desire, as discussed next. For a look at a common Web activity today—cloud computing—see the How It Works box.

## Using URLs and Hyperlinks

To navigate to a new Web page for which you know the URL, type that URL in the browser's *Address bar* (shown in Figure 1-25) and press Enter. Once that page is displayed, you can use the hyperlinks—graphics or text linked to other Web pages—located on that page to display other Web pages. In addition to Web pages, hyperlinks can also be linked to other types of files, such as to enable Web visitors to view or download images, listen to or download music files, play videos, or download software programs.

**FIGURE 1-25**
**Surfing the Web with Chrome.**

**BACK AND FORWARD BUTTONS**
Move between Web pages that have been recently viewed.

**ADDRESS BAR**
Type a URL in the Address bar and press Enter to display the corresponding Web page.

**STATUS BAR**
Displays URLs as you point to hyperlinks.

**HYPERLINKS**
Point to a hyperlink to see the corresponding URL on the status bar; click the hyperlink to display that page.

**TABS**
Click the rightmost tab to open a new tab.

**CHROME MENU**
Contains options to view or manage bookmarks, history, settings, closed tabs, and more.

**BOOKMARKS BUTTON**
Click to create a bookmark or access other bookmarks.

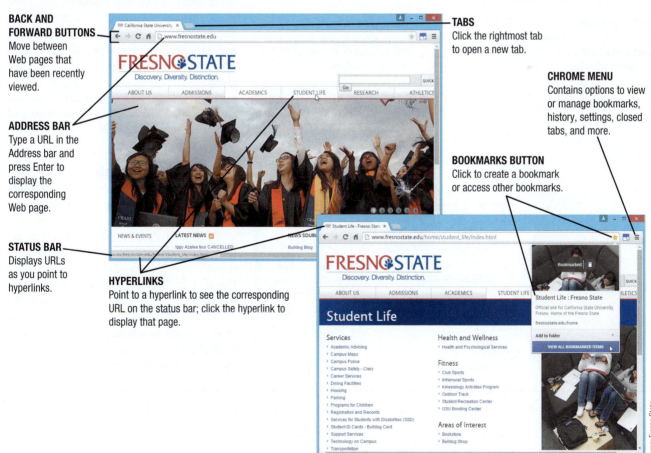

Source: Fresno State

**TIP**

If you accidentally close a browser window in Chrome, open a new tab and use the *History and recent tabs* option on the Chrome menu to redisplay the page.

**TIP**

If you get an error message when typing a URL, first check to make sure you typed it correctly. If it is correct, edit the URL to remove any folder or filenames and press Enter to try to load the home page of that site.

The most commonly used Web browsers include Chrome (shown in Figure 1-25), Edge (shown in Figure 1-26), Internet Explorer, Safari, and Firefox. Most browsers today include *tabbed browsing* (which allows you to have multiple Web pages open at the same time and to drag a tab to move that window), the ability to search for Web pages using the Address bar, and tools for *bookmarking* and revisiting Web pages, as discussed shortly. Browsers today also typically include security features to help notify you of possible threats as you browse the Web, *download managers* to help you manage your downloaded files, and *crash recovery* features, such as the ability to open the last set of Web pages that were open before you accidentally closed your browser or before the browser or computer *crashed* (stopped working). In any browser, you can use the Back button to return to a previous page and the Home button to display your browser's home page. To print the current Web page, look for a *Print* option on a menu or press *Ctrl+P*.

## Using Favorites/Bookmarks and the History List

All Web browsers have a feature (usually called **Favorites** or **Bookmarks** and accessed via a Favorites or Bookmarks menu, button, or bar) that you can use to save Web page URLs (refer again to Figure 1-25). Once a Web page is saved as a favorite or a bookmark, you can redisplay that page without typing its URL—you simply select its link from the Favorites or Bookmarks list. You can also use this feature to save a group of tabbed Web pages in order to open the entire group again at a later time. Web browsers also maintain a *History list*, which is a record of all Web pages visited during the period of time specified in the browser settings; you can revisit a Web page located on the History list by displaying the History list and selecting that page.

Most Web browsers today allow you to delete, move into folders, and otherwise organize your favorites/bookmarks, as well as to search your favorites/bookmarks or History list to help you find pages more easily. If you use a browser in conjunction with an online account (such as *Google*), your bookmarks and history can be *synched* between your computer and your smartphone so they are always available on either device. If there is e-mail associated with your account (such as Gmail for Google users), your contacts and e-mail are synched as well.

## Searching the Web

People typically turn to the Web to find specific types of information. There are a number of special Web pages, called *search sites*, available to help you locate what you are looking for on the Internet. One of the most popular search sites—Google—is shown in Figure 1-26. To conduct a search, you typically type one or more *keywords* into the search box on a search site, and a list of links to Web pages matching your search criteria is displayed. There are also numerous *reference sites* available on the Web to look up

**FIGURE 1-26**
**Google displayed in the Edge browser.**

**KEYWORD SEARCHES**
Type keywords here and press Enter to see a list of Web pages matching your search criteria.

**OTHER APPS**
Provide access to other Google apps, such as Google+, Images, Gmail, Drive, Calendar, and Docs.

Source: Google Inc.

>**Favorite.** A link to a Web page saved within a browser to facilitate quick access to that Web page; also called a **bookmark**.

addresses, phone numbers, ZIP codes, maps, and other information. To find a reference site, type the information you are looking for (such as "ZIP code lookup" or "topographical maps") in a search site's search box to see links to sites containing that information. Searching the Web is discussed in more detail in Chapter 8.

## E-Mail

**Electronic mail** (more commonly called **e-mail**) is the process of exchanging electronic messages between individuals over a network—usually the Internet. E-mail is one of the most widely used Internet applications—Americans alone send billions of e-mail messages daily. You can send an e-mail message from any Internet-enabled device (such as a computer or smartphone) to anyone who has an Internet e-mail address. As illustrated in Figure 1-27, e-mail messages travel from the sender's device to his or her ISP's mail server, and then through the Internet to the mail server being used by the recipient. When the recipient's device retrieves new e-mail (typically on a regular basis as long as the device is powered up and connected to the Internet), the e-mail message is displayed on the device he or she is using. In addition to text, e-mail messages can include attached files, such as documents, photos, and videos.

E-mail can be sent and received via an installed *e-mail program*, such as *Microsoft Outlook* or *OS X Mail* (sometimes referred to as *conventional e-mail*) or via a *Web mail* service or app such as *Gmail* or *Outlook.com*. Using an installed e-mail program is convenient if you want to have copies of sent and received e-mail messages stored on your computer. To use an installed e-mail program, however, it must first be set up with the user's name, e-mail address, incoming mail server, and outgoing mail server information. Web mail allows you to access your e-mail from any device with an Internet connection as long as you are logged in to your Web mail account. Consequently, Web-based e-mail is more flexible than conventional e-mail. However, you may not be able to view your Web mail messages when you are offline.

Web-based e-mail is typically free and virtually all ISPs used with personal computers include e-mail service in their monthly fee. Mobile e-mail may be counted against your data usage, unless you are using Wi-Fi when you retrieve it. Other types of mobile communications, such as text messages and multimedia messages that typically use the *Short Message Service* (*SMS*) and *Multimedia Message Service* (*MMS*) protocols, respectively, may also incur a fee. Messaging and other types of online communications are discussed in Chapter 8.

**FIGURE 1-27**
How e-mail works.

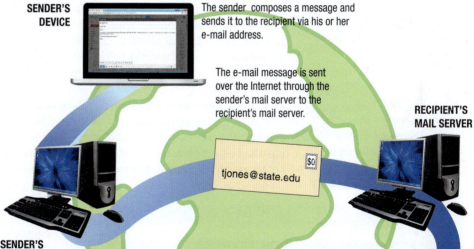

SENDER'S DEVICE

The sender composes a message and sends it to the recipient via his or her e-mail address.

The e-mail message is sent over the Internet through the sender's mail server to the recipient's mail server.

RECIPIENT'S MAIL SERVER

tjones@state.edu

SENDER'S MAIL SERVER

The message is displayed when the recipient's device checks for new mail.

RECIPIENT'S DEVICE

anderspphoto/Shutterstock.com; 300dpi/Shutterstock.com; Roman Samokhin/Shutterstock.com; Google Inc.

>**Electronic mail (e-mail).** Electronic messages sent from one user to another over the Internet or other network.

# TECHNOLOGY AND SOCIETY

The vast improvements in technology over the past decade have had a distinct impact on daily life. Computers have become indispensable tools at home, at work or school, and while on the go, and related technological advancements have changed the way our everyday items—cars, microwaves, coffeepots, toys, exercise bikes, telephones, televisions, and more—look and function. As computers and everyday devices become smarter, they tend to do their intended jobs faster, better, and more reliably than before, as well as take on additional capabilities. In addition to affecting individuals, computerization and technological advances have changed society as a whole. Without computers, banks would be overwhelmed by the job of tracking all the transactions they process, moon exploration and the International Space Station would still belong to science fiction, and some scientific advances—such as DNA analysis and gene mapping—would be nonexistent. In addition, we as individuals are getting accustomed to the increased automation of everyday activities, such as shopping and banking, and we depend on having fast and easy access to information via the Internet and rapid communications via e-mail and messaging. In addition, many of us would not think about making a major purchase without first researching it online. In fact, it is surprising how fast the Internet and its resources have become an integral part of our society. But despite all its benefits, *cyberspace* has some risks. Some of the most important societal implications related to computers and the Internet are introduced next; many of these issues are covered in more detail in later chapters of this text.

## Benefits of a Technology-Oriented Society

The benefits of having such a technology-oriented society are numerous, as touched on throughout this chapter. The capability to virtually design, build, and test new buildings, cars, and airplanes before the actual construction begins helps professionals create safer end products. Technological advances in medicine allow for earlier diagnosis and more effective treatment of diseases than ever before. The benefit of beginning medical students performing virtual surgery using a computer instead of performing actual surgery on a patient is obvious. The ability to shop, pay bills, research products, participate in online classes, and look up vast amounts of information 24 hours a day, 7 days a week, 365 days a year via the Internet is a huge convenience. In addition, a technology-oriented society generates new opportunities. For example, technologies—such as *speech recognition software* and Braille input and output devices—enable physically- or visually-challenged individuals to perform necessary job tasks and to communicate with others more easily.

In general, technology has also made a huge number of tasks in our lives go much faster. Instead of experiencing a long delay for a credit check, an applicant can get approved for a purchase, loan, or credit card almost immediately. Documents and photographs can be e-mailed in mere moments, instead of taking at least a day to be mailed physically. We can watch many of our favorite TVs shows online (such as *Survivor* via the Web site shown in Figure 1-28) and access up-to-the-minute news at our convenience. And we can download information, programs, music files, movies, and more on demand when we want or need them, instead of having to order them and then wait for delivery or physically go to a store to purchase the desired items.

**▼ FIGURE 1-28**
Episodes of many television shows are available online to be viewed at the user's convenience.

Source: CBS Interactive

## Risks of a Technology-Oriented Society

Although there are a great number of benefits from having a technology-oriented society, there are risks as well. A variety of problems have emerged from our extensive use of computers and related technology, ranging from stress and health concerns, to the proliferation of *spam* (unsolicited e-mails) and *malware* (harmful programs that can be installed on our computers without our knowledge), to security and privacy issues, to legal and ethical dilemmas. Many of the security and privacy concerns stem from the fact that so much of our personal business takes place online—or at least our personal data ends up as data in a computer database somewhere—and the potential for misuse of this data is enormous. Another concern is the repercussions of collecting such vast amounts of information electronically. Some people worry about creating a "Big Brother" situation, in which the government or another organization is watching everything that we do. Although the accumulation and distribution of information is a necessary factor of our networked economy, it is one area of great concern to many individuals. And some Internet behavior, such as downloading music or movies from an unauthorized source or viewing pornography on an office computer, can get you arrested or fired.

## Security Issues

One of the most common online security risks today is your computer becoming infected with a malware program. Malware often causes damage to the infected computer, such as erasing data or bogging down the computer so it does not function well. It can also be used to try to locate sensitive data on your computer (such as Web site passwords or credit card numbers) and send that data to the malware creator or to take control of your computer for criminal activities. Malware is typically installed by downloading a program that secretly contains malware or by clicking a link on a Web page or in an e-mail message that then installs malware. In addition to computers, malware and other security threats are increasingly being directed toward smartphones and other mobile devices. To help protect your computer or mobile device, never open an e-mail attachment from someone you do not know and be careful about what files you download from the Internet. In addition, it is crucial to install security software on your computer and mobile devices and to set up the program to monitor your devices on a continual basis (see Figure 1-29). If a virus or other type of malware attempts to install itself on your computer or mobile device (such as through an e-mail message attachment or a Web link), the security program will block it. If malware does find its way onto your computer or mobile device, the security program will detect it during a regular scan, notify you, and attempt to remove it.

**FIGURE 1-29**
**Security software.**

Malware and other security concerns, as well as precautions you can take to protect yourself and your devices, are discussed in detail in Chapter 9.

## Privacy Issues

Some individuals view the potential risk to personal privacy as one of the most important issues regarding our networked society. As more and more data about our everyday activities is collected and stored on devices accessible via the Internet, our privacy is at risk because the potential for privacy violations increases. Today, data is collected about practically anything we buy online or offline, although offline purchases may not be associated with our identity unless we use a credit card or a membership or loyalty card. At issue is not that data is collected—with virtually all organizations using computers for recordkeeping, that is unavoidable—but rather how the collected data is used and how secure it is. Data collected by businesses may be used only by that company or, depending on the businesses' *privacy policy*, may be shared with others. Data shared with others often results in spam, which is considered by many to be a violation of personal privacy. Privacy concerns and precautions are discussed in detail in Chapter 9.

> **CAUTION CAUTION CAUTION CAUTION CAUTION CAUTION CAUT**
>
> Using your primary e-mail address when shopping online or signing up for a sweepstake or other online activity will undoubtedly result in spam being sent to that e-mail address. Using a *throwaway e-mail address* (a free e-mail address from Gmail or another free e-mail provider that you can change easily) for these activities instead helps protect your privacy and cut back on the amount of spam delivered to your regular e-mail account.

## Differences in Online Communications

There is no doubt that e-mail and other online communications methods have helped speed up both personal and business communications and have made them more efficient (such as avoiding the telephone tag problem). As you spend more and more time communicating online, you will probably notice some differences between online communications methods (such as e-mail and social media posts) and traditional communications methods (such as telephone calls and written letters). In general, online communications tend to be much less formal and, in fact, many people compose and send e-mail messages quickly, without taking the time to reread the message content or check the spelling or grammar. However, you need to be careful not to be so casual—particularly in business—that your communications appear unprofessional or become too personal with people you do not know.

To help in that regard, a special etiquette—referred to as *netiquette*—has evolved to guide online behavior. A good rule of thumb is always to be polite and considerate of others and to refrain from offensive remarks. This holds true whether you are asking a question via a company's e-mail address, posting a message on someone's Facebook page, or messaging a friend. With business communications, you should also be very careful with your grammar and spelling to avoid embarrassing yourself. Some specific guidelines for proper online behavior are listed in Figure 1-30.

Another trend in online communications is the use of abbreviations and *emoticons*. Abbreviations or *acronyms*, such as BTW for "by the way," are commonly used to save time in all types of communications today. They are being used with increased frequency in text messaging and e-mail exchanged via mobile phones to speed up the text entry process. Emoticons are illustrations of faces showing smiles, frowns, and other expressions that are created with keyboard symbols—such as the popular :-) smile emoticon—and allow people to add an emotional tone to written online communications. Without these symbols, it is sometimes difficult to tell if the person who sent the online communication is serious or joking because you cannot see the individual's face or hear his or her tone of voice. While most people would agree that using abbreviations and emoticons with personal communications is fine, they are usually viewed as inappropriate for formal business communications.

**▼ FIGURE 1-30**

**Netiquette.** Use these netiquette guidelines and common sense when communicating online.

| RULE | EXPLANATION |
|---|---|
| Use descriptive subject lines | Use short, descriptive subject lines for e-mail messages and online posts. For example, "Question regarding your online classes" is much better than a vague title, such as "Question." |
| Don't shout | SHOUTING REFERS TO TYPING YOUR ENTIRE E-MAIL MESSAGE OR ONLINE POST USING CAPITAL LETTERS. Use capital letters only when it is grammatically correct to do so or for emphasizing a few words. |
| Watch what you say | Things that you say or write online can be interpreted as being sexist, racist, or in just general bad taste. Also check spelling and grammar—typos look unprofessional and nobody likes wading through poorly written materials. |
| Don't spam your contacts | Don't hit *Reply All* to an e-mail when a simple *Reply* will do. The same goes for forwarding e-mail chain letters, reposting every joke you run across, or sending every funny YouTube video you find—to everyone you know. |
| Be cautious | Don't give out personal information—such as your real name, telephone number, or credit card information—to people you meet online. |
| Think before you send or post | Once you send an e-mail or text message or post something online, you lose control of it. Don't include content (such as compromising photos of yourself) that you would not want shared with others, and don't tag people in photos that are unflattering to them. In addition, don't e-mail or post anything if emotions are running high—wait until you calm down. |

## The Anonymity Factor

By their very nature, online communications lend themselves to *anonymity*. Because recipients usually do not hear senders' voices or see their handwriting, it is difficult to know for sure who the sender is. Particularly in online discussions, online worlds, and other online activities where individuals use made-up names instead of real names, there is an anonymous feel to being online.

Being anonymous gives many individuals a sense of freedom, which makes them feel able to say or do anything online. This sense of true freedom of speech can be beneficial. For example, a reserved individual who might never complain about a poor product or service in person may feel comfortable lodging a complaint by e-mail. In online discussions, many people feel they can be completely honest about what they think and can introduce new ideas and points of view without inhibition. Anonymous e-mail is also a safe way for an employee to blow the whistle on a questionable business practice, or for an individual to tip off police to a crime or potential terrorist attack.

But, like all good things, online anonymity can be abused. Using the Internet as their shield, some people use rude comments, ridicule, profanity, and even slander to attack people, places, and things they do not like or agree with. Others may use multiple online identities in online discussions to give the appearance of increased support for their points of view. Still others may use multiple identities to try to manipulate stock prices (by posting false information about a company to drive the price down, for instance), to get buyers to trust an online auction seller (by posting fictitious positive feedback about themselves), or to commit other illegal or unethical acts.

It is possible to hide your true identity while browsing or sending e-mail by removing personal information from your browser and e-mail program or by using privacy software that acts as a middleman between you and Web sites and hides your identity, as discussed in Chapter 9. But, in fact, even when personal information is removed, ISPs and the government may still be able to trace communications back to a particular computer when a crime has occurred, so it is difficult—perhaps impossible—to be completely anonymous online.

**FIGURE 1-31**

**Snopes.com.** This Web site can be used to check out online rumors.

## Information Integrity

The Web contains a vast amount of information on a wide variety of topics. While much of the information is factual, other information may be misleading, biased, or just plain wrong. As more and more people turn to the Web for information, it is crucial that they take the time to determine if the information they obtain and pass on to others is accurate. There have been numerous cases of information intended as a joke being restated on a Web site as fact, statements being quoted out of context (which changed the meaning from the original intent), and hoaxes circulated via e-mail. Consequently, use common sense when evaluating what you read online, and double-check information before passing it on to others.

One way to evaluate online content is by its source. If you obtain information from a news source that you trust, you should feel confident that the accuracy of its online information is close to that of its offline counterpart. For information about a particular product, go to the originating company. For government information, government Web sites are your best source for fact checking. There are also independent Web sites (such as the *Snopes.com* Web site shown in Figure 1-31) that report on the validity of current online rumors and stories.

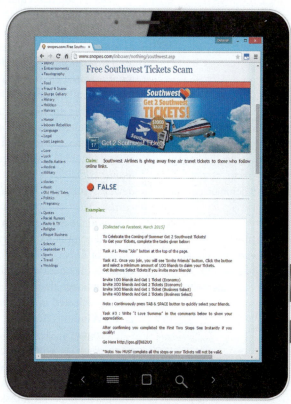

robert_s/Shutterstock.com; Snopes.com

# SUMMARY

## TECHNOLOGY IN YOUR LIFE

Computers and other techology appear almost everywhere in today's world, and most people need to use a computer or a computerized device frequently on the job, at home, at school, or while on the go. **Computer literacy**, which is being familiar with basic computer concepts, helps individuals feel comfortable using computers and is a necessary skill for everyone today.

Computers abound in today's homes, schools, workplaces, and other locations. Most students and employees need to use a computer for productivity, research, or other important tasks. Individuals often use computers at home and/or carry portable computers or smartphones with them to remain in touch with others or to use Internet resources on a continual basis. Individuals also frequently encounter computers while on the go, such as *consumer kiosks* and *point-of-sale (POS) systems*.

## WHAT IS A COMPUTER AND WHAT DOES IT DO?

A **computer** is a *programmable* electronic device that accepts **input**; performs **processing** operations; **outputs** the results; and provides **storage** for data, programs, or output when needed. Most computers today also have **communications** capabilities. This progression of input, processing, output, and storage is sometimes called the *information processing cycle*.

**Data** is the raw, unorganized facts that are input into the computer to be processed. Data that the computer has processed into a useful form is called **information**. Data can exist in many forms, representing text, graphics, audio, and video.

One of the first calculating devices was the *abacus*. Early computing devices that predate today's computers include the *slide rule*, the *mechanical calculator*, and Dr. Herman Hollerith's *Punch Card Tabulating Machine and Sorter*. *First-generation computers*, such as *ENIAC* and *UNIVAC*, were powered by *vacuum tubes*; *second-generation computers* used *transistors*; and *third-generation computers* were possible because of the invention of the *integrated circuit (IC)*. Today's *fourth-generation computers* use *microprocessors* and are frequently connected to the *Internet* and other *networks*. *Fifth-generation computers* are emerging and are, at the present time, based on *artificial intelligence*.

A computer is made up of **hardware** (the actual physical equipment that makes up the computer system) and **software** (the computer's programs). Common hardware components include the *keyboard* and *mouse (input devices)*, the *CPU (a processing device)*, *monitors/display screens* and *printers (output devices)*, and *storage media* and *storage devices* (such as *DVDs, DVD drives, hard drives, USB flash drives*, and *flash memory cards*). Most computers today also include a *modem*, *network adapter*, or other type of *communications device* to allow users to connect to the Internet or other network.

All computers need *system software*, namely an **operating system** (usually *Windows*, *OS X*, or *Linux*), to function. The operating system assists with the **boot** process, and then controls the operation of the computer, such as to allow users to run other types of software and to manage their files. Most software programs today use a variety of graphical objects that are selected to tell the computer what to do. The basic workspace for Windows' users is the **Windows desktop**.

Programs designed to allow people to perform specific tasks or applications, such as word processing, Web browsing, photo touch-up, and so on are called **application software (apps)**. Software programs are written using a *programming language*. Programs are written by *programmers*; *computer users* are the people who use computers to perform tasks or obtain information.

## COMPUTERS TO FIT EVERY NEED

**Embedded computers** are built into products (such as cars and household appliances) to give them added functionality. **Mobile devices** are small devices (such as *mobile phones* and **tablets**) with computing or Internet capabilities; an Internet-enabled mobile phone is called a **smartphone**.

Small computers used by individuals at home or work are called **personal computers** (**PCs**) or **microcomputers**. Most personal computers today are either **desktop computers** or **portable computers** (**notebook computers, laptop computers, tablet computers, hybrid notebook-tablet computers,** and **netbooks**) and typically conform to either the *PC-compatible* or *Mac* standard. **Thin clients** are designed solely to access a network; **Internet appliances** are ordinary devices that can be used to access the Internet.

Medium-sized computers, or **servers**, are used in many businesses to host data and programs to be accessed via the company network. A growing trend is **virtualization**, such as creating separate virtual environments on a single server that act as separate servers or delivering each users' desktop to his or her device. The powerful computers used by most large businesses and organizations to perform the information processing necessary for day-to-day operations are called **mainframe computers**. The very largest, most powerful computers, which typically run one application at a time, are **supercomputers**.

**Chapter Objective 6:**
List the six basic types of computers, giving at least one example of each type of computing device and stating what that type of device might be used for.

## COMPUTER NETWORKS AND THE INTERNET

**Computer networks** are used to connect individual computers and related devices so that users can share hardware, software, and data as well as communicate with one another. The **Internet** is a worldwide collection of networks. Typically, individual users connect to the Internet by connecting to computers belonging to an **Internet service provider** (**ISP**)—a company that provides Internet access, usually for a fee. One resource available through the Internet is the **World Wide Web** (**Web**)—an enormous collection of **Web pages** located on **Web servers**. The starting page for a **Web site** (a related group of Web pages) is called the *home page* for that site. Web pages are viewed with a **Web browser**, are connected with **hyperlinks**, and can be used for many helpful activities.

To access a computer network, you need some type of *modem* or *network adapter*. To access the Internet, an Internet service provider (ISP) is also used. **Internet addresses** are used to identify resources on the Internet and include numerical **IP addresses** and text-based **domain names** (used to identify computers), **Uniform Resource Locators** or **URLs** (used to identify Web pages), and **e-mail addresses** (a combination of a **username** and domain name that is used to send an individual e-mail messages).

Web pages are displayed by clicking hyperlinks or by typing appropriate URLs in the browser's *Address bar. Favorites/Bookmarks* and the *History list* can be used to redisplay a previously visited Web page and *search sites* can be used to locate Web pages matching specified criteria. **Electronic mail** (**e-mail**) is used to send electronic messages over the Internet.

**Chapter Objective 7:**
Explain what a network, the Internet, and the World Wide Web are, as well as how computers, people, and Web pages are identified on the Internet.

**Chapter Objective 8:**
Describe how to access a Web page and navigate through a Web site.

## TECHNOLOGY AND SOCIETY

Computers and devices based on related technology have become indispensable tools for modern life, making ordinary tasks easier and quicker than ever before and helping make today's worker more productive than ever before. In addition to the benefits, however, there are many risks and societal implications related to our heavy use of the Internet and the vast amount of information available through the Internet. Issues include privacy and security risks and concerns (such as *malware* and *spam*), the differences in online and offline communications, the anonymity factor, and the amount of unreliable information that can be found on the Internet.

**Chapter Objective 9:**
Discuss the societal impact of computers and technology, including some benefits and risks related to their prominence in our society.

# REVIEW ACTIVITIES

## KEY TERM MATCHING

a. computer

b. hardware

c. Internet

d. processing

e. software

f. storage

g. supercomputer

h. tablet computer

i. Uniform Resource Locator (URL)

j. Web site

**Instructions:** Match each key term on the left with the definition on the right that best describes it.

1. _____ A collection of related Web pages usually belonging to an organization or individual.

2. _____ An Internet address, usually beginning with http:// or https://, that uniquely identifies a Web page.

3. _____ A programmable, electronic device that accepts data input, performs processing operations on that data, and outputs and stores the results.

4. _____ A portable computer about the size of a notebook that is designed to be used with a digital pen or touch input.

5. _____ Performing operations on data that has been input into a computer to convert that input to output.

6. _____ The operation of saving data, programs, or output for future use.

7. _____ The fastest, most expensive, and most powerful type of computer.

8. _____ The instructions, also called computer programs, that are used to tell a computer what it should do.

9. _____ The largest and most well-known computer network, linking billions of devices all over the world.

10. _____ The physical parts of a computer system, such as the keyboard, monitor, printer, and so forth.

## SELF-QUIZ

**Instructions:** Circle **T** if the statement is true, **F** if the statement is false, or write the best answer in the space provided. **Answers for the self-quiz are located in the References and Resources Guide at the end of the book.**

1. **T   F**   A mouse is one common input device.

2. **T   F**   Software includes all the physical parts of a computer.

3. **T   F**   A computer can run without an operating system if it has good application software.

4. **T   F**   One of the most common types of home computers is the notebook computer.

5. **T   F**   Apple Watch is an example of a netbook.

6. _____ is the operation in which data is entered into the computer.

7. A(n) _____ computer is a portable computer designed to function as both a notebook and a tablet PC.

8. _____ is frequently used with servers today to create several separate environments on a single server that function as separate servers.

9. Text or an image on a Web page that is clicked to access additional Web resources is called a(n) _____.

**10.** Write the number of the term that best matches each of the following descriptions in the blank to the left of its description.

**a.** _____ Allows access to resources located on the Internet.

**b.** _____ Supervises the running of all other programs on the computer.

**c.** _____ Enables users to perform specific tasks on a computer.

**d.** _____ Allows the creation of application programs.

1. Application software
2. Operating system
3. Programming language
4. Web browser

---

---

**1.** For the following list of computer hardware devices, indicate the principal function of each device by writing the appropriate letter—I (input device), O (output device), S (storage device), P (processing device), or C (communications device)—in the space provided.

**a.** CPU _____     **d.** Keyboard _____     **g.** Speakers _____

**b.** Monitor _____     **e.** Hard drive _____     **h.** DVD drive _____

**c.** Mouse _____     **f.** Modem _____     **i.** GPU _____

**2.** Supply the missing words to complete the following statements.

**a.** The Internet is an example of a(n) _____, a collection of computers and other devices connected together to share resources and communicate with each other.

**b.** The starting page for a Web site is called the site's _____.

**c.** For the e-mail address *jsmith@cengage.com*, *jsmith* is the _____ and *cengage.com* is the _____ name.

**d.** The e-mail address pronounced *bill gee at microsoft dot com* is written _____.

**3.** What are three differences between a desktop computer and a portable computer?

**4.** List two reasons why a business may choose to network its employees' computers.

**5.** If a computer manufacturer called Apex created a home page for the Web, what would its URL likely be? Also, supply an appropriate e-mail address for yourself, assuming that you are employed by that company.

---

**1.** There is usually a positive side and a negative side to each new technological improvement. Select a technology you use every day and consider its benefits and risks. What benefits does the technology provide? Are there any risks involved and, if so, how can they be minimized? If you chose not to use this technology because of the possible risks associated with it, how would your life be affected? Who should determine if the benefits of a new technology outweigh the potential risks? Consumers? The government?

**2.** The ubiquitous nature of mobile phones (and, soon, wearables) today brings tremendous convenience to our lives, but will misuse of new improvements to this technology result in the loss of that convenience? For instance, camera phones are now banned in many fitness centers, park restrooms, and other similar facilities because some people have used them inappropriately to take compromising photos, and smartphones are banned in many classrooms because of the use of phones by dishonest students to cheat on exams. Do you think these reactions to the misuse of technology are justified? Is there another way to ensure the appropriate use of technology without banning its use for all individuals? Should there be more stringent consequences for those who use technology for illegal or unethical purposes?

# PROJECTS

1. **Wearables** As discussed in this chapter, wearables (computing devices that you wear on your body instead of carry) are a hot trend today.

   For this project, select one type of wearable to research, such as a smart watch, fitness band, or smart glasses. Determine the main purpose of your selected wearable, such as the type of data it collects, any notifications it provides, and if it is designed to work alone or in conjunction with another device. Select two possible products and compare and contrast them considering features such as battery life, compatibility with other devices, how they are recharged, how they share the data they collect, and cost. Do you think this type of wearable would be useful? Are there any privacy risks with the way it collects and shares data? Would you want to buy any of the products you researched? Why or why not? At the conclusion of your research, prepare a one-page summary of your findings and opinions and submit it to your instructor.

2. **Buying a New PC** New personal computers are widely available directly from manufacturers, as well as in retail, computer, electronic, and warehouse stores. Some stores carry only standard configurations as set up by the manufacturers; others allow you to customize a system.

   For this project, assume that you are in the market for a new personal computer. Give some thought to the type of computer (such as desktop, notebook, tablet, or hybrid notebook-tablet) that best fits your lifestyle and the tasks you need it to perform (such as the application programs you plan to use, how many programs you expect to use at one time, and how fast you desire the response time to be). Make a list of your hardware and software requirements (refer to the "Guide to Buying a PC" in the References and Resources Guide at the end of this book, if needed), being as specific as possible. By researching newspaper ads, manufacturer Web sites, and/or systems for sale at local stores, find three computing devices that meet your minimum requirements. Prepare a one-page comparison chart, listing each requirement and how each device meets or exceeds it. Also include any additional features each device has, and information regarding the brand, price, delivery time, shipping, sales tax, and warranty for each device. On your comparison sheet, mark the computing device that you would prefer to buy and write one paragraph explaining why. Turn in your comparison sheet and summary to your instructor, stapled to copies of the printed ads, specifications printed from Web sites, or other written documentation that you collected during this project.

3. **The Internet** The Internet and World Wide Web are handy tools that can help you research topics covered in this textbook, complete many of the projects, and perform the online activities available via the textbook's Web site that are designed to enhance your learning and help you prepare for exams on the content covered in this textbook.

   For this project, use an Internet-enabled device to perform the following tasks, then submit your results and printout to your instructor. (Note: Some of the answers will vary from student to student.)

   a. Open a browser and the Google search site. Enter the search terms *define: Internet* to search for definitions of that term. Click on one result to display the definition. Use your browser's *Print* option (or *Ctrl+P*) to print the page.

   b. Click your browser's *Back* button to return to the Google home page. Use your browser's Bookmark or Favorites feature to bookmark the page. Close your browser.

   c. Reopen your browser and use its Bookmark or Favorites feature to redisplay the Google home page.

   d. Google yourself to see if you can find any information online. On your printout from part a, indicate how many hits were returned for this search and if any of the hits on the first page really contained information about you.

4. **Gossip Sites** A recent trend on college campuses today is the use of campus gossip sites, where students can post campus-related news, rumors, and basic gossip. These sites were originally set up to promote free speech and to allow participants to publish comments anonymously without repercussions from school administrators, professors, and other officials. However, they are now being used to post vicious comments about others. What do you think of campus gossip sites? Is it ethical to post a rumor about another individual on these sites? How would you feel if you read a posting about yourself on a gossip site? School administrators cannot regulate the content because the sites are not sponsored or run by the college, and federal law prohibits Web hosts from being liable for the content posted by its users. Is this ethical? What if a posting leads to a criminal act, such as a rape, murder, or suicide? Who, if anyone, should be held responsible?

For this project, form an opinion about the ethical ramifications of gossip Web sites and be prepared to discuss your position (in class, via an online class forum, or via a class blog, depending on your instructor's directions). You may also be asked to write a short paper expressing your opinion.

**ETHICS IN ACTION**

5. **Online Education** The amount of distance learning available through the Internet and World Wide Web has exploded in the last couple of years. A few years ago, it was possible to take an occasional course online—now, an entire college degree can be earned online.

For this project, look into the online education options available at your school and two other colleges or universities. Compare and contrast the programs in general, including whether or not the institution is accredited, the types of courses available online, whether or not an entire certificate or degree can be earned online, and the required fees. Next, select one online course and research it more closely. Find out how the course works in an online format—including whether or not any face-to-face class time is required, whether assignments and exams are submitted online, which software programs are required, and other course requirements—and determine if you would be interested in taking that course. Share your findings with the class in the form of a short presentation. The presentation should not exceed 10 minutes and should make use of one or more presentation aids, such as a whiteboard, handouts, or a computer-based slide presentation (your instructor may provide additional requirements). You may also be asked to submit a summary of the presentation to your instructor.

**PRESENTATION/ DEMONSTRATION**

6. **Should Social Media Activity Cost You a Job?** When you apply for a new job, there's a good chance that the company will take a look at your social media activity, such as your Facebook page, blog activity, and even Craigslist listings. In fact, many companies now require job applicants to pass a social media background check before offering them a job. Companies are trying to protect themselves by looking for such things as racist remarks and illegal activities, as well as get a feel for whether or not an individual would be a good fit for the company. But should individuals have to risk losing a job if they post a photo of themselves in a racy Halloween costume or make an offhand comment that an employer may misinterpret? What if a company denies you a job based on inaccurate information or information they wouldn't be allowed to ask in a job interview, such as information relating to your age, race, gender, religion, and so forth? And what if someone else posts and tags a questionable photo of you— should a potential employer be able to use that or other third-party information to make a decision about your future? To be safe, should job applicants have to abstain from social media activity in order to protect themselves, even though such sites are typically viewed as places to casually interact with others on personal free time? Or is everything a potential employer finds online fair game?

Pick a side on this issue, form an opinion and gather supporting evidence, and be prepared to discuss and defend your position in a classroom debate or in a one- to two-page paper, depending on your instructor's directions.

**BALANCING ACT**

# Computers and Technology

Courtesy of D-Link Systems

**D-Link®**
Building Networks for People

Daniel Kelley is the Vice President of Marketing for D-Link Systems, Inc. and is responsible for connectivity solutions tailored for home and business users. He has more than 15 years of professional marketing experience and holds a Bachelor of Arts degree in communications. As a result of Daniel's leadership and thriving marketing programs, many of the programs initiated in North America, including the implementation of numerous social media campaigns hosted on D-Link's social media platforms, have been adopted worldwide.

**A conversation with DANIEL KELLEY**
**Vice President, Marketing, D-Link Systems, Inc.**

*"Technology advancements, such as the use of 3D printers to create live tissue that can be used for replacing lost body parts, can have a very positive impact on our health and wellness."*

### My Background . . .

As the Vice President of Marketing for D-Link Systems, Inc., I am responsible for the overall marketing and branding of the company and its products. My focus is on creating demand and loyalty from customers through a range of disciplines including advertising, sponsorships, press relations, social media, and channel marketing. Although I hold a degree in communications, which helped launch my career in marketing, I attribute most of my skills to real-world marketing experience and constantly challenging myself to learn and stay on top of the latest marketing tactics, platforms, and trends.

### It's Important to Know . . .

**The evolution from the first massively sized computers to today's small devices, such as the iPhone, has created a major shift in the industry.** Once the average consumer could get a powerful PC in his or her home, it started what we now view as the natural integration of technology in our daily lives. Putting a full-fledged computer with virtually unlimited potential into one's pocket has changed how we interact with information and with others in ways we're still discovering.

**Software is the interactive way a customer sees and uses a device, such as a PC, tablet, or phone.** Software—in the form of applications (or apps)—allows us to utilize the hardware of the machine itself in ways that are seemingly unending.

**Social media's influence will continue to grow and impact how we communicate.** The noticeable shift from customers trusting impersonal third-party reviews of products and services to those of friends, family members, and others via social media sites is changing the way businesses market themselves and communicate with customers. We've also seen a rapid adoption of photo-focused and short video platforms such as Vine and Instagram, which is a key indicator that individuals are looking to capture and share more photos and videos not only for entertainment but also for everyday interactions.

### How I Use this Technology . . .

Growing up, I always had an interest in all things creative and spent much of my time drawing, painting, and doing other creative projects. I carried this interest through my education, learning design graphics, animation, video, and Web development programs. The knowledge of these programs and my eye for design helps me provide direction on creative projects and allows me to dive in and give more specific examples or direction as needed. Today, I also use a laptop, tablet, and my smartphone every day to work and communicate with others from home, the office, and while traveling. My most used app is Evernote, which helps me create and keep track of notes and ideas across all of my devices.

## What the Future Holds . . .

One of the trends I personally find the most interesting is the rapid evolution of wearable technology. With the introduction of Google Glass and wellness-focused products such as FitBit, I see a very rapid adoption of new solutions designed to integrate technology with our clothing and accessories, which will lead to an entirely new way of interacting with information in our daily lives. We've become empowered in ways never dreamed of just decades ago, with endless information and new communication vehicles at our fingertips, and we've seen a rapid and dramatic shift from face-to-face conversations and phone calls to texting, e-mail, and social media as preferred ways to communicate. This shift will continue to accelerate, with video calls and video messages becoming a primary communication medium. However, we have to be careful we don't become more isolated and detached from others in public social situations so we can continue to interact positively with each other in the future.

Another concern for the future is privacy. As we put more of ourselves out there in the cloud, we make ourselves more vulnerable. With any new technology or service, there are going to be those looking to exploit it and cause harm to others for personal gain and we've seen how private information doesn't necessarily remain private. This should encourage individuals to protect themselves as much as possible, such as using strong online passwords and just using common sense when determining what to share online.

I'm hoping that one of the biggest impacts of technology in the future is in the medical field or solving big problems like world hunger. Technology advancements, such as the use of 3D printers to create live tissue that can be used for replacing lost body parts, can have a very positive impact on our health and wellness. This same 3D printing technology has the potential to create a large food supply (utilizing protein "ink" from meal worms, for instance) for third-world countries where food is desperately needed. As much as technology advances our entertainment and social interaction, I am more interested to see how it can actually improve how we take care of those in need.

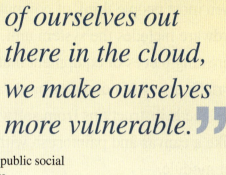

**❝** *As we put more of ourselves out there in the cloud, we make ourselves more vulnerable.* **❞**

## My Advice to Students . . .

Jump in with both feet. Take things apart, build things, and constantly learn new things through education and resources such as the Internet and books. We are living in a truly remarkable time where opportunities abound in the tech field, and those who apply themselves and commit to learning, trying, and doing will have an upper hand for building a career or leading the next wave of where technology can take us.

---

### Discussion Question

Daniel Kelley views emerging technology, such as 3D printers, as a possible way to solve world hunger and to facilitate medical advancements. What technological, legal, and ethical issues may need to be resolved before we use 3D printers to print replacement body parts or food? How, if at all, should use of these devices be regulated? What if people want to use the technology to create additional body parts for a fashion statement—do you foresee that becoming an issue in the future? Why or why not? Be prepared to discuss your position (in class, via an online class forum, or via a class blog, depending on your instructor's directions). You may also be asked to write a short paper expressing your opinion.

---

**>** **For more information about D-Link, visit the official Web site at us.dlink.com. D-Link also communicates through social sites (facebook.com/dlink and twitter.com/dlink), and has a resource center located at resource.dlink.com.**

# module

# Hardware

When most people think of computers, images of hardware usually fill their minds. Hardware includes the system unit, keyboard, mouse, monitor, printer, and all the other interesting pieces of equipment that make up a computer system. This module explores the rich variety of computer hardware available today. But, as you already know, hardware needs instructions from software in order to function. Hardware without software is like a canvas and paintbrush without an artist. Software is discussed in detail in the next module.

This module divides coverage of hardware into three parts. Chapter 2 describes the hardware located inside the system unit, which is the main box of the computer and where most of the work of a computer is performed. Chapter 3 discusses the different types of devices that can be used for storage. Chapter 4 covers the wide variety of hardware that can be used for input and output.

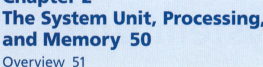

*"Hardware will continue to shrink in size while increasing in capabilities."*

For more comments from Guest Expert **Ali Moayer** of Logitech, see the **Expert Insight on . . . Hardware** feature at the end of the module.

# chapter 2

# The System Unit, Processing, and Memory

**After completing this chapter, you will be able to do the following:**

1. Understand how data and programs are represented to a computing device and be able to identify a few of the coding systems used to accomplish this.

2. Explain the functions of the hardware components commonly found inside the system unit, such as the CPU, GPU, memory, buses, and expansion cards.

3. Describe how peripheral devices or other hardware can be added to a computer or mobile device.

4. Understand how the CPU and memory components process program instructions and data.

5. Name and evaluate several strategies that can be used today for speeding up the operations of a computer.

6. List some processing technologies that may be used in future computing devices.

## outline

# OVERVIEW

The system unit of a computing device is sometimes thought of as a mysterious "black box" and often the user does not have much understanding of what happens inside it. In this chapter, we demystify the system unit by looking inside the box and closely examining the functions of the parts. Consequently, the chapter gives you a feel for what the CPU, memory, and other devices commonly found inside the system unit do and how they work together to perform the tasks that the user requests.

To start, we discuss how a computing device represents data and program instructions. Specifically, we talk about the codes that computers and mobile devices use to translate data back and forth from the symbols that these devices can manipulate to the symbols that people are accustomed to using. These topics lead to a discussion of how the CPU and memory are arranged with other components inside the system unit and the characteristics of those components. Next, we discuss how a CPU performs processing tasks. Finally, we look at strategies that can be used today to speed up a computer, plus some strategies that may be used to create faster and better devices in the future.

Many of you will apply this chapter's content to conventional personal computers, such as desktop and portable computers. However, it is important to realize that the principles and procedures discussed in this chapter apply to other types of computers as well, such as those embedded in toys, consumer devices, household appliances, cars, and other devices, and those used with mobile devices, servers, mainframes, and supercomputers. ■

## DATA AND PROGRAM REPRESENTATION

In order to be understood by a computer, data and software programs need to be represented appropriately. Consequently, *coding systems* are used to represent data and programs in a manner that can be understood by the computer. These concepts are discussed in the next few sections.

### Digital Data Representation

Virtually all computers today—such as the embedded computers, mobile devices, personal computers, servers, mainframes, and supercomputers discussed in Chapter 1—are *digital computers*. Digital computers can understand only two (*binary*) states, usually thought of as *off* and *on* and represented by the digits 0 and 1. Consequently, all data processed by a computer must be in binary form (0s and 1s). The 0s and 1s used to represent data can be represented in a variety of ways, such as with an open or closed circuit, the absence or presence of electronic current, two different types of magnetic alignment on a storage medium, and so on (see Figure 2-1).

Regardless of their physical representations, these 0s and 1s are commonly referred to as bits, a computing term

**FIGURE 2-1**

**Ways of representing 0 and 1.** Computers recognize only two states—off and on—usually represented by 0 and 1.

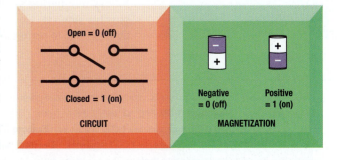

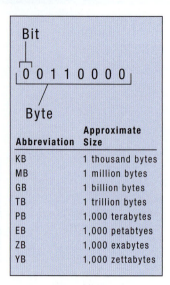

| Abbreviation | Approximate Size |
|---|---|
| KB | 1 thousand bytes |
| MB | 1 million bytes |
| GB | 1 billion bytes |
| TB | 1 trillion bytes |
| PB | 1,000 terabytes |
| EB | 1,000 petabtyes |
| ZB | 1,000 exabytes |
| YB | 1,000 zettabytes |

**FIGURE 2-2**

**Bits and bytes.**
Document size, storage capacity, and memory capacity are all measured in bytes.

derived from the phrase *binary digits*. A **bit** is the smallest unit of data that a computer can recognize. Therefore, the input you enter via a keyboard, the software program you use to play your music collection, the term paper stored on your USB flash drive, and the digital photos located on your smartphone are all just groups of bits. Representing data in a form that can be understood by a digital computer is called *digital data representation*.

Because most computers can only understand data and instructions in binary form, binary can be thought of as the computer's *natural language*. People, of course, do not speak in binary. For example, you are not likely to go up to a friend and say,

0100100001001001

which translates into the word "HI" using the ASCII binary coding system, which is discussed shortly. People communicate with one another in their natural languages, such as English, Chinese, Spanish, and French. For example, this book is written in English, which uses a 26-character alphabet. In addition, most countries use a numbering system with 10 possible symbols—0 through 9. As already mentioned, however, computers understand only 0s and 1s. For us to interact with a computer, a translation process from our natural language to 0s and 1s and then back again to our natural language is required. When we enter data into a computer, it  translates the natural-language symbols we input into binary 0s and 1s. After processing the data, the computer translates and outputs the resulting information in a form that we can understand.

A bit by itself typically represents only a fraction of a piece of data. Consequently, large numbers of bits are needed to represent a written document, computer program, digital photo, music file, or virtually any other type of data. Eight bits grouped together are collectively referred to as a **byte**. It is important to be familiar with this concept because *byte* terminology is frequently used in a variety of computer contexts, such as to indicate the size of a document or digital photo, the amount of memory a computer has, or the amount of room left on a storage medium. Because these quantities often involve thousands or millions of bytes, prefixes are commonly used in conjunction with the term *byte* to represent larger amounts of data (see Figure 2-2). For instance, a **kilobyte** (**KB**) is approximately 1,000 bytes; a **megabyte** (**MB**) is about 1 million bytes; a **gigabyte** (**GB**) is about 1 billion bytes; a **terabyte** (**TB**) is about 1 trillion bytes; a **petabyte** (**PB**) is about 1,000 terabytes; an **exabyte** (**EB**) is about 1,000 petabytes; a **zettabyte** (**ZB**) is about 1,000 exabytes; and a **yottabyte** (**YB**) is about 1,000 zettabytes. Using these definitions, 5 KB is about 5,000 bytes, 10 MB is about 10 million bytes, and 2 TB is about 2 trillion bytes.

Computers represent programs and data through a variety of binary-based coding systems. The coding system used depends primarily on the type of data that needs to be represented; the most common coding systems are discussed in the next few sections.

## Representing Numerical Data: The Binary Numbering System

A *numbering system* is a way of representing numbers. The numbering system we commonly use is called the **decimal numbering system** because it uses 10 symbols—the digits 0, 1, 2, 3, 4, 5, 6, 7, 8, and 9—to represent all possible numbers. Numbers greater than nine, such as 21 and 683, are represented using combinations of these 10 symbols. The **binary numbering system** uses only two symbols—the digits 0 and 1—to represent all possible numbers. Consequently, computers use the binary numbering system to represent numbers and to perform math computations.

---

> **Bit.** The smallest unit of data a digital computer can recognize; represented by a 0 or a 1. > **Byte.** A group of 8 bits. > **Kilobyte (KB).** Approximately 1 thousand bytes. > **Megabyte (MB).** Approximately 1 million bytes. > **Gigabyte (GB).** Approximately 1 billion bytes. > **Terabyte (TB).** Approximately 1 trillion bytes. > **Petabyte (PB).** Approximately 1,000 terabytes. > **Exabyte (EB).** Approximately 1,000 petabytes. > **Zettabyte (ZB).** Approximately 1,000 exabytes. > **Yottabyte (YB).** Approximately 1,000 zettabytes. > **Decimal numbering system.** The numbering system that represents all numbers using 10 symbols (0–9). > **Binary numbering system.** The numbering system that represents all numbers using just two symbols (0 and 1).

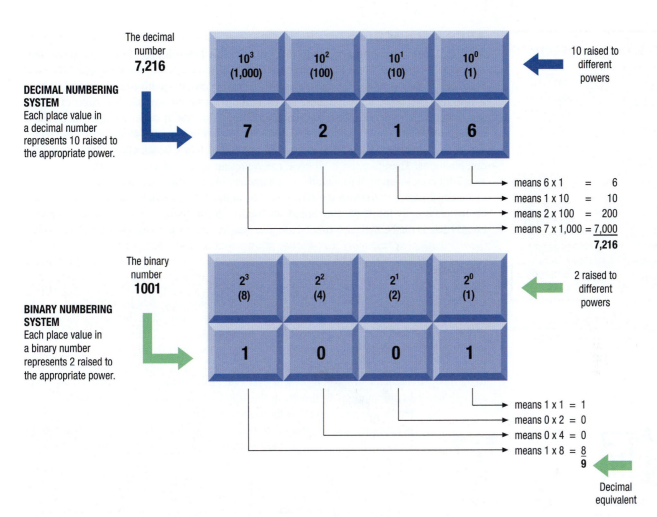

**HW**

In both numbering systems, the position of each digit determines the power, or exponent, to which the *base number* (10 for decimal or 2 for binary) is raised. In the decimal numbering system, going from right to left, the first position or column (the ones column) represents $10^0$ or 1; the second column (the tens column) represents $10^1$ or 10; the third column (the hundreds column) represents $10^2$ or 100; and so forth. Therefore, as Figure 2-3 shows, the decimal number 7,216 is understood as follows: $7 \times 10^3 + 2 \times 10^2 + 1 \times 10^1 + 6 \times 10^0$ or $7,000 + 200 + 10 + 6$ or 7,216.

In binary, the concept is the same but the columns have different place values. For example, the far-right column is the ones column (for $2^0$), the second column is the twos column ($2^1$), the third column is the fours column ($2^2$), and so on. Therefore, although 1001 represents "one thousand one" in decimal notation, 1001 represents "nine" ($1 \times 2^3 + 0 \times 2^2 + 0 \times 2^1 + 1 \times 2^0$ or $8 + 0 + 0 + 1$ or 9) in the binary numbering system, as illustrated in the bottom half of Figure 2-3.

**FIGURE 2-3**
**Examples of using the decimal and binary numbering systems.**

## Coding Systems for Text-Based Data

While numeric data is represented by the binary numbering system, text-based data is represented by binary coding systems specifically developed for text-based data—namely, ASCII, EBCDIC, and Unicode. These codes are used to represent all characters that can appear in text data—such as numbers, letters, and special characters and symbols like the dollar sign, comma, percent symbol, and mathematical symbols.

**TIP**

For more information about and examples of converting between numbering systems, see the "A Look at Numbering Systems" section in the References and Resources Guide at the end of this book.

| CHARACTER | ASCII |
|---|---|
| 0 | 00110000 |
| 1 | 00110001 |
| 2 | 00110010 |
| 3 | 00110011 |
| 4 | 00110100 |
| 5 | 00110101 |
| A | 01000001 |
| B | 01000010 |
| C | 01000011 |
| D | 01000100 |
| E | 01000101 |
| F | 01000110 |
| + | 00101011 |
| ! | 00100001 |
| # | 00100011 |

**FIGURE 2-4**
Some extended ASCII code examples.

CHINESE        GREEK        HEBREW

AMHARIC        TIBETAN        RUSSIAN

**FIGURE 2-5**
Unicode. Many characters, such as these, can be represented by Unicode but not by ASCII or EBCDIC.

## ASCII and EBCDIC

**ASCII (American Standard Code for Information Interchange)** is the coding system traditionally used with personal computers. *EBCDIC (Extended Binary-Coded Decimal Interchange Code)* was developed by IBM, primarily for use with mainframes. ASCII is a 7-digit (7-bit) code, although there are several different 8-bit *extended versions* of ASCII that contain additional symbols not included in the 7-bit ASCII code. The extended ASCII character sets (see some examples of 8-bit ASCII codes in Figure 2-4) and EBCDIC represent each character as a unique combination of 8 bits (1 byte), which allows 256 ($2^8$) unique combinations. Therefore, an 8-bit code can represent up to 256 characters (twice as many as a 7-bit code)—enough to include the characters used in the English alphabet, as well as some non-English characters, the 10 digits used in the decimal numbering system, the other characters usually found on a keyboard, and many special characters not included on a keyboard such as mathematical symbols, graphic symbols, and additional punctuation marks.

## Unicode

Unlike ASCII and EBCDIC, which are limited to only the Latin alphabet used with the English language, **Unicode** is a universal international coding standard designed to represent text-based data written in any ancient or modern language, including those with different alphabets, such as Chinese, Greek, Hebrew, Amharic, Tibetan, and Russian (see Figure 2-5). Unicode uniquely identifies each character using 0s and 1s, no matter which language, program, or computer platform is being used. It is a longer code, consisting of 8 to 32 bits per character, and can represent over one million characters, which is more than enough unique combinations to represent the standard characters in all the world's written languages, as well as thousands of mathematical and technical symbols, punctuation marks, and other symbols and signs. The biggest advantage of Unicode is that it can be used worldwide with consistent and unambiguous results.

Unicode is quickly replacing ASCII as the primary text-coding system. In fact, Unicode includes the ASCII character set so ASCII data can be converted easily to Unicode when needed. Unicode is used by most Web browsers and is widely used for Web pages and Web applications (Google data, for instance, is stored exclusively in Unicode). Most recent software programs, including the latest versions of Microsoft Windows, OS X, and Microsoft Office, also use Unicode, as do modern programming languages, such as Java and Python. Unicode is updated regularly to add new characters and new languages not originally encoded—the most recent version is *Unicode 8.0.*

## Coding Systems for Other Types of Data

So far, our discussion of coding systems has focused on numeric and text-based data, which consists of alphanumeric characters and special symbols, such as the comma and dollar sign. Multimedia data, such as graphics, audio, and video data, must also be represented in binary form in order to be used with a computer, as discussed next.

### Graphics Data

*Graphics data* consists of still images, such as photographs or drawings. One of the most common methods for storing graphics data is in the form of a bitmap image—an image made up of a grid of small dots, called pixels (short for *picture elements*), that are colored appropriately to represent an image. The color to be displayed at each pixel is represented by some combination of 0s and 1s, and the number of bits required to store the color for each pixel ranges from 1 to 24 bits. For example, each pixel in a *monochrome graphic* can be only one of two possible colors (such as black or white). These monochrome images require only one bit of storage space per pixel (for instance, the bit would contain a 1 when representing a pixel that should display as white, and the bit would contain a 0 for a pixel that should display as black). Images with more than two colors can use 4, 8, or 24 bits to store the color data for each pixel—this allows for 16 ($2^4$), 256 ($2^8$), or 16,777,216 ($2^{24}$) colors respectively, as shown in Figure 2-6.

The number of bits used per pixel depends on the type of image being stored; for instance, the *JPEG* images taken by most digital cameras today use 24-bit *true color images*. While this can result in large file sizes, images can typically be *compressed* to a smaller file size when needed, such as to send a lower-resolution version of an image via e-mail. Other common image formats include *TIF* (used with scanned images), *BMP* (created with some painting programs), *GIF* (an older format for Web page images), and *PNG* (a newer format for Web page images).

One sample pixel:
1110

**16-BIT IMAGE**
The color of each pixel is represented using 4 bits.

One sample pixel:
01110110

**256-BIT IMAGE**
The color of each pixel is represented using 8 bits.

One sample pixel:
101001100100110111001011

**TRUE COLOR IMAGE**
**(16.8 million colors)**
The color of each pixel is represented using 24 bits.

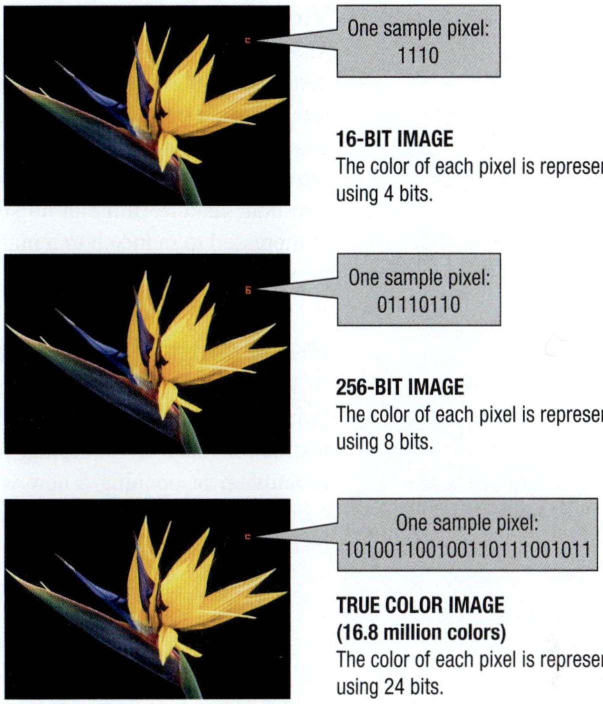

Source: United States Department of Agriculture

**FIGURE 2-6**

**Representing graphics data.**
With bitmapped images, the color of each pixel is represented by bits; the more bits used, the better the image quality.

## Audio Data

Like graphics data, *audio data*—such as a song or the sound of someone speaking—must be in digital form in order to be stored on a storage medium or processed by a computer. To convert analog sound to digital sound, several thousand *samples*—digital representations of the sound at particular moments—are taken every second. When the samples are played back in the proper order, they re-create the sound of the voice or music. For example, audio CDs record sound using 2-byte samples, which are sampled at a rate of 44,100 times per second. When these samples are played back at a rate of 44,100 samples per second, they sound like continuous voice or music. With so many samples, however, sound files take up a great deal of storage space—about 32 MB for a 3-minute stereo song (44,100 times × 2 bytes × 180 seconds × 2 channels).

Because of its large size, audio data is usually compressed to reduce its file size when it is transmitted over the Internet or stored on a smartphone or another device. For example, files that are *MP3-encoded*—that is, compressed with the *MP3 compression algorithm* developed by the *Motion Pictures Expert Group* (*MPEG*)—are about 10 times smaller than their uncompressed digital versions, so they download 10 times faster and take up one-tenth of the storage space. The actual storage size required depends on the *bit rate*—the number of bits to be transferred per second when the file is played—used when the file is initially created; audio files using the common bit rate of 128 *Kbps* (thousands of bits per second) are about one-tenth the size of the original CD-quality recording.

## ASK THE EXPERT

Courtesy Unicode Inc.

**Mark Davis,** President, The Unicode Consortium

**What should the average computer user know about Unicode?**

Whenever you read or write anything on a computer, you're using Unicode. Whenever you search on Google, Yahoo!, MSN, Wikipedia, or other Web sites, you're using Unicode. It's the way that text in all the world's languages can be stored and processed on computers.

### Video Data

*Video data*—such as home movies, feature films, video clips, and television shows—is displayed using a collection of frames; each frame contains a still image. When the frames are projected one after the other (typically at a rate of 24 *frames per second* (*fps*) for film-based video and 30 or 60 fps for video taken with digital video cameras), the illusion of movement is created. With so many frames, the amount of data involved in showing a two-hour feature film can be substantial. Fortunately, like audio data, video data can be compressed to reduce it to a manageable size. For example, a two-hour movie can be compressed to fit on a single DVD disc or to be delivered over the Web.

### Representing Software Programs: Machine Language

Just as numbers, text, and multimedia data must be represented by 0s and 1s, software programs must also be represented by 0s and 1s. Before a computer can execute any program instruction, such as requesting input from the user, moving a file from one storage device to another, or opening a new window on the screen, it must convert the instruction into a binary code known as **machine language**. An example of a typical machine language instruction is as follows:

$$01011000011100000000000100000010$$

A machine language instruction might look like a meaningless string of 0s and 1s, but it actually represents specific operations and storage locations. The 32-bit instruction shown here, for instance, moves data between two specific memory locations on one type of computer. Early computers required programs to be written in machine language, but today's computers allow programs to be written in a programming language, which is then translated by the computer into machine language in order to be understood by the computer. Programming languages and *language translators* are discussed in Chapter 11.

## INSIDE THE SYSTEM UNIT

The **system unit** is the main case of a computer or mobile device. It houses the processing hardware for that device, as well as other components, such as storage devices, the power supply, and cooling hardware. The system unit for a desktop computer often looks like a rectangular box, as in Figure 2-7. The system units for all-in-one computers, notebooks, tablets, and mobile devices are much smaller and are usually combined with the device's display screen to form a single piece of hardware (see one example in Figure 2-8). However, these system units have components that are similar to those found in desktop computers, the components just tend to be smaller and more integrated into the system unit. A system unit usually contains one or more processors, several types of memory, interfaces to connect external peripheral devices (such as printers), and other components all interconnected through sets of wires called buses on the motherboard. These components are discussed in detail in the next few sections.

### The Motherboard

A *circuit board* is a thin board containing *computer chips* and other electronic components. Computer chips, also called *integrated circuits* (*ICs*), contain interconnected components (such as *transistors*) that enable electrical current to perform particular functions. The main circuit board inside the system unit is called the **motherboard**.

---

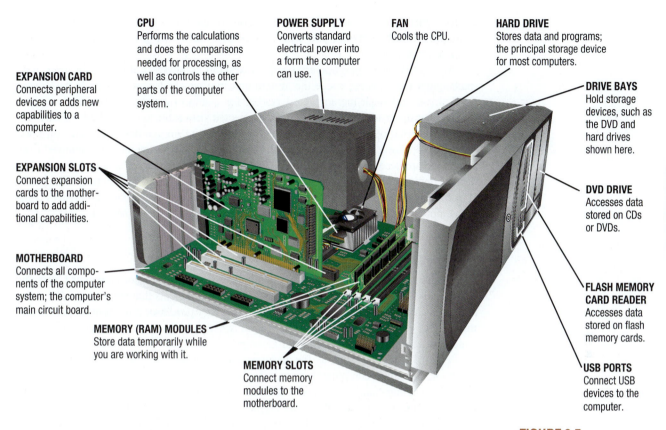

**CPU**
Performs the calculations and does the comparisons needed for processing, as well as controls the other parts of the computer system.

**POWER SUPPLY**
Converts standard electrical power into a form the computer can use.

**FAN**
Cools the CPU.

**HARD DRIVE**
Stores data and programs; the principal storage device for most computers.

**EXPANSION CARD**
Connects peripheral devices or adds new capabilities to a computer.

**EXPANSION SLOTS**
Connect expansion cards to the motherboard to add additional capabilities.

**MOTHERBOARD**
Connects all components of the computer system; the computer's main circuit board.

**MEMORY (RAM) MODULES**
Store data temporarily while you are working with it.

**MEMORY SLOTS**
Connect memory modules to the motherboard.

**DRIVE BAYS**
Hold storage devices, such as the DVD and hard drives shown here.

**DVD DRIVE**
Accesses data stored on CDs or DVDs.

**FLASH MEMORY CARD READER**
Accesses data stored on flash memory cards.

**USB PORTS**
Connect USB devices to the computer.

HW

As shown in Figure 2-7, the motherboard has a variety of chips, boards, and connectors attached to it. All devices used with a computer need to be connected via a wired or wireless connection to the motherboard. Typically, *external devices* (such as monitors, keyboards, mice, and printers) connect to the motherboard by plugging into a port—a special connector exposed through the exterior of the system unit case. The port is either built directly into the motherboard or created via an expansion card inserted into an expansion slot on the motherboard. Wireless external devices use either a *transceiver* that plugs into a port on the computer to transmit data between the wireless device and the motherboard or wireless networking technology (such as Bluetooth or Wi-Fi) that is integrated into the system unit. Ports and system expansion are discussed in more detail later in this chapter; wireless networking is covered in Chapter 7.

**FIGURE 2-7**
Inside a desktop system unit.

**FIGURE 2-8**
Inside a tablet system unit.

## The Power Supply and Drive Bays

Most personal computers plug into a standard electrical outlet. The *power supply* inside a computer delivers electricity to the computer via a power cord. Portable computers and mobile devices contain *rechargeable battery packs*, which are charged via a power outlet; some devices can be charged via a computer as well. One issue with newer portable computers and mobile devices is the growing use of built-in batteries. Although these batteries allow the devices to be lighter and are supposed to last for the typical life of the device, they are more difficult and expensive to replace if they fail. In fact, consumers often decide to just discard a device when its built-in battery fails, resulting in an increase

**CAMERA MODULE**

**PROCESSOR**
Contains a CPU and GPU.

**CHIPS**
Provide memory, storage, Wi-Fi and Bluetooth connectivity, and GPS capability.

**BATTERY**

**PORTS**
Connect HDMI and USB devices.

Source: NVIDIA Corporation

in electronic waste (e-waste). The ramifications of the growing amount of e-waste, such as discarded mobile phones and other electronics, that is being generated worldwide is discussed in Chapter 13.

Most conventional computers (such as desktop computers) also contain *drive bays* (rectangular metal racks) inside the system unit into which storage devices (a hard drive, DVD drive, and flash memory card reader, for instance) can be inserted and secured. Storage devices inside the system unit are connected via a cable to the motherboard, as well as to the internal power supply if the device requires it. Storage devices (such as a DVD drive) that are used with removable media that need to be inserted into and removed from the device are accessible through the front of the system unit (refer again to Figure 2-7). Storage devices (such as an internal hard drive) that are not used in conjunction with removable storage media are not visible outside the system unit. Many desktop computers come with empty drive bays so users can add additional storage devices as needed.

## Processors

Computers and mobile devices today contain one or more **processors** (such as CPUs and GPUs), which consist of a variety of circuitry and components that are packaged together and connected directly to the motherboard. The primary processor is the **central processing unit (CPU)**—also called the **microprocessor** when talking about personal computers—which does most of the processing for a computer. CPUs are typically designed for a specific type of computer, such as for desktop computers, servers, portable computers (like notebook and tablet computers), or mobile devices (like tablets and smartphones). Most desktop computers and servers today use Intel or Advanced Micro Devices (AMD) CPUs. Portable computers and mobile devices typically use an Intel or AMD *mobile processor* or a mobile processor manufactured by ARM or another company that makes mobile CPUs based on ARM CPU designs. In fact, many mobile processors (such as the *Snapdragon 800 series processors* from Qualcomm, the *Tegra X1* from NVIDIA, the *Exynos 7 Octa* from Samsung, and the *A8X* from Apple) are based on ARM processors, such as the ARM *Cortex-A72*. Some examples of common processors are shown in Figure 2-9.

Most CPUs today are **multi-core CPUs**; that is, CPUs that contain the processing components or *cores* of multiple independent processors on a single CPU. For example, **dual-core CPUs** contain two cores and **quad-core CPUs** contain four cores. Up until just a few years ago, most CPUs designed for desktop computers had only a single core; as a result, a common way to increase the amount of processing performed by the CPU was to increase the speed of the CPU. However, heat constraints are making it progressively more difficult to continue to increase CPU speed, so CPU manufacturers today are focusing on multi-core CPUs to increase the amount of processing that a CPU can do in a given time period.

Multi-core CPUs allow computers to work simultaneously on more than one task at a time, such as burning a DVD while surfing the Web, as well as to work faster within a single application if the software is designed to take advantage of multiple cores. Another benefit of multi-core CPUs is that they typically experience fewer heat problems than *single-core CPUs* because each core typically runs slower than a single-core CPU, although the total processing power of the multi-core CPU is greater. Multi-core CPUs also increase the performance of mobile devices while, at the same time, delivering better battery life. In addition, some CPUs are designed to turn individual parts of the processor off when they

---

>**Processor.** A chip (such as the CPU or GPU) that performs processing functions. >**Central processing unit (CPU).** The chip located on the motherboard of a computer that performs most of the processing for a computer. >**Microprocessor.** A central processing unit (CPU) for a personal computer. >**Multi-core CPU.** A CPU that contains the processing components or cores of more than one processor in a single CPU. >**Dual-core CPU.** A CPU that contains two separate processing cores. >**Quad-core CPU.** A CPU that contains four separate processing cores.

Four cores

Shared Level 3 cache memory

**SERVER PROCESSORS**     **DESKTOP PROCESSORS**

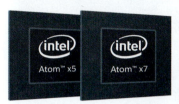

**MOBILE PROCESSORS**

| TYPE OF CPU | NAME | NUMBER OF CORES |
|---|---|---|
| SERVER | Intel Xeon (E7 family) | 4–18 |
| | AMD Opteron (6300 series) | 4–16 |
| DESKTOP | Intel Core i7 (6th gen) | 4–8 |
| | AMD FX | 4–8 |
| MOBILE (NOTEBOOKS) | Intel Core M | 2 |
| | Intel Atom x7 | 4 |
| | Intel Celeron | 1–4 |
| MOBILE (MOBILE DEVICES) | Intel Atom x5 | 4 |
| | ARM Cortex-A17 | 4 |
| | NVIDIA Tegra 4* | 4 |

\* Based on ARM Cortex-A15

Source: Intel Corporation; NVIDIA Corporation

HW

**FIGURE 2-9**
CPU examples.

are not needed to save power and then wake them up again as soon as they are needed, or to slow down the CPU whenever possible, in order to save power. Most CPUs today also support virtualization and other recent technologies.

CPUs used in desktop computers typically have 4 cores; server processors may have 15 cores or more. Mobile processors typically run a little slower than comparable desktop CPUs, but they are often multi-core and they run cooler and consume less power to allow devices to run longer on battery power without a recharge.

Another processor located inside the system unit is the **graphics processing unit (GPU)**, which takes care of the processing needed to display images (including still images, animations, and video)—and particularly 3D images—on the screen. While GPUs (one example of a *mobile GPU* is shown in Figure 2-10) can be located on the motherboard or on a video graphics card (as discussed later in this chapter), a growing trend is to integrate both the CPU and GPU into the CPU package. For instance, many AMD, Intel, and Qualcomm processors have integrated GPUs; AMD calls their integrated processors *APUs* or *accelerated processing units*. Mobile processors tend to integrate other capabilities into the processor package as well, such as support for multimedia capture and playback, GPS capabilities, and connectivity (cellular, Wi-Fi, USB, and/or Bluetooth capabilities, for instance). A processor that contains all the necessary capabilities for a single device is sometimes referred to as a *system-on-a-chip (SoC)*; the processor shown in Figure 2-8 is an SoC.

In addition to computers and mobile devices, processors are incorporated into a variety of products today, such as TVs, smart meters, cars, gaming consoles, exercise machines, electric toothbrushes, and ATM machines, as well as other computing hardware such as printers, digital cameras, and modems. The CPUs for these devices are typically different

**FIGURE 2-10**
A GPU.

Source: NVIDIA Corporation

>**Graphics processing unit (GPU).** The chip that does the processing needed to display images on the screen; can be located on the motherboard, inside the CPU, or on a video graphics board.

# TECHNOLOGY AND YOU

## Modular Phones

Want to easily replace your cracked smartphone screen or add a new feature? You may soon be in luck if *modular phones* become a reality. Currently in the development and testing stages, modular phones (such as Google's *Project Ara* prototype shown in the accompanying photo) allow individuals to create custom phones with the functions, modules, and appearance they wish. Modular phones start with basic modules (such as modules for the processor, memory, battery, camera, and screen) and then additional modules can be added as needed. Modules can be safely inserted and removed from the phone's basic *endoskeleton*, even while the device is powered on. In addition to enabling individuals to initially build the phone they want, modular phones give the user flexibility to add new modules whenever they are needed and only for as long as they are needed, such as to use a telephoto lens or heart rate monitor temporarily. Modular phones also reduce e-waste by enabling individuals to upgrade just the modules they need or replace only the module that is broken (such as sliding out a cracked screen module and inserting a new one), instead of discarding an old phone for an entirely new one.

Source: Google ATAP

**Google's modular smartphone prototype.**

from the ones used in personal computers and determine the processing capabilities of the device. For a look at an emerging type of smartphone that uses modules for the processor and other components, see the Technology and You box.

## Processing Speed

One measurement of the *processing speed* of a CPU is the *CPU clock speed*, which is typically rated in *megahertz* (*MHz*) or *gigahertz* (*GHz*). A CPU with a higher CPU clock speed means that more instructions can be processed per second than the same CPU with a lower CPU clock speed. For instance, a Core i7 processor running at 3.2 GHz would be faster than a Core i7 processor running at 2.66 GHz if all other components remain the same. CPUs for the earliest personal computers ran at less than 5 MHz; today's fastest CPUs designed for PCs have a clock speed of more than 5 GHz. Although CPU clock speed is an important factor in computer performance, other factors (such as the number of cores, the amount of memory, the speed of external storage devices, the GPU being used, and the bus width and bus speed) greatly affect the overall processing speed of the computer. As a result, computers today are typically classified less by CPU clock speed and more by the computer's overall processing speed or performance.

One measurement of overall processing speed is the maximum number of instructions the CPU can process per second—such as *megaflops*, *gigaflops*, and *teraflops* (millions, billions, and trillions of floating point operations per second, respectively). It is also common for experts associated with computer journals, technical Web sites, and other organizations to test the performance of CPUs. These tests—called *benchmark tests*—typically run the same series of programs on several computer systems that are identical except for one component (such as the CPU) and measure how long each task takes in order to determine the overall relative performance of the component being tested. Because the large number of factors affecting computer performance today makes it increasingly difficult for consumers to evaluate the performance of CPUs and computers, benchmark tests are becoming an extremely important resource for computer shoppers.

## Word Size

A computer *word* is the amount of data (typically measured in bits or bytes) that a CPU can manipulate at one time. In the past, CPUs used 32-bit words (referred to as *32-bit processors*); today, most CPUs are *64-bit processors* (that is, they can simultaneously process 64 bits, or 8 bytes, at one time). Usually, a larger word size allows for faster processing and the use of more RAM, provided the software being used is written to take advantage of 64-bit processing. For instance, a computer with a 64-bit processor running the 64-bit version of the Windows operating system can use more RAM and has a higher performance than the same computer running the regular 32-bit version of Windows. However, much of today's software is still 32-bit software.

## ASK THE EXPERT

*Courtesy ARM*

**ARM** **James Bruce,** Lead Mobile Strategist, ARM

**Does a smartphone need a multi-core processor?**

Multi-core processors allow smartphones to deliver increased performance, while delivering better battery life. The reason for this is that the tasks that run on a smartphone have widely different performance needs; for instance, compare writing an SMS text message with playing a 3D game.

To provide this scalability of performance and power in today's advanced chip manufacturing processes, it is better to have multiple smaller cores versus one large monolithic core. With multi-core processors, you can switch one core off for tasks such as SMS (to save power), and then you can switch both cores on when maximum performance is needed.

## Cache Memory

**Cache memory** is a special group of very fast memory circuitry usually built into the CPU. Cache memory is used to speed up processing by storing the data and instructions that may be needed next by the CPU in handy locations. In theory, it works the same way you might work at your desk; that is, with the file folders or documents you need most often placed within an arm's length and with other useful materials placed farther away but still within easy reach. The computer works in a similar manner. Although it can access items (data, instructions, and programs, for instance) in RAM relatively quickly, it can work much faster if it places the most urgently needed items into areas—cache memory—that allow even faster access. When cache memory is full and the CPU calls for additional data or a new instruction, the system overwrites as much data in cache memory as needed to make room for the new data or instruction. This allows the data and instructions that are most likely still needed to remain in cache memory.

Cache memory today is usually *internal cache* (built right into the CPU chip). In the past, some cache memory was *external cache* (located close to, but not inside, the CPU), but that is less common today. Cache memory level numbers indicate the order in which

> **Cache memory.** A group of fast memory circuitry usually built into the CPU and used to speed up processing.

the various levels of cache are accessed by the CPU when it requires new data or instructions. *Level 1 (L1) cache* (which is the fastest type of cache but typically holds less data than other levels of cache) is checked first, followed by *Level 2 (L2) cache*, followed by *Level 3 (L3) cache* if it exists. If the data or instructions are not found in cache memory, the computer looks for them in RAM, which is slower than cache memory. If the data or instructions cannot be found in RAM, then they are retrieved from the hard drive—an even slower operation. Typically, more cache memory results in faster processing. Most multi-core CPUs today have some cache memory (such as an L1 and L2 cache) dedicated to each core; they may also use a larger shared cache memory (such as L3 cache) that can be accessed by any core as needed.

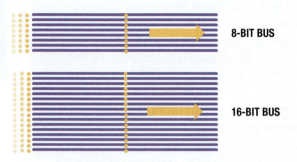

**8-BIT BUS**

**16-BIT BUS**

### Bus Width, Bus Speed, and Bandwidth

A *bus* is an electronic path over which data can travel. There are buses inside the CPU, as well as on the motherboard. You can picture a bus as a highway with several lanes; each wire in the bus acts as a separate lane, transmitting one bit at a time. The number of bits being transmitted at one time is dependent on the *bus width*—the number of wires in the bus over which data can travel. Just as a wider highway allows more cars to travel at one time, a wider bus allows more data to be transferred at one time (see Figure 2-11). The *bus speed* is also a very important factor because the bus width and bus speed together determine the bus's **bandwidth**—that is, the amount of data that can be transferred via the bus in a given time period. The amount of data actually transferred under real-life conditions is called **throughput**.

**FIGURE 2-11**
**Bus width.** A wider bus can transfer more data at one time than a narrower bus.

### Memory

**Memory** refers to chip-based storage. When the term *memory* is used alone, it refers to locations, usually inside the system unit (typically random access memory or RAM, discussed next) that a computer uses to store data on a temporary basis. In contrast, the term *storage* refers to the more permanent storage a computer uses—usually in the form of the computer's internal hard drive or removable storage media (such as DVDs and flash memory storage systems, which are discussed in the next chapter), but it can also be in the form of chip-based *internal storage*—especially in mobile devices.

In addition to RAM, computer users should be familiar with four other types of computer memory. Two of these—cache memory and registers—are **volatile** like RAM, which means that their content is erased when power to the memory ceases; the other two—read-only memory (ROM) and flash memory—are **nonvolatile**. Cache memory has already been discussed; these other types of memory are explained next.

**TIP**

To avoid confusion, when you are referring to the amount of storage space on your hard drive or other device, use the proper term—*storage*, not *memory*.

### Random Access Memory (RAM)

**RAM** (**random access memory**), also called *main memory* or *system memory*, is used to store the essential parts of the operating system while the computer is running, as well as the programs and data that the computer is currently using. When someone uses the term *memory* in reference to computers, he or she is usually referring to RAM. Because RAM is volatile, its content is lost when the computer is shut off. Data in RAM is also deleted

---

>**Bandwidth.** The amount of data that can be theoretically transferred through a communications medium in a given period of time.
>**Throughput.** The amount of data that is actually transferred through a communications medium under real-life conditions. >**Memory.** Chip-based storage. >**Volatile.** A characteristic of memory or storage in which data is not retained when the power to the computer is turned off.
>**Nonvolatile.** A characteristic of memory or storage in which data is retained even when the power to the computer is turned off.
>**RAM (random access memory).** Memory used to provide a temporary location for the computer to hold data and program instructions while they are needed.

when it is no longer needed, such as when the program using that data is closed. If you want to retrieve a document later, you need to save the document on a storage medium before closing it or before closing the program used to create the document, as discussed in more detail in Chapter 3. After the document is saved to a storage medium, it can be retrieved from the storage medium when it is needed.

Like the CPU, RAM consists of electronic circuits etched onto chips. While smartphones and other mobile devices typically use *embedded memory chips*, the memory chips for servers and personal computers are typically arranged onto circuit boards called *memory modules*, which, in turn, are plugged into the motherboard (see Figure 2-12). Most desktop and server memory modules today are *dual in-line memory modules* or *DIMMs*. Notebook computers typically use the smaller *small-outline DIMMs* or *SO-DIMMs*; even smaller devices may use the even smaller *Mini-DIMMs* or *Micro-DIMMs*. Most personal computers sold today have slots for two to four memory modules and at least one slot will be filled. For example, in the motherboard shown in Figure 2-7, there are two memory modules already installed and room to add an additional two modules, if needed. If you want to add more RAM to a computer and no empty slots are available, you must replace at least one of the existing memory modules with a higher capacity module in order to increase the amount of RAM in that computer.

RAM capacity is measured in bytes. The amount of RAM that can be installed in a computer depends on both the CPU in that computer and the operating system being used. For instance, while computers with older 32-bit CPUs can use up to only 4 GB of RAM, computers with 64-bit CPUs and a 64-bit operating system can use significantly more RAM. In addition, different versions of computers with 64-bit CPUs and a 64-bit operating system may support different amounts of RAM. Consequently, when you are considering adding more RAM to a computer, it is important to first determine that your computer can support it. More RAM allows more applications to run at one time and the computer to respond more quickly when a user switches from task to task. Most computers sold today for personal use have between 4 and 16 GB of RAM; mobile devices typically have between 1 and 4 GB of RAM.

In addition to knowing the type of memory module and the amount of memory your computer can support, it is important to select the proper type and speed of RAM when adding new memory. Most personal computers today use *SDRAM* (*synchronous dynamic RAM*). SDRAM is available in several *DDR* (*double-data rate*) versions, including *DDR2*, *DDR3*, and *DDR4*. DDR memory sends data twice as often as ordinary SDRAM (or prior versions of DDR RAM); the most common types of DDR RAM today are DDR3 and DDR4 (which are about twice as fast as DDR2 and DDR3, respectively). Each type of SDRAM is also usually available in a variety of speeds (measured in MHz)—for optimal performance, you should use the type and speed of RAM your computer was designed to use.

To further improve memory performance, memory typically uses a *dual-channel memory architecture*, which has two paths that go to and from memory and so it can transfer twice as much data at one time as *single-channel memory architecture* of the same speed. *Tri-channel* (three paths) and *quad-channel* (four paths) *memory architecture* can be used for higher performance. In order to take advantage of the improved performance of using multiple paths, multi-channel RAM typically needs to be installed in matched sets, such as two 4 GB dual-channel memory modules instead of a single 8 GB dual-channel memory

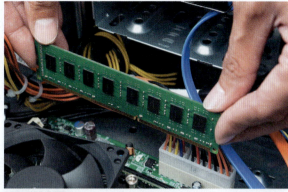

**DESKTOP RAM**

**NOTEBOOK RAM**

Source: Kingston Technology Corporation

**FIGURE 2-12**
Inserting RAM memory modules.

**TIP**

With smartphones and other devices that use embedded memory chips instead of memory modules, you typically cannot expand or replace the RAM.

**HW**

## ASK THE EXPERT

**Kingston** TECHNOLOGY

**Mark Tekunoff,** Senior Technology Manager, Kingston Technology

### How can I find out if more memory can be added to my computer?

The best way to upgrade memory is to go to a memory manufacturer's Web site (such as Kingston.com) and look up your PC to see which memory upgrade options are available. In general, basic users typically need 4 GB to 8 GB of memory, advanced users see advantages when using 8 GB to 16 GB of RAM, and power users who create or manipulate content such as large photos, stitching panoramic images, or processing video content will benefit from using 16 GB to 32 GB of system memory.

> **FIGURE 2-13**
> Memory addressing.

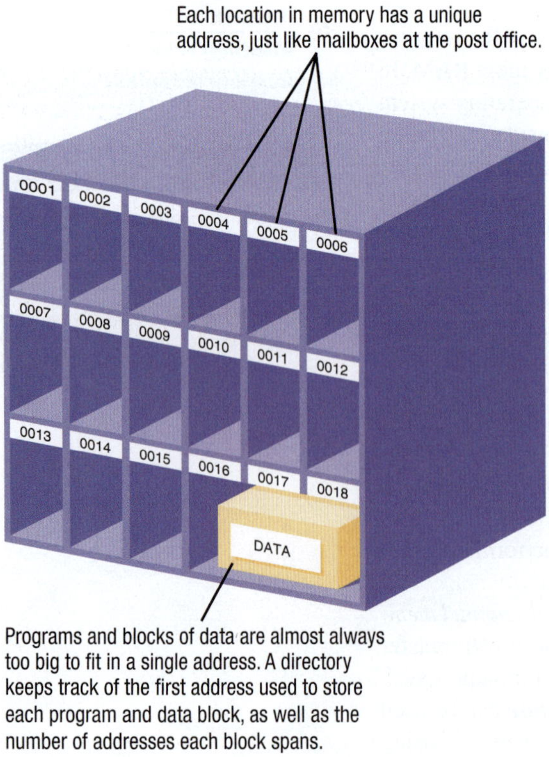

Each location in memory has a unique address, just like mailboxes at the post office.

DATA

Programs and blocks of data are almost always too big to fit in a single address. A directory keeps track of the first address used to store each program and data block, as well as the number of addresses each block spans.

module. As the number of cores used with CPUs grows, RAM performance is becoming increasingly important to ensure that data can be delivered to the CPU fast enough to match its processing capabilities.

While RAM as we know it today is volatile, *nonvolatile RAM* (*NVRAM*) retains its data when the power to the device is off. Consequently, devices consume less power when using NVRAM instead of traditional RAM, which can extend battery life. NVRAM is also usually faster than current flash memory.

There are several types of nonvolatile RAM becoming available or under development. For instance, *magnetic RAM* (*MRAM*) uses *magnetic polarization* rather than an electrical charge to store data, *memristor-based RAM* uses *memristors* (short for *memory resistors*) that change their resistance in response to current flowing through them, *resistive RAM* (*RRAM*) uses three layers with the middle layer having a different resistance than the outer layers, *NRAM* uses *carbon nanotubes* (discussed later in this chapter), and *PRAM* (*phase change random access memory*) has a special coating that changes its physical state when heat is applied (similar to the rewritable CDs and DVDs discussed in Chapter 3).

The most common applications for nonvolatile RAM today include storing critical data for enterprise systems as they operate to guard against data loss and saving the data necessary to help industrial automation and robotics systems recover quickly from a power loss. Emerging applications include "instant-on" computers and mobile devices that use NVRAM as both memory and storage. To facilitate this, capacities of NVRAM chips are increasing. In fact, a 1 TB RRAM nonvolatile RAM chip the size of a postage stamp is expected to be available by the end of 2016.

Regardless of the type of RAM used, the CPU must be able to find data and programs located in memory when they are needed. To accomplish this, each location in memory has an address. Whenever a block of data, instruction, program, or result of a calculation is stored in memory, it is usually stored in one or more consecutive addresses, depending on its size. The computer system sets up and maintains directory tables that keep track of where data is stored in memory in order to facilitate the retrieval of that data. When the computer has finished using a program or set of data, it frees up that memory space to hold other programs and data. Therefore, the content of each memory location constantly changes. This process can be roughly compared with the handling of the mailboxes in your local post office: the number on each P.O. box (memory location) remains the same, but the mail (data) stored inside changes as patrons remove their mail and as new mail arrives (see Figure 2-13).

## Registers

A **register** is high-speed memory built into the CPU. Registers are used by the CPU to store data and intermediary results temporarily during processing. Registers are the fastest type of memory used by the CPU, even faster than Level 1 cache. Generally, more registers and larger registers result in increased CPU performance. Most CPUs contain multiple registers; registers are discussed in more detail later in this chapter.

## Read-Only Memory (ROM)

**ROM** (**read-only memory**) consists of nonvolatile chips that permanently store data or programs. Like RAM, these chips are attached to the motherboard inside the system unit, and the data or programs are retrieved by the computer when they are needed. An important difference, however, is that you can neither write over the data or programs in ROM chips (which is the reason ROM chips are called *read-only*) nor erase their content when you shut off the computer's power. Traditionally, ROM was used to store the permanent instructions used by a computer (referred to as *firmware*). However, ROM is increasingly being replaced with flash memory, as discussed next, for any data that may need to be updated during the life of the computer.

## Flash Memory

**Flash memory** consists of nonvolatile memory chips that can be used for storage by the computer or the user. Flash memory chips have begun to replace ROM for storing system information, such as a computer's *BIOS* (*basic input/output system*) or, in recent versions of Windows, *Unified Extensible Firmware Interface* (*UEFI*), which is the sequence of instructions the computer follows during the boot process. For instance, one of the computer's first activities when you turn on the power is to perform a *power-on self-test* or *POST*. The POST takes an inventory of system components, checks each component to see if it is functioning properly, and initializes system settings, which produces the beeps you may hear as your computer boots. Traditionally, these instructions have been stored in ROM. By storing this information in flash memory instead of ROM, however, the boot sequence can be updated as needed. Similarly, firmware for personal computers and other devices (such as smartphones and networking hardware) are now typically stored in flash memory that is embedded in the device so the firmware can be updated over the life of the product.

Flash memory chips are also built into many types of devices (such as tablets, handheld gaming devices, and smartphones) for user storage, as well as built into storage media and devices (such as flash memory cards and USB flash drives). Flash memory media and devices used for storage purposes are discussed in more detail in Chapter 3.

## Fans, Heat Sinks, and Other Cooling Components

One by-product of packing an increasing amount of technology into a smaller system unit is heat, an ongoing problem for CPU and computer manufacturers. Because heat can damage components and cooler chips run faster, computers and mobile devices today employ cooling techniques to cool the inside of the system unit. Computers traditionally use *fans* and *heat sinks* (small components typically made out of aluminum with fins that help to dissipate heat). For instance, desktop computers often include a fan on the power supply that can be seen on the back of the computer, a fan on the video graphics board, and a fan and a heat

> **TIP**
>
> Product descriptions for smartphones and tablets that use built-in flash memory for storage sometimes refer to that storage capacity as *memory*—it's important for shoppers to realize that this quantity refers to storage, not RAM.

> **Register.** High-speed memory built into the CPU that temporarily stores data during processing. > **ROM (read-only memory).** Nonvolatile chips located on the motherboard into which data or programs have been permanently stored. > **Flash memory.** Nonvolatile memory chips that can be used for storage by the computer or user; can be built into a computer or a storage medium.

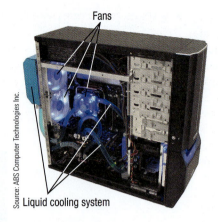

Fans

Liquid cooling system

**DESKTOP COMPUTERS**
Can use fans, heat sinks, and liquid cooling systems to cool the inside of the computer.

**SERVERS**
Often use liquid cooling systems; an immersion cooling system is shown here.

Built-in fan is powered by a USB cable that connects to the notebook.

**NOTEBOOK COMPUTERS**
Often have at least one internal fan; notebook cooling stands can be used to cool the underside of the computer.

**FIGURE 2-14**
Computer cooling methods.

sink on top of the CPU. As devices continue to shrink in size, however, finding room for cooling components is an issue. For example, the newest and thinnest notebook computers (such as the MacBook), as well as smartphones and other mobile devices, don't include a fan. Instead, these devices often use mobile CPUs (such as the Intel Core M) that run cooler than desktop CPUs, as well as thermal transfer materials (such as sheets of metal or graphite) inside the system unit to spread out the heat generated by the device components.

For servers and other computers that require a greater degree of cooling, *liquid cooling systems* can be used. Conventional liquid cooling systems consist of liquid (often a water solution) filled tubes that draw heat away from processors and other critical components. While more expensive than fans and requiring more room inside the system unit, these systems can cool specific components to a greater degree than fans, can significantly reduce air-conditioning costs in server rooms, and are quieter. As shown in Figure 2-14, some desktop computers use a combination of fans and water cooling systems. An emerging possibility for cooling the servers in large data centers—such as the ones used to provide cloud services—is *immersion cooling* where the hardware is actually submerged into units filled with a liquid cooling solution (refer again to Figure 2-14). Notebook computers and smartphones may use a thin liquid-filled *heat pipe* to transfer heat from the CPU and other hot areas to cooler areas inside the system unit. To cool the underside of a notebook computer—one of the problem areas—a *notebook cooling stand* (such as the one shown in Figure 2-14) can be used.

Because heat is an ongoing problem with computers, new cooling technologies are continually being developed. One emerging possibility is a cooling system—such as a liquid cooling system or an *ion pump cooling system*, which continuously cools the air with no moving parts—built directly into the CPU design.

## Expansion Slots and Expansion Cards

**Expansion slots** are locations on the motherboard into which **expansion cards** (also called *interface cards*) can be inserted to connect those cards to the motherboard. Expansion cards are used to give computers additional capabilities, such as to connect a computer to

---

a network, to connect a smartphone or external hard drive to a computer, or to connect a monitor to a computer. Today, some basic capabilities (such as the necessary connectors for speakers and monitors) are often integrated directly into the motherboard instead of requiring the use of an expansion card. However, an expansion card can be added and used when needed. For instance, a video graphics card can be added to a computer to add additional capabilities not allowed by the computer's integrated graphics feature. Most new desktop computers come with a few empty expansion slots on the motherboard so that new expansion cards can be added when new capabilities are needed. There are different types of expansion cards, such as PCI and the various sizes of PCIe—each corresponds to a specific type of expansion slot, as discussed in the next section, and they are not interchangeable.

It is much less common to add an expansion card to a notebook or other portable computer because many capabilities (such as graphics and networking capabilities) are integrated directly into the motherboard or CPU. Capabilities may also be added during manufacturing using an expansion card designed specifically for smaller devices, such as a *PCIe Mini Card* or the newer *M.2* interface (see Figure 2-15). When additional functionality is needed for a portable computer or mobile device, you can plug a USB adapter (such as the wireless networking USB adapter shown in Figure 2-15) into one of those ports. Most adapters (such as network adapters) are available in USB versions and so can be used with any desktop or portable computer that has a USB port. Because a USB port is the only available port on some devices, adapters are available to convert a USB port to another format (such as Ethernet or HDMI) so that the USB port can be used with devices that would normally connect via a different type of port (such as an Ethernet or HDMI port). Ports are discussed in more detail shortly.

Figure 2-15 shows a full-sized and a mini expansion card, as well as a USB adapter. Regardless of their form, expansion devices designed to connect external devices (such as a monitor or a wired networking device) have a port accessible to connect that device; those expansion devices that do not need to connect to additional hardware (such as a hard drive card or wireless networking card) do not have an exposed port.

**FIGURE 2-15**
**Expansion cards and adapters.**

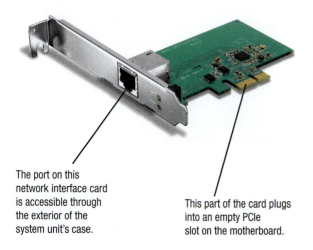

The port on this network interface card is accessible through the exterior of the system unit's case.

This part of the card plugs into an empty PCIe slot on the motherboard.

This part of this wireless networking card plugs into an empty M.2 slot; the card is not visible from the outside.

There is no port because this is a wireless networking adapter.

This end of this wireless networking adapter is inserted into an empty USB port.

**FULL-SIZED PCIe CARDS**
(for desktop computers)

**M.2 MINI CARDS**
(for portable computers)

**USB ADAPTERS**
(for any device with an available USB port)

Source: TRENDnet; Intel Corporation

## Buses

As already discussed, a **bus** in a computer is an electronic path over which data travels. There are buses located within the CPU to move data between CPU components; there are also a variety of buses etched onto the motherboard to tie the CPU to memory and to peripheral devices (one possible *bus architecture* for a desktop computer is shown in Figure 2-16). The buses that connect peripheral (typically input and output) devices to the motherboard are often called **expansion buses**. Expansion buses connect directly to

**FIGURE 2-16**

**Buses and expansion slots.**

Buses transport data from one component to another.

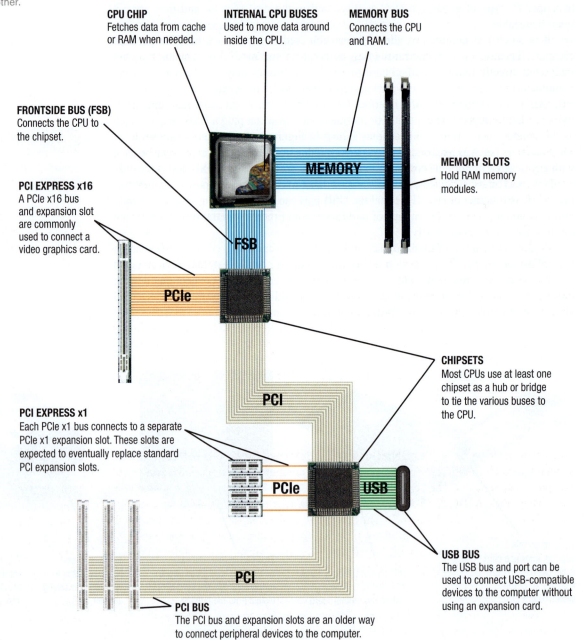

**CPU CHIP**
Fetches data from cache or RAM when needed.

**INTERNAL CPU BUSES**
Used to move data around inside the CPU.

**MEMORY BUS**
Connects the CPU and RAM.

**FRONTSIDE BUS (FSB)**
Connects the CPU to the chipset.

**PCI EXPRESS x16**
A PCIe x16 bus and expansion slot are commonly used to connect a video graphics card.

**MEMORY SLOTS**
Hold RAM memory modules.

**CHIPSETS**
Most CPUs use at least one chipset as a hub or bridge to tie the various buses to the CPU.

**PCI EXPRESS x1**
Each PCIe x1 bus connects to a separate PCIe x1 expansion slot. These slots are expected to eventually replace standard PCI expansion slots.

**USB BUS**
The USB bus and port can be used to connect USB-compatible devices to the computer without using an expansion card.

**PCI BUS**
The PCI bus and expansion slots are an older way to connect peripheral devices to the computer.

---

**> Bus.** An electronic path on the motherboard or within the CPU or other computer component along which data is transferred. **> Expansion bus.** A bus on the motherboard used to connect peripheral devices.

ports on the system unit case or to expansion slots on the motherboard (some of the most common expansion buses and expansion slots for a desktop computer are illustrated in Figure 2-16). It is important to realize that expansion slots are not interchangeable—that is, each type of expansion slot is designed for a specific type of expansion card, such as a full-sized PCIe card or a PCIe mini card. The specific buses shown in Figure 2-16 are discussed next. Portable computers and mobile devices have at least some of the buses discussed next, but typically not as many.

### Memory Bus

One relatively recent change in the bus architecture used with most personal computers today is connecting the CPU directly to RAM, as shown in Figure 2-16. This change allows for increased performance; the bus used to connect the CPU to RAM is typically called the **memory bus**.

### Frontside Bus (FSB)

The **frontside bus** (**FSB**) connects the CPU to the *chipset*—a set of chips that connects the various buses together and connects the CPU to the rest of the bus architecture. Because of the importance of the FSB connection, CPU manufacturers typically use special high-speed technologies; for instance, Intel uses its *QuickPath Interconnect* (*QPI*) technology and AMD uses its *HyperTransport Technology*.

### PCI and PCI Express (PCIe) Bus

The *PCI* (*Peripheral Component Interconnect*) *bus* has been one of the most common types of expansion buses in past years. Today, however, the **PCI Express** (**PCIe**) **bus** (which connects to the PCI bus) is more often used for expansion. The PCIe bus is available in several different widths. The 16-bit version of PCIe (referred to as *PCIe x16*) is commonly used with video graphics cards to connect a monitor to a desktop computer; expansion cards for other peripherals often connect via the 1-bit PCIe bus (referred to as *PCIe x1*). PCIe is extremely fast—the current version (*PCIe 4.0*) transfers data at 16 *Gbps* (billions of bits per second) per lane, which is significantly faster than the standard PCI bus. For example, with 16 lanes, PCIe x16 transfers data at 256 Gbps.

### USB Bus

One of the more versatile bus architectures is the **Universal Serial Bus** (**USB**). The USB standard allows 127 different devices to connect to a computer via a single USB port on the computer's system unit. The original USB standards, called USB 1.0 and 2.0, are relatively slow. They transfer data at 12 *Mbps* (millions of bits per second), and 480 Mbps, respectively. The newest *USB 3.0* and *3.1* standards (also called *SuperSpeed USB*) are much faster (5 Gbps and 10 Gbps, respectively). USB 3 also supports faster and more powerful charging, so it can be used to charge larger devices (such as laptops and monitors) in addition to smartphones and other mobile devices. The convenience and universal support of USB have made it one of the most widely used standards for connecting peripherals (such as keyboards, mice, printers, and storage devices) today. In fact, some portable computers now come with only USB ports for connecting devices to the computer, as well as to power the computer. To help you identify USB 3 ports, they are colored blue.

>**Memory bus.** The connection between the CPU and RAM. >**Frontside bus (FSB).** The bus that connects the CPU to the chipset that connects to the rest of the bus architecture. >**PCI Express (PCIe) bus.** One of the buses most commonly used to connect peripheral devices. >**Universal Serial Bus (USB).** A universal bus used to connect up to 127 peripheral devices to a computer without requiring the use of additional expansion cards.

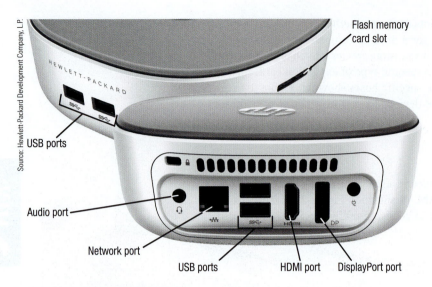

Flash memory card slot

USB ports

Audio port

Network port

USB ports

HDMI port

DisplayPort port

Source: Hewlett-Packard Development Company, L.P.

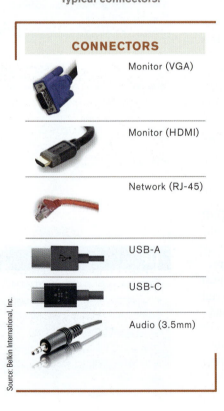

**CONNECTORS**

Monitor (VGA)

Monitor (HDMI)

Network (RJ-45)

USB-A

USB-C

Audio (3.5mm)

Source: Belkin International, Inc.

⚠ **FIGURE 2-17**
**Typical ports.**

▼ **FIGURE 2-18**
**Typical connectors.**

## Ports and Connectors

As already mentioned, **ports** are the connectors located on the exterior of a system unit that are used to connect external hardware devices. Each port is attached to the appropriate bus on the motherboard so that when a device is plugged into a port, the device can communicate with the CPU and other computer components. Several of the original ports used with desktop computers—such as the *parallel ports* traditionally used to connect printers, as well as the *keyboard* and *mouse ports* traditionally used to connect keyboards and mice—are now considered *legacy ports* and so are not typically included on newer computers. Ports often found on a desktop or notebook computer are illustrated on the mini desktop computer shown in Figure 2-17; some of the most common connectors used with these ports are shown in Figure 2-18. Instead of these full-sized connectors, mobile devices often use smaller versions, such as micro-USB and micro-HDMI. The various types of ports you might find on a computer are discussed next.

> *Monitor ports* are used to connect a monitor to a computer. Traditionally, monitors connected via a *VGA connector* or *Digital Video Interface* (*DVI*) connector. Today, monitors more commonly connect to a desktop or notebook computer via an *HDMI* (*High-Definition Multimedia Interface*); to connect an additional monitor to a tablet or other mobile device, a *Mini-HDMI port* or the even smaller *Micro-HDMI port* is often used instead. Additional options for connecting monitors, such as DisplayPort and wireless options, are discussed in Chapter 4.

> *Network ports* are used to connect a computer to a computer network via a networking cable—typically a cable using an *RJ-45 connector*, which looks similar to a telephone connector (refer again to Figure 2-18) but is larger. Networks and networking hardware are discussed in detail in Chapter 7.

> *USB ports* are used to connect USB devices (such as keyboards, mice, printers, hard drives, and digital cameras) to a computer via a USB connector. Smaller *mini-USB* ports or the even smaller *micro-USB* ports are often included on mobile devices instead of a full-sized USB port to connect USB devices. In addition to the traditional *USB-A* ports, there is now a newer *USB-C* port that is a different size and shape. (For a look at USB-C and how it is being used today, see the How It Works box.) To connect multiple USB devices to a single USB port, a *USB hub* (such as the one shown in Figure 2-19) can be used. USB hubs are growing in importance as an increasing number of computers and mobile devices are including only USB ports and not many of them. For example, the newest MacBook has only a single USB-C port that is used to connect peripheral devices as well as to power the device.

> **Port.** A connector on the exterior of a computer to which a device may be attached.

➤ *IrDA* (*Infrared Data Association*) *ports* and *Bluetooth ports* are used to receive wireless transmissions from devices; because the transmissions are wireless, these ports do not use a plug. IrDA ports are commonly used to "beam" data from a portable computer or mobile device to a computer. Bluetooth ports are most often used with wireless keyboards, mice, speakers, and headsets. Bluetooth and wireless data transmission is discussed in more detail in Chapter 7.

➤ *Flash memory card slots* are used to connect flash memory cards or other hardware using a flash memory card interface.

➤ *Audio ports* are used to connect speakers, headphones, or a microphone to the computer.

Source: Nonda

**FIGURE 2-19**
**USB hubs.** This USB hub is used to connect multiple USB-A and USB-C devices to a single USB-C port.

➤ *eSATA* (*external SATA*) *ports* are used to connect external SATA devices (most commonly, an external hard drive). External hard drives that connect via eSATA are much faster than external hard drives that connect via a USB. Hard drives are discussed in detail in Chapter 3.

➤ *Thunderbolt ports* (available primarily on some Apple devices) are used to connect peripheral devices (such as storage devices and monitors) via Thunderbolt cables. At 40 Gbps, the latest version of Thunderbolt, *Thunderbolt 3*, is extremely fast. Up to six devices can be daisy-chained together to connect them via a single Thunderbolt port, and adapters are available to connect USB devices to a Thunderbolt port and vice versa.

Most computers today support the *Plug and Play* standard, which means the computer automatically configures new devices as soon as they are installed and the computer is powered up. If you want to add a new device to your computer and there is an available port for the device you want to add, then you just need to plug it in. If the appropriate port is not available, you need to either install the appropriate expansion card to create the necessary port or use a USB or Thunderbolt version of the device, if you have one of those two ports available on your computer.

USB and Thunderbolt devices are *hot-swappable*, meaning they can be plugged into their respective ports while the computer is powered up. Hot-swappable devices—along with some removable storage media, such as flash memory cards—are recognized by the computer as soon as they connected to it and can be used right away. Other devices are recognized by the computer when the computer is first powered up after the device has been added.

Tablets have ports similar to desktop and notebook computers, but they often have fewer of them. As shown in Figure 2-20, connecting a tablet to a *tablet dock* (a docking station containing ports that can be used with the tablet whenever the tablet is connected to the dock) can provide additional connectivity options. Smartphones tend to have a more limited amount of expandability. However, they almost always have a USB port;

**TIP**

The ports for an all-in-one desktop computer are built into the monitor because the monitor is also the system unit.

**TIP**

USB-C, HDMI, and Thunderbolt cables can be used to transmit both audio and video data; USB-C and Thunderbolt cables can transfer power as well.

**HW**

# HOW IT WORKS

## USB-C

USB cables used with traditional USB ports have two different connectors on the ends: *USB-A* (the end that goes into the computer) and *USB-B* (the end that goes into the device being connected to the computer). The newest type of USB port and cable is *USB-C* (see the accompanying illustration).

USB-C has many advantages over traditional USB and is expected to eventually replace it. One advantage is its flexibility—both ends of a USB-C cable are the same, so it doesn't matter which end goes into which device, and the ends have no up or down orientation, so you don't have to flip the connection in order to have it line up properly. Another advantage is speed and power—many USB-C ports support the USB 3.1 standard, so they are not only very fast but can also be used to charge and power portable computers.

To connect a non-USB-C device to a USB-C port and vice versa, many types of adapters are available. For example, a USB-A to USB-C cable connects a USB-C device to a traditional USB-A port, and a USB-C to VGA or USB-C to HDMI

cable connects a VGA or HDMI monitor, respectively, to a USB-C port. Similar to conventional USB, there are hubs that can be used to connect multiple USB-C devices to a single USB-C port. In addition, multiport adapter cables are available that have a USB-C connector on one end (to connect to a computer) and a collection of ports (such as for power, HDMI, and USB-A) on the other.

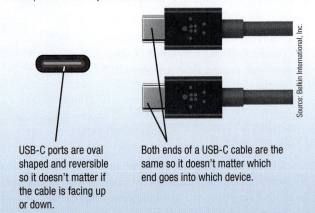

Source: Belkin International, Inc.

USB-C ports are oval shaped and reversible so it doesn't matter if the cable is facing up or down.

Both ends of a USB-C cable are the same so it doesn't matter which end goes into which device.

---

**FIGURE 2-20**

Typical ports for tablets and tablet docks.

some also have a flash memory card slot. Flash memory cards are discussed in more detail in Chapter 3. Some mobile devices also have a *Subscriber Identify Module* (*SIM*) slot to hold a *SIM card* used to connect that device to a mobile phone network.

Source: Microsoft Corporation

Headset jack

MicroSD card slot     USB port

Micro USB port

Mini DisplayPort

**TABLET**

Source: Toshiba

Tablet being docked

USB and networking ports

VGA port     HDMI port     Keyboard and touch pad

**TABLET DOCK**

# HOW THE CPU WORKS

As already discussed, a CPU consists of a variety of circuitry and components packaged together. The key element of the processor is the *transistor*—a device made of semiconductor material that controls the flow of electrons inside a chip. Today's CPUs contain hundreds of millions of transistors, and the number doubles approximately every 18 months. This phenomenon is known as Moore's Law and is explained in the Inside the Industry box. The other primary components of a typical CPU are discussed next.

## Typical CPU Components

To begin to understand how a CPU works, you need to know how the CPU is organized and what components it includes. This information will help you understand how electronic impulses move from one part of the CPU to another to process data. The architecture and components included in a CPU (referred to as *microarchitecture*) vary from processor to processor. A simplified example of the principal components that might be included in a single core of a typical CPU is shown in Figure 2-21 and discussed next. There are also additional components that are typically located inside the CPU, but not within each core. For instance, there are buses to connect the CPU cores to each other (typically via QuickPath Interconnect (QPI) or HyperTransport Technology connections), buses to connect each core to the CPU's *memory controller* (which controls the communication between the CPU cores and RAM), and buses to connect each core to any cache memory that is shared between the cores. If the CPU contains a graphics processing unit (GPU), as many do today, that would be located inside the CPU package as well.

**FIGURE 2-21**
Inside a CPU core.

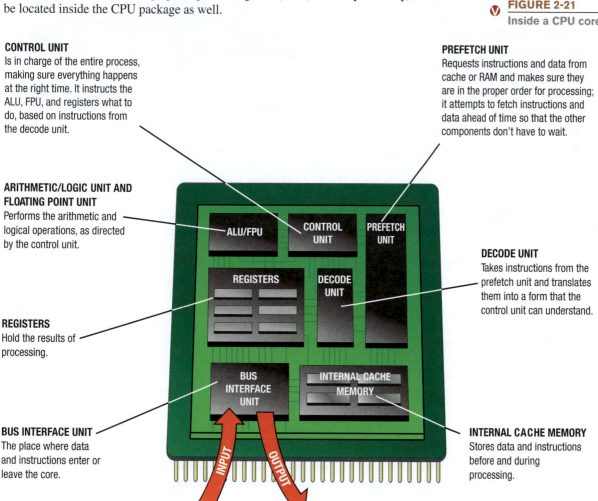

**CONTROL UNIT**
Is in charge of the entire process, making sure everything happens at the right time. It instructs the ALU, FPU, and registers what to do, based on instructions from the decode unit.

**PREFETCH UNIT**
Requests instructions and data from cache or RAM and makes sure they are in the proper order for processing; it attempts to fetch instructions and data ahead of time so that the other components don't have to wait.

**ARITHMETIC/LOGIC UNIT AND FLOATING POINT UNIT**
Performs the arithmetic and logical operations, as directed by the control unit.

**DECODE UNIT**
Takes instructions from the prefetch unit and translates them into a form that the control unit can understand.

**REGISTERS**
Hold the results of processing.

**BUS INTERFACE UNIT**
The place where data and instructions enter or leave the core.

**INTERNAL CACHE MEMORY**
Stores data and instructions before and during processing.

ALU/FPU  CONTROL UNIT  PREFETCH UNIT
REGISTERS  DECODE UNIT
BUS INTERFACE UNIT  INTERNAL CACHE MEMORY
INPUT  OUTPUT

# INSIDE THE INDUSTRY

### Moore's Law

In 1965, Gordon Moore, the co-founder of Intel and shown in the accompanying photograph, observed that the number of transistors per square inch on chips had doubled every two years since the integrated circuit was invented. He then made a now-famous prediction—that this doubling trend would continue for at least 10 more years. Here we are, more than 50 years later, and transistor density still doubles about every 18 months. Due to technological breakthroughs, *Moore's Law* has been maintained for far longer than the original prediction and most experts, including Moore himself, expect the doubling trend to continue for at least another decade. In fact, Intel states that the mission of its technology development team is to continue to break barriers to Moore's Law.

Interestingly, other computer components also follow Moore's Law. For example, storage capacity doubles approximately every 20 months, and chip speed doubles about every 24 months. Consequently, the term *Moore's Law* has been expanded and is now used to describe the amount of time it takes components to double in capacity or speed. Many experts predict that, eventually, a physical limit to the number of transistors that can be crammed onto a chip will end Moore's Law for current CPU technology. But new technology is being developed all the time and, as an Intel executive recently stated, "Engineers love a challenge."

Source: Intel Corporation

**Gordon Moore (1970)**

### Arithmetic/Logic Unit (ALU) and Floating Point Unit (FPU)

The **arithmetic/logic unit** (**ALU**) is the section of a CPU core that performs arithmetic (addition, subtraction, multiplication, and division) involving integers and logical operations (such as comparing two pieces of data to see if they are equal or determining if a specific condition is true or false). Arithmetic requiring decimals is usually performed by the **floating point unit** (**FPU**). Arithmetic operations are performed when mathematical calculations are requested by the user, as well as when many other common computing tasks are performed. For example, editing a digital photograph in an image editing program, running the spell checker in a word processing program, and burning a music CD are all performed by the ALU, with help from the FPU when needed, using only arithmetic and logical operations. Most CPUs today have multiple ALUs and FPUs that work together to perform the necessary operations.

### Control Unit

The **control unit** coordinates and controls the operations and activities taking place within a CPU core, such as retrieving data and instructions and passing them on to the ALU or

---

> **Arithmetic/logic unit (ALU).** The part of a CPU core that performs logical operations and integer arithmetic. > **Floating point unit (FPU).** The part of a CPU core that performs decimal arithmetic. > **Control unit.** The part of a CPU core that coordinates its operations.

FPU for execution. In other words, it directs the flow of electronic traffic within the core, much like a traffic cop controls the flow of vehicles on a roadway. Essentially, the control unit tells the ALU and FPU what to do and makes sure that everything happens at the right time in order for the appropriate processing to take place.

## Prefetch Unit

The **prefetch unit** orders data and instructions from cache or RAM based on the current task. The prefetch unit tries to predict what data and instructions will be needed and retrieves them ahead of time in order to help avoid delays in processing.

## Decode Unit

The **decode unit** takes the instructions fetched by the prefetch unit and translates them into a form that can be understood by the control unit, ALU, and FPU. The decoded instructions go to the control unit for processing.

## Registers and Internal Cache Memory

As mentioned earlier, registers and cache memory are both types of memory used by the CPU. Registers are groups of high-speed memory located within the CPU that are used during processing. The ALU and FPU use registers to store data, intermediary calculations, and the results of processing temporarily. CPU registers are also used for other purposes, such as to hold status information, program counters, or memory addresses. Internal cache memory (such as the Level 1 and Level 2 cache typically built into each core of a CPU and the Level 3 cache that is often shared by all cores of the CPU) is used to store instructions and data for the CPU in order to avoid retrieving them from RAM or the hard drive.

## Bus Interface Unit

The **bus interface unit** allows a core to communicate with other CPU components, such as the memory controller and other cores. As previously mentioned, the memory controller controls the flow of instructions and data going between the CPU cores and RAM.

## The System Clock and the Machine Cycle

As mentioned at the beginning of this chapter, every instruction that you issue to a computer, such as by typing a command or clicking something with the mouse, is converted into machine language. In turn, each machine language instruction in a CPU's *instruction set* (the collection of basic machine language commands that the CPU can understand) is broken down into several smaller, machine-level instructions called *microcode*. Microcode instructions, such as moving a single piece of data from one part of the computer system to another or adding the numbers located in two specific registers, are built into the CPU and are the basic instructions used by the CPU.

To synchronize all of a computer's operations, a **system clock**, which is located on the motherboard, is used. The system clock sends out a signal on a regular basis to all other computer components, similar to a musician's metronome or a person's heartbeat. Each signal is referred to as a *cycle*. The number of cycles per second is measured in *hertz* (*Hz*). One megahertz (MHz) is equal to one million ticks of the system clock. Many personal computers today

---

>**Prefetch unit.** The part of a CPU core that attempts to retrieve data and instructions before they are needed for processing in order to avoid delays. >**Decode unit.** The part of a CPU core that translates instructions into a form that can be processed by the ALU and FPU.
>**Bus interface unit.** The part of a CPU core that allows it to communicate with other CPU components. >**System clock.** The timing mechanism within a computer system that synchronizes the computer's operations.

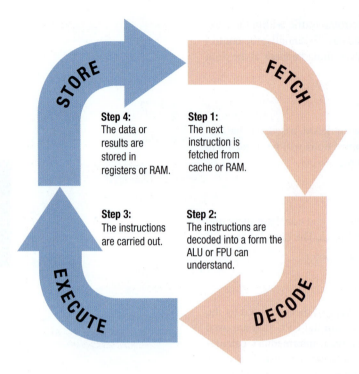

**STORE**

**Step 4:**
The data or results are stored in registers or RAM.

**FETCH**

**Step 1:**
The next instruction is fetched from cache or RAM.

**Step 3:**
The instructions are carried out.

**Step 2:**
The instructions are decoded into a form the ALU or FPU can understand.

**EXECUTE**

**DECODE**

◭ **FIGURE 2-22**
**A machine cycle.**
A machine cycle is typically accomplished in four steps.

have a system clock that runs at 200 MHz, and each device (such as a CPU) that is synchronized with the system clock runs at either the system clock speed or at a multiple of or a fraction of the system clock speed. For example, a CPU with a *CPU clock speed* of 2 GHz uses a multiplier of 10, meaning that the CPU clock essentially "ticks" 10 times during each system clock tick. During each CPU clock tick, the CPU can execute one or more pieces of microcode. Virtually all CPUs today can process more than one piece of microcode at one time—a characteristic known as *superscalar*, which is the ability to process multiple *instructions per cycle* (*IPC*). A CPU with a higher CPU clock speed processes more instructions per second than the same CPU with a lower CPU clock speed.

Whenever the CPU processes a single piece of microcode, it is referred to as a **machine cycle**. Each machine cycle consists of the four general operations illustrated in Figure 2-22 and discussed next.

1. *Fetch*—the program instruction is fetched.

2. *Decode*—the instructions are decoded so the control unit, ALU, and FPU can understand them.

3. *Execute*—the instructions are carried out.

4. *Store*—the original data or the result from the ALU or FPU execution is stored in the CPU's registers.

Because each machine cycle processes only a single microcode instruction, many seemingly simple commands (such as multiplying two numbers) might require more than one machine cycle, and a computer might need to go through thousands, millions, or even billions of machine cycles to complete a user command or program instruction. For instance, a CPU processing the command 2 + 3 would typically require at least four machine cycles, such as to:

1. Fetch the number 2 from RAM, decode it, and store it in register X.

2. Fetch the number 3 from RAM, decode it, and store it in a register Y.

3. Fetch and decode the addition instruction, then add the two numbers (currently stored in registers X and Y) and store the sum in register Z.

4. Fetch and decode the instruction to display the sum, and then output the sum (currently stored in register Z) to RAM.

## MAKING COMPUTERS FASTER AND BETTER NOW AND IN THE FUTURE

Over the years, computer designers have developed a number of strategies to achieve faster, more powerful, and more reliable computers. Researchers are also constantly working on ways to improve the performance of computers of the future. Some strategies for both are discussed next.

---

> **Machine cycle.** The series of operations involved in the execution of a single machine-level instruction.

## Improving the Performance of Your System Today

Several strategies you can use to try to improve the performance of your current computer are discussed next.

### Add More Memory

With today's graphic-intensive interfaces and applications, much more memory is required than was necessary even a couple of years ago. If your computer is just a few years old, slows down significantly when you have multiple programs open, and has less than 4 GB of RAM installed, you should consider adding more memory to your system. To accomplish this, first check to see if there is room inside your computer for any additional memory modules (either by looking inside the computer or by using a scanning utility like the one shown in Figure 2-23 that is available on some memory manufacturers' Web sites). You can then determine (either by the scan information or by checking your computer's specifications) the maximum amount of memory that can be added to your computer and what type and speed of RAM your computer requires. If you do not have enough empty memory slots in your computer, you will need to remove some of the old memory modules and replace them with newer, higher capacity ones in order to add more memory to your system. For example, the computer being scanned in Figure 2-23 has two memory slots (one slot currently has 2 GB of RAM and the other has 4 GB) and the maximum RAM for this computer is 8 GB. In order to add more memory to this computer, the 2 GB memory module would need to be removed and replaced with a 4 GB memory module.

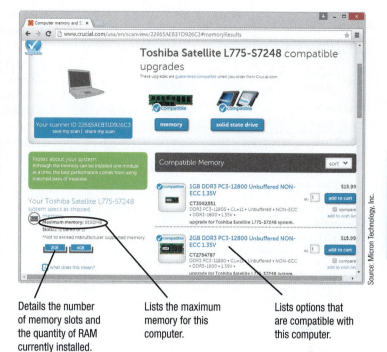

Details the number of memory slots and the quantity of RAM currently installed.

Lists the maximum memory for this computer.

Lists options that are compatible with this computer.

*Source: Micron Technology, Inc.*

⚠ **FIGURE 2-23**

**Online memory scanners can help you determine what memory can be added to your computer.**

**CAUTION** CAUTION CAUTION CAUTION CAUTION CAUTION CAUT

Never open the case of your computer when it is powered up or plugged into an electrical outlet. To avoid damaging your computer with the static electricity stored in your body, consider wearing an *antistatic wristband*.

### Perform System Maintenance

As you work and use your hard drive to store and retrieve data, and as you install and uninstall programs, most computers tend to become less efficient. One reason for this is because as large documents are stored, retrieved, and then stored again, they often become *fragmented*—that is, not stored in contiguous (adjacent) storage areas. Because the different pieces of the document are physically located in different places, it may take longer for the computer to retrieve or store them. Another reason a computer might become inefficient is that when programs are uninstalled, pieces of the program are sometimes left behind or references to these programs are left in operating system files, such as the *Windows registry*. In addition, as a hard drive begins to get full, it takes longer to locate the data stored on the hard drive. All of these factors can result in a system performing more slowly than it should.

To avoid some of these problems, regular system maintenance should be performed. Some system maintenance tips every computer user should be aware of are listed next.

**TIP**

If your computer is running slowly and you have many programs and windows open, close a few to see if your performance improves; if not, try rebooting your PC to reset the system files and RAM.

**TIP**

On Windows computers, many maintenance options are accessed through the Control Panel.

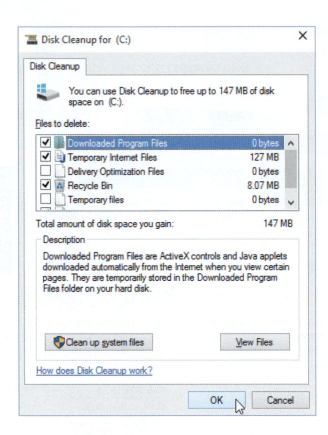

**FIGURE 2-24**
**Windows Disk Cleanup.** Can help free up room on your hard drive.

➤ Uninstall any programs that you no longer want on your computer in order to free up space on your hard drive. Be sure to use the proper removal process, such as the *Uninstall a program* option in the Windows Control Panel or an *Uninstall* option for that program located on the Start menu. Windows users can also periodically use a *registry cleaner* (a number of free registry cleaners are available online) to clean the Windows registry by removing references to non-existent programs.

➤ Remove any unnecessary programs from the startup list so they don't run every time the PC boots. Users with recent versions of Windows can use the Startup tab on the Task Manager to view and change the programs that run automatically, as discussed in more detail in Chapter 5.

➤ If you have large files (such as digital photos or videos) stored on your computer that you do not need on a regular basis but want to keep, consider moving them to a DVD disc, an external hard drive, or a cloud storage site and then deleting them from your hard drive to free up space. Make sure the files open on the storage medium before deleting the files from your hard drive, and consider copying important files to two different storage media or sites. Backing up files, deleting files, and types of storage media are discussed in more detail in later chapters.

➤ Delete the temporary files (such as installation files, Web browsing history, and files in the Recycle Bin) stored by your computer and Web browser to free up room on your hard drive. You can delete these files manually, if desired, but the *Windows Disk Cleanup* program shown in Figure 2-24 can locate and delete these temporary files for you.

➤ *Error-check* and *defragment* your hard drive periodically to make it work more efficiently. Windows users can right-click a hard drive icon in File Explorer, select *Properties*, and then select the *Check* option on the Tools tab to check that hard drive for errors, or select *Optimize* to defragment that hard drive. Many computers are set up to defragment hard drives automatically on a regular basis.

➤ Scan for computer viruses and spyware continually. A computer that suddenly slows down might be the result of a computer virus, spyware program, or other threat. As discussed in Chapter 9, security software can help detect and correct these problems.

➤ Clean out the dust from inside the system unit of desktop computers once or twice a year using a can of compressed air or a small vacuum cleaner designed for this purpose. Although the dust may not slow down your system by itself, it can slow down the fans that cool your computer as well as cause the components inside your computer to run hotter than they should, which can cause problems with your computer such as overheating, burned out components, and periodic shutting down without warning. Notebook users should also clean their fans when needed, especially if their fans don't automatically reverse periodically to blow out dust, which some newer notebooks do.

### Buy a Larger or Second Hard Drive

As already mentioned, hard drives become less efficient as they fill up. If your hard drive is almost full and you do not have any data or programs that you can remove, consider buying and installing a second hard drive. The new hard drive can be an internal hard drive if you have an empty drive bay inside your computer. It can also be an external hard drive that connects via a USB port or wireless connection. Hard drives are discussed in detail in Chapter 3.

### Upgrade Your Internet Connection

If your system seems slow primarily when you are using the Internet, consider upgrading to a faster type of connection. The different types of Internet connections available today are described in Chapters 7 and 8.

### Upgrade Your Video Graphics Card

If you are using a desktop computer and programs, documents, and other items seem sluggish as they are displayed on your monitor, you can check to see if a video upgrade might help. First, determine if your computer has the GPU integrated into the motherboard, into the CPU, or on a separate video graphics card. If it uses *integrated graphics*, then installing a separate video card containing adequate video memory may speed up your system and it will free up the RAM currently being used for video memory. You may also want to buy and install a new video card if your video graphics card isn't adequate and you are a gamer, computer artist, engineer, or otherwise use 3D-graphic-intensive applications. Users of notebooks that have *switchable graphics* capabilities can select integrated graphics when they are working on battery power to save power, and then switch to using an installed video graphics card when extra performance is needed or when the computer is plugged in.

> **TIP**
>
> While it is sometimes possible to upgrade the video graphics card in a notebook computer, the decision of whether to have integrated graphics or a video graphics card is typically made when you buy a notebook computer.

## Strategies for Making Faster and Better Computers

Researchers and manufacturers are continually developing strategies to build faster and better personal computers, as well as devices that better fit changing needs. Some relate to technology in general; others are techniques used specifically to speed up the CPU. Some of these strategies are described in the next few sections.

### Pipelining

In older, single-core computer systems, the CPU had to finish processing one instruction completely before starting another. Today's computers, however, can process multiple instructions at one time. One way to accomplish this within each core is through **pipelining**. With pipelining, a new instruction begins executing as soon as the previous one reaches the next stage of the pipeline. Figure 2-25 illustrates this process with a 4-stage pipeline. Notice that while the pipelined CPU is executing one instruction, it is simultaneously fetching and getting the next instruction ready for execution. Without a pipeline, the ALU and FPU would be idle while an instruction is being fetched and decoded.

Pipelines for CPUs today usually have between 4 and 20 stages, and the machine cycle is broken down into as many parts as needed to match the number of stages used. For example, with a 10-stage pipeline, the 4 steps of the machine cycle would be broken down into a total of 10 steps so that all stages of the pipeline can be used at one time. Pipelining increases the number of machine cycles completed per second, which increases the number of instructions performed per second, which improves performance.

> **Pipelining.** The capability of a CPU or CPU core to begin processing a new instruction as soon as the previous instruction completes the first stage of the machine cycle.

**FIGURE 2-25**

**Pipelining.** Pipelining streamlines the machine cycle by executing different stages of multiple instructions at the same time so that the different parts of the CPU are idle less often.

**Stages**

| Fetch Instruction 1 | Decode Instruction 1 | Execute Instruction 1 | Store Result Instruction 1 | Fetch Instruction 2 | Decode Instruction 2 | Execute Instruction 2 |
|---|---|---|---|---|---|---|

**WITHOUT PIPELINING**
Without pipelining, an instruction finishes an entire machine cycle before another instruction is started.

**Stages**

| Fetch Instruction 1 | Fetch Instruction 2 | Fetch Instruction 3 | Fetch Instruction 4 | Fetch Instruction 5 | Fetch Instruction 6 | Fetch Instruction 7 |
|---|---|---|---|---|---|---|
| | Decode Instruction 1 | Decode Instruction 2 | Decode Instruction 3 | Decode Instruction 4 | Decode Instruction 5 | Decode Instruction 6 |
| | | Execute Instruction 1 | Execute Instruction 2 | Execute Instruction 3 | Execute Instruction 4 | Execute Instruction 5 |
| | | | Store Result Instruction 1 | Store Result Instruction 2 | Store Result Instruction 3 | Store Result Instruction 4 |

**WITH PIPELINING**
With pipelining, a new instruction is started when the preceding instruction moves to the next stage of the pipeline.

## Multiprocessing and Parallel Processing

The use of more than one processor or processing core in a computer (such as using multiple CPUs in a server, mainframe, or supercomputer, or using a multi-core CPU in a personal computer or smartphone) is common today. When two or more processors or processing cores are located within a single device, techniques that perform operations simultaneously—such as **multiprocessing** (where each processor or core typically works on a different job) and **parallel processing** (where multiple processors or cores work together to make one single job finish sooner)—are possible.

The use of multiprocessing and parallel processing can increase astronomically the number of calculations performed in any given time period. For example, the Titan supercomputer (shown in Figure 1-19 in Chapter 1) uses 299,008 CPU cores and more than 18,000 GPUs and operates at more than 27 *petaflops* or 27,000 trillion floating point operations per second; that is, it is able to process more than 27,000 trillion calculations per second. To increase efficiency in multiprocessing systems, many CPUs include direct links between the processors to improve communications.

A concept related to multiprocessing is *multithreading*—the ability of a CPU (or software) to execute multiple streams of instructions (called *threads*) within a single program at the same time. For instance, many Intel CPUs are capable of running 2 threads per core, so a 4-core CPU could simultaneously execute 8 threads, providing the software being used supported it. Because this technique (called *Hyper-Threading Technology* by Intel) utilizes processing power in the chip that would otherwise go unused, it lets the chip operate more efficiently, resulting in faster processing.

## Improved Architecture

Computer manufacturers are continually working to improve the basic architecture of computers, such as to make them faster, cooler, quieter, more energy efficient, and more reliable. For example, new designs for motherboards and CPUs are always under development, and computer components are continually being built smaller, so more power and capabilities can be

>**Multiprocessing.** The capability of a single computer to use multiple processors or multiple processing cores, usually to process multiple jobs at one time and to process those jobs faster than could be performed with a single processor. >**Parallel processing.** A processing technique that uses multiple processors or multiple processing cores simultaneously, usually to process a single job as fast as possible.

contained in the same size package. In fact, today's CPUs—which are formed using a process called *lithography* that imprints patterns on semiconductor materials—contain transistors as small as 14 *nanometers* (*nm*) in size (1 nanometer is a billionth of a meter). CPUs using 7 nm chips are expected to be available by 2018, and transistors as small as a single atom have been created in lab settings. As lithography techniques continue to improve, transistors will likely continue to shrink, allowing more transistors to fit on the same-sized CPU. Creating components smaller than 100 nm fits the definition of nanotechnology, which is discussed in more detail shortly.

Other improvements include developing faster memory and faster bus speeds to help speed up processing and to help reduce or eliminate bottlenecks, as well as creating CPUs with an increasing number of cores and integrated GPUs. CPUs are also increasingly including additional technology to meet new needs, such as support for virtualization and increased 3D graphics processing. Improvements to CPU instruction set designs are made as needed to expand the instruction set design for new applications—particularly the growing use of multimedia applications, such as editing digital movies and photos and streaming online content.

## Improved Materials

Traditionally, CPU chips used aluminum circuitry etched onto a silicon chip. As the number of aluminum circuits that can be packed onto a silicon chip without heat damage or interference approached its limit, chipmakers began to look for alternate materials. Copper was one of the next choices because it is a far better electrical conductor, and it can produce chips containing more circuitry at a lower price. As transistors have continued to shrink (which results in an increased leakage of current), CPU manufacturers have looked to new materials that reduce current leakage to allow more reliable high-speed operation. For instance, Intel switched to a material called *high-k* for some of the silicon components in its CPUs. Intel is also combining silicon with materials, such as *germanium*, that are based on elements from the third and fifth columns of the periodic table and collectively referred to as *III-V materials*.

A new material with great possibilities is **graphene**—flat sheets of carbon that are one atom tall. Graphene is the lightest and strongest known material and is the best known conductor of electricity. According to Georgia Tech physics professor Walter de Heer, one of the leading researchers in this area, silicon can't keep up with the current growth in chip technology and graphene may be the answer. Because electrons move through graphene with almost no resistance, they generate little heat; graphene also allows any heat that is generated to dissipate quickly. As a result, *graphene chips* (which are made out of strips of graphene) can operate at much higher speeds than silicon and require less power. For example, during the initial tests of the first graphene CPU to be developed, it ran a tablet for 3 months before requiring a battery recharge.

**FIGURE 2-26**
Flexible smartphone.

For integrating computer components into clothing and other flexible materials (such as to create clothing, backpacks, and other objects that can control your electronic devices or display content on demand), as well as for creating flexible devices (such as the Portal flexible smartphone shown in Figure 2-26), *flexible electronic components* are needed. Flexible circuits and other flexible components are currently being developed by a number of companies. In addition to the ability to be bent without damaging the circuitry, flexible circuits are thinner, lighter, generate little heat, and consume significantly less energy than

Courtesy Arubixs, Inc.

>**Graphene.** Flat sheets of carbon that are one atom thick, are extremely light and strong, and are a great conductor of electricity.

# TREND

## Smart Clothing

The next trend in wearable technology isn't your smartwatch or fitness band. It's your clothes—*smart clothes* to be precise.

Smart clothes usually contain flexible circuitry and sensors, as well as wireless connectivity and a battery. One category of smart clothing is fitness apparel. Similar to fitness bands, smart clothing (most commonly *smart shirts*) monitors your physical activity, sleep, heart rate, and other health and fitness data. For more serious athletes, some smart apparel transmits 3D information about your activities so you can monitor your form as you work out, or an app or live coach can provide feedback on your technique. Smart clothing is washable and, in a manner that is similar to fitness bands, usually syncs your data to your smartphone, typically via Bluetooth.

For more versatile smart clothes, *smart fabric* is under development. Integrating conductive fibers into fabric allows whatever garment is made from that fabric to have smart properties. For even more versatility, Google's *Project Jacquard* is developing conductive yarn that can be woven on any industrial loom to enable clothing manufactures to create smart clothing using their normal techniques (see the accompanying photos). Tiny connectors and circuits can then be attached to the garments in the appropriate locations to provide the desired smart functions. Google's first partner in this project is Levi's and the goal of the project is to create smart clothes-based interfaces for smartphones and other mobile devices.

Next up? Smart shoes that buzz when you deviate from a custom route or pace.

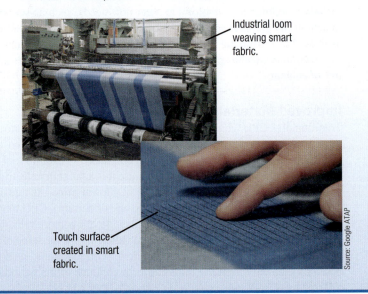

Industrial loom weaving smart fabric.

Touch surface created in smart fabric.

Source: Google ATAP

---

conventional processors. Some flexible circuits, such as the ones used in the smartphone shown in Figure 2-26, are made out of plastic. Others use conductive yarn, which can be integrated into clothing more easily (for a look at the emerging trend of smart clothes, see the Trend box).

## 3D Chips

*Three-dimensional* (*3D*) *chips* are a technique for packing an increasing number of components onto small chips. With 3D chips, the components are layered, which cuts down on the surface area required. This is especially important with notebook computers and mobile devices that have limited room inside the system unit. By one estimate, the capacities of solid-state drives using *planar* technology (where chips are laid out within one plane), has reached its limit of 1 TB for today's notebooks. By using 3D technology, however, the same-sized drive could hold at least 10 TB.

To create 3D RAM or flash memory chips, the memory cells are stacked on top of one another in layers. For example, both Samsung and Intel make flash memory chips containing 32 layers and Toshiba has created the first 48-layer chip. For CPUs, the transistors are layered. For example, recent Intel CPUs include 3D *Tri-Gate transistors* in which electrical current flows on three sides of vertical fins (see the illustration in Figure 2-27). Tri-Gate transistors provide increased performance and low voltage, making them ideal for use in small devices, such as mobile devices.

**∨ FIGURE 2-27**

**Tri-Gate transistor.**

In this 3D transistor, the electrical current (represented by the yellow dots) flows on three sides of a vertical fin.

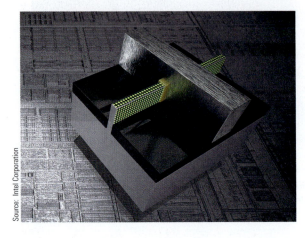

Source: Intel Corporation

## Nanotechnology

Although there are varying definitions, most agree that **nanotechnology** involves creating computer components, machines, and other structures that are less than 100 nanometers in size. Many of today's components (such as transitors) already fit that definition. However, some experts believe that, eventually, current technology will reach its limits. At that point, transistors and other computer components may need to be built at the atomic and molecular level; that is, starting with single atoms or molecules to construct the components. Prototypes of computer products built in this fashion include the *single atom transistor*, which is a single switch that can be turned on and off like a transistor but is made from a single organic molecule, and a tiny *nanogenerator* that generates power with vibrations, such as vibrations from a moving car or a simple body movement like walking.

One nanotechnology development that is already being used in a variety of products available today is **carbon nanotubes (CNTs)**, which are tiny, hollow tubes made by rolling up sheets of graphine. The wall of a single-walled carbon nanotube is only one carbon atom thick and the tube diameter is approximately 10,000 times smaller than a human hair. Carbon nanotubes have great potential for many applications because they conduct electricity better than copper, are 100 times stronger than steel at one-sixth the weight, conduct heat better than diamonds, and transmit electronic impulses faster than silicon. For example, because they can transmit electricity and are transparent, CNTs are used in products such as TVs, solar cells, and light bulbs. Because of their strength and lightness for their size, they are also integrated into products that benefit from those characteristics, such as automobile panels, airplanes, tennis rackets, and racing bikes. Carbon nanotubes are also beginning to be combined with other materials, such as plastic, to increase the durability of materials used to produce other consumer items, such as surfboards.

Carbon nanotubes also have great potential for computing products and are already used today in display screen and memory products. One possibility for the future is replacing the silicon used in chips today with carbon nanotubes. For example, Stanford researchers recently built a computer consisting of 178 transistors made from carbon nanotubes; the computer was able to perform basic tasks, such as counting and number sorting (the wafer containing the CNT transistors is shown in Figure 2-28). In an even more recent development, Stanford researchers built a 3D chip that layers CNT transistors with memory in the same chip package and uses nanoscale electronic "elevators" instead of wires to connect the layers—this design speeds up communications between the processors and memory. Another recent development is *carbon nanotube fibers* that look and act like thread but conduct heat and electricity like a metal wire (see Figure 2-29). According to the researchers, these fibers are expected to eventually be used in new products for the aerospace, automotive, medical, and smart clothing markets.

Two other recent developments are *nanofilters* that can remove contaminants from water sources and *nanosensors* that can detect cancer-causing toxins or cancer drugs inside single living cells. Possible future applications of nanotechnology include disposing of e-waste by rearranging dangerous components at the atomic level into inert substances, *nanosponges* that can enter the bloodstream and soak up toxins, and improved military uniforms that protect against bullets and germ warfare.

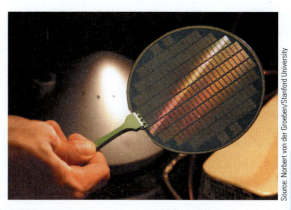

**FIGURE 2-28**
**Wafer containing CNT transistors.**

**FIGURE 2-29**
**Carbon nanotube fibers.** This light bulb is powered and held in place by two carbon nanotube fibers.

*Source: Norbert von der Groeben/Stanford University*

*Source: Jeff Fitlow/Rice University*

---

> **Nanotechnology.** The science of creating tiny computers and components by working at the individual atomic and molecular levels.
> **Carbon nanotubes (CNTs).** Tiny, hollow tubes made by rolling up sheets of graphene.

## Terascale and Exascale Computing

As demand by consumers and businesses for online software, services, and media-rich experiences continues to increase, *high-performance computing* (*HPC*) is becoming more necessary. With supercomputers currently reaching teraflop and petaflop speeds, **terascale computing**—the ability of a computer to process one trillion floating point operations per second (teraflops)—has arrived and is expected to become more common. Much of today's terascale research is focusing on creating multi-core processors with tens to hundreds of cores used in conjunction with multithreaded hardware and software to achieve teraflop performance. The research also includes working on developing higher-speed communications between computers, such as between Web servers and high-performance mobile devices or computers, to help facilitate high-performance cloud computing.

Intel, one of the leaders in terascale research, has created a CPU designed for use with supercomputers that contains 72 cores and integrated memory, and that operates at 3 teraflops per CPU. To deliver even faster speeds in the future, the next development is expected to be **exascale computers** that can process data at *exaflop* (1,000 petaflops) speed.

## Quantum Computing

The idea of **quantum computing** emerged in the 1970s, but it has received renewed interest lately. Quantum computing applies the principles of quantum physics and quantum mechanics to computers, going beyond traditional physics to work at the subatomic level. Quantum computers differ from conventional computers in that they utilize atoms or nuclei working together as *quantum bits* or *qubits*. Qubits function simultaneously as both the computer's processor and memory, and each qubit can represent more than just the two states (one and zero) available to today's electronic bits; a qubit can even represent many states at one time. Quantum computers can perform computations on many numbers at one time, making them, theoretically, exponentially faster than conventional computers. Physically, quantum computers in the future might consist of a thimbleful of liquid whose atoms are used to perform calculations as instructed by an external device.

**Ⓥ FIGURE 2-30**

**Quantum computers.**

This vial of liquid contains a 7-qubit computer.

Source: IBM Research, Almaden Research Center.

While fully-functioning quantum computers are still many years away, working quantum computers do exist. For instance, in 2001 the researchers at IBM's Almaden Research Center created a 7-qubit quantum computer (see Figure 2-30) composed of the nuclei of seven atoms that can interact with each other and be programmed by radio frequency pulses. This quantum computer successfully factored the number 15—not a complicated computation for a conventional computer, but the fact that a quantum computer was able to understand the problem and compute the correct answer is viewed as a highly significant event in the area of quantum computer research.

Some of the obstacles to creating a fully functional quantum computer include the inability of qubits to hold information for long periods of time and their susceptibility to errors due to heat, noise, and other factors. Recently, UCLA scientists developed a new technique for cooling molecules, which may be applied to future quantum computers in order to bring the molecules to the state at which they can be manipulated to store and transmit data. In addition, IBM recently developed a new error-detection process to be used with quantum computers. In another recent development, scientists in Australia

---

> **Terascale computing.** The ability of a computer to process data at teraflop speeds.  > **Exascale computing.** The ability of a computer to process data at exaflop (1,000 petaflops) speeds.  > **Quantum computing.** A technology that applies the principles of quantum physics and quantum mechanics to computers to direct atoms or nuclei to work together as quantum bits (qubits), which function simultaneously as the computer's processor and memory.

have created a silicon quantum bit using a single atom—this development is viewed as a big step forward in the development of silicon-based quantum computers. These break-throughs are viewed as significant steps toward the ability to create more sophisticated working quantum computers in the future.

Quantum computing is not well suited for general computing tasks but is ideal for, and expected to be widely used in, highly data-intensive applications, such as encryption (discussed in Chapter 9) and code breaking.

## Optical Computing and Silicon Photonics

Using light is the fastest way to transmit data. While light is commonly used to transmit data (such as via fiber-optic cabling, discussed in Chapter 7), converting optical data so that it is able to work with electronic hardware (such as a computer) significantly slows down the overall speed. To avoid this delay, the computer of the future may be an **optical computer**—a computer that uses light, such as from laser beams or infrared beams, to perform digital computations. Because light beams do not interfere with each other, optical computers can be much smaller and faster than electronic computers. For instance, according to one NASA senior research scientist, an optical computer could solve a problem in one hour that would take an electronic computer 11 years to solve.

Using light for ultra-fast data transfers within and among silicon chips is called *silicon photonics* (photonics is the control and manipulation of light). Silicon photonics is expected to be used to transfer large quantities of data at very high speeds between computer chips in servers, mainframes, and supercomputers. In fact, IBM recently tested a *silicon photonics chip* that is fast enough to transfer an entire high-definition movie in just two seconds. Another recent development was invented by engineering researchers at University of Utah. They created a tiny *beamsplitter* (shown in Figure 2-31), which divides light waves into two separate channels of information; it is designed to be placed on a silicon chip to direct light waves. At about one-fiftieth the width of a human hair, it is expected that millions of beamsplitters could be placed on a single chip.

While all-optical computers are not expected for quite some time, silicon photonics is being used today to create hybrid *opto-electronic processors* (that are part optical and part electronic) for supercomput-ers. In addition to increased speed, another benefit of opto-electronic chips is reduced power consumption. While increased bandwidth (such as between servers, between CPU cores, or between the CPU and memory) increases power consumption using electrical connections, the impact is much less with opto-electronic chips because they move data with light instead of electricity.

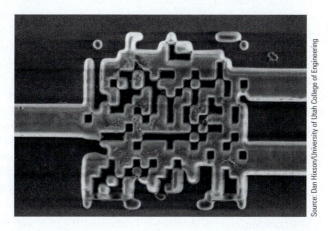

Source: Dan Hixson/University of Utah College of Engineering

**FIGURE 2-31**
Silicon photonics beamsplitter.

---

>**Optical computer.** A computer that uses light, such as from laser beams or infrared beams, to perform digital computations.

# SUMMARY

## DATA AND PROGRAM REPRESENTATION

*Digital computers* work in a two-state, or *binary*, fashion. It is convenient to think of these binary states in terms of 0s and 1s. Computer people refer to these 0s and 1s as bits. Converting data to these 0s and 1s is called *digital data representation.*

While most individuals use the **decimal number system** to represent numbers and perform numeric computations, computers use the **binary numbering system**. Text-based data can be represented with one of several fixed-length binary codes (such as **ASCII** (**American Standard Code for Information Interchange**) or **Unicode**) that represent single characters of data—a numeric digit, alphabetic character, or special symbol—as strings of **bits**. Each string of eight bits is called a **byte**. Use of Unicode is growing because it can represent text in all written languages, including those that use alphabets different from English, such as Chinese, Greek, and Russian.

The storage capacity of computers is often expressed using prefixes in conjunction with the term *byte* to convey the approximate quantity being represented, such as using **kilobyte (KB)**, about one thousand bytes; **megabyte (MB)**, about one million bytes; **gigabyte (GB)**, about one billion bytes; or **terabyte (TB)**, about one trillion bytes. Other possibilities are **petabyte (PB)**, about 1,000 terabytes; **exabyte (EB)**, about 1,000 petabytes; **zettabyte (ZB)**, about 1,000 exabytes; and **yottabyte (YB)**, about 1,000 zettabytes.

The binary system can represent not only text but also graphics, audio, and video data. **Machine language** is the binary-based code through which computers represent program instructions. A program must be translated into machine language before the computer can execute it.

## INSIDE THE SYSTEM UNIT

Personal computers typically contain a variety of hardware components located inside the **system unit**. For instance, *chips* are mounted onto *circuit boards*, and those boards are positioned in slots on the **motherboard**—the main circuit board for a computer. Every computer (and most mobile devices) has one or more **processors**, such as a **central processing unit** (**CPU**)—also called a **microprocessor** when referring to personal computers—and a **graphics processing unit** (**GPU**), that perform the processing for the computer. CPU chips differ in many respects, such as what types of computer the CPU is designed for, *clock speed*, and *word size*. They can also be **multi-core CPUs**, such as the **dual-core** (two cores) and **quad-core** (four cores) **CPUs** now available. Another difference is the amount of **cache memory**—memory located on or very close to the CPU chip to help speed up processing. Other important differences are the general architecture of the CPU and the bus speed and width being used. The overall *processing speed* of the computer determines its performance. One of the most consistent measurements of overall performance is a *benchmark test.*

**Memory** refers to chip-based storage. The main memory for a personal computer is **RAM (random access memory)**. Traditional RAM is **volatile** and is used to hold programs and data temporarily while they are needed; **nonvolatile** RAM is under development. RAM is available in different types and speeds, and is measured in bytes. **ROM (read-only memory)** is a type of nonvolatile memory that stores nonerasable programs. **Flash memory** is a type of nonvolatile memory that can be used for storage by the computer or the user. Flash memory chips can be found in many personal computers and mobile devices; flash memory chips are also integrated into storage media and devices. **Registers** are memory built into the CPU chip to hold data before or during processing. *Fans*, *heat sinks*, and other techniques are used to compensate for the heat that CPUs and other components generate.

Desktop computers contain internal **expansion slots**, into which users can insert **expansion cards** to give the computer added functionality. Expansion of portable computers and mobile devices is more limited and typically obtained via external ports.

A computer **bus** is an electronic path along which bits are transmitted. The **memory bus** moves data between the CPU and RAM. The **frontside bus** (**FSB**) connects the CPU to the *chipset*, which connects the CPU and memory to the rest of the *bus architecture*. Common **expansion buses** include the *PCI* and **PCI Express** (**PCIe**) **buses**, and **Universal Serial Bus** (**USB**). The performance of a bus can be measured by the bus's **bandwidth** or **throughput**; that is, the amount of data that can (theoretically and under real-life conditions, respectively) be transferred via the bus in a given time period.

System units typically have external **ports** that are used to connect peripheral devices to the computer. Notebook, tablet, and netbook computers may have fewer ports than desktop computers. Mobile device users often add new capabilities via USB ports.

**Chapter Objective 3:**
Describe how peripheral devices or other hardware can be added to a computer or mobile device.

## HOW THE CPU WORKS

CPUs today include at least one **arithmetic/logic unit** (**ALU**), which performs integer arithmetic and logical operations on data, and most include at least one **floating point unit** (**FPU**), which performs decimal arithmetic. The **control unit** directs the flow of electronic traffic between memory and the ALU/FPU and also between the CPU and input and output devices. Registers—high-speed temporary holding places within the CPU that hold program instructions and data immediately before and during processing—are used to enhance the computer's performance. The **prefetch unit** requests data and instructions before or as they are needed, the **decode unit** decodes the instructions input into the CPU, internal cache stores frequently used instructions and data, and the **bus interface unit** allows the various parts of the CPU to communicate with each other.

The CPU processes instructions in a sequence called a **machine cycle**, consisting of four basic steps. Each machine language instruction is broken down into several smaller instructions called *microcode*, and each piece of microcode corresponds to an operation (such as adding two numbers located in the CPU's registers) that can be performed inside the CPU. The computer system has a built-in **system clock** that synchronizes all of the computer's activities.

**Chapter Objective 4:**
Understand how the CPU and memory components process program instructions and data.

## MAKING COMPUTERS FASTER AND BETTER NOW AND IN THE FUTURE

There are several possible remedies for a computer that is performing too slowly, including adding more memory, performing system maintenance to clean up the computer's hard drive, buying a larger or additional hard drive, and upgrading the computer's Internet connection or video card, depending on the primary role of the computer and where the processing bottleneck appears to be. To make computers work faster overall, computer designers have developed a number of strategies over the years, and researchers are continually working on new strategies. Some of the strategies already being implemented include improved architecture, **pipelining**, **multiprocessing**, **parallel processing**, and the use of new materials, such as **graphene**, and *3D chips*.

One possibility for both current and future computers is **nanotechnology** research, which focuses on building computer components at the individual atomic and molecular levels. Some computer and consumer products (such as NRAM, solar cells, tennis rackets, and bikes) using **carbon nanotubes** or **CNTs** (tiny hollow tubes made of graphene) are currently on the market. **Quantum computing** and **optical computers** are other possibilities being researched, along with *silicon photonics*, **terascale computing,** and **exascale computing**.

**Chapter Objective 5:**
Name and evaluate several strategies that can be used today for speeding up the operations of a computer.

**Chapter Objective 6:**
List some processing technologies that may be used in future computing devices.

# REVIEW ACTIVITIES

## KEY TERM MATCHING

a. ASCII

b. binary numbering system

c. byte

d. central processing unit (CPU)

e. control unit

f. graphene

g. motherboard

h. nanotechnology

i. RAM (random access memory)

j. Universal Serial Bus (USB)

**Instructions:** Match each key term on the left with the definition on the right that best describes it.

1. _____ A fixed-length, binary coding system used to represent text-based data for computer processing on many types of computers.

2. _____ A group of 8 bits.

3. _____ A universal bus used to connect up to 127 peripheral devices to a computer without requiring the use of additional expansion cards.

4. _____ Flat sheets of carbon that are one atom thick, are extremely light and strong, and are a great conductor of electricity.

5. _____ Memory used to provide a temporary location for the computer to hold data and program instructions while they are needed.

6. _____ The chip located on the motherboard of a computer that performs most of the processing for a computer.

7. _____ The main circuit board of a computing device, located inside the system unit, to which all computer system components connect.

8. _____ The numbering system that represents all numbers using just two symbols (0 and 1).

9. _____ The part of the CPU that coordinates its operations.

10. _____ The science of creating tiny computers and components by working at the individual atomic and molecular levels.

## SELF-QUIZ

**Instructions:** Circle **T** if the statement is true, **F** if the statement is false, or write the best answer in the space provided. **Answers for the self-quiz are located in the References and Resources Guide at the end of the book.**

1. **T  F**  A storage medium that can hold 256 GB can hold about 256 billion characters.

2. **T  F**  The amount of data that can be transferred over a bus in a given time period determines the bus's volatility.

3. **T  F**  Cache memory is typically built into a CPU.

4. **T  F**  A bus is a pathway, such as on the motherboard or inside the CPU, along which bits can be transferred.

5. **T  F**  Computers that process data with light are referred to as quantum computers.

6. The ability of a computer to process data at teraflop speeds is referred to as _____.

7. A CPU with four separate processing cores is referred to as a(n) _____ CPU.

8. A(n) _____ is a connector on the exterior of a computer into which a peripheral device may be plugged.

9. Multi-core CPUs allow _____, in which the CPU is able to work on multiple jobs at one time.

10. Number the following terms from 1 to 9 to indicate their size from smallest to largest.

a. _____ Petabyte     d. _____ Yottabyte     g. _____ Zettabyte

b. _____ Kilobyte     e. _____ Exabyte     h. _____ Terabyte

c. _____ Gigabyte     f. _____ Byte     i. _____ Megabyte

---

**EXERCISES**

1. What do each of the following acronyms stand for?

a. KB _____     c. GPU _____     e. PCIe _____

b. RAM _____     d. USB _____     f. CPU _____

2. Using the ASCII code chart in this chapter or in the References and Resources Guide at the end of the book, decode the following word. What does it say?

01000011       01000001       01000110       01000101

_____        _____        _____        _____

3. Supply the missing words to complete the following statements.

a. The smallest piece of data (a 0 or 1) that can be represented by a computer is called a(n) _____.

b. _____ is an international coding system for text-based data using any written language.

c. L1 is a type of _____.

d. The part of the CPU that performs logical operations and integer arithmetic is the _____.

4. Assume you have a USB mouse, USB keyboard, and USB printer to connect to a computer, but you have only two USB ports. Explain one solution to this problem that does not involve buying a new mouse, keyboard, or printer.

5. If your computer seems sluggish, list two things you could do to try to speed it up without resorting to purchasing an entirely new system.

---

**DISCUSSION QUESTIONS**

1. As discussed in the chapter, one push by computer manufacturers is making computers run as efficiently as possible to save battery power and electricity. What do you think is the motivation behind this trend? Is it social responsibility or a response to consumer demands? Should the energy consumption of electronic devices be regulated and controlled by the government or another organization? Why or why not? How responsible should consumers be for energy conservation in relation to electronic use? In your opinion, what, if anything, should all computer users do to practice green computing?

2. In addition to being used with computers and consumer products, there are also processors and other components designed to be implanted inside the human body, such as the *VeriChip* (discussed in Project 4), implantable wafers containing medication and a processor that delivers the medication at the appropriate time and dosage, *camera pills* that are swallowed to transmit images of an individual's digestive system to a receiving unit, and pacemakers designed to regulate an individual's heart rate. One step further is *brain-to-computer interfacing (BCI)*, which involves implanting electrodes directly into the human brain to restore lost functionality or to facilitate the communications ability of severely disabled individuals, such as by enabling them to control a mouse using only their thoughts. What do you think about these implantable chip applications? Are the benefits worth the risk of something going wrong with the chips implanted inside your body? Are there any privacy risks? Would you consider using an implanted device? Why or why not?

# PROJECTS

**HOT TOPICS**

1. **Modular Phones** As mentioned in the Technology and You box, modular phones are under development. You can slide new modules in to replace obsolete or broken modules; you can also insert a module temporarily and then remove it when you are done with it.

   For this project, research modular phones. Are there any currently on the market? If not, when are they expected to be available? What are the advantages of using a modular phone? Are there any disadvantages? Would you want to have a modular phone? Why or why not? At the conclusion of your research, prepare a one-page summary of your findings and opinions and submit it to your instructor.

**SHORT ANSWER/
RESEARCH**

2. **Adding Memory** Adding additional RAM to a computer is one of the most common computer upgrades. Before purchasing additional memory, however, it is important to make sure that the memory about to be purchased is compatible with the computer.

   For this project, select a computer (such as your own computer, a school computer, or a computer at a local store) and then determine the manufacturer and model number, CPU, current amount of memory, total memory slots, operating system, and the number of available memory slots. (You can look at the computer, research online, or ask an appropriate individual, such as a lab aide in a school computer lab or a salesperson at a local store.) Once you have the necessary information, use your information and a memory supplier's Web site to determine the appropriate type of memory needed for your selected computer. What choices do you have in terms of capacity and configuration? Can you add just one memory module, or do you have to add memory in pairs? Can you keep the old memory modules, or do they have to be removed? At the conclusion of your research, prepare a one-page summary of your findings and recommendations and submit it to your instructor.

**HANDS ON**

3. **Intel Museum Tour** Intel Corporation has a great deal of interesting information about processors on its Web site, including details about its processors, chipsets, motherboards, wireless products, and other components Intel manufactures, as well as information about new technological developments and research that Intel is working on. In addition, an interesting collection of exhibits related to the history of processors and how processing technology works is available through its online museum.

   For this project, go to the Intel Museum at **www.intel.com/museum/index.htm** (if this URL no longer works, go to the Intel home page at www.intel.com and search for "Intel Museum"). Once you are at the Intel Museum home page, visit the online museum exhibits to locate an exhibit or documents related to processors or memory, such as *From Sand to Circuits*, *Making Silicon Chips*, or *Moore's Law*, and then tour the exhibit or read through the available information, making a note of at least three interesting facts you didn't know before. At the conclusion of this task, prepare a short summary listing the tour you took and the interesting facts you recorded and submit it to your instructor.

ETHICS IN ACTION

**4. People Chips** The first RFID chip approved to be implanted into a person was the *VeriChip*. While no longer a current product, VeriChips were designed to be used primarily for identification purposes—the unique number contained in a VeriChip can be read by a proprietary scanner and can be used in conjunction with a database, such as to provide hospital emergency room personnel with health information about an unconscious patient. Today, implanted chips are being used to control access to secure areas and for electronic payment purposes. For example, employees working at one company in Sweden have implanted RFID chips that are used to gain access through security doors, unlock copy machines, and pay for lunch at the facility. What do you think of implanted devices being used for access control (such as for government buildings or highly secure facilities), for expediting passage through security check points (such as at airports), or for making electronic payments (such as at a grocery store)? Would you be willing to be "chipped" if it made some tasks (such as unlocking your home or car) easier or some types of transactions (such as ATM withdrawals) more secure? Is it ethical for a government to require its citizens to be chipped, similar to a national ID card? Is it ethical for a business to request or require that its employees be chipped for security purposes?

For this project, form an opinion about the ethical use and ramifications of human-implantable chips and be prepared to discuss your position (in class, via an online class forum, or via a class blog, depending on your instructor's directions). You may also be asked to write a short paper expressing your opinion.

PRESENTATION/ DEMONSTRATION

**5. Binary Conversions** As discussed in the chapter, all numbers processed by the CPU must be represented in a binary format. Binary (base 2) represents all numbers using 2 digits, decimal uses 10 digits, and hexadecimal uses 16 digits.

For this project, research how to convert a three-digit decimal number to both binary and hexadecimal and back again, without the use of a calculator (see the "A Look at Numbering Systems" feature located in the References and Resources Guide at the end of this book). Next, determine how to represent the decimal number 10 in base 3 (the numbering system that uses only the digits 0, 1, and 2). Share your findings with the class in the form of a short presentation, including a demonstration of the conversions between binary and hexadecimal and the representation of the decimal number 10 in base 3. The presentation should not exceed 10 minutes and should make use of one or more presentation aids such as a whiteboard, handouts, or a computer-based slide presentation (your instructor may provide additional requirements). You may also be asked to submit a summary of the presentation to your instructor.

BALANCING ACT

**6. Should Computers Run Vital Systems Like the Stock Market?** In 2013, the stock market tumbled in response to a tweet from the Associated Press that President Obama had been injured by explosions at the White House. One problem? It never happened. Another problem? The computers that analyze natural language to allow high-speed trading saw the words "explosion," "Obama," and "White House" and caused the reaction. Today, computers run a number of vital systems and are viewed by many as the safer alternative to avoid human error. But, the AP Twitter account was hacked by humans to cause the Wall Street incident, so what is to prevent hackers from using the nation's computerized systems to do harm? What types of safeguards are needed to continue to use computers to run vital systems? Or should there always be a human ultimately in charge? What if cyberterrorists gain control over the country's financial or defense systems? What about the computers that run water purification and other health-related systems? Could computerized systems be endangering our lives instead of helping them?

Pick a side on this issue, form an opinion and gather supporting evidence, and be prepared to discuss and defend your position in a classroom debate or in a one- to two-page paper, depending on your instructor's directions.

# chapter 3

# Storage

**After completing this chapter, you will be able to do the following:**

1. Name several general characteristics of storage systems.

2. Describe the three most common types of hard drives and what they are used for today.

3. Discuss the various types of optical discs available today and how they differ from each other.

4. Identify some flash memory storage devices and media and explain how they are used today.

5. List at least three other types of storage systems.

6. Summarize the storage alternatives for a typical personal computer.

# OVERVIEW

In Chapter 2, we discussed the role of RAM, the computer's main memory. RAM temporarily holds program instructions, data, and output while they are needed by the computer. For instance, when you first create a letter or other word processing document on your computer, both the word processing program and the document are temporarily stored in RAM. But when the word processing program is closed, the computer no longer needs to work with the program or the document, and so they are both erased from RAM. Consequently, anything (such as your word processing document) that needs to be preserved for future use needs to be stored on a more permanent medium. Storage systems fill this role.

We begin this chapter with a look at the characteristics common among all storage systems. Then, we discuss the primary storage for most personal computers—the hard drive. From there, we turn our attention to optical discs, including how they work and the various types of optical discs available today. Next, we discuss flash memory storage systems, followed by a look at a few other types of storage systems, including network and cloud storage, smart cards, and the storage systems used with large computer systems. The chapter concludes with a discussion about evaluating the storage alternatives for a typical personal computer. ∎

## STORAGE SYSTEMS CHARACTERISTICS

All *storage systems* have specific characteristics, such as having both a storage medium and a storage device, how portable and volatile the system is, how data is accessed and represented, and the type of storage technology used. These characteristics are discussed in the next few sections.

### Storage Media and Storage Devices

There are two parts to any storage system: the **storage medium** and the **storage device**. A storage medium is the hardware where data is actually stored (for example, a DVD or a flash memory card); a storage medium is inserted into its corresponding storage device (such as a DVD drive or a flash memory card reader) in order to be read from or written to. Often the storage device and storage medium are two separate pieces of hardware (that is, the storage medium is *removable*), although with some systems—such as a hard drive or most USB flash drives—the two parts are permanently sealed together to form one piece of hardware.

Storage devices can be *internal* (located inside the system unit), *external* (plugged into an external port on the system unit), or *remote* (located on another computer, such as a network server or Web server). Internal devices have the advantage of requiring no additional

---

> **Storage medium.** The part of a storage system, such as a DVD disc, where data is stored. > **Storage device.** A piece of hardware, such as a DVD drive, into which a storage medium is inserted to be read from or written to.

The letter C is usually assigned to the first hard drive.

CD/DVD drives are usually assigned letters after the hard drives, such as D for this computer.

AS-kom/Shutterstock.com

Any storage devices attached to the computer via USB ports are typically assigned next, such as E for this USB flash drive.

Other letters, beginning with F for this computer, are used for any other storage devices attached to the computer, such as via this built-in flash memory card reader.

 **FIGURE 3-1**

**Storage device identifiers.** To keep track of storage devices in an unambiguous way, the computer system assigns letters of the alphabet or names to each of them.

desk space and are usually faster than their external counterparts. External devices, however, can be easily transported from one location to another (such as to share data with others, to transfer data between a work computer and a home computer, or to take digital photos to a photo store). They can also be removed from the computer and stored in a secure area (such as for backup purposes or to protect sensitive data). Remote devices are accessed over a network. Some remote storage devices, such as those accessed via the Internet, have the additional advantage of being accessible from any computer with an Internet connection.

Regardless of how storage devices are connected to a computer, letters of the alphabet and/or names are typically assigned to each storage device so that the user can identify each device easily when it needs to be used (see Figure 3-1). Some drive letters, such as the letter C typically used with the primary hard drive, are usually consistent from computer to computer and do not change even if more storage devices are added to the computer. The rest of the drive letters on a computer may change as new devices are added either permanently (such as when an additional hard drive is installed inside the computer) or temporarily (such as when a USB flash drive, digital camera, external hard drive, or smartphone is connected to the computer). When a new storage device is detected, the computer just assigns and reassigns drive letters, as needed.

## Volatility

As discussed in Chapter 2, conventional RAM is volatile so programs and documents held in RAM are erased when they are no longer needed by the computer or when the power to the computer is turned off. Storage media, however, are nonvolatile, so the data remains on the media even when the power to the computer or storage device is off. Consequently, storage media are used for anything that needs to be saved for future use.

## Random vs. Sequential Access

When the computer receives an instruction that requires data located on a storage medium, it must go to the designated location on the appropriate storage medium and retrieve the requested data. This procedure is referred to as *access*. Two basic access methods are available: random and sequential.

*Random access*, also called *direct access*, means that data can be retrieved directly from any location on the storage medium, in any order. A random access device works in a manner similar to a DVD player used to play music or movies; that is, it can jump directly to a particular location on the medium when data located at that location is needed. Virtually all storage devices used with computers today for day-to-day storage—including hard drives, DVD drives, and USB flash drives—are random access devices.

Media that allow random access are sometimes referred to as *addressable* media. This means that the storage system can locate each piece of stored data at a unique *address*, which is determined by the computer system. With *sequential access*, however, the data can only be retrieved in the order in which it is physically stored on the medium. One type of storage device that is sometimes used with computers for backup purposes and that uses sequential access is a *magnetic tape drive*. Computer magnetic tapes work like audiocassette tapes or videotapes—to get to a specific location on the tape, you must play or fast forward through all of the tape that comes before the location you want to access.

## Logical vs. Physical Representation

Anything (such as a program, letter, digital photograph, or song) stored on a storage medium is referred to as a **file**. Data files are also often called *documents*. When a document that was just created (such as a memo or letter in a word processing program) is saved, it is stored as a new file on the storage medium designated by the user. During the storage process, the user is required to give the file a name, called a **filename**; that filename is used to retrieve the file when it is needed at a later time.

To keep files organized, related documents are often stored in **folders** (also called *directories*) located on the storage medium. For example, one folder might contain memos to business associates while another might hold a set of budgets (see Figure 3-2). To organize files further, you can create *subfolders* (*subdirectories*) within a folder. For instance, you might create a subfolder within the *Budgets* subfolder for each fiscal year. In Figure 3-2, both *Budgets* and *Memos* are subfolders inside the *Documents* folder; the *Budgets* subfolder contains two additional subfolders (*Current year* and *Next year*).

Although both the user and the computer use drive letters, folder names, and filenames to save and retrieve documents, they perceive them differently. The user typically views how data is stored (what has been discussed so far in this section and what appears in the File Explorer file management program screen shown in Figure 3-2) using *logical file representation*. That is, individuals view a document stored as one complete unit in a particular folder on a particular drive. Computers, however, use *physical file representation*; that is, they access a particular document stored on a storage medium using its physical location or locations. For example, the *ABC Industries Proposal Memo* file shown in Figure 3-2 is *logically* located in the *Memos* folders in the *Documents*, *Debbie*, and *Users* folders on the hard drive C, but the content of this file could be *physically* stored in many different pieces scattered across that hard drive. When this occurs, the computer keeps track of the various physical locations used to store that file, as well as the logical representations (filename, folder names, and drive letter) used to identify that file, in order to retrieve the entire file when needed. Fortunately, users do not have to be concerned with how files are physically stored on a storage medium because the computer keeps track of that information and uses it to retrieve files whenever they are requested.

 **FIGURE 3-2**

**Organizing data.**
Folders are used to organize related items on a storage medium.

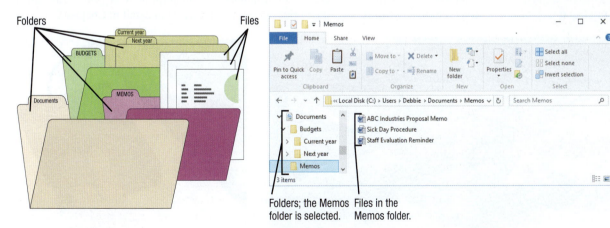

Folders

Files

Folders; the Memos folder is selected.

Files in the Memos folder.

---

>**File.** Something stored on a storage medium, such as a program, a document, or an image. >**Filename.** A name given to a file by the user; it is used to retrieve the file at a later time. >**Folder.** A named place on a storage medium into which the user can place files in order to keep the files stored on that medium organized.

## Type of Storage Technology Used

Data is stored *magnetically* or *optically* on many types of storage media. With magnetic storage systems, such as conventional hard drives, data is stored magnetically on the storage medium, which means the data (0s and 1s) is represented using different magnetic alignments. The storage device can change the magnetic alignment when needed, so data can be written to the medium, deleted from the medium, or rewritten to the medium. Optical storage media (such as DVDs) store data optically using laser beams. On some optical media, the laser burns permanent marks to represent 0s and 1s into the surface of the medium so the data cannot be erased or rewritten. With rewritable optical media, the laser changes the reflectivity of the medium to represent 0s and 1s but it does not permanently alter the disc surface so the reflectivity of the medium can be changed back again as needed. Consequently, the data stored on a rewritable optical disc can be changed.

Some storage systems use a combination of magnetic and optical technology. Others use a different technology altogether, such as flash memory storage systems that represent data using *electrons* inside *flash memory cells* to represent 0s and 1s. Some of the most widely used storage systems are discussed next.

## HARD DRIVES

With the exception of computers designed to use only network storage devices (such as thin clients and some Internet appliances), virtually all personal computers come with a **hard drive** that is used to store most programs and data. *Internal hard drives* (those located inside the system unit) are not designed to be removed, unless they need to be repaired or replaced. *External hard drives* typically connect to a computer via an external port (such as a USB or Thunderbolt port) or a wireless connection and are frequently used for additional storage (such as for digital photos, videos, and other large multimedia files—particularly for users of tablets and other devices with limited internal storage, as discussed in the How It Works box), to move files between computers, and for backup purposes. Hard drives are also incorporated into other consumer products, such as smartphones, digital video recorders (DVRs), gaming consoles, digital camcorders, and more, although some devices today use only flash memory chips for internal storage.

For security purposes, both internal and external hard drives today are available with built-in encryption that automatically encrypts (essentially scrambles) all data stored on the hard drive and limits access to the hard drive to only authorized users, typically via a password, PIN (personal identification number), or fingerprint scan (see Figure 3-3). Encryption, passwords, and fingerprint readers are discussed in detail in Chapter 9.

**FIGURE 3-3**

**Encrypted hard drives.** The data stored on these external hard drives is accessed via a fingerprint scan (left) or PIN (right).

*Source: Apricorn*

> **Hard drive.** The primary storage system for most computers; used to store most programs and data used with a computer.

## Magnetic Hard Drives, Solid-State Drives (SSDs), and Solid-State Hybrid Drives (SSHDs)

Traditional hard drives are magnetic hard drives in which particles on the metal disks inside the drive are magnetized to represent the data's 0s and 1s (see Figure 3-4). The particles retain their magnetic orientation until the orientation is changed again, so files can be stored, rewritten, and deleted as needed.

Newer types of hard drives are solid-state drives (SSDs), which use flash memory technology instead of magnetic technology to store data, and solid-state hybrid drives (SSHDs), which use a combination of magnetic disks and flash memory. These three types of hard drives are discussed next.

### Magnetic Hard Drives

A **magnetic hard drive** (the traditional type of hard drive, also called a **hard disk drive** or an **HDD**) contains one or more metal *hard disks* or *platters* that are coated with a magnetizable substance. These hard disks are permanently sealed inside the hard drive case, along with the *read/write heads* used to store (*write*) and retrieve (*read*) data and an *access mechanism* used to move the read/write heads in and out over the surface of the hard disks (see Figure 3-5). Hard drives designed for desktop computers (sometimes referred to as *desktop hard drives*) typically use 2.5-inch or 3.5-inch hard disks and notebook hard drives typically use 2.5-inch hard disks. Portable digital media players, digital cameras, and other small devices that include a magnetic hard drive typically use tiny 1.5-inch or smaller hard drives instead. Regardless of the size, one hard drive usually contains a stack of two or more hard disks; if so, there is a read/write head for each hard disk surface (top and bottom), as illustrated in Figure 3-5, and these heads move in and out over the disk surfaces simultaneously.

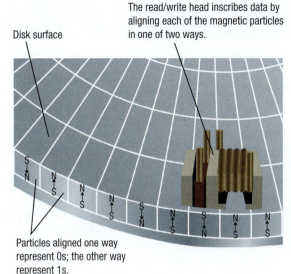

Disk surface

The read/write head inscribes data by aligning each of the magnetic particles in one of two ways.

Particles aligned one way represent 0s; the other way represent 1s.

**FIGURE 3-4**
Storing data on magnetic disks.

**FIGURE 3-5**
Magnetic hard drives.

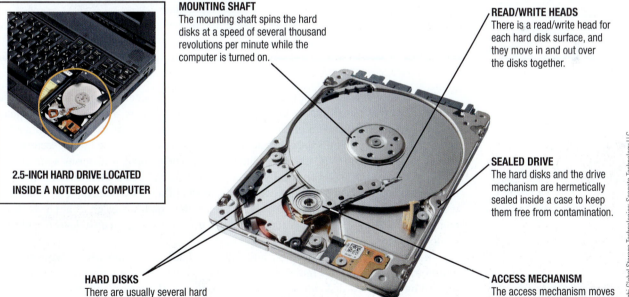

**2.5-INCH HARD DRIVE LOCATED INSIDE A NOTEBOOK COMPUTER**

**MOUNTING SHAFT**
The mounting shaft spins the hard disks at a speed of several thousand revolutions per minute while the computer is turned on.

**READ/WRITE HEADS**
There is a read/write head for each hard disk surface, and they move in and out over the disks together.

**SEALED DRIVE**
The hard disks and the drive mechanism are hermetically sealed inside a case to keep them free from contamination.

**HARD DISKS**
There are usually several hard disk surfaces on which to store data. Most hard drives store data on both sides of each disk.

**INSIDE A 3.5-INCH HARD DRIVE**

**ACCESS MECHANISM**
The access mechanism moves the read/write heads in and out together between the hard disk surfaces to access required data.

Source: Hitachi Global Storage Technologies; Seagate Technology LLC

>**Magnetic hard drive.** A hard drive consisting of one or more metal magnetic disks permanently sealed, along with an access mechanism and read/write heads, inside its drive; also called a **hard disk drive (HDD)**.

# HOW IT WORKS

### More Storage for Your Tablet

For many users, the internal storage capacity of a tablet (usually between 16 GB and 128 GB of storage) just doesn't cut it. While ultra-slim SSDs, which can bring tablet storage up to 500 GB, are becoming available, the hard drives are not cheap. Minimizing the built-in storage of tablets and other mobile devices is necessary to keep the cost and size down, but many users want more. While some users connect their device to a desktop or notebook computer to transfer content (such as movies, music, and photos) to and from their mobile devices, there is another, easier option—going wireless.

A number of new storage products are emerging that connect directly to your devices (including tablets, smartphones, and computers) via Wi-Fi so that you don't have to worry about cables or how to connect to a device that doesn't have a USB port. Sizes and configurations vary widely—from the 32 GB SanDisk *Connect Wireless Flash Drive* to the 2 TB Seagate *Wireless Plus* magnetic hard drive (shown in the accompanying photograph) that can hold up to 1,000 high-definition movies. These storage devices have built-in Wi-Fi capabilities and data can be transferred in both directions (such as to stream a movie from the hard drive to your tablet or smart TV, or to transfer photos or videos taken with your smartphone to the hard drive). Unlike cloud storage, these drives can be used in locations (such as while traveling in a car or an airplane) where you don't

have Internet access and, because the drives are accessed locally, you can play back full HD video without any buffering or stuttering. The Wireless Plus even allows up to eight devices to access the hard drive at one time and it has a 10-hour battery life, which makes it even more useful while you are on the go.

To use one of these wireless hard drives with your mobile device, you need to download the appropriate app from your app store (such as the *App Store* for iPad and iPhone users or *Google Play* for Andriod users) and launch it. You should then have quick and easy wireless access to the wireless drive. You can also connect these drives to your computer, if you wish, via Wi-Fi.

Source: Seagate Technology LLC

The surface of a hard disk is organized into **tracks** (concentric rings) and pie-shaped groups of **sectors** (small pieces of a track), as shown in Figure 3-6. On most computer systems, the smallest amount of disk space on a hard drive that can be used to store a file is a **cluster**—one or more adjacent sectors. The computer numbers the tracks, sectors, and clusters so it can keep track of where data is stored. The computer also uses a *file system* to record where each file is physically stored on the hard drive and what filename the user has assigned to it. When the user requests a document (always by filename), the computer uses its file system to retrieve it. Because a cluster is the smallest area on a hard drive that a computer can access, everything stored on a hard drive always takes up at least one cluster of storage space.

In addition to tracks, sectors, and clusters, hard drives are also organized into **cylinders** (refer again to Figure 3-6). A cylinder is the collection of one specific track located on each hard disk surface. In other words, it is the area on all of the hard disks inside a hard drive that can be accessed without moving the read/write access mechanism, once it has been moved to the proper position. For example, the hard drive shown

> **Track.** A concentric path on a disk where data is recorded. > **Sector.** A small piece of a track. > **Cluster.** One or more sectors; the smallest addressable area of a disk. > **Cylinder.** The collection of tracks located in the same location on a set of hard disk surfaces.

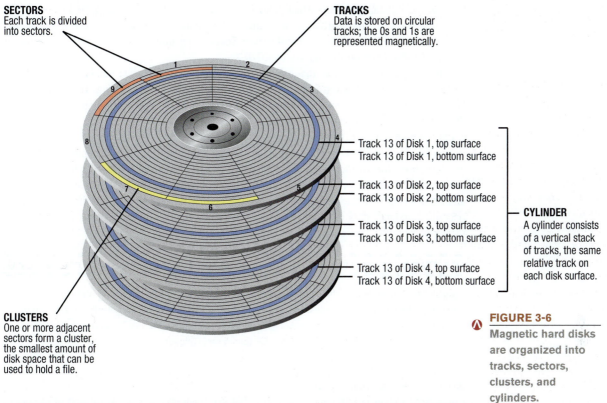

**SECTORS**
Each track is divided into sectors.

**TRACKS**
Data is stored on circular tracks; the 0s and 1s are represented magnetically.

Track 13 of Disk 1, top surface
Track 13 of Disk 1, bottom surface
Track 13 of Disk 2, top surface
Track 13 of Disk 2, bottom surface
Track 13 of Disk 3, top surface
Track 13 of Disk 3, bottom surface
Track 13 of Disk 4, top surface
Track 13 of Disk 4, bottom surface

**CYLINDER**
A cylinder consists of a vertical stack of tracks, the same relative track on each disk surface.

**CLUSTERS**
One or more adjacent sectors form a cluster, the smallest amount of disk space that can be used to hold a file.

**FIGURE 3-6**
Magnetic hard disks are organized into tracks, sectors, clusters, and cylinders.

in Figure 3-6 contains four hard disks, which means there are eight possible recording surfaces (using both sides of each hard disk). Consequently, a cylinder for that hard drive would consist of eight tracks, such as track 13 on all eight surfaces. Because all of the read/write heads move together, all of the tracks in a cylinder are accessible at the same time.

Traditionally, the magnetic particles on a hard disk have been aligned horizontally, parallel to the hard disk's surface (referred to as *longitudinal magnetic recording*). To increase capacity and reliability, most new hard drives today use *perpendicular magnetic recording* (*PMR*), in which the bits are placed upright (as in Figure 3-4) to allow them to be closer together than is possible with a horizontal layout.

To allow for even higher capacities, hard drives using *shingled magnetic recording* (*SMR*), which squeezes more data onto disks by overlapping the data tracks on them like the shingles on a roof, are available. While SMR offers increased capacities, it may have reduced performance, particularly when writing data to the disk. Another option becoming available is hard drives filled with helium gas instead of air to reduce friction and vibration. In fact, hard drive manufacturer Western Digital recently announced that it will produce only helium-filled drives by 2017. An emerging option is *Heat-Assisted Magnetic Recording* (*HAMR*), which uses lasers to temporarily heat the surface of the hard disks when storing data in order

**ASK THE EXPERT**

Courtesy Seagate Technology LLC

**Josh Tinker,** Product Planning Manager, Seagate Technology

**Should my next computer have a magnetic hard drive or an SSD?**

Your storage options for a new computer include traditional hard drives (HDDs), solid-state drives (SSDs), and solid-state hybrid drives (SSHDs). Selecting what is right for you is a trade-off between price, performance, and capacity.

> HDDs have the lowest cost and high capacity, but have only good performance.

> SSDs have faster computer performance and better shock resistance, but are expensive.

> SSHDs have SSD-like performance and high capacity, but are more expensive than HDDs (though less expensive than SSDs at the same capacity).

to pack more data onto the surface than is normally possible—it is expected to boost the storage capacity of hard drives significantly. The capacity of magnetic hard drives is currently up to 10 TB; hard drive manufacturer Seagate has announced that it hopes to have a 20 TB HAMR drive on the market by 2020.

It is important to realize that a magnetic hard drive's read/write heads never touch the surface of the hard disks at any time, even during reading and writing. If the read/write heads do touch the surface (for example, if a desktop computer is bumped while the hard drive is spinning or if a foreign object gets onto the surface of a hard disk), a *head crash* occurs, which can permanently damage the hard drive. Because the read/write heads are located extremely close to the surface of the hard disks (less than one-half millionth of an inch above the surface), the presence of a foreign object the width of a human hair or even a smoke particle on the surface of a hard disk is like placing a huge boulder on a road and then trying to drive over it with your car. When hard drives containing critical data become damaged, data recovery firms may be able to help out, as discussed in the Inside the Industry box.

**CAUTION  CAUTION  CAUTION  CAUTION  CAUTION  CAUTION  CAUT**

Because you never know when a head crash or other hard drive failure will occur—there may be no warning whatsoever—be sure to back up the data on your hard drive on a regular basis. Backing up data—that is, creating a second copy of important files—is critical not only for businesses but also for individuals and is discussed in detail in Chapter 5 and Chapter 9.

### Solid-State Drives (SSDs)

**Solid-state drives (SSDs)** are hard drives that use flash memory chips instead of magnetic disks (see Figure 3-7); consequently, SSDs have no moving parts and data is stored as electrical charges on the flash memory media located within the SSD. These characteristics mean that SSDs are not subject to mechanical failures like magnetic hard drives, and are, therefore, more resistant to shock and vibration. They also consume less power, generate less heat, make no noise, and are much faster than magnetic hard drives. Consequently, SSDs are becoming the norm for netbooks, mobile devices, and other very portable devices. They are also being used with notebooks and other portable computers instead of, or in addition to, a magnetic hard drive. While SSDs are faster than HDDs, they are more expensive.

SSDs are most often 2.5-inch drives so they can easily be used instead of conventional magnetic hard drives in notebooks, netbooks, and other personal computers (most come with a bracket so the drive can also be used in a 3.5-inch drive bay of a desktop computer). There are also smaller 1.8-inch SSDs available that can be used when a smaller physical size is needed, such as for a portable digital media player or smartphone. SSDs are also available as expansion card drives. SSDs are available in capacities up to 4 TB today.

While small-capacity SSDs are affordable, high-capacity SSDs are extremely expensive. Consequently, one recent trend is utilizing both an SSD and a magnetic hard drive inside a single computer. A smaller, less expensive SSD (such as 128 GB)

**FIGURE 3-7**

**Solid-state drives (SSDs).** Contain only flash memory.

Source: Transcend Information USA

Data is stored in flash memory chips located inside the drive; unlike magnetic drives, there are no moving parts.

---

> **Solid-state drive (SSD).** A hard drive that uses flash memory chips instead of metal magnetic hard disks.

# INSIDE THE INDUSTRY

## Data Recovery Experts

It happens far more often than most people imagine. A home computer crashes and all the family's digital photos are lost, a tablet computer is dropped and the files are no longer accessible, a smartphone falls into a pool and no longer works, or a business is flooded and the computers storing the business's critical files are damaged. If the data on a damaged device is backed up, then it is fairly easy and inexpensive to restore it onto a new hard drive or device. If the data is not backed up, however, it is time to seek help from a data recovery expert.

Professional *data recovery firms*, such as DriveSavers in California, specialize in recovering critical data from damaged storage devices (see the accompanying photos). Engineers open the damaged device (in a *Class 100 clean room* to minimize contamination and maximize data recovery) and then make an image of the data located on that device, bit by bit, onto a target drive. The target drive is then used to reconstruct the data; if the file directory is not recovered, engineers try to match the jumbled data to file types in order to reconstruct the original files. Once the data recovery process is complete, the customer receives the data on a new hard drive. To ensure data is safe and remains confidential, DriveSavers has numerous security certifications; in fact, it is used by government agencies to recover critical data.

Professional data recovery firms are also used when hard drives and other storage media simply stop working. In fact, DriveSavers estimates that 75% of its business is due to malfunctioning devices. With the vast amounts of digital data (such as photos, music, home videos, personal documents, and school papers) that the average person stores today, data recovery firms are increasingly being used by individuals to recover personal data, in addition to being used by businesses to recover critical company data.

Data loss can happen to any business or individual, even to the rich and famous. A few celebrity clients of DriveSavers include Bruce Willis, Conan O'Brien, Harrison Ford, Sean Connery, and Bill Oakely, the executive producer of *The Simpsons*, whose computer crashed taking scripts for 12 episodes of the show with it. In some cases, data loss is a result of a natural disaster or an unusual circumstance; for instance an iMac computer that contained the only digital pictures of a survivor's family was destroyed by a Japanese tsunami; a laptop was trapped for two days beneath a sunken cruise ship in the Amazon River; and a server went down at a Fortune 500 company, which caused that company to lose all its financial data and stockholder information. In all of these cases, DriveSavers was able to recover all of the lost data.

Data recovery firms stress the importance of backing up data to avoid data loss. According to Scott Gaidano, founder and former president of DriveSavers, "The first thing we tell people is back up, back up, back up. It's amazing how many people don't back up." It is also important to make sure the backup procedure is working. For instance, the Fortune 500 company mentioned previously performed regular backups and kept the backup media in a fire-resistant safe, but it wasn't known until after its server crashed that all the backup media were blank.

Because potentially losing all the data on a storage medium can be so stressful and traumatic, DriveSavers has its own data-crisis counselor, a former suicide hotline worker. Fortunately for its clients, DriveSavers has an extremely high recovery rate. While the services of data recovery experts are not cheap, when the data on a damaged device is critical data, using a data recovery expert is your best chance for getting your data back.

Source: DriveSavers Data Recovery

**Data recovery.** The data on this destroyed computer (left) was recovered by data recovery experts in a clean room (right).

**MAGNETIC HARD DRIVE**
This 2 TB drive contains 2 hard disks and 4 read/write heads that operate in a manner similar to a conventional hard drive.

**FLASH MEMORY CHIPS**
This drive contains 8 GB of flash memory to increase performance.

Source: Seagate Technology LLC

**FIGURE 3-8**
**Solid-state hybrid drives (SSHDs).**
Contain both magnetic hard disks and flash memory.

can be used for the operating system and important applications to speed up the system, and a larger magnetic hard drive can be used for data storage and lesser-used applications. Computers with both types of drives and Intel's *Smart Response* technology can go one step further by monitoring the programs and files used most frequently and storing them on the SSD for faster access.

## Solid-State Hybrid Drives (SSHDs)

**Solid-state hybrid drives (SSHDs)**, also called **hybrid drives**, contain both flash memory chips and magnetic hard drives (see Figure 3-8). With an SSHD, the data that is most directly associated with performance (such as boot data and frequently accessed data) is stored in the flash memory. The flash memory (usually about 8 GB) allows the hard drive to be faster. It is used to reduce the number of times the hard disks need to be read, as well as to temporarily store data to be written to the hard disks, both of which can extend the battery life of portable computers and mobile devices. The flash memory can also allow encryption or other security measures to be built into the drive. SSHDs are considered a good balance between price and performance because they are nearly as fast as solid-state drives (SSDs) but are just slightly more expensive per gigabyte than magnetic hard disk drives (HDDs).

## Internal vs. External Hard Drives

*Internal hard drives* are permanently located inside a computer's system unit and typically are not removed unless there is a problem with them. Virtually all computers have at least one internal hard drive (an HDD, SSD, or SSHD) that is used to store programs and data. In addition, a variety of *external hard drives* are available (see Figure 3-9). External hard drives are commonly used for transporting a large amount of data from one computer to another (by moving the entire hard drive to another computer), for backup purposes, and for additional storage.

Today, because of their large capacity, full-sized external hard drives are often used by individuals to store their digital photos, digital music, home movies, recorded TV shows, and other multimedia content. To distribute multimedia to the computers and entertainment devices located in the home, special hard drive products (typically called *home servers* or *media servers*) are available. These special hard drives are designed to be connected to a home network to serve as a centralized storage device for all the computers in the home, as well as to back up the data on those computers automatically. There are also *DVR expanders*—hard drives designed to add additional storage to an individual's digital video recorder (DVR).

Full-sized external hard drives can be moved from computer to computer when needed; however, *portable hard drives* are smaller external hard drives specifically designed for that purpose. Unlike full-sized external hard drives (which typically need to be plugged into a power outlet to be used), portable hard drives are typically powered via the computer they are being used with instead. The capacity of portable hard drives is typically smaller than full-sized external hard drives. Most external desktop and portable hard drives connect to the computer via a USB connection. However, some can connect via a wired or wireless networking connection instead, and Thunderbolt drives are also available.

>**Solid-state hybrid drive (SSHD).** A hard drive that uses a combination of flash memory chips and magnetic hard disks; also called a **hybrid drive**.

**FULL-SIZED EXTERNAL HARD DRIVES**
This drive is about the size of a 5 by 7-inch picture frame, but thicker, and holds 6 TB.

**PORTABLE HARD DRIVES**
This drive is about the size of a 3 by 5-inch index card, but thicker, and holds 2 TB.

**WIRELESS HARD DRIVES**
This drive connects via Wi-Fi and holds 500 GB.

**FIGURE 3-9**
External hard drives.

## Hard Drive Speed and Disk Caching

The hard disks inside a magnetic hard drive typically spin continually at a rate of between 5,400 and 15,000 revolutions per minute. The total time that it takes for a hard drive to read or write data is called the **disk access time** and requires the following three steps:

1. Move the read/write heads to the cylinder that contains (or will contain) the desired data—called *seek time*.

2. Rotate the hard disks into the proper position so that the read/write heads are located over the part of the cylinder to be used—called *rotational delay*.

3. Move the data, such as reading the data from the hard disk and transferring it to memory, or transferring the data from memory and storing it on the hard disk—called *data movement time*.

A typical magnetic disk access time is around 8 milliseconds (ms). To minimize disk access time, magnetic hard drives usually store related data on the same cylinder. This strategy reduces seek time and, therefore, improves the overall access time. Because SSDs do not have to move any parts to store or retrieve data, they don't require seek time or rotational delay and their access time is much faster than magnetic hard drives—essentially instantaneous at about 0.1 ms on some benchmark tests.

To speed up magnetic hard drive performance, *disk caching* is often used. A *cache* (pronounced "cash") is a place to store something temporarily. For instance, in Chapter 2, you learned that cache memory is very fast memory used by the CPU to store data and instructions that might be needed in order to speed up processing. A **disk cache** is similar in concept—it stores copies of data or programs that are located on the hard drive and that might be needed soon in memory in order to avoid having to retrieve the data or programs from the hard drive when they are requested. Because the hard disks do not have to be accessed if the requested data is located in the disk cache and because retrieving data from memory is much faster than from a magnetic hard disk, disk caching can speed up performance. Disk caching also saves wear and tear on the hard drive and, in portable computers, can extend battery life.

While the memory used for disk caching can be a designated portion of RAM, today's hard drives typically use a disk cache consisting of memory chips located on a circuit board inside the hard drive case. When a magnetic hard drive uses disk caching (as most do today), any time the hard drive is accessed the computer copies the requested data, as

>**Disk access time.** The time it takes to locate and read data from (or position and write data to) a storage medium. >**Disk cache.** Memory used in conjunction with a magnetic hard drive to improve system performance.

well as extra data located in neighboring areas of the hard drive (such as all of the data located on the cylinder being accessed), to the disk cache. When the next data is requested, the computer checks the disk cache first to see if the data it needs is already there. If it is, the data is retrieved for processing; if not, the computer retrieves the requested data from the hard disks. Most conventional magnetic hard drives today include a RAM-based disk cache ranging in size from 16 MB to 128 MB; hybrid hard drives may have a small RAM-based disk cache in addition to their much larger amount of flash memory.

## Hard Drive Partitioning and File Systems

*Partitioning* a hard drive enables you to divide the physical capacity of a single hard drive logically into separate areas, called *partitions* or *volumes*. Partitions function as independent hard drives and are sometimes referred to as *logical drives* because each partition is labeled and treated separately (such as C drive and D drive) when viewed in a file management program (such as File Explorer for Windows computers), but they are still physically one hard drive. One or more partitions are created when a hard drive is first *formatted* (that is, prepared for data storage). For instance, some new personal computers come with two partitions: a C drive partition ready to use for programs and data and a D drive partition set up as a *recovery partition*. A recovery partition contains the data necessary to restore a hard drive back to its state at the time the computer was purchased and is designed to be used only if the computer malfunctions.

In the past, operating systems could only use hard drives up to 512 MB, so hard drives larger than that limit had to use multiple partitions. While today's operating systems can use much larger hard drives and, therefore, do not require the use of multiple partitions, partitioning a large magnetic hard drive can make it function more efficiently. This is because operating systems typically use a larger cluster size with a larger hard drive. Because even tiny files have to use up one entire cluster of storage space, disk space is often wasted when a large cluster size is used. When a hard drive is partitioned, each logical drive can use a smaller cluster size because each logical drive is smaller than the original hard drive.

Users can create additional partitions on a hard drive if desired, but they should be careful when partitioning a hard drive because deleting a partition erases all data contained on that partition. One reason advanced users may partition a primary hard drive is to be able to use two different operating systems on the same hard drive—such as Windows and Linux (these and other operating systems are discussed in detail in Chapter 5). With a *dual-boot system* such as this, the user specifies the operating system to be run each time the computer boots. Another reason for partitioning a hard drive is to create the appearance of having separate hard drives for file management, multiple users, or other purposes. For instance, some users choose to create a separate partition on which to store their data, as in Figure 3-10. Storing data files on a separate physical hard drive or logical partition makes it easier for the user to locate data files. It also enables users to back up all data files simply by backing up the entire hard drive or partition containing the data, as well as change or upgrade the operating system in one partition without disturbing their data partitions.

The partition size, cluster size (on magnetic hard drives), maximum drive size, and maximum file size that can be used with a hard drive are determined by the *file system* being used. For instance, most Windows computers typically use *NTFS*, which supports much larger hard drives and files than the older *FAT32* and includes better security and error-recovery capabilities. Computers with older versions of Windows and some removable storage devices like USB flash drives use FAT32, which has a maximum partition size of 32 GB and a maximum file size of 4 GB.

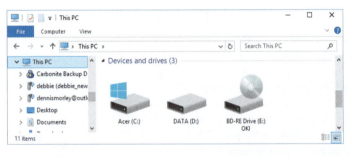

**FIGURE 3-10**

Hard drive partitions.

**TIP**

Windows servers may use the new file system *Resilient File System (ReFS)* instead of NTFS.

## Hard Drive Interface Standards

Hard drives connect, or interface, with a computer using one of several different standards. The most common internal *hard drive interface standard* for desktop computers today is *serial ATA (SATA)*. The SATA standard was designed to replace the older, slower *parallel ATA (PATA)* standard, which is also referred to as *Fast ATA* and *EIDE (Enhanced Integrated Drive Electronics)*. SATA is faster (up to 6 Gbps for *SATA III* devices) than PATA and uses thinner cables, which means SATA hard drives take up less room inside the system unit. Internal SSDs may use the SATA interface but many plug directly into a PCIe port or use the faster *serial attached SCSI (SAS)* interface standard. External hard drives most often connect to the computer via a USB or Thunderbolt port.

In addition to SATA and SAS, servers may use *Fibre Channel*, which is a reliable, flexible, and very fast standard geared for long-distance, high-bandwidth applications. For network storage, newer standards, such as *Internet SCSI (iSCSI)* that communicates over the Internet or another network using the TCP/IP networking standard, have evolved. Networks and networking standards are discussed in Chapter 7.

> **TIP**
>
> You can transfer the data from the hard drive of an old or broken computer if the hard drive is still functioning—just use an appropriate transfer cable (such as SATA to USB) to connect the drive to a USB port on your new computer.

> **HW**

## OPTICAL DISCS AND DRIVES

Data on **optical discs** (such as CDs and DVDs) is stored and read *optically*; that is, by using laser beams. General characteristics of optical discs are discussed next, followed by a look at the various types of optical discs available today.

### Optical Disc Characteristics

Optical discs are thin circular discs made out of *polycarbonate substrate*—essentially a type of very strong plastic—that are topped with layers of other materials and coatings used to store data and protect the disc. Data can be stored on one or both sides of an optical disc, depending on the disc design, and some types of discs use multiple recording layers on each side of the disc to increase capacity. An optical disc contains a single spiral track (instead of multiple tracks like magnetic disks), and the track is divided into sectors to keep data organized. As shown in Figure 3-11, this track (sometimes referred to as a *groove* in order to avoid confusion with the term *tracks* used to refer to songs on an audio CD) begins at the center of the disc and spirals out to the edge of the disc.

**FIGURE 3-11**
How recorded optical discs work.

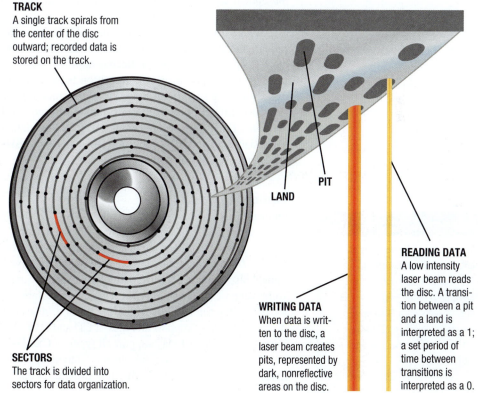

**TRACK**
A single track spirals from the center of the disc outward; recorded data is stored on the track.

**SECTORS**
The track is divided into sectors for data organization.

**LAND**

**PIT**

**WRITING DATA**
When data is written to the disc, a laser beam creates pits, represented by dark, nonreflective areas on the disc.

**READING DATA**
A low intensity laser beam reads the disc. A transition between a pit and a land is interpreted as a 1; a set period of time between transitions is interpreted as a 0.

> **Optical disc.** A type of storage medium read from and written to using a laser beam.

Advantages of optical discs include large capacity for their size (as discussed shortly) and durability (they are more durable than magnetic media and don't degrade with use like some magnetic media do). However, the discs should be handled carefully and stored in their cases when they are not in use in order to protect the recorded surfaces of the discs from scratches, fingerprints, and other marks that can interfere with the usability of the discs. Optical discs are the standard today for packaged software; they are also commonly used for backup purposes, and for storing and/or transporting music, photos, videos, and other large files.

### Representing Data on an Optical Disc

Data is written to an optical disc in one of two ways. With read-only optical discs like movie, music, and software CDs and DVDs, the surface of the disc is molded or stamped appropriately to represent the data. With recordable or rewritable optical discs that can be written to using an optical drive such as a DVD drive, as discussed shortly, the reflectivity of the disc is changed using a laser to represent the data. In either case, the disc is read with a laser and the computer interprets the reflection of the laser off the disc surface as 1s and 0s.

To accomplish this with molded or stamped optical discs, tiny depressions (when viewed from the top side of the disc) or bumps (when viewed from the bottom) are created on the disc's surface. These bumps are called *pits*; the areas on the disc that are not changed are called *lands*. Although many people think that each individual pit and land represents a 1 or 0, that idea is not completely accurate—it is actually the transition between a pit and land that represents a 1. When the disc is read, the amount of laser light reflected back from the disc changes when the laser reaches a transition between a pit and a land. When the optical drive detects a transition, it is interpreted as a 1; no transition for a specific period of time indicates a 0.

With a disc that is recorded using a DVD drive, the recording laser beam changes the reflectivity of the appropriate areas on the disc to represent the data stored there—dark, nonreflective areas are pits; reflective areas are lands, as illustrated in Figure 3-11. As with molded or stamped discs, the transition between a pit and a land represents a 1 and no transition for a specific distance along the track represents a 0. Different types of optical discs use different types of laser beams. Conventional **CD discs** use *infrared lasers*; conventional **DVD discs** use *red lasers*, which allow data to be stored more compactly on the same size disc; and high-definition **Blu-ray Discs (BDs)** use *blue-violet lasers*, which can store data even more compactly on a disc.

### Optical Drives

Optical discs in each of the three categories (CD, DVD, and BD) can be read-only, recordable, or rewritable; they can use the + or – standard; and they can be either single-layer or dual-layer (DL) discs. Optical discs are designed to be read by **optical drives**, such as *CD*, *DVD*, and *BD drives*, and the type of optical drive being used must support the type of optical disc being used. Most optical drives today support multiple types of optical discs— some support all possible types. Optical drives are almost always *backward-compatible*, meaning they can be used with older types of discs but not newer ones. So, while a DVD drive would likely support all types of CD and DVD discs, it cannot be used with BD discs, but most BD drives today support all types of CD, DVD, and BD discs.

To use an optical disc, it is inserted into an appropriate optical drive. Purchased optical discs often have a title and other text printed on one side; if so, they are inserted into the

>**CD disc.** A low capacity (typically 700 MB) optical disc that is often used to deliver music and software, as well as to store user data.
>**DVD disc.** A medium capacity (typically 4.7 GB or 8.5 GB) optical disc that is often used to deliver software and movies, as well as to store user data. >**Blu-ray Disc (BD).** A high-capacity (typically 25 GB or 50 GB) disc that is often used to deliver high-definition movies, as well as to store user data. >**Optical drive.** A drive used with optical discs, such as CD or DVD discs.

optical drive with the printed side facing up. Two-sided commercial discs typically identify each side of a disc by printing that information on the disc close to the inner circle.

The process of recording data onto a recordable or rewritable optical disc is called *burning*. To burn an optical disc, the optical drive being used must support burning and the type of disc being used. In addition, *CD-burning* or *DVD-burning* software is required. Many burning programs are available commercially, and recent versions of operating systems (including Windows and OS X) include burning capabilities. In addition, most CD and DVD drives come bundled with burning software. Some optical drives—such as *LightScribe-enabled drives*—are even capable of burning label information on the surface of a disc after the content has been recorded. (To do this, you first burn the data to the disc, and then you flip the disc over and burn the desired label information on the other side of the disc.) Most personal computers today come with an internal optical drive; however, netbooks and mobile devices typically do not include an optical drive. An *external optical drive* that connects via a USB port (see Figure 3-12) can be used with most computers and some tablets whenever an optical drive is temporarily needed.

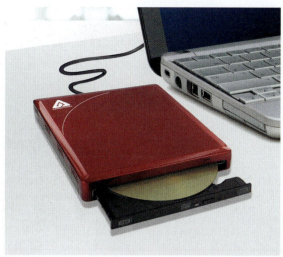

**FIGURE 3-12**

**External optical drives.** Can be connected as needed, typically via a USB port, such as to the netbook shown here.

## Optical Disc Shapes, Sizes, and Capacities

Standard-sized optical discs are 120-mm (approximately 4.7-inch) discs. As shown in Figure 3-13, there are also smaller 80-mm (approximately 3-inch) *mini discs* that use that smaller form factor. Because the track starts at the center of the disc and the track just stops when it reaches an outer edge of the disc, optical discs theoretically can be made into a variety of sizes and shapes—such as a heart, a triangle, an irregular shape, or a hockey-rink shape appropriate for *business card CDs* (discs that have business card information printed on the top surface or label of the disc and that contain a résumé, portfolio, or other digital documents stored on the disc). However, an ongoing patent battle over changing the shape of any normally round storage media (a process an individual claims to have patented) has resulted in some of these custom shapes not being available at the present time. Instead of a custom shape, sometimes a clear background is used around a colored design to make it appear that the disc is custom shaped even though it is a standard disc, as in the right-most image in Figure 3-13. The practice of using optical discs to replace ordinary objects, such as business cards and mailed advertisements, is becoming more common.

**FIGURE 3-13**

**Optical discs are available in a variety of sizes, appearances, and capacities.**

**STANDARD 120 MM (4.7 INCH) SIZED DISC**

**MINI 80 MM (3.1 INCH) SIZED DISC**

Back of disc

Front of disc

**MINI 80 MM (3.1 INCH) SIZED DISC**
(with a clear background to be standard size)

| TYPE OF DISC | CAPACITY | USED FOR |
|---|---|---|
| CD | 700 MB | Audio music delivery; custom CDs containing music, photos, etc. |
| DVD | 4.7 GB | Movie and software delivery; |
| DVD-DL | 8.5 GB | custom DVDs containing videos, music, photos, etc. |
| BD | 25 GB | Primarily movie delivery |
| BD-DL | 50 GB | |
| BDXL (3 layers) | 100 GB | Primarily video archiving |
| BDXL (4 layers) | 128 GB | |
| Ultra HD (4K) (2 layers) | 66 GB | Primarily 4K movie delivery |
| Ultra HD (4K) (3 layers) | 100 GB | |

**FIGURE 3-14**
Summary of optical discs.

**TIP**

To use BDXL or Ultra HD Blu-ray discs, you need to use a drive that supports that format.

One of the biggest advantages of optical discs is their large capacity (see Figure 3-14). To further increase capacity, many discs are available as *dual-layer (DL) discs* (also called *double-layer discs*) that store data in two layers on a single side of the disc, so the capacity is approximately doubled. For an even larger capacity, *triple-layer discs* are becoming available. Standard-sized CD discs are normally single-layer and usually hold 700 MB (though some hold 650 MB). Standard-sized DVD discs hold 4.7 GB (single-layer discs) or 8.5 GB (dual-layer discs), and standard-sized BD discs hold either 25 GB (single-layer discs) or 50 GB (dual-layer discs). The newer *BDXL* standard uses even more layers to boost capacity up to 128 GB. As discussed in the Trend box, the newest BD discs are *Ultra HD Blu-ray discs* that hold up to 100 GB and are designed to deliver *Ultra HD (4K)* movies. Discs can also be *double sided*, which doubles the capacity; however, unlike hard disks, optical discs are only read on one side at a time and so must be turned over to access the second side. Double-sided discs are most often used with movies and other prerecorded content, such as to store a *widescreen version* of a movie on one side of a DVD disc and a *standard version* on the other side. Small optical discs have a smaller storage capacity than their larger counterparts: typically, single-layer, single-sided 3-inch mini CD, DVD, and BD discs hold about 200 MB, 1.4 GB, and 7.5 GB, respectively, and business card-sized CD and DVD discs hold about 50 MB and 325 MB, respectively.

## Read-Only Optical Discs: CD-ROM, DVD-ROM, and BD-ROM Discs

**CD-ROM** (*compact disc read-only memory*) **discs** and **DVD-ROM** (*digital versatile disc read-only memory*) **discs** are *read-only optical discs* that come prerecorded with commercial products, such as software programs, clip art and other types of graphics collections, music, and movies. For high-definition content (such as feature films), **BD-ROM** (*Blu-ray Disc read-only memory*) **discs** are available; for 4K movies, read-only Ultra HD Blu-ray discs can be used. There are also additional read-only disc formats for specific gaming devices, such as the proprietary discs used with the Wii, Xbox, and PlayStation gaming consoles. The data on a read-only disc cannot be erased, changed, or added to because the pits that are molded into the surface of the disc when the disc is produced are permanent.

## Recordable Optical Discs: CD-R, DVD-R, DVD+R, and BD-R Discs

*Recordable optical discs* (also sometimes called *write-once discs*) can be written to, but the discs cannot be erased and reused. Recordable CDs are referred to as **CD-R discs**. Single-layer recordable DVDs are called either **DVD-R discs** or **DVD+R discs**, depending

> **CD-ROM disc.** A CD that can be read from, but not written to, by the user. > **DVD-ROM disc.** A DVD that can be read from, but not written to, by the user. > **BD-ROM disc.** A Blu-ray Disc that can be read from, but not written to, by the user. > **CD-R disc.** A recordable CD.
> **DVD-R/DVD+R discs.** Recordable DVDs.

on the standard being used, and dual-layer recordable DVDs are called *DVD+R DL* or *DVD-R DL discs*. Recordable BD discs are also available in single-layer, dual-layer, and XL discs (**BD-R discs**, *BD-R DL discs*, and *BD-R XL* discs, respectively). The capacities of recordable optical discs are the same as the read-only formats.

Instead of having physically molded pits, most recordable optical discs have a recording layer containing organic light-sensitive dye embedded between the disc's plastic and reflective layers. One exception to this is the BD-R disc, which has a recording layer consisting of inorganic material. When data is written to a recordable disc, the recording laser inside the recordable optical drive burns the dye (for CD and DVD discs) or melts and combines the inorganic material (for BD-R discs), creating nonreflective areas that function as pits. In either case, the marks are permanent so data written to the disc cannot be erased or rewritten.

Recordable CDs are commonly used for backing up files, sending large files to others, and creating custom music CDs (for example, from MP3 files legally downloaded from the Internet or from songs located on a music album purchased on CD). DVD-Rs can be used for similar purposes when more storage space is needed, such as for backing up large files and for storing home movies, digital photos, and other multimedia files. BD-R discs can be used when an even greater amount of storage is needed, such as very large backups or high-definition multimedia files.

## Rewritable Optical Discs: CD-RW, DVD-RW, DVD+RW, and BD-RE Discs

*Rewritable optical discs* can be written to, erased, and overwritten just like magnetic hard disks. The most common types of rewritable optical discs are **CD-RW**, **DVD-RW**, **DVD+RW**, and **BD-RE discs**; BD-RE discs are also available as dual-layer discs (*BD-RE DL discs*) and XL discs (*BD-RE XL*). The capacities of rewritable discs are the same as their read-only and recordable counterparts. An additional, but not widely used, rewritable DVD format is *DVD-RAM*. DVD-RAM and DVD-RAM DL discs are supported by *DVD-RAM drives*, as well as by some DVD and BD drives.

To write to, erase, or overwrite rewritable optical discs, *phase change* technology is used. With this technology, the rewritable disc is coated with layers of a special metal alloy compound that can have two different appearances after it has been heated and then cooled, depending on the heating and cooling process used. With one process, the material *crystallizes* and that area of the disc is reflective. With another process, the area cools to a nonreflective *amorphous* state. Before any data is written to a rewritable optical disc, the disc is completely reflective. To write data to the disc, the recording laser heats the metal alloy in the appropriate locations on the spiral track and then uses the appropriate cooling process to create either the nonreflective areas (pits) or the reflective areas (lands). To erase the disc, the appropriate heating and cooling process is used to change the areas to be erased back to their original reflective state.

Rewritable optical discs are used for many of the same purposes as recordable optical discs. However, they are particularly appropriate for situations in which data written to the optical disc can be erased at a later time so the disc can be reused (such as for transferring large files from one computer to another or temporarily storing TV shows recorded on your computer that you will later watch using your living room TV and DVD player).

>**BD-R disc.** A recordable Blu-ray Disc. >**CD-RW disc.** A rewritable CD. >**DVD-RW/DVD+RW discs.** Rewritable DVDs. >**BD-RE disc.** A rewritable Blu-ray Disc.

## TREND

### Ultra HD (4K)

*Ultra HD* (*Ultra High Definition* or *4K*) is the next big step in high-definition (HD) TVs and content. It has four times the resolution of ordinary HD and is changing how HD content is delivered to the consumer.

Currently, many movies, TV shows, and sporting events are filmed and delivered in HD. While much of this content will be filmed in 4K in the near future, today's hardware and streaming services are not designed to support 4K content because it requires four times as much data as regular HD video. Cable and satellite providers already compress content to enable it to be delivered more efficiently and some online streaming services, such as Netflix, allow subscribers to reduce the quality of the content they stream in order to speed up delivery and save Internet bandwidth. In addition, many Internet connections are not fast enough to support the large amounts of data required for 4K quality (by one estimate, a season of *House of Cards* delivered in 4K will eat up at least 75 GB of data). However, streaming 4K is becoming available for those individuals who have the speed and bandwidth to support it. For the rest of us, 4K content is expected to be delivered via high capacity Ultra

HD (4K) Blu-ray discs. In addition to high capacity (100 GB), Ultra HD discs offer other improvements in color, frames per second, and other specifications to better deliver 4K content.

Courtesy 4K Ultra HD Movies 4k-ultra-hd-movies.com

## FLASH MEMORY STORAGE SYSTEMS

▼ **FIGURE 3-15**
Embedded flash memory.

As previously discussed, **flash memory** is a chip-based storage medium that represents data using electrons. It is used in a variety of storage systems, such as the SSDs and SSHDs already discussed and the additional storage systems discussed next.

Source: Samsung Electronics Co., Ltd

**TABLET**
Contains 64 GB of embedded flash memory.

Source: SanDisk Corporation

**EMBEDDED FLASH MEMORY CHIP**

### Embedded Flash Memory

**Embedded flash memory** refers to flash memory chips embedded into products. Because flash memory media are physically very small, they are increasingly being embedded directly into a variety of consumer products—such as smartphones, tablets, smart watches, and even sunglasses and wristwatches—to provide built-in data storage. In fact, flash memory is usually the primary storage for mobile devices, such as tablets and smartphones. While embedded flash memory can take the form of small SSDs or memory cards, it is increasingly being implemented with small stand-alone *embedded flash memory chips*, such as the one shown in Figure 3-15.

> **Flash memory.** Nonvolatile memory chips that can be used for storage by the computer or user; can be built into a computer or a storage medium.
> **Embedded flash memory.** Flash memory chips embedded into products, such as consumer devices.

## Flash Memory Cards and Readers

One of the most common types of flash memory media is the **flash memory card**—a small card containing one or more flash memory chips, a controller chip, other electrical components, and metal contacts to connect the card to the device or reader being used. Flash memory cards are available in a variety of formats, such as *CompactFlash* (*CF*), *Secure Digital* (*SD*), *MultiMedia Card* (*MMC*), *xD Picture Card* (*xD*), *XQD*, and *Memory Stick* (*MS*) (see Figure 3-16). These formats are not interchangeable, so the type of flash memory card used with a device is determined by the type and size of flash media card that device can accept. Flash memory cards are the most common type of storage media for digital cameras, smartphones, and other portable devices. Flash memory cards can also be used to store data for a personal computer, as needed, as well as to transfer data from a portable device (digital camera or tablet, for instance) to a computer. Consequently, most personal computers and many mobile devices today have a built-in *flash memory card reader* capable of reading flash memory cards; an external flash memory card reader (such as the ones shown in Figure 3-16) that connects via a USB port can be used when the destination device doesn't have a built-in reader. Flash memory cards are available in capacities up to 512 GB.

One of the most widely used types of flash memory media—Secure Digital (SD)—is available in different physical sizes, as well as in different capacities. For instance, standard-sized SD cards are often used in digital cameras and computers; the smaller *microSD* cards (about one-quarter the size of a standard SD card, as shown in Figure 3-16) are typically used with smartphones and other mobile devices. However, as shown in Figure 3-16, there are adapters that can be used to enable a smaller card to be used in a larger slot of the same type. There are also different versions of SD cards based on capacity. For example, *Secure Digital High Capacity* (*SDHC*) and *Secure Digital Extended Capacity* (*SDXC*) hold more data than standard SD cards.

**FIGURE 3-16**
Flash memory cards, readers, and adapters.

Can read both CompactFlash and SD cards.

CompactFlash card

Source: Micron Consumer Products Group, Inc

microSD card goes into the adapter to fit into an SD card slot.

Source: Micron Consumer Products Group, Inc.

microSD card goes into the reader to fit into a USB port.

SD card

microSD card

Source: SanDisk Corporation

**FLASH MEMORY CARD READERS AND ADAPTERS**

**FLASH MEMORY CARDS**

> **Flash memory card.** A small, rectangular flash memory storage medium, such as a Secure Digital (SD) card.

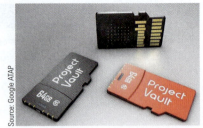

While general-purpose flash memory cards can be used for most applications, there are also flash memory cards designed for specific uses. For instance, *professional flash memory cards* designed for professional photographers are faster and more durable than consumer cards (some professional flash memory cards support 4K video) and *gaming flash memory cards* are specifically designed for gaming consoles and devices, such as the Nintendo Wii or Sony PSP. There are even Wi-Fi-enabled flash memory cards that can wirelessly upload digital photos taken with a camera using that card for storage, as discussed in the Technology and You box in Chapter 7.

For more secure data storage, there are also encrypted flash memory cards that can be used with smartphones and other devices. For example, Google recently announced *Project Vault*, an encrypted microSD card shown in Figure 3-17. Vault is essentially a computer on a flash memory card with an ARM processor, 4 GB of storage space, and an antenna. It encrypts all data stored on the card so if the card or device with the card is lost, the data isn't compromised. In addition, two devices that contain Vault cards can communicate over a secure connection.

**FIGURE 3-17**
Google Project Vault encrypted microSD card.

## USB Flash Drives

**USB flash drives** (sometimes called *USB drives* or *flash drives*) consist of flash memory media integrated into a self-contained unit that connects to a computer or other device via a USB port and is powered via that port. USB flash drives are designed to be very small and very portable. In order to be appropriate for a wide variety of applications, USB flash drives are available in a host of formats—including those designed to be attached to backpacks or worn on a lanyard around the neck; those built into pens, necklaces, wristbands, or wristwatches; those thin enough to fit easily into a wallet; and those made into custom shapes for promotional or novelty purposes. There are also *low-profile USB flash drives* that are designed to remain in a computer at all times, as well as *micro USB flash drives* designed to be used with smartphones and other mobile devices that have a micro USB port (see Figure 3-18). When a USB flash drive is built into a consumer product (such as a watch, sunglasses, or a Swiss Army knife), a retractable cord is typically used to connect the device to a computer when needed. Because they are becoming so widely used, additional hardware related to USB flash drives is becoming available, such as *USB duplicator systems* used by educators to copy assignments or other materials to and from a large collection of USB flash drives at one time.

**FIGURE 3-18**
USB flash drives.

**CONVENTIONAL DRIVE**

**LOW-PROFILE DRIVE**

**CUSTOM LANYARD DRIVE**

**MICRO DRIVE**

>**USB flash drive.** A small storage device that plugs into a USB port and contains flash memory media.

# TECHNOLOGY AND YOU

### Tiny PCs

Computers have shrunk again. Forget small notebooks, tablets, or even the small mini desktop computers available now. If you want portability, look no further than today's tiny PCs that are the size of a USB flash drive.

Tiny PCs typically connect to a TV via an HDMI port to turn that TV into a fully-functional computer or at least a smart TV capable of delivering Internet content. Many tiny PCs have USB ports to connect a keyboard or mouse or to power the device if external power is required. Some include Bluetooth capabilities to more easily connect a keyboard or mouse. They may also have built-in storage and a microSD slot for transferring photos, videos, or other content to the device.

The capabilities of these devices vary from device to device. Some devices (such as *Amazon Fire TV Stick* and *Roku Streaming Stick*) are designed to transform a traditional TV into a smart TV capable of displaying Internet content (such as YouTube videos and Netflix movies) via apps installed on the device, as well as displaying photos and videos from a smartphone, tablet, or Windows PC. Others (such as *Google Chromecast*) are designed to stream videos, movies, music, and other content from, and control the device via, a computer, smartphone, or tablet, though the latest version of Chromecast also includes support for Netflix, Hulu, Pandora, and other popular online media apps.

The newest tiny PCs (such as *Google Chromebit* and *Intel Compute Stick*, shown in the accompanying illustration) go one step further and are fully functioning "computers-on-a-stick." After you plug one of these devices into the HDMI port on a TV or monitor and connect a USB or Bluetooth mouse and keyboard, you can use it as a traditional PC, accessing both Internet content and running software that you would typically run on a personal computer.

The flexibility of these tiny PCs and the apps they can run vary from device to device, based on the operating system they use and the amount of storage available. For example, the Windows version of the Intel Compute stick has 32 GB of built-in storage. But for turning a TV at any location into your own personal computer, gaming device, or video player, tiny PCs are definitely the way to go.

Micro SD card slot

USB port

Power port

Power switch

Contains a quad-core Atom processor, built-in memory and storage, and Wi-Fi and Bluetooth connectivity.

Connects to a display device via an HDMI port.

Source: Intel Corporation

**Intel Compute Stick**

To read from or write to a USB flash drive, you just plug it into a USB port. If the USB flash drive is being used with a computer, it is assigned a drive letter by the computer, just like any other type of attached drive, and files can be read from or written to the USB flash drive until it is unplugged from the USB port. USB flash drives today can store up to 1 TB. USB flash drive use has become commonplace for individuals, students, and employees to transport files from one computer to another, as well as to quickly back up important files. For a look at tiny USB flash drive-sized PCs, see the Technology and You box.

## ASK THE EXPERT

**Kingston** TECHNOLOGY

**Mark Tekunoff,** Senior Technology Manager, Kingston Technology

**Is it better to copy a file from a USB flash drive to a hard drive for extensive editing instead of working directly on the USB flash drive?**

For performance processing work, it is better to process work on a hard drive as it is better designed for this type of activity. Depending on the type of work being performed, it can be done on a USB flash drive, but the overall processing time or the time it takes to complete a task may be longer—although flash technology continues to evolve and capacities increase. In fact, thanks to the USB 3.0 specification, USB flash drives up to 1 TB and beyond of storage and high read/write speeds can now be found.

For most people, a USB flash drive is still a portable storage solution, designed to take data from one place to another, rather than as a working storage medium.

In addition to providing basic data storage and data portability, USB flash drives can provide additional capabilities. For instance, they can be used to lock a computer and to issue Web site passwords; *secure USB flash drives* are encrypted to protect the data stored on the drive and allow access to only authorized individuals via a password or a built-in fingerprint reader or number pad.

## OTHER TYPES OF STORAGE SYSTEMS

Other types of storage systems used with personal and business computers today include network storage, cloud storage, and smart cards. There are also storage systems and technologies designed for large computer systems and for archiving data. These storage systems are discussed next.

### Network and Cloud Storage Systems

*Remote storage* refers to using a storage device that is not connected directly to the user's computer; instead, the device is accessed through a local network or through the Internet. Using a remote storage device via a local network (referred to as **network storage**) works in much the same way as using *local storage* (the storage devices and media that are directly attached to the user's computer). To read data from or write data to a network storage device (such as a hard drive being accessed via a network), the user just selects it (see Figure 3-19) and then performs the necessary tasks in the normal fashion. Network storage is common in businesses; it is also used by individuals with home networks for backup purposes or to share files with other devices in the home.

Because of the vast amount of data shared and made available over networks today, network storage has become increasingly important. Two common types of network storage used today are **network attached storage (NAS)** devices and **storage area networks (SANs)**. NAS devices are high-performance storage systems that are connected individually to a network to provide storage for the computers connected to that network. Some (such as the one shown in Figure 3-19) are designed for small business use; others are geared for home use instead. A growing trend, in fact, is home NAS devices designed to store multimedia data (such as downloaded music, recorded TV shows, and downloaded movies) to be distributed over a home entertainment network. NAS devices typically have room for two to eight hard disk drives and connect to the network via a wired or wireless networking connection; networking is explained in detail in Chapter 7.

A storage area network (SAN) also provides storage for a network, but it consists of a separate network of hard drives or other storage devices, which is connected to the main network. The primary difference between an NAS and an SAN is how the storage

> ✓ **TIP**
>
> NAS and SAN devices typically require an operating system to function; many also include software to provide additional features, such as automatic backups or security scans.

> ✓ **TIP**
>
> If the router used to connect devices to your home network includes a USB port, you can create a NAS by plugging a USB storage device (such as an external hard drive) directly into the router.

---

>**Network storage.** The use of a storage device that is accessed through a local network. >**Network attached storage (NAS).** A high-performance storage device individually connected to a network to provide storage for computers on that network. >**Storage area network (SAN).** A network of hard drives or other storage devices that provide storage for a network of computers.

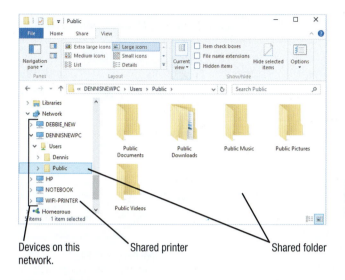

Devices on this network.　　　Shared printer　　　Shared folder

**LOCAL NETWORKS**
Network devices appear and are accessed in a manner similar to local resources.

Hard drives are located inside the NAS device.

**NETWORK ATTACHED STORAGE (NAS) DEVICES**
This NAS device holds up to 12 TB of data on two magnetic hard drives.

**FIGURE 3-19**
Network storage.

devices interface with the network—that is, whether the storage devices act as individual network nodes, just like computers, printers, and other devices on the network (NAS), or whether they are located in a completely separate network of storage devices that is accessible via the main network (SAN). SANs can be more appropriate when a larger amount of network storage is needed; however, in terms of functionality, the distinction between NAS and SAN is blurring because they both provide storage services to the network. Typically, both NAS and SAN systems are *scalable*, which means that new devices can be added as more storage is needed, and devices can be added or removed without disrupting the network.

Remote storage services accessed via the Internet are often referred to as **cloud storage** or **online storage**. Cloud storage can be provided either as a stand-alone service or as part of a cloud computing service. For instance, most cloud applications (such as Google Docs, the Flickr photo sharing service, and social networking sites like Facebook) provide online storage for these services. There are also sites whose primary objective is to allow users to store documents online, such as *Box, Dropbox, iCloud, Google Drive,* or Microsoft

## ASK THE EXPERT

**Sven Rathjen,** Vice President of Marketing Content Solutions, Western Digital

### Do home networks today need network hard drives?

Absolutely! Adding an external hard drive to your home network (or using an external hard drive with built-in Wi-Fi) enables you to share data among your devices without having to plug devices into your computer or use a USB flash drive to transfer files from one device to another. For example, you can use a network hard drive to access stored files using your computer or tablet, stream audio and video to your smart TV or smartphone, and back up files, photos, and videos from all of your devices. Some network hard drives even let you create a personal cloud that you can access from any device, from anywhere that you have an Internet connection. In a nutshell, network hard drives can keep your important digital content safe, while allowing you to easily access that content using any of your personal devices.

> **Cloud storage.** Refers to using a storage device that is accessed via the Internet; also called **online storage**.

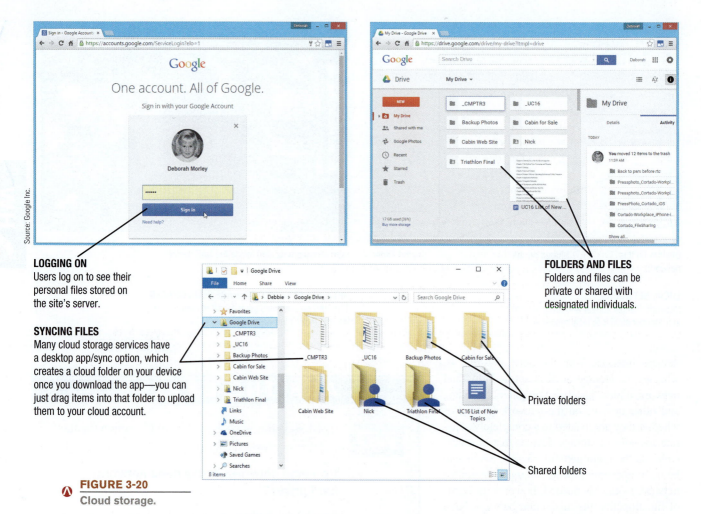

Source: Google Inc.

**LOGGING ON**
Users log on to see their personal files stored on the site's server.

**SYNCING FILES**
Many cloud storage services have a desktop app/sync option, which creates a cloud folder on your device once you download the app—you can just drag items into that folder to upload them to your cloud account.

**FOLDERS AND FILES**
Folders and files can be private or shared with designated individuals.

Private folders

Shared folders

**FIGURE 3-20**
Cloud storage.

*OneDrive*. Cloud storage sites allow users to share uploaded files or folders with others via an e-mail message or a link to the shared content. For security purposes, cloud storage sites are usually password protected (see Figure 3-20) and you can specify the individuals that are allowed to view shared files.

The ability to store documents online (or "in the cloud") is growing in importance as more and more applications are becoming cloud based and as individuals increasingly want access to their files from anywhere with any Internet-enabled device, such as a portable computer, tablet, or smartphone. Cloud storage is also increasingly being used for backup purposes—some sites have an automatic backup option that uploads the files in designated folders on your computer to your cloud account at regular specified intervals, as long as your computer is connected to the Internet. Many Web sites providing cloud storage to individuals offer the service for free (for instance, OneDrive and Google Drive both give individuals 15 GB of free storage space); additional storage space can be purchased if needed.

Business cloud storage services are also available, such as those offered in conjunction with cloud computing services that allow subscribers to access a flexible amount of both storage and computing power as needed on demand. For instance, *Amazon Simple Storage Service* (*Amazon S3*)—one of the leaders in *enterprise cloud storage*—charges a monthly fee per GB of storage used plus a fee based on the amount of data transferred that month. This service can be used alone or in conjunction with Amazon's cloud computing service, *Amazon Elastic Compute Cloud* (*Amazon EC2*). In addition to these *public cloud storage services*, businesses can also create *private clouds* that are hosted in the business's data center and are designed to be accessed only by that business's designated users.

## Smart Cards

A **smart card** is a credit card-sized piece of plastic that has built-in computer circuitry and components—typically a processor, memory, and storage. Smart cards today store a relatively small amount of data (typically 64 KB or less) that can be used for payment or identification purposes. For example, a smart card can store a prepaid amount of *digital cash*, which can be used for purchases at a smart card-enabled vending machine or to pay transit fares—the amount of cash available on the card is reduced each time the card is used. Smart cards are also commonly used worldwide for national and student ID cards, credit and debit cards adhering to the global *EMV* standard to increase security and decrease fraudulent use, as discussed in the Chapter 9 Inside the Industry box, and access cards for facilities or computer networks. Although these applications have all used conventional *magnetic stripe* technology in the past, the processor integrated into a smart card can perform computations—such as to authenticate the card, encrypt the data on the card to protect its integrity, and secure it against unauthorized access—and can allow data to be added to the card or modified on the card as needed. Smart cards can also store the identifying data needed to accelerate airport security and to link patients to the *electronic health records* (*EHRs*) increasingly being used by hospitals.

To use a smart card (see Figure 3-21), it must either be inserted into a *smart card reader* (if it is the type of card that requires contact) or placed close to a smart card reader (if it is a *contactless* card) built into or attached to a computer, door lock, ATM machine,

**FIGURE 3-21**
Uses for smart cards.

**LOGGING ONTO A COMPUTER**

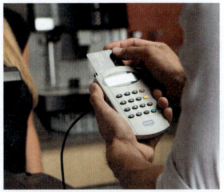

**MAKING A STORE PURCHASE**

**ACCESSING A SECURE FACILITY**

**USING TRANSIT TICKETS**

Source: HID Global Corporation

> **Smart card.** A storage medium consisting of a credit card-sized piece of plastic with built-in computer circuitry and other components.

vending machine, or other device. Once a smart card has been verified by the card reader, the transaction—such as making a purchase or unlocking a door—can be completed. For an even higher level of security, some smart cards today store biometric data in the card and use that data to authenticate the card's user before authorizing the smart card transaction (biometrics, encryption, and other security procedures are discussed in more detail in Chapter 9). An emerging trend is the use of *mobile smart cards*—smart microSD cards that are designed to add smart card capabilities to any device that contains a microSD slot—though it is likely that NFC (Near Field Communications) will be the eventual technology of choice for mobile payments (as well as possibly for mobile access control), as discussed in later chapters.

## Storage Systems for Large Computer Systems

Businesses and other organizations (particularly cloud providers) have tremendous storage needs. In addition to regular business data storage (such as employee files, customer and order data, business documents, and Web site content), new regulations are continually increasing the types and amounts of data that many businesses need to archive. For instance, the *Health Insurance Portability and Accountability Act* (*HIPAA*) requires healthcare providers to archive huge amounts of medical data, and the *Sarbanes-Oxley Act* requires certain accounting records and work papers to be archived for five years. In addition, a recent *e-discovery* federal mandate requires businesses to locate and provide to the courts in a timely manner any document stored electronically (such as e-mail messages, text messages, and text documents) that is needed for evidence in civil litigation involving their companies. All of these requirements mean that business storage needs are growing exponentially—in fact, the amount of digital data produced is expected to double every two years through 2020, according to one estimate—and the documents must be stored in a manner in which they can be readily retrieved as needed.

Storage for large computer systems (such as for mainframes and servers) utilizes much of the same storage hardware, standards, and principles as those used with personal computers, but on a much larger scale. However, instead of finding a single magnetic or SSD hard drive installed within the system unit, you will likely find a large storage system (sometimes called a *storage server*)— a separate piece of hardware containing multiple high-speed hard drives—connected to the computer system or network. While some NAS devices today are classified as storage servers, large storage systems typically contain drawers of hard drives for a significantly larger total capacity. For instance, the storage system shown in Figure 3-22 can include up to 240 hard drives for a total capacity of 432 TB. These types of storage systems—also referred to as *enterprise storage systems*— typically use fast Fibre Channel or iSCSI connections and are scalable so more hard drives can be added as needed up to the maximum system capacity. In addition to being used as stand-alone storage for large computer systems, large storage systems may also be used in network attached storage (NAS), storage area network (SAN), and the RAID (redundant arrays of independent disks) systems, which are discussed next. Most large storage systems are based on magnetic hard disks, although some systems (such as the one shown in Figure 3-22) can use a combination of magnetic and SSD drives.

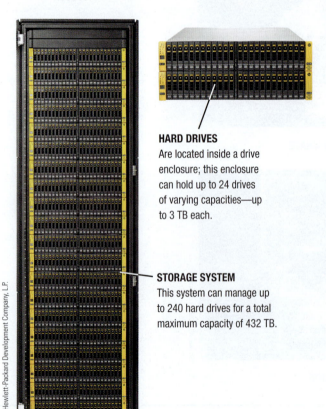

**FIGURE 3-22**

**Large storage systems.** Large storage systems are usually scalable so additional hard drives can be added as needed.

**HARD DRIVES**
Are located inside a drive enclosure; this enclosure can hold up to 24 drives of varying capacities—up to 3 TB each.

**STORAGE SYSTEM**
This system can manage up to 240 hard drives for a total maximum capacity of 432 TB.

Source: Hewlett-Packard Development Company, L.P.

## RAID

**RAID (redundant arrays of independent disks)** is a method of storing data on two or more hard drives that work together. Although RAID can be used to increase performance, it is most often used to protect critical data on a large storage system. Because RAID usually involves recording redundant (duplicate) copies of stored data, the copies can be used, when necessary, to reconstruct lost data. This helps to increase the *fault tolerance*— the ability to recover from an unexpected hardware or software failure, such as a system crash—of a storage system.

There are several different RAID designs or levels that use different combinations of RAID techniques. For example, *RAID 0* uses *disk striping*, which spreads files over two or more hard drives (see the leftmost part of Figure 3-23). Although striping improves performance because multiple hard drives can be accessed at one time to store or retrieve data, it does not provide fault tolerance. Another common RAID technique is *disk mirroring*, in which data is written to two duplicate hard drives simultaneously (see the rightmost part of Figure 3-23). The objective of disk mirroring is to increase fault tolerance—if one of the hard drives fails, the system can instantly switch to the other hard drive without any loss of data or service. *RAID 1* uses disk mirroring. Levels beyond RAID 1 use some combination of disk striping and disk mirroring, with different types of error correction provisions.

One disadvantage of RAID in the past is the difficulty traditionally involved with setting up and maintaining the system. New storage systems—such as *Drobo* storage systems (see Figure 3-24 on the next page) and some of today's NASs—eliminate this concern. For instance, Drobo devices connect to an individual computer or a network via a USB cable similar to an external hard drive and have a number of empty drive bays into which hard drives can be inserted (for example, the system shown in Figure 3-24 can hold four drives for a total storage capacity of up to 24 TB). Like many RAID systems, Drobo systems offer continuous data redundancy, but they are much easier to use than conventional RAID

**FIGURE 3-23**

**RAID.** Two primary RAID techniques are striping and mirroring.

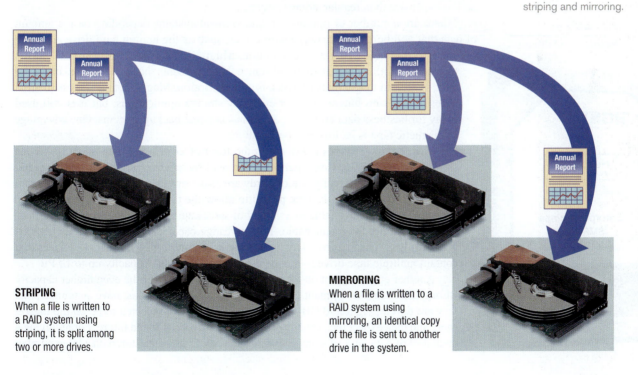

**STRIPING**
When a file is written to a RAID system using striping, it is split among two or more drives.

**MIRRORING**
When a file is written to a RAID system using mirroring, an identical copy of the file is sent to another drive in the system.

>**RAID (redundant arrays of independent disks).** A storage method that uses several hard drives working together, typically to increase performance and/or fault tolerance.

Source: Drobo, Inc.

systems and no special skills are needed to manage, repair, or upgrade them. For example, indicator lights tell you the capacity status of each hard drive and drives just slide in and out of Drobo devices to make it easy to replace a bad hard drive or to increase capacity, even while the devices are being used. When a drive is replaced, the system automatically copies data as needed to the new hard drive to restore the system back to its configuration before the hard drive failed or was removed. The new hard drives don't even have to match the others—they can be different types, speeds, capacities, and brands. In addition, Drobo has additional features (called *thin provisioning* and *automatic tiering*) that allow applications more control over the storage system than usual. This flexibility and ease of use makes the Drobo systems particularly appropriate for individuals and small businesses that need the security of data redundancy but have no IT personnel to assign to a RAID system.

**FIGURE 3-24**
A Drobo storage system.

### Archival Storage Systems

*Data archiving* is the process of identifying and moving data that is no longer actively being used from regular storage systems to a separate long-term archival storage system. Data archiving is important because, while there is a great deal of data that needs to be retained for future reference or regulatory compliance, this data doesn't need to be accessed very frequently. Moving this data out of the regular storage systems improves performance of the regular systems while still meeting data storage needs. It also reduces backup time because less regular data needs to be backed up. As a bonus, data archival systems tend to be less expensive than regular storage systems.

There are a number of options for data archival systems depending on the amount of data that will be archived. Large hard drives, such as the helium hard drive shown in Figure 3-25 that holds 10 TB, is one option. **Magnetic tape**, which consists of plastic tape coated with a magnetizable substance that represents the bits and bytes of digital data, similar to magnetic hard disks, is another option. Magnetic tape uses sequential access so it is no longer used for everyday storage applications, but it is still used today for business data archiving, as well as in some backup systems. One advantage of magnetic tape is its low cost per terabyte.

**FIGURE 3-25**
Helium hard drive.

Source: HGST, Inc.

Most computer tapes today are in the form of *cartridge tapes*, such as the one shown in Figure 3-26. Computer tapes are read by *tape drives*, which can be either an internal or an external piece of hardware. Tape drives contain one or more read/write heads over which the tape passes to allow the tape drive to read or write data. Cartridge tapes are available in a variety of sizes and formats; tape sizes and formats generally are not interchangeable. Tape cartridge capacity varies widely, up to 5 TB per cartridge. When an even larger capacity is required, *tape libraries*—devices that contain multiple tape drives—can be used to boost storage capacity up to 10 PB.

Another emerging option for data archiving is the use of the even higher capacity Blu-ray Discs in development. For example, Sony and Panasonic have announced that they are developing a 300 GB BD *Archival Disc* that is expected to be on the market soon, and they expect the capacity of BDs to grow to 1 TB in the future. For archiving a great deal of data, optical storage systems that can access data stored on a large number

---

>**Magnetic tape.** Storage media consisting of plastic tape with a magnetizable surface that stores data as a series of magnetic spots; typically comes as a cartridge.

of high-capacity optical discs can be used. For example, Facebook has developed an *optical jukebox archival system* that can hold 10,000 100 GB Blu-ray Discs per cabinet. The system is designed to archive data for up to 50 years. The optical discs used for archiving are often recordable discs.

As cloud storage options continue to grow, some businesses are turning to cloud storage providers for their data archival needs. While the business using the cloud storage services doesn't have any hardware on site, the cloud provider would use one of the archival options (such as hard drives, optical discs, or tape) to archive the data at its location.

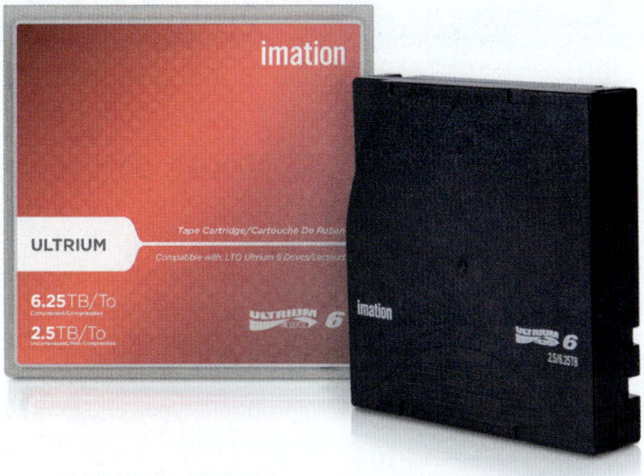

# EVALUATING YOUR STORAGE ALTERNATIVES

Storage alternatives are often compared by weighing a number of product characteristics and cost factors. Some of these product characteristics include speed, compatibility, storage capacity, convenience, and the portability of the media. Keep in mind that each storage alternative normally involves trade-offs. For instance, most systems with removable media are slower than those with fixed media, and external drives are typically slower than internal ones. Although cost is a factor when comparing similar devices, it is often not the most compelling reason to choose a particular technology. For instance, although USB flash drives are relatively expensive per GB compared to optical discs and external hard drives, many users find them essential for transferring files between work and home or for taking presentations or other files with them as they travel. For drives that use a USB interface, the type of USB port is also significant. For example, storage devices that connect via a USB 3.0 or 3.1 port operate significantly faster than devices plugged into a USB 1.0 or USB 2.0 port.

With so many different storage alternatives available, it is a good idea to research which devices and media are most appropriate to use with your personal devices. In general, most computer users need a hard drive (for storing programs and data), some type of recordable or rewritable optical drive (for installing programs, backing up files, and sharing files with others), and a flash memory card reader (for transferring photos, music, and other content between portable devices and the computer). Users who plan to use flash memory cards with their other devices—such as a digital camera or smartphone—will want to select and use the flash memory media that are compatible with those devices as well as obtain any necessary adapters. In addition, virtually all computer users will need at least one convenient USB port to be used to connect external hard drives, USB flash drives, printers, mice, and other USB-based hardware, as well as USB devices that contain storage media, such as digital cameras and smartphones. Several convenient USB ports are even better, though a USB hub can be used to connect multiple devices to a single USB port, if needed.

Mobile device users have fewer options for storage alternatives, so users should consider the available options when selecting a mobile device to ensure it can perform the functions the user deems necessary, such as the ability to back up data and contacts in the cloud or onto a medium the user can access with another device, the ability to transfer photos and other data to a computer or printer, and the ability to connect to any desired storage devices or other hardware. In addition, mobile device users will want to ensure that the device has the appropriate wireless connectivity (such as Wi-Fi) to connect to the desired wireless storage devices and other resources.

**FIGURE 3-26**
**Magnetic tape.**
This cartridge holds 2.5 TB of uncompressed data.

**TIP**

Because most netbooks don't come with an optical drive, netbook users may want to obtain an external DVD drive to use when needed.

# SUMMARY

## STORAGE SYSTEMS CHARACTERISTICS

**Chapter Objective 1:**
Name several general characteristics of storage systems.

*Storage systems* make it possible to save programs, data, and processing results for later use. They provide nonvolatile storage, so when the power is shut off, the data stored on the storage medium remains intact. All storage systems involve two physical parts: a **storage device** (such as a DVD drive) and a **storage medium** (such as a DVD disc). Data is often stored *magnetically* or *optically* on storage media, and storage media are read by the appropriate types of drive. Drives can be *internal*, *external*, or *remote*. Drives are typically assigned letters by the computer; these letters are used to identify the drive.

Sequential access allows a computer system to retrieve the records in a file only in the same order in which they are physically stored. *Random access* (also called *direct access*) allows the system to retrieve records in any order. In either case, **files** (sometimes called *documents*) stored on a storage medium are given a **filename** and can be organized into **folders**. This is referred to as *logical file representation*. *Physical file representation* refers to how the files are physically stored on the storage medium by the computer.

## HARD DRIVES

**Chapter Objective 2:**
Describe the three most common types of hard drives and what they are used for today.

**Hard drives** are used in most computers to store programs and data. Conventional hard drives are **magnetic hard drives** (also called **hard disk drives** or **HDDs**); a newer type of hard drive that uses flash memory instead of magnetic disks is the **solid-state drive** (**SSD**). **Solid-state hybrid drives** (also called **SSHDs** or **hybrid drives**) are a combination of a magnetic hard drive and an SSD. Hard drives can be *internal* or *external*; external hard drives can be full-sized or portable.

Magnetic hard drives contain metal hard disks that are organized into concentric **tracks** encoded with magnetized spots representing 0s and 1s. **Sector** boundaries divide a magnetic disk surface into pie-shaped pieces. A **cluster**, which is the smallest amount of disk space that can be allocated to hold a file, contains one or more sectors. All tracks in the same position on all surfaces of all disks in a hard drive form a **cylinder**. A separate *read/write head* that corresponds to each disk surface is used to read and write data. Hard drives can be divided into multiple *partitions* (logical drives) for efficiency or to facilitate multiple users or operating systems. SSDs are increasingly used for portable computers and mobile devices because they are more shock-resistant and energy-efficient.

The total time it takes for a magnetic hard drive to read from or write to disks is called **disk access time**. **Disk caching**, which is the process of transferring data to memory whenever disk content is retrieved, can help to speed up access time. Hard drives connect to a computer using wireless networking or standards such as *serial ATA (SATA)*, *parallel ATA (PATA)*, *serial attached SCSI (SAS)*, *eSATA*, *Fibre Channel*, Thunderbolt, or USB.

## OPTICAL DISCS AND DRIVES

**Chapter Objective 3:**
Discuss the various types of optical discs available today and how they differ from each other.

**Optical discs**, such as **CD discs**, **DVD discs**, and **Blu-ray Discs** (**BDs**), store data *optically* using laser beams, and they can store data much more densely than magnetic disks. They are divided into tracks and sectors like magnetic disks, but they use a single spiral track instead of concentric tracks. Data is represented by *pits* and *lands* permanently formed on the surface of the disk. Optical discs are available in a wide variety of sizes, shapes, and capacities and are read by **optical drives**, such as *CD* or *DVD drives*. **CD-ROM discs**

come with data already stored on the disc. CD-ROM discs cannot be erased or overwritten—they are *read-only*. **DVD-ROM discs** are similar to CD-ROM discs, but they hold much more data (at least 4.7 GB instead of 700 MB). High-capacity read-only optical discs designed for high-definition content are **BD-ROM discs** (*BDXL* and *Ultra HD Blu-ray discs* have an even greater capacity). *Recordable discs* (**CD-R**, **DVD-R/DVD+R**, and **BD-R discs**, for example) and *rewritable disks* (**CD-RW**, **DVD-RW/DVD+RW**, and **BD-RE discs**, for instance) can all be written to, but only rewritable discs can be erased and rewritten to, similar to a hard drive. Recordable CDs and DVDs store data by burning permanent marks onto the disc, similar to CD-ROM and DVD-ROM discs; rewritable discs typically use *phase change* technology to temporarily change the reflectivity of the disc to represent 1s and 0s.

## FLASH MEMORY STORAGE SYSTEMS

**Flash memory** is used in a variety of storage systems. It can be **embedded flash memory**, which is embedded into products to provide storage capabilities, or it can take the form of *flash memory media* like flash memory cards and USB flash drives. **Flash memory cards**, one of the most common types of flash memory media, are commonly used with digital cameras, portable computers, smartphones, and other portable devices, as well as with desktop computers. Flash memory cards come in a variety of formats—the most common are the various types of *Secure Digital (SD) cards*. **USB flash drives** connect to a computer or other device via a USB port and are a convenient method of transferring files between computers. They can also provide other capabilities, such as to lock a computer or control access to the data stored on the USB flash drive.

**Chapter Objective 4:**
Identify some flash memory storage devices and media and explain how they are used today.

## OTHER TYPES OF STORAGE SYSTEMS

*Remote storage* involves using a storage device that is not directly connected to your computer. One example is using a **network storage** device, such as a **network attached storage (NAS)** or **storage area network (SAN)**. Another is **cloud storage** or **online storage**; that is, storage available via the Internet. **Smart cards** contain a chip or other circuitry usually used to store data or a monetary value.

Storage systems for larger computers implement many of the same standards as the hard drives used with personal computers. However, instead of a single set of hard disks inside a hard drive permanently installed within a system unit, a large *storage server* is often used. **RAID (redundant arrays of independent disks)** technology can be used to increase *fault tolerance* and performance. **Magnetic tape** systems store data on plastic tape coated with a magnetizable substance. Magnetic tapes are usually enclosed in cartridges and are inserted into a *tape drive* in order to be accessed. Magnetic tape is typically used today only for backup and archival purposes. Other options for *data archiving* include high-capacity hard drives or optical discs, as well as online data archival services.

**Chapter Objective 5:**
List at least three other types of storage systems.

## EVALUATING YOUR STORAGE ALTERNATIVES

Most personal computers today include a hard drive, some type of optical drive, a flash memory card reader, and multiple USB ports that can be used to connect USB-based storage devices, such as external hard drives and USB flash drives, as well as other USB hardware. The type of optical drive and any additional storage devices are often determined by weighing a number of factors, such as cost, speed, compatibility, storage capacity, removability, and convenience. Most devices will also include some type of wireless connectivity in order to access storage devices and other hardware via a wireless connection.

**Chapter Objective 6:**
Summarize the storage alternatives for a typical personal computer.

# REVIEW ACTIVITIES

## KEY TERM MATCHING

a. cloud storage

b. disk cache

c. file

d. flash memory card

e. folder

f. hard drive

g. optical disc

h. RAID

i. solid-state drive (SSD)

j. storage area network (SAN)

**Instructions:** Match each key term on the left with the definition on the right that best describes it.

1. _____ A named place on a storage medium into which the user can place files in order to keep the files stored on that medium organized.

2. _____ A hard drive that uses flash memory chips instead of metal magnetic hard disks.

3. _____ A type of storage medium read from and written to using a laser beam.

4. _____ A small, rectangular flash memory storage medium, such as a Secure Digital (SD) card.

5. _____ A network of hard drives or other storage devices that provide storage for a network of computers.

6. _____ Refers to using a storage device that is accessed via the Internet.

7. _____ A storage method that uses several hard drives working together, typically to increase performance and/or fault tolerance.

8. _____ Memory used in conjunction with a magnetic hard drive to improve system performance.

9. _____ Something stored on a storage medium, such as a program, a document, or an image.

10. _____ The primary storage system for most computers; used to store most programs and data used with that computer.

## SELF-QUIZ

**Instructions:** Circle **T** if the statement is true, **F** if the statement is false, or write the best answer in the space provided. **Answers for the self-quiz are located in the References and Resources Guide at the end of the book.**

1. **T  F**  A computer system with a C drive and a D drive must have two physical hard drives.

2. **T  F**  The smallest amount of space a file on a hard drive can use is one cluster.

3. **T  F**  External hard drives typically connect via a flash memory reader.

4. **T  F**  A CD-R disc can be written to by the user.

5. **T  F**  A hybrid hard drive contains both magnetic hard disks and optical discs.

6. The drive letter that would most likely be assigned to the primary hard drive on a typical personal computer is _____.

7. Storage media are not _____, meaning they do not lose their contents when the power is shut off.

8. CDs, DVDs, and BDs are examples of _____ discs.

9. A(n) _____ looks similar to a credit card but contains a chip and other circuitry that can store data.

10. Secure Digital (SD) cards are one type of _____ medium.

1. Assume, for simplicity's sake, that a kilobyte is 1,000 bytes, a megabyte is 1,000,000 bytes, and a gigabyte is 1,000,000,000 bytes. You have a 500-gigabyte hard drive with the following content:

| ITEM | STORAGE SPACE USED |
|---|---|
| Operating system | 15 GB |
| Other software | 1,350 MB |
| Digital photos and videos | 50 GB |
| Other documents | 85 MB |

    How much storage space is currently being used? _____ How much is left? _____

2. Supply the missing words to complete the following statements.

    a. A(n) _____ disc typically holds either 25 GB or 50 GB and is designed for high-definition content, such as movies.

    b. SSD uses _____ for storage.

    c. A hard drive that contains both a magnetic hard drive and flash memory is called a(n) _____ hard drive.

3. Explain why DVD-ROM discs are not erasable, but DVD+RW discs are.

4. List two possible advantages and two possible disadvantages for using cloud storage.

5. Which types of storage media would be appropriate for someone who needed to exchange large (5 MB to 75 MB) files with another person? List at least three different types, stating why each might be the most appropriate under specific conditions.

1. There are a number of types of flash memory cards available, such as SD, CF, XD, XQD, and memory stick. Is there an advantage to having multiple standards or would it be beneficial to consumers if there was only one flash memory standard, such as just the various sizes of SD cards? Would having a single standard be less expensive and more convenient for consumers? If so, will a single standard naturally evolve or should it be mandated by the storage industry or the government? If you use multiple types of flash memory cards with your devices, would you prefer they all used the same type? Why or why not?

2. People send their digital photos over the Internet in different ways. For instance, digital photos are often e-mailed to others, posted on Facebook pages and other social networking sites, and uploaded to a server (such as one belonging to Snapfish, Walmart, or Costco) in order to order prints, enlargements, or other photo-based items. If you have ever sent photos over the Internet, were you concerned about someone other than the intended recipient intercepting or viewing your photo files? If you have ever uploaded files to a processing service for printing, did you check to see if the Web server being used was secure? Should individuals be concerned about sending their personal photos over the Internet? There are a number of advantages, but are there privacy risks, as well?

# PROJECTS

1. **4K** As discussed in the chapter Trend box, 4K (Ultra HD) is the newest standard for high-definition content and TVs.

    For this project, research the current state of 4K. Are there 4K movies available on disc? If so, what additional features, if any, are included with 4K versions of movies? Are 4K movies available via streaming services like Netflix? If so, what Internet speed is required? What are the advantages of watching 4K content over traditional HD content? Are you considering upgrading to a 4K TV to view 4K content? Why or why not? At the conclusion of your research, prepare a one-page summary of your findings and opinions and submit it to your instructor.

2. **Big Brother?** Some of the storage technology used today, such as smart cards, can help facilitate fast and secure access to locked facilities, can protect against the use of stolen credit card numbers, and, when used in conjunction with a biometric characteristic, can unequivocally identify an individual. They can also be used for employee monitoring, such as to identify the location of an employee carrying or wearing his or her smart card at any time. While some people find benefits to the applications just discussed, others worry that smart cards and other devices will be used to track our movements.

    For this project, write a short essay expressing your opinion about the use of smart cards and similar technology to identify individuals for various applications. Is the convenience of smart card technology worth the possible loss of privacy? Do you think employers or the government have the right to track individuals' movements? If so, under what conditions? What are some advantages and disadvantages for the government and your employer always knowing where you are? Have you ever used a smart card or been identified with a biometric system? If so, how do you rate the experience? Submit your opinion on this issue to your instructor in the form of a one-page paper.

3. **Cloud Storage** There are a number of cloud storage services (such as ADrive, Microsoft OneDrive, Google Drive, and Box) designed to allow individuals to back up files online and share specific files with others; specialty online storage services designed for digital photo sharing include Flickr, Photobucket, and Snapfish.

    For this project, visit at least one cloud storage site designed for backup and file exchange, and at least one site designed for digital photo sharing. You can try the sites listed above or use a search site to find alternative sites. Tour your selected sites to determine the features each service offers, the cost, the amount of storage space available, and the options for sending uploaded files to others. Do the sites password-protect your files, or are they available for anyone with an Internet connection to see? What are the benefits for using these types of storage services? Can you think of any drawbacks? Would you want to use any of the storage sites you visited? Why or why not? At the conclusion of this task, prepare a short summary of your findings and submit it to your instructor.

4. **Lost and Found** Portable computers, tablets, smartphones, USB flash drives, and other portable devices are lost all the time today. They can be dropped out of a pocket or bag, inadvertently left on a table, and so forth. If the owner has identifying information (name, phone number, or e-mail address, for instance) printed on the device, the individual who finds the device can attempt to return it to the owner. But what if there is no identifying information clearly visible on the device? Should the finder look at the contents of the device to try to determine the owner? If the device is lost in a location where there is a responsible party (such as an airplane or a restaurant), the finder can turn over the device to that authority (such as a flight attendant or manager), but is it ethical for the responsible party to look at the contents in order to identify the owner? If you lost a device, would you want someone to look at the contents to try to determine your identity? Why or why not? Is looking at the contents on a found device ever ethical? Should it be illegal?

For this project, form an opinion about the ethical ramifications of lost devices and be prepared to discuss your position (in class, via an online class forum, or via a class blog, depending on your instructor's directions). You may also be asked to write a short paper expressing your opinion.

**ETHICS IN ACTION**

**HW**

5. **Flash Cards** There are a wide variety of flash memory card products available today and they can be used with a variety of devices.

For this project, find at least two different examples of flash memory card products in each of the following three categories: user storage; software, music, or movie delivery; and an interface for a peripheral device. Share your findings with the class in the form of a short presentation, including the products that you found, their purpose, what devices they are intended to be used with, and their cost. Be sure to also mention any additional categories or applications using flash cards (in addition to the three categories listed here) that you found doing your research. The presentation should not exceed 10 minutes and should make use of one or more presentation aids, such as a whiteboard, handouts, or a computer-based slide presentation (your instructor may provide additional requirements). You may also be asked to submit a summary of the presentation to your instructor.

**PRESENTATION/ DEMONSTRATION**

6. **Is E-Hording Bad for Us?** With large amounts of storage available to us at a reasonable cost or even for free, many computer users today are sloppy about deleting e-mails, old photos, and other digital data that they may no longer want or need. The average worker alone sends and receives more than 100 e-mails per day and about 90 billion spam e-mails are sent each day. With that kind of volume, it's hard for anyone to keep a clean Inbox. But should we try? Most workers are governed by policies regarding what e-mails and documents they are allowed to delete, but what about our personal documents? Is there anything wrong with saving everything in case it might be needed again? Or does having that much clutter create unnecessary stress and waste our time? If we have the necessary storage, are we prudent to keep everything in case we need it again? Or are we just lazy?

Pick a side on this issue, form an opinion and gather supporting evidence, and be prepared to discuss and defend your position in a classroom debate or in a one- to two-page paper, depending on your instructor's directions.

**BALANCING ACT**

# chapter 4

# Input and Output

**After completing this chapter, you will be able to do the following:**

1. Explain the purpose of a computer keyboard and the types of keyboards widely used today.

2. List several different pointing devices and describe their functions.

3. Describe the purposes of scanners and readers and list some types of scanners and readers in use today.

4. Explain what digital cameras are and how they are used today.

5. Understand the devices that can be used for audio input.

6. Describe the characteristics of a display device and explain some of the technologies used to display images.

7. List several types of printers and explain their functions.

8. Identify the hardware devices typically used for audio output.

## outline

# OVERVIEW

In Chapter 2, we learned how data is processed by a computer. The focus of this chapter is on the hardware designed for inputting data into the computer and for outputting results to the user after the data has been processed. We begin with a look at input. First, we discuss the most common input devices used with computers and mobile devices today—mainly, keyboards, pointing devices (such as a mouse or pen), and touch devices. Next, we discuss hardware designed for capturing data in electronic form (such as scanners, barcode readers, and digital cameras), followed by an overview of audio input, including the voice input increasingly being used with mobile devices today.

The second part of this chapter explores output devices. Most output today occurs on a screen (via a display device) or on paper (via a printer). Display devices are covered first, including their basic properties and the various types of display devices that are in use today. Next, we discuss printers and then devices used for audio output. Due to the vast number of different types of input and output devices that can be used for various needs, this chapter focuses on the most common types of input and output devices in use today. ■

# KEYBOARDS

Most computers today are designed to be used with a **keyboard**—a device used to enter characters at the location on the screen marked by the *insertion point* or *cursor* (typically a blinking vertical line). Keyboards can be built into a device, attached by inserting the keyboard's wired cable or *wireless receiver* into a USB port, or connected via a wireless networking connection (such as Bluetooth, which is discussed in Chapter 7). A typical desktop computer keyboard is shown in Figure 4-1. Like most keyboards, this keyboard contains standard *alphanumeric keys* to input text and numbers, as well as additional keys used for various purposes. For instance, this keyboard contains a *numeric keypad* (for entering numbers), *function keys* (for issuing commands in some programs), *Delete* and *Backspace keys* (for deleting characters), *Ctrl* and *Alt keys* (for issuing commands in conjunction with other keys on the keyboard, such as [Ctrl]+[S] to save the current document in some programs), and *arrow keys* (for moving around within a document). Some keyboards also contain special keys that are used for a specific purpose, such as to control the speaker volume or DVD playback, or to launch an e-mail program or favorite Web site. To allow individuals to work under a variety of lighting conditions (such as in a dark living room or in an airplane), keyboards today are increasingly using *illuminated keys* to light up the characters on the keyboard.

Many computer keyboards today include touch pads, scroll wheels, and other components for easier control over some functions, such as gesture input (discussed shortly) or scrolling through documents. Some keyboards also include a fingerprint reader or other biometric reader that can be used for identification purposes, as discussed in more detail

---

>**Keyboard.** An input device containing numerous keys that can be used to input letters, numbers, and other symbols.

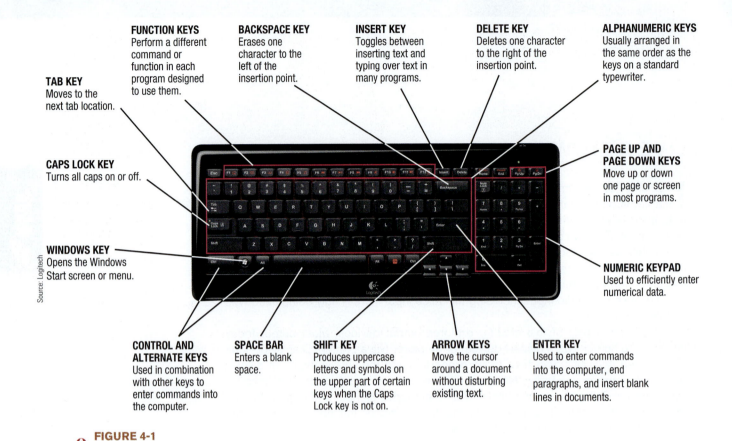

**TAB KEY**
Moves to the next tab location.

**FUNCTION KEYS**
Perform a different command or function in each program designed to use them.

**BACKSPACE KEY**
Erases one character to the left of the insertion point.

**INSERT KEY**
Toggles between inserting text and typing over text in many programs.

**DELETE KEY**
Deletes one character to the right of the insertion point.

**ALPHANUMERIC KEYS**
Usually arranged in the same order as the keys on a standard typewriter.

**CAPS LOCK KEY**
Turns all caps on or off.

**PAGE UP AND PAGE DOWN KEYS**
Move up or down one page or screen in most programs.

**WINDOWS KEY**
Opens the Windows Start screen or menu.

**NUMERIC KEYPAD**
Used to efficiently enter numerical data.

Source: Logitech

**CONTROL AND ALTERNATE KEYS**
Used in combination with other keys to enter commands into the computer.

**SPACE BAR**
Enters a blank space.

**SHIFT KEY**
Produces uppercase letters and symbols on the upper part of certain keys when the Caps Lock key is not on.

**ARROW KEYS**
Move the cursor around a document without disturbing existing text.

**ENTER KEY**
Used to enter commands into the computer, end paragraphs, and insert blank lines in documents.

**FIGURE 4-1**
**A typical desktop keyboard.**

later in this chapter and in Chapter 9. In addition, some keyboards are made for languages other than English and some keyboards are designed for special purposes, such as to allow easy input for specific systems (such as a library electronic card catalog or a company database), to input music into a computer (such as a MIDI keyboard used for piano compositions), or to be regularly and easily sterilized (such as keyboards used in hospitals).

Notebook and netbook computers usually have a keyboard that is similar to a desktop keyboard, but it is typically smaller, contains fewer keys (it often has no numeric keypad, for instance), and the keys are typically placed somewhat closer together. To make inputting data easier, notebook, netbook, and tablet computer users can also connect and use a conventional keyboard if their computer contains an appropriate port (such as a USB port) or Bluetooth capabilities.

While some mobile devices have a built-in physical keyboard, many tablets, smartphones, and other mobile devices have only an *on-screen keyboard* that can be used with touch or pen input, which is discussed shortly (see Figure 4-2). The order and layout of the keys on a mobile device keyboard may be different from the order and layout on a conventional keyboard, and the keyboard layout may vary from device to device. For easier data entry, an external keyboard (either a keyboard built into a tablet case or a stand-alone keyboard) that connects to the device via a wired or wireless connection when needed (see the universal keyboard in Figure 4-2) can often be used. New input methods for mobile devices are under development as well. For instance, tiny keyboards (such as those used on smart watches, refer again to Figure 4-2) can automatically zoom in on the part of the keyboard you touch to allow you to touch a larger key for your final selection, as well as try to predict what you are typing to save keystrokes. And the *Swype* app enables users with compatible on-screen keyboards to continuously drag through the letters in a word to spell that word, instead of having to type each letter separately. For instance, on the tablet shown in the left image of Figure 4-2, the user dragged through the letters that spell *Seattle* to enter that data in the map app.

**ON-SCREEN KEYBOARD**
This keyboard is using the Swype app in which the user continuously drags through the letters in a word for faster input.

**UNIVERSAL KEYBOARD**
This keyboard can connect wirelessly to three devices at once and the user can switch between those devices.

**ONE-ROW KEYBOARD**
This on-screen keyboard uses software to try to determine and predict what the user is typing.

**HW**

**FIGURE 4-2**
Keyboards for mobile devices.

# POINTING AND TOUCH DEVICES

In addition to a keyboard, most computers today are used in conjunction with some type of **pointing device**. Pointing devices are used to select and manipulate objects, to input certain types of data (such as handwritten data), and to issue commands to the computer. The most common pointing devices are the mouse, the pen/stylus, and devices that use touch input. For a look at a possible input option for the future—perceptual computing—see the Trend box.

## Mice

The **mouse** (see Figure 4-3) is the most common pointing device for a desktop computer. It typically rests on the desk or other flat surface close to the user's computer, and it is moved across the surface with the user's hand in the appropriate direction to point to and select objects on the screen. As it moves, an on-screen *mouse pointer*—usually an arrow— moves accordingly. Once the mouse pointer is pointing to the desired object on the screen, the buttons on the mouse are used to perform actions on that object (such as to open a hyperlink, to select text, or to resize an image). Similar to keyboards, mice today typically connect via a USB port or via a wireless connection.

Older *mechanical mice* have a ball exposed on the bottom surface of the mouse to control the pointer movement. Virtually all mice today are *optical mice* or *laser mice* that track movements with light (*LED* or *laser light*, respectively). There are also mice that support two-dimensional gestures, such as *touch mice* (refer again to Figure 4-3) designed for Windows devices. Instead of buttons, these mice include a touch surface on top of the mouse in order to support *finger swipes* and other gestures for convenient

**FIGURE 4-3**
Mice.

**TRADITIONAL MICE**
Support pointing, clicking, and scrolling.

**TOUCH MICE**
Support swiping, tapping, and other navigational gestures.

> **Pointing device.** An input device that moves an on-screen pointer, such as an arrow, to allow the user to select objects on the screen.
> **Mouse.** A common pointing device that the user slides along a flat surface to move a pointer around the screen and clicks its buttons to make selections.

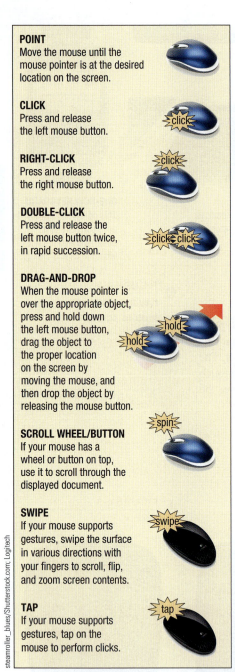

**POINT**
Move the mouse until the mouse pointer is at the desired location on the screen.

**CLICK**
Press and release the left mouse button.

click

**RIGHT-CLICK**
Press and release the right mouse button.

click

**DOUBLE-CLICK**
Press and release the left mouse button twice, in rapid succession.

click click

**DRAG-AND-DROP**
When the mouse pointer is over the appropriate object, press and hold down the left mouse button, drag the object to the proper location on the screen by moving the mouse, and then drop the object by releasing the mouse button.

hold    hold

**SCROLL WHEEL/BUTTON**
If your mouse has a wheel or button on top, use it to scroll through the displayed document.

spin

**SWIPE**
If your mouse supports gestures, swipe the surface in various directions with your fingers to scroll, flip, and zoom screen contents.

swipe

**TAP**
If your mouse supports gestures, tap on the mouse to perform clicks.

tap

steamroller_blues/Shutterstock.com; Logitech

**FIGURE 4-4**
Common mouse operations.

navigation. In addition to being used with desktop computers, mice can also be used with portable computers (such as notebooks, tablets, and netbooks), as long as an appropriate port (such as a USB port) is available or the mouse can connect via Bluetooth. There are also special *cordless presenter* mice that can be used by presenters to control on-screen slide shows.

Mice are used to start programs; open, move around, and edit documents; draw or edit images; and more. Some of the most common mouse operations are described in Figure 4-4.

## Pens/Styluses

Many devices today, including computers, tablets, and smartphones, can accept *pen input*; that is, input by writing, drawing, or tapping on the screen with a pen-like device called a **stylus**. Sometimes, the stylus (also called a *digital pen*, *electronic pen*, or *pen*) is simply a plastic device with no additional functionality; other times, it is a pressure-sensitive device that transmits the pressure applied by the user to the device that the stylus is being used with in order to allow more precise input. These more sophisticated styluses are typically powered by the device with which they are being used, have a smooth rounded tip so they don't scratch the screen, and contain buttons or switches to perform actions such as erasing content or right-clicking.

The idea behind pen input and *digital writing* in general is to make using a computer or other device as convenient as writing with a pen, while adding the functionality that pen input can provide (such as converting handwritten pen input to editable typed text). Pen input is being used increasingly for photography, graphic design, animation, industrial design, document processing, and healthcare applications. In addition to supporting handwritten input (referred to as *inking*), digital pens can be used to navigate through a document and issue commands to the computer. Pens can also be used to provide easier touch input for mobile device users who have long fingernails, who wear gloves in the winter, or who have a device with a screen that is too small to have accurate touch input via a finger. Some of the most common devices that use pen input are discussed next.

### Pen-Based Computers and Mobile Devices

Although their capabilities depend on the type of device and software being used, pen input can be used with a variety of computers and mobile devices today (see Figure 4-5). Most often, pens are used with mobile devices and tablet computers to both input handwritten text and sketches and to manipulate objects (such as to select an option from a menu, select text, or resize an image). They can also be used with a desktop or notebook computer if the device supports pen input. Recent versions of Windows support both pen and touch input, but the display screen being used with the Windows device must support this type of input in order for you to use it. To enable a regular Windows computer to function as a pen-enabled touch screen computer, new digital pens that use a USB receiver to transmit the pen's location information to a computer are available. Depending on the software being used, handwritten input can issue commands to the computer, be stored as an image, be

> **Stylus.** An input device that is used to write electronically on the display screen; also called a digital pen, electronic pen, or pen.

# TREND

### Perceptual Computing

In the 2002 futuristic movie *Minority Report*, Tom Cruise changes the images on his display by gesturing with his hands. While it was fiction in the movie, it is now just about a reality. Enter the trend of *perceptual computing* where users control their devices with three dimensional (3D) gestures, voice commands, and facial expressions instead of with traditional input devices like the keyboard and mouse.

Gesture input itself isn't new—it's been used in various forms for several years with devices such as the Nintendo Wii, Xbox Kinect, and the Apple iPhone and in large screen consumer gaming and advertising applications; it is also an important component of the Windows operating system. But the gesture-input systems of the future are expected to be much more sophisticated and combined with other types of input to allow users to more naturally control their computers and to allow the devices to adapt to each individual's need. For example, a computer or smartphone could offer to make a game easier if a player appears frustrated or could offer to turn the page on a tablet displaying a recipe if the hands of the person cooking are covered with flour.

One recent step in this direction is the *Leap 3D System* shown in the accompanying photograph. It is a box about the size of a USB flash drive that connects to a computer via a USB port and creates an eight-cubic-foot 3D interactive space inside which users can swipe, grab, pinch, and move objects around as if they were using a touch screen, except that they are not actually touching the screen. Instead, the device tracks hand and finger movement in 3D and in real time to provide input to the app being used, such as creating the sculpture shown in the accompanying photo. Noncontact systems like this have additional advantages, such as being able to use 3D gestures instead of just 2D gestures, avoiding the fingerprint and germ issues related to public keyboard and touch screen use, allowing for full body input, and enabling input to be performed from a slight distance (such as from a nearby chair or through a glass storefront window).

Courtesy Leap Motion

stored as handwritten characters that can be recognized by the computer, or be converted to editable, typed text. For the latter two options, software with **handwriting recognition** capabilities must be used.

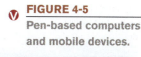

**FIGURE 4-5**
**Pen-based computers and mobile devices.**

Source: Samsung Electronics Co., Ltd

**SMARTPHONES**

Source: Microsoft Corporation

**TABLET COMPUTERS**

Source: Wacom Company

**DESKTOP COMPUTERS**

>**Handwriting recognition.** The ability of a device to identify handwritten characters.

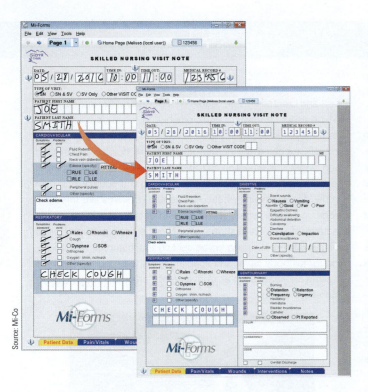

Source: Mi-Co

With handwriting recognition, the computer interprets data handwritten with a digital pen as individual characters. For instance, handwritten notes can be converted by the computer to typed notes and data written on a *digital form* (such as the patient assessment form shown in Figure 4-6) can be handwritten on the screen using a stylus and then automatically converted into typed text. The use of handwriting recognition technology in conjunction with digital forms saves time, reduces paper waste, and increases data accuracy. The use of digital forms is growing rapidly and is expected to continue to grow as companies increasingly move toward digital records and digital documents, such as electronic health records (EHRs). In addition, the U.S. government is converting many paper forms to electronic forms. For example, the U.S. Department of Defense (DoD) has announced a new forms management system that allows nearly 1,000 electronic forms used by DoD entities (including the Army, Navy, Air Force, Marines, Coast Guard, Joint Chiefs of Staff, and the Office of the Secretary of Defense) to be filled out, saved, digitally signed, and submitted electronically. This new system is expected to save time and minimize the need for printed copies.

**FIGURE 4-6**

**Digital forms.** If the software supports it, the text handwritten on a digital form can be converted by the computer to typed text.

## Digital Writing Systems

*Digital writing systems* are pen-based systems that capture handwritten input as it is being written. Some digital writing systems are handwriting apps that allow you to create handwritten documents that can be stored on the device or in a cloud account. Others (such as the one in Figure 4-7 and sometimes referred to as *smartpens*) require the use of special paper that contains a grid of dots so the pen (which contains a camera) can determine what is being written or drawn on the paper and where that data was written on the paper. The handwritten input is transferred to a computer, tablet, smartphone, or cloud account via a Bluetooth or Wi-Fi wireless connection. If the digital writing system being used supports handwriting recognition, the handwritten text can be converted to typed text. The digital writing system shown in Figure 4-7 has an extra feature to facilitate student note taking—it records audio and can play back a recording made at the time a note was written by just tapping the appropriate words with the pen.

**FIGURE 4-7**

**Other uses for digital pens.**

Source: Livescribe, Inc.

**DIGITAL WRITING SYSTEMS**
Record all input written on the paper and transfer it to a device either in real time or when directed by the user.

Source: Wacom Company

**GRAPHICS/PEN TABLETS**
Transfer all input written or drawn on the tablet to the computer in real time and allow the use of pen navigation tools.

Courtesy Verifone

**SIGNATURE CAPTURE DEVICES**
Record signatures for purchases, deliveries, and other applications that require recorded authorization.

## Graphics Tablets

A **graphics tablet**—also called a *pen tablet* or *digitizing tablet*—is a flat, touch-sensitive tablet used in conjunction with a digital pen (refer again to Figure 4-7). The graphics tablet is typically connected to a computer via a USB port or a wireless connection and anything drawn or written on the graphics tablet is automatically transferred to the connected computer. The graphics tablet can also be used to issue commands to the computer. Graphic artists, photographers, and other graphics professionals often use graphics tablets in conjunction with image editing software to create original images or to modify digital photographs. Graphics tablets can also be used to add overall pen capabilities to a computer.

## Signature Capture Devices

Another type of pen-based input device is the *signature capture device* (one example is shown in Figure 4-7). These devices are found most often at checkout counters to record signatures used to authorize credit card purchases electronically. Delivery companies, restaurants, retail stores, and other service businesses may also use a signature capture device—or a mobile device with a stylus and appropriate software—to record authorizing signatures.

## Touch Screens

**Touch screens** allow the user to touch the screen with his or her finger to select commands or otherwise provide input to the device associated with the touch screen. Touch screens are common on computers, as well as on smartphones and other mobile devices (see Figure 4-8), in order to provide easy input. While desktop monitors, all-in-one PCs, and conventional notebook computers can also use touch input, it is most practical (and comfortable) when the touch screen is not vertical; as a result, extensive touch input is most appropriate with hybrid notebook-tablet computers, mobile devices, and other devices that can be held in a more horizontal position. Many touch screens

**FIGURE 4-8**
Touch screens.

**PERSONAL COMPUTERS**
Courtesy of Dell Inc.

**MOBILE DEVICES**
Source: Amazon.com, Inc.

**SURFACE HUBS**
Source: Microsoft Corporation

**TABLE PCS**
Source: Lenovo

>**Graphics tablet.** A flat, rectangular input device that is used in conjunction with a stylus to transfer drawings, sketches, and anything written on the device to a computer. >**Touch screen.** A display device that is touched with the finger to issue commands or otherwise provide input to the connected device.

## ASK THE EXPERT

**Microsoft** **Stephen Rose,** Senior Product Marketing Manager and Industry Vertical Lead for U.S. Windows and Devices, Microsoft

### How is touch input changing personal computing today?

In the past, we were chained to a desk and our computers in order to have access to the services and resources required to do our jobs. As we moved into the laptop era, mobility and the opportunity to work from almost anywhere became the vision. We are now in the tablet and smartphone era, and these thin, light, mobile consumption devices allow us to truly work from anywhere using just the touch of a finger.

What I find interesting is that touch has not taken over the way I work but it has enabled me to perform actions faster than I can with a mouse. In addition, I see touch input creating a convergence of platforms. People expect their smartphone to give them information about meetings, phone calls, texts, and other timely items, as well as view Word and PDF documents and other items traditionally accessed with their laptop. With the worlds of personal computing and mobile computing merging and users moving between screens of all sizes, touch becomes key to bridging these worlds and giving us a more personalized, intimate computing experience not available in a non-touch environment.

today are *multi-touch*; that is, they can recognize input from more than one finger at a time, such as using two fingers to enlarge or rotate an image on the screen. Similar multi-touch products are used for large wall displays, such as for use in museums, government command centers, and newsrooms. For instance, news anchors can use large multi-touch screens to display maps, photos, videos, charts, and other data during broadcasts, and businesses can use them in conference rooms (see the *Surface Hub* display in Figure 4-8, which supports both touch and pen input).

Another touch screen option is the *table PC*—a large screen computer either built into a table or designed to be used on a table (such as the 27-inch table PC shown in Figure 4-8) that allows multi-touch input from multiple users. Table PCs can be used by several individuals at once to play games together, work together on a project, participate in an interactive museum display together, and so forth.

Touch screens are also used in consumer kiosks, restaurant order systems, and other point-of-sale (POS) systems, and they are useful for on-the-job applications (such as factory work) where it might be impractical to use a keyboard or mouse. A growing trend is to use touch screens that provide *tactile feedback*— a slight movement or other physical sensation in response to the users' touch so they know their input has been received by the computer. For a closer look at another emerging trend for mobile device displays—augmented reality— see the How It Works box. While touch screens make many devices today (such as computers, smartphones, televisions, and many other consumer electronics) more convenient for the majority of individuals to use, there is concern that these devices and their applications are not accessible to blind individuals, users with limited mobility, and other individuals with a disability. There are also concerns about the possible health ramifications of using vertical touch screens extensively. Ergonomic issues related to touch screens and other computing hardware, as well as accessibility issues, are discussed in detail in Chapter 13.

### Other Pointing Devices

A few other common pointing devices are described next and shown in Figure 4-9. In addition to these and the other pointing devices discussed in this chapter, pointing devices specifically designed for users with limited mobility are available. These pointing devices—along with ergonomic keyboards, Braille keyboards, and other types of input devices designed for users with special needs—are discussed in Chapter 13.

### Gaming Devices

A variety of gaming devices today (such as the ones shown in Figure 4-9) can be used as controllers to supply input to a computer. For instance, the stick of a *joystick* can be moved with the hand to move an on-screen object (such as a player or vehicle in a game) and the buttons pressed to perform their assigned functions (such as jumping or firing a weapon). *Gamepads* perform similar functions but are held in the hand instead; *steering wheels* are also available for driving games. There are also input devices designed to be used with gaming devices, such as Wii, Xbox, and PlayStation gaming consoles. These include gamepads and steering wheels; guitars, drums, and other musical instruments; dance pads, balance boards, and other motion sensitive controllers; and proprietary controllers such as the *Wii Remote*, *Xbox Kinect*, and *PlayStation Move*.

Guitar controller · Joystick · Gamepad · Steering wheel

Source: Logitech

**GAMING DEVICES**
Most often used for gaming applications.

## Trackballs

Similar to an upside-down mechanical mouse, a *trackball* has the ball mechanism on top, instead of on the bottom. The ball is rotated with the thumb, hand, or finger to move the on-screen pointer. Because the device itself does not need to be moved, trackballs take up less space on the desktop than mice and they can be used on a variety of surfaces.

Source: Logitech

**TRACKBALLS**
An alternative to a mouse that has all tracking mechanisms on the top surface.

byggarn.se/Shutterstock.com; Logitech

**TOUCH PADS**
Commonly found on notebook and netbook computers (left); also available as stand-alone devices (right).

▲ **FIGURE 4-9**
Other common pointing devices.

## Control Buttons and Wheels

Many consumer devices today, such as smart watches, GPS devices, and handheld gaming devices, use special control buttons and wheels to select items and issue commands to the device. For instance, the Apple Watch has a *Digital Crown* button that is used as a pointing device to zoom and scroll; pressing the button returns to the Watch Home screen.

## Touch Pads

A **touch pad** is a touch-sensitive pad across which a fingertip or thumb slides to move the on-screen pointer; tapping the touch pad (or one of its associated buttons) typically performs clicks and other mouse actions. Touch pads are the most common pointing device for notebook and netbook computers. They are used to point to and select objects, to scroll through documents or other content, and to perform gestures such as *swiping* and *pinching*. Because touch is so integrated into the newest operating systems (such as the most recent versions of Windows and OS X), there are also stand-alone touch pads available (see Figure 4-9) that can be used with computers that don't have a touch screen. Touch pads are also built into some keyboards.

>**Touch pad.** A small touch-sensitive input device, often found on notebook and netbook computers, that is touched with the finger or thumb to control an on-screen pointer and make selections.

# HOW IT WORKS

## Augmented Reality

While *virtual reality* (*VR*) immerses you into a virtual world and blocks out the real world, *augmented reality* refers to overlaying computer-generated images on top of real-time images. Some of the earliest applications were industrial, such as displaying wiring diagrams on top of the actual wiring of an airplane or other item via a headset. Today, augmented reality is going mobile—being used with smartphones, as well as other mobile devices. To accomplish this, content is displayed over the images seen through the device's camera and displayed on the device. Some content is based on the user's location (such as overlaying information about the location that the user is currently viewing); other content is based on the physical objects being viewed (such as overlaying a movie trailer or a 3D image over a magazine ad or book page being viewed).

Some initial mobile augmented reality apps designed for consumers include overlaying home listing information (such as pricing and photos) over the video images displayed as a smartphone is pointing at houses in a neighborhood, displaying information (such as real-time game stats and player information) as a smartphone is pointing at a sporting event, and displaying activity opportunities (such as restaurant, movie, museum, or shopping information) as a smartphone is pointing at a business district (see the accompanying illustration). Travelers can use apps designed to overlay directions on top of a street map corresponding to what the camera sees, as well as apps to display sightseeing information as the camera is pointing at a historical building, a statue, or another landmark. Mobile augmented reality can also work indoors, such as identifying displays, concession stands, restrooms, and more at conventions or displaying exhibit information at museums.

Emerging mobile augmented reality opportunities for businesses include displaying the exact physical location of a business and relevant information or ads when an individual points his or her smartphone in the vicinity of the business. Information displayed could include room photos and pricing (for hotels), dining room photos and menus (for restaurants), or merchandise photos and specials (for stores). And augmented reality is moving beyond smartphones to glasses (such as Google Glass) and other head-mounted computing devices (such as Microsoft HoloLens, discussed later in this chapter).

Source: Nokia

# SCANNERS, READERS, AND DIGITAL CAMERAS

There are a variety of input devices designed to capture data in digital form so a computer can manipulate it. Some devices (such as scanners and readers) convert data that already exists in physical form (such as on *source documents* like photographs, checks, or product labels); other devices (such as digital cameras) capture data initially in digital form. Automating the data entry process is referred to as *source data automation* and can refer to capturing data electronically from a source document or entering data directly into a computer at the time and place the data is generated (see Figure 4-10).

Source data automation is widely used today because it can save a great deal of time and is much more accurate than recording the data on paper and then later entering it into a computer via a keyboard. It also allows the people who know the most about the events that the data represents to be the ones who input the data, which helps increase accuracy during the data entry process. For instance, an insurance adjuster or auto mechanic entering data directly into a computer about the condition of a car involved in an accident will likely have fewer input errors than if he or she records that data on paper, and then has an assistant key the data into a computer later.

Many devices used in source data automation are *scanning* or *reading devices*; that is, devices that scan or read printed text, codes, or graphics, and then translate the results into digital form. The next few sections discuss several different types of scanning and reading devices, followed by a look at digital cameras.

## Scanners

A **scanner**, more officially called an *optical scanner*, captures an image of an object (usually a flat object, such as a printed document or photograph) in digital form, and then transfers that data to a computer. Typically, the entire document (including both text and images) is input as a single image that can be resized, inserted into other documents, posted on a Web page, e-mailed to someone, printed, or otherwise treated like any other graphical image. The text in the scanned image, however, cannot be edited unless optical character recognition (OCR) software is used in conjunction with the scanner to input the scanned text as individual text characters.

Individuals frequently use scanners to input printed photographs and other personal documents into a computer. Businesses are increasingly using scanners to convert paper documents into electronic format for archival or document processing purposes. Most scanners scan in color and some are *duplex scanners*—that is, they can scan both sides of a document at one time. Scanners with networking capabilities can be used to scan images to other devices on that network, such as a computer or smartphone; some can scan directly to a cloud storage account or an e-mail address. The most common types of scanners are discussed next.

### Types of Scanners

**Flatbed scanners** are designed to scan flat objects one page at a time, and they are the most common type of scanner. Flatbed scanners work in much the same way that photocopiers do—whatever is being scanned remains stationary while the scanning mechanism moves underneath it to capture the image (see Figure 4-11). Some scanners can scan slides and

**RECORDING DATA DIRECTLY INTO A COMPUTER**

**CAPTURING DATA FROM ITS SOURCE DOCUMENT**

Source: Motion Computing

Courtesy Honeywell International Inc.

**FIGURE 4-10**

**Source data automation.** Recording data initially in digital form or capturing data directly from a source document can help reduce data input errors and save time.

**FIGURE 4-11**

**Scanners.**

BlueSkyImage/Shutterstock.com

Source: Wizcomtech LTD

Courtesy Creaform

**FLATBED SCANNERS**
Used to input digital copies of photos, sketches, slides, book pages, and other relatively flat documents into the computer.

**PORTABLE SCANNERS**
Used to capture digital copies of documents while on the go; the data is typically transferred to a computer at a later time.

**PORTABLE 3D SCANNERS**
Used to capture 3D digital images of a person or an object.

>**Scanner.** An input device that reads printed text and graphics and transfers them to a computer in digital form. >**Flatbed scanner.** An input device that scans flat objects one at a time.

film negatives, in addition to printed documents. Scanners designed for high-volume business processing come with automatic document feeders so that large quantities of paper documents can be scanned (one page after the other) with a single command.

**Portable scanners** are designed to capture text and other data while on the go. Some are *full-page portable scanners* that can capture images of an entire document (such as a printed document or receipt); others (such as the one shown in Figure 4-11) are *handheld scanners* designed to capture text one line at a time. In either case, the scanner is typically powered by batteries, the scanned content is stored in the scanner, and the content is transferred to a computer (via a cable or a wireless connection) when needed. Some handheld scanners have OCR capabilities and some of these can also be used to translate scanned text from one language to another. One recent option is a scanner built into a mouse to enable users to switch between mouse actions and scanning as needed.

Multimedia, medical, and some business applications may require the use of a *three-dimensional* (*3D*) *scanner*, which can scan an item or person in 3D (refer again to Figure 4-11). Task-specific scanners, such as *receipt scanners* and *business card scanners*, are also available. In addition, scanning hardware is being incorporated into a growing number of products, such as ATM machines to scan the images of checks deposited into the machine; typically, the check images are printed on the deposit receipt and can be viewed online via online banking services.

### Scanning Quality and Resolution

The quality of scanned images is indicated by *optical resolution*, usually measured in the number of *dots per inch* (*dpi*). When a document is scanned (typically using scanning software, though some application programs allow you to scan images directly into that program), the resolution of the scanned image can often be specified. The resolution can also be reduced if needed (such as to *compress* an image to reduce its file size before posting it on a Web page) using an image editing program. Scanners today usually scan at between 75 dpi and 6,400 dpi. A higher resolution results in a better image but also results in a larger file size, as illustrated in Figure 4-12. Images need to be scanned at a higher resolution, however, if the image (or a part of it) will be enlarged significantly. The file size of a scanned image is also determined in part by the physical size of the image. Once an image has been scanned, it can usually be resized and then saved in the appropriate file format and resolution for the application with which the image is to be used.

### Readers

A variety of readers are available to read the different types of codes and marks used today, as well as to read an individual's biometric characteristics. Some of the most common types of readers are discussed next.

### Barcode Readers

A **barcode** is an *optical code* that represents data with bars of varying widths or heights. Two of the most familiar barcodes are *UPC* (*Universal Product Code*), which is the type of barcode found on packaged goods in supermarkets and other retail stores, and *ISBN* (*International Standard Book Number*), which is the type of barcode used with printed books (see Figure 4-13). A newer barcode designed for small consumer goods like fresh food is *DataBar*. Businesses and organizations can also create and use custom barcodes to fulfill their unique needs. For instance, shipping organizations (such as FedEx and UPS) use

**FIGURE 4-12**
**Scanning resolution.**

96 dpi
(833 KB)

300 dpi
(1,818 KB)

600 dpi
(5,374 KB)

**RESOLUTION**
Most scanners let you specify the resolution (in dpi) to use for the scan. High-resolution images look sharper but result in larger file sizes.

custom barcodes to mark and track packages, retailers (such as Target and Walmart) use custom barcodes added to customer receipts to facilitate returns, hospitals use custom barcodes to match patients with their charts and medicines, libraries use custom barcodes for checking out and checking in books, and law enforcement agencies use custom barcodes to mark evidence. In fact, any business with a *barcode printer* and appropriate software can create custom barcodes for use with its products or to classify items (such as paper files or equipment) used within its organization. The most popular barcode for these types of nonfood use is *Code 39*, which can encode both letters and numbers. Examples of the Code 39 barcode and the *Intelligent Mail barcode* (used by the U.S. Postal Service to represent destination ZIP Codes, as well as shipper IDs and other identifying data specified by the shipper) are shown in Figure 4-13.

These conventional types of barcodes are referred to as *one-dimension (1D) barcodes* because they contain data in only one direction (horizontally). Newer *two-dimensional (2D) barcodes* store information both horizontally and vertically and can hold significantly more data—up to several hundred times more. One of the most common 2D barcodes—the *QR (Quick Response) code* that represents data with a matrix of small squares—is shown in Figure 4-13. Most QR codes today are designed to be used by consumers and so are located on items such as magazine and newspaper ads, promotional posters, store displays, and package delivery notices. QR codes are read using a mobile app that displays the embedded information (such as package tracking information, a video clip, or a photo) or performs an assigned action (such as entering a contest, displaying a Web page, or downloading a coupon or ticket) when the QR code is captured. These types of information or assigned actions can also be invisibly embedded into print media using *digital watermarks* that can be read by a mobile app, as discussed in Chapter 13. Digital watermarks embedded into print media often use a barcode or an icon (such as the *Women's Day* magazine icon shown in Figure 4-13) to show consumers where to point their smartphones to capture the embedded data.

Barcodes are read with **barcode readers**. Barcode readers (see Figure 4-14) use either light reflected from the barcode or imaging technology to interpret the bars contained in the barcode as the numbers or letters they represent. Then, data associated with that barcode—typically identifying data, such as to uniquely identify a product, shipped package, or other item—can be retrieved. *Fixed barcode readers* are frequently used in point-of-sale (POS) systems; *portable barcode readers* are also available for individuals who need to scan

**ISBN CODES**

**UPC (UNIVERSAL PRODUCT CODE) CODES**

**CODE 39 CODES**

**INTELLIGENT MAIL CODES**

**QR CODES**

**DIGITAL WATERMARK ICONS**

Source: Motorola Solutions

**FIGURE 4-13**
Barcodes and digital watermark icons.

**FIGURE 4-14**
Barcode readers.

**FIXED BARCODE READERS**
Used most often in retail point-of-sale applications.

**PORTABLE BARCODE READERS**
Used when portability is needed.

**INTEGRATED BARCODE READERS**
Used most often for consumer applications.

iStock.com/mtreasure

Courtesy Honeywell International Inc.

Bloomua/Shutterstock.com

>**Barcode reader.** An input device that reads barcodes.

barcodes while on the go, such as while walking through a warehouse, retail store, hospital, or other facility. In addition, with the appropriate mobile app, smartphones and tablets can read barcodes and digital watermarks, such as to access information and features offered by a QR code or digital watermark, or to comparison shop for products by capturing UPC codes.

## Radio Frequency Identification (RFID) and Near Frequency Identification (NFC) Readers

**Radio frequency identification (RFID)** is a technology that can store, read, and transmit data located in **RFID tags**. RFID tags contain tiny chips and radio antennas (see Figure 4-15); they can be attached to objects, such as products, price tags, shipping labels, ID cards, assets (such as livestock, vehicles, computers, and other expensive items), and more. The data in RFID tags is read by **RFID readers**. Whenever an RFID-tagged item is within range of an RFID reader (up to 300 feet or more, depending on the type of tag and the radio frequency being used), the tag's built-in antenna allows the information located within the RFID tag to be sent to the reader.

Unlike barcodes, RFID tags only need to be within range (not within line of sight) of a reader. This enables RFID readers to read the data stored in many RFID tags at the same time and read them through cardboard and other materials—a definite advantage for shipping and inventory applications. Another advantage over barcodes is that the RFID tag attached to each item is unique (unlike UPC codes, for instance, that have the same code on all instances of a single product), so each tag can be identified individually and the data can be updated as needed. In addition, the data stored in RFID chips can be updated during the life of a product (such as to record information about a product's origin, shipping history, and the temperature range the item has been exposed to) and that information can be read when needed (such as at a product's final destination). One disadvantage of RFID technology is cost, though the chipless, printable RFID tags in development are expected to eventually drop the cost to less than a tenth of a cent per tag. This reduced cost plus the many advantages of RFID over barcodes make it possible that RFID may eventually replace barcodes on product labels and price tags. Because RFID technology can read numerous items at one time, it is also possible that, someday, RFID will allow a consumer to perform self-checkout at a retail store by just pushing a shopping cart past an RFID reader, which will ring up all items in the cart at one time.

RFID is used today for many different applications (see Figure 4-16 for some examples). Some of the initial RFID applications were tracking the movement of products and shipping containers during transit, tagging pets and livestock, and tracking tractors and other large assets. Many of these applications use GPS technology in conjunction with RFID to provide location information for the objects to which the RFID tags are attached. RFID is also used by prescription drug manufacturers to comply with government requirements that drugs be tracked throughout their life cycles and to track food products and sources. For example, all cows, sheep, and goats in Australia are required to have RFID ear tags so that animals can be traced from birth to slaughter and diseased animals can be tracked back to their ranches.

Other RFID applications include *electronic toll collection* (automatically deducting highway tolls from a payment account when an RFID-tagged car drives past a tollbooth), tracking patients at hospitals, increasing efficiency in ticketing applications (such as train passes, concert tickets, and ski lift tickets), and speeding up the identification process of travelers at border crossings. In the United States, for instance, several states are issuing *enhanced driver's licenses* that contain RFID chips, and all *U.S. Passports* and *U.S. Passport Cards* issued today contain RFID chips.

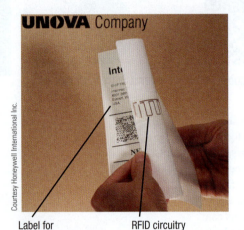

Courtesy Honeywell International Inc.

Label for shipping carton

RFID circuitry (chip and antenna)

**FIGURE 4-15**
RFID tags.

> **Radio frequency identification (RFID).** A technology used to store and transmit data located in RFID tags. > **RFID tag.** A device containing a tiny chip and a radio antenna that is attached to an object so it can be identified using RFID technology. > **RFID reader.** A device used to read RFID tags.

To facilitate electronic payments and other short-range transactions, **Near Field Communications (NFC)**—a short-range wireless communication standard that is based on RFID—is increasingly being used. For example, NFC-enabled credit cards and smartphones allow for contactless electronic payments via NFC-enabled payment terminals (refer again to Figure 4-16). Because the credit card or smartphone has to be within an inch or so of the NFC-enabled reader, using NFC is more secure, and therefore more appropriate, than conventional RFID for electronic payment applications.

A variety of RFID readers, including *handheld*, *portal*, and *stationary RFID readers*, are available to fit the various RFID applications in use today. Handheld RFID readers are used by workers to read RFID tags on the go or to read RFID-enabled tickets at a venue entrance. Portal RFID

**SHIPPING**
This portal RFID reader reads RFID tags attached to the shipping container or to items inside the container as it passes through the portal.

**WAREHOUSING**
This handheld RFID reader is used to read the RFID tags located on the warehouse shelves, as well as on the pallets currently stored there.

**MOBILE PAYMENTS**
This stationary NFC reader is used at checkout locations to process payments via NFC-enabled credit cards or smartphones.

**TICKETING**
This stationary RFID reader is used to automatically open ski lift entry gates for valid lift ticket holders at a ski resort in Utah.

readers are used to read all the RFID tags on all the products located inside sealed shipping boxes on a palette at one time when the palette passes through the portal. Stationary RFID readers are used at checkstands, border crossings, and other locations where RFID tags need to be read on a continual basis. NFC devices are read by NFC-enabled payment terminals or other NFC readers. For a closer look at mobile payments, see the Technology and You box.

Despite all its advantages, RFID growth in the retail industry has been slower than initially expected. This is primarily because of cost constraints and a number of privacy and security issues, such as concerns that others might be able to read the data contained in an RFID tag attached to your clothing, passport, or other personal item, or they might be able to make fraudulent charges via your smartphone. Precautions against fraudulent use—such as requiring a PIN code, signature, or other type of authorization when an RFID or NFC payment system is used—are becoming available. For example, when iPhone 6 users make a payment with *Apple Pay* (an NFC-based payment system built into Apple Watch and

**FIGURE 4-16**
RFID and NFC applications.

**TIP**

NFC can also be used to transfer data (such as contact info, photos, and payments) between two NFC-enabled smartphones.

> **Near Field Communication (NFC).** A short-range wireless technology based on RFID and used to transfer payments or other information from a smartphone to another smartphone or to a payment terminal.

some iPhones), they can authorize the payment via a fingerprint swipe. Privacy advocates are also concerned about linking RFID tag data with personally identifiable data contained in corporate databases, such as to track consumer movements or shopping habits.

**CAUTION** **CAUTION** **CAUTION** **CAUTION** **CAUTION** **CAUTION** **CAUT**

Keep your enhanced driver's license and passport in the supplied protective sleeve when not in use to protect against unauthorized reading or tracking. While currently no personal data is stored in the RFID chips embedded in these items, hackers have demonstrated the ability to read the RFID chips embedded in these items if they are not properly shielded. Because of this, privacy advocates recommend taking this precaution with any RFID-enabled identity item.

**▼ FIGURE 4-17**

**Optical mark readers (OMRs).**

Are commonly used to score tests and tally questionnaires.

Source: Scantron Corporation

## Optical Mark Readers (OMRs)

*Optical mark readers* (*OMRs*) input data from *optical mark forms* to score or tally exams, questionnaires, ballots, and so forth. Typically, you use a pencil to fill in small circles or other shapes on the form to indicate your selections, and then the form is inserted into an optical mark reader (such as the one shown in Figure 4-17) to be scored or tallied. The results can be input into a computer system if the optical mark reader is connected to a computer.

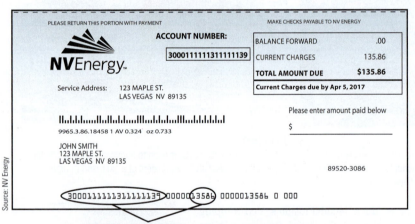

Source: NV Energy

**OPTICAL CHARACTERS**
These OCR characters indicate the customer account number and amount due and can be read by both computers and human beings.

**▲ FIGURE 4-18**

**Optical characters.**

Are often used in turnaround documents, such as on this utility bill.

## Optical Character Recognition (OCR) Devices

**Optical character recognition** (**OCR**) refers to the ability of a computer to recognize text characters printed on a document. The characters are read by a compatible scanning device, such as a flatbed scanner or dedicated *OCR reader*, and then *OCR software* is used to identify each character and convert it to editable text. While OCR systems can recognize many different types of printed characters, *optical characters*—which are characters specifically designed to be identifiable by humans as well as by an OCR device—are often used on documents intended to be processed by an OCR system. For example, optical characters are widely used in processing *turnaround documents*, such as the monthly bills for credit card and utility companies (see Figure 4-18). These documents contain optical characters in certain places on the bill to aid processing when consumers send it back with payment—or "turn it around."

## Magnetic Ink Character Recognition (MICR) Readers

*Magnetic ink character recognition* (*MICR*) is a technology used primarily by the banking industry to facilitate check processing. MICR characters (such as those located on the bottom of a check that represent the bank routing number, check number, and account number) are inscribed on checks with magnetic ink when the checks are first printed.

> **Optical character recognition (OCR).** The ability of a computer to recognize scanned text characters and convert them to electronic form as text, not images.

# TECHNOLOGY AND YOU

### Mobile Payments and Digital Wallets

*Digital wallets*, like *Apple Pay* and *Google Wallet*, store payment information to help individuals pay for purchases more conveniently. Mobile digital wallets are stored on smartphones, smart watches, and other mobile devices. Mobile digital wallet transactions today typically use NFC technology; if an NFC-enabled smartphone is used, payments can be made by simply moving the smartphone very close to or touching the NFC-enabled payment terminal (see the accompanying photo). Advantages of NFC digital wallets include faster and easier checkouts (because you don't have to open your wallet or even unlock your smartphone in some cases to pay for a purchase), the ability to add digital copies of other items often found in a wallet (such as your identification cards, loyalty cards, discount cards, medical insurance cards, and so forth) to your digital wallet in order to replace your physical wallet with your smartphone, the ability to store digital coupons and other offers to be used at checkout, the ability to secure your digital wallet with a passcode or PIN, and the ability of some digital wallets to mask your credit card numbers during the transaction. Disadvantages include having a variety of competing systems with different NFC readers and the inability to use the wallet if your smartphone's battery dies.

Other forms of mobile payments include *mobile payment processing* (taking credit card payments via a credit card reader attached to your smartphone or tablet, like the one shown in the Technology and You box in Chapter 1), as well as paying bills and sending money to others via a mobile banking app or mobile payment app, such as *Square Cash* or *PayPal*.

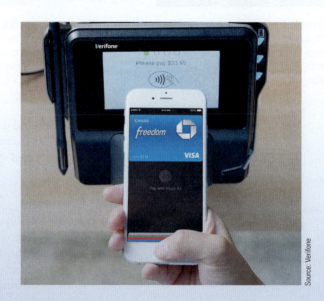

Source: Verifone

---

These characters can be read and new characters (such as to reflect the check's amount) can be added by an *MICR reader* (also called a *check scanner*) when needed. High-volume MICR readers are used by banks to process checks deposited at the bank. Smaller units (such as the one shown in Figure 4-19) can be used by many businesses to deposit paper checks remotely (referred to as *remote deposit* and permitted by the *Check 21 Law*, which allows financial institutions to exchange digital check images and process checks electronically). To make a remote deposit using an MICR reader, the check is scanned and then the check data is transmitted to the bank electronically for payment. There are also MICR readers incorporated in most new ATM machines today to enable the MICR information located on checks inserted into the ATM machine to be read at the time of the deposit.

Remote deposit and electronic check processing is a growing trend. It is faster and more convenient for businesses and individuals. It also helps the environment because, according to one estimate, a paper check travels 48 miles during processing, which results in an annual cost to the environment for check processing of more than 80,000 tons of paper used and more than 160 million gallons of fuel consumed. In addition to MICR readers, remote deposit can be performed via your smartphone by transmitting photos of the front and back of an endorsed check via your bank's mobile app. After the software optimizes the image and verifies it meets the *Check 21 Law* image standards, the check images and deposit data are transmitted to your bank and the check is deposited into your bank account.

**FIGURE 4-19**

Magnetic ink character recognition (MICR) readers are used primarily to process checks.

Source: Epson America, Inc.

Fingerprint
reader

Fingerprint
reader is built
into the Home
button.

**PERSONAL COMPUTERS**
Often used to control access to the device (such as the notebook computer shown here), as well as to log on to secure Web sites.

**MOBILE DEVICES**
Often used to verify an individual's identity (such as via the iPhone Touch ID fingerprint reader shown here).

**FIGURE 4-20**
Biometric readers.

## Biometric Readers

*Biometrics* is the science of identifying individuals based on measurable biological characteristics. **Biometric readers** are used to read biometric data about a person so that the individual's identity can be verified based on a particular unique physiological characteristic (such as a fingerprint or a face) or personal trait (such as a voice or a signature). Biometric readers can be stand-alone or built into a computer or mobile device (see Figure 4-20); they can also be built into another piece of hardware, such as a keyboard, an external hard drive, or a USB flash drive. Biometric readers can be used to allow only authorized users access to a computer or facility or to the data stored on a storage device, as well as to authorize electronic payments, log on to secure Web sites, or punch in and out of work. Biometrics used for access control is covered in more detail in Chapter 9.

## Digital Cameras

**Digital cameras** work much like conventional film cameras, but instead of recording images on film, they record them on a digital storage medium, such as a flash memory card, embedded flash memory, or a built-in hard drive. Digital cameras are usually designated either as still cameras (which take individual still photos) or video cameras (which capture moving video images), although many cameras today take both still images and video. In addition to stand-alone still and video cameras, digital camera capabilities are integrated into many portable computers and mobile devices today.

## Digital Still Cameras

*Digital still cameras* are available in a wide variety of sizes and capabilities, such as inexpensive point-and-shoot digital cameras designed for consumers, professional digital cameras, and digital cameras integrated into smartphones and other mobile devices (see Figure 4-21). Consumer digital cameras start at about $50; professional digital cameras can cost several thousand dollars each.

The primary appeal of digital still cameras is that the images are immediately available for viewing or printing, instead of having to have the film developed first as was the case with conventional film cameras. One disadvantage of digital cameras is the slight delay between when the user presses the button and when the camera takes the photo, which is especially important when taking action shots. Although not yet as quick as conventional film cameras, the delay typically associated with digital cameras is getting shorter. Digital still cameras most often use flash memory cards for storage; the number of digital photos that can be stored at one time depends on the capacity of the card being used, as well as the photo resolution being used.

Photos taken with a digital camera are typically transferred to a computer or printer via the flash memory card containing the images or by connecting the camera to the

> **Biometric reader.** A device used to input biometric data, such as an individual's fingerprint or voice. > **Digital camera.** An input device that takes pictures and records them as digital images.

computer or printer using a wired or wireless connection. Some digital cameras and flash memory cards can connect directly to photo sharing Web sites via a Wi-Fi connection, as discussed in the Chapter 7 Technology and You box, to upload your photos automatically as they are taken. Once the photos have been transferred to a computer, they can be retouched with image editing software, saved, printed, posted to a Web page, or burned onto a CD or DVD disc, just like any other digital image. The images on the flash memory card or other storage medium being used with the camera can be deleted at any time to make room for more photos.

One factor affecting digital camera quality is the number of pixels (measured in *megapixels* or millions of pixels) used to store the data for each image. Today's cameras typically use between 8 and 36 megapixels. Although other factors—such as the quality of the lens and the technology used inside the camera to capture and process images—also affect the quality of digital photographs, the number of pixels does impact how large the digital photos can be printed. For instance, to print high-quality 8 by 10-inch or larger prints, a 5-megapixel camera is needed as a minimum.

Most smartphones today have a built-in digital camera. This has many advantages, such as the ability to keep your friends up to date about your current activities (such as by uploading photos to Facebook, Instagram, or other social media); to take photos of car accidents and other incidents for authorities; and to read barcodes, remotely deposit checks, and facilitate gesture input. However, they have also created new ethical problems in our society, such as the ability to take and distribute compromising photos of others, as well as to send compromising photos of oneself to others (a form of sexting, as discussed in more detail in Chapter 9).

## Digital Video Cameras

*Digital video cameras* (see Figure 4-22) include *digital camcorders* and small digital video cameras used in conjunction with computers and other devices. Digital video cameras are often built into portable computers and mobile devices; they are also available

**PREVIEWS**
Virtually all digital cameras let you display and erase images.

**STORAGE MEDIA**
Most cameras use removable storage media in addition to, or instead of, built-in storage.

**TYPICAL CONSUMER DIGITAL CAMERAS**

**PROFESSIONAL DIGITAL CAMERAS**

**DIGITAL CAMERAS INTEGRATED INTO SMARTPHONES**

**FIGURE 4-21**
Digital still cameras.

**ASK THE EXPERT**

**Louis Kaneshiro,** Senior Technology Manager, Kingston Digital, Inc.

**Is the speed of a flash memory card important?**

Faster SD card speed is only important if your device is designed to take advantage of it. This is becoming more important with digital video cameras, action cameras, and the latest SLRs as many of these devices start at Class 10 speeds. The more recent SDXC UHS-I capacity and speed specifications are designed for the newest SLR and action cameras that require faster throughput for burst mode photography, RAW files, and HD video capture. We recommend that customers buy the speed class advised by the manufacturer in the device's manual, as this will typically satisfy their needs at the lowest cost.

Source: Sony Electronics

**DIGITAL CAMCORDERS**
Typically store video on a built-in hard drive (as in this camera) or on embedded flash memory.

Built-in video camera

Source: Tango

**INTEGRATED VIDEO CAMERAS**
Commonly used to deliver video over the Internet, such as during a video phone call as shown here.

**FIGURE 4-22**
Digital video cameras.

as stand-alone devices (commonly called *PC cams* or *webcams*) that connect to a desktop computer or a network. Digital camcorders are similar to conventional *analog* camcorders, but they store images on digital media—typically on built-in hard drives or embedded flash memory. Video taken on a device with a built-in camera is typically stored on the device's internal storage. Once a video is recorded, it can be transferred to a computer, edited with software as needed, and saved to a DVD or other type of storage medium. It can also be *compressed* (made smaller), if needed, and then uploaded to social media sites, such as YouTube, Facebook, or *Vine*. Some digital video cameras today can take high-definition (HD) and Ultra HD (4K) video, and some include wide angle lenses and microphones to facilitate video phone calls and videoconferences with multiple individuals.

Both individuals and businesses commonly use digital video cameras today. Both can set up a webcam to share a video feed of a scenic location, zoo, or other place with the public via a Web site. Typical personal applications include recording home movies with a digital camcorder and making video phone calls via a computer or smartphone (as in Figure 4-22). An emerging personal application is using special *home surveillance video cameras* for security purposes—such as to monitor an empty house from work or keep an eye on a sleeping baby from another room in the home. Typically, these systems transmit the video either via the Internet to a computer or smartphone or via a wireless connection to a special display device located in the home. Their use is growing and can give homeowners and parents the peace of mind of being able to watch their home surveillance video via the Internet in order to know that their home or children are safe, as well as give them the opportunity to notify the police immediately if they see their house is in the process of being burglarized or their children are being mistreated by a nanny or babysitter. Businesses also often use digital video cameras for security applications, as well as to create videos for marketing purposes and to perform videoconferences and Webinars (seminars that take place via the Web). Digital video cameras can also be used for identification purposes, such as with the face recognition technology used to authorize access to a secure facility or computer resource via an individual's face, as discussed in more detail in Chapter 9.

## AUDIO INPUT

*Audio input* is the process of entering audio data into the computer. The most common types of audio input are voice and music.

### Voice Input and Speech Recognition Systems

*Voice input*—inputting spoken words and converting them to digital form—is typically performed via a *microphone*, which is often built into the computer or mobile device being used. It can be used in conjunction with *sound recorder software* to store the voice in an audio file, such as to create a podcast or perform legal or medical dictation. It can also be used to place voice phone calls, as well as in conjunction with *speech recognition software* to provide spoken instructions to a computer.

**Speech recognition systems** enable the device being used to recognize voice input as spoken words. It requires appropriate software, such as *Dragon NaturallySpeaking* or *Windows Speech Recognition*, in addition to a microphone. With speech recognition, voice input can be used to control the computer, such as opening and closing programs, selecting options from a menu or list, and moving the insertion point. It can also be used to input and edit text, including dictating text to be typed, selecting text to be formatted or edited, deleting text, correcting errors, and so forth. Speech recognition systems are used by individuals who cannot use a keyboard, as well as by individuals who prefer not to use a keyboard or who can generate input faster via a voice input system. For instance, medical and legal transcription is one of the most frequently used speech recognition applications at the present time.

To enable hands-free operation and faster input, speech recognition capabilities are usually incorporated into smartphones, GPS systems, and other mobile devices. They are also commonly built into cars to enable hands-free control of navigation systems and sound systems, as well as to allow hands-free mobile phone calls to take place via the car's voice interface. Specialty speech recognition systems are frequently used to control machines, robots, and other electronic equipment, such as by surgeons during surgical procedures.

With a typical speech recognition system (see Figure 4-23), a microphone is used to input the spoken words into the computer, and then the sounds are broken into digital representations of *phonemes*—the basic elements of speech, such as *duh*, *aw*, and *guh* for the word *dog*. Next, the speech recognition software analyzes the content of the speech to convert the phonemes to words. Once words are identified, they are displayed on the screen. If a match is questionable or a homonym is encountered (such as the choice between *two*, *too*, and *to*), the program analyzes the context in which the word is used in an attempt to identify the correct word. If the program inserts a wrong word while converting the user's voice input to text, the user can correct it. To increase accuracy, most speech recognition software can be trained by individual users to allow the program to become accustomed to the user's speech patterns, voice, accent, and pronunciation.

The basic concept of speech recognition is also being applied to other audio input applications that enable computers and devices to recognize sounds other than voice. For instance, one type of *sound recognition system* located inside a computer could monitor the sound a hard drive is making to detect a possible malfunction before it happens, and another type could be used in conjunction with security systems to "listen" for the sound of a door opening or other suspicious sounds in order to alert security personnel.

**FIGURE 4-23**
Speech recognition systems.

1. The user speaks into a microphone that cancels out background noise and inputs the speech into the computer.

2. An analog-to-digital converter on the sound card or integrated sound component located inside the system unit converts the spoken words to digital form.

3. Voice recognition software converts the words to phonemes and then determines the words that were spoken.

4. The spoken words appear on the screen in the application program (such as a word processor or an e-mail program) being used.

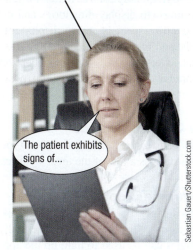

The patient exhibits signs of...

The patient exhibits signs of

Sebastian Gauert/Shutterstock.com

OmniArt/Shutterstock.com

---

>**Speech recognition system.** A system, consisting of appropriate hardware and software, used to recognize voice input, such as dictation or spoken computer commands.

Gines Romero/Shutterstock.com

**▲ FIGURE 4-24**

**Music input systems.** Musicians can input original compositions into a computer via microphones, MIDI keyboards and guitars, and other devices.

## Music Input Systems

*Music input systems* are used to input music into a computer, such as to create an original music composition or arrangement, or to create a custom music CD. Existing music can be input into a computer via a music CD or a Web download. For original compositions, microphones, *keyboard controllers*, and *guitar controllers* can be used to input the music into the computer—a *MIDI interface* is often used to connect musical instruments (such as the guitar shown in Figure 4-24) to a computer. Original music compositions can also be created using a conventional computer keyboard with appropriate software or a special device (such as a microphone or digital pen) designed to input music and convert it to a printed musical score. Once music is input into a computer, it can be saved, modified, played, inserted into other programs, or burned to a CD or DVD.

## DISPLAY DEVICES

A **display device**—the most common form of output device—presents output visually on some type of screen. Because the output appears temporarily on a display device, it is sometimes referred to as *soft copy*. The display device for a desktop computer is more formally called a **monitor**; the display device for a notebook, tablet, smartphone, smart watch, or other device for which the screen is built into the device is typically called a **display screen**. In addition to being used with computers and mobile devices, display screens are also built into handheld gaming devices, home entertainment devices (like remote controls, televisions, and portable DVD players), kitchen appliances, *e-book readers* or *e-readers* (which display e-books), and other products (see Figure 4-25).

Display screens also appear in public locations on *digital signage systems*—digital signs whose content can be changed throughout the day as needed. The content displayed on a digital sign can be graphics or video sent from a computer, video streamed via a camera, live Internet content, and more. For instance, the digital signage system shown in Figure 4-25 is located inside a convention center and displays information about events taking place at the convention center in the main part of the screen, and real-time stock quotes and other information in the ticker area at the bottom part of the screen. Digital signage systems are also frequently used as outdoor digital billboards (to display advertisements), in office buildings (to display directories and other information), in retail stores and restaurants (to advertise specials and to display menus, for instance), on consumer kiosks, in lecture halls, and in sporting arenas. Digital signage systems are even found in displays used to target advertising to consumers when they are waiting in a checkout line, riding in an elevator or taxi, stopped at a traffic light, or some other location where they are captive for a few minutes—a trend referred to as *captive marketing*.

### Display Device Characteristics

Several characteristics and features differentiate one type of display device from another. The following sections discuss a few of the most significant characteristics.

#### Color vs. Monochrome Displays

Display devices form images by lighting up the proper configurations of **pixels** (the smallest colorable areas on a display device—essentially tiny dots on a display screen). A variety of technologies can be used to light up the appropriate pixels needed to display

**PORTABLE COMPUTERS**

Source: Apple, Inc.

**E-READERS**

Source: Barnesandnoble.com llc

**HOME APPLIANCE CONTROL PANELS**

Source: General Electric Company

**MOBILE DEVICES**
Include smart watches (left) and smartphones (right).

Source: LG

Source: HTC

**DIGITAL SIGNAGE SYSTEMS**

Source: Planar Systems, Inc.

HW

a particular image, as discussed shortly. Display devices can be *monochrome displays* (in which each pixel can only be one of two colors, such as black or white) or *color displays* (in which each pixel can display a combination of three colors—red, green, and blue—in order to display a large range of colors). Most monitors and display devices today are color displays.

**FIGURE 4-25**
**Uses for display devices.**

## CRT Monitors vs. Flat-Panel Displays

The *CRT monitor* used to be the norm for desktop computers. CRT monitors use the same *cathode-ray tube* technology used in conventional televisions in which an electron gun sealed inside a large glass tube projects an electron beam at a screen coated with red, green, and blue phosphor dots; the beam lights up the appropriate colors in each pixel to display the necessary image. As a result, CRTs are large, bulky, and heavy.

While CRT monitors are still in use, most computers today (as well as most television sets, smartphones, and other consumer devices containing a display screen) use the thinner and lighter **flat-panel displays**. As discussed in more detail shortly, flat-panel displays form images by manipulating electronically charged chemicals or gases sandwiched between thin panes of glass or other transparent material. Flat-panel displays take up less desk space, which makes it possible to use multiple monitors working together to increase the amount of data the user can view at one time, increasing productivity without filling up an entire desk (see the left image in Figure 4-26). Flat-panel displays also consume less power than CRTs and most use digital signals to display images (instead of the analog

> **Flat-panel display.** A slim type of display device that uses electronically charged chemicals or gases instead of an electron gun to display images.

**MULTIPLE MONITOR SETUPS**
Can be used with a single computer to extend a desktop, which can increase productivity.

**SECOND DISPLAY FOR PORTABLE COMPUTERS**
Can be used to extend the desktop when needed; this curved screen has a wider viewing angle than a traditional display.

**FIGURE 4-26**
Flat-panel displays.

signals used with CRT monitors), which allows for sharper images. One disadvantage of a flat panel display is that the images sometimes cannot be seen clearly when viewed from a wide angle. To correct this, some newer monitors today are curved, such as the larger monitor in the right image in Figure 4-26. To use multiple monitors, you must have the necessary hardware to support it, such as the appropriate monitor ports, as discussed shortly. Multiple displays can be used with both desktop and portable computers; typically, you will use the displays to *extend* your desktop as in Figure 4-26, instead of duplicate it.

### Size and Aspect Ratio

Display device size is measured diagonally from corner to corner, in a manner similar to the way TV screens are measured. Most desktop computer monitors today are between 19 inches and 30 inches (though larger screens—up to 80 inches and more—are becoming increasingly common); notebook displays are usually between 14 inches and 17 inches; netbooks typically have 10- or 11-inch displays; and tablet displays are typically between 7 inches and 11 inches. To better view DVDs and other multimedia content, most monitors sold today are *widescreen displays*, which conform to the *16:9 aspect ratio* of widescreen televisions, instead of the conventional *4:3 aspect ratio*.

### Screen Resolution

Regardless of the technology used, the screen of a display device is divided into a fine grid of tiny pixels, as previously discussed. The number of pixels used on a display screen determines the *screen resolution*, which affects the amount of information that can be displayed on the screen at one time. When a higher resolution is selected, such as 1,920 pixels horizontally by 1,080 pixels vertically for a widescreen computer monitor (written as $1,920 \times 1,080$ and read as *1920 by 1080*), more information can fit on the screen, but everything will be displayed smaller than with a lower resolution, such as $1,024 \times 768$. The screen resolution on many computers today can be changed by users to match their preferences and the software being used. On Windows computers, display options are changed using the Control Panel. When multiple monitors are used, typically the screen resolution of each display can be set independently of the others. Very high-resolution monitors are available for special applications, such as viewing digital X-rays.

### Video Adapters, Interfaces, and Ports

The *video card* or *graphics card* installed inside a computer or the integrated graphics component built directly into the motherboard or the CPU of the computer houses the graphics processing unit (GPU)—the chip devoted to rendering images on a display device. The video card or the integrated graphics component determines the graphics capabilities of the computer, including the screen resolutions available, the number of bits used to store color information about each pixel (called the *bit depth*), the total number of colors that can be used to display images, the number of monitors that can be connected to the computer via that video card or component, and the types of connectors that can be used to connect a monitor to the computer. Video cards typically contain a fan and other cooling components to cool the card. Most video cards also contain memory chips (typically called *video RAM* or *VRAM*) to support graphics display, although some are designed to use a portion of the computer's regular RAM as video RAM instead. To support higher resolutions, higher bit depths, and a greater number of colors, a sufficient amount of video RAM is required. Most video cards today contain between 512 MB and 12 GB of video RAM. A typical video card is shown in Figure 4-27.

**GPU**
Renders images on the display screen (this GPU is located inside the fan enclosure for cooling purposes).

**FAN**
Cools the components on the video card.

**VGA    HDMI    DVI**

**VIDEO RAM CHIPS**
Provide memory for video display (this card contains 2 GB of video RAM inside the fan enclosure).

**PORTS**
Determine how a monitor can connect.

**PCI EXPRESS (PCIe) CONNECTOR**
Plugs into the PCIe slot on the motherboard.

Source: NVIDIA Corporation

**FIGURE 4-27**
**Video cards.** Provide a connection to a monitor, as well as determine video capabilities.

The three most common types of interfaces used to connect a monitor to a computer are *VGA* (*Video Graphics Array*), *DVI* (*Digital Visual Interface*), and *HDMI* (*High-Definition Multimedia Interface*), all shown in Figure 4-27. VGA is an older connection traditionally used with CRT monitors and many flat-panel monitors to transfer analog images to the monitor. DVI uses a more rectangular connector and it is used with flat-panel displays to allow the monitor to receive clearer, more reliable digital signals than is possible with a VGA interface. HDMI is a newer type of digital connection that uses a smaller connector. It transfers audio signals as well as video signals and can be used with display devices that support high-definition content. Another option is *DisplayPort*, which supports HD and 4K resolutions and is available in regular-sized, as well as the smaller *Mini DisplayPort*, formats.

A video card or an integrated video component in a desktop computer will have at least one port exposed through the system unit case to connect a monitor. Notebook computers and other computers with a built-in display typically contain a monitor port to connect a second monitor to the computer. If the needed port is not available on the computer, often an adapter can be used to connect the monitor to an available port. For example, to connect a DVI monitor to a notebook computer that only has an HDMI port, an *HDMI to DVI adapter* could be used. There are also adapters to connect monitors to a computer using the computer's USB port (see Figure 4-28). These adapters often use *DisplayLink USB graphics* technology, which uses an embedded chip in the adapter and the processors in the attached computer to process and display the graphical information. DisplayLink USB technology also allows multiple monitors to be connected to a single USB port on a computer using multiple adapters and a USB hub, or by using a USB docking station that contains multiple monitor ports. Monitors with DisplayLink USB graphics technology built in can be connected without using an adapter—just a USB cable is needed.

**FIGURE 4-28**
**A USB to DisplayPort 4K adapter.**

Courtesy StarTech.com

DisplayPort cable connects the display device.

USB 3.0 cable connects the adapter to the computer.

## Wired vs. Wireless Displays

Traditionally, computer monitors are *wired displays*; that is, monitors that are physically connected to the system unit via a cable. However, an increasing number of display devices today—including digital photo frames, e-readers, computer monitors, and television sets—are designed to be wireless. *Wireless displays* connect to a computer or other

device (such as to a smartphone, as in Figure 4-29) using a wireless networking connection such as Wi-Fi, Bluetooth, or a special wireless standard designed for transmitting multimedia (as discussed in more detail in Chapter 7). Once connected, either all content or selected content from the source device is displayed on the wireless display.

### High-Definition Displays

Most displays today are *high-definition* (*HD*) displays. The most common HD format is *1080p*, which uses a screen resolution of 1,920 × 1,080 and displays screen images one line at a time (called *progressive display*). In contrast, *interlaced displays* (like *1081i*) display every other line each pass, which produces screen images that are not as sharp or defined as progressive displays. The newest HD format is **Ultra HD (4K)**, which displays progressive images using about four times as many pixels as 1080p displays. As discussed in Chapter 3, 4K content requires a very fast connection and may be compressed for Internet delivery. HD and 4K displays are available for both home entertainment and productivity applications and are essential for professionals who work with photos, video, and other multimedia.

**FIGURE 4-29**
**Wireless displays.**
Display content from a device (such as the smartphone shown here) to the display via a wireless signal.

### Wearable Displays

While most displays are designed to be looked at from at least several inches away, some displays are designed to be wearable. *Wearable displays* can project images from a smartphone or directly from the Internet. Typically, wearable displays have control buttons on the side for input, which allow the user to see images as if they are on a distant large screen display. Many wearable displays overlay the projected image on top of what the user is seeing in real time to provide augmented reality. One type of wearable display is **smart glasses**, such as *Google Glass* and the smart glasses shown in Figure 4-30. Smart glasses are used by athletes, mobile workers, soldiers, and other individuals for hands-free communication and notifications. A growing trend is using smart glasses with other professions, such as engineering, transportation, oil and gas, and healthcare. For example, medical personnel can use them to view vital signs, test results, and patient health record information, as well as consult with other medical personnel, while they are evaluating and treating patients. For a look at another type of wearable display (wearable holographic displays), see the Inside the Industry box.

Notifications and other content appear in your line of vision.

Display is built into the frame of the smart glasses.

**FIGURE 4-30**
**Smart glasses.**

### Touch and Gesture Capabilities

As discussed earlier in this chapter, it is increasingly common for monitors and display screens to support touch input. Touch screen displays are commonly used with personal computers, as well as with consumer kiosks, portable gaming devices, smartphones, tablets, and other consumer devices. Large screen (such as 55-inch) touch screen displays are also available for conference room and other group locations. Gesture input is widely used with these products, as well as with large screen interactive displays and smart TVs.

**TIP**

Smart glasses with prescription lenses are now available.

> **Ultra HD (4K).** A high-definition display format that uses four times as many pixels as traditional HD displays. > **Smart glasses.** A wearable display device that looks like a pair of glasses but has a built-in display.

# Flat-Panel Display Technologies

The most common flat-panel technologies include liquid crystal display (LCD), various types of light emitting diode (LED), gas plasma, and e-paper. One emerging flat-panel technology is interferometric modulator display (IMOD). These display technologies are discussed next.

## Liquid Crystal Displays (LCDs)

A **liquid crystal display** (**LCD**) uses charged liquid crystals located between two sheets of clear material (usually glass or plastic) to light up the appropriate pixels to form the image on the screen. Several layers of liquid crystals are used, and, in their normal state, the liquid crystals are aligned so that light passes through the display. When an electrical charge is applied to the liquid crystals (via an electrode grid layer contained within the LCD panel), the liquid crystals change their orientation or "twist" so that light cannot pass through the display, and the liquid crystals at the charged intersections of the electrode grid appear dark. Color LCDs use a color filter that consists of a pattern of red, green, and blue *subpixels* for each pixel. The voltage used controls the orientation (twisting) of the liquid crystals and the amount of light that gets through, affecting the color and shade of that pixel—the three different colors blend to make the pixel the appropriate color.

LCDs can be viewed only with reflective light, unless light is built into the display. Consequently, LCD panels used with computer monitors typically include a light, usually at the rear of the display device—a technique referred to as *backlighting*. Many newer LCDs use *IPS* (*In-Plane Switching*) technology to display images with a broader range of color and brightness, with a better viewing angle, and with less blurring when the display is touched. However, LCDs using the older *TN* (*Twisted Nematic*) technology are less expensive.

## Light Emitting Diode (LED) and Organic Light Emitting Diode (OLED) Displays

**Light emitting diode (LED) displays** are another common type of flat-panel display. LED displays consist of LCD panels that are backlit with LEDs, which are the same type of lights that are commonly used with consumer products, such as alarm clocks and Christmas lights. In addition to standard LED displays, there are several emerging types of LEDs, which are discussed next.

**Organic light emitting diode (OLED) displays** use layers of organic material, which emit a visible light when electric current is applied. As shown in Figure 4-31, each pixel on an OLED display emits visible light in the necessary color. Because OLED displays emit a visible light, they do not use backlighting. This characteristic makes OLEDs more energy efficient than LCDs and LEDs and lengthens the battery life of portable devices using OLED displays. Other advantages of OLEDs are that

**V** **FIGURE 4-31**
**How OLED displays work.**

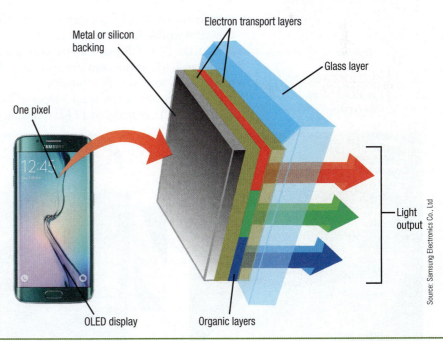

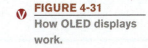

Source: Samsung Electronics Co., Ltd

> **Liquid crystal display (LCD).** A type of flat-panel display that uses charged liquid crystals to display images. > **Light emitting diode (LED) display.** An LCD display that is backlit with LEDs. > **Organic light emitting diode (OLED) display.** A type of flat-panel display that uses emissive organic material to display brighter and sharper images than LCDs.

# INSIDE THE INDUSTRY

## Wearable Holographic Displays

In addition to smart glasses, there are other head-mounted wearable displays that project images on top of what the person wearing the display is already seeing. One example is *Microsoft HoloLens*, which projects 3D *holograms* (light-based images) on top of the user's physical environment. HoloLens is essentially a head-mounted Windows computer and so it does not need to connect to a smartphone or computer to function. Unlike VR (where the user is completely immersed in a computer-generated reality) or traditional AR (where data is just overlaid on top of real world images), HoloLens is designed for *holographic computing* where holographic objects are anchored to specific physical locations or objects in the real world that the wearer is viewing.

HoloLens can project 3D images throughout an entire room. As shown in the accompanying photo, it can also project images via video chat to another individual who can then draw on top of the images the HoloLens wearer is seeing and both individuals see both the images and the notes. While still in the development stages, HoloLens has great potential for training and customer support, as well as for entertainment and productivity.

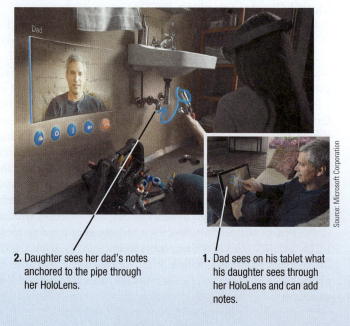

Source: Microsoft Corporation

2. Daughter sees her dad's notes anchored to the pipe through her HoloLens.

1. Dad sees on his tablet what his daughter sees through her HoloLens and can add notes.

**Microsoft HoloLens**

---

they are thinner than LCDs, they have a wider viewing angle than LCDs and so displayed content is visible from virtually all directions, and their images are brighter and sharper than LCDs. OLED displays are incorporated into many consumer devices, including digital cameras, televisions, and smartphones (refer again to Figure 4-31). White OLEDs are beginning to be used with lightbulbs.

There are also a few special types of OLEDs that support applications not possible with CRT, LCD, or traditional LED technology. For instance, *flexible OLED* (*FOLED*) displays are OLED displays built on flexible surfaces, such as plastic or metallic foil. Flexible displays using FOLED technology—such as displays for portable computers, smartphones, and televisions that can roll up when not in use (see Figure 4-32)—are being developed by several companies. Other possible uses for flexible screens include making lighter displays for computers and mobile devices, integrating displays on military uniform sleeves, and allowing retractable wall-mounted large screen displays.

**V FIGURE 4-32**
Special types of OLEDs.

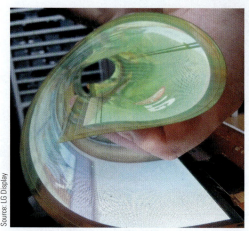

Source: LG Display

**FLEXIBLE OLEDS**
Used to create flexible displays on plastic or another type of flexible material.

**TRANSPARENT OLEDS**
Used to create transparent displays.

Another form of OLED is *transparent OLED* (*TOLED*). TOLED displays are transparent. The portion of the display that does not currently have an image displayed (and the entire display device when it is off) is nearly as transparent as glass, so the user can see through the screen (refer again to Figure 4-32). Transparent OLED technology opens up the possibility of displays on home windows, car windshields, helmet face shields, and other transparent items. A third type of OLED being developed by Universal Display Corporation is *Phosphorescent OLED* or *PHOLED*. The term *phosphorescence* refers to a process that results in much more conversion of electrical energy into light instead of heat; with phosphorescence, OLEDs can be up to four times more efficient than without it. Consequently, PHOLED technology is especially appropriate for use on mobile devices, consumer electronics, and other devices where power consumption is an important concern.

## Electronic Paper (E-Paper) Displays

**Electronic paper** (**e-paper**) is a technology used with *electronic paper displays* (*EPDs*) that attempts to mimic the look of ordinary printed paper on the display screen. EPDs are high-contrast, so they can be viewed in direct sunlight. They also require much less electricity than other types of displays because they don't require backlighting and they don't require power to maintain the content shown on the display—they only need power to change the content. E-paper displays were originally used for e-readers but they are beginning to appear in a wide variety of products, such as on electronic signs, smart watches, and smartphones, as well as displays built into USB flash drives, tools, credit cards, remote controls, and smartphone cases (see Figure 4-33).

EPDs use *electronic ink*—essentially charged ink that consists of millions of tiny beads or *microcapsules* about half the diameter of a human hair—to display images. For monochrome displays, these beads contain positively charged white particles and negatively charged black particles suspended in a clear fluid. When voltage is applied to the beads (through the circuitry contained within the display), either the white or the black particles rise to the top and the opposite colored particles are pulled to the bottom of the bead, depending on the polarity of the charge applied. Consequently, the beads in each pixel appear to be either white or black (refer again to Figure 4-33) and remain in that state until another transmission changes the pattern. Color e-ink displays work in a similar manner but typically include a color filter to make the images appear in color.

## Interferometric Modulator (IMOD) Displays

Another emerging flat-panel display technology is *interferometric modulator* (*IMOD*) *displays*. Designed initially for mobile phones and other portable devices, an IMOD display is essentially a complex mirror that uses external light—such as from the sun or artificial light inside a building—to display images. Because IMOD displays are utilizing light instead of fighting it the way LCD displays do, images are bright and clear even in direct sunlight (see Figure 4-34). And, because backlighting isn't used, power consumption is much less than what is needed for LCD displays. In fact, similar to e-paper, devices using IMOD displays use no power unless

**FIGURE 4-33**
How e-paper works.

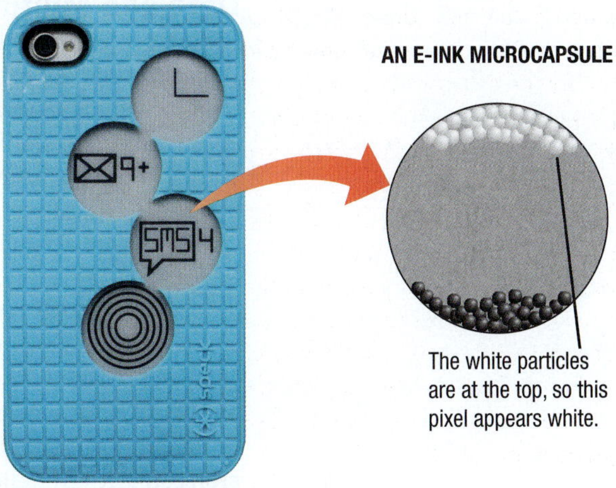

AN E-READER

**AN E-INK MICROCAPSULE**

The white particles are at the top, so this pixel appears white.

Source: E Ink Corporation a subsidiary of E Ink Holdings, Inc.

**FIGURE 4-34**
IMOD displays.

Source: Qualcomm Technologies, Inc.

> **Electronic paper (e-paper).** A technology that attempts to mimic the look of ordinary printed paper on a display screen.

the image changes so they can remain on at all times without draining the device battery. Beginning to be used with mobile devices, IMODs could eventually be used for large digital signs and other outdoor display devices that normally consume a great deal of power.

## Plasma Displays

**Plasma displays** use a layered technology like LCD and OLED and look similar to LCD displays, but they use a layer of gas between two plates of glass instead of liquid crystals or organic material. A phosphor-coated screen (with red, green, and blue phosphors for each pixel) is used, and an electrode grid layer and electronic charges are used to make the gas atoms light up the appropriate phosphors to create the image on the screen. While plasma technology has traditionally been used with the very large displays used by businesses, as well as with many large screen televisions, it is being replaced by LEDs.

## Data and Multimedia Projectors

A **data projector** is used to display output from a computer to a wall or projection screen. Projectors that are designed primarily to display movies and other multimedia are sometimes called *multimedia projectors*. Data projectors are often found in classrooms, conference rooms, and similar locations and can be portable units, freestanding larger units, or units that are permanently mounted onto the ceiling (see Figure 4-35). While larger data projectors typically connect via cable to a computer, *wireless projectors* that use a Wi-Fi connection are available to more easily project content located on a company network, the Internet, or a smartphone.

For projecting content to a small audience while on the go, small *pico projectors* are available. These pocket-sized projectors typically connect to a smartphone, portable computer, or other device to enable the device to project an image (such as a document, presentation, or movie) onto a wall or other flat surface. Projection capabilities are also beginning to be integrated directly into smartphones and smartphone cases in order to project images from the smartphone. In addition, stand-alone *keyboard projectors*, such as the one shown in Figure 4-35, project a *virtual keyboard* that can be used with Bluetooth-compatible smartphones or tablets for easier input. An emerging type of data projector is

**FIGURE 4-35**
Data projectors.

**CONVENTIONAL DATA PROJECTORS**
The projector shown here is ceiling mounted and Wi-Fi-enabled.

**PICO PROJECTORS**
Are very portable; images from the device connected to the projector can be displayed on any surface.

**KEYBOARD PROJECTORS**
The projector shown here projects a virtual keyboard that can be used with any Bluetooth-compatible device.

Source: Epson America, Inc.

Source: Philips Communications

Source: Celluon

>**Plasma display.** A type of flat-panel display that uses layers of gas to display images; most often used on large displays. >**Data projector.** A display device that projects output to a wall or projection screen.

the *3D projector*. Some 3D projectors are designed to project 3D images that are viewed with 3D glasses, similar to 3D televisions. Others are designed to project holograms. For instance, holograms of individuals and objects can be projected onto a stage for a presentation and hologram display devices can be used in retail stores, exhibitions, and other locations to showcase products or other items in 3D.

# PRINTERS

Instead of the temporary, ever-changing soft copy output that a monitor produces, **printers** produce *hard copy*; that is, a permanent copy of the output on paper. Most desktop computers are connected to a printer; portable computers and some mobile devices can use printers as well.

## Printer Characteristics
Printers differ in a number of important respects, such as the technology used, size, print quality, speed, and type of connection used. Some general printer characteristics are discussed next, followed by a look at the most common types of printers.

### Printing Technology
Printers produce images through either impact or nonimpact technologies. *Impact printers*, like old ribbon typewriters, have a print mechanism that actually strikes the paper to transfer ink to the paper. For example, a *dot-matrix printer* (see Figure 4-36) uses a *printhead* consisting of pins that strike an inked ribbon to transfer the ink to the paper—the appropriate pins are extended (and, consequently, strike the ribbon) as the printhead moves across the paper in order to form the appropriate words or images. Impact printers are used today primarily for producing multipart forms, such as invoices, packing slips, and credit card receipts.

Most printers today are *nonimpact printers*, meaning they form images without the print mechanism actually touching the paper. Nonimpact printers usually produce higher-quality images and are much quieter than impact printers are. The two most common types of printers today—laser printers and ink-jet printers—are both nonimpact printers. As discussed in more detail shortly, laser printers form images with toner powder (essentially ink powder) and ink-jet printers form images with liquid ink. Both impact and nonimpact printers form images with dots, in a manner similar to the way monitors display images with pixels. Because of this, printers are very versatile and can print text in virtually any size, as well as print photos and other graphical images. In addition to paper, both impact and nonimpact printers can print on transparencies, envelopes, mailing labels, and more.

## Color vs. Black and White
Both *color printers* and *black-and-white printers* are available. Color printers work similarly to black-and-white printers, except that, instead of using just black ink or toner, they also use cyan (blue), magenta (red), and yellow ink or toner (see Figure 4-37). Color printers either apply all of the colors in one pass or go through the entire printing process multiple times, applying one color during each pass. Color printers are often used in homes (to print photographs, greeting cards,

Source: InfoPrint Solutions Company

**FIGURE 4-36**
**Dot-matrix printers.**

**FIGURE 4-37**
**Color printing.**
Requires four colors.

Paul Broadbent/Shutterstock.com

flyers, and more). Businesses may use black-and-white printers for output that does not need to be in color (because it is less expensive and faster to print in black and white) and color printers for output that needs to be in color (such as product brochures and other colorful marketing materials).

### Print Resolution

Most printing technologies today form images with dots of liquid ink or flecks of toner powder. The number of dots per inch (dpi)—called the *print resolution*—affects the quality of the printed output. Printers with a higher print resolution tend to produce sharper text and images than printers with a lower resolution tend to produce, although other factors (such as the technology and number of colors used) also affect the quality of a printout. Guidelines for acceptable print resolution are typically 300 dpi for general-purpose print-outs, 600 dpi for higher-quality documents, and 2,400 dpi for professional applications.

### Print Speed

*Print speed* is typically measured in *pages per minute* (*ppm*). How long it takes a document to print depends on the actual printer being used, the selected print resolution, the amount of memory inside the printer, and the content being printed. For instance, pages containing photographs or other images typically take longer to print than pages containing only text, and full-color pages take longer to print than black-and-white pages. Because of these variations, the standard of *images per minute* (*IPM*) was developed as a more uniform measurement of print speed to allow consumers to more easily compare printers from different manufacturers.

### Personal vs. Network Printers

Printers today can be designated as *personal printers* (printers designed to be connected directly to a single computer, typically via a USB cable) or *network printers* (printers designed to be connected directly to a home or an office network). Network printers can be used by anyone connected to the network via a wired or wireless connection and they are increasingly being used in homes as well as in businesses. *Enterprise network printers* are designed for high-volume office printing, typically support multiple paper trays to print various sized documents, and often include other capabilities, such as the ability to collate, staple, hole-punch, and print on both sides of the page (referred to as *duplex printing*). Networks are discussed in detail in Chapter 7.

### Connection Options

Most personal printers today connect to a computer via a USB connection; many have the option of connecting via a wired or wireless networking connection as well (printers that use a Wi-Fi connection are also referred to as *wireless printers* or *Wi-Fi printers*). In addition, some personal printers can receive data to be printed via a flash memory card. Network printers are connected directly to a wired or wireless network and can be used by any device on the network, or via the Internet if *cloud printing* (see Figure 4-38) is available and enabled. For example, network printers can be accessed via the Internet using an appropriate app, an assigned e-mail address for that printer, or a cloud printing service such as *Google Cloud Print*. So, if your printer has Internet access, you can print content from your smartphone, tablet, or other mobile device to your home or office printer from any location with Internet access; you can also send printouts wirelessly to public printers, such as those located at airports, libraries, office stores, and shipping stores such as FedEx Office and The UPS Store.

**FIGURE 4-38**

**Cloud printing.**

Allows you to send documents to a printer via the Internet.

Source: Epson America, Inc.

## Multifunction Capabilities

Many printers today offer more than just printing capabilities. These units—referred to as **multifunction devices (MFDs)** or *all-in-ones*—typically copy, scan, fax, and print documents (see Figure 4-39). MFDs can be based on ink-jet printer or laser printer technology, and they are available as both color and black-and-white devices. Although multifunction devices have traditionally been desktop units used in small offices and home offices, it is common today for enterprise printers to be multifunction devices.

## Laser Printers

**Laser printers** (see Figure 4-40) are the standard for business documents and come in both personal and network versions; they are also available as both color and black-and-white printers. To print a document, the laser printer first uses a laser beam to charge the appropriate locations on a drum to form the page's image, and then *toner powder* (powdered ink) is released from a *toner cartridge* and sticks to the drum. The toner is then transferred to a piece of paper when the paper is rolled over the drum, and a heating unit fuses the toner powder to the paper to permanently form the image. Laser printers print one entire page at a time and are typically faster and have better quality output than ink-jet printers, discussed next.

Source: Epson America, Inc.

**HW**

**FIGURE 4-39**
A multifunction device (MFD).

**FIGURE 4-40**
Laser printers.

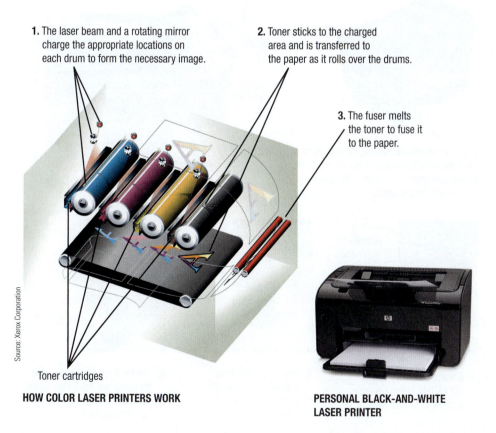

**1.** The laser beam and a rotating mirror charge the appropriate locations on each drum to form the necessary image.

**2.** Toner sticks to the charged area and is transferred to the paper as it rolls over the drums.

**3.** The fuser melts the toner to fuse it to the paper.

Source: Xerox Corporation

Toner cartridges

**HOW COLOR LASER PRINTERS WORK**

**PERSONAL BLACK-AND-WHITE LASER PRINTER**

Source: Hewlett-Packard Development Company, L.P.

**ENTERPRISE COLOR LASER PRINTER**

> **Multifunction device (MFD).** A device that offers multiple functions (such as printing, scanning, and faxing) in a single unit. > **Laser printer.** An output device that uses toner powder and technology similar to that of a photocopier to produce images on paper.

## Ink-Jet Printers

**Ink-jet printers** form images by spraying tiny drops of liquid ink from one or more *ink cartridges* onto the page, one printed line at a time (see Figure 4-41). Some printers print with one single-sized ink droplet; others print using different-sized ink droplets and using multiple nozzles or varying electrical charges for more precise printing. The printhead for an ink-jet printer typically travels back and forth across the page, which is one reason why ink-jet printers are slower than laser printers. However, some ink-jet printers use a printhead that is the full width of the paper, which allows the printhead to remain stationary while the paper feeds past it, significantly increasing the speed of the printer. These printers are designed primarily for business use.

Because they are relatively inexpensive, have good-quality output, and can print in color, ink-jet printers are often the printer of choice for home use. With the use of special photo paper, ink-jet printers can also print photograph-quality digital photos. Starting at less than $50 for a simple home printer, ink-jet printers are affordable, although the cost of the replaceable ink cartridges can add up, especially if you do a lot of color printing.

In addition to being used in computer printers, ink-jet technology is being applied to a number of other applications. For instance, ink-jet technology may eventually be used for dispensing liquid metals, aromas, computer chips and other circuitry, and even "printing" human tissue and other organic materials for medical purposes. For example, researchers are developing *silk ink* to be used as a base for medical products (such as medical gloves that change color when they are contaminated with bacteria and smart bandages that are embedded with antibiotics), as well as *protein ink* that could be used in implants or to stimulate bone growth.

**FIGURE 4-41**
**How ink-jet printers work.**

Each ink cartridge is made up of multiple tiny ink-filled firing chambers; to print images, the appropriate color ink is ejected through the appropriate firing chamber.

Source:. Hewlett-Packard Development Company, L.P.

**INK-JET PRINTER**

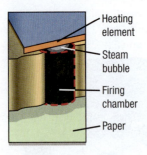

Heating element
Steam bubble
Firing chamber
Paper

**1.** A heating element makes the ink boil, which causes a steam bubble to form.

Steam bubble
Ink droplet

**2.** As the steam bubble expands, it pushes ink through the firing chamber.

Steam bubble
Ink droplet

**3.** The ink droplet is ejected onto the paper and the steam bubble collapses, pulling more ink into the firing chamber.

> **Ink-jet printer.** An output device that sprays droplets of ink to produce images on paper.

## Special-Purpose Printers

Although both laser and ink-jet printers can typically print on a variety of media—including sheets of labels, envelopes, transparencies, photo paper, and even fabric, in addition to various sizes of paper—some printers are designed for a particular purpose. Some of the most common *special-purpose printers* are discussed next.

### Barcode, RFID, Label, and Postage Printers

**Barcode printers** enable businesses and other organizations to print custom barcodes on price tags, shipping labels, and other documents for identification or pricing purposes. Most barcode printers can print labels in a variety of barcode standards; some (called *RFID printers*) can also encode RFID tags embedded in labels (see Figure 4-42). For other types of labels, such as for envelopes, packages, and file folders, regular *label printers* may come in handy. Some special-purpose label printers referred to as *postage printers* can print *electronic postage* (also called *e-stamps*). E-stamps are valid postage stamps that can be printed via an account from an e-stamp vendor; postage values are charged to your account as you print the e-stamps. E-stamp services typically allow stamps to be printed directly onto shipping labels and envelopes using laser or ink-jet printers.

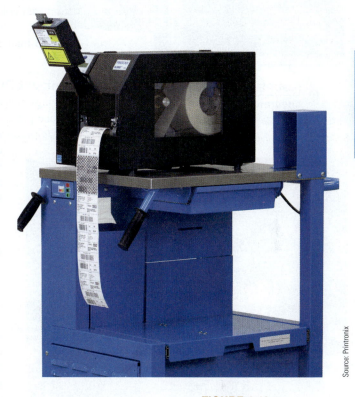

Source: Printronix

### Photo Printers

**Photo printers** are color printers designed to print photographs. They can be connected to a computer to print photos stored on the hard drive; most photo printers also can print photos directly from a digital camera, smartphone, or storage medium (such as a flash memory card) by connecting that device either physically or wirelessly to the printer. Often, photo printers have a preview screen to allow for minor editing and cropping before printing, but it is usually more efficient to do extensive editing on a computer. Some photo printers can print a variety of photo paper sizes; others—sometimes called *snapshot* or *pocket printers*—print only on standard 4 by 6-inch photo paper. In addition to photo printers designed for home use, there are also professional photo printers used by businesses and photo processing companies. Although home photo printers offer the convenience of printing digital photos at home and whenever the need arises, the cost per photo is typically higher than using a photo printing service at a retail store or an Internet photo printing service.

**FIGURE 4-42**
RFID printers.

### Portable and Integrated Printers

**Portable printers** are small, lightweight printers that can be used on the go, usually with a notebook computer or mobile device, and they connect via either a wired or wireless connection. Portable printers that can print on regular-sized (8.5 by 11-inch) paper are used by businesspeople while traveling; portable receipt, label, and barcode printers are used in some service professions. Printers can also be integrated into other devices, such as smartphones, smartphone cases, and digital cameras (see Figure 4-43). And some portable and integrated printers don't use conventional ink-jet or laser technology.

> **TIP**
>
> In addition to printing your digital photos, many retail and Internet photo services can print digital photos on shirts, mugs, playing cards, calendars, mouse pads—even valid U.S. postage stamps.

---

>**Barcode printer.** An output device that prints barcoded documents. >**Photo printer.** An output device designed for printing digital photographs. >**Portable printer.** A small, lightweight printer designed to be used while on the go.

Source: Polaroid

For instance, the printer built into the digital camera shown in Figure 4-43 uses a technology developed by *ZINK* (for "zero ink") *Imaging*. ZINK printers use no ink; instead, they use special paper that is coated with special color dye crystals. Before printing, the embedded dye crystals are clear, so the paper looks like regular white photo paper. The printer uses heat to activate and colorize these dye crystals when a photo is printed, creating a full-color image. The printer shown in Figure 4-43 prints 2 by 3-inch color photos.

**⋀ FIGURE 4-43**
**Integrated printers.**

### Large-Format Ink-Jet Printers

To print charts, drawings, maps, blueprints, posters, signs, advertising banners, and other large documents in one piece, a larger printer (such as the one shown in Figure 4-44) is needed. Today, most *large-format printers* (sometimes called *plotters*) are ink-jet printers and are designed to print documents up to about 120 inches in width. Although typically used to print on paper, some large-format ink-jet printers can print directly on fabric and other types of materials.

Source: Hewlett-Packard Development Company, L.P.

### 3D Printers

When 3D output is required, **3D printers** can be used. Instead of printing on paper, these printers typically form output in layers using materials such as plastic, metal, ceramic, wood, or glass during a series of passes to build a 3D version of the desired output—a process referred to as *additive manufacturing* because material is added instead of being taken away as in traditional *subtractive manufacturing*. Some printers can produce multicolor output; others print in only one color and need to be painted by hand if color output is desired. 3D printers can even print objects containing moving parts, such as gears and action figures with movable joints. 3D printers are available in a variety of sizes, from personal printers for printing smartphone cases, toys, jewelry, and other personal objects to professional printers for printing working product prototypes or custom manufacturing parts (one example of a 3D printer is shown in Figure 4-45). They can even print custom medical and dental prosthetics and implants using FDA-approved 3D material, as well as edible products printed from sugar or chocolate. In fact, the FDA recently approved a 3D-printed epilepsy medication built with layers of powdered medication. This drug is the first 3D-printed product approved for use inside the human body and has the advantage of dissolving instantly to make it considerably easier for patients to swallow than the typically large traditional epilepsy pills.

**⋀ FIGURE 4-44**
**Large-format printers.** Are used to print documents that are too large for a standard-sized printer.

The ability of 3D printers to print customized objects on demand is a distinct advantage. For example, NASA has installed a 3D printer at the International Space Station and is testing its ability to print tools and other objects that astronauts may need on demand. In the future, it is possible that 3D printers will be used by consumers on a regular basis to print everyday items on demand (you can already order 3D-printed shoes or insoles custom printed to fit to your feet or 3D-printed earbuds custom printed to fit your ears). One issue with the increased availability of 3D printers is the risk of them being used to print dangerous or illegal items, such as working plastic guns. In fact, the first 3D-printed gun firing standard bullets was

>**3D printer.** An output device designed to print three-dimensional objects, such as product prototypes.

demonstrated in 2013 and more than 100,000 copies of the open-source blueprint were downloaded before the file was taken offline per a U.S. State Department request. In some countries, such as Japan, 3D-printed guns are illegal and the first person convicted of making a 3D-printed gun is currently serving a two-year prison sentence.

## AUDIO OUTPUT

*Audio output* includes voice, music, and other audible sounds. **Computer speakers**, the most common type of audio output device, are either connected to or built into a computer in order to provide audio output for computer games, music, video clips and TV shows, Web conferencing, and other applications. Computer speaker systems resemble their stereo system counterparts and are available in a wide range of prices. Some speaker systems (such as the one shown in Figure 4-46) consist of only a pair of speakers. Others include additional speakers and a subwoofer to create better sound (such as surround sound) for multimedia content. Instead of being stand-alone units, the speakers for some desktop computers are built directly into, or permanently attached to, the monitor. Portable computers and mobile devices typically have speakers integrated into the device; these devices can also be connected to a home or car stereo system, portable speakers, or a consumer device (such as a treadmill) that contains a compatible *dock* and integrated speakers in order to play music stored on or streamed to the device through those speakers. Typically, mobile devices are connected to a speaker system via the device's headphone jack, dock connection, USB port, or wireless connection. For example, the portable wireless speaker shown in Figure 4-46 can play music from a smartphone whenever that phone is within range.

**Headphones** can be used instead of speakers when you don't want the audio output to disturb others (such as in a school computer lab or public library). **Headsets** are headphones with a built-in microphone and are often used when dictating, making phone calls, or participating in Web conferences using a computer; wireless headsets are commonly used in conjunction with mobile phones. Even smaller than headphones are the **earbuds** often used with smartphones, handheld gaming devices, and other mobile devices.

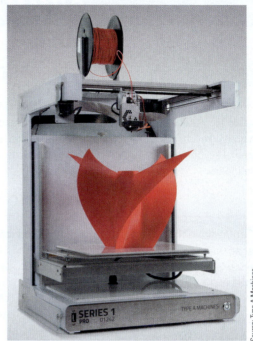

Source: Type A Machines

**FIGURE 4-45**
**3D printers.** Can print using a variety of materials (plastic is shown here).

**FIGURE 4-46**
**Audio output devices.**

Source: Altec Lansing/AL Infinity, LLC

**COMPUTER SPEAKERS**
Used to output sound from a computer.

Source: Mova Systems SAS

**PORTABLE SPEAKERS**
Connect wirelessly to output sound from a smartphone or tablet.

Source: Altec Lansing/AL Infinity, LLC

**EARBUDS**
Used to deliver sound from a smartphone or other mobile device to one individual.

>**Computer speakers.** Output devices connected to computers that provide audio output. >**Headphones.** A personal audio output device used by an individual so only he or she can hear the sound; headphones with a built-in microphone are typically referred to as **headsets**. >**Earbuds.** A very small audio output device worn inside the ear.

# SUMMARY

## KEYBOARDS

Most people use a **keyboard** to input data into a personal computer. Keyboards typically include the standard alphanumeric keys, plus other keys for special purposes. Many smartphones and other mobile devices include a keyboard today—if not, a *portable keyboard* can often be used. *Wireless keyboards* are also available.

## POINTING AND TOUCH DEVICES

**Pointing devices** are hardware devices that move an on-screen *mouse pointer* or similar indicator. The most widely used pointing device is the **mouse**. Another common pointing device is the **stylus**, which is used with pen-based computers, many mobile devices, and *digital writing systems* to input handwritten data and to select options; with **handwriting recognition** technology, the input can be converted to typed text. Use of *digital forms* in conjunction with handwriting recognition is a growing trend. **Touch screens** are monitors that are touched with the finger to select commands or provide input. Touch screens are widely used today with personal computers, smartphones, mobile devices, and other consumer devices. Other pointing devices include **graphics tablets**, gaming devices, and **touch pads**. Some pointing devices also support *gestures*.

## SCANNERS, READERS, AND DIGITAL CAMERAS

There are many different input devices that can be used to convert data that already exists (such as *source documents*) into digital form or to initially capture data in digital form. A **scanner** allows users to input data that exists in physical form, such as photographs, drawings, and printed documents, into a computer. Most scanners are **flatbed scanners** or **portable scanners**. *Receipt*, *3D*, and *business card scanners* are also available. When used with **optical character recognition** (**OCR**) software, the computer can recognize scanned text characters as editable text; if not, the scanned page is input as a single image.

**Barcode readers** are used to read **barcodes**, such as *UPC codes*; the cameras in mobile devices are used to read *QR codes*. **Radio frequency identification** (**RFID**) is a technology used to store and transmit data located in **RFID tags**, which contain tiny chips and antennas and which are attached to items. RFID tags are read by **RFID readers** and are most often used in conjunction with shipping containers and other large assets. RFID technology can also be used to track individuals, assets, and other items, as well as be used for electronic payment systems using **Near Field Communications** (**NFC**), a short-range wireless technology based on RFID.

*Optical mark readers* (*OMRs*) read specific types of marks on certain forms, such as on testing forms and voter ballots. *OCR readers* read characters, such as the specially printed *optical characters* used on bills and other *turnaround documents*. *Magnetic ink character recognition* (*MICR*) is used by the banking industry to rapidly sort, process, and route checks to the proper banks. **Biometric readers** read *biometric* characteristics (such as a fingerprint, hand geometry, or a face) in order to identify individuals.

**Digital cameras** work much like conventional film cameras, but they record digital images on a digital storage medium (such as a flash memory card, built-in hard drive, or DVD disc), instead of on conventional film or videotape. The images are immediately available without processing and can be transferred to a computer for manipulation or printing, or sent directly to some printers for printing. *Digital still cameras* take still photos; *digital video cameras* can be *digital camcorders*, *PC cams/webcams*, or cameras that are integrated into personal computers or mobile devices.

## AUDIO INPUT

**Speech recognition systems**, which enable computer systems to recognize spoken words, are one means of *audio input*. Speech recognition can be used for data input, as well as for controlling a computer or other device (such as a smartphone, car navigation system, or surgical robot). *Music input systems* are used to input music, such as original music compositions, into a computer. Music can also be input via a CD, DVD, or Web download.

**Chapter Objective 5:**
Understand the devices that can be used for audio input.

## DISPLAY DEVICES

**Display devices** (also called **monitors** and **display screens**) are the most common type of output device for a computer; they are also incorporated into a wide variety of other electronic devices such as **Ultra HD (4K)** displays and **smart glasses**. Display devices are available in a wide variety of sizes and are typically **flat-panel displays**, though older *CRT monitors* still exist. Flat-panel displays can be **liquid crystal displays (LCDs)** or **plasma displays**, but they are more commonly **light emitting diode (LED) displays** or **organic light emitting diode (OLED) displays**. Other display technologies include *interferometric modulator* (*IMOD*) displays, special types of OLEDs (such as *flexible*, *transparent*, and *Phosphorescent OLEDs*), and **electronic paper (e-paper)**. Regardless of the technology used, the screen of a display device is divided into a fine grid of small areas or dots called **pixels**. Monitors can be *color* or *monochrome*, *wired* or *wireless*, and are available in a wide variety of sizes. Some monitors support 3D images, and many include touch screen capabilities. The *video card* or integrated graphics component being used determines many of the graphics capabilities of the computer. **Data projectors** connect to a computer and project any output sent to the computer's monitor through the projector onto a wall or projection screen. Some projectors are integrated into mobile devices; others project *holograms* or other 3D images.

**Chapter Objective 6:**
Describe the characteristics of a display device and explain some of the technologies used to display images.

## PRINTERS

**Printers** produce *hard copy* output through either *impact* or *nonimpact* printing technology. Most printers today form images as matrices of dots, although with many technologies, the dots are too small to be visible. Printer quality is usually measured in *dots per inch* (*dpi*); speed is typically measured in *pages per minute* (*ppm*). Both *personal* and *network printers* are available and there are a number of options for connecting a printer to a network, computer, or other device. Some printers print in color and others print in just black and white. **Multifunction devices** (**MFDs**) incorporate the functions of multiple devices—typically a printer, scanner, and fax machine—into a single unit.

The most common printers are **laser printers** (which use *toner powder*) and **ink-jet printers** (which use liquid ink). Special-purpose printers include **photo printers**, **barcode printers**, **portable printers**, *large-format ink-jet printers*, and **3D printers**. Some printers are integrated into other devices, such as digital cameras or smartphone cases.

**Chapter Objective 7:**
List several types of printers and explain their functions.

## AUDIO OUTPUT

**Computer speakers**, which output music or spoken voice, are the most common *audio output* device. **Headphones**, **headsets**, or **earbuds** can be used to prevent the sound from disturbing other people. Speakers are also integrated into some consumer devices (such as treadmills); portable speakers and *docks* are available for use with mobile devices.

**Chapter Objective 8:**
Identify the hardware devices typically used for audio output.

# REVIEW ACTIVITIES

## KEY TERM MATCHING

a. digital camera

b. ink-jet printer

c. light emitting diode (LED) display

d. mouse

e. OLED display

f. optical character recognition (OCR)

g. RFID tag

h. scanner

i. smart glasses

j. touch screen

**Instructions:** Match each key term on the left with the definition on the right that best describes it.

1. _____ A common pointing device that the user slides along a flat surface to move a pointer around the screen and clicks its buttons to make selections.

2. _____ A device containing a tiny chip and a radio antenna that is attached to an object so it can be identified using radio frequency identification technology.

3. _____ A display device that is touched with the finger to issue commands or otherwise provide input to the connected device.

4. _____ An input device that reads printed text and graphics and transfers them to a computer in digital form.

5. _____ An LCD display that is backlit with LEDs.

6. _____ An input device that takes pictures and records them as digital images.

7. _____ A wearable display device that looks like a pair of glasses but has a built-in display.

8. _____ A type of flat-panel display that uses emissive organic material to display brighter and sharper images than LCDs.

9. _____ An output device that sprays droplets of ink to produce images on paper.

10. _____ The ability of a scanning device to recognize scanned text characters and convert them to electronic form as text, not images.

## SELF-QUIZ

**Instructions:** Circle **T** if the statement is true, **F** if the statement is false, or write the best answer in the space provided. **Answers for the self-quiz are located in the References and Resources Guide at the end of the book.**

1. **T  F**  A keyboard is an example of a pointing device.

2. **T  F**  Near Field Communications (NFC) is most commonly used for electronic payments.

3. **T  F**  UPC is a type of barcode.

4. **T  F**  Consumer kiosks located in retail stores commonly use touch screens for input.

5. **T  F**  An ink-jet printer normally produces a better image than a laser printer.

6. With _____ software, pen-based computers can convert handwritten text into editable, typed text.

7. A(n) _____ can be used to convert flat printed documents, such as a drawing or photograph, into digital form.

8. The smallest colorable area in an electronic image (such as a scanned document, digital photograph, or image displayed on a display screen) is called a(n) _____.

9. Virtually all portable computers and mobile devices, and most desktop computers today, use _____ displays, which are smaller, thinner, and lighter than the _____ monitors used with desktop computers in the past.

10. Match each input device to its input application, and write the corresponding number in the blank to the left of the input application.

a. _____ Pen-based computing     1. Keyboard

b. _____ Smartphone              2. Stylus

c. _____ Text-based data entry   3. RFID tag

d. _____ Secure facility access  4. Biometric reader

e. _____ Tracking goods          5. Touch screen

1. For the following list of computer input and output devices, write the appropriate abbreviation (I or O) in the space provided to indicate whether each device is used for input (I) or output (O).

a. _____ Biometric reader      f. _____ Digital camera

b. _____ E-paper               g. _____ Data projector

c. _____ Speaker               h. _____ Microphone

d. _____ 3D printer            i. _____ OLED monitor

e. _____ Flat-panel display    j. _____ Touch pad

2. Write the number of the type of printer that best matches each of the printing applications in the blank to the left of each printing application.

a. _____ To print inexpensive color printouts for a wide variety of documents.

b. _____ To print all output for an entire office.

c. _____ To print receipts for jet-ski rentals at the beach.

d. _____ To print high-quality black-and-white business letters and reports at home.

1. Personal laser printer

2. Network laser printer

3. Ink-jet printer

4. Portable printer

3. List three advantages of RFID technology over barcode technology.

4. Would an OLED display or an LCD display use more battery power? Explain why.

5. What type of printer would be used to create a fully-functioning product prototype?

1. While gaming and texting are both popular pastimes, it is possible to become injured by performing these activities. For instance, some Wii users have developed tennis elbow and other ailments from some Wii Sports games and heavy texters have developed problems with their thumbs. Think of the devices you use regularly. Have you ever become sore or injured from their use? If so, was it the design of the input device being used, overuse, or both? What responsibilities do hardware manufacturers have with respect to creating safe input devices? If a user becomes injured due to overuse of a device, whose fault is it? Should input devices come with warning labels?

2. The choice of an appropriate input device for a product is often based on both the type of device being used and the target market for that device. For instance, a device targeted to college students and one targeted to older individuals may use different input methods. Suppose that you are developing a device to be used primarily for Internet access that will be marketed to senior citizens. What type of hardware would you select as the primary input device? Why? What are the advantages and disadvantages of your selected input device? How could the disadvantages be minimized?

# PROJECTS

1. **Wearable Displays** As discussed in the Inside the Industry box, wearable displays today include smart glasses and wearable holographic displays. While both project images on top of what the user is seeing, their functions and features differ.

   For this project, select one type of wearable display and research it. Determine the main purpose and features of your selected device. Does it display information from a smartphone? Can it connect to the Internet? Who is this type of device targeted to? Individuals? Workers? Gamers? Is there more than one product available today? If so, do their features differ? Is the product designed to be worn continuously or just for certain activities? Would you be willing to wear this display in public? Why or why not? At the conclusion of your research, prepare a one-page summary of your findings and opinions and submit it to your instructor.

2. **Biometrics and Personal Privacy** Biometric input devices, such as fingerprint readers and iris scanners, are increasingly being used for access purposes. They are also being built into smartphones and other devices to authorize payments and other transactions. While viewed as a time-saving tool by some, other individuals may object to their biometric characteristics being stored in a database. Is the convenience of biometric systems worth compromising some personal privacy?

   For this project, research one use of biometric input today (such as mobile payments, airport screening systems, or company access control) and form an opinion about its use and any potential impact it may have on personal privacy. At the conclusion of your research, prepare a one-page summary of your findings and opinions and submit it to your instructor.

3. **Keyboarding Speed Test** Although voice and other alternative means of input are emerging, most data input today is still performed via the keyboard. Proper keyboarding technique can help increase speed and accuracy. Online keyboarding tests can help to evaluate your keyboarding ability.

   For this project, find a site (such as **TypingTest.com**) that offers a free online typing test and test your keyboarding speed and accuracy. At the conclusion of the test, rate your keyboarding ability and determine whether a keyboarding course or tutor program, or just keyboarding practice, will help you improve if your score is not at least 20 correct words per minute (cwpm). Take the test one more time to see if your speed improves now that you are familiar with how the test works. If your speed is fast, but accuracy is low, take the test once more, concentrating on accuracy. If you still test less than 20 cwpm, locate a free typing tutor program or Web site and evaluate it to see if it would help you to increase your speed and accuracy. At the conclusion of this task, prepare a short summary of your experience, including the typing test site used and your best score.

4. **Green Technology Mandates** This chapter discusses e-paper—an erasable, reusable alternative to traditional paper and ink. While e-paper has many societal benefits (such as reducing the use of traditional paper and ink, as well as the resources needed to create and dispose of them), it has been slow to catch on beyond e-readers. When a new technology, such as e-paper, that has obvious benefits to society is developed, who (if anyone) should be responsible for making sure it gets implemented in a timely fashion? Do we, as a society, have an ethical responsibility to ensure the new product succeeds? Should the government mandate the use of beneficial technology? Will businesses or individuals choose to use e-paper products if the only incentive is a cleaner environment? Would you be willing to switch to a new technology (such as e-paper) that is beneficial to society if it costs more than the existing technology? Is it ethical for an industry or the government to mandate the use of new technologies if they create an additional cost or inconvenience to individuals?

For this project, form an opinion about the ethical obligations individuals, businesses, and the government have with respect to the development and implementation of beneficial new technologies and be prepared to discuss your position (in class, via an online class forum, or via a class blog, depending on your instructor's directions). You may also be asked to write a short paper expressing your opinion.

5. **Assistive Computing** In addition to the conventional input and output hardware mentioned in the chapter, there are a variety of assistive input and output devices that physically challenged individuals can use to make computing easier and more efficient.

For this project, select one type of disability, such as being blind, deaf, paraplegic, quadriplegic, or having the use of only one arm or hand. Research the hardware and software options that could be used with a new computer for someone with the selected disability. Make a list of potential limitations of any standard computing hardware and the assistive hardware and software that would be appropriate for this individual. Research each assistive option, comparing the ease of use, cost, and availability, and then prepare a recommendation for the best computer system for your selected hypothetical situation. Share your findings with the class in the form of a short presentation. The presentation should not exceed 10 minutes and should make use of one or more presentation aids, such as a whiteboard, handouts, or a computer-based slide presentation (your instructor may provide additional requirements). You may also be asked to submit a summary of the presentation to your instructor.

6. **Should Printers Be Used to Print Body Parts?** As discussed in this chapter, researchers are looking to ink-jet printers and 3D printers as a means to create body parts for the future. Possibilities include replacement joints, blood vessels, skin, muscles, organs, and implants. Instead of ink, these printers print with living cells. It is looking like this technology will eventually be feasible, but do we want it to be? Possible advantages include quickly printing new skin on a burn victim's wound, printing new organs on demand when needed, and creating custom implants from the patient's cells so they won't be as easily rejected. But what about the ethical ramifications, such as selling manufactured body parts or surgeons adding extra body parts (such as an extra ear or arm) on demand for a fashion statement or for added productivity? What if replacing our failing organs as needed leads to virtual immortality—will we end up an overcrowded society of essentially mutants? Or are the potential benefits worth the risks?

Pick a side on this issue, form an opinion and gather supporting evidence, and be prepared to discuss and defend your position in a classroom debate or in a one- to two-page paper, depending on your instructor's directions.

# Hardware

Courtesy Logitech

# logitech

**Ali Moayer is a Senior Director at Logitech and the head of engineering for developing audio/ video communications products for the Unified Communications (UC) market. He has worked on many innovative ideas and designs, many of which were patented. Ali has more than 30 years of engineering experience and holds a Bachelor of Science degree in Electrical Engineering and an MBA in Technology Management.**

## A conversation with ALI MOAYER
### Senior Director of Engineering, Logitech

*" . . . augmented reality technology in products such as Google Glass will transform the way we look at the world and interact with each other. "*

### My Background . . .

I have been curious about technology from my childhood. I studied engineering and technology management in college and then started my career developing office messaging and networking equipment. I am now a Senior Director of Engineering in the Logitech for Business (LFB) group. As part of my responsibilities, I am the head of engineering for developing audio/video communications products for the Unified Communications (UC) market; my group also develops webcams and security cameras for the electronics retail market. Throughout my career, my college background, together with my work experiences developing medical imaging instruments, video cameras, and a wide variety of computer peripherals, has helped me be successful in the computer hardware industry. I also believe that my ability to understand electronics and consumer needs has been a contributing factor in my success in developing some of the best-in-class products for the PC peripheral market.

### It's Important to Know . . .

**The importance of input/output devices.** Interface devices used with computers, such as audio/ video capture and playback control devices and human interface control devices like mice and touch screens, are essential for providing a good user experience. We will continue to see computer interfaces enhanced with voice and gesture recognition, as well as new interfaces evolving to enable the human-to-machine interface to be more natural and intuitive.

**Hardware will continue to shrink in size while increasing in capabilities.** Computation power and memory capacity in devices will continue to increase and hardware systems will have access to remote sensors and robots. In addition, expect to see products that accommodate organic shapes with forms that no longer have to be rigid.

**Our interactions with smart devices will intensify.** We will rely on smart devices to act as our intelligent personal assistant and we will start to expect much more from computers to relieve us from mundane tasks. In addition, augmented reality technology in products such as Google Glass will transform the way we look at the world and interact with each other. However, before wearable products become mainstream, the industry will need to break technology barriers in the areas of miniature electronics, very low energy devices, and wireless connectivity.

### How I Use this Technology . . .

Like most people, I use computer systems for my personal life and, in fact, feel detached from our world if I don't have my smartphone next to me. I use audio/video communications tools, such as Skype and FaceTime, with my computing devices to enable me to have closer relationships with people around the world. I also use my smartphone to capture audio/video clips and pictures to share on social networking sites, as well as to read the latest news and conduct business over interactive Web sites. At home, I am starting to build electronic control systems that will be accessed with my smartphone to make my home smarter and more energy efficient, and I imagine that we will all have smart digital homes in the near future that will save us money and make our lives easier.

## What the Future Holds . . .

Electronic systems will continue to expand in many sectors, such as wearable electronics, smartphones and personal computers, smart home and business appliances, robotics, and Internet servers. The intelligence and capabilities of these systems will grow rapidly and be challenged with being energy efficient, compact, and low cost. Audio, video, and control interfaces for home and business appliances will improve and Internet servers will provide analytic capabilities for making decisions and monitoring and controlling our environment, in addition to storing, searching, and exchanging data.

Another difference in the future will be in the intelligence and fluidity of the interactions between users and computers. The Internet initially provided access to stored data and services that were provided by large organizations. Now the majority of information is authored and shared by individuals but is still in a pre-recorded or stored form. Soon it will be common for people to interact with each other and with computer-generated artificial intelligence in real time.

One ongoing risk for the future is privacy. Our personal information is now mostly in the form of digital records, and our lives are being tracked by electronic sensors and cameras all over the world. We all need to understand that our private data can be accessed easily by hackers and we should try our best to secure it with passwords, data encryption, and firewalls. We should also all be careful not to post sensitive information about our personal lives and our family members on social networking Web sites, and should become educated about the "social engineering" techniques that criminals are increasingly using. Unfortunately, hackers have become creative in manipulating people as the human interactions shift more toward electronic systems and we all should do what we can to protect ourselves.

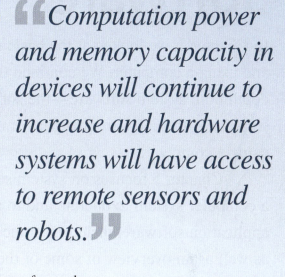

*"Computation power and memory capacity in devices will continue to increase and hardware systems will have access to remote sensors and robots."*

## My Advice to Students . . .

Participate in as many hands-on projects or internship programs that your time allows. This will help you to learn valuable problem-solving techniques, as well as retain the knowledge that you gain in school.

---

## Discussion Question

Ali Moayer believes that we will rely on smart devices to act as our intelligent personal assistant and relieve us from mundane tasks in the near future. Think about the routine tasks that you need to do on a daily basis—which tasks could be performed by a smart device? Are there any tasks that you wouldn't feel comfortable trusting to that device? If so, what technological improvements would need to be made in order for you to assign those tasks to your device? Would a more natural and intuitive human-to-computer interface make a difference? Are there some routine tasks that you don't see ever being turned over to your computer? Be prepared to discuss your position (in class, via an online class forum, or via a class blog, depending on your instructor's directions). You may also be asked to write a short paper expressing your opinion.

---

**>For more information about Logitech, visit www.logitech.com.**

# module

## Software

In Chapter 1, we looked at the basic software concepts involved with starting up and using a computer. We continue that focus in this module, discussing in more depth both system software—the software used to run a computer—and application software—the software that performs the specific tasks users want to accomplish using a computer.

Chapter 5 focuses on system software and how it enables the hardware of a computer system to operate and to run application software. Chapter 6 discusses application software, including some important basic concepts and characteristics, as well as an overview of some of the most common types of application software used today—namely, word processing, spreadsheet, database, presentation graphics, and multimedia software.

Solis Images/Shutterstock.com

> *"We are moving to a 'cloud first, mobile first' world."*

For more comments from Guest Expert **Stephen Rose** of Microsoft, see the **Expert Insight on . . . Software** feature at the end of the module.

# chapter 5

# System Software: Operating Systems and Utility Programs

**After completing this chapter, you will be able to do the following:**

1. Understand the difference between system software and application software.

2. Explain the different functions of an operating system and discuss some ways that operating systems enhance processing efficiency.

3. List several ways in which operating systems differ from one another.

4. Name today's most widely used operating systems for personal computers and servers.

5. Name today's most widely used operating systems for smartphones and other mobile devices.

6. Discuss the operating systems used with mainframes and supercomputers.

7. Discuss the role of utility programs and outline several tasks that these programs perform.

8. Describe what the operating systems of the future might be like.

# OVERVIEW

**A**s you already know, all computers require software in order to operate and perform basic tasks. For instance, software is needed to translate your commands into a form the computer can understand, to open and close other software programs, to manage your stored files, and to locate and set up new hardware as it is added to a computer. The type of software used to perform these tasks is system software—the focus of this chapter. System software runs in the background at all times, making it possible for you to use your computer.

We begin this chapter by looking at the difference between system software and application software. System software, the primary topic of this chapter, is usually divided into two categories: operating systems and utility programs. First, we examine the operating system—the primary component of system software. We discuss the functions of and general differences between operating systems, and then we explore the specific operating systems most widely used today. Next, we look at utility programs. Utility programs typically perform support functions for the operating system, such as allowing you to manage your files, perform maintenance on your computer, check your computer for viruses, or uninstall a program you no longer want on your computer. Chapter 5 closes with a look at what the future of operating systems may hold. ∎

## SYSTEM SOFTWARE VS. APPLICATION SOFTWARE

Computers run two types of software: system software and application software.

> **System software** consists of the operating system and utility programs that control your computer and allow you to use it. These programs enable the computer to boot, to launch application programs, and to facilitate important jobs, such as transferring files from one storage medium to another, configuring your computer to work with the hardware connected to it, connecting your computer to a network, managing files on your hard drive, and protecting your computer from unauthorized use.

> **Application software** includes all the programs that allow you to perform specific tasks on your computer, such as writing a letter, preparing an invoice, viewing a Web page, listening to a music file, checking the inventory of a particular product, playing a game, preparing financial statements, designing a home, and so forth. Application software is discussed in detail in Chapter 6.

In practice, the difference between system and application software is not always straightforward. Some programs, such as those used to burn DVDs, were originally viewed as utility programs. Today, these programs typically contain a variety of additional features,

---

>**System software.** Programs, such as the operating system, that control the operation of a computer and its devices and that enable the computer to run application software. >**Application software.** Programs that enable users to perform specific tasks on a computer, such as writing a letter or playing a game.

such as the ability to organize and play music and other media files, transfer videos and digital photos to a computer, edit videos and photos, create DVD movies, and create slide shows. Consequently, these programs now fit the definition of application software more closely. On the other hand, system software today typically contains several application software components. For example, the Microsoft Windows operating system includes a variety of application programs including a Web browser, a calculator, a calendar program, a photo editing program, an e-mail program, and a text editing program. A program's classification as system or application software usually depends on the principal function of the program, and the distinction between the two categories is not always clear cut.

## THE OPERATING SYSTEM

A computer's **operating system** is a collection of programs that manage and coordinate the activities taking place within the computer and it is the most critical piece of software installed on the computer. The operating system boots the computer, launches application software, and ensures that all actions requested by a user are valid and processed in an orderly fashion. For example, when you issue the command for your computer to store a document on your hard drive, the operating system must perform the following steps: 1) make sure that the specified hard drive exists, 2) verify that there is adequate space on the hard drive to store the document and then store the document in that location, and 3) update the hard drive's directory with the filename and disk location for that file so that the document can be retrieved again when needed. In addition to managing all of the resources associated with your local computer, the operating system also facilitates connections to the Internet and other networks.

In general, the operating system serves as an intermediary between the user and the computer, as well as between application programs and the computer system's hardware (see Figure 5-1). Without an operating system, no other program can run, and the computer cannot function. Many tasks performed by the operating system, however, go unnoticed by the user because the operating system works in the background much of the time.

### Functions of an Operating System

Operating systems have a wide range of functions—some of the most important are discussed next.

**FIGURE 5-1**

The intermediary role of the operating system.

**1. USER**
The user instructs the operating system to start an application program.

**2. OPERATING SYSTEM**
The operating system starts the requested program.

**3. USER**
The user instructs the application program to open a document and then print it.

**4. APPLICATION PROGRAM**
The application program hands the document over to the operating system for printing.

**5. OPERATING SYSTEM**
The operating system sends the document to the printer.

**6. PRINTER**
The printer prints the document.

Martin Novak/Shutterstock.com

>**Operating system.** The main component of system software that enables a computer to operate, manage its activities and the resources under its control, run application programs, and interface with the user.

## Interfacing with Users

As Figure 5-1 illustrates, one of the principal roles of every operating system is to translate user instructions into a form the computer can understand. It also translates any feedback from hardware—such as a signal that the printer has run out of paper or that a new hardware device has been connected to the computer—into a form that the user can understand. The means by which an operating system or any other program interacts with the user is called the *user interface*; user interfaces can be text-based or graphics-based, as discussed in more detail shortly. Most, but not all, operating systems today use a graphical user interface (GUI).

## Booting the Computer

As discussed in Chapter 1, the first task your operating system performs when you power up your computer is to boot the computer. During the boot process, the essential portion, or core, of the operating system (called the **kernel**) is loaded into memory. The kernel remains in memory the entire time the computer is on so that it is always available; other parts of the operating system are retrieved from the hard drive and loaded into memory when they are needed. Before the boot process ends, the operating system determines the hardware devices that are connected to the computer and configured properly, and it reads an opening batch of instructions. These startup instructions (which the user can customize to some extent when necessary) assign tasks for the operating system to carry out each time the computer boots, such as launching a security program to run continually in the background to detect possible threats.

Typically, many programs are running in the background all the time, even before the user launches any application software. The Windows *Task Manager* (shown in Figure 5-2) lists all the programs and *processes* (program tasks) currently running on a computer. Some of these programs are *startup programs* that are launched automatically by the operating system during the boot process; regardless of how programs are launched, they all consume memory and processing power. To view the programs that will run each time the computer boots or to remove a program from this *startup list*, Windows users can use the *Startup* tab on the Task Manager, as shown in Figure 5-2. To avoid creating a problem with your computer, however, do not disable a program from the startup list without knowing absolutely what the program does and that it can be safely disabled. Other system configuration information is stored in the *Windows registry* files, which should be modified only by the Windows program or by advanced Windows users.

**FIGURE 5-2**
**Windows Task Manager.** Shows all running programs and processes and allows you to specify startup programs.

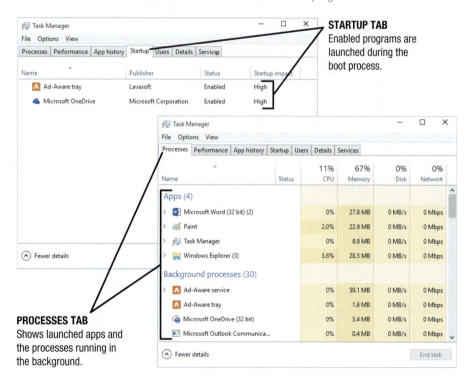

**STARTUP TAB**
Enabled programs are launched during the boot process.

**PROCESSES TAB**
Shows launched apps and the processes running in the background.

---

> **Kernel.** The essential portion, or core, of an operating system.

**FIGURE 5-3**

**Finding new hardware.** Most operating systems are designed to detect new hardware and to try to configure it automatically.

## Configuring Devices

The operating system also configures all devices connected to a computer. Small programs called **device drivers** (or simply **drivers**) are used to communicate with peripheral devices, such as monitors, printers, portable storage devices, and keyboards. Most operating systems today include the drivers needed for the most common peripheral devices. In addition, drivers often come on a CD packaged with the peripheral device or they can be downloaded from the manufacturer's Web site. Most operating systems today look for and recognize new devices each time the computer boots. If a new device is found, the operating system typically tries to install the appropriate driver automatically in order to get the new hardware ready to use (see Figure 5-3). Because USB devices can be connected to a computer when the computer is running, those devices are recognized and configured, as needed, each time they are plugged in to the computer.

Once a device and its driver have been installed properly, they usually work fine. If the device driver file is deleted, becomes *corrupted*, or has a conflict with another piece of software, then the device will no longer work. Usually, the operating system detects problems like this during the boot process and notifies the user, and then tries to reinstall the driver automatically. If the operating system is unable to correct the problem, the user can reinstall the driver manually. You may also need to update or reinstall some device drivers if you *upgrade* your operating system to a newer version. To keep your system up to date, many operating systems have an option to check for operating system updates automatically—including updated driver files—on a regular basis. Enabling these *automatic updates* is a good idea to keep your system running smoothly and protected from new threats (like the computer viruses discussed in Chapter 9).

## Managing Network Connections

The operating system is also in charge of managing your network connections, such as a wired connection to a home or office network or wireless connections at home, school, work, or on the go. For instance, as you move into range of a wireless network, the operating system will notify you that a new wireless network is available and then either connect your device to that network or wait for your instruction to connect to the network, depending on your device's wireless network settings. If at any time you lose a network connection, the operating system can try to fix it, such as by resetting your device's network adapter (see Figure 5-4). If your device connects to a secure network, the operating system will prompt you for the appropriate password when needed and then connect your device to the network after verifying the password is correct.

**FIGURE 5-4**

**Network connections.** Most operating systems can repair network connections when needed.

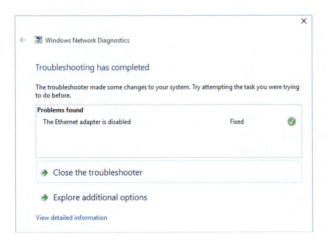

## Managing and Monitoring Resources and Jobs

As you work on your computer, the operating system continuously manages your computer's resources (such as software, disk space, and memory) and makes them available to devices and programs when they are needed. If a problem occurs—such as a program stops functioning or too many programs are open for the amount of memory installed in the computer—the operating system notifies the user and tries to correct the problem, often by closing the offending program. If the problem cannot be corrected by the operating system, then the user typically needs to reboot the computer.

>**Device driver.** A program that enables an operating system to communicate with a specific hardware device; often referred to simply as a **driver**.

As part of managing system resources, the operating system schedules jobs (such as documents to be printed or files to be retrieved from a hard drive) to be performed using those resources. *Scheduling routines* in the operating system determine the order in which jobs are carried out, as well as which commands get executed first if the user is working with more than one program at one time or if the computer (such as a server or mainframe) supports multiple users.

## File Management

Another important task that the operating system performs is *file management*—keeping track of the files stored on a computer so that they can be retrieved when needed. As discussed in Chapter 3, you can organize the files on a storage medium into folders to simplify file management. Usually the operating system files are stored inside one folder (such as the *Windows* folder), and each application program is stored in its own separate folder inside a main programs folder (such as *Program Files*). Other folders designed for storing data files are typically created by the operating system for each user (such as *Documents*, *Music*, and *Pictures* folders); individuals may create additional folders, as desired, to keep their files organized. Folders can contain both files and other folders (called *subfolders*).

Files and folders are usually viewed in a hierarchical format; the top of the hierarchy for any storage medium is called the *root directory* (such as C: for the root directory of the hard drive C shown in Figure 5-5). The root directory typically contains both files and folders. To access a file, you generally navigate to the folder containing that file by opening the appropriate drive, folder, and subfolders. Alternatively, you can specify the *path* to a file's exact location. For example, as Figure 5-5 shows, the path

C:\Documents\Letters\Mary

leads through the root directory of the C drive and the *Documents* and *Letters* folders to a file named *Mary*. A similar path can also be used to access the files *John* and *Bill*. As discussed in Chapter 3, you specify a filename for each file when you initially save the file on a storage medium; there can be only one file with the exact same filename in any particular folder on a storage medium.

Filename rules vary with each operating system. For instance, Windows supports filenames that are from 1 to 260 characters long (the length includes the entire path to the file's location) and may include numbers, letters, spaces, and any special characters except \ / : * ? " < > and |. Filenames typically include a *file extension* (usually three or four characters preceded by a period) at the end of the filename, which indicates the type of file (see Figure 5-6). File extensions are automatically added to a filename by the program in which that file was created, although sometimes the user may have a choice of file extensions supported by a program.

File extensions should not be changed by the user because the operating system uses them to identify the program that should be used to open the file. For instance, if you issue a command to open a file named *Letter to Mom.docx*, the file will open using the Microsoft Word program (assuming the device being used has access to a recent version of that program) because the *.docx* file extension is associated with

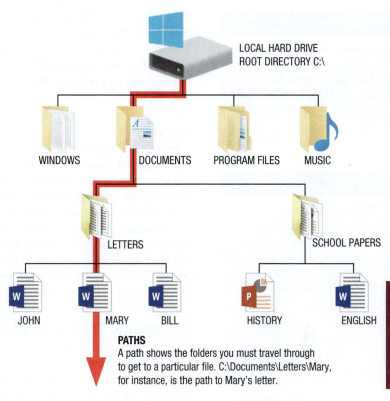

LOCAL HARD DRIVE
ROOT DIRECTORY C:\

WINDOWS    DOCUMENTS    PROGRAM FILES    MUSIC

LETTERS    SCHOOL PAPERS

JOHN    MARY    BILL    HISTORY    ENGLISH

**PATHS**
A path shows the folders you must travel through to get to a particular file. C:\Documents\Letters\Mary, for instance, is the path to Mary's letter.

**FIGURE 5-5**
A sample hard drive organization.

**FIGURE 5-6**
Common file extensions.

**DOCUMENTS**

.doc  .docx  .txt  .rtf  .htm  .html

.mhtml  .xml  .xls  .xlsx  .mdb.  .accdb

.ppt  .pptx  .pdf  .sxc  .sxi  .odf

**PROGRAMS**

.com  .exe

**GRAPHICS**

.bmp  .tif  .tiff  .jpg  .jpe  .jpeg  .eps

.gif  .png  .pcx  .svg  .dib

**AUDIO**

.wav  .au  .mp3  .snd  .aiff  .midi

.aac  .wma  .ra  .m4a

**VIDEO**

.mpg  .mp2  .mp4  .mpe  .mov  .avi

.rm  .wmv  .wm  .asf

**COMPRESSED FILES**

.zip  .sit  .sitx  .tar

SW

recent versions of the Microsoft Word program. Files can be opened, as well as moved, copied, renamed, and deleted, using a file management program such as File Explorer. You may not be able to see file extensions in your file management program, however, because they are usually hidden by default. The File Explorer file management program and other utilities typically included in an operating system are discussed near the end of this chapter.

## Security

A computer's operating system can use passwords, biometric characteristics (such as fingerprints), and other security procedures to limit access to the computer and other system resources to only authorized users. Most operating systems also include other security features, such as an integrated firewall to protect against unauthorized access via the Internet or an option to download and install *security patches* (small program updates that correct known security problems) automatically from the operating system's manufacturer on a regular basis. Operating system passwords can also be used to ensure that *administrative level* operating system tasks (such as installing programs or changing system settings) are performed only by authorized users. Passwords, biometrics, and other security issues related to networks and the Internet are discussed in detail in Chapter 9.

## Processing Techniques for Increased Efficiency

Operating systems often utilize various processing techniques in order to operate more efficiently and increase the amount of processing the computer can perform in any given time period. Some of the techniques most commonly used by operating systems to increase efficiency are discussed in the next few sections.

### Multitasking

**Multitasking** refers to the ability of an operating system to have more than one program (also called a *task*) open at one time. For example, multitasking allows a user to edit a spreadsheet file in one window while loading a Web page in another window or to retrieve new e-mail messages in one window while a word processing document is open in another window. Without the ability to multitask, an operating system would require the user to close one program before opening another program. Virtually all operating systems today support multitasking.

Although multitasking enables a user to work with multiple programs at one time, a single CPU core cannot execute more than one task at one time (unless Intel's Hyper-Threading Technology or another technology that allows a single core to function as two cores is used, as discussed in Chapter 2). Consequently, the CPU rotates between processing tasks, but it works so quickly that it appears to the user that all programs are executing at the same time. However, CPUs with multiple cores can execute multiple tasks at one time, as discussed shortly.

### Multithreading

A *thread* is a sequence of instructions within a program that is independent of other threads, such as spell checking, printing, and opening documents in a word processing program. Operating systems that support *multithreading* have the ability to rotate between multiple threads (similar to the way multitasking can rotate between multiple programs) so that processing is completed faster and more efficiently, even though only one thread is executed by a single core at one time. Most operating systems support multithreading.

> **Multitasking.** The capability of an operating system to run more than one program at one time.

**SEQUENTIAL PROCESSING**
Tasks are performed one right after the other.

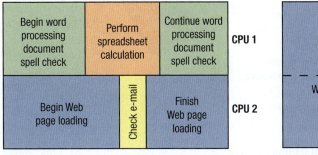

(multitasking and multithreading)

**SIMULTANEOUS PROCESSING**
Multiple tasks are performed at the exact same time.

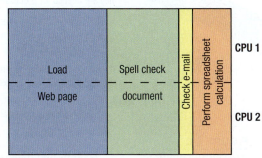

(multiprocessing)

(parallel processing)

**FIGURE 5-7**
Sequential vs. simultaneous processing.

## Multiprocessing and Parallel Processing

As discussed in Chapter 2, both multiprocessing and parallel processing involve using two or more CPUs (or multiple cores in a single CPU) in one computer to perform work more efficiently. The primary difference between these two techniques is that, with multiprocessing, each CPU or core typically works on a different job; with parallel processing, the CPUs or cores usually work together to complete one job more quickly. In either case, tasks are performed *simultaneously* (at exactly the same time); in contrast, multitasking and multithreading use a single CPU or core and process tasks *sequentially* (by rotating through tasks), as discussed previously. Figure 5-7 illustrates the difference between sequential and simultaneous processing, using tasks typical of a personal computer.

Multiprocessing is supported by most operating systems and is used with personal computers that have multi-core CPUs, as well as with servers and mainframe computers that have multi-core CPUs and/or multiple CPUs. Parallel processing is used most often with supercomputers.

## Memory Management

Because many of today's programs are memory intensive, good *memory management*, which involves optimizing the use of main memory (RAM), can help speed up processing. The operating system allocates RAM to programs as needed and then reclaims that memory when the program is closed. Because each additional running program or open window consumes memory, users can also help with memory management by limiting the number of startup programs to only the ones that are absolutely necessary, as well as by closing windows when they are no longer needed.

One memory-management technique frequently used by operating systems is **virtual memory**, which uses a portion of the computer's hard drive as additional RAM. All programs and data located in RAM are divided into fixed-length *pages* or variable-length

>**Virtual memory.** A memory-management technique that uses hard drive space as additional RAM.

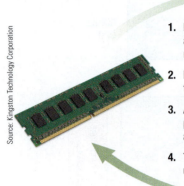

1. Pages of programs or data are copied from RAM to the virtual memory area of the hard drive.

2. Pages are copied back to RAM as they are needed for processing.

3. As more room in RAM is needed, pages are copied to virtual memory and then deleted from RAM.

4. The swapping process continues until the program finishes executing.

Source: Kingston Technology Corporation

Source: Seagate Technology LLC

**FIGURE 5-8**
**How virtual memory works.**

*segments*, depending on the operating system being used. When the amount of RAM required exceeds the amount of RAM available, the operating system moves pages from RAM to the virtual memory area of the hard drive (this area is called the *page file* or *swap file*). Consequently, as a program is executed, some of the program may be stored in RAM and some in virtual memory. As RAM gets full, pages are moved to virtual memory, and as pages stored in virtual memory are required, they are retrieved from virtual memory and moved to RAM (see Figure 5-8). This *paging* or *swapping* process continues until the program finishes executing. Virtual memory allows you to use more memory than is physically available on your computer, but using virtual memory is slower than just using RAM. Most operating systems today allow the user to specify the total amount of hard drive space to be used for virtual memory.

## Buffering and Spooling

Some input and output devices are exceedingly slow, compared to today's CPUs. If the CPU had to wait for these slower devices to finish their work, the computer system would experience a horrendous bottleneck. For example, suppose a user sends a 100-page document to the printer. Assuming the printer can output 20 pages per minute, it would take 5 minutes for the document to finish printing. If the CPU had to wait for the print job to be completed before performing other tasks, the computer would be tied up for 5 minutes.

To avoid this problem, most operating systems use buffering and spooling. A **buffer** is an area in RAM or on the hard drive designated to hold data that is waiting to be used by the computer, typically on its way in or out of the computer system. For instance, a *keyboard buffer* stores characters as they are entered via the keyboard, and a *print buffer* stores documents that are waiting to be printed. The process of placing items in a buffer so they can be retrieved by the appropriate device when needed is called **buffering** or **spooling**. One common use of buffering and spooling is *print spooling*. Print spooling allows multiple documents to be sent to the printer at one time and to print, one after the other, in the background while the computer and user are performing other tasks. The documents waiting to be printed are said to be in a *print queue*, which designates the order the documents will be printed. While in the print queue, most operating systems allow the user to cancel print jobs and pause the printer (see Figure 5-9); some also allow the user to prioritize the documents in the print queue.

**FIGURE 5-9**
**A print queue.**

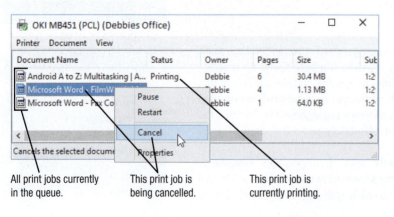

All print jobs currently in the queue.

This print job is being cancelled.

This print job is currently printing.

---

> **Buffer.** An area in RAM or on the hard drive designated to hold data that is waiting to be used by the computer. > **Buffering.** The process of placing items in a buffer so the appropriate device can retrieve them when needed; also called **spooling**, particularly when used in conjunction with a printer.

Although originally used primarily for keyboard input and print jobs, most computers and operating systems today use several other buffers to speed up operations. For instance, it is common today for computers to use buffers to assist in redisplaying images on the screen and to temporarily store data that is in the process of being burned onto a DVD or being streamed from the Internet (such as videos and other multimedia content).

## Differences Among Operating Systems

There are different types of operating systems available to meet different needs. Some of the major distinctions among operating systems include the type of user interface utilized, the category of device the operating system will be used with, and the type of processing the operating system is designed for.

**FIGURE 5-10**
Graphical user vs. command line interfaces.

### Graphical User vs. Command Line Interface

As mentioned earlier in this chapter, a user interface is the manner in which an operating system interacts with its users. Most operating systems today use a **graphical user interface** (**GUI**). The older DOS operating system and some versions of the UNIX and Linux operating systems use a **command line interface** (see Figure 5-10), although graphical versions of UNIX and Linux are available. Command line interfaces require users to input commands using the keyboard; graphical user interfaces allow the user to issue commands by selecting icons, buttons, menu items, and other graphical objects—typically with a mouse, pen, or finger.

**GRAPHICAL USER INTERFACE**
Objects (such as icons, buttons, menus, and tiles) are selected with the mouse, pen, or finger to issue commands to the computer.

### Categories of Operating Systems

Operating systems are typically designed for a particular type of device. For example, operating systems used with personal computers are typically referred to as **personal operating systems** (also called **desktop operating systems**) and they are designed to be installed on a single computer. In contrast, **server operating systems** (also called **network operating systems**) are designed to be installed on a network server to grant multiple users access to a network and its resources. Each computer on a network has its own personal operating system installed (just as with a stand-alone computer) and that operating system controls the activity on that computer, while the server operating system controls access to network resources. Computers on a network may also need special *client* software to access the network and issue requests to the server.

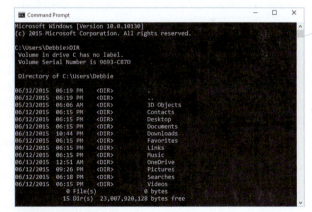

**COMMAND LINE INTERFACE**
Commands are entered using the keyboard.

Server operating systems are typically used with large networks, such as those found in businesses and schools. Home networks don't require a server operating system, though some home network devices (such as a media server or an NAS) come with networking software designed for that device. For both large and home networks, network resources (such as a shared network hard drive or printer) generally look like *local* (non-network) resources to any device that is connected to the network. For example, you will see a network hard drive listed with its own identifying letter (such as F or G) along with the drives located on your computer, and you will see a network printer included in your list of available printers whenever you open a Print dialog box. If

---

1. The client software provides a shell around your desktop operating system. The shell program enables your computer to communicate with the server operating system, which is located on the network server.

2. When you request a network activity, such as printing a document using a network printer, your application program passes the job to your desktop operating system, which sends it to the client shell, which sends it on to the server operating system, which is located on the network server.

3. The server operating system then lines up your job in its print queue and prints the job when its turn comes.

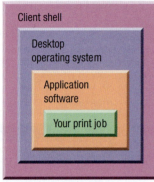

Client shell

Desktop operating system

Application software

Your print job

Desktop computer running Windows and client software for the server operating system being used.

Your print job

Your print job

Your print job

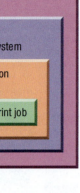

Pryzmat/Shutterstock.com

Network server running a server operating system.

Igor Klimov/Shutterstock.com

kavione/Shutterstock.com

Network printer

4. Your print job

3. Job C

2. Job B

1. Job A

**PRINT QUEUE**

**FIGURE 5-11**
How network operating systems work.

you do not log on to the network or if the network is down, you cannot access network resources, such as to launch a program located on the network server, save a document to a network hard drive, print using a shared printer, or access the Internet via a shared Internet connection. However, you can still work locally on that computer, just as you would on a stand-alone computer. An overview of how a typical personal operating system and a server operating system interact on a business computer network is illustrated in Figure 5-11.

In addition to personal operating systems and server operating systems, there are **mobile operating systems** that are designed to be used with smartphones and other mobile devices, and **embedded operating systems** that are built into consumer kiosks, cash registers, cars, consumer electronics, and other devices. Specific examples of operating systems are covered later in this chapter.

## The Types of Processors Supported

Most operating systems today are designed to be used with specific types of processors (such as mobile, desktop, or server processors), as well as with specific numbers of processors. In addition, most operating systems are designed for either 32-bit or 64-bit CPUs (many operating systems have a version for each). Because 64-bit processors can process up to twice as much data per clock cycle as 32-bit processors (depending on the extent to which the application being used supports 64-bit processing) and can address more than 4 GB of RAM, using a 64-bit operating system with a 64-bit computer can help to speed up processing. Operating systems that support 64-bit CPUs often include other architectural improvements that together may result in a more efficient operating system and, consequently, faster operations. Details about Windows, OS X, Linux, and other operating systems are discussed shortly.

# TREND

## Amazon Echo

At first glance, *Amazon Echo* (see the accompanying photo) looks like just a Bluetooth speaker. While it does have speaker capabilities, it is much more than that. It is a voice-controlled assistant for your home.

At the heart of Echo is *Alexa*—the cloud-based software that controls Echo. Echo connects to the Internet and devices via Wi-Fi and Bluetooth. It is designed to understand spoken commands and provide the requested information. For example, you can ask Echo for music, news, traffic, weather, and more and you will get results instantly. To ensure you can be heard and understood from across the room, Echo uses an array of seven microphones and combines the signals from the individual microphones to suppress noise, reverberation, and even competing speech.

To initially set up the device, you download the Echo app to your smartphone or tablet, or access it via your computer's browser. You can set up your favorite music resources (including Amazon Music, Pandora, iTunes, and iHeartRadio), your audio book resources (such as Audible), your Google Calendar, and Gmail. In addition, you can add items to your shopping list and to-do lists, as well as control lights, smart appliances (such as the WeMo smart coffeemaker shown in Figure 7-26 in Chapter 7), and other devices connected to a *Philips Hue* or *Belkin WeMo* smart home system. You can also request general information to be retrieved from the Web, as well as weather, news, and sports scores. As you talk to your Echo, Alexa provides the information or performs the task you request via your

Echo and, with each command, Alexa learns your voice to continually improve voice recognition.

One of the newest Echo additions is support for *If This Then That* (*IFTTT*) recipes, which connect Echo to your desired apps and enable you to specify triggers and what you want to happen when that trigger occurs. For example, you can use IFTTT to have your Echo send you an e-mail when you receive a direct message on Twitter, add new to-do items to your Evernote list as you speak them, or e-mail you your current shopping list when you ask what is on your shopping list.

Source: Amazon.com, Inc.

## Support for Virtualization and Other Technologies

As new technologies or trends (such as a new CPU characteristic or a new type of bus, virtualization, mobility and wearable computers, security concerns, power consumption concerns, touch and gesture input, and the move to cloud software) emerge, operating systems must be updated or new operating systems developed in order to support those new technologies or trends. For example, the latest versions of Windows added support for touch and pen input, which is commonly used today, and new operating systems are being developed for wearables and smart appliances. On the other hand, as technologies become obsolete, operating system manufacturers need to decide when support for those technologies will cease. Alternatively, hardware manufacturers also need to respond to new technologies introduced by operating systems. For instance, because the latest versions of Windows and OS X support multi-touch input, a flurry of new devices that have touch screens and that support gesture input have been introduced. For a look at one new product resulting from the trend of speech recognition—Amazon Echo—see the Trend box.

> **TIP** ✓
>
> When a new version of a program that you use (such as an operating system or application program) becomes available, you can typically buy a version *upgrade* that installs over your existing version. Upgrades are usually less expensive than buying a new full version.

# OPERATING SYSTEMS FOR PERSONAL COMPUTERS AND SERVERS

As previously discussed, many operating systems today are designed for specific types of devices. The operating systems most commonly used with personal computers and servers are discussed next. Operating systems for mobile devices and larger computers are discussed later in this chapter.

## DOS

During the 1980s and early 1990s, **DOS (Disk Operating System)** was the dominant operating system for microcomputers. DOS traditionally used a command line interface, although later versions of DOS supported a menu-driven interface. There are two primary forms of DOS: *PC-DOS* and *MS-DOS*. PC-DOS was created originally for IBM PCs (and is owned by IBM), whereas MS-DOS was created for use with IBM-compatible PCs. Both versions were originally developed by Microsoft Corporation, but neither version is updated any longer. DOS is considered obsolete today because it does not utilize a graphical user interface and does not support modern processors and processing techniques. However, computers running the Windows operating system can still execute DOS commands via the *Command Prompt* window, as shown in Figure 5-12. DOS commands can be used to quickly determine specific information or perform tasks, such as the *ipconfig* command used to display your computer's IP address or the *ping* command used to check your Internet connection.

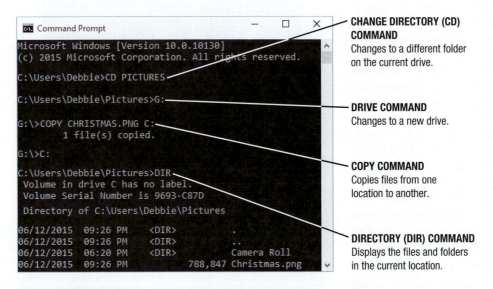

**CHANGE DIRECTORY (CD) COMMAND**
Changes to a different folder on the current drive.

**DRIVE COMMAND**
Changes to a new drive.

**COPY COMMAND**
Copies files from one location to another.

**DIRECTORY (DIR) COMMAND**
Displays the files and folders in the current location.

**FIGURE 5-12**
**DOS.** Even though DOS has become technologically obsolete, Windows users can still issue DOS commands via the Command Prompt.

## Windows

Microsoft Windows has been the predominant personal operating system for many years and still holds about 90% of the market. There have been many different versions of **Windows** over the years; the next few sections chronicle the main developments of this operating system.

### Windows 1.0 Through Windows 7

Microsoft created the original version of Windows—*Windows 1.0*—in 1985 in an effort to meet the needs of users frustrated by having to learn and use DOS commands. Windows 1.0 through *Windows 3.x* (*x* stands for the version number of the software, such as Windows 3.0, 3.1, or 3.11) were not, however, full-fledged operating systems.

Instead, they were *operating environments* for the DOS operating system; that is, graphical shells that operated around the DOS operating system and were designed to make DOS easier to use.

In 1994, Microsoft announced that all versions of Windows after 3.11 would be full-fledged operating systems instead of just operating environments. The next three versions of Windows designed for personal computers were *Windows 95*, *Windows 98*, and *Windows Me* (*Millennium Edition*). *Windows NT* (*New Technology*) was the first 32-bit version of Windows designed for high-end workstations and servers. It was built from the ground up using a different kernel than the other versions of Windows and was eventually replaced by *Windows 2000*. *Windows XP* replaced both Windows 2000 (for business use) and Windows Me (for home use). Throughout this progression of Windows releases, support for new hardware (such as DVD drives and USB devices), networking and the Internet, multimedia applications, and voice and pen input were included. Support for all of these early versions of Windows has been discontinued.

*Windows Vista* replaced Windows XP. One of the most obvious initial changes in Windows Vista was the *Aero* interface, a visual graphical user interface that uses transparent windows and dynamic elements. Windows Vista also introduced the *Sidebar* feature that contained *gadgets*—small applications that are used to perform a variety of tasks, such as displaying weather information, a calendar, and news headlines. Other features new to Vista included the *Windows Media Center* and *Windows Speech Recognition*. Support for Windows Vista is scheduled to end in 2017.

*Windows 7* was released next. It required less memory and processing power than previous versions of Windows, and it was designed to start up and respond faster than Vista so it could run well on netbooks and tablets. Windows 7 also added *jump lists* that show your most recent documents, *live thumbnails* of open programs that can be displayed by pointing to the taskbar buttons, and virtual folders called *Libraries* that display together in one location the files that the user specifies, regardless of where those files are physically located on the hard drive. In addition, Windows 7 included a *HomeGroup* feature for improved home networking; one-click Wi-Fi connections; support for multi-touch, voice, and pen input; and improved accessory programs (such as a more versatile Calculator and a Paint program that uses the Ribbon interface found in recent versions of Microsoft Office).

## Windows 8

*Windows 8* was released in 2012. According to Microsoft, it is a "reimaging of Windows, from the chip to the interface." It is designed to be used with a wide range of devices, from smartphones to desktop computers, as well as with or without a keyboard or mouse because it supports multi-touch input. The new Windows 8 *Start screen* (the initial screen you see when you boot your computer, though if

**SW**

## ASK THE EXPERT

*Courtesy Strike Fighter Weapons School Pacific, NAS Lemoore*

**Tony Onorati,** Former Naval Aviator and Former Commanding Officer, Strike Fighter Weapons School Pacific, NAS Lemoore

### What computer experience is needed to be a U.S. Navy pilot?

While no computer experience is necessarily required to enter flight school, failure to have a solid knowledge of the Windows operating system will put the candidate well behind his/her contemporaries when they finally do reach the fleet as a pilot. All the tactical planning tools for preflight preparation, navigation, ordnance delivery, and mission planning, as well as all aircraft-specific publications, manuals, and training, are all computer based. For the FA-18 Hornet, all mission data is created on the computer, copied to a mission computer card, and plugged into the jet where it is downloaded into the aircraft's computer for use in flight. Becoming a naval aviator without computer skills is like entering flight school without ever having flown before—it can be done but it places you well behind the power curve.

you have a password you'll see the *lock screen* until you enter your password) uses **tiles** to represent apps, folders, Web sites, and more; tiles are selected with the mouse or finger to launch the corresponding content (see Figure 5-13). Windows 8 apps run full-screen; conventional programs run inside windows that can be sized as in previous versions of Windows. Some tiles are *live tiles*, which show up-to-date information and notifications (such as social media activity, news, weather, and new e-mail messages). Both conventional programs and apps from the *Windows Store* are represented by tiles; users can pin and unpin apps to and from the Start screen, as well as rearrange and name groups of tiles. Although you launch most programs via the Start screen, users can work with the more traditional Windows desktop if they prefer. To display the desktop from the Start screen, click the *Desktop tile*; to return to the Start screen, press the Windows key on the keyboard, click the bottom left corner of the screen, or use the Start charm (discussed shortly). The Windows 8 desktop is similar to the desktops in previous versions of Windows, with a taskbar, taskbar buttons, and windows.

Another new feature of Windows 8 is *charms*. The *charms bar* (refer again to Figure 5-13) is displayed by pointing to the upper or lower right corner of the screen or by swiping in from the right edge of the screen. The *Search charm* allows you to search your computer, the Web, and the Windows Store. The *Share charm* allows you to send links, photos, and other content to your friends. The *Start charm* takes you to the Start screen (or if you are on the Start screen, it takes you to your last app). The *Devices charm* helps you manage the devices that are connected to your computer. The *Settings charm* is used to configure settings (such as networks and speaker volume) and to shut down your PC. To easily launch other system management programs, point to the lower left corner of the screen to display the *Start screen preview* and then right-click.

**FIGURE 5-13**
Windows 8.

**WINDOWS 8 START SCREEN**

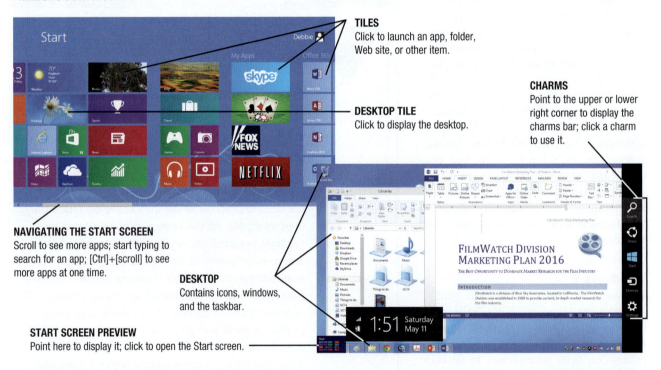

**TILES**
Click to launch an app, folder, Web site, or other item.

**DESKTOP TILE**
Click to display the desktop.

**CHARMS**
Point to the upper or lower right corner to display the charms bar; click a charm to use it.

**NAVIGATING THE START SCREEN**
Scroll to see more apps; start typing to search for an app; [Ctrl]+[scroll] to see more apps at one time.

**DESKTOP**
Contains icons, windows, and the taskbar.

**START SCREEN PREVIEW**
Point here to display it; click to open the Start screen.

**WINDOWS 8 DESKTOP**

>**Tiles.** Components of the Windows Start screen interface; tiles represent apps, folders, Web sites, and other items, and they are clicked to launch the corresponding item.

In addition to desktop versions of Windows 8 and earlier versions of Windows that are designed for personal computers, there are server versions of Windows. For example, the various versions of *Windows Server* and *Windows Home Server* are used with servers and preinstalled on home server devices designed to provide services for a home network, respectively.

## Windows 10

The latest version of Windows is **Windows 10**. The most significant change from previous versions of Windows is that Windows 10 is a universal operating system that will run on any device, from smartphones to tablets to personal computers to servers. Consequently, Windows 10 replaces all previous versions of Windows. The look and features of Windows 10 are consistent regardless of the devices used, although the experience is automatically adjusted to be optimized for each device and screen size, such as working with a keyboard and mouse when a notebook is used or working with pen and touch input when a tablet is used. In addition, apps developed for Windows 10 can run on any device that has Windows 10 installed.

Windows 10 looks similar to Windows 8. However, some features have been adjusted to make them work better with both touch devices and conventional computers. For example, the **Start menu** contains a menu of shortcuts as well as tiles (like those found on the Windows 8 Start screen) that can be used to launch applications, folders, Web sites, and more, as shown in Figure 5-14. In addition, apps downloaded from the Windows Store run in a resizable window instead of full screen as in Windows 8. One discontinued feature is the Windows 8 charms bar.

**SW**

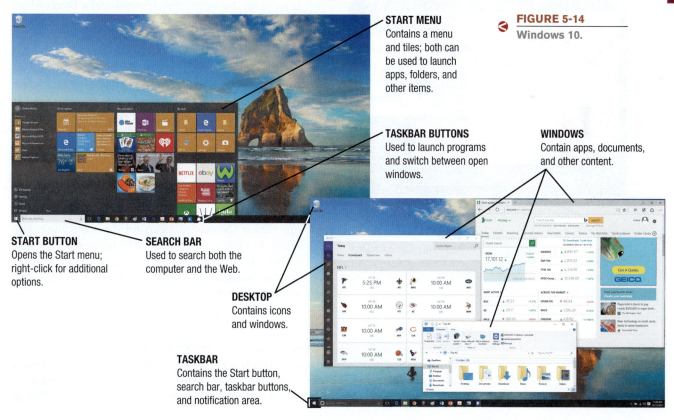

**START MENU**
Contains a menu and tiles; both can be used to launch apps, folders, and other items.

**TASKBAR BUTTONS**
Used to launch programs and switch between open windows.

**WINDOWS**
Contain apps, documents, and other content.

**START BUTTON**
Opens the Start menu; right-click for additional options.

**SEARCH BAR**
Used to search both the computer and the Web.

**DESKTOP**
Contains icons and windows.

**TASKBAR**
Contains the Start button, search bar, taskbar buttons, and notification area.

**FIGURE 5-14**
Windows 10.

>**Windows 10.** The current version of Windows. >**Start menu.** The main menu for Windows computers; in Windows 10, it contains both a menu and tiles that can be used to launch applications.

One new feature of Windows 10 is *Task View*, which enables each user to create personalized, virtual desktops. Each virtual desktop includes the programs the user specifies (such as programs used for work in one desktop and programs used for gaming and other personal activities in another desktop), and the user can switch between the desktops as needed. Windows 10 also includes a new Web browser called *Edge* that replaces Internet Explorer, and a new virtual assistant called *Cortana* (available via the taskbar *Search bar*).

Windows 10 is being offered as a free upgrade for one year for all Windows 7 and 8 users. As a result, it is expected that individuals and businesses will transition to Windows 10 much faster than they have upgraded to a new version of Windows in the past.

## OS X

The proprietary operating system for Mac computers made by Apple Corporation was *Mac OS*. It was based on the UNIX operating system (discussed shortly) and originally set the standard for graphical user interfaces. Many of today's operating systems follow the trend that Mac OS started and, in fact, use GUIs that highly resemble the one used with Mac OS.

Starting with version 10 of Mac OS, the operating system was renamed **OS X** and includes a release name instead of a release number (such as *OS X El Capitan* and *OS X Yosemite* shown in Figure 5-15). Similar to Windows, OS X supports multithreading, multitasking, multiprocessing, and 64-bit processors, and has a high level of multimedia functions and connectivity. It includes the *Safari* Web browser and a *Dock*, which you can use to launch programs and open frequently used files and folders (refer again to Figure 5-15). New features include a cleaner look and a new *Notification Center* that displays and lets you interact with notifications such as e-mail, messages, and calendar items. In addition, with the new *Continuity* feature, you can place iPhone calls or send and receive texts via your Mac. You can also switch from one device to another and continue your work seamlessly, as long as the two devices are within range, and you can sync all your Apple devices via *iCloud*. The *menu bar* at the top of an OS X desktop contains icons that can be used to open the *Apple menu* (used to access a variety of tools), *app menus* (containing items for the applications currently in use), *status menus* (used to view a variety of information), *Spotlight* (used to search your computer), and the Notification Center. *OS X Server* is the server version of OS X.

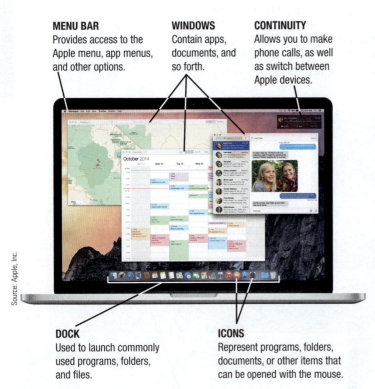

**V FIGURE 5-15**
OS X Yosemite.

**MENU BAR**
Provides access to the Apple menu, app menus, and other options.

**WINDOWS**
Contain apps, documents, and so forth.

**CONTINUITY**
Allows you to make phone calls, as well as switch between Apple devices.

**DOCK**
Used to launch commonly used programs, folders, and files.

**ICONS**
Represent programs, folders, documents, or other items that can be opened with the mouse.

## UNIX

**UNIX** was originally developed in the late 1960s at AT&T Bell Laboratories as an operating system for midrange servers. UNIX is a multiuser, multitasking operating system. Computer systems ranging from microcomputers to mainframes can run UNIX, and it can support a variety of devices from different manufacturers. This flexibility gives UNIX an

---

>**OS X.** The operating system used on Apple computers; the most recent version is OS X El Capitan. >**UNIX.** An operating system developed in the late 1960s for midrange servers and mainframes; many variations of this operating system are in use today.

advantage over competing operating systems in some situations. However, UNIX is more expensive, requires a higher level of technical knowledge, and tends to be harder to install, maintain, and upgrade than most other commonly used operating systems.

There are many versions of UNIX available, as well as many other operating systems that are based on UNIX. These operating systems—such as OS X—are sometimes referred to as *UNIX flavors*. In fact, the term *UNIX*, which initially referred to the original UNIX operating system, has evolved to refer today to a group of similar operating systems based on UNIX. Many UNIX flavors are not compatible with each other, which creates some problems when a program written for one UNIX computer system is moved to another computer system running a different flavor of UNIX. To avoid this incompatibility problem, the *Open Group* open source consortium has overseen the development of the *Single UNIX Specification*—a standardized programming environment for UNIX applications—and certifies UNIX systems if they conform to the Single UNIX Specification. Both personal and server versions of UNIX-based operating systems are available.

## Linux

**Linux** is an operating system developed by *Linus Torvalds* in 1991 when he was a student at the University of Helsinki in Finland. The operating system resembles UNIX but was developed independently from it. Linux was released to the public as open source software; that is, a program whose source code is available to the public and can be modified to improve it or to customize it to a particular application, as discussed in more detail in Chapter 6. Over the years, the number of Linux users has grown, and volunteer programmers from all over the world have collaborated to improve it, sharing their modified code with others over the Internet. Although Linux originally used a command line interface, most recent versions of Linux programs use a graphical user interface and operate similarly to other desktop operating systems, such as Windows and OS X. For instance, the version of Linux shown in Figure 5-16 (*Ubuntu*) has icons, menus, windows, and an app dock. Linux is widely available as a free download via the Internet; companies are also permitted to customize Linux and sell it as a retail product. Commercial Linux distributions come with maintenance and support materials (something that many of the free versions do not offer), making the commercial versions more attractive for corporate users.

**FIGURE 5-16**

**Linux.** This version is Ubuntu, one of the most widely-used Linux operating systems.

Source: Canonical Ltd.

Over the years, Linux has become a widely accepted operating system with strong support from mainstream companies, such as IBM, NVIDIA, HP, and Dell. Versions of Linux are available for a wide variety of devices, from personal computers to servers to mobile devices and smart TVs.

One reason individuals and organizations are switching to Linux and other open source software is cost. Typically, using the Linux operating system and a free or low-cost office suite, Web browser, and e-mail program can save several

>**Linux.** An open source operating system that is available without charge over the Internet and is increasingly being used with mobile devices, personal computers, servers, mainframes, and supercomputers.

## ASK THE EXPERT

**Jim Zemlin,** Executive Director, The Linux Foundation

**Is there a downside to installing Linux on a personal computer?**

We encourage people to install Linux on their personal computers. People who install Linux on their desktops learn by using Linux and grow to become the world's best Linux users and developers. Tinkering on your Linux desktop can translate into major breakthroughs for your personal computing experience and for the greater community at large; it can also lead to widespread recognition. And, even if you're not running Linux on your desktop today, you're using it every time you're using your browser because Linux runs Google, Amazon, Facebook, and most of the Internet. In addition, Chrome OS, Android, and other operating systems are based on Linux. We see no downside in sight and, furthermore, Linux offers you flexibility, customization, and choice on your desktop. This freedom is important, as your PC is your personal property and you should be able to use it exactly how you see fit. Linux allows you to do that.

hundreds of dollars per computer. Other reasons include the ability to customize the user interface and to directly control the computer much more than is possible with Windows and OS X. In addition, Linux computers can run faster than Windows and OS X, due to Linux's much lower hardware requirements. For example, the Ubuntu version of Linux shown in Figure 5-16 requires only 512 MB of RAM and 5 GB of hard drive space versus the 1 GB of RAM and 16 GB of hard drive space required by recent versions of Windows.

### Chrome OS

*Chrome OS* is the first *cloud operating system*; that is, an operating system designed for devices that will be used entirely online. Chrome OS is essentially the Chrome Web browser redesigned to run a computer, in addition to accessing Web resources. It replaces traditional desktop operating systems like Windows but it is currently only available preinstalled on Chrome devices, such as *Chromebooks*.

## OPERATING SYSTEMS FOR MOBILE DEVICES

While notebook, hybrid notebook-tablets, and other portable personal computers typically use the same operating systems as desktop computers, smartphones, tablets, and other mobile devices usually use mobile operating systems—either mobile versions of personal operating systems (such as Windows or Linux) or special operating systems (such as Android or Apple iOS) that are designed specifically for mobile devices. There are also embedded operating systems designed to be used with everyday objects, such as home appliances, gaming consoles, digital cameras, e-readers, digital photo frames, ATMs, toys, watches, GPS systems, home medical devices, voting terminals, and cars (for a look at some current and emerging smart car features, see the Technology and You box). Most users select a smartphone by considering the wireless provider, hardware, and features associated with the smartphone. However, users should also consider the operating system used with a smartphone or other device because it determines some of the capabilities of the device, the interface used, and the applications that can run on that device. The operating systems most commonly used with mobile devices today are discussed next.

### Windows 10 Mobile

As previously mentioned, Windows 10 is designed to work on smartphones, tablets, and other mobile devices in addition to personal computers. While the display is smaller on a smartphone or tablet than on a desktop, Windows on a mobile device uses the same kernel, user interface, and other features as desktop installations (see Figure 5-17). One new feature, dubbed *Continuum*, allows Windows to provide the most appropriate

# TECHNOLOGY AND YOU

### Smart Cars

Computers have been integrated into cars for years to perform specific tasks, such as assisting with gear shifting and braking. Lately, however, the use of computers in cars has skyrocketed because they are being used to add additional convenience and safety to the driving experience. Some *smart car* features, such as GPS navigation systems and smart air bag systems that adjust the deployment of an air bag based on the weight of the occupant, are fairly standard today. Integrated *infotainment systems* that use Bluetooth and USB ports to tie smartphones to the car stereo system, as well as to steering wheel and voice control systems, are also widely available. Some other new and emerging trends in smart cars are discussed next.

➤ *Self-driving systems*—use sensors, radar, and video cameras to drive the car via an autopilot system; prototypes are currently being tested and self-driving vehicles are expected to be on the market by 2020.

➤ *Self-parking/parking assist systems*—use cameras and/or sensors to assist with parking; the onboard computer completely controls the car's steering wheel during the parking process and instructs the driver when any action (such as changing gears) is needed in order to park the car correctly. Systems that enable drivers to control the parking system via a mobile app in order to have the car park itself after the passengers have left the vehicle or to have it pull out of a parking space to pick up its passengers (see the accompanying photo) are currently in the prototype stage.

➤ *Lane departure systems*—use cameras to view the markings on the road and vibrate the steering wheel if the car begins to veer out of its lane.

➤ *Drowsiness detection systems*—use cameras to evaluate the driver's blinking pattern and eyelid movements and vibrate the seat or otherwise alert the driver if the driver becomes drowsy.

➤ *Blind spot detection systems*—use cameras mounted on the car's side mirrors to detect vehicles in the driver's blind spot and display a warning light near the mirror to notify the driver that something is in the blind spot.

➤ *Adaptive cruise control and distance alert systems*—use a radar system installed on the front of the car to detect the speed and distance of the vehicle ahead of it, and then automatically decrease or increase the speed of the car to maintain a safe distance from that vehicle.

➤ *Windshield displays*—project images from car instruments, GPS systems, and infotainment systems to enable the driver to see instrument readings, maps, incoming calls, and more without looking away from the windshield; some systems can also read speed limit signs and display that information (along with notifications, such as excessive speed for the current conditions) on the windshield.

➤ *Collision warning and auto brake systems*—use radar and camera systems installed on the front of the car to warn the driver when they are too close to the car in front of them; if a collision is imminent, the brakes are automatically activated at that point. Some systems can detect pedestrians as well as other vehicles.

➤ *Keyless entry and ignition systems*—use the owner's fingerprint or a key fob to unlock and start the car; smartphone applications that perform these tasks are beginning to become available.

➤ *Distraction-prevention systems*—delay or prevent mobile phone calls and other distractions while the car is in motion or during intense steering, braking, or acceleration, depending on the settings.

One of the biggest challenges for smart car technologies is the safe use of all the smart gadgets being incorporated into cars. The concern stems from studies consistently showing that distracted drivers are the cause of a vast majority of crashes. Voice-controlled dashboard components, smartphones, and other devices help because they are hands-free, although studies have found that your risk of an accident requiring a trip to the hospital quadruples when you are talking on a smartphone—hands-free or not.

Source: BMW Group

**SMARTPHONE**  **PERSONAL COMPUTER**

 **FIGURE 5-17**
Windows 10 has a
universal appearance.

interface (such as supporting keyboard and mouse input when your device is attached to a keyboard and using a touchscreen interface when it is not). It even enables some smartphones to function as a Windows 10 PC when the smartphone is connected to an external monitor, a mouse, and a keyboard via a wired or wireless connection. Windows 10 (shown in Figure 5-17) replaces older mobile versions of Windows, including *Windows Phone 8* and *Windows RT*, as well as older embedded versions of Windows.

 **FIGURE 5-18**
Android is used with
a variety of devices.

## Android

**Android** (see Figure 5-18) is a Linux-based operating system developed by the *Open Handset Alliance*, a group that includes Google and more than 30 technology and mobile companies. The most widely used mobile operating system in the United States, Android was built from the ground up with current mobile device capabilities in mind, which enables developers to create mobile applications that take full advantage of all the features a mobile device has to offer. It is an open platform, so anyone can download and use Android, although hardware manufacturers must adhere to certain specifications in order to be called "Android compatible." The current version of Android is *Android 6.0*, also known as *Marshmallow*. Similar to previous versions of Android, Android Marshmallow supports multi-touch input and has a variety of built-in Google apps (such as the Chrome Web browser, Gmail, and the *Google Now* virtual assistant) with more than one million additional apps available via the *Google Play* store. It also includes

> **Android.** A Linux-based operating system designed for mobile devices and developed by the Open Handset Alliance, which is a group of companies led by Google.

the *Android Device Manager* to help users locate, lock, or remotely wipe a lost or stolen Android phone; support for *Android Pay* for mobile purchases; and the ability to unlock the phone via a PIN, password, pattern, or face recognition. One feature new to Marshmallow is the ability to access Google Now from any screen (called *Google on Tap*). In addition to being used with Android smartphones and tablets, there are versions of Android designed for other devices, such as *Android Wear* for wearables, *Android TV* for smart TVs, and *Android Auto* for cars.

## iOS

The mobile operating system designed for Apple mobile devices, such as the iPhone and the iPad, is **iOS** (see Figure 5-19). This operating system is based on Apple's OS X operating system, supports multi-touch input, and has a variety of built-in apps with more than one million additional apps available via the *App Store*. The current version of iOS is *iOS 9*. It includes *Touch ID* and *Apple Pay* for secure purchases; the Safari Web browser; the *Siri* virtual assistant that lets users perform searches, place calls, and perform other tasks via voice commands; *FaceTime* for video calls; and *iCloud* for online storage. It also includes a *Find My iPhone* app to help users locate, lock, or remotely wipe a lost or stolen iPhone, as well as support for Apple Watch. The embedded operating system used with Apple Watch is *watchOS* (the current version is *watchOS2*); *tvOS* is the new embedded operating system for Apple TV.

## BlackBerry OS and BlackBerry PlayBook OS

*BlackBerry OS* is the operating system designed for BlackBerry devices. It supports multitasking and, like other mobile operating systems, it includes e-mail and Web browsing support, music management, video recording, calendar tools, and more. The latest version is *BlackBerry 10 OS*. Blackberry's tablet operating system is *BlackBerry PlayBook OS*. There is a wide range of software available for BlackBerry devices, from business and syncing software to games and other apps available through *BlackBerry World*.

Source: Apple, Inc.

**FIGURE 5-19**
iOS.

## Additional Linux-Based Mobile Operating Systems

In addition to Android and iOS, there are other Linux-based mobile operating systems used with mobile devices today. For instance, Ubuntu has versions available for phones and tablets, and HP recently made its *webOS* product an open source program. Two newer Linux-based mobile operating systems are *Firefox OS* and *Tizen*. Firefox OS was developed by Mozilla and includes a customizable Home screen and a number of built-in apps (including the Firefox Web browser) with additional apps available via the *Firefox Marketplace*. In addition to being used with smartphones, Firefox OS is used with some tablets and smart TVs. Tizen is also used with a variety of devices, including smartphones, wearables, tablets, and smart TVs. For a look at another product increasingly using a Linux-based operating system—drones—see the Inside the Industry box.

>**iOS.** The operating system designed for Apple mobile devices, such as the iPhone and iPad.

# INSIDE THE INDUSTRY

### Drones

A *drone* is an unmanned aircraft. Drones usually are remote controlled, run an operating system and other software, and look like small airplanes or multi-rotor helicopters (for example, a drone with four rotors is called a *quadcopter*). Drones are commonly used today for aerial filming; these drones are equipped with cameras and transmit video to the operator's base station, such as to capture video footage for feature films and real estate marketing or to enable farmers and ranchers to remotely check the conditions of crops, irrigation, or cattle. Drones can also be programmed to fly predetermined paths via GPS in order to create 3D maps, perform surveillance for firefighters, or assist with search and rescue operations, as shown in the accompanying illustration.

The use of drones for both personal and business use is skyrocketing. In response, many countries are developing regulations for the use of unmanned aircraft (in the United States, the FAA is charged with regulating drone use and is drafting new policies to address both current and future use of drones). While flying a drone for personal use in the United States doesn't require a license at the present time, operators must register their drones with the government, as well as follow safety rules including flying no higher than 400 feet and always being in sight of their drone. In addition, there are regulations regarding how close drones can get to airports, sporting arenas, and other no-fly zones. Use of drones is expected to keep growing as the potential uses for these aircraft are discovered. In fact, Amazon is currently testing a drone-based *Amazon Prime Air* delivery system.

Source: Airwave

## OPERATING SYSTEMS FOR LARGER COMPUTERS

Larger computers—such as high-end servers, mainframes, and supercomputers—sometimes use operating systems designed solely for that type of system. For instance, IBM's *z/OS* is designed for IBM mainframes. In addition, many servers and mainframes today run conventional operating systems, such as Windows, UNIX, and Linux. Linux in particular is increasingly being used with both mainframes and supercomputers. Larger computers may also use a customized operating system based on a conventional operating system; for instance, many IBM mainframes and Cray supercomputers use versions of UNIX developed specifically for those computers.

## UTILITY PROGRAMS

A **utility program** is a software program that performs a specific task, usually related to managing or maintaining a computer system. Many utility programs—such as programs for finding files, diagnosing and repairing system problems, cleaning up a hard drive, viewing images, playing multimedia files, and backing up files—are built into operating systems. There are also many stand-alone utility programs available as an alternative to

> **Utility program.** A type of software that performs a specific task, usually related to managing or maintaining a computer system.

the operating system's utility programs or to provide additional utility features not built into the operating system being used. Stand-alone utility programs are often available in a *suite* of related programs (such as a collection of maintenance programs or security programs, as shown in Figure 5-20). Some of the most commonly used integrated and stand-alone utility programs are discussed next.

## File Management Programs

**File management programs** allow you to perform file management tasks such as looking to see which files are stored on a storage medium, as well as copying, moving, deleting, and renaming folders and files. The file management program incorporated into recent versions of Windows is **File Explorer** (previous versions of Windows use *Windows Explorer*); some common file management tasks using this program are summarized next.

### Looking at the Folders and Files Stored on a Computer

Once a file management program is open, you can look at the folders and files stored on your computer. For instance, you can do the following in File Explorer (see Figure 5-21):

➤ To see the folders and files stored on your hard drive, USB flash drive, or any other storage medium, click the appropriate letter or name for that medium in the left pane (called the *Navigation pane*).

➤ To look inside a folder, click it (in the left pane) or double-click it (in the right pane). To go back to the previous location, click the Back toolbar button.

➤ To open a file in its associated program, double-click it.

➤ To create a new folder in the current location, click the *New folder* button and then type the name for the new folder.

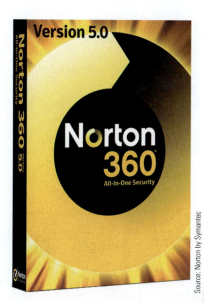

Source: Norton by Symantec

**FIGURE 5-20**
Utility suites contain a number of related programs.

**FIGURE 5-21**
Using File Explorer to look at the files stored on a computer.

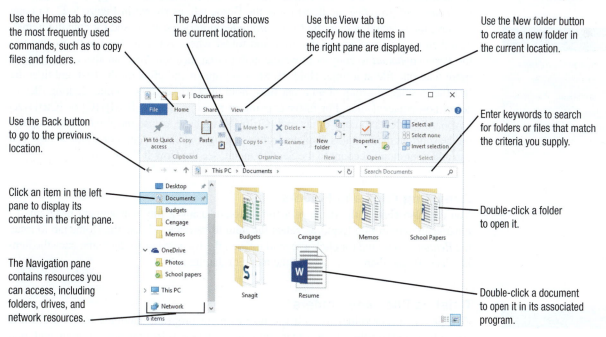

Use the Home tab to access the most frequently used commands, such as to copy files and folders.

The Address bar shows the current location.

Use the View tab to specify how the items in the right pane are displayed.

Use the New folder button to create a new folder in the current location.

Use the Back button to go to the previous location.

Enter keywords to search for folders or files that match the criteria you supply.

Click an item in the left pane to display its contents in the right pane.

Double-click a folder to open it.

The Navigation pane contains resources you can access, including folders, drives, and network resources.

Double-click a document to open it in its associated program.

> **File management program.** A utility program that enables the user to perform file management tasks, such as copying and deleting files.
> **File Explorer.** The file management program built into the Windows operating systems; older versions of Windows use Windows Explorer.

2. Click *Copy* to copy the file to the Clipboard.

3. Navigate to the drive and folder where you want the file to go.

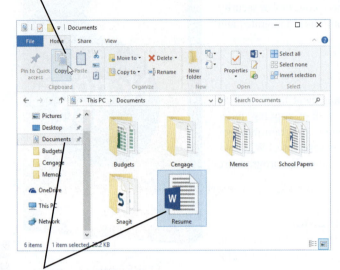

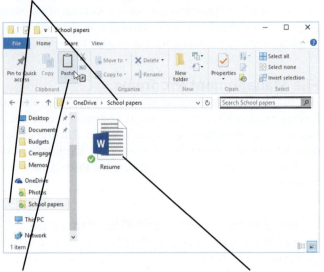

1. Navigate to the drive and folder containing the file you want to copy or move, and then select the file.

4. Click *Paste* to copy the file to the current location.

5. The file is copied.

 **FIGURE 5-22**
Using File Explorer to copy files.

## Copying and Moving Files and Folders

To copy or move a file or folder using a file management program such as File Explorer, you first need to navigate to the drive and folder where the item is located and then select the desired file or folder. Next, issue either the *Copy command* (to copy the item) or the *Cut command* (to move the item) using the Home tab, as shown in Figure 5-22, to copy or move the selected item to the *Clipboard* (a temporary location used for copying items). You then need to navigate to the drive and folder where you want the file to go, and use the *Paste command* to copy or move the item to that location. You can also copy or move more than one file at a time: Hold the Shift key down and click on the first and then the last file to select a group of adjacent files; hold the Ctrl key down while clicking files to select non-adjacent files. For faster copying or moving, use the [Ctrl]+[C] or [Ctrl]+[X] keyboard shortcuts to copy or cut and [Ctrl]+[V] to paste, or use the *Send to menu* option on the shortcut menu that is displayed when you right-click an item. For a look at how you can add your cloud account to the Send to menu, see the How It Works box.

## Renaming Files and Folders

You can also change the name of a file or folder using a file management program. To rename an item in File Explorer, select the item to be renamed, use the Home tab to issue the *Rename command* (or click a second time on the filename or folder name once the item is selected), and then retype or edit the name of that item.

## Deleting Files and Folders

To delete a file or folder using a file management program, navigate to the drive and folder that contains the file or folder you want to delete, select the desired item, and then press the Delete key on the keyboard. You will need to select *Yes* when the Confirm File/Folder Delete dialog box opens to finish the deletion process. Deleting a folder deletes all of the contents located inside that folder. Deleted files go to the *Recycle Bin*. To *restore* a file or folder deleted from your computer's hard drive, open the Recycle Bin and restore the file.

**TIP**

You can also copy, move, rename, or delete a file or folder in File Explorer by right-clicking the item and selecting the desired action from the shortcut menu that is displayed.

**TIP**

To free up room on your hard drive, periodically empty the Recycle Bin. However, be sure to check the files first to make sure that none need to be restored.

## Search Tools

As the amount of e-mail, photos, documents, and other important data individuals store on their computers continues to grow, **search tools**—utility programs that search for documents and other files on a user's hard drives—are becoming more important. Search tools are often integrated into file management programs and they are highly improved in recent versions of some operating systems, such as OS X and Windows. There are also a number of third-party search tools available.

Search tools typically are used to find files located somewhere on the specified storage medium that meet specific criteria, such as being in a certain folder, including certain characters in the filename, being of a particular type (a song, digital photo, or spreadsheet, for instance), and/or having a particular date associated with the file. If a document has been manually or automatically assigned *metadata tags* (information about the file, such as author, artist, or keywords), some search programs can search by those tags as well.

In Windows, for instance, users can use the *search box* located at the upper-right corner of the File Explorer window (refer again to Figure 5-21) to search for files and folders in the current location that match the keywords entered into the search box. You can also use the Search box on the taskbar; start typing search terms to display matching content as shown in Figure 5-23 (the default search is to search for apps and documents on your computer, as well as to search the Web). The taskbar Search box also doubles as an interface for the Cortana virtual assistant so you can use it to issue commands to Cortana (such as to set a reminder) in addition to using it for traditional searches.

## Diagnostic and Disk Management Programs

*Diagnostic programs* evaluate your system, looking for problems and making recommendations for fixing any errors that are discovered. *Disk management programs* diagnose and repair problems related to your hard drive. Diagnostic and disk management utilities built into the Windows operating system (see Figure 5-24) include programs to check your hard drive for errors, as well as programs to optimize your hard drive (by rearranging the data on the hard drive so all files are stored in contiguous locations—called *disk defragmentation*) so it works more efficiently. Third-party utility programs can perform these and other related tasks, as well.

Start typing search terms to see matching content.

Click an app to launch it or a document to open it.

**FIGURE 5-23**
Using the taskbar search box in Windows 10.

**FIGURE 5-24**
Windows disk tools.

To avoid deleting any system files used by other programs when uninstalling a program, be sure to keep all files (such as *.dll* files) that an uninstall utility asks you about and says might be needed by another program. As an extra precaution, you can create a *System Restore point* (using the *Recovery* tools) before uninstalling a program (if you are using a Windows computer) so you can roll the computer's settings back to that point if a problem occurs after the program is uninstalled.

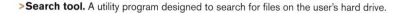

>**Search tool.** A utility program designed to search for files on the user's hard drive.

# HOW IT WORKS

## Sending to the Cloud

The Windows *Send to* menu is a great shortcut for sending files to a USB flash drive, external hard drive, or other resource listed on the shortcut menu that is displayed when you right-click on a file or folder. But what if the resource you use all the time—like your cloud storage account—isn't listed? Simple. You add it.

To add a cloud resource to the Send to menu, do the following (refer to the accompanying illustrations):

1. Type this command in the File Explorer Address bar and press Enter.

1. Open a File Explorer window and type the following command in the Address bar and press Enter:
   **%APPDATA%/Microsoft/Windows/SendTo**

2. The SendTo folder will then be displayed showing the current available options for the Send to menu. Add your desired Send to location to the SendTo folder, such as by dragging a cloud account into the folder and choosing the appropriate option to create a link or shortcut if a menu is displayed asking what you would like to do with the item.

3. The next time you right-click on an item, all of your specified Send to locations will be displayed.

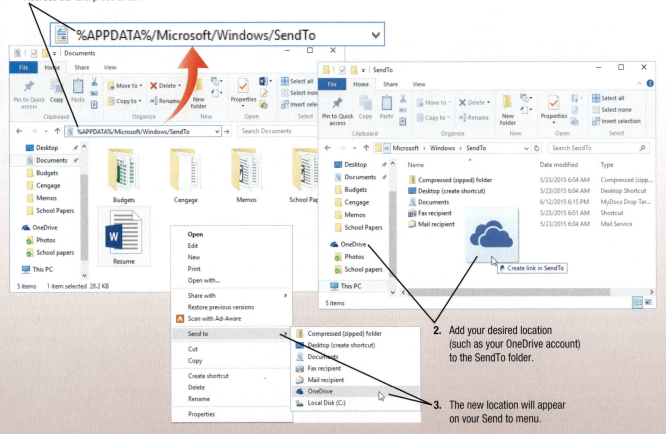

2. Add your desired location (such as your OneDrive account) to the SendTo folder.

3. The new location will appear on your Send to menu.

## Uninstall and Cleanup Utilities

As programs are used, temporary data is often created. When programs are *uninstalled* (removed from the hard drive), this data and other remnants of that program can be left behind on the hard drive or in system files unless an *uninstall utility* is used. If a user removes programs by deleting the program's folder (which is not the recommended method for removing programs), the extraneous data is left behind, using up valuable disk space and, sometimes, slowing down the computer. Uninstall utilities remove the programs along with related extraneous data, such as references to those programs in your system files. Some uninstall capabilities are built into most operating systems; often an uninstall option is also included in a program's folder when that program is originally installed.

*Cleanup utilities* (such as Windows *Disk Cleanup* shown in Figure 2-24 in Chapter 2) are designed to delete temporary files (such as deleted files still in the Recycle Bin, temporary Internet files, temporary installation files, and so forth) in order to free up disk space. Some specialty cleanup programs (called *registry cleaners*) are designed to locate unnecessary information in the Windows registry and other system files (such as from uninstalled programs) and delete it, making your computer run more efficiently.

## File Compression Programs

**File compression programs** reduce the size of files so they take up less storage space on a storage medium or can be transmitted faster over the Internet. The most common format for user-compressed files in the Windows environment is the *.zip* or *.zipx* format, which is created by file compression programs such as *WinZip* and the free 7-Zip program, as well as by the file compression features built into recent versions of Windows (see Figure 5-25). Mac users typically use *StuffIt* (which creates files in the *.sit* or *.sitx* format) or a similar program, although many file compression programs can open files compressed with other programs. A file compression program is required to both compress (*zip*) and decompress (*unzip*) files, unless the zipped file is made *executable*. Executable zipped files have the extension *.exe* and decompress automatically when they are opened, even if the appropriate file compression program is not installed on the recipient's computer. File compression programs can compress either a single file or a group of files into a single compressed file. When multiple files are compressed, they are separated back into individual files when the file is decompressed. Some file compression programs can also *encrypt* your zipped files so that a password is needed to unzip them. Encryption is discussed in detail in Chapter 9.

# ASK THE EXPERT

**Mike Cobb,** Director of Engineering, DriveSavers Data Recovery

**How important are disk-maintenance procedures—such as defragmenting a hard drive—in preventing a hard drive failure?**

It's important to run a disk maintenance program occasionally to fix minor directory corruption and repair incorrect disk or file permissions. In addition, defragmenting files—or optimizing as it is sometimes called—can help improve the performance of a hard drive.

Computer users who create large high-resolution graphics, professional audio recordings, and video production files should defragment regularly; these users will see the most benefit from a regular defragmenting routine.

**FIGURE 5-25**

**File compression.** Reduces the size of files so they can be more efficiently stored or transmitted.

Click to compress the selected files into a single file.

Compressed folder was created and contains these individual files.

Click to extract all files in the compressed folder to a location you specify.

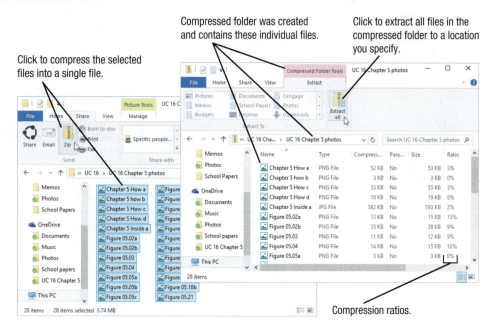

Compression ratios.

---

>**File compression program.** A program that reduces the size of files, typically to be stored or transmitted more efficiently.

## Backup and Recovery Utilities

Virtually every computer veteran will warn you that, sooner or later, you will lose some critical files. This could happen due to a power outage (if the file you are working on has not yet been saved), a hardware failure (such as if your computer or hard drive stops functioning), a major disaster (such as a fire that destroys your computer), or a user error (such as accidentally deleting or overwriting a file).

Creating a **backup** means making a duplicate copy of important files so that when a problem occurs, you can restore those files using the backup copy to avoid data loss. Performing a backup can include backing up an entire computer (so it can be restored at a later date, if needed), backing up all data files (in order to restore them in case the computer is lost or damaged), or backing up only selected files (to make sure you have a clean copy of each file if the original is accidentally lost or destroyed). Depending on its size, backup data can be placed on a recordable or rewritable DVD disc, an external hard drive, a USB flash drive, or virtually any other storage medium. To protect against fires and other natural disasters, backup media should be stored in a different physical location than your computer or inside a fire-resistant safe. Creating a backup is illustrated in Figure 5-26.

It is critical for a business to have backup procedures in place that back up all data on a frequent, regular basis—such as every night. A rotating collection of backup media should be used so it is possible to go back beyond the previous day's backup, if needed. While individuals tend to back up in a less formal manner, personal backups are becoming increasingly necessary as the amount of important information that users store digitally (such as home movies, music, digital photos, and tax returns) grows. Personal backups can be as simple as copying important documents to a USB flash drive or uploading them to a cloud storage site, or as comprehensive as backing up the entire contents of your computer.

**FIGURE 5-26**
**Using a backup program.**

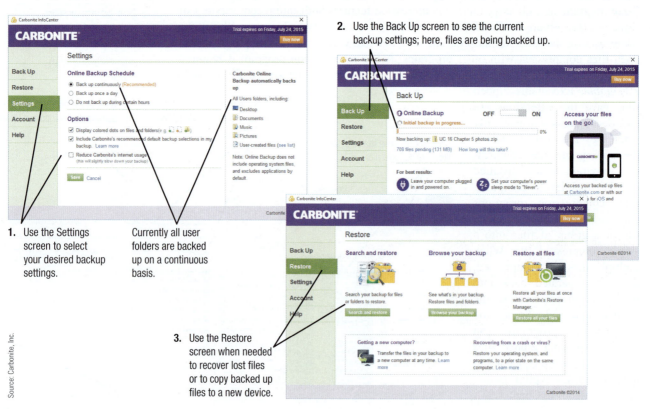

1. Use the Settings screen to select your desired backup settings.

Currently all user folders are backed up on a continuous basis.

2. Use the Back Up screen to see the current backup settings; here, files are being backed up.

3. Use the Restore screen when needed to recover lost files or to copy backed up files to a new device.

Source: Carbonite, Inc.

> **Backup.** A duplicate copy of data or other computer content in case the original version is destroyed.

You can perform backups by manually copying files using your file management program, but there are *backup utility* programs (both stand-alone and built into operating systems) that make the backup process easier, such as the *File History* program used in recent versions of Windows that backs up your files to an external drive and the *Carbonite* cloud backup program shown in Figure 5-26 that backs up your data continuously to the cloud. One advantage of cloud backup programs is that your files can be accessed with any Web-enabled device. However, in either case, you can recover your data using the backup if the originals are lost, corrupted, or accidentally deleted.

**TIP** ✓

System failure and disaster recovery are discussed in detail in Chapter 9.

### Antivirus, Antispyware, Firewalls, and Other Security Programs

A computer virus is a software program that is designed to cause damage to a computer or perform some other malicious act, and spyware is a software program installed without the user's knowledge that secretly collects information and sends it to an outside party via the user's Internet connection. Other security concerns today include phishing schemes that try to trick users into supplying personal information that can be used for credit card fraud, identity theft, and other criminal acts. Because of these threats, it is critical that all computer users today protect themselves and their computers. There are many security programs available, such as antivirus programs and antispyware programs (that protect against malicious software being installed on your computer) and firewall programs (that protect against someone accessing your computer via the Internet or a wireless connection). Increasingly, operating systems are including security software integrated into the operating system. For instance, recent versions of Windows include a variety of security utilities, such as *Windows Defender* and *Windows SmartScreen* (to protect against viruses) and *Windows Firewall*, shown in Figure 5-27 (to protect against intrusions). Because network and Internet security is such an important topic today, Chapter 9 is dedicated to these topics.

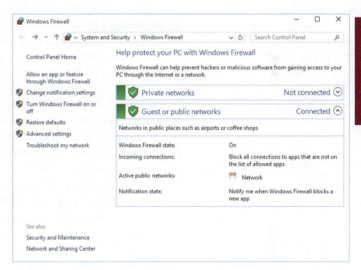

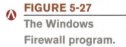

**FIGURE 5-27**
**The Windows Firewall program.**

## THE FUTURE OF OPERATING SYSTEMS

The future configuration of operating systems is anyone's guess, but it is expected that they will continue to become more user-friendly and, eventually, be driven primarily by a voice, touch, and/or gesture interface. Operating systems are also likely to continue to become more stable and self-healing, repairing or restoring system files as needed. In addition, they are expected to continue to include security and technological improvements as they become available.

Improvements will almost certainly continue to be made in the areas of synchronizing and coordinating data and activities among a person's various computing devices, such as his or her personal computer, smartphone, and wearable devices. Desktop and mobile operating systems will also likely continue to converge into a single operating system as those devices continue to converge. In addition, with the pervasiveness of the Internet, operating systems in the future may be used primarily to access software available through the Internet or other networks, instead of accessing software on the local computer.

# SUMMARY

## SYSTEM SOFTWARE VS. APPLICATION SOFTWARE

**System software** consists of the programs that coordinate the activities of a computer system. The basic role of system software is to act as a mediator between **application software** (programs that allow a user to perform specific tasks on a computer, such as word processing, playing a game, preparing taxes, browsing the Web, and so forth) and the computer system's hardware, as well as between the computer and the user.

## THE OPERATING SYSTEM

A computer's **operating system** is the primary system software program; it manages the computer system's resources and interfaces with the user. The essential portion, or core, of an operating system is called its **kernel**. The functions of the operating system include booting the computer, configuring devices and **device drivers** (often simply called **drivers**), communicating with the user, managing and monitoring computer resources, file management, and security. File management programs allow the user to manage the enormous collection of files typically found on a computer's hard drive by organizing files hierarchically into folders. To access a file in any directory, the user can specify the *path* to the file; the path identifies the drive and folders the user must navigate through in order to access the file.

A variety of processing techniques can be built into operating systems to help enhance processing efficiency. **Multitasking** allows more than one program to be open at one time; *multithreading* allows for rotation between program *threads*; and multiprocessing and parallel processing involve using two or more CPUs (or CPU cores) to perform work at the same time. Operating systems typically use **virtual memory** to extend conventional memory by using a portion of the hard drive as additional memory, and **buffering** and **spooling** free up the CPU from delays by storing data that is waiting to be used in a **buffer**.

Some of the differences among operating systems center around whether they use a **graphical user interface** (**GUI**) or **command line interface**, whether they are a **personal (desktop) operating system** designed for individual users or a **server (network) operating system** designed for multiple users, and the types and numbers of processors supported. Operating systems that are used with mobile devices or are embedded in other devices are called **mobile operating systems** or **embedded operating systems**, respectively.

## OPERATING SYSTEMS FOR PERSONAL COMPUTERS AND SERVERS

One of the original operating systems for IBM and IBM-compatible personal computers was **DOS** (**Disk Operating System**), which is still in existence but not widely used. Most desktop computers today run a version of **Windows**. *Windows 3.x*, the first widely used version of Windows, was an *operating environment* that added a GUI shell to DOS, replacing the DOS command line interface with a system of menus, icons, and screen boxes called *windows*. *Windows 95*, *Windows 98*, *Windows NT*, *Windows Me*, *Windows 2000*, *Windows XP*, *Windows Vista*, and *Windows 7*—all full-fledged operating systems and successors to Windows 3.x—each included an increasing number of enhancements, such as multitasking, a better user interface, and more Internet, multimedia, and communications functions. *Windows Server* is the server version of the various Windows operating systems. The most recent versions of Windows are *Windows 8*, which introduced a **tile** interface, and **Windows 10**, which uses the **Start menu** and is a universal operating system that can be used with a variety of devices, including computers and mobile devices.

**OS X** is the operating system used on Apple computers. The most recent personal versions include *OS X Yosemite* and *OS X El Capitan*); *Mac OS X Server* is designed for server use. **UNIX** is a flexible operating system that was originally developed for use with mid-range servers, but is now available for a variety of devices. UNIX comes in many versions or *UNIX flavors* and is the basis of several other operating systems, including OS X. The open source **Linux** operating system has gathered popularity because it is distributed free over the Internet and can be used as an alternative to Windows and OS X. Linux has earned support as a mainstream operating system in recent years and is being used in computers of all sizes, from netbooks to supercomputers.

## OPERATING SYSTEMS FOR MOBILE DEVICES

Smartphones and mobile devices usually require a different operating system than a desktop computer or server, although many mobile operating systems are mobile versions of desktop operating systems. Operating systems commonly used with mobile devices today include Windows 10, **Android**, **iOS**, and other operating systems based on Linux.

## OPERATING SYSTEMS FOR LARGER COMPUTERS

High-end servers, mainframes, and supercomputers may use an operating system designed specifically for that type of system, but are increasingly using customized versions of conventional operating systems, such as Windows, UNIX, and Linux.

## UTILITY PROGRAMS

A **utility program** is a type of system software written to perform specific tasks usually related to maintaining or managing the computer system. **File management programs** enable users to perform file management tasks, such as copying, moving, and deleting files. The file management system built into Windows is **File Explorer**. **Search tools** are designed to help users find files on their hard drives; *diagnostic* and *disk management programs* are used mainly to diagnose and repair computer problems, such as hard drive errors and files deleted accidentally, as well as maintenance tasks, such as performing *disk defragmentation*. *Uninstall utilities* remove programs from a hard drive without leaving annoying remnants behind, **file compression programs** reduce the stored size of files so they can be more easily archived or sent over the Internet, and **backup** programs make it easier for users to back up the contents of their hard drive. There are also a number of security-oriented utility programs, such as antivirus, antispyware, and firewall programs.

## THE FUTURE OF OPERATING SYSTEMS

In the future, operating systems will likely become even more user-friendly, voice-driven, and stable, repairing themselves when needed and causing errors and conflicts much less frequently. They will also likely continue to include improved security features, support for new technologies, and assistance for coordinating data and activities among a user's various computing devices. Operating systems for various devices will likely continue to converge and they may also more often be designed primarily for accessing cloud applications.

**Chapter Objective 5:**
Name today's most widely used operating systems for smartphones and other mobile devices.

**SW**

**Chapter Objective 6:**
Discuss the operating systems used with mainframes and supercomputers.

**Chapter Objective 7:**
Discuss the role of utility programs and outline several tasks that these programs perform.

**Chapter Objective 8:**
Describe what the operating systems of the future might be like.

# REVIEW ACTIVITIES

## KEY TERM MATCHING

a. Android

b. backup

c. device driver

d. kernel

e. multitasking

f. operating system

g. spooling

h. utility program

i. virtual memory

j. Windows

**Instructions:** Match each key term on the left with the definition on the right that best describes it.

1. _____ A duplicate copy of data or other computer content for use in the event that the original version is destroyed.

2. _____ A Linux-based operating system designed for mobile devices and developed by the Open Handset Alliance, which is a group of companies led by Google.

3. _____ A memory-management technique that uses hard drive space as additional RAM.

4. _____ A program that enables an operating system to communicate with a specific hardware device.

5. _____ A type of software that performs a specific task, usually related to managing or maintaining a computer system.

6. _____ The capability of an operating system to run more than one program at one time.

7. _____ The essential portion, or core, of an operating system.

8. _____ The main component of system software that enables a computer to operate, manage its activities and the resources under its control, run application programs, and interface with the user.

9. _____ The primary personal computer operating system developed by Microsoft Corporation.

10. _____ The process of placing items in a buffer so the appropriate device (such as a printer) can retrieve them when needed.

## SELF-QUIZ

**Instructions:** Circle **T** if the statement is true, **F** if the statement is false, or write the best answer in the space provided. **Answers for the self-quiz are located in the References and Resources Guide at the end of the book.**

1. **T   F**   Windows 10 is an example of an operating system.

2. **T   F**   Most operating systems today use a graphical user interface.

3. **T   F**   Mobile devices, such as tablets and smartphones, do not require an operating system.

4. **T   F**   File Explorer is an example of an operating system.

5. **T   F**   OS X is a versatile operating system designed to be used on a variety of computer types, such as mainframes, servers, personal computers, and smartphones.

6. _____ is an open-source operating system that is available without charge over the Internet.

7. _____ is the operating system used with iPhones and iPads.

8. To decrease the size of a file, a(n) _____ utility program can be used.

9. To guard against losing your data if a computer problem occurs, you should _____ your data files on a regular basis.

**10.** Match each device to the most appropriate operating system and write the corresponding number in the blank to the left of the device.

a. _____ Home office computer      1. Android

b. _____ Mainframe computer      2. Windows 10

c. _____ Tablet      3. UNIX

---

**EXERCISES**

**1.** For the following path, identify the drive the document is located on, the name of the file (including its file extension), and whether or not the document is stored inside a folder. If the file is stored inside one or more folders, list the folder name(s).

**C:\Documents\Resume.docx**

**2.** Match each program or processing technique with the appropriate term and write the corresponding number in the blank to the left of each term.

a. _____ Zipped file      1. Spooling

b. _____ Printer      2. File management program

c. _____ Swap file      3. File compression program

d. _____ Folder      4. Virtual memory

**3.** Would a new smartphone more likely have Windows 8, OS X, or Android installed as its operating system? Explain your answer.

**4.** What type of utility program is designed to automatically make duplicate copies of your hard drive content for safekeeping?

**5.** Identify the purpose of each of the following types of utility programs.

a. File management program _____

b. Uninstall utility _____

c. File compression program _____

d. Antivirus program _____

---

**DISCUSSION QUESTIONS**

**1.** There are a few companies, such as Microsoft and Google, that have moved into many different areas of computing, such as operating systems, application software, cloud software, search, and more, and some of these companies have been accused of monopolistic procedures. Is there a risk for the consumer or for businesses if one company is involved with so many different aspects of computing? Should this be prohibited or should the natural order of the free market be trusted to prevent areas of computing from being monopolized by one company?

**2.** As discussed in the chapter, many everyday devices—including cars and other vehicles—are controlled by operating systems. There are advantages, such as avoiding possible driver errors and the ability to change the speed of or reroute trains automatically to avoid collisions. But are there potential risks, as well? For example, Thailand's Finance Minister once had to be rescued from inside his limousine after the onboard computer malfunctioned, leaving the vehicle immobilized and the door locks, power windows, and air conditioning not functioning. Do you think the benefits of increased automation of devices that could put us in danger if they malfunction outweigh the risks? What types of safeguards should be incorporated into computer-controlled cars, subway trains, and other automated vehicles? What about medication dispensers and other automated medical devices?

**SW**

# PROJECTS

**1. Drones** As discussed in the Inside the Industry box, drones are a hot trend today.

For this project, research the current status of drone use. What tasks are they being used for? Are they being used just as a hobby or do business applications exist? Are there any new regulations for personal or commercial drone pilots? Have there been any recent incidents regarding drone use, such as security scares or interference with airplanes? Do you think the level of safety regulations is adequate? Why or why not? At the conclusion of your research, prepare a one-page summary of your findings and opinions and submit it to your instructor.

**2. File Compression** As described in the chapter, compression programs can be used to reduce the size of files before they are stored or sent over the Internet. The most common compression programs create files with the file extensions *.zip*, *.sit*, *.sitx*, and *.exe*. Self-extracting compressed files decompress automatically when you download them, while compressed files must be decompressed with a version of the program that compressed them.

For this project, identify compression programs associated with each of the file extensions listed above and determine which extensions represent a self-extracting format, as well as which extensions are associated with the Windows and OS X operating systems. For the type of computer you use most often, find at least two compression programs that you might use and compare their costs and capabilities. At the conclusion of your research, prepare a one-page summary of your findings and submit it to your instructor.

**3. File Practice** As discussed in the chapter, all operating systems have a file management system, such as the File Explorer program illustrated in Figures 5-21 and 5-22.

For this project, obtain a removable storage medium (such as a USB flash drive) appropriate for a computer you have access to, connect it to that computer, and perform the following tasks.

  **a.** Open the file management program and select the icon representing the removable storage medium being used to display its contents. Are there any files on the storage medium? How much room is available on the storage medium?

  **b.** Open any word processing program available on your computer (such as Word or Notepad for a Windows computer). Create a new document consisting of just your name, then save the document to your storage medium (be sure to change the save location to the appropriate drive and use an appropriate filename). In the file management program, view the content of your storage medium to see the new document. What is the file size and how much room is now left on your storage medium?

  **c.** Prepare a short summary of your work to submit to your instructor, listing the software programs and storage medium used, the name and size of the file, and the amount of space left on your storage medium once the file was stored on it.

  **d.** Return to your file management program and delete the file from your storage medium.

4. **Operating System Bugs** Most software, including operating systems, is not error free when it is first released. Some programs, in fact, contain thousands of problems, called *bugs*. Software companies regularly release fixes (called *patches*) to correct known issues with released software. Is it ethical for software companies to release products that have known problems? Many hackers and other criminals target these bugs with computer viruses or other attacks, frequently on the day a new vulnerability is announced—called a *zero-day attack*. Obviously, the acts by these criminals are not ethical, but what responsibility does a software company have to consumers if they are put at risk due to the company's carelessness or rush to market? What responsibility do consumers have to make sure they keep their computers patched against new vulnerabilities?

For this project, form an opinion about the ethical ramifications of software bugs and be prepared to discuss your position (in class, via an online class forum, or via a class blog, depending on your instructor's directions). You may also be asked to write a short paper expressing your opinion.

5. **OS Support** No matter which operating system you have, it's likely you will eventually need to get some help resolving a problem. Support options typically include the following: searchable knowledge bases, technical support phone numbers and e-mail addresses, online chat, FAQs, and user discussion groups.

For this project, select one operating system and go to the manufacturer's Web site to determine which of the support options listed in the previous paragraph are available. Select one support option and find out how it is used and what type of information can be obtained. Share your findings with the class in the form of a short presentation. The presentation should not exceed 10 minutes and should make use of one or more presentation aids, such as a whiteboard, handouts, or a computer-based slide presentation (your instructor may provide additional requirements). You may also be asked to submit a summary of the presentation to your instructor.

6. **Are Computerized Cars a Cyber Threat?** As discussed in this chapter, cars are continually getting smarter and these features are supposed to help make us safer. But do they put us at risk as well? Today's cars are essentially computers on wheels and computers can be hacked. What if a hacker infects a car with malware or takes control of the car's speed, braking, and other vital systems? Researchers have already shown that hacking into a car to take control is possible. There are a number of access points available to hackers, such as the car's entertainment system, the car's Internet connection—even the acceleration and braking systems. Could hackers be hired as hit men to murder selected individuals by taking control of their cars? What about terrorists introducing a virus to large numbers of cars as a terrorist act? Do we need new laws to make hacking cars illegal? Should security companies be developing antivirus software for cars? Will we get to the point where we'll need to run a virus scan before we can safely use our vehicles? What about self-driving cars? Are the benefits of computerized cars worth the potential risks?

Pick a side on this issue, form an opinion and gather supporting evidence, and be prepared to discuss and defend your position in a classroom debate or in a one- to two-page paper, depending on your instructor's directions.

# chapter 6

# Application Software: Desktop and Mobile Apps

**After completing this chapter, you will be able to do the following:**

1. Describe what application software is, the different types of ownership rights, and the difference between installed and cloud software.

2. Detail some concepts and commands that many software programs have in common.

3. Discuss word processing and explain what kinds of documents are created using this type of program.

4. Explain the purpose of spreadsheet software and the kinds of documents created using this type of program.

5. Identify some of the vocabulary used with database software and discuss the benefits of using this type of program.

6. Describe what presentation graphics and electronic slide shows are and when they might be used.

7. List some types of graphics and multimedia software that consumers use frequently.

8. Name several other types of application software programs and discuss what functions they perform.

# OVERVIEW

**A**s discussed in previous chapters, application software consists of programs designed to perform specific tasks or applications. Today, a wide variety of application software is available to meet virtually any user need. Individuals and businesses use software to perform hundreds of tasks, including to write letters, keep track of their finances, participate in videoconferences, watch videos, learn a foreign language, entertain themselves or their children, create music CDs or home movie DVDs, manage business inventories, create greeting cards and flyers, make business presentations, process orders, prepare payrolls and tax returns, touch up digital photos, and access Web-based resources.

This chapter begins with a discussion of some general characteristics of application software. Then we look at five of the most widely used types of application software: word processing, spreadsheet, database, presentation graphics, and graphics/multimedia software. The chapter concludes with an overview of some of the other types of application software you may encounter in your personal and professional life. ■

## THE BASICS OF APPLICATION SOFTWARE

All computer users should be familiar with the basic characteristics and concepts related to **application software (apps)**—for instance, the different possible ownership rights and delivery methods used with application software, how software for personal computers and mobile devices differs, and the basic commands that are common to most types of application software. Although these topics are discussed next in the context of application software, they also apply to other types of software, such as system software (discussed in Chapter 5) and programming languages (discussed in Chapter 11).

### Software Ownership Rights

The *ownership rights* of a software program specify the allowable use of that program. After a software program is developed, the developer (typically an individual or an organization) holds the ownership rights for that program and decides whether or not the program can be sold, shared with others, or otherwise distributed. When a software program is purchased, the buyer is not actually buying the software. Instead, the buyer is acquiring a **software license** that permits him or her to use the software. This license, also called an *end user license agreement* (*EULA*), specifies the conditions under which a buyer can use the software, such as the number of devices on which it may be installed. Mobile apps may instead display a *terms of use* agreement that lists what smartphone resources the app will access. In either case, the licensing agreement or terms of use agreement is usually displayed and must be agreed to by the end user at the beginning of the software installation process (see Figure 6-1).

> **Application software (apps).** Programs that enable users to perform specific tasks on a computer, such as writing a letter or playing a game.
> **Software license.** An agreement, either included in a software package or displayed on the screen when the software is installed or launched, that specifies the conditions under which the program can be used.

BY USING THE SOFTWARE, YOU ACCEPT THESE TERMS. IF YOU DO NOT ACCEPT THEM, DO NOT USE THE SOFTWARE.

MICROSOFT PRE-RELEASE SOFTWARE LICENSE TERMS
MICROSOFT ... KTOP PREVIEW
These license ter... re an agreement between Microsoft Corporation (or based on where you live, one of its affiliate... nd you. Please read them. They apply to the pre-release software named above, which includes th... edia on which you received it, if any. The terms also apply to any Microsoft
• updates,
• supplements,
• Internet-base... ervices, and
• support ser... es
for this software, unless other terms accompany those items. If so, those terms apply.
BY USING THE SOFTWARE, YOU ACCEPT THESE TERMS. IF YOU DO NOT ACCEPT THEM, DO NOT USE THE SOFTWARE.
AS DESCRIBED BELOW, USING SOME FEATURES ALSO OPERATES AS YOUR CONSENT TO THE TRANSMISSION OF CERTAIN STANDARD COMPUTER INFORMATION FOR INTERNET-BASED SERVICES.
IF YOU COMPLY WITH THESE LICENSE TERMS, YOU HAVE THE RIGHTS BELOW.
1. INSTALLATION AND USE RIGHTS.
a. Installation and Use.
• You may install and test any number of copies of the software on your premises. You may use as many copies of the software as the product key permits.
• You may not test the software in a live operating environment unless Microsoft permits you to do

< Back

OK

**COMMERCIAL SOFTWARE**

These Terms affect your legal rights and obligations, so if you do not agree to these Terms, do not use the Services.

‹ Terms of Use

**Terms of Use**

Last updated: November 17, 2014

Please read these Terms of Use ("Terms") carefully. By downloading, accessing, or using the mobile applications, websites, or other products or services of Snapchat, Inc. and our affiliates ("Snapchat", "we" or "us"), or the services, features, or functionality jointly offered with other companies through our mobile application or website (collectively, the "Services"), you agree to be bound by these Terms. These Terms affect your legal rights and obligations, so if you do not agree to these Terms, do not use the Services.

In the event you use a service, feature, or

Snapchat
needs access to
Identity
Contacts
Location
SMS
Photos/Media/Files
Camera
Microphone
Wi-Fi connection information
Google play   ACCEPT

Source: Snapchat

**MOBILE APP**

**FIGURE 6-1**

**Software licenses and terms of use.**

Are typically displayed and must be agreed to during the installation process.

Regardless of the device being used, software typically falls into four basic categories of software: *commercial software*, *shareware*, *freeware*, and *public domain software* (see Figure 6-2). Each of these types of software has different ownership rights, as discussed next. In addition, software that falls into any of these four categories can also be **open source software**, which are programs made up of source code that is available to the public. An open source program can be copyrighted, but individuals and businesses are allowed to modify the program and redistribute it—the only restrictions are that changes must be shared with the open source community and the original copyright notice must remain intact. For more information about open source software, see the Inside the Industry box.

**FIGURE 6-2**

**Software ownership rights.**

## Commercial Software

**Commercial software** is software that is developed and sold for a profit. When you buy a commercial software program, it typically comes with a *single-user license*, which means you cannot legally make copies of the installation program or CD to give to your friends and you cannot legally install the software on their computers using your copy. You cannot even install the software on a second computer that you own, unless allowed by the license. For example, some software licenses state that the program can be installed on only one device; others can be installed on one desktop computer and one portable computer belonging to the same individual. To determine which activities are allowable for a particular commercial software program, refer to its software license. Schools or businesses that need to install software on a large number of computers or need to have the software available to multiple users over a network can usually obtain a *site license* or *network license* for the number of users needed.

| TYPE OF SOFTWARE | EXAMPLES |
| --- | --- |
| Commercial software | Microsoft Office (office suite) <br> Norton AntiVirus (antivirus program) <br> Adobe Photoshop CC (image editing program) <br> Minecraft - Pocket Edition (game) |
| Shareware | WinZip (file compression program) <br> Video Edit Magic (video editing program) <br> Image Shrinker (image optimizer) <br> Deluxe Ski Jump 3 (game) |
| Freeware | Chrome (Web browser) <br> LibreOffice (office suite) <br> VLC Media Player (media player) <br> Evernote Basic (notetaking/archiving software) |
| Public domain software | Lynx (text-based Web browser) <br> Quake 3 (game) |

> **Open source software.** Software programs made up of source code that is made available to the public. > **Commercial software.** Copyrighted software that is developed, usually by a commercial company, for sale to others.

# INSIDE THE INDUSTRY

### Open Source Software

The use of open source software has grown over the past few years, primarily for cost reasons. One of the first widely known open source programs was the Linux operating system, which was discussed in Chapter 5. However, there are also low-cost or no-cost open source alternatives for a wide selection of application programs today. For instance, the free LibreOffice office suite can be used as an alternative to Microsoft Office, and the free *GIMP* program (see the accompanying screenshot) can be used to retouch photos instead of Adobe Photoshop or another pricey image editing program. In addition to saving you money, these alternative programs often require less disk space and memory than their commercial software counterparts require.

Other possible benefits of using open source software include increased stability and security (because they are tested and improved by a wide variety of programmers and users), and the ability to modify the application's source code. Perceived risks of using open source software include lack of support and compatibility issues. However, both Linux and open source application programs are continuing to gain acceptance and their use is growing. Some insiders feel that the open source movement is finally gathering the momentum it deserves.

A recent survey of executives found that most executives view open source software as beneficial to both innovation and collaboration. Another recent study revealed that the use of open source software is at an all-time high with 78% of companies using open source software for part or all of their operations; the majority of the companies believe that open source software affords the greatest ability to scale and nearly half of the companies said open source options are considered first.

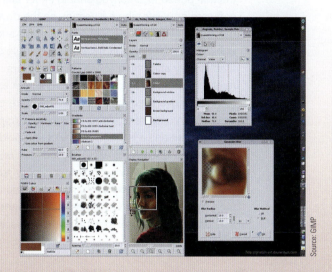

Source: GIMP

In addition to their full versions, some commercial software is available in a *demo* or *trial version*. Typically, these versions can be used free of charge and distributed to others, but often they are missing some key features (such as the ability to save or print a document) or they will not run after the trial period expires. Because these programs are not designed as replacements for the fee-based version, it is ethical to use them only to determine if you would like to buy the full program. If the decision is made against purchasing the product, the demo or trial version should be uninstalled from your computer.

Recent trends in computing—such as multiprocessing, virtualization, mobile computing, and cloud computing, all discussed in earlier chapters of this book—are leading to new software licensing issues for commercial software companies. For example, software companies must decide whether the number of installations allowed by the license is counted by the number of computers on which the software is installed, the total number of processors or CPU cores used by those computers, or the number of individuals using installed or virtual copies of the software at any given time. Some Microsoft software, for instance, is licensed per processor, regardless of the number of cores each processor has. And, for some server software used within a virtual environment, Microsoft computes the number of users based on a *per running instance*—that is, the number of software instances (installed or virtual) being used at any given time—instead of how many virtual environments the software is actually available to. Another option is using *license tokens* that are drawn from a central license server when the application is running and returned

> **TIP**
> Ownership rights for original creative works are referred to as *copyrights* and are discussed in more detail in Chapter 13.

> **TIP**
> Businesses should periodically audit their software licenses to ensure they are paying only for the number of installs actually being used. They should also consider negotiating new types of licensing agreements that best fit the company, such as concurrent-user pricing instead of per-computer pricing.

## ASK THE EXPERT

**Stacy Reed,** Managing Editor/Software Librarian, Tucows

**Why should an individual or business pay for shareware?**

Ethically and legally, it's the right thing to do. Software publishers offer trial versions of their software for free because it allows users ample opportunity to evaluate the software to ensure it meets their needs. After the trial period expires, you should either uninstall the software or pay for the full version so the developer can continue to provide technical support and product enhancements. Some software may disable or cripple functionality after the trial has ended; others may remind you to pay by displaying nag screens, watermarks, or advertisements. Though there are sneaky ways to circumvent licensing, doing so is copyright infringement and it is illegal. Conviction could include jail time and/or fines for each infringement and, if you or your company willfully profit from stolen software, you stand to face maximum penalties—in some countries, that could mean hundreds of thousands of dollars in fines per instance or several years in prison.

to the server when the application is finished. This system allows the number of tokens used by an individual computer to vary depending on the computing hardware (such as number of cores) being used, but still ensures that the number of users accessing the software at any one time does not exceed the limits specified in the software license. Software vendors are expected to continue to develop and implement new licensing models to address these and other trends in the future.

### Shareware

**Shareware** programs are software programs that are distributed on the honor system. Most shareware programs are available to try free of charge, but typically require a small fee if you choose to use the program regularly. By paying the requested registration fee, you can use the program for as long as you want to use it and may be entitled to product support, updates, and other benefits. You can legally and ethically copy shareware programs to pass along to friends and colleagues for evaluation purposes, but those individuals are expected to pay the shareware fee if they decide to keep the product.

Many shareware programs have a specified trial period, such as one month. Although it is not illegal to use shareware past the specified trial period, it is unethical to do so. Ethical use of shareware dictates either paying for the program or uninstalling it from your computer at the end of the trial period. Shareware is typically much less expensive than commercial versions of similar software because it is often developed by a single programmer and because it uses the shareware marketing system to sell directly to consumers (typically via a variety of software download sites, such as the one shown in Figure 6-3) with little or no packaging or advertising expenses. Shareware authors stress that the ethical use of shareware helps to cultivate this type of software distribution. Legally, shareware and demo versions of commercial software are similar, but shareware is typically not missing key features.

### Freeware

**Freeware** programs are software programs that are given away by the author for others to use free of charge. Although freeware is available without charge and can be shared with

**✔ FIGURE 6-3**
**Download sites.**

---

> **Shareware.** Copyrighted software that is distributed on the honor system; consumers should either pay for it or uninstall it after the trial period.
> **Freeware.** Copyrighted software that may be used free of charge.

others, the author retains the ownership rights to the program, so you cannot do anything with it—such as sell it or modify it—that is not expressly allowed by the author. Freeware programs are frequently developed by individuals; commercial software companies sometimes release freeware as well. Like shareware programs, freeware programs are widely available over the Internet. In fact, many apps available at the *app stores* used with mobile devices (see Figure 6-4) are freeware.

### Public Domain Software

**Public domain software** is not copyrighted; instead, the ownership rights to the program have been donated to the public domain. Consequently, it is free and can be used, copied, modified, and distributed to others without restrictions.

### Desktop vs. Mobile Software

Notebook computers, tablet computers, and other portable computers typically run the same application software as desktop computers. However, smartphones and other mobile devices (such as iPads and other tablets) typically require *mobile software* (also called *mobile apps*); that is, software specifically designed for a specific type of mobile device and operating system, such as an iPhone or Android tablet. A wide variety of apps are available today. For instance, there are mobile versions of popular programs like Word or PowerPoint, games and other entertainment apps, business and reference tools, calendars and communications apps, location-based apps, financial and banking apps, health and fitness apps, Web browsers, and more (see Figure 6-5). In fact, there are more than one million apps available via the *Google Play* store (shown in Figure 6-4) and the Apple *App Store*. Many mobile apps are available free of charge or for a minimal cost, such as 99 cents. For a look at a recent trend in mobile apps—mobile ticketing—see the Trend box.

In addition to having a more compact, efficient appearance, many mobile apps include features for easier data input, such as an on-screen keyboard, a phrase list, voice input capabilities, or handwriting recognition capabilities. Some mobile apps are designed to be compatible with popular *desktop software*, such as Microsoft Office; *Windows Apps* go one step further by being able to run on any Windows 10 device. Windows programs that run only on PCs are called *Windows desktop applications*; the desktop versions of the most common Microsoft Office programs are illustrated later in this chapter.

### Installed vs. Cloud Software

Software also differs in how it is accessed by the end user. It can be installed on and run from the end user's computer (or installed on and run from a network server in a network setting), or it can be cloud software that is accessed by the end user over the Internet.

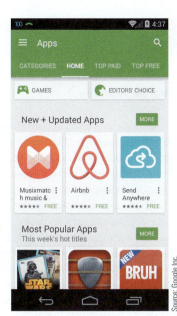

⚠ **FIGURE 6-4**
Many apps at app stores are freeware.

🔻 **FIGURE 6-5**
Mobile apps.

---

>**Public domain software.** Software that is not copyrighted and may be used without restriction.

# TREND

## Mobile Ticketing

A relatively new trend in mobile apps is *mobile ticketing*. Mobile ticketing goes beyond just using your smartphone or other mobile device to locate and purchase tickets that are then mailed to you. From concerts to sporting events to movie tickets, you can now use your mobile device as your admission ticket.

To buy a mobile ticket, you typically use a mobile app, such as an individual app for a particular application or organization (such as the *Fandango app* for movie tickets) or a generalized app (such as *StubHub*) for tickets to sporting events, concerts, and more. In either case, you use the app to select the desired event, date, time, and seat location, if applicable, and pay, and then your tickets are sent to your smartphone or tablet via e-mail or text message. Typically, mobile tickets have a barcode on them; to enter the venue, you just display the ticket on your mobile device for an attendant to scan. For example, the *mobile boarding pass* shown in the accompanying photo allows you to use your smartphone or tablet as your airline boarding pass at airport security checkpoints or at the gate during boarding. NFC mobile tickets are also available and are expected to be more common in the near future.

There are also Web sites (such as *InstantSeats*) that allow you to easily sell and distribute mobile tickets to custom events, such as a fundraiser or conference. You just publish an event (including details, ticket prices, and payment options) on the ticketing Web site and you're in business!

robert_s/Shutterstock.com; Source: American Airlines

---

**FIGURE 6-6**

**Installed software.**
Is often purchased via the Internet.

Source: Norton by Symantec

Once purchased, the installation program will be downloaded to the buyer's computer.

## Installed Software

**Installed software** must be installed on the device being used before it is run. Desktop software can be purchased in physical form (such as on a DVD) or downloaded via an app store (such as *Windows Store* or *Mac App Store*) or a Web site (such as the one shown in Figure 6-6); mobile software is almost always downloaded from an app store, such as the App Store or Google Play. In either case, the program is installed using its *installation program*. Once the software is installed, it is ready to use. Whether or not installed software requires a fee depends on whether the program is a commercial, demo/trial, shareware, freeware, or public domain program. For a look at an ongoing issue with software downloads today—crapware—see the Technology and You box.

## Cloud Software

Instead of being available in an installed format, some software is run directly from the Internet as **cloud software**, also referred to as *Web-based software*, *Software as a Service* (*SaaS*), and

---

> **Installed software.** Software that must be installed on a computer in order to be used. > **Cloud software.** Software that is delivered on demand via the Web; also referred to as Web-based software, Software as a Service (SaaS), and cloudware.

*cloudware.* Cloud software is delivered on demand via the Web to wherever the user is at the moment, provided he or she has an Internet connection (and has paid to use the software if a payment is required). The use of cloud software is growing rapidly and a recent study estimates that SaaS spending worldwide will exceed $100 billion in 2016. Typically, documents created using cloud software are stored online so that they are accessible via any Internet-enabled device.

There is a wide range of cloud software available (see Figure 6-7 for some examples). Some software is offered in both installed and cloud versions. For instance, the latest version of Microsoft Office is available as a traditional installed version (*Office 2016*) or a subscription-based cloud version (*Office 365*). There is also a free cloud version of Office available (called *Office Online* and shown in Figure 6-7). In addition, many business software services are offered as SaaS, including applications geared for collaboration, scheduling, customer service, accounting, project management, and more. Typically, business SaaS applications use a subscription (often per user, per month) pricing scheme. As it evolves, cloud software is beginning to move from single stand-alone applications to

**FIGURE 6-7**

**Cloud software.** Is commonly used with both computers and mobile devices.

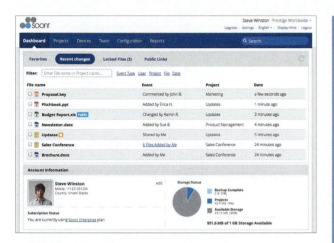

**BUSINESS SAAS APPLICATIONS**
This program allows you to share documents and collaborate on projects online.

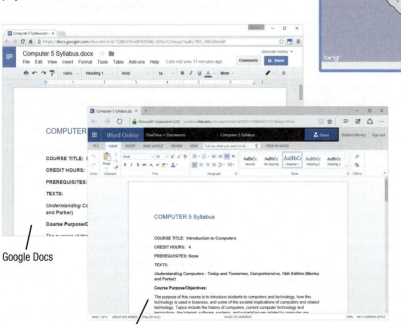

Google Docs

Office Online

**WEB DATABASE APPLICATIONS**
This application allows you to retrieve property information, such as home values and homes for sale.

**CLOUD PRODUCTIVITY APPLICATIONS**
These programs allow you to create documents online.

Source: Soonr; Zillow; Google Inc.

# TECHNOLOGY AND YOU

### Dealing with Crapware

*Crapware*, also called *bloatware*, most commonly refers to programs that are preinstalled on a new PC. With the costs of computers getting lower all the time, many computer manufacturers are accepting payments to preinstall third-party software on new PCs. So, while in the past, a new PC was fast and pristine, today it is often loaded with trial software that takes up valuable hard disk space and often slows down the system. With smartphones, crapware apps can also eat into your data use. Another way you can end up with crapware on your device is when it is bundled with a software program you download.

The crapware issue really came to light in 2015 when it was revealed that the *Superfish* software program, which PC manufacturer Lenovo included on new PCs, was a security risk. In addition to inserting its ads in the user's Web search results, Superfish exposed the user's Internet traffic to potential hackers. As a result of this fiasco, Lenovo and security companies released Superfish removal tools, but, by the time the tools were released, potentially millions of users were already at risk. This incident focused attention on the risks and ethics surrounding crapware.

You can avoid installing crapware by downloading software from the manufacturer's site whenever possible and by reading each installation screen carefully. If you see a screen indicating that other programs or services are being installed (see the accompanying screen shot taken during an Ad-Aware installation), uncheck the additional programs to prevent those programs from being installed or cancel the installation. For a new

PC, immediately uninstall the programs that you do not want and then run security scans (such as by using the free MalwareBytes program) and remove all programs identified as *PUPs* (*potentially unwanted programs*). Once you have uninstalled the crapware and have installed any new software you need, perform a full backup so you can restore your system back to this installation state (instead of the factory settings) if needed.

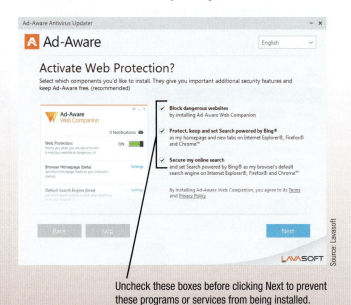

Uncheck these boxes before clicking Next to prevent these programs or services from being installed.

**Pay close attention to the options listed on installation screens to avoid installing crapware.**

---

**TIP**

A cloud version of LibreOffice is under development and is expected to be available by 2016.

groups of products that can work together to fulfill a wide variety of needs. For instance, the Google Docs Home page provides access to the Google Docs applications, but it also allows easy access to other Google online apps and services, such as Gmail, Calendar, Drive, Photos, and Web search.

One advantage of cloud software over installed software is that the programs and your files can be accessed from any computer with an Internet connection regardless of the type of computer or operating system used; some can also be accessed via a smartphone, tablet, or other type of Internet-enabled mobile device. This makes cloud software especially appropriate for applications like shared scheduling and collaboration applications that are time-critical because documents and other data can be shared regardless of an individual's location or device. Other advantages of cloud software include ease of implementation, potential lower cost of ownership, improved collaboration capabilities, and always working with the most current version of the software without having to perform software updates on company computers. In addition, cloud applications can easily interface with existing online databases, such as online maps and property records (for instance, the real estate applications accessible via the Zillow Web site shown in Figure 6-7 utilize maps, property record information, and real estate listing information pulled from various online databases).

Some potential disadvantages of cloud software are that online applications tend to run more slowly than applications stored on a local hard drive, that many online applications have a limit regarding the file size of the documents you create, and that the cost may eventually exceed the cost of buying a similar installed software program. In addition, you cannot access cloud software and your data if the server on which they reside goes down or if you are in a location with no Internet access, such as while traveling or in a rural area. To eliminate this last concern, a growing trend is for online applications to also function, at least in part, offline like installed software. For instance, Google Docs users can access the Google Docs applications and their documents locally on their computers, when needed. Edits are stored locally on the computer when a user is offline and, when the user reconnects to the Internet, the changes are synchronized with the documents stored on the Google Docs servers.

## Software Suites

Related software programs (such as a group of graphics programs, utility programs, or office-related software) are sometimes sold bundled together as a **software suite**. Businesses and many individuals often use *office suites*, sometimes called *productivity software suites*, to produce written documents. Typically, office suites contain the following programs:

> ➤ Word processing software—allows users to easily create and edit complex text-based documents that can also include images and other content.

> ➤ Spreadsheet software—provides users with a convenient means of creating documents containing complex mathematical calculations.

> ➤ Database software—allows users to store and organize vast amounts of data and retrieve specific information when needed.

> ➤ Presentation graphics software—allows users to create visual presentations to convey information more easily to others.

One of the most widely used office software suites is **Microsoft Office**. The latest version is Microsoft Office 2016 (called Office 365 when purchased as an online subscription). Similar suites are available from Corel (*WordPerfect Office* and *Corel Office*) and Apple (*iWork*). Free alternative installed office suites are *LibreOffice* and *Apache OpenOffice*; free cloud office suites include Google Docs and Office Online. Many office suites are available in a variety of versions, such as a home or student version that contains fewer programs than a professional version. Increasingly, software suites are becoming available for multiple operating systems. For example, Microsoft Office and LibreOffice are available for both Windows and OS X computers, as well as for Android and iOS devices (see Figure 6-8).

The primary advantages of using a software suite include a common interface among programs in the suite and a total cost that is often lower than buying the programs included in the suite individually. Although most programs written for the same operating system (such as Windows or OS X) use similar interfaces and commands, the entire command interface for a software suite is usually very

TIP

Some office suites also contain additional productivity tools, such as a calendar, an e-mail or a messaging program, or collaboration tools.

**FIGURE 6-8**

**Office suites.** Many suites, such as Microsoft Office shown here, are available for a variety of devices.

MacBook

iPad

Windows tablet

Android phone

Source: Microsoft Corporation

---

> **Software suite.** A collection of software programs bundled together and sold as a single software package. > **Microsoft Office.** One of the most widely used office software suites.

similar from program to program. This similarity is not only for basic commands (such as *Save* and *Print*) but also for all commands (such as adding borders and shading or inserting a row or column) that appear in more than one program in the suite. The standardization of the user interface across all programs in a suite means that once you are familiar with how to use one program in a suite, you will probably find it easy to learn another program in that suite.

## Common Software Commands

One of the greatest advantages of using software instead of paper and pencil to create a document is that you do not have to recreate the entire document when you want to make changes to it. This is because the document is created in RAM and then saved on a storage medium, instead of being created directly on paper. Consequently, the document can be retrieved, modified, saved, and printed as many times as needed. The types of commands used to perform these tasks are similar in most application programs; the most common ways to issue commands to application programs are discussed next.

### Toolbars, Menus, Keyboard Shortcuts, and the Ribbon

Most commands in an application program are issued through *menus*, *keyboard shortcuts*, or *command buttons* located on a toolbar or Ribbon. The *menu bar* appears at the top of many windows and contains text-based lists (menus), which provide access to commands that can be selected to perform actions in that program. Many programs also have *toolbars*—sets of icons or command buttons that are selected with the mouse, pen, or finger to issue commands. To save time, many programs support **keyboard shortcuts**, which are key combinations that correspond to specific commands, such as [Ctrl]+[S] for the Save command (this keyboard shortcut is issued by holding down the Ctrl key and pressing the S key). A list of common keyboard shortcuts used in Microsoft Office and many other programs is shown in Figure 6-9, along with examples of the command buttons typically used to perform these operations and a description of each operation. As shown in this figure, some keyboard shortcuts include function keys, such as [Alt]+[F4] to close a document.

**FIGURE 6-9**
Common application software commands.

| COMMAND | COMMAND BUTTON | KEYBOARD SHORTCUT | DESCRIPTION |
|---|---|---|---|
| Open |  | [Ctrl]+[O] | Opens a dialog box so you can choose a saved document to open from a storage medium so it can be edited or printed. |
| Save |  | [Ctrl]+[S] | Saves the current version of the document to a storage medium. |
| Print |  | [Ctrl]+[P] | Prints the current version of the document onto paper. |
| Cut |  | [Ctrl]+[X] | Moves the selected item to the Clipboard. |
| Copy |  | [Ctrl]+[C] | Copies the selected item to the Clipboard. |
| Paste |  | [Ctrl]+[V] | Pastes the last item copied or cut to the Clipboard to the current location. |
| Undo |  | [Ctrl]+[Z] | Undoes the last change to the document. |
| Close |  | [Alt]+[F4] | Closes the document. Any changes made to the document are lost if the document wasn't saved first. |

>**Keyboard shortcut.** A combination of keyboard keys that are pressed in unison to issue a specific software command.

**FILE TAB**
Contains common document commands, such as Save and Print.

**QUICK ACCESS TOOLBAR**
Contains command buttons for frequently used commands; can be modified by the user.

**TABS**
Organize related groups of commands; the Home tab is currently selected.

**TELL ME BOX**
Suggests a Ribbon command or provides help related to the description you type.

**SIGN IN/SHARE**
Used to store documents online and collaborate with others, respectively.

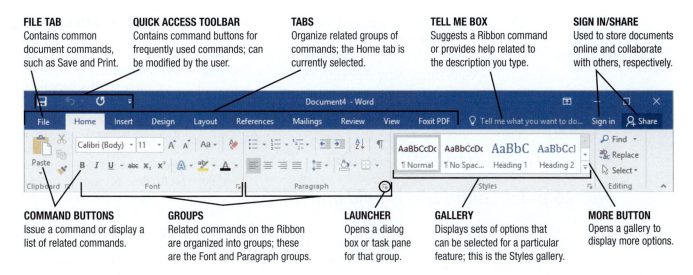

**COMMAND BUTTONS**
Issue a command or display a list of related commands.

**GROUPS**
Related commands on the Ribbon are organized into groups; these are the Font and Paragraph groups.

**LAUNCHER**
Opens a dialog box or task pane for that group.

**GALLERY**
Displays sets of options that can be selected for a particular feature; this is the Styles gallery.

**MORE BUTTON**
Opens a gallery to display more options.

**FIGURE 6-10**
The Microsoft Office Ribbon.

The **Ribbon** is a tool in recent versions of Microsoft Office, starting with Office 2007. The Ribbon (see Figure 6-10) consists of *tabs*, which contain *groups* of related command buttons for the program being used. For convenience, most programs have a *Home tab* that contains the most frequently used commands in that program. In addition to the standard Ribbon tabs that are available whenever the program is open, additional *contextual tabs* are displayed as needed, depending on the action being taken. For instance, selecting a picture or other graphic in Word displays the *Picture Tools tab* that contains commands you might use to edit a picture, such as to crop, resize, rotate, or recolor the picture. Clicking a command button on the Ribbon either carries out that command or displays a *gallery* of choices from which the user can select the desired action. The *File tab* replaces the Microsoft Office Button and the File menu used in older versions of Office and opens the *Backstage*, which contains commands commonly used with all documents, such as to open, save, print, or share a document.

> **TIP**
>
> Right-click a command button on the Ribbon and select *Add to Quick Access Toolbar* to add that command to your Quick Access toolbar.

### Editing a Document

**Editing** a document refers to changing the content of the document, such as adding or deleting text or moving a block of text from one location in a document to another location in that document. Most application programs that allow text editing have an **insertion point** that looks like a blinking vertical line on the screen and shows where the next change will be made to the document currently displayed on the screen. To insert text, just start typing and the text will appear at the insertion point location. To delete text, press the Delete key to delete one character to the right of the insertion point or press the Backspace key to delete one character to the left of the insertion point. If the insertion point is not in the proper location for the edit, it must be moved to the appropriate location in the document by using the arrow keys on the keyboard or by pointing and selecting that location with the mouse, pen, or finger. To select an object or block of text, click the object or drag over the text. Usually, once an object or some text is selected, it can be manipulated, such as to be moved, deleted, copied, or *formatted*.

> **Ribbon.** A feature found in recent versions of Microsoft Office that uses tabs to organize groups of related commands. > **Editing.** Changing the content of a document, such as inserting or deleting words. > **Insertion point.** An on-screen character that looks like a blinking vertical line; indicates the current location in a document, which is where the next change will be made.

This is 10-point Arial.

This is 12-point Times New Roman.

*This is 16-point Lucida Handwriting.*

This is 20-point Calibri.

**This 16-point Calibri text is bold and italic.**

This 16-point Calibri text is red and underlined.

**FIGURE 6-11**

**Fonts.** The font face, size, style, and color used with text can be specified in many application programs.

## Formatting a Document

While editing changes the actual content of a document, **formatting** changes the appearance of the document. One common type of formatting is changing the appearance of selected text in a document. You can change the *font face* or *typeface* (a named collection of text characters that share a common design, such as Calibri or Times New Roman), *font size* (which is measured in *points*), *font style* (such as bold, italic, or underline), and *font color* (see Figure 6-11). Other common types of formatting include changing the line spacing or margins of a document; adding page numbers; and adding shading or borders to a paragraph, image, or other item; formatting is discussed in more detail shortly.

## Getting Help

Most people have an occasional question or otherwise need some help as they work with a software program. There are various options for getting help when you need it. For instance, most application programs have a built-in help feature, typically available through a *Help button* or a *Help* option on a menu. The type and amount of built-in help available varies from program to program, but typically includes one or more of the following forms.

➤ *Table of Contents*—works much like the table of contents in a book; that is, with related help topics organized under main topics. With most help systems, selecting a main topic reveals the subtopics related to that main topic; subtopics can then be selected until the desired help topic is displayed. Selecting a help topic displays information related to that topic on the screen.

➤ *Browsing*—allows you to click hyperlinks related to major help categories, similar to a Table of Contents but each time a topic is clicked, a new page containing links appears, similar to the way Web pages work. Clicking a link representing a help topic displays information related to that topic on the screen.

## ASK THE EXPERT

**LibreOffice** The Document Foundation

**Cor Nouws,** Founding Member and Volunteer Contributor, The Document Foundation

**Can a student use the free LibreOffice office suite at home and the Microsoft Office suite at school for the same documents?**

Yes, absolutely. You can save LibreOffice documents in many different formats, including Microsoft Office (such as .docx or .doc for word processing documents or .xlsx or .xls for spreadsheet files), as well as CorelDraw and Visio. While some formatting can be lost in the translation process between file formats, most features that you use in LibreOffice are also found in Office.

For complex documents, you can use styles, tables, and other formatting features to help your work look the same in both programs. You can also save your documents in either suite using the OpenDocument (ODF) file formats.

>**Formatting.** Changing the appearance of a document, such as changing the margins or font size.

➤ *Search*—allows you to search for help topics by typing a keyword or phrase, and then the help system displays a list of links to possible matching help topics; clicking a help topic link displays information related to that topic on the screen (see Figure 6-12).

Some help systems automatically search for online help from the manufacturer's Web site if the program detects an Internet connection. In addition, there is a vast amount of additional information about application software programs available via the Web, such as online articles, tutorials, and forums for particular software programs, as well as e-mail support from software companies. Of course, online and offline books are also available for many software programs.

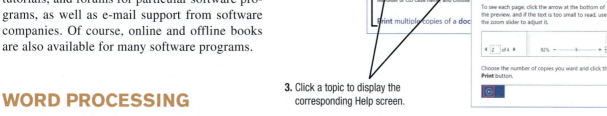

1. Type search terms here.

2. Matching help content is then displayed.

3. Click a topic to display the corresponding Help screen.

**FIGURE 6-12**

**Getting help.** Most application programs have built-in help systems.

# WORD PROCESSING CONCEPTS

Word processing is one of the most widely used application programs today. Although the actual commands and features vary somewhat from program to program, it is important to be familiar with the general concept of what word processing enables you to do, as well as the basic features of word processing. The following sections discuss these concepts and features.

## What Is Word Processing?

**Word processing** refers to using a computer and **word processing software** to create, edit, save, and print written documents, such as letters, contracts, manuscripts, newsletters, invoices, marketing material, and reports. At its most basic level, word processing is used to do what was done on a typewriter before computers were commonplace. Many documents created with word processing software also include content that was not possible to create using a typewriter, such as photos, drawn objects, clip art images, hyperlinks, video clips, and text in a variety of sizes and appearances. Like any document created with software instead of paper and pencil, word processing documents can be retrieved, modified, and printed as many times as needed.

Word processing programs today typically include improved collaboration, security, and *rights-management tools* (tools used to protect original content from misuse by others). Rights management and intellectual property rights are discussed in more detail in Chapter 13; digital signatures, encryption, and other security tools that can be used to secure word processing documents are discussed in Chapter 9. Word processing programs today also typically include a variety of Web-related tools, as well as support for speech, pen, and touch input. For a look at how to use gesture input with Microsoft Word and other Microsoft Office programs on touch screen devices, see the How It Works box.

**TIP** ✓

To open Help in Office 2016, click the File tab and then click the question mark located near the upper right corner.

**TIP** ✓

When selecting font size in a document, 72 points equals one-inch-tall text.

> **Word processing.** Using a computer and word processing software to create, edit, save, and print written documents, such as letters, contracts, and manuscripts. > **Word processing software.** Application software used to create, edit, save, and print written documents.

# HOW IT WORKS

## Gesture Input with Microsoft Office

The newest versions of Word and other Microsoft Office products support gestures on touch screen devices.

You may wonder if using touch can be handy in Office applications. The answer is yes. But, before you can use touch gestures in Office programs, you need to master a few basic gestures (see the following table and the illustrations below).

| GESTURE | HOW TO PERFORM | USE IN OFFICE |
|---------|----------------|---------------|
| *Tap* | Using one finger, tap the screen in the appropriate location (tap twice for a *double-tap*). | Similar to clicking with the mouse. Examples:<br>➤ Move the insertion point (to the location where you tap).<br>➤ Select/open what you tap (such as a Ribbon tab or button, or the Show Keyboard button).<br>➤ Select text (tap in the desired text and then drag a selection handle).<br>➤ Select multiple objects (tap and hold the first object, then tap other objects).<br>➤ Resize/rotate an object (tap and then drag the resize/rotate handle). |
| *Press and hold* | Press one finger down on the screen and leave it there for a few seconds. | Similar to right-clicking with the mouse. Examples:<br>➤ Show information about the selected item.<br>➤ Open a menu specific to the item and what you are doing. |
| *Slide* | Using one finger, touch the appropriate location on the screen and move your finger across the screen. | Similar to scrolling or dragging with the mouse. Examples:<br>➤ Scroll the contents of the screen.<br>➤ Move an object (tap and hold on an object and then drag it to the appropriate new location). |
| *Swipe* | Using one finger, touch the appropriate location on the screen and move your finger across the screen a short distance; also called a *flick*. | Show more options/items (such as when swiping a Gallery). |
| *Pinch* | Using two or more fingers, touch the appropriate location on the screen and move your fingers closer together. | Zoom in on your document. |
| *Stretch* | Using two or more fingers, touch the appropriate location on the screen and move your fingers farther apart. | Zoom out on your document. |

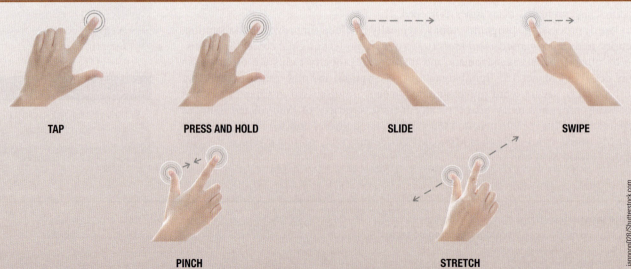

TAP          PRESS AND HOLD          SLIDE          SWIPE

PINCH                    STRETCH

jannoon028/Shutterstock.com

Virtually all formal writing today is performed using a word processing program. Among today's most frequently used word processing programs are *Microsoft Word, Corel WordPerfect, Google Docs,* and *Apple Pages* (all part of software suites). Most word processing programs offer hundreds of features, but virtually all support a core group of features used to create, edit, and format documents. Some of these basic features are described in the next few sections, using Microsoft Word 2016 as the example. Recent versions of Word save documents using the *.docx* extension by default, although other file formats (including the original *.doc* Word format for files that may need to be opened in older versions of Word, the more universal *Rich Text Format* (*.rtf*) and *OpenDocument* formats, the standardized *Portable Document* (*PDF*) format, and several Web page formats) can be used instead when needed.

## Creating a Word Processing Document

Every word processing program contains an assortment of operations for creating and editing documents, including commands to insert text, graphics, and other items, and then move, copy, delete, or otherwise edit the content, as needed. Some features in a typical word processing program are shown in Figure 6-13.

When entering text in a word processing document, it is important to know when to press the Enter key. Word processing programs use a feature called **word wrap**, which means the insertion point automatically moves to the beginning of the next line when the

**FIGURE 6-13**
**Some features in a typical word processing program.**

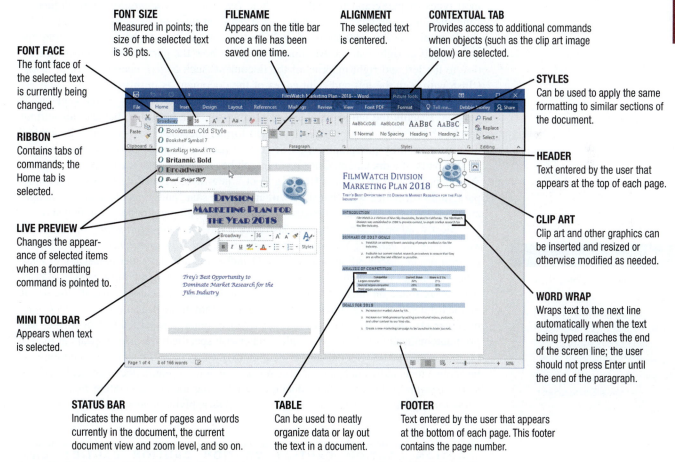

**FONT SIZE**
Measured in points; the size of the selected text is 36 pts.

**FILENAME**
Appears on the title bar once a file has been saved one time.

**ALIGNMENT**
The selected text is centered.

**CONTEXTUAL TAB**
Provides access to additional commands when objects (such as the clip art image below) are selected.

**FONT FACE**
The font face of the selected text is currently being changed.

**RIBBON**
Contains tabs of commands; the Home tab is selected.

**LIVE PREVIEW**
Changes the appearance of selected items when a formatting command is pointed to.

**MINI TOOLBAR**
Appears when text is selected.

**STYLES**
Can be used to apply the same formatting to similar sections of the document.

**HEADER**
Text entered by the user that appears at the top of each page.

**CLIP ART**
Clip art and other graphics can be inserted and resized or otherwise modified as needed.

**WORD WRAP**
Wraps text to the next line automatically when the text being typed reaches the end of the screen line; the user should not press Enter until the end of the paragraph.

**STATUS BAR**
Indicates the number of pages and words currently in the document, the current document view and zoom level, and so on.

**TABLE**
Can be used to neatly organize data or lay out the text in a document.

**FOOTER**
Text entered by the user that appears at the bottom of each page. This footer contains the page number.

>**Word wrap.** The feature in a word processing program that automatically returns the insertion point to the next line when the end of the screen line is reached.

end of the screen line is reached. Consequently, the Enter key should not be pressed until it is time to begin a new paragraph or leave a blank line. With word wrap, when changes are made to the document—such as adding, modifying, or deleting text or changing the text size or page margins—the program will automatically adjust the amount of text on each screen line, as long as the Enter key was not pressed at the end of each line.

In most word processing programs, formatting can be applied at the character, paragraph, and document levels. *Character formatting* changes the appearance of individual characters, such as to change the font face, size, style, or color. To format characters, you usually select them and then apply the appropriate format. In recent versions of Word, for instance, you can use the command buttons on the Ribbon's Home tab or the *Mini toolbar* (which appears when text is selected and is designed to allow easy text formatting). To see additional character formatting options, click the *Launcher* (a small arrow at the lower-right corner of the *Font group* on the Home tab) to open the *Font dialog box*. As shown in Figure 6-13, Word includes a *Live Preview* feature, which allows the user to see the results of many formatting commands before they are applied, such as watching selected text change as the user scrolls through a list of font faces or sizes.

*Paragraph formatting* changes an entire paragraph at one time, such as specifying the line spacing for a particular paragraph. To format paragraphs, you usually select the paragraph and then apply the appropriate format. In Word, for instance, you can use the command buttons in the *Paragraph group* on the Ribbon's Home tab or you can click the Launcher in the *Paragraph group* to open the *Paragraph dialog box*. The most common types of paragraph formatting include *line spacing*, *indentation*, and *alignment*. Line spacing is the amount of blank space between lines of text—usually set to 1 for single spacing or 2 for double spacing. Indentation is the distance between the paragraph and the left or right margin. Alignment indicates how the paragraph is aligned in relation to the left and right margins of the document, such as *left*, *center*, *right*, or *justify* (flush with both the left and right edges of the document as in this textbook). *Tabs* are set locations to which the insertion point is moved when the Tab key on the keyboard is pressed. Usually the tab settings are preset to every one-half inch, but the tab settings can be changed by the user. *Styles*—named format specifications—can also be applied on a paragraph-by-paragraph basis. Styles are used to keep a uniform appearance for related parts of a document. Once a paragraph has been assigned a style (such as one of Word's predefined styles, like Heading 1, or a new style defined by the user), all other paragraphs formatted with that style will appear the same and, if any formatting changes are made to the style, those changes will be applied to all paragraphs using that style.

Most word processing programs also have a variety of *page formatting* options, such as changing the *margins*, the *paper size* being used, and *page orientation*—the traditional *portrait orientation* is 8.5 inches wide by 11 inches tall and the wider *landscape orientation* is 11 inches wide by 8.5 inches tall. In recent versions of Word, most page formatting options are found on the *Page Layout tab* on the Ribbon. You can also use the *Insert tab* on the Ribbon to add page numbers at the top or bottom of the page, or to specify a *header* or *footer*. As shown in Figure 6-13, a header or a footer is specified text or images that print automatically on every page unless otherwise specified; a header appears at the top of every page and a footer appears at the bottom of every page. Many of these options can be applied to an individual page as page formatting or to the entire document (called *document formatting*). Other types of document formatting include generating *footnotes* and *endnotes*, a *table of contents*, or an *index*, as well as applying a *background* or a *theme* to the entire document.

**CAUTION** CAUTION CAUTION CAUTION CAUTION CAUTION CAUT

To avoid the embarrassment of distributing a document with hidden text, internal comments, personal information, and other data you may not want to pass on to others, click *File*, *Info*, *Check for Issues*, and then *Inspect Document* to check for and remove this data before distribution.

**INSERT TAB**
Used to insert a table, picture, shape, or other object into the document.

**TABLE TOOLS CONTEXTUAL TABS**
Used to change the design or layout of a table; available only when a table is selected.

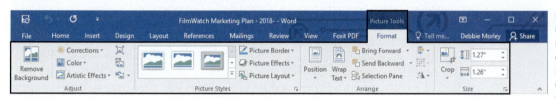

**PICTURE TOOLS CONTEXTUAL TAB**
Used to format a picture object, such as to crop it or change its size, color, or border; available only when an image is selected.

## Tables, Graphics, and Templates

Most word processing programs today have advanced features to help users create documents or add special features to documents. For instance, a *table* feature allows content to be organized in a table consisting of *rows* and *columns*. Tables can be used to organize basic data, such as the table shown in Figure 6-13; they can also be used to lay out documents, such as when creating a newsletter, résumé, or Web page. Once a table has been created, shading, borders, and other formatting can be applied to the table and/or its contents, and rows and columns can be inserted or deleted, as needed. There are a number of Ribbon tabs that can be used in Word to help users insert and modify tables. For instance, the Insert tab (shown in Figure 6-14) is used to insert tables (as well as pictures, shapes, charts, text boxes, and other objects). Once a table is created and selected, the *Table Tools* contextual tabs (*Design* and *Layout*—Layout is the active tab in Figure 6-14) appear on the Ribbon and contain commands that can be used to modify the table.

Graphics or drawing features are also commonly found in word processing programs. Virtually all word processing programs allow images (such as a photograph, a drawing from another program, a geometric shape, or a *clip art image* like the one in Figure 6-13) to be inserted into a document. Once an image is inserted into a document, it can be modified (such as changing the brightness or contrast of a digital photo, cropping an image, converting a color image to grayscale, compressing an image to reduce the file size of the document, or adding borders). The *Picture Tools* contextual tab, which is used in Word for these purposes and is displayed on the Ribbon whenever an image is selected, is shown in Figure 6-14. Once images are inserted into a document, they can be copied, moved, deleted, or otherwise modified, just like any other object in the document.

To help users create new documents quickly, many word processing programs have a variety of *templates* available. A template is a document that is already created and formatted to fit a particular purpose, such as a fax cover sheet, résumé, memo, calendar, invoice, newsletter, or Web page. Usually placeholder text is included for text that can be customized so that all the user needs to do is to replace that text with the appropriate content.

## Word Processing and the Web

Most word processing programs today include Web-related features, such as the ability to send a document as an e-mail message or post to a blog via the word processing program, the inclusion of Web page hyperlinks in documents, and the ability to create or modify Web pages. The latest versions of Office also include the ability to collaborate with others online, as well as stream Office apps from and store Office documents in the cloud.

**FIGURE 6-14**
**Ribbon tabs used to insert and modify tables and images.**

**TIP**
When using a table for layout purposes, change the table borders to *None* after the document is finished to make the table outline invisible.

**TIP**
Additional templates are often available free of charge through software manufacturer Web sites, such as Microsoft's *Office.com* Web site.

**TIP**
To open the Web page associated with a hyperlink included in a document (assuming you have an active Internet connection), hold down the Ctrl key and then click the hyperlink.

# SPREADSHEET CONCEPTS

Another widely used application program is spreadsheet software. Spreadsheet software is commonly used by a variety of businesses and employees, including CEOs, managers, assistants, analysts, and sales representatives. Basic spreadsheet concepts and features are described next.

## What Is a Spreadsheet?

A **spreadsheet** is a group of values and other data organized into rows and columns, similar to the ruled paper worksheets traditionally used by bookkeepers and accountants. **Spreadsheet software** is the type of application software used to create computerized spreadsheets, which typically contain a great deal of numbers and mathematical calculations. Most spreadsheets include formulas that are used to compute calculations based on data entered into the spreadsheet. All formula results are updated automatically whenever any changes are made to the data. Consequently, no manual computations are required, which increases accuracy. In addition, the automatic recalculation of formulas allows individuals to modify spreadsheet data as often as necessary either to create new spreadsheets or to experiment with various possible scenarios (called what-if analysis, as discussed shortly) to help make business decisions. Spreadsheet software typically includes a variety of data analysis tools, as well as the ability to generate charts.

The most widely used spreadsheet programs today are *Microsoft Excel*, *Corel Quattro Pro* (which is part of the WordPerfect Office X7 Professional Edition), *Google Sheets*, and *Apple Numbers* (all are part of their respective software suites). Some of the basic features supported by all spreadsheet programs are described in the next few sections, using Microsoft Excel 2016 as the example. Recent versions of Excel save spreadsheet files with the *.xlsx* extension by default.

## Creating a Spreadsheet

A single spreadsheet document is often called a **worksheet**. Most spreadsheet programs allow multiple worksheets to be saved together in a single spreadsheet file, called a **workbook**. Worksheets are divided into **rows** and **columns**. The intersection of a row and a column is called a **cell**. Each cell is identified by its *cell address*, which consists of the column letter followed by the row number, such as B4 or E22. The *cell pointer* is used to select a cell; the selected cell is called the *active cell* or *current cell* and has a border around it so it is easy to identify. You can enter content into the active cell, as well as apply formatting to content already in the active cell. The cell pointer can be used to select more than one cell; if so, the selected cells are called a *range* or *block*. Ranges are always rectangular and are identified by specifying two opposite corners of the range, such as D8 through E9 for the four cells in the range shown in Figure 6-15 (and usually typed as *D8:E9* or *D8..E9*, depending on the spreadsheet program being used). As with Word, the Excel interface uses the Ribbon, contextual tabs, the Mini toolbar, and Live Preview for editing and formatting.

## Entering Data into a Spreadsheet Cell

Data is entered directly into worksheet cells by clicking a cell to make it the active cell and then typing the data to be contained in that cell. The contents of the active cell can be erased by pressing the Delete key or by typing new content, which replaces the old contents of that cell. The data entered into a cell is usually a label, a constant value, a formula,

>**Spreadsheet.** A document containing a group of values and other data organized into rows and columns. >**Spreadsheet software.** Application software used to create spreadsheets, which typically contain a great deal of numbers and mathematical computations organized into rows and columns.
>**Worksheet.** A single spreadsheet document in a spreadsheet program. >**Workbook.** A collection of worksheets saved in a single spreadsheet file.
>**Row.** In a spreadsheet program, a horizontal group of cells on a worksheet. >**Column.** In a spreadsheet program, a vertical group of cells on a worksheet.
>**Cell.** The location at the intersection of a row and column on a worksheet into which data can be typed.

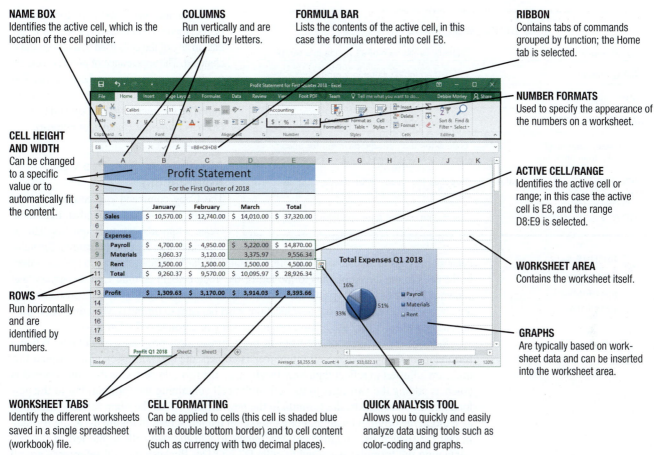

**NAME BOX**
Identifies the active cell, which is the location of the cell pointer.

**COLUMNS**
Run vertically and are identified by letters.

**FORMULA BAR**
Lists the contents of the active cell, in this case the formula entered into cell E8.

**RIBBON**
Contains tabs of commands grouped by function; the Home tab is selected.

**NUMBER FORMATS**
Used to specify the appearance of the numbers on a worksheet.

**CELL HEIGHT AND WIDTH**
Can be changed to a specific value or to automatically fit the content.

**ACTIVE CELL/RANGE**
Identifies the active cell or range; in this case the active cell is E8, and the range D8:E9 is selected.

**WORKSHEET AREA**
Contains the worksheet itself.

**ROWS**
Run horizontally and are identified by numbers.

**GRAPHS**
Are typically based on work-sheet data and can be inserted into the worksheet area.

**WORKSHEET TABS**
Identify the different worksheets saved in a single spreadsheet (workbook) file.

**CELL FORMATTING**
Can be applied to cells (this cell is shaded blue with a double bottom border) and to cell content (such as currency with two decimal places).

**QUICK ANALYSIS TOOL**
Allows you to quickly and easily analyze data using tools such as color-coding and graphs.

**FIGURE 6-15**
Some features in a typical spreadsheet program.

**FIGURE 6-16**
Universal mathematical operators.

| SYMBOL | OPERATION |
| --- | --- |
| + | Addition |
| − | Subtraction |
| * | Multiplication |
| / | Division |
| ^ | Exponentiation |

or a function. **Labels** are words, column headings, and other nonmathematical data, such as *Profit Statement* and *January* in Figure 6-15. **Constant values** are numbers (such as *105* or *12740.25*) and are entered into a cell without any additional characters (such as a dollar sign or comma). A **formula** performs mathematical operations using the content of other cells (such as adding or multiplying the values in the specified cells) and displays the result in the cell containing the formula. A **function** is a named, preprogrammed formula, such as to compute the average of a group of cells or to calculate a mortgage payment amount. There are literally hundreds of functions that can be used in spreadsheets for statistical, engineering, math, logical, and text-based computations. The standard mathematical operators used in formulas and functions are shown in Figure 6-16; some examples of commonly used spreadsheet functions are listed in Figure 6-17 on the next page.

When entering a formula or function into a cell, most spreadsheet programs require that you begin with some type of mathematical symbol—usually the equal sign (=). You can then enter the cell addresses and mathematical operators to create the formula, or you can type the appropriate function name and *arguments* (such as a cell or range address). When creating formulas and functions, it is important to always use the cell addresses of the numbers you want to include in the calculation (such as =B8+C8+D8 for the formula used to calculate the value displayed in cell E8 in Figure 6-15), rather than the numbers themselves (such as =4700+4950+5220). If the actual numbers are used in a formula instead of the cell addresses, the result of that formula (such as the total in cell E8) will not be correctly updated if one of the numbers (such as January payroll expenses in cell B8) is changed. When a proper formula (using the cell references instead of

> **Label.** A text-based entry in a worksheet cell that identifies data on the worksheet. > **Constant value.** A numerical entry in a worksheet cell.
> **Formula.** An entry in a worksheet cell that performs computations on worksheet data and displays the results. > **Function.** A named formula that can be entered into a worksheet cell to perform some type of calculation or to extract information from other cells in the worksheet.

| EXAMPLES OF FUNCTIONS | |
|---|---|
| =SUM(range) | Calculates the sum of all values in a range. |
| =MAX(range) | Finds the highest value in a range. |
| =MIN(range) | Finds the lowest value in a range. |
| =AVERAGE(range) | Calculates the average of values in a range. |
| =PMT(rate, number of payments, loan amount) | Calculates the periodic payment for a loan. |
| =IF(conditional expression, value if true, value if false) | Supplies the values to be displayed if the conditional expression is true or if it is false. |
| =NOW( ) | Inserts the current date and time. |

**FIGURE 6-17**

Common spreadsheet functions.

**FIGURE 6-18**

Relative vs. absolute cell referencing.

the actual numbers) is used, the formula will be recomputed automatically every time any data in any of the cells used in that formula is changed. The appearance of numeric content (such as constant values or the result of a formula or numeric function) in a cell is determined by the *number format* applied to a cell (such as *Currency*, *Comma*, or *Percent*).

## Absolute vs. Relative Cell Referencing

The Copy command can be used to copy content from one cell to another, in order to create a spreadsheet more quickly. This is especially true for cells containing formulas because the cells in a column or row often contain similar formulas (such as to add the values in the cells in the three columns to the left of the Total cells in column E in the spreadsheet shown in Figure 6-15) and typing formulas can be time consuming. Labels and constant values are always copied exactly to the new location; what happens to formulas when they are copied depends on whether they use relative cell referencing or absolute cell referencing.

*Relative cell references* are used in most spreadsheet programs by default. When a formula containing relative cell references is copied, the cell addresses in the copied formula are adjusted to reflect their new location, so the formula performs the same operation (such as adding the two cells to the left of the cell containing the formula) but in the new location. In other words, the formula in the new location does the same *relative* operation as it did in the original location. For example, in the left screen in Figure 6-18, the formula in cell D2 (which uses relative cell references to add the two cells to the left of the cell containing the formula) is copied to cells D3 and D4. Because the cell references are all relative, when the formula is copied to the new cells, the cell references are adjusted to continue to add the two cells to the left of the cell containing the formula. For instance, the formula in cell D3 is updated automatically to =B3+C3 and the formula in cell D4 is

**COPYING WITH RELATIVE CELL REFERENCES**
In most formulas, cell addresses are relative and will be adjusted as the formula is copied.

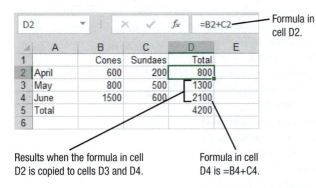

Formula in cell D2.

Results when the formula in cell D2 is copied to cells D3 and D4.

Formula in cell D4 is =B4+C4.

**COPYING WITH ABSOLUTE CELL REFERENCES**
A dollar sign ($) marks a cell reference as absolute; it will be copied exactly as it appears in the source cell.

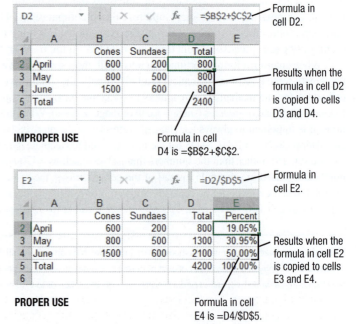

Formula in cell D2.

Results when the formula in cell D2 is copied to cells D3 and D4.

**IMPROPER USE**

Formula in cell D4 is =$B$2+$C$2.

Formula in cell E2.

Results when the formula in cell E2 is copied to cells E3 and E4.

**PROPER USE**

Formula in cell E4 is =D4/$D$5.

updated automatically to =B4+C4. Relative cell references are also adjusted automatically when a row or column is inserted or deleted.

In contrast, when *absolute cell references* are used, formulas are copied exactly as they are written (see the rightmost screens in Figure 6-18). It is appropriate to use an absolute cell reference when you want to use a specific cell address in all copies of the formula—such as always multiplying by a constant value (perhaps a sales tax rate located in a particular cell on the worksheet) or always dividing by a total in order to compute a percentage. In other words, whenever you do not want a cell address to be adjusted when the formula is copied, you must use an absolute cell reference in the formula. To make a cell reference in a formula absolute, a special symbol—usually a dollar sign ($)—is placed before each column letter and row number that should not change. For example, both of the cell references in the formula in cell D2 in the upper-right screen in Figure 6-18 are absolute, resulting in the formula =$B$2+$C$2 being placed in both cells D3 and D4 when the formula is copied. Obviously, this is not the correct formula for these cells—the formula in cell D2 needs to use relative cell references for both cell references in order to display the proper totals in cells D3 and D4 when the formula is copied to those cells. In cells E2 through E4 in the lower-right screen, however, an absolute cell reference is correctly used for cell D5 (and written as $D$5) in order to divide the total sales for each month (located in cells D2, D3, and D4, respectively) by the total sales for all three months (located in cell D5) to compute the percent of total sales. The reference to cell D5 must be absolute if the formula in cell E2 is to be copied to other cells because the denominator in that formula should always be the value in D5.

## Charts and What-If Analysis

Most spreadsheet programs include some type of *charting* or *graphing* capability. Because the data to be included in many business charts is often already located on a spreadsheet, using that program's charting feature eliminates reentering that data into another program. Instead, the cells containing the data to be charted are selected, and then the type of chart—as well as titles and other customizations—can be specified. Charts are inserted into an Excel spreadsheet using the commands in the *Charts group* on the Insert tab on the Ribbon. Finished charts (like the one included in the spreadsheet shown in Figure 6-15) can be moved like other graphical objects to the desired location on the worksheet. Selecting an existing chart displays two *Chart Tools* contextual tabs on the Ribbon. These tabs can be used to change the design or format of the chart.

Because spreadsheet programs automatically recalculate all formulas on a worksheet every time the content of a cell on the worksheet is edited, spreadsheet programs are particularly useful for *what-if analysis* (also called *sensitivity analysis*)—a tool frequently used to help make business decisions. For example, suppose you want to know *what* profit would have resulted for January in Figure 6-15 *if* sales had been $15,000 instead of $10,570. You can simply enter the new value (15000) into cell B5, and the spreadsheet program automatically recalculates all formulas, allowing you to determine (from looking at the new value in cell B13) that the profit would have been $5,739.63. This ability to enter new numbers and immediately see the result allows businesspeople to run through many more possibilities in a shorter period of time before making decisions than in the past when all such calculations had to be performed by hand. Another type of sensitivity analysis (called *goal seeking* in Microsoft Excel) involves having the spreadsheet compute the amount a constant value would need to be in order for the result of a particular formula to become a specified amount (such as the total sales required to obtain a January profit of $5,000 if all of the expenses stayed the same).

## Spreadsheets and the Web

As with word processors, most spreadsheet programs have built-in Web capabilities. Although they are used less commonly to create Web pages, many spreadsheet programs include the option to save the current worksheet as a Web page, and hyperlinks can be inserted into worksheet cells. Microsoft Excel includes the ability to send a workbook as an e-mail message and to collaborate online; ranges of cells can also be copied to a Web publishing or word processing program to insert spreadsheet data into a document as a table.

# DATABASE CONCEPTS

People often need to retrieve specific data rapidly while on the job. For example, a customer service representative may need to locate a customer's order status quickly while the customer is on the telephone. The registrar at a university may have to look up a student's grade point average or rapidly determine if the student has any outstanding fees before processing his or her class registration. A librarian may need to determine if a particular book is available to check out and, if not, when it is scheduled to be returned. The type of software used for such tasks is a database management system. Computer-based database management systems are rapidly replacing the paper-based filing systems that people used in the past to find information. The most common type of database used with personal computers today is a relational database. The basic features and concepts of this type of database software are discussed next. Relational databases and other types of database programs are discussed in detail in Chapter 12.

## What Is a Database?

A **database** is a collection of related data that is stored on a computer and organized in a manner that enables information to be retrieved as needed. A *database management system* (*DBMS*)—also called **database software**—is the type of program used to create, maintain, and organize data in a database, as well as to retrieve information from it. Typically data in a database is organized into fields, records, and files. A **field** (today more commonly called a **column**) is a single type of data, such as last name or telephone number, to be stored in a database. A **record** (today more commonly called a **row**) is a collection of related fields—for example, the ID number, name, address, and major of Phyllis Hoffman (see Figure 6-19).

**FIGURE 6-19**

**Paper-based vs. computerized databases.** Data is organized into fields (columns), records (rows), and tables.

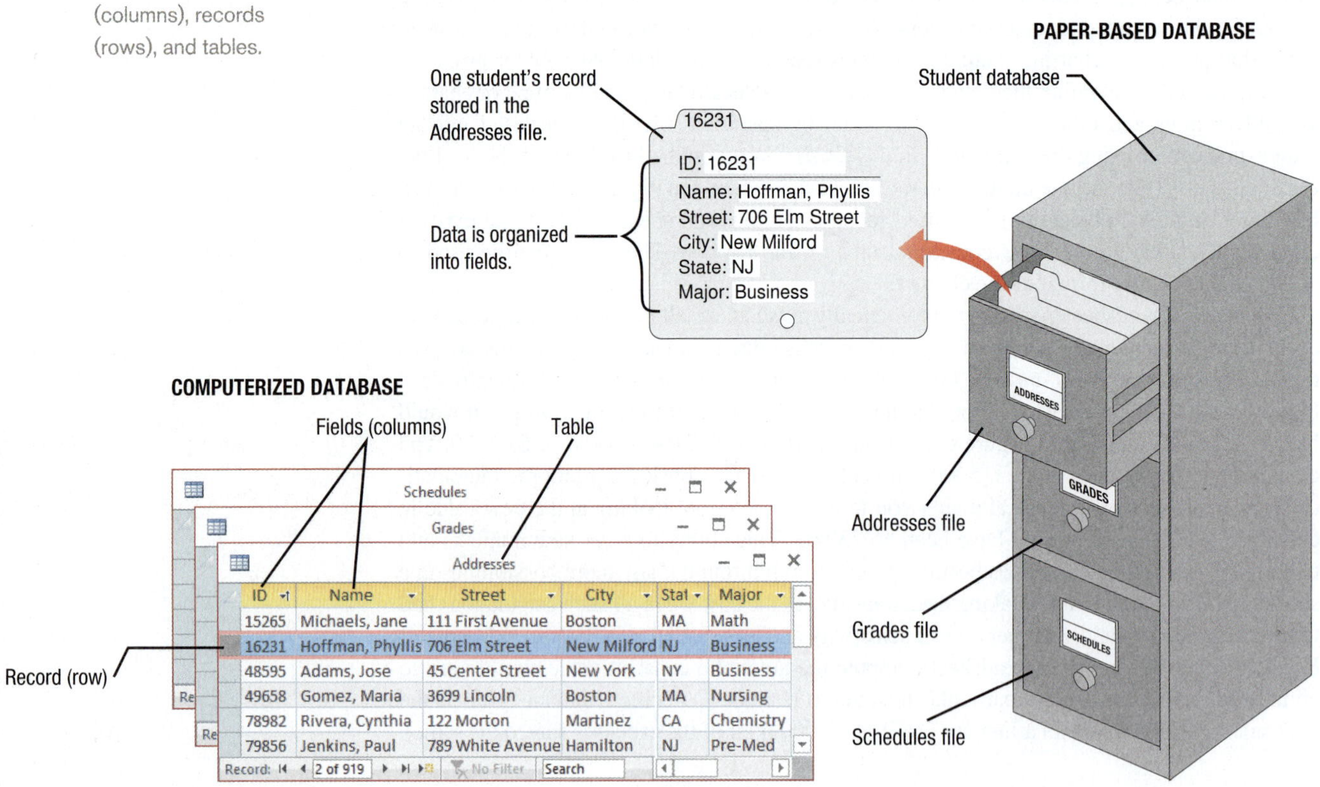

One student's record stored in the Addresses file.

16231

ID: 16231
Name: Hoffman, Phyllis
Street: 706 Elm Street
City: New Milford
State: NJ
Major: Business

Data is organized into fields.

PAPER-BASED DATABASE

Student database

Addresses file

Grades file

Schedules file

COMPUTERIZED DATABASE

Fields (columns)    Table

Record (row)

| ID | Name | Street | City | Stat | Major |
|----|------|--------|------|------|-------|
| 15265 | Michaels, Jane | 111 First Avenue | Boston | MA | Math |
| 16231 | Hoffman, Phyllis | 706 Elm Street | New Milford | NJ | Business |
| 48595 | Adams, Jose | 45 Center Street | New York | NY | Business |
| 49658 | Gomez, Maria | 3699 Lincoln | Boston | MA | Nursing |
| 78982 | Rivera, Cynthia | 122 Morton | Martinez | CA | Chemistry |
| 79856 | Jenkins, Paul | 789 White Avenue | Hamilton | NJ | Pre-Med |

Record: 2 of 919    No Filter    Search

---

>**Database.** A collection of related data that is stored in a manner enabling information to be retrieved as needed; in a relational database, a collection of related tables. >**Database software.** Application software that allows the creation and manipulation of an electronic database. >**Field.** A single category of data to be stored in a database, such as a person's last name or phone number; also called a **column**. >**Record.** A collection of related fields in a database; also called a **row**.

A **table** is a collection of related records (such as all student address data, all student grade data, or all student schedule data). One or more related tables can be stored in a database file.

The most commonly used *relational database management systems* (*RDBMSs*) include *Microsoft Access* and *Corel Paradox* (both part of their respective software suites), *Oracle Database,* and IBM's *DB2*. Some of the basic features of relational database programs in general are described in the next few sections, using Microsoft Access 2016 as the example. Recent versions of Access save database files with the *.accdb* extension by default.

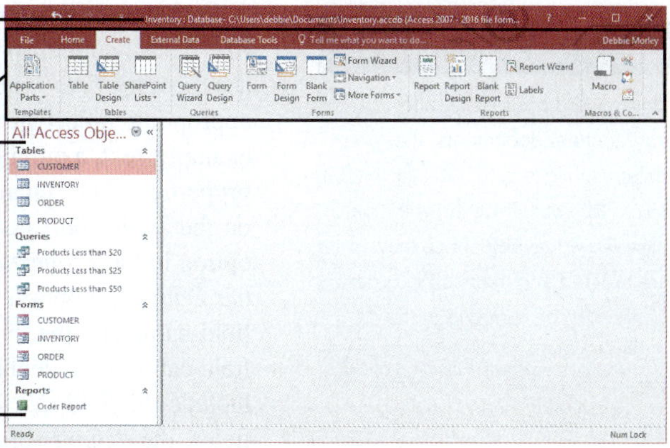

## Creating a Database

An Access database can contain a variety of *objects*. Tables are the objects that contain the database data. Other types of objects (such as forms, queries, and reports, discussed shortly) can be created and used in conjunction with tables when needed. As shown in Figure 6-20, a list of the various objects stored in a database file is displayed when the file is opened. However, you do not see the content of a database object until you open that object.

To create a database, you create the database file first, and then you create the database objects you want that database to contain. Each time Access is launched, you have the option of creating a new blank database file, creating a database file from a template, or opening an existing database file. If you choose to create a new blank database file, a new blank table opens in the table's *Datasheet view* (which displays the table in rows and columns similar to a spreadsheet—see the left screen in Figure 6-21).

**DATABASE FILE**
Contains the Inventory database objects.

**RIBBON**
Contains tabs of commands grouped by function; the Create tab, which is used to create new database objects, is selected.

**DATABASE OBJECTS**
Include Tables (for storing data), Forms (for viewing and editing table data), and Queries and Reports (for retrieving information from tables).

**FIGURE 6-20**
**Typical database objects.** Common database objects include tables, forms, queries, and reports. The first object to be created is the table.

**FIGURE 6-21**
**Creating a database table.**

**TABLE DATASHEET VIEW**

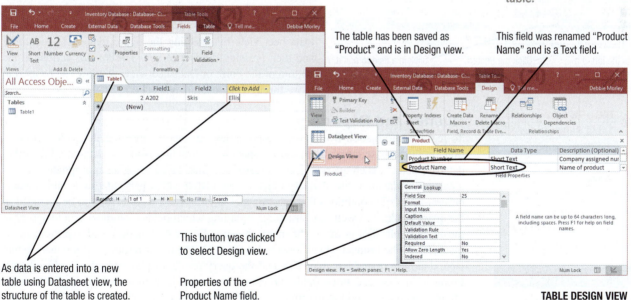

As data is entered into a new table using Datasheet view, the structure of the table is created.

This button was clicked to select Design view.

Properties of the Product Name field.

The table has been saved as "Product" and is in Design view.

This field was renamed "Product Name" and is a Text field.

**TABLE DESIGN VIEW**

> **Table.** In a relational database, a collection of related records.

**TIP**

Unlike word processing and spreadsheet documents, the database file is automatically saved for you. However, you must save individual objects as they are created and modified in order for them to be included in the database file.

As data is entered into a new table using Datasheet view, the *structure* of the table (the fields and their properties) is created. Each column becomes a new field and is given a temporary *field name* (a unique identifying name, such as *Field1*) and is assigned an appropriate *data type* (which identifies the type of data to be contained in the field; for example, text, a number, or a date) based on the data initially entered into that field. These properties can be changed by selecting the field and using the commands on the *Fields tab* on the *Table Tools* contextual tab on the Ribbon (such as selecting the *Name & Caption* option in the *Properties* group to rename the field or selecting a different data type using the *Data Type* option in the *Formatting* group). Each field should be given a descriptive field name and the data type should be changed if the default data type is not correct. A field can also be declared a *required* field if it cannot be left blank. Other field properties include the *field size* (the maximum number of characters allowed for the content of that field), the *default value* (the initial content of that field that remains until it is changed),

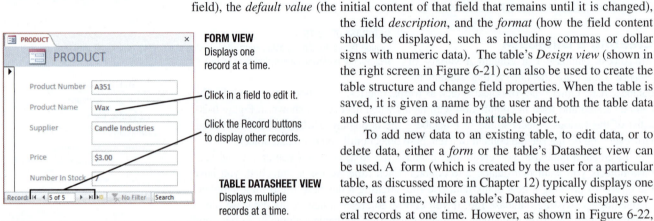

**FORM VIEW**
Displays one record at a time.

Click in a field to edit it.

Click the Record buttons to display other records.

**TABLE DATASHEET VIEW**
Displays multiple records at a time.

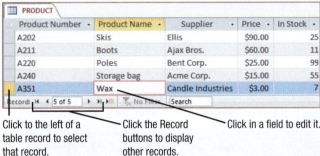

Click to the left of a table record to select that record.

Click the Record buttons to display other records.

Click in a field to edit it.

the field *description*, and the *format* (how the field content should be displayed, such as including commas or dollar signs with numeric data). The table's *Design view* (shown in the right screen in Figure 6-21) can also be used to create the table structure and change field properties. When the table is saved, it is given a name by the user and both the table data and structure are saved in that table object.

To add new data to an existing table, to edit data, or to delete data, either a *form* or the table's Datasheet view can be used. A form (which is created by the user for a particular table, as discussed more in Chapter 12) typically displays one record at a time, while a table's Datasheet view displays several records at one time. However, as shown in Figure 6-22, either Datasheet view or *Form view* can be used to change the data in the table. Data can be edited by clicking inside the appropriate field and then making the necessary edits. A record can be deleted in a table's Datasheet view by clicking to the left of the first field in the appropriate row and then pressing the Delete key. A field can be deleted in a table's Datasheet view by selecting the appropriate field (column), and then pressing the Delete key. The *Record buttons* at the bottom of the Form or Datasheet view window can be used to move through the records as needed.

**FIGURE 6-22**
Table data can be modified using Form view or Datasheet view.

## Queries and Reports

To retrieve information from a database, queries and reports are used. A *query* is a question, or, in database terms, a request for specific information from the database. Like other database objects, each query object is created and then saved using an appropriate name as a part of the database file. A query object is associated with a particular table and contains *criteria*—specific conditions that must be met in order for a record (row) to be included in the query results—as well as instructions regarding which fields (columns) should appear in the query results. For instance, the query shown in Figure 6-23 is designed to retrieve information from the Product table shown in Figure 6-22. The query retrieves all products in that table that have prices less than $25, and the query results display only the Product Name, Product Number, and Price fields. Whenever the query is opened, only the records meeting the specified criteria at the time the query is opened are displayed, and only the specified fields for those records are listed. For instance, the query results shown in Figure 6-23 contain only two records from the Product table in Figure 6-22 because only two records in that table contain products with prices less than $25. If a new product priced less than $25 is added to the database, three records will be displayed the next time the query is opened.

When a more formal output is required, *reports* are used. Reports can contain page and column headings, as well as a company logo or other graphics, and can be formatted and

**TIP**

For a database object, use Datasheet view, Form view, or Report view to show the current content for that object, and use Design view to modify the structure of that object.

customized as desired. Reports are associated with a database table or query and can be easily created using the *Report button* or *Report Wizard button* on the *Create tab* on the Ribbon. Existing reports can be modified using the report's Design view. Whenever a report object is opened, the corresponding data is displayed in the specified location in the report. Consequently, just as with queries, reports always display the data contained in a table at the time the report is generated. Queries and reports are discussed in more detail in Chapter 12.

## Databases and the Web

Databases are often used on the Web. Many Web sites use one or more databases to keep track of inventory; to allow searching for people, documents, or other information; to place real-time orders; and so forth. For instance, any time you type keywords in a search box on a search site or hunt for a product on a retail store's Web site using its search feature, you are using a Web database. Web databases are explained in more detail in Chapter 12.

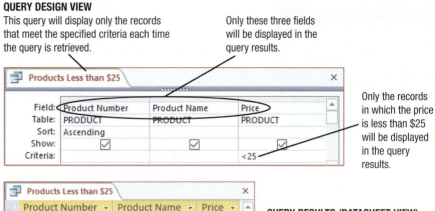

**QUERY DESIGN VIEW**
This query will display only the records that meet the specified criteria each time the query is retrieved.

Only these three fields will be displayed in the query results.

Only the records in which the price is less than $25 will be displayed in the query results.

**QUERY RESULTS (DATASHEET VIEW)**
The two records meeting the specified criteria are displayed.

**FIGURE 6-23**
Creating and using a database query.

**FIGURE 6-24**
Examples of presentation graphics.

# PRESENTATION GRAPHICS CONCEPTS

If you try to explain to others what you look like, it may take several minutes. Show them a color photograph, on the other hand, and you can convey the same information within seconds. The saying "a picture is worth a thousand words" is the cornerstone of presentation graphics. The basic concepts and features of presentation graphics are discussed in the next few sections.

## What Is a Presentation Graphic?

A **presentation graphic** (see Figure 6-24) is an image designed to enhance a presentation (such as an *electronic slide show* or a printed report) visually, typically to convey information more easily to people. A variety of software (including spreadsheet programs, image editing programs, and presentation graphics software) can be used to create presentation graphics. Presentation graphics often take the form of electronic **slides** containing images, text, video, and more that are displayed

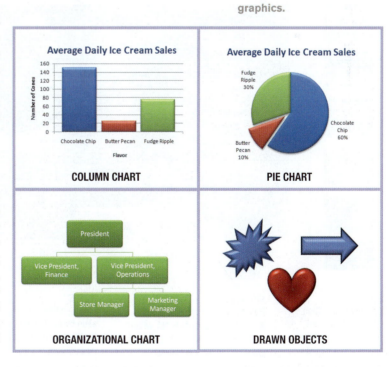

---

>**Presentation graphic.** An image, such as a graph or drawn object, designed to visually enhance a presentation. >**Slide.** A one-page presentation graphic that can be displayed in a group with others to form an electronic slide show.

one after the other in an **electronic slide show**. Electronic slide shows are created with **presentation graphics software** and can be run on individual computers or presented to a large group using a data projector; for instance, they are frequently used for business and educational presentations. Some of today's most common presentation graphics programs are *Microsoft PowerPoint*, *Corel Presentations*, *Google Slides*, and *Apple Keynote* (again, all part of their respective software suites). The next few sections discuss creating an electronic slide show, using Microsoft PowerPoint 2016 as the example. Recent versions of PowerPoint save files with the *.pptx* extension by default.

## Creating a Presentation

A presentation graphics program, such as the one shown in Figure 6-25, contains an assortment of tools and operations for creating and editing slides. For instance, new slides can be added to a new or existing presentation (preformatted *slide layouts* containing placeholders for text and charts and other elements in a slide can be used, if desired). Text, photographs, tables, shapes, charts, and more can then be added to slides using the Insert tab and formatted as needed. To create more exciting and dynamic presentations, multimedia objects and animation effects can be used. For instance, video and audio clips can be inserted into a slide and set up to play automatically each time the slide containing those elements is displayed, or, alternatively, to play when certain objects on the slide

**FIGURE 6-25**

Some features in a typical presentation graphics program.

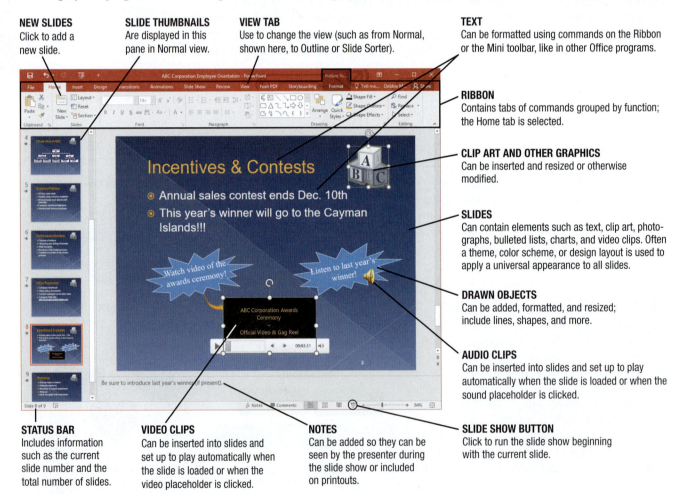

**NEW SLIDES**
Click to add a new slide.

**SLIDE THUMBNAILS**
Are displayed in this pane in Normal view.

**VIEW TAB**
Use to change the view (such as from Normal, shown here, to Outline or Slide Sorter).

**TEXT**
Can be formatted using commands on the Ribbon or the Mini toolbar, like in other Office programs.

**RIBBON**
Contains tabs of commands grouped by function; the Home tab is selected.

**CLIP ART AND OTHER GRAPHICS**
Can be inserted and resized or otherwise modified.

**SLIDES**
Can contain elements such as text, clip art, photographs, bulleted lists, charts, and video clips. Often a theme, color scheme, or design layout is used to apply a universal appearance to all slides.

**DRAWN OBJECTS**
Can be added, formatted, and resized; include lines, shapes, and more.

**AUDIO CLIPS**
Can be inserted into slides and set up to play automatically when the slide is loaded or when the sound placeholder is clicked.

**STATUS BAR**
Includes information such as the current slide number and the total number of slides.

**VIDEO CLIPS**
Can be inserted into slides and set up to play automatically when the slide is loaded or when the video placeholder is clicked.

**NOTES**
Can be added so they can be seen by the presenter during the slide show or included on printouts.

**SLIDE SHOW BUTTON**
Click to run the slide show beginning with the current slide.

> **Electronic slide show.** A group of electronic slides that are displayed one after the other on a computer monitor or other display device.
> **Presentation graphics software.** Application software used to create presentation graphics and electronic slide shows.

are clicked. Text or other objects can be *animated* so that a special effect (such as *flying* the text in from the edge of the screen or *dissolving* the text in or out on a slide) is used to display that text or object each time the slide is viewed. *Animation settings* can be specified to indicate the sequence in which objects are displayed (such as to build a bulleted list one item at a time), whether or not a video loops continuously, and more.

In addition to formatting the individual items located on slides, the overall appearance of the entire slide show can be changed by applying a *theme* (a combination of colors, fonts, and effects that can be applied to an entire slide show at one time) to the presentation using the *Design tab*. In addition, *transitions*—special effects used between slides—can be applied to specific slides, or random transitions can be selected for the entire slide show. In PowerPoint, animations and transitions are specified using the *Animations tab* and *Transitions tab,* respectively.

## Finishing a Presentation

Once all of the slides in a slide show have been created and the desired animation and transition effects have been applied, the slide show is ready to be finalized. To preview the slides and rearrange them if needed, presentation graphics programs typically have a special view, such as PowerPoint's *Slide Sorter view*, that shows thumbnails of all the slides in a presentation. Using this view, slides can easily be rearranged by dragging them to their new location in the presentation. When the slide show is run, the slides are displayed in the designated order. The slides advance either automatically or manually, depending on how the presentation is set up. For an *automatic slide show*, the amount of time each slide should be displayed before moving on to the next slide is specified using the *Slide Show tab* on the Ribbon. For a *manual slide show*, the speaker (or person viewing the slide show for a stand-alone presentation) moves to the next slide by pressing the spacebar or by clicking or tapping anywhere on the screen. If desired, PowerPoint allows narration to be recorded and played back when the slide show is run, and *speaker notes* can be added to the slides, as needed.

PowerPoint, like many other presentation software programs, also has a variety of *speaker tools*. For instance, the speaker can choose a laser pointer, pen, or highlighter tool and point to items or "write" on the slides while the slide show is running, perhaps to circle a particular sentence for emphasis or to draw an arrow pointing to one part of the slide. Recent versions of PowerPoint also include a *Presenter view* (see Figure 6-26) that can be used when two display devices are available (such as when a data projector is connected to the notebook computer being used to run the presentation). The regular slide show is projected in full screen for the audience on one display device (such as onto a large screen via the data projector), while a special Presenter view version of the slide show (containing a smaller version of the current slide along with speaker notes, a preview of the next slide, a timer, and so forth) is displayed for the presenter on the second display device (such as on the notebook computer's display screen). Most presentation software programs can also print the speaker notes, as well as the slides (either full-sized or miniature versions printed several to a page) to create audience handouts.

## Presentation Graphics and the Web

As with the other application programs discussed so far, presentation graphics programs can be used to generate Web pages or Web page content, and slides can include hyperlinks. When a slide show is saved as a series of Web pages and displayed using a Web browser, generally forward and backward navigational buttons are displayed on the slides to allow the user to control the presentation.

**FIGURE 6-26**
**Running an electronic slide show.**

**SLIDE SHOW VIEW**
Displays the slide show for the audience in full screen with the software interface hidden. Slides can be advanced at predetermined intervals, by clicking or tapping on the screen, or by pressing the spacebar.

**PRESENTER VIEW**
Seen only by the presenter on a different display device; includes a preview of the next slide or animation, a timer, speaker notes, annotation tools, and so forth.

# GRAPHICS AND MULTIMEDIA CONCEPTS

**Graphics** are digital representations of images, such as digital photos, clip art, scanned drawings, and original images created using a software program. **Multimedia** technically refers to any application that contains more than one type of media (such as graphics, audio, video, and/or animation), but is most often used to refer to audio and video content. There are a variety of software programs designed to help individuals create or modify graphics, edit digital audio or video files, play media files, burn CDs and DVDs, and so forth, as discussed next. Some programs focus on just one task; others are designed to perform multiple tasks, such as to import and edit images, audio, and video, and then create a finished DVD.

## Graphics Software

**Graphics software**—also called *digital imaging software*—is used to create or modify images. Graphics software programs are commonly distinguished by whether they are primarily oriented toward painting, drawing, or image editing, although these are general categories, not strict classifications, and some products fit into more than one category.

*Painting programs* traditionally create *bitmap images*, which are created by coloring the individual pixels in an image. One of the most common painting programs is *Microsoft Paint* (shown in Figure 6-27). Painting programs are often used to create and modify simple

**FIGURE 6-27**
Graphics software.

**PAINTING PROGRAMS**
Typically create images pixel by pixel so the images cannot be layered or resized without losing quality.

**DRAWING PROGRAMS**
Typically create images using mathematical formulas and layers so the images can be resized without distortion.

**PHOTO EDITING PROGRAMS**
Allow users to edit digital photos from their computer (left) or smartphone (right).

Source: Corel Corporation; Adobe Systems Incorporated; Bloomua/Shutterstock.com

>**Graphic.** A digital representation of a photograph, drawing, chart, or other visual image. >**Multimedia.** The integration of a variety of media, such as text, images, video, animation, and sound. >**Graphics software.** Application software used to create or modify images.

images but, unless the painting program supports *layers* and other tools discussed shortly, use for these programs is relatively limited. This is because when something is drawn or placed on top of a bitmap image, the pixels in the image are recolored to reflect the new content so whatever was beneath the new content is lost. In addition, bitmapped images cannot be enlarged and still maintain their quality because the pixels in the images just get larger, which makes the edges of the images look jagged. Some painting programs today do support layers and so are more versatile. Painting tools are also increasingly included in other types of software, such as in office suites and the drawing programs discussed next.

*Drawing programs* (also referred to as *illustration programs*) typically create *vector graphics*, which use mathematical formulas to represent image content instead of pixels. Unlike bitmap images, vector images can be resized and otherwise manipulated without loss of quality. Typically, objects in drawing programs can also be *layered* so, if you place one object on top of another, you can later separate the two images if desired. Drawing programs are often used by individuals and small business owners to create original art, logos, business cards, and more; they are also used by professionals to create corporate images, Web site graphics, and so forth. Popular drawing programs include *Adobe Illustrator CC, CorelDRAW,* and *Corel Painter* (shown in Figure 6-27).

*Image editing* or *photo editing programs* are drawing or painting programs that are specifically designed for touching up or modifying images, such as original digital images and digital photos. Editing options include correcting brightness or contrast, eliminating red eye, cropping, resizing, and applying filters or other special effects. Most programs also include options for *optimizing* images to reduce the file size. Optimization techniques include reducing the number of colors used in the image, reducing the resolution of the image, and converting the image to another file format. Some of the most widely used consumer image editing and photo editing programs are *Adobe Photoshop Elements, Adobe Photoshop Express* (shown in Figure 6-27), *Apple Photos, Corel PaintShop Pro* (also shown in Figure 6-27), *GIMP,* and the free *Picasa* program. For professional image editing, the full *Adobe Photoshop CC* program is the leading program.

## Audio Capture and Editing Software

For creating and editing audio files, *audio capture* and *audio editing* software is used. To capture sound from a microphone, *sound recorder* software is used; to capture sound from a CD, *ripping software* is used. In either case, once the audio is captured, it can then be modified, as needed. For instance, background noise or pauses can be removed, portions of the selection can be edited out, multiple segments can be spliced together, and special effects such as fade-ins and fade-outs can be applied. There are also specialized audio capture and editing programs designed for specific applications, such as creating podcasts

## ASK THE EXPERT

**Ben Bardens,** Professional Animator and Motion Graphics Artist

### What computer skills should an individual obtain to prepare for a career in computer animation?

First and foremost, a solid understanding of different operating systems and how to navigate and manage files within them is crucial. It is not uncommon for digital artists to be expected to work proficiently on both Macintosh and Windows platforms and sometimes switch between the two.

Second, all digital artists (including graphic designers, motion graphics artists, animators, illustrators, and photographers) should be proficient with Adobe Photoshop. Photoshop is considered by many to be the foundation computer graphics program, and it has a broad range of uses and applications within several related fields. Any aspiring computer animator or artist should start by learning Photoshop. Once a student knows how to create and edit composite images within Photoshop, it is much easier to transition to learning other computer graphics and animation programs, such as Adobe Illustrator, After Effects, or Flash.

**SW**

**TIP**

You can often do some photo editing in apps designed to be used with smartphone photos; for instance, with Instagram, you can straighten a crooked photo, crop it, or apply a filter before sharing it online.

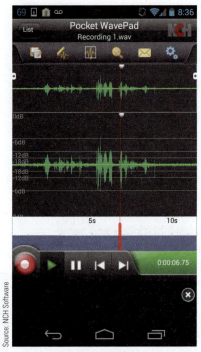

**FIGURE 6-28**
Audio editing
software.

or musical compositions. Professional audio capture and editing software (such as *Sony Creative Software Sound Forge Pro* and *Adobe Audition CC*) is used to create professional audio for end products, Web pages, commercial podcasts, presentations, and so forth. Common consumer audio capture and editing programs include *Windows Voice Recorder*, *Apple GarageBand*, and the free *Audacity* program. The free *WavePad Audio Editor* mobile app that can be used to record and edit voice recordings while you are on the go is shown in Figure 6-28.

## Video Editing and DVD Authoring Software

It is common today for individuals to want to create finished videos, such as to create a video to upload to YouTube or to edit home videos and transfer them to a DVD. Businesses also often find the need for *video editing*, such as to prepare video clips for presentations, Web sites, or the company's YouTube channel. Most video capture today is in digital form; if so, the video can be imported directly into a video editing program by connecting the camera to the computer or by inserting the storage media containing the video (such as a DVD) into the computer. Once the video has been imported, video editing tasks (such as deleting or rearranging scenes, adding voice-overs, and adding other special effects) can be performed (see Figure 6-29). Some video editing software today can edit video in high-definition format. There are also mobile apps (such as *Vine* and *Instagram*) designed to help you create and share short videos taken with a smartphone.

DVD authoring refers to organizing content to be transferred to DVD, such as importing video clips and then creating the desired menu structure for the DVD to control the playback of those videos. *DVD burning* refers to recording data (such as a collection of songs or a finished video) on a recordable or rewritable DVD. DVD authoring and burning capabilities can be included in *video editing software*, and there are standalone *DVD authoring programs* as well. DVD burning capabilities are often preinstalled on computers containing a recordable or rewritable optical drive. Some file management programs and media players (discussed next) include CD and DVD burning capabilities, as well.

Consumer video editing software includes *Adobe Premiere Elements*, *Roxio Creator*, *Apple iMovie*, and *Corel VideoStudio*. Professional products include *Adobe Premiere Pro CC* (shown in Figure 6-29), *Corel VideoStudio Ultimate*, and *Sony Creative Software Vegas Pro*.

**FIGURE 6-29**
Video editing
software.

All content for this
project is listed here.

Video clips are
previewed here.

Video clips can be edited
as needed; the timeline
is used to crop out sections
of the current video clip.

Audio clips can
be edited in a
manner similar
to video clips.

## Media Players

*Media players* are programs designed to play audio and video files. They are used to play media available via your device—such as music CDs, downloaded music, or video streamed from the Internet. Many media players are available for free, such as *RealPlayer, iTunes* (see Figure 6-30), *VLC Media Player*, and *QuickTime Player*. Media players typically allow you to arrange your stored music and videos into *playlists*, and then transfer them to a CD or mobile phone. Some players also include the ability to purchase and download music via an associated *music store*.

It is important when using digital music to adhere to copyright laws, such as only transferring music from CDs that you have purchased and only downloading digital music files from sites that are authorized to distribute the music. While most music download sites today are legal and charge around $1 per title, illegal peer-to-peer (P2P) MP3 file exchanges do exist. Copyrights and P2P networks are discussed in more detail in later chapters.

Current library content is listed here.

Additional music and videos can be purchased via the iTunes Store.

Source: Apple, Inc.

**FIGURE 6-30**
**A typical media player program.**

## Graphics, Multimedia, and the Web

Graphics and multimedia software are often used by individuals and businesses to create content to be included on a Web site or to be shared via the Web. For instance, company logos, Web site banners, games, tutorials, videos, demonstrations, and other multimedia content available on the Web are created with multimedia software. In addition to the graphics software already discussed, other software used to create Web multimedia content include *Adobe Flash, Adobe After Effects CC, Adobe Edge Animate CC, Microsoft Silverlight*, and other programs used to create *animations* (a series of images that are displayed one after the other to simulate movement). *Multimedia authoring software* (such as *Adobe Director*) can be used to create large multimedia applications, such as complex games and training simulations.

# OTHER TYPES OF APPLICATION SOFTWARE

There are many other types of application software available today. Some are geared for business or personal productivity; others are designed for entertainment or educational purposes. Still others are intended to help users with a particular specialized application, such as preparing financial reports, issuing prescriptions electronically, designing buildings, controlling machinery, and so forth. A few of the most common types of application software not previously covered are discussed next.

> **TIP**
>
> More cloud applications are featured in Chapter 8; security software is discussed in Chapter 9.

## Desktop, Personal, and Web Publishing Software

*Desktop publishing* refers to using a personal computer to combine and manipulate text and images to create attractive documents that look as if they were created by a professional printer. Although many desktop publishing effects can be produced using a word processing program, users who frequently create publication-style documents usually find a desktop publishing program more efficient. Some popular desktop publishing programs are *Adobe InDesign CC* and *Microsoft Publisher*. *Personal publishing* refers to creating desktop-publishing-type documents—such as greeting cards, invitations, flyers, and certificates—for personal use. There are also specialized personal publishing programs for particular purposes,

Click to publish the Web site.

Content is contained in modules, which can be edited, moved, or deleted.

Drag a new module to the page and then specify the content.

Source: Webs

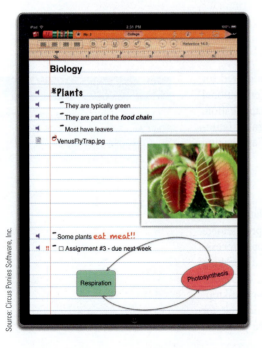

Source: Circus Ponies Software, Inc.

**FIGURE 6-31**

**Web site builders.**

Allow users to create Web sites quickly and easily.

**FIGURE 6-32**

**Note taking software.**

Allows individuals to record and organize important data.

such as to create scrapbook pages, cross-stitch patterns, CD and DVD labels, and so forth.

*Web publishing software* (also called *Web site builders* when referring to a cloud service) is used to create complete Web sites. Most of these programs automatically generate Web pages as the user specifies what the content of each Web page should contain and what it should look like. They also typically allow users to choose a theme for the Web site to ensure it has a consistent appearance from page to page. After a site is created, most programs have the option of publishing it directly to a Web server. Web publishing programs include *Adobe DreamWeaver CC*, *Adobe Contribute*, and cloud software such as *Webs* shown in Figure 6-31.

## Educational, Entertainment, and Reference Software

A wide variety of educational and entertainment application programs are available. *Educational software* is designed to teach one or more skills, such as reading, math, spelling, or a foreign language, or to help prepare for standardized tests. *Entertainment software* includes games, simulations, and other programs that provide amusement. A hybrid of these two categories is called *edutainment*—educational software that also entertains. *Reference software* includes encyclopedias, mapping/travel programs, cookbook programs, nutrition or fitness programs, and other software designed to provide valuable information. Although still available as stand-alone programs, reference information today is often cloud software or obtained via reference Web sites.

## Note Taking Software and Web Notebooks

*Note taking software* is used by both students and businesspeople to take notes during class lectures, meetings, and similar settings. It is used most often with tablet computers and other devices designed to accept pen input. Typically, note taking software (such as Microsoft *OneNote* or the Circus Ponies *Notebook* program shown in Figure 6-32) supports both typed and handwritten input; handwritten input can usually be saved in its handwritten form as an image or converted to typed text. The Notebook program also includes a voice recorder so you can record a lecture or meeting—tapping the speaker icon next to a note replays the voice recorded at the time that particular note was taken. Note taking software typically contains features designed specifically to make note taking—and, particularly, retrieving information from the notes—easier. Like a paper notebook, tabbed sections can usually be created (such as one tab per course) and files, notes, Web links, and any other data are stored under the appropriate tabs. In addition, search tools that allow you to find the information you need quickly and easily are usually included. Online versions of these programs (such as *Zoho Notebook* and *Evernote*) are sometimes referred to as *Web notebooks*. Web notebooks are designed to help organize your online research (including text, images, Web links, search results, and other Web resources), as well as other content (including notes, documents, and scanned images) that you want to save.

## CAD and Other Types of Design Software

As discussed in more detail in Chapter 10, *computer-aided design* (*CAD*) *software* enables designers to design objects on the computer. For example, engineers or architects can create designs of buildings or other objects and modify the designs as often as needed. Increasingly, CAD programs are including capabilities to analyze designs in terms of how well they meet a number of design criteria, such as testing how a building design will hold up during an earthquake or how a car will perform under certain conditions. Besides playing an important role in the design of finished products, CAD is also useful in fields such as art, advertising, architecture, and movie production. In addition to professional CAD programs, there are also design programs intended for home and small business use, such as for designing new homes, and for making remodeling plans, interior designs, and landscape designs.

## Accounting and Personal Finance Software

*Accounting software* is used to automate some of the accounting activities that need to be performed on a regular basis. Common tasks include recording purchases and payments, managing inventory, creating payroll documents and checks, preparing financial statements, keeping track of business expenses, and creating and managing customer accounts and invoices (see Figure 6-33). *Personal finance software* is commonly used at home by individuals to write checks and balance checking accounts, track personal expenses, manage stock portfolios, and prepare income taxes. Increasingly, personal finance activities are becoming Web-based, such as the online banking and online portfolio management services available through many banks and brokerage firms and discussed in more detail in Chapter 8.

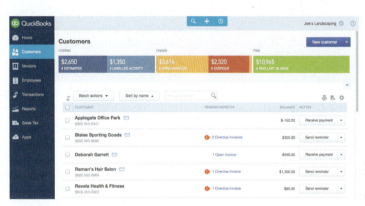

**FIGURE 6-33**

**Accounting software.** This QuickBooks Online for iPad app allows you to create and keep track of customer invoices while on the go.

Source: Intuit

## Project Management, Collaboration, and Remote Access Software

*Project management software* is used to plan, schedule, track, and analyze the tasks involved in a project, such as the construction of a building or the schedule for preparing a large advertising campaign for a client. Project management capabilities are often included in *collaboration software*—software that enables a group of individuals to work together on a project—and are increasingly available as cloud software programs.

*Remote access software* enables individuals to access content on another computer they are authorized to access via the Internet. Some programs allow you to control the remote computer directly; others allow you to access your media files (such as recorded TV shows or music) from any Web-enabled device while you are away from home. For instance, the *Slingbox* product gives you access to and control over your cable box and DVR via the Internet, and *TeamViewer* software (see Figure 6-34) allows you to access a computer (such as a home or an office PC), including controlling the computer and accessing files, from any Web-enabled device while you are away from home (provided you have the remote access software running on your PC). Other remote access software automatically backs up all data files on your main computer to a secure Web server so they can be accessed from any Web-enabled device (such as a portable computer, smartphone, or tablet), as well as shared with others for collaboration purposes. Some companies (such as Microsoft) offer a remote access feature for technical support, where the technician will access your computer remotely to resolve your problem if you grant permission.

**FIGURE 6-34**

**Remote access software.** Allows you to use a computer from a remote Internet-enabled device.

This Windows computer is being accessed remotely via this smartphone.

Source: TeamViewer; Chardchanin/Shutterstock.com; Bombaert Patrick/Shutterstock.com

# SUMMARY

## THE BASICS OF APPLICATION SOFTWARE

**Application software** (**apps**) are programs designed to carry out a specific task. Common types of application software include games, Web browsers, word processing programs, multimedia software, and more. Many application software programs today are **commercial software** programs that are developed and sold for a profit. When a software program is purchased, individual users receive a **software license** authorizing them to use the software. Some mobile apps have a *terms of use* instead. Commercial software is sometimes available in a *demo* or *trial version*. Other software is available as **shareware**, **freeware**, or **public domain software**. **Open source software** is the term for programs whose source code is available to the general public. Software is designed as either *desktop software* or *mobile software*. **Installed software** is installed on a local computer or network server; **cloud software**, which is also called *Web-based software*, *Software as a Service (SaaS)*, and *cloudware*, is run from the Internet instead.

Many office-oriented programs are sold bundled together as a **software suite**. One of the most widely used software suites is **Microsoft Office**. Although they are used for different purposes, most application software programs share some of the same concepts and functions, such as similar document-handling operations and help features. For instance, documents are commonly opened, saved, printed, edited, and formatted in a similar manner. **Editing** a document changes its content; **formatting** a document changes its appearance (such as by changing the *font face*, *font size*, or *font style* of text or by changing the *line spacing* or *margins*). Commands can be issued via a variety of methods, such as by using *menus*, *toolbars*, **keyboard shortcuts**, or the Microsoft Office **Ribbon**—the **insertion point** typically looks like a blinking vertical line and identifies the current position in a document. Online help is available in many programs.

## WORD PROCESSING CONCEPTS

**Word processing** refers to using a computer and **word processing software** to create, manipulate, and print written documents, such as letters, contracts, and so forth. When creating or editing a word processing document, the **word wrap** feature automatically moves the insertion point to the next line when the end of the screen line is reached. Formatting can be applied at the character, paragraph, or document level. Other enhancements found in most word processing programs include the ability to include graphical images and *tables*, and to use *styles*, *templates*, or *wizards* for more efficient document creation. Documents can also include hyperlinks and be saved as Web pages in many programs. Most word processors also include a spelling and grammar check feature and other useful tools.

## SPREADSHEET CONCEPTS

**Spreadsheet software** is used to create documents (**spreadsheets** or **worksheets**) that typically include a great deal of numbers and mathematical computations; a collection of worksheets stored in the same spreadsheet file is called a **workbook**. A worksheet is divided into **rows** and **columns** that intersect to form **cells**, each of which can be accessed through a *cell address*, such as B3. A rectangular group of cells is referred to as a *range*.

Content is entered into individual cells and may consist of **labels**, **constant values**, **formulas**, or **functions**. Formulas can be typed using *relative cell* or *absolute cell references*, depending on the type of computation required. Once created, the content of individual cells may be edited and formatted. *Numeric formats* are used to change the appearance of numbers, such as adding a dollar sign or displaying a specific number of decimal places. Spreadsheet programs commonly include a *charting* or *graphing* feature and the ability to perform *what-if analysis*. Some spreadsheet programs allow worksheets to be saved as a Web page and the inclusion of hyperlinks in cells.

## DATABASE CONCEPTS

A *database management system (DBMS)* or **database software** program enables the creation of a **database**—a collection of related data stored in a manner so that information can be retrieved as needed. In a relational DBMS (the most common type found on personal computers), a **field** or **column** is a collection of characters that make up a single piece of data, such as a name or phone number; a **record** or **row** is a collection of related fields; and a **table** is a collection of related records. One or more tables can be stored in a database file.

A relational database typically contains a variety of *objects*, such as tables, *forms* to input or view data, *queries* to retrieve specific information, and *reports* to print a formal listing of the data stored in a table or the results of a query. When a table is created, the table fields are specified along with their characteristics, such as *field name*, *field size*, and *data type*. This structure, as well as the data, are saved in the table and can be modified when needed. Databases are commonly integrated into the Web, such as to keep track of inventory and to facilitate online ordering.

**Chapter Objective 5:**
Identify some of the vocabulary used with database software and discuss the benefits of using this type of program.

## PRESENTATION GRAPHICS CONCEPTS

**Presentation graphics** are images used to visually enhance the impact of information communicated to other people. **Presentation graphics software** can be used to create presentation graphics and **electronic slide shows** consisting of electronic **slides**. The individual slides in the slide show are created, and then they can be edited and formatted, as can the overall appearance of the presentation. Multimedia elements, such as images and video clips, can also be included. After all slides have been created for a presentation, the order of the slides can be rearranged and *transitions* between the slides can be specified. It is becoming increasingly common to find slide-based presentations available through the Web. Web-based slide shows can include multimedia elements, as well as hyperlinks and other navigational buttons.

**Chapter Objective 6:**
Describe what presentation graphics and electronic slide shows are and when they might be used.

## GRAPHICS AND MULTIMEDIA CONCEPTS

**Graphics** are graphical representations of images, such as digital photographs, clip art, and original art. **Multimedia** refers to applications that include more than one type of media, but often refers to audio and video content. To create graphics, **graphics software**—such as a *painting*, a *drawing*, or an *image editing program*—can be used. *Audio editing*, *video editing*, and *DVD authoring software* are common types of multimedia programs, as are the *media player* programs used to play audio and video files. *CD* and *DVD burning software* can be used to burn songs or other data on a CD or DVD disc.

**Chapter Objective 7:**
List some types of graphics and multimedia software that consumers use frequently.

## OTHER TYPES OF APPLICATION SOFTWARE

Other types of application software include *desktop*, *personal*, and *Web publishing* programs, *computer-aided design (CAD)* and other types of *design software*, *accounting software*, *personal finance software*, and *project management software*. The use of *collaboration*, *remote access*, and *note taking software* is growing. *Educational*, *entertainment*, and *reference software* are very popular with home users.

**Chapter Objective 8:**
Name several other types of application software programs and discuss what functions they perform.

# REVIEW ACTIVITIES

## KEY TERM MATCHING

a. cell

b. database

c. field

d. formula

e. label

f. public domain software

g. record

h. shareware

i. software license

j. workbook

**Instructions:** Match each key term on the left with the definition on the right that best describes it.

1. _____ A collection of related data that is stored in a manner enabling information to be retrieved as needed.

2. _____ A collection of related fields in a database; also called a row.

3. _____ A collection of worksheets saved in a single spreadsheet file.

4. _____ An agreement, either included in a software package or displayed on the screen when the software is installed or launched, that specifies the conditions under which the program can be used.

5. _____ An entry in a worksheet cell that performs computations on worksheet data and displays the results.

6. _____ A single category of data to be stored in a database, such as a person's name or phone number; also called a column.

7. _____ A text-based entry in a worksheet cell that identifies data on the worksheet.

8. _____ Copyrighted software that is distributed on the honor system; consumers should either pay for it or uninstall it after the trial period.

9. _____ Software that is not copyrighted and may be used without restriction.

10. _____ The location at the intersection of a row and column on a worksheet into which data can be typed.

## SELF-QUIZ

**Instructions:** Circle **T** if the statement is true, **F** if the statement is false, or write the best answer in the space provided. **Answers for the self-quiz are located in the References and Resources Guide at the end of the book.**

1. **T  F**  Microsoft Office is one example of a software suite.

2. **T  F**  Changing the font size in a document is an example of a formatting operation.

3. **T  F**  In a word processing document, the Enter key is always pressed at the end of each screen line to move down to the next line.

4. **T  F**  The formula =A2+B2 located in cell C2 would multiply the two cells to the left of cell C2.

5. **T  F**  Graphics are animated sequences of images.

6. With a(n) _____ program, the source code for the program is made available to the public and so it can be legally modified by others.

7. The blinking vertical line displayed on the screen that indicates the current location in a document, such as where the next change will be made to the document in a word processing program, is called the _____.

8. Software that is delivered via the Web is called _____.

9. In a relational database, the database object that contains the actual data is the _____.

**10.** Match each application with its type of application program, and write the corresponding number in the blank to the left of each application.

a. _____ Listening to a music CD.

b. _____ Creating a child's birthday invitation.

c. _____ Creating a home movie DVD.

d. _____ Creating a Web site.

**1.** DVD authoring software

**2.** Media player

**3.** Web site builder

**4.** Personal publishing software

---

**1.** List the programs included in the Microsoft Office software suite that fit in the following categories.

a. Spreadsheet software _____

b. Presentation graphics software _____

c. Word processing software _____

d. Database software _____

**2.** Match each spreadsheet element with its term and write the corresponding number in the blank to the left of each term.

a. _____ An absolute cell address

b. _____ A relative cell address

c. _____ A function

**1.** =SUM(A1:A2)

**2.** $D$4

**3.** B6

**3.** For a customer database containing 50 customers and recording data about the customer's number, last name, street, city, state, ZIP code, and current balance, answer the following questions.

a. How many records are in the database? _____

b. How many fields are in the database? _____

c. To display a list of all customers who live in Texas and have a current balance of less than $10, what database tool should be used? _____

**4.** Write the number of the presentation graphic that best matches each of the following possible uses in the blank to the left of each use.

a. _____ Adding an arrow to highlight a point located on a slide.

b. _____ Illustrating the percent of sales coming from each sales territory.

c. _____ Conveying the key points in an educational lecture.

**1.** Pie chart
**2.** Slide
**3.** Drawn object

**5.** Would rearranging the paragraphs in a document using a word processing program be an editing operation or a formatting operation? Explain your answer.

---

**1.** There are an increasing number of cloud applications available and the current version of Office is available in both installed and cloud versions. What are the advantages and disadvantages of cloud software? Which do you prefer to use for school-related documents? Why? If you prefer installed software, what would have to change about cloud software in the future to change your opinion?

**2.** Open source software is usually reviewed and improved at no cost. Proponents of open source software believe that if programmers who are not concerned with financial gain work on an open source program, they will produce a more useful and error-free product much faster than the traditional commercial software development process. As open source use continues to grow, will it force existing commercial software companies to cut costs to better compete with open source products? Or will they strive to produce products that are better and more reliable than open source competitors? Or will commercial software companies simply go out of business? Will commercial software manufacturers be justified in raising their prices to make up for revenue lost to open source competitors? Do you think open source software will have an overall positive or negative impact on the quality of software?

# PROJECTS

1. **Crapware** As discussed in the Technology and You box, crapware is a growing problem on new PCs, as well as with software downloads.

   For this project, research crapware and its use today. How frequently is it installed on new desktop and portable computers? Does it come installed on mobile devices? Does software available through common download sites include crapware components? Have there been any additional examples in the media since Superfish? Have you found crapware on a new PC or included in a download? If so, was it a problem? Explain. Do you think dealing with crapware is a fair exchange for lower prices of hardware and software? Why or why not? At the conclusion of your research, prepare a one-page summary of your findings and opinions and submit it to your instructor.

2. **Software Search** Just as with toys, movies, and music, the price of a software program can vary tremendously, based on where you buy it, sales, rebates, and more. Although most software has a manufacturer's suggested retail price, it is almost always possible to beat that price—sometimes by a huge amount—with careful shopping.

   For this project, select one software program (such as an office suite or a security suite) that you might be interested in buying and research it. By reading the program specifications either in a retail store or on a Web page, determine the program's minimum hardware and software requirements. By checking in person, over the phone, or via the Internet, locate three price quotes for the program, including any sales tax and shipping, and check availability and estimated delivery time. Do any of the vendors have the option to download the software? If so, do you have to register the program online or enter a code to activate the product after it is downloaded? At the conclusion of this task, prepare a one-page summary of your research and submit it to your instructor. Be sure to include a recommendation of where you think it would be best to buy your chosen product and why.

3. **Online Tours** There are many online tours and tutorials for application programs. Some are available through the software company's Web site; others are located on third-party Web sites. Many are free.

   For this project, select one common software program (such as Word, Excel, PowerPoint, Chrome, Google Docs, or Paint). Locate a free online tour or tutorial for the program you selected and work your way through one tour or tutorial. How useful is it? Is it easy to use and understand? Did you learn anything new? Did you encounter any errors or other problems? Are there multiple versions for varying levels of difficulty? Would you recommend this tour or tutorial to others? At the conclusion of this task, prepare a one-page summary of your efforts and submit it to your instructor.

**ETHICS IN ACTION**

4. **Emotion Recognition Software** An emerging application is *emotion recognition software*, which uses camera input to try to read a person's current emotion. The first expected application of such a system is for ATM machines because they already have cameras installed. Possibilities include changing the advertising display based on the customer's emotional response to displayed advertising, and enlarging the screen text if the customer appears to be squinting. Is it ethical for businesses using emotion recognition software to read the emotions of citizens without their consent? Proponents of the technology argue that it is no different than when human tellers or store clerks interpret customers' emotions and modify their treatment of the customer accordingly. Do you agree? Why or why not? Is this a worthy new technology or just a potential invasion of privacy? Would you object to using an ATM machine with emotion recognition capabilities? Why or why not?

   For this project, form an opinion about the ethical ramifications of emotion recognition systems and be prepared to discuss your position (in class, via an online class forum, or via a class blog, depending on your instructor's directions). You may also be asked to write a short paper expressing your opinion.

**PRESENTATION/ DEMONSTRATION**

5. **Compatibility** Files created by an application program are often upward compatible but not always downward compatible. For example, a *.docx* file created in Microsoft Word 2016 cannot be opened in Word 2003, but a Word 2003 *.doc* file can be opened in Word 2016. Most application programs feature a "Save As" option that can be used to save a file in one of several formats.

   For this project, select one widely used software program and determine in which file formats the program can save documents and which file formats the program can open. If there are older versions of the program, are documents upward compatible? Downward compatible? Research *plain text* (*.txt*), *Portable Document Format* (*PDF*), *OpenDocument format*, and the *Rich Text Format* (*.rtf*) and determine their purposes, the programs that can open documents saved in each of these formats, and any disadvantages for using these formats. Have you ever experienced a compatibility problem with a document? If so, how was the problem resolved? Share your findings with the class in the form of a short presentation. The presentation should not exceed 10 minutes and should make use of one or more presentation aids, such as a whiteboard, handouts, or a computer-based slide presentation (your instructor may provide additional requirements). You may also be asked to submit a summary of the presentation to your instructor.

**BALANCING ACT**

6. **Should Computers Grade Essay Tests?** Using computers and other automated tools to grade true-false and multiple-choice tests is widespread, but grading essays has been reserved for instructors. Until now. Software developed by a nonprofit enterprise founded by Harvard and MIT recently released software that can grade student essays and short written answers. Students answer online instead of in a blue book and immediately receive their grade after clicking a Send button. The software uses artificial intelligence (it initially "learns" how to grade an instructor's test by reviewing 100 essay exams that the instructor scored) and is designed to free up professors for other tasks, as well as give students the opportunity to immediately revise their graded essays for an improved grade. But does the system work? Are the automated grades similar to what a human grader would award? Skeptics (including the National Council of Teachers of English) say no. Objections include a lack of tests to support the validity of the grading system and the inability of the software to leave in-depth comments in the margin of a paper like a professor would. But does the immediate feedback, as well as the ability to improve your writing and grade, offset these objections? Would you prefer that your essays be graded immediately via software or wait for a human score? Is this an advancement in education or a mistake?

   Pick a side on this issue, form an opinion and gather supporting evidence, and be prepared to discuss and defend your position in a classroom debate or in a one- to two-page paper, depending on your instructor's directions.

Courtesy Microsoft, Inc.

## Microsoft

**Stephen Rose is the Senior Product Marketing Manager and Industry Vertical Lead on the U.S. Windows and Devices team in Redmond. Before that, he spent five years managing content for the programs, such as the Springboard Series on TechNet, that drive Windows adoptions. Stephen has spoken at over 100 IT conferences, and he participates in numerous blogs, webinars, videos, and podcasts. He has been an MCSE, MCITP, and MCT (Microsoft Certified Trainer) for 20 years, as well as a two-time Microsoft Most Valuable Professional (MVP).**

## A conversation with STEPHEN ROSE

**Senior Product Marketing Manager and Industry Vertical Lead for U.S. Windows and Devices, Microsoft**

> *The hardware matters less and less every year—what matters is the delivery system.*

### My Background . . .

It's funny how things work out. I received a bachelor's degree in Film and Video production from Columbia College in Chicago in the late '80s. By 1996, I was burned-out and decided to follow my passion for computers and IT by becoming a technical trainer with New Horizons. Within two years I got my MCT and MCSE, and I started my own IT consulting company that designed, built, and managed software and services for companies worldwide (including many Fortune 500 companies) for 15 years. I'm now the Senior Product Marketing Manager and Industry Vertical Lead for U.S. Windows and Devices at Microsoft. There are 22.6 million IT pros in the world and my job is to help support them within the workplace. I oversee and manage the Windows content on Microsoft TechNet, as well as on a number of forums, newsletters, and blogs. I also speak at conferences, roundtables, and the North American and European Springboard Series Tours.

### It's Important to Know . . .

**We are moving to a "cloud first, mobile first" world.** Businesses, as well as individuals, are moving into the cloud with amazing speed. This has dramatically changed the business model for many companies. In addition, we are now able to offer identical experiences to Windows, iOS, and Android users. The hardware matters less and less every year—what matters is the delivery system.

**Software is not always a one-size-fits-all situation.** Apps will need to run on many different form factors, such as phones, tablets, and touch-based devices, in addition to laptops and desktops. And these devices are not always interchangeable. In addition, an overblown app on a device without a keyboard can be hard to use—if an app is difficult to use, no one will adopt it.

**Computers are inherently secure.** It is the choices that users make (such as clicking on links in e-mails and downloading music, movies, and software illegally) that make their devices not secure. If users use their best judgment when surfing the Web, they will be safer. If something sounds too good to be true, it usually is. At Microsoft, we are adding many new features to our operating system and browser to help users make smart decisions.

### How I Use this Technology . . .

Windows 10 has several key features that leverage this "cloud first, mobile first" focus of our customer base and that I use on a regular basis. For example, I use the EDP (Enterprise Data Protection) feature to encrypt my data, to separate my work and personal applications so they do not cross pollinate, and to prevent me (and my employees) from accidentally launching apps not approved for corporate use from business applications. Security features such as this give businesses greater control over their employees, which is especially important with cloud storage, without inhibiting the creative, business process. For example, an employee about to lose his or her job could stash gigs of data into a free cloud storage in a matter of minutes. With Windows 10 and EDP, access to any corporate document can be removed no matter where the document is located (such as in e-mail or cloud storage, or on an external storage medium) simply by revoking the document's encryption key.

## What the Future Holds . . .

The cloud is one of the major technologies changing our future. It is going to dramatically change how we do business and how we perceive data. The physical PC is no longer part of the equation and the idea of "my data anywhere on the planet from any computer" is very powerful. Not storing data locally reduces risk, lowers costs, and adds more productivity via flexibility. In addition, cloud computing—along with new form factors, the need for social media accessibility, the emergence of location-aware applications, and the increased availability of app stores—have changed how we view devices. The lines between tablets, smartphones, and PCs are already blurring.

We are also in the process of killing the password, something that I believe is long overdue. We are moving from "what you know" security methods to "what you have" security methods. Devices now can log you in with your face, a fingertip, or a wearable device. Not needing a password is less stressful for the end user and a far more secure solution for IT because end users often aren't very smart about picking secure passwords. This is a key area that I see growing into everyday life. Within the next few years, your face will be your key for such everyday activities as buying groceries and paying the check at your local diner.

> *" . . . technology shapes us but, like any tool, it's how we leverage it and use it for the better that is important. "*

## My Advice to Students . . .

Understanding the cloud, as well as where and when it makes sense to use it, is key to being a successful IT pro. Whatever career you choose, remember that technology shapes us but, like any tool, it's how we leverage it and use it for the better that is important.

---

### Discussion Question

Stephen Rose believes that cloud computing will impact both individuals and businesses and change how we perceive data and do business. Think about the computing and communications tasks you use today. What is the benefit of being able to perform them via the cloud? Are there any disadvantages? Do you currently use multiple devices to access your data and apps? If so, are the data and apps stored in the cloud, on each device, or both? If not, would the ability to access your data and apps via any device, anywhere, be an advantage in your life? Would a cloud-based world change how you use data or apps on a daily basis? If a person or business decides not to utilize the cloud, will this be a disadvantage for that person or business? Why or why not? Be prepared to discuss your position (in class, via an online forum, or via a class blog, depending on your instructor's directions). You may also be asked to write a short paper expressing your opinion.

**>For more information about Microsoft, visit www.windows.com/ltpro and follow Stephen on his Twitter feed @stephenlrose.**

# module

# Networks and the Internet

From telephone calls, to home and business networks, to Web surfing and online shopping, networking and the Internet are deeply embedded in our society today. Because of this, it is important for individuals to be familiar with basic networking concepts and terminology, as well as with the variety of activities that take place today via networks—including the Internet, the world's largest network. It is also important for all individuals to be aware of the potential problems and risks associated with networks and our networked society.

The purpose of Chapter 7 is to introduce basic networking principles, including what a computer network is, how it works, and what it can be used for. The Internet and World Wide Web are the topics of Chapter 8. Although these topics were introduced in Chapter 1, Chapter 8 explains in more detail how the Internet and World Wide Web originated, and looks more closely at common Internet activities, including how to search the Web effectively for information. Chapter 8 also discusses the various options for connecting to the Internet, as well as how to select an Internet service provider (ISP). Chapter 9 takes a look at some of the risks related to computer, network, and Internet use, and explains measures computer users can take to lessen these risks.

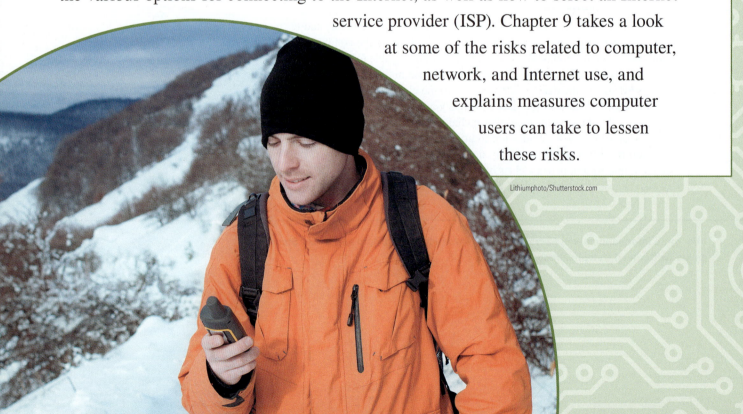

Lithiumphoto/Shutterstock.com

# in this module

*"In the digital world, you are your digital identity."*

For more comments from Guest Expert **Shishir Singh** of Intel Security Group, see the **Expert Insight on . . . Networks and the Internet** feature at the end of the module.

# chapter 7

# Networks and Communication Devices

**After completing this chapter, you will be able to do the following:**

1. Define a computer network and its purpose.

2. Describe several uses for networks.

3. Understand the various characteristics of a network, such as topology, architecture, and size.

4. Understand characteristics about data and how it travels over a network.

5. Name specific types of wired and wireless networking media and explain how they transmit data.

6. Identify the most common communications protocols and networking standards used with networks today.

7. List several types of networking hardware and explain the purpose of each.

# OVERVIEW

The term *communications*, when used in a computer context, refers to *telecommunications*; that is, data sent from one device to another using communications media, such as telephone lines, privately owned cables, and the airwaves. Communications usually take place over a private (such as a home or business) computer network, the Internet, or a telephone network, and are an integral part of our personal and professional lives today.

The purpose of Chapter 7 is to introduce you to the concepts and terminology associated with computer networks. First, a computer network is defined, followed by a look at some common networking applications. Next, a number of technical issues related to networks are discussed, including general characteristics of networks and data transmission, as well as the types of transmission media in use today. We then proceed to an explanation of the various communications protocols and networking standards used today, which help explain the ways networked devices communicate with one another. The chapter closes with a look at the various types of hardware used in a computer network. ■

## WHAT IS A NETWORK?

A *network*, in general, is a connected system of objects or people. As discussed in Chapter 1, a **computer network** is a collection of computers and other hardware devices connected together so that network users can share hardware, software, and data, as well as communicate with each other electronically. Today, computer networks are converging with *telephone networks* and other *communications networks*, with both data and voice being sent over these networks. Computer networks range from small private networks to the Internet and are widely used by individuals and businesses today (see Figure 7-1).

In most businesses, computer networks are essential. They enable employees to share expensive resources, access the Internet, and communicate with each other, as well as with business partners and customers. They facilitate the exchange and collaboration of documents and they are often a key component of the ordering, inventory, and fulfillment systems used to process customer orders. In homes, computer networks enable individuals to share resources, access the Internet, and communicate with others. In addition, they allow individuals to access a wide variety of information, services, and entertainment, as well as share data (such as digital photos, downloaded movies, and music) among the networked

**FIGURE 7-1**
Common uses for computer networks.

### USES FOR COMPUTER NETWORKS

Sharing an Internet connection among several users.

Sharing application software, printers, and other resources.

Facilitating Voice over IP (VoIP), e-mail, videoconferencing, messaging, and other communications applications.

Working collaboratively; for example, sharing a company database or using collaboration tools to create or review documents.

Exchanging files among network users and over the Internet.

Connecting the computers and the entertainment devices (such as TVs, gaming consoles, and stereo systems) located within a home.

NET

---

> **Computer network.** A collection of computers and other hardware devices that are connected together to share hardware, software, and data, as well as to communicate electronically with one another.

# HOW IT WORKS

### Wireless Power

Imagine recharging your notebook computer or smartphone just by setting it down in the right place, or using your kitchen blender just by placing it on a countertop but not plugging it in. After many years of development, these scenarios are now possible with *wireless power*.

The first wireless power application to become available is *wireless charging*, which allows your smartphone or other mobile device to be charged by just placing it on a charging surface. Wireless charging uses *magnetic induction* (similar to cordless electric toothbrushes that have a charging base) to transfer power wirelessly from the charging device to the target device. It usually adjusts the power transmitted to each device being charged automatically in order to meet the needs of that device, and it deactivates the charging process when the device is fully charged. Charging works with the target device's regular battery, but the device needs an embedded or attached charging receiver. Smartphones and other mobile devices are beginning to include built-in wireless charging capabilities, and several new CPUs support wireless power to enable portable computers using those CPUs to be charged wirelessly. These devices can be used with stand-alone wireless chargers, as well as with the integrated charging stations beginning to appear at locations where individuals normally place their devices during the day, such as cars, IKEA furniture, and customer tables at McDonald's and Starbucks (see the accompanying photo).

There are currently two competing wireless charging standards, PMA and Qi (pronounced "chee"). *PMA* is supported by the *Power Matters Alliance*, which recently merged with the *Alliance for Wireless Power*. Members include Intel, Broadcom, and AT&T. *Qi* is supported by the *Wireless Power Consortium*, which includes

Panasonic, Verizon Wireless, Sony, Energizer, Motorola Mobility, Nokia, and LG Electronics. These two standards are not compatible with each other, but some products (such as Samsung phones) support both standards so consumers can use wireless chargers based on either technology.

It is expected that wireless charging capabilities based on one or both of these standards will soon be expanded to other objects, such as kitchen countertops, hotel nightstands, airline tray tables, and other locations where it is common to place your devices. Future wireless power applications could even include charging transmitters built into walls to power all of the devices located in the home on a continual basis, as well as into garage floors and parking lots to wirelessly recharge electric vehicles.

Because there is a cost associated with providing the wireless power, it is expected that businesses providing wireless charging services may eventually charge for these services or include a certain amount of recharge with a purchase, similar to when Wi-Fi hotspots first started appearing in public locations.

Source: Powermat Technologies Ltd.

devices in a home. On the go, networks enable individuals to work from remote locations, locate information whenever and wherever it is needed, and stay in touch with others.

## NETWORKING APPLICATIONS

Today, there are a wide variety of important networking applications used by businesses and individuals for communications, information retrieval, and other applications. Some of the most common networking applications are described next. For a look at an emerging networking application—wireless power—see the How It Works box.

### The Internet

As previously discussed, the Internet is the largest computer network in the world. Many networking applications today (such as information retrieval, shopping, entertainment, and e-mail) take place via the Internet. Accessing Web pages and exchanging e-mail were discussed in Chapter 1; additional Internet-based activities are covered in Chapter 8.

## Telephone Service

The original telephone network, sometimes called the *plain old telephone service* (*POTS*), was one of the first communications networks. This network is still used today to provide telephone service to conventional *landline phones*, and is used for some types of Internet connections.

**Mobile phones** (also called *wireless phones*) are phones that use a wireless network for communications instead of the regular telephone network. Billions of mobile phones are in use worldwide and more than 90% of Americans own a mobile phone. In fact, mobile phones may be the only telephone alternative in developing countries

**CELLULAR PHONES**
Can be used wherever cellular phone coverage is available.

**SATELLITE PHONES**
Can be used virtually anywhere.

and other locations with a poor landline telephone infrastructure. Even in developed countries, however, many individuals (nearly one half of all Americans, according to a recent report) have dropped their conventional landline telephone service and are using their mobile phones as their primary telephones. Companies that provide mobile phone services are commonly called *wireless providers*.

In addition to making telephone calls, most mobile phones today are smartphones and so can be used for a wide variety of purposes, such as exchanging e-mail and text messages, viewing Web pages, and watching TV shows. Some smartphones can also be used to pay for goods or services and to unlock doors. These types of smartphone applications are more prominent in countries like Asia and Europe that have a longer history of mobile phone use than the United States, but they are now available in the United States as well.

The most common type of mobile phone is the **cellular (cell) phone** (see Figure 7-2), which communicates via *cellular technology*. Cell phone service is available in most populated areas of the United States, but coverage varies depending on location because cell phones need to be within range of a cell tower to function, as described later in this chapter. Some cell phones today are **dual-mode phones**—phones that allow users to make telephone calls using more than one communications network, such as via two different cellular standards or via both a cellular and a Wi-Fi network. This allows users to carry a single device and, at any given time, use the network that is available, least expensive, or has the needed capabilities. For example, service from the wireless provider Republic Wireless is designed to work with a *cellular/Wi-Fi dual-mode phone*. When a subscriber makes a phone call, the phone first tries to connect via a Wi-Fi network, such as using a home or office Wi-Fi network (in order to use that network's Internet connection to make the call); if a Wi-Fi network is not available or the signal becomes too weak, the phone places or continues the call via a cellular network. Cellular/Wi-Fi dual-mode phones and *Wi-Fi calling* are also becoming available via other wireless providers, such as T-Mobile. They allow callers to save on cell phone minutes because they can receive and place calls

NET

**FIGURE 7-2**
Types of mobile phones.

**TIP**

Even if your cell phone can't place phone calls via Wi-Fi, it may be able to connect to Wi-Fi networks for browsing and other Web applications.

---

>**Mobile phone.** A phone, such as a cellular or satellite phone, that uses a wireless telephone network. >**Cellular (cell) phone.** A mobile phone that communicates via a cellular network. >**Dual-mode phone.** A mobile phone that can be used with more than one communications network, such as with both a cellular and a Wi-Fi network.

via Wi-Fi when they are in range of a Wi-Fi network, and via a cellular network when they are out of range of a Wi-Fi network.

Another, but less common, type of mobile phone is the **satellite phone** (refer again to Figure 7-2), which communicates via *satellite technology*, also described in detail later in this chapter. Although more expensive than cellular service, satellite phone coverage is typically much broader, often on a country-by-country basis, and some satellite phone services cover the entire earth. Consequently, satellite phones are most often used by individuals—such as soldiers, journalists, wilderness guides, and researchers—traveling in remote areas where continuous cellular service might not be available. They are also useful during times when cellular service might be interrupted, such as during a hurricane or other emergency. An emerging option is the *cellular/satellite dual-mode phone* that can be used with cellular service when it is available and then switches to satellite service when cellular service is not available.

## Television and Radio Broadcasting

Two other original communications networks are *broadcast television networks* and *radio networks*. These networks are still used to deliver TV and radio content to the public, though some of this content is also available via the Internet today, as discussed in Chapter 8. Other networks involved with video content delivery are *cable TV networks*, *satellite TV networks*, and the private *closed-circuit television* (*CCTV*) systems used by businesses for surveillance and security purposes. Cable and satellite TV networks are also used today to provide access to the Internet.

## Global Positioning System (GPS) Applications

The **global positioning system** (**GPS**) network consists of 24 Department of Defense *GPS satellites* (in orbit approximately 12,000 miles above the earth) that are used for location and navigation purposes. A *GPS receiver* measures the distance between the receiver and four GPS satellites simultaneously (based on how long radio signals, which travel at the speed of light, take to travel between the receiver and satellite) to determine the receiver's exact geographic location; these receivers are accurate to within 3 meters (less than 10 feet).

GPS receivers (see some examples in Figure 7-3) are commonly used by individuals to determine their geographic location while hiking and to obtain driving directions while traveling. GPS receivers are also commonly used on the job, such as by surveyors, farmers, fishermen, and public safety personnel. In addition to relaying location information, GPS can be used to guide vehicles and equipment (for example, to locate and dispatch ambulances, police cars, and other emergency vehicles, or to guide bulldozers and other construction equipment automatically using that device's preprogrammed instructions). GPS is used by the military to guide munitions and trucks, as well as to track military aircraft, ships, and submarines. Most smartphones today include GPS capabilities, which allow the use of location-specific services and applications such as using your location in driving directions, Web searches, social media activities, and other *location-aware apps* (see the Foursquare app in Figure 7-3). GPS capabilities are also built into consumer devices that are designed for specific purposes, such as wearable fitness devices (refer again to Figure 7-3) that use GPS technology to record workout data for runners or bicyclists.

>**Satellite phone.** A mobile phone that communicates via satellite technology. >**Global positioning system (GPS).** A system that uses satellites and a receiver to determine the exact geographic location of the receiver.

**CAR-MOUNTED GPS RECEIVERS**

Source: Toyota Motor Sales, U.S.A., Inc.

**GPS RECEIVERS INTEGRATED INTO SMARTPHONES**

Chardchanin/Shutterstock.com; Foursquare

**WEARABLE GPS RECEIVERS**

Source: Garmin Ltd.

One recent concern regarding GPS technology is the possibility that the aging GPS satellites might fail (and, consequently, interrupt GPS services) before new replacement satellites can be launched. There must be 24 GPS satellites in orbit at any given time in order to have at least four satellites in view from anywhere on the planet. Currrently, there are 31 GPS satellites in orbit so that satellites can be serviced or decommissioned as needed. The current GPS system is *GPS II*. The next generation GPS system (*GPS III*) is currently under development and will be more powerful and more accurate than the current system. The first GPS III satellite is scheduled to launch in 2017.

**FIGURE 7-3**
**GPS receivers.** Allow people to determine their exact geographical location, usually for safety or navigational purposes.

## Monitoring Systems

*Monitoring systems* use networking technology to determine the current location or status of an object. Some monitoring systems in use today use the RFID tags and RFID readers discussed in Chapter 4 to monitor the status of the objects (such as shipping boxes, livestock, or expensive equipment) to which the RFID tags are attached. Other monitoring systems use GPS technology. For instance, many law enforcement *ankle bracelet monitoring systems* use GPS to detect if the offender has left his or her authorized areas, and the *OnStar* system built into many GM cars uses GPS to locate vehicles when the occupant activates the service or when sensors indicate that the car was involved in an accident. There are also *vehicle monitoring systems* that are installed in cars by parents and employers to monitor the location and use of the vehicles (by children or employees, respectively) using networking technology; *child monitoring systems* allow parents to monitor the physical locations of their children. Both types of monitoring systems typically record a location history; many also allow the location of a vehicle or child to be tracked in real time via a Web site or mobile app (see Figure 7-4). Some systems can even be used to set up a "virtual fence" for a child or a car or a maximum allowable car speed; the parent or employer is notified (usually via a text message) anytime the child or vehicle leaves the prescribed geographical area or the vehicle being monitored (or that the child being monitored is riding in) exceeds the designated speed. Child monitoring systems often include additional features, such as the ability to have the child's location pushed to the parent's device at regular intervals, the ability to have the parent notified if the child is within 500 feet of a registered sex offender, and an "SOS" button that the child can press if he or she is lost or afraid. The child monitoring system shown in Figure 7-4 also is available as a smartphone app for teenagers. Similar GPS systems are designed to be used to track elderly parents or by individuals who are hiking or traveling so they can be located if they become lost or injured.

**FIGURE 7-4**
**GPS-based child monitoring systems.** Allow parents to track their children in real time.

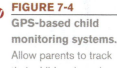

Locations of registered offenders.

Child's current (green) and past (red) locations.

Source: Amber Alert GPS; Chardchanin/Shutterstock.com

**NET**

Source: Nest Labs

**⚠ FIGURE 7-5**

**Smart thermostats.**
This thermostat (left)
contains a variety of
sensors and can be
controlled remotely via
a mobile app (right).

> **TIP**
>
> It has been predicted that 50
> billion devices (essentially anything
> with an on-off switch) will be
> connected by 2020, creating an
> Internet of Things (IoT), discussed
> more in Chapter 8.

**▼ FIGURE 7-6**

**Placeshifting.** Used
to transfer multimedia
content to the user's
current location.

Another area in which monitoring systems are frequently used is home healthcare. With the U.S. population aging, a variety of home medical monitoring systems are available to monitor elderly or infirm individuals and to notify someone if a possible problem is detected. For instance, *electronic medical monitors* take the vital signs of an individual (such as weight, blood-sugar readings, or blood pressure) or prompt an individual to answer questions (such as if he or she has eaten yet that day or has taken prescribed medication). These monitors then transfer readings or the individual's responses to a healthcare provider via the Internet or a telephone network for evaluation and feedback and to detect potential problems as early as possible.

Other monitoring systems use *sensors*—devices that respond to a stimulus (such as heat, light, or pressure) and generate an electrical signal that can be measured or interpreted. The sensors are usually small and lightweight; contain the necessary hardware and software to sense and record the appropriate data, as well as transmit the data to other devices in the network; and include a power source (typically a battery). Sensors can be included in a network anytime there is a situation with measurable criteria that needs precise, automatic, and continual monitoring. For example, *sensor networks* can be used during transport to monitor the temperature inside cargo containers to ensure that products stay within their allowable temperature range, in pharmaceutical plants to monitor temperature and relative humidity in the drug development process, and in homes to manage and control devices such as smart appliances and heating/cooling systems. For example, the thermostat shown in Figure 7-5 contains temperature, humidity, activity, and light sensors; can be controlled via a mobile app; and can program itself based on the activity within the home. IBM expects to see the use of sensor technology expanding to additional areas in the future, such as nano-sized sensors embedded in paint that help manage the energy use of a building or as a coating applied to plumbing systems to detect leaks and other potential problems.

## Multimedia Networking

A growing use of home networks is to deliver digital multimedia content (such as digital photos, digital music, home movies, streaming movies, and recorded TV shows) to devices (such as computers, mobile devices, televisions, and home entertainment systems) on that network. Home networks are also used to connect smart TVs to the Internet. While sometimes the necessary networking capabilities are built into the devices being used (such as smart TVs with wireless technology built in), a *streaming media player* (such as an *Apple TV* or a *Roku* device) can be used to connect a conventional television to your home network to deliver content from your networked devices or the Internet to that television. The most common multimedia networking standards available today are discussed later in this chapter.

Other multimedia networking devices (such as the *Slingbox* shown in Figure 7-6) are designed to *placeshift* multimedia content; that is, to allow individuals to view their multimedia content at a more convenient location. For instance, an individual with a Slingbox installed at home can both control and view programs from their home TV or DVR via a portable computer or mobile device, in order to watch local news while out of town, watch a recorded TV show while at the beach, or start recording a TV show from the office. The newest Slingboxes also allow you to wirelessly transfer photos and videos from your mobile devices to your home TV via your home network.

**1.** Slingbox device is connected to the user's home cable or satellite set-top box, as well as to the home Wi-Fi network.

**2.** SlingPlayer software allows the user to watch and control his or her home TV system from anywhere with an Internet connection.

Source: Sling Media, Inc.

## Videoconferencing, Collaborative Computing, and Telecommuting

**Videoconferencing** is the use of networking technology to conduct real-time, face-to-face meetings between individuals physically located in different places. Videoconferencing can take place between individuals using their personal computers and the Internet (as discussed in more detail in Chapter 8) or it can take place using two smartphones or other mobile devices with videoconferencing (sometimes called *video calling* or *video chat*) capabilities. Larger business videoconferences often take place via a dedicated videoconferencing setup using *telepresence videoconferencing*, in which participants appear life-sized to more closely mimic a real-time meeting environment (see Figure 7-7). Although telepresence videoconferencing setups are expensive, with travel becoming increasingly more expensive and time consuming, many businesses view videoconferencing as a viable replacement for face-to-face meetings. Telepresence videoconferencing is also used in educational settings (to hold live classes in multiple locations simultaneously, for instance) and in public locations such as airports and hospitals to provide language translation services for nonverbal languages such as American Sign Language.

Networking technology is also widely used today with collaborative software tools to enable individuals to work together on documents and other project components. This trend toward online collaboration is usually called *workgroup computing* or *collaborative computing*. For many industries, collaboration is a very important business tool. For example, engineers and architects commonly collaborate on designs; advertising firms and other businesses often route proposals, presentations, and other important documents to several individuals for comments before preparing the final version for a client; and newspaper, magazine, and book editors must read and edit drafts of articles and books before they are published. Instead of these types of collaborations taking place on paper, as in the past, collaboration tools (such as the Microsoft Office *markup tools* and specialized *collaboration software*) are used in conjunction with networking technology (typically a company network or the Internet) to allow multiple individuals to edit and make comments in a document without destroying the original content. Once a document has been reviewed by all individuals, the original author can read the comments and accept or reject changes that others have made. Some collaboration software also includes shared calendars, project scheduling, and videoconferencing tools.

Source: Cisco Systems, Inc.

**FIGURE 7-7**
Telepresence videoconferencing.

## ASK THE EXPERT

Courtesy D-Link Systems, Inc.

**D-Link** Building Networks for People

**Daniel Kelley,** Vice President, Marketing, D-Link Systems, Inc.

### How will the Internet of Things (IoT) affect our daily lives?

The Internet of Things (IoT) is already having an impact on our daily lives and that impact will only increase as more and more existing devices and new products become integrated into the IoT in order to interact with other devices. While the IoT will touch nearly every aspect of our society in some way or another over time, I hope and trust that the major advancements will be in terms of improving health and safety. While it's always cool to see new applications focused on entertainment, I foresee big advancements in safety such as cars that are able to avoid both traffic and collisions by getting "smarter" and having constant dialogue with other cars and the environment around them.

NET

>**Videoconferencing.** The use of computers, video cameras, microphones, and networking technologies to conduct face-to-face meetings over a network.

The availability of videoconferencing, collaborative computing, and other tools (such as the Internet, e-mail, and smartphones) has made **telecommuting** a viable option for many individuals. With telecommuting, individuals work from a remote location (typically their home) and communicate with their place of business and clients via networking technologies. Telecommuting allows the employee to be flexible, such as to work nontraditional hours or remain with the company after a relocation. It also enables a company to save on office and parking space, as well as office-related expenses such as electricity. As an environmental plus, telecommuting helps cut down on the traffic and pollution caused by traditional work commuting. In addition, it gives a business the possibility to continue operations during situations that may affect an employee's ability to get to the office, such as during hurricanes, during a bridge or highway closure, or during a flu outbreak. As a result, many experts suggest businesses include telecommuting procedures in their *business continuity plans*, even if they don't intend to use telecommuting on a regular basis. Business continuity plans and disaster recovery are discussed in detail in Chapter 9.

**FIGURE 7-8**

Examples of telemedicine applications.

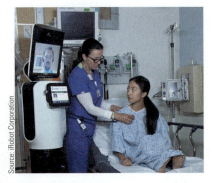

**REMOTE DIAGNOSES**
Teleconferencing systems and remote diagnostic equipment enable physicians to receive and review patient data and interact with patients and/or on-site medical staff in order to make remote diagnoses.

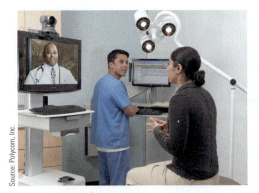

**REMOTE CONSULTATIONS**
Teleconferencing systems enable physicians to talk with patients and consult with other physicians.

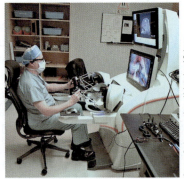

**TELESURGERY**
Telesurgery systems enable surgeons to control a surgical robot remotely in order to operate via the Internet or a private network.

## Telemedicine

**Telemedicine** is the use of networking technology to provide medical information and services. At its simplest level, it includes Web sites that patients can access to contact their physicians, make appointments, view lab results, and more. More complex telemedicine systems are used to provide care to individuals who may not otherwise have access to that care. For instance, physicians can use telemedicine to perform remote diagnoses of patients—for example, healthcare workers at rural locations, childcare facilities, and other locations can use video cameras, electronic stethoscopes, and other devices to send images and vital statistics of a patient to a physician located at a medical facility, and individuals can get a medical consultation from their homes (see Figure 7-8). Videoconferencing robots or systems can also be used to allow physicians to communicate remotely with other physicians or with hospitalized patients, enabling individuals living in remote areas to consult with a specialist or otherwise receive medical care.

Another example of telemedicine is **telesurgery**—a form of *robot-assisted surgery* (where a robot controlled by a physician operates on the patient) in which at least one of the surgeons performs the operation by controlling the robot remotely over the Internet or another network (refer again to Figure 7-8). Robot-assisted surgery systems typically use cameras to give the human surgeon an extremely close view of the surgical area. As a result, robot-assisted surgery is typically more precise and results in smaller incisions than those made by a human surgeon, allowing for less invasive surgery (for example, not having to crack through the rib cage to access the heart) and resulting in less pain for the patient, a faster recovery time, and fewer potential complications.

Telemedicine has enormous potential for providing quality medical care to individuals who live in rural or underdeveloped areas and who do not have access to sufficient medical care. Telemedicine will also be necessary for future long-term space explorations—such as a trip to Mars and back that may take two years or more—because astronauts will undoubtedly need medical care while on the journey. In fact, NASA astronauts and physicians have performed telesurgery experiments in the Aquarius Undersea Laboratory 50 feet below the ocean surface to help in the development of a robotic unit that will eventually allow physicians to perform surgery remotely on patients who are in outer space. Some individuals envision the eventual use of portable robot-assisted telesurgery units in space, war zones, and other environments where access to surgeons is extremely limited.

## NETWORK CHARACTERISTICS

Networks can be identified by a variety of characteristics, including whether they are designed for wired or wireless access, their topology, their architecture, and their size or coverage area. These topics are described in the next few sections.

### Wired vs. Wireless Networks

Networks can be designed for access via wired and/or wireless connections. With a **wired network** connection, the computers and other devices on the network are physically connected (via cabling) to the network. With a **wireless network** connection, wireless (usually radio) signals are used to send data through the air between devices, instead of using physical cables. Wired networks include conventional telephone networks, cable TV networks, and the wired networks commonly found in schools, businesses, and government facilities. Wireless networks include conventional television and radio networks, cellular telephone networks, satellite TV networks, and the wireless networks commonly found in homes, schools, and businesses. Wireless networks are also found in many public locations (such as coffeehouses, businesses, airports, hotels, and libraries) to provide Internet access to users while they are on the go via public wireless **hotspots**. For a look at how wireless networks and other technologies are being used at baseball and football stadiums today, see the Inside the Industry box.

Many networks today are accessible via both wired and wireless connections. For instance, a business may have a wired main company network to which the computers in employee offices are always connected, as well as provide wireless access to the network for visitors and employees to use while in waiting rooms, conference rooms, and other locations within the office building. A home network may have a wired connection to the Internet (such as via a modem and router), plus wireless access for the devices in the home (such as computers, printers, televisions, and gaming devices) that will access the home network wirelessly.

Wired networks tend to be faster and more secure than wireless networks, but wireless networks have the advantage of allowing easy connections in locations where physical wiring is impractical or inconvenient (such as inside an existing home or outdoors),

**TIP** ✓

A fast and stable Internet connection is a critical component of a telesurgery system. A recent study found that surgeons didn't notice a lag time of up to 200 milliseconds (about the blink of an eye), but a lag time of more than 500 milliseconds was too risky.

**TIP** ✓

The first surgery broadcast live via the surgeon's Google Glass smart glasses occurred in 2014 and was watched by 13,000 medical students.

**NET**

---

>**Wired network.** A network in which computers and other devices are connected to the network via physical cables. >**Wireless network.** A network in which computers and other devices are connected to the network without physical cables; data is typically sent via radio waves. >**Hotspot.** A location that provides wireless Internet access.

# INSIDE THE INDUSTRY

### High-Tech Stadiums

Beginning with the 2004 Opening Day of the San Francisco Giants baseball team, when AT&T Park became the first professional sports venue to provide continuous universal wireless access to fans in all concourses and seating areas, wireless networks and sports stadiums have been intertwined. Today, technology is a big factor when designing or updating stadiums. The $1.2 billion Levi's Stadium in Santa Clara, home to the San Francisco 49ers football team, is one example of cutting-edge technology integrated into a new stadium design. The stadium (shown in the accompanying photo) opened in 2014 and is the host stadium for Super Bowl 50 in 2016. It was designed with technology in mind and as a showcase for Silicon Valley innovation, featuring services and technology from Sony, Comcast, Intel, Yahoo!, and other companies. The stadium includes 200 miles of data cable and more than 12,000 network ports. All sound and video is delivered via the network, which supports 40 gigabits per second of data traffic and is considered the foundation of the stadium. Fans can enjoy free Wi-Fi (using both 2.4 and 5 GHz channels and in a variety of Wi-Fi standards, including 802.11ac) available throughout the stadium, via more than 1,000 access points. Other high-tech features include tablet holders on the seats, and more than 2,000 screens inside the stadium, including high-definition video boards measuring over 19,000 square feet total. Games are captured in 4K using 10 video cameras,

which allows up to six replays to be played per live play. The Levi's Stadium mobile app allows fans to view exclusive 49ers content, video replays after live plays, in-seat ordering and delivery of food and beverages, and paperless ticketing.

The technology-rich Levi's Stadium has kick-started discussion about including consumer-oriented technology in stadiums across the country. According to Baltimore Ravens President Dick Cass, "It's what our fans want. They want the ability to take out their tablet, send a Facebook picture, and check the fantasy football scores, so we have to provide that." Based on recent trends, they likely will.

Courtesy of LevisStadium.com

as well as giving users much more freedom regarding where they can use their computers. With wireless networking, for example, you can surf the Web on your notebook computer from anywhere in your house, access the Internet with your tablet or smartphone while you are on the go, and create a home network without having to run wires among the rooms in your house.

## Network Topologies

The physical *topology* of a computer network indicates how the devices in the network are arranged. Three of the most common physical topologies are star, bus, and mesh (see Figure 7-9).

> ➤ **Star network**—uses a central device (such as a server or a switch, discussed later in this chapter) to which all network devices connect and through which all network data is sent. If the central device fails, then the network cannot function.

> **Star network.** A network that uses a central device to connect all network devices and through which all network data is sent.

➤ **Bus network**—uses a central cable to which all network devices connect. All data is transmitted down the bus line from one device to another so, if the bus line fails, then the network cannot function.

➤ **Mesh network**—uses a number of different connections between network devices so that data can take any of several possible paths from source to destination. With a *full mesh topology* (such as the one shown in Figure 7-9), each device on the network is connected to every other device on the network. With a *partial mesh topology*, some devices are connected to all other devices, but some are connected only to those devices with which they exchange the most data. Consequently, if one device on a mesh network fails, the network can still function, assuming there is an alternate path available. Mesh networks are used most often with wireless networks.

Many networks, however, don't conform to a standard topology. Some networks combine topologies and connect multiple smaller networks, in effect turning several smaller networks into one larger one. For example, two star networks may be joined together using a bus line.

## Network Architectures

Networks also vary by their *architecture*; that is, the way they are designed to communicate. The two most common network architectures are client-server and peer-to-peer (P2P).

### Client-Server Networks

*Client-server networks* include both *clients* (computers and other devices on the network that request and utilize network resources) and *servers* (computers that are dedicated to processing client requests). Network servers are typically powerful computers with lots of memory and a very large hard drive. They provide access to software, files, and other resources that are being shared via the network. Servers typically perform a variety of tasks. For example, a single server can act as a *network server* to manage network traffic, a *file server* to manage shared files, a *print server* to handle printing-related activities, and/or a *mail server* or *Web server* to manage e-mail and Web page requests, respectively. For instance, there is only one server in the network illustrated in Figure 7-10 on the next page, and it is capable of performing all server tasks for that network. When a client retrieves files from a server, it is called *downloading*; transferring data from a client to a server is called *uploading*.

### Peer-to-Peer (P2P) Networks

With a *peer-to-peer* *(P2P) network*, a central server is not used (see Figure 7-11 on the next page). Instead, all the computers on the network work at the same functional level, and users have direct access to the computers and other devices attached to the network. For instance, users can access files stored on a peer computer's hard drive and print using a peer computer's printer, provided those devices have been designated as *shared devices*. Peer-to-peer networks are less expensive and less complicated to implement than client-server networks because there are no dedicated servers, but they may not have the same performance as client-server networks under heavy use.

**STAR NETWORKS**
Use a central device to connect each device directly to the network.

**BUS NETWORKS**
Use a central cable to connect each device in a linear fashion.

**MESH NETWORKS**
Each computer or device is connected to multiple (sometimes all of the other) devices on the network.

**FIGURE 7-9**
Basic network topologies.

**NET**

---

> **Bus network.** A network consisting of a central cable to which all network devices are connected and through which all network data is sent.
> **Mesh network.** A network in which there are multiple connections among the devices on the network so that data can take any of several possible paths.

CLIENT

CLIENT

THE INTERNET

**NETWORK SERVER**
(provides client devices with
network services, such as file,
print, e-mail, and Internet access)

ROUTER

CLIENT

**SHARED NETWORK
PRINTER**

⚠ **FIGURE 7-10**

**Client-server networks.**
Client computers
communicate through one
or more servers.

⚠ **FIGURE 7-11**

**Peer-to-peer networks.**
Computers communicate
directly with one another.

THE INTERNET

**P2P HOME NETWORKS**
Devices connect and communicate via the
home network.

**INTERNET P2P NETWORKS**
Devices connect and communicate
via the Internet.

Peer-to-peer capabilities are built into many personal operating systems and are often used with small office or home networks.

Another type of peer-to-peer networking—sometimes called *Internet peer-to-peer* (*Internet P2P*) *computing*—is performed via the Internet. Instead of placing content on a Web server for others to view via the Internet, content is exchanged over the Internet directly between individual users via a peer-to-peer network. For instance, one user can copy a file from another user's hard drive to his or her own computer via the Internet. Internet P2P networking is commonly used for exchanging music and video files with others over the Internet—an illegal act if the content is copyright-protected and the exchange is unauthorized, although legal Internet P2P networks exist. Copyright law, ethics, and other topics related to peer-to-peer file exchanges are covered in Chapter 13.

**CAUTION  CAUTION  CAUTION  CAUTION  CAUTION  CAUTION  CAUT**

Do not enable sharing for folders that you do not want others on your network to see. And, if you choose to use a P2P network, be sure to designate the files in your shared folder as *read-only* to prevent your original files from being overwritten by another P2P user.

## Network Size and Coverage Area

Networks are also frequently classified by their size and their coverage area. This classification impacts the types of users the network is designed to service. The most common categories of networks are discussed next; these networks can use both wired and wireless connections.

## Personal Area Networks (PANs)

A **personal area network (PAN)** is a small network of two or more personal devices for one individual

> **Personal area network (PAN).** A network that connects two or more of an individual's personal devices when they are located close together.

(such as a personal computer, smartphone, headset, tablet, portable speaker, smart watch, and/or printer) that is designed to enable those devices to communicate and share data. PANs can be set up on demand or set up to work together automatically as soon as the devices get within a certain physical distance of each other. For instance, a PAN can be used to sync a mobile device automatically with a personal computer whenever the devices are in range of each other, to connect a tablet to a portable speaker, or to connect a smartphone and other devices to a smart watch or fitness band (see Figure 7-12). PANs are typically wireless and are implemented via Bluetooth or another short-range networking standard (discussed shortly) or via the Internet using Google or another cloud service.

**FIGURE 7-12**
**A fitness PAN.**

## Local Area Networks (LANs)

A **local area network (LAN)** is a network that covers a relatively small geographical area, such as a home, an office building, or a school. LANs allow users on the network to exchange files and e-mail, share printers and other hardware, and access the Internet. The client-server network shown in Figure 7-10 is an example of a LAN.

## Metropolitan Area Networks (MANs)

A **metropolitan area network (MAN)** is a network designed to service a metropolitan area, typically a city or county. Most MANs are owned and operated by a city or by a network provider in order to provide individuals in that location access to the MAN. Some wireless MANs are created by cities (such as Riverside, California—see Figure 7-13) or large organizations (such as Google in downtown Mountain View, California) to provide free or low-cost Internet access to area residents; these are often referred to as *municipal Wi-Fi projects*. In addition, some Internet service providers have free wireless MANs or hotspots in select metropolitan areas for their subscribers to use for Internet access when they are on the go.

**FIGURE 7-13**
**Municipal Wi-Fi.**
This MAN covers downtown Riverside, California.

## Wide Area Networks (WANs)

A **wide area network (WAN)** is a network that covers a large geographical area. Typically, a WAN consists of two or more LANs that are connected together using communications technology. The Internet, by this definition, is the world's largest WAN. WANs may be publicly accessible, like the Internet, or they may be privately owned and operated. For instance, a company may have a private WAN to transfer data from one location to another, such as from each retail store to the corporate headquarters. Large WANs, like the Internet, typically use a mesh topology.

## Intranets and Extranets

An **intranet** is a private network (such as a company LAN) that is designed to be used by an organization's employees and is set up like the Internet (with data posted on Web pages that are accessed with a Web browser). Consequently, little or no employee training is required to use an intranet, and intranet content can be accessed using a variety of devices. Intranets today are used for many purposes, including coordinating internal e-mail and communications, making company publications (such as contact information, manuals, forms, job announcements, and so forth) available to employees, facilitating collaborative computing,

> **Local area network (LAN).** A network that connects devices located in a small geographical area, such as within a building. > **Metropolitan area network (MAN).** A network designed to service a metropolitan area. > **Wide area network (WAN).** A network that connects devices located in a large geographical area. > **Intranet.** A private network that is set up similar to the Internet and is accessed via a Web browser.

## ASK THE EXPERT

Norton by Symantec

**David Lee,** Senior Manager, Mobile Product Management, Norton by Symantec Corporation

**How can an individual surf safely at a public Wi-Fi hotspot?**

First, be sure you are connecting to an official Wi-Fi hotspot, not a similarly named imposter, with a password required to join the network. It's also important to have comprehensive security software on your device, including antivirus, firewall, and intrusion protection.

In addition, avoid doing any sensitive financial transactions, such as online banking or shopping, while using a public Wi-Fi hotspot. If you must do these types of transactions, use a Virtual Private Network (VPN), which provides stronger protection against a variety of risks. A VPN will encrypt your connection, so your usernames, passwords, credit card numbers, and other confidential information are safe.

and providing access to shared calendars and schedules.

A company network that is accessible to authorized outsiders is called an **extranet**. Extranets are usually accessed via the Internet, and they can be used to provide customers and business partners with access to the data they need. Access to intranets and extranets is typically restricted to employees and other authorized users, similar to other company networks.

### Virtual Private Networks (VPNs)

A **virtual private network (VPN)** is a private, secure path across a public network (usually the Internet) that is set up to allow authorized users private, secure access to a network. For instance, a VPN can allow a traveling employee, business partner, or employee located at a satellite office or public wireless hotspot to connect securely to the company network via the Internet. It can also be used by individuals to secure their connection to a public hotspot and can protect any device that connects to a hotspot via Wi-Fi, including notebook computers, tablets, and smartphones. VPNs typically use a process called *tunneling* to carry the data over the Internet and special encryption technology to protect the data so it cannot be understood if it is intercepted during transit (encryption is explained in Chapter 9). Without a VPN, passwords, credit card numbers, and other sensitive data sent to or from a hotspot could be intercepted.

## DATA TRANSMISSION CHARACTERISTICS

Data transmitted over a network has specific characteristics, and it can travel over a network in various ways. These and some other characteristics related to data transmission are discussed next.

### Bandwidth

As discussed in Chapter 2, bandwidth refers to the amount of data that can be transferred (such as via a bus or over a certain type of networking medium) in a given time period and throughput is the amount of data that is actually transferred under real-life conditions. Text data requires the least amount of bandwidth; video data requires the most. Just as a wide fire hose allows more water to pass through it per unit of time than a narrow garden hose allows, a networking medium with a high bandwidth allows more data to pass through it per unit of time than a networking medium with a low bandwidth. Bandwidth is usually measured in the number of *bits per second* (*bps*), *Kbps* (thousands of bits per second), *Mbps* (millions of bits per second), or *Gbps* (billions of bits per second).

> **Extranet.** An intranet that is at least partially accessible to authorized outsiders. > **Virtual private network (VPN).** A private, secure path over a public network, typically the Internet.

## Analog vs. Digital Signals

Data can be represented as either analog or digital signals. Voice and music data in its natural form, for instance, is analog, and data stored on a computer is digital. Most networking media send data using **digital signals**, in which data is represented by only two *discrete states*: 0s and 1s (see Figure 7-14). **Analog signals**, such as those used by conventional telephone systems, represent data with *continuous waves*. The data to be transmitted over a networking medium must match the type of signal (analog or digital) that the medium supports; if it doesn't originally, then it must be converted before the data is transmitted. For instance, analog data that is to be sent using digital signals (such as analog music broadcast by a digital radio station) must first be converted into digital form, and digital data to be sent using analog signals (such as computer data sent over a conventional analog telephone network) must be converted into analog form before it can be transmitted. The conversion of data between analog and digital form is performed by networking hardware.

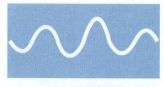

**ANALOG SIGNALS**

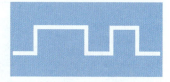

**DIGITAL SIGNALS**

**FIGURE 7-14**
Analog vs. digital signals.

## Transmission Type and Timing

Networking media can also use either serial transmission or parallel transmission. With **serial transmission**, data is sent one bit at a time, one after the other along a single path (see Figure 7-15). When **parallel transmission** is used, a group of bits are sent at the same time, and each bit takes a separate path (refer again to Figure 7-15). While parallel transmission is frequently used within computer components (such as buses) and is used for some wireless networking applications, networking media typically use serial transmission.

When data is sent using serial transmission, a technique must be used to organize the bits being transferred so the data can be reconstructed after it is received. Three ways of timing serial transmissions are by using synchronous, asynchronous, and isochronous connections (see Figure 7-16 on the next page). Although all three of these methods send data one bit at a time, the methods vary with respect to how the bits are organized for transfer.

➤ *Synchronous transmission*—data is organized into groups or blocks of data, which are transferred at regular, specified intervals. Because the transmissions are synchronized, both devices know when data can be sent and when it should arrive. Most data transmissions within a computer and over a network are synchronous transmissions.

➤ *Asynchronous transmission*—data is sent when it is ready to be sent, without being synchronized. To identify the bits that belong in each byte, a *start bit* and *stop bit* are used at the beginning and end of the byte, respectively. This overhead makes asynchronous transmission less efficient than synchronous transmission and so it is not as widely used as synchronous transmission.

➤ *Isochronous transmission*—data is sent when it is ready but all data must be delivered at the time that it is needed. For example, when transmitting a video file, the audio data must be received at the proper time in order for it to be played with its corresponding video data. To accomplish this with isochronous transmission, the sending and receiving devices first communicate to determine the bandwidth and other factors needed for the transmission, and then the necessary bandwidth is reserved just for that transmission.

**FIGURE 7-15**
Serial vs. parallel transmissions.

 01000001

**SERIAL TRANSMISSIONS**
The bits follow one another over a single path.

**PARALLEL TRANSMISSIONS**
The bits are transmitted over separate paths at the same time.

**SYNCHRONOUS TRANSMISSIONS**
Data is sent in blocks and the blocks are timed so that the receiving device knows when they will arrive.

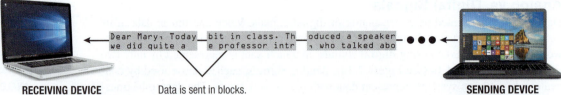

RECEIVING DEVICE     Data is sent in blocks.     SENDING DEVICE

**ASYNCHRONOUS TRANSMISSIONS**
Data is sent one byte at a time, along with a start bit and a stop bit.

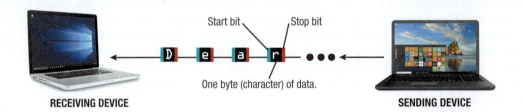

Start bit     Stop bit

One byte (character) of data.

RECEIVING DEVICE     SENDING DEVICE

**ISOCHRONOUS TRANSMISSIONS**
Data is sent when it is ready but only after requesting and being assigned the bandwidth necessary for all the data to arrive at the correct time.

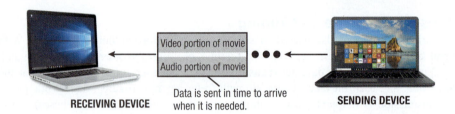

Video portion of movie
Audio portion of movie

Data is sent in time to arrive when it is needed.

RECEIVING DEVICE     SENDING DEVICE

Igor Lateci/Shutterstock.com; You can more/Shutterstock.com

 **FIGURE 7-16**

**Transmission timing.** Most network transmissions use synchronous transmission.

Another distinction between types of transmissions is the direction in which transmitted data can move.

> *Simplex transmission*—data travels in a single direction only (like a doorbell). Simplex transmission is relatively uncommon in data transmissions because most devices that are mainly one-directional, such as a printer, can still transmit error messages and other data back to the computer.

> *Half-duplex transmission*—data can travel in either direction, but only in one direction at a time (like a walkie-talkie where only one person can talk at a time). Some network transmissions are half-duplex.

> *Full-duplex transmission*—data can move in both directions at the same time (like a telephone). Many network and most Internet connections are full-duplex; sometimes two connections between the sending device and receiving device are needed to support full-duplex transmissions.

## Delivery Method

When data needs to travel across a large network (such as a WAN), typically one of three methods is used (see Figure 7-17). With *circuit switching*, a dedicated path over a network is established between the sender and receiver and all data follows that path from the sender to the receiver. Once the connection is established, the physical path or circuit is dedicated to that connection and cannot be used by any other device until the transmission is finished. The most common example of a circuit-switched network is a conventional telephone system.

The technique used for data sent over the Internet is *packet switching*. With packet switching, messages are separated into small units called *packets*. Packets contain information about the sender and the receiver, the actual data being sent, and information about how to reassemble the packets to reconstruct the original message. Packets travel along the network separately, based on their final destination, network traffic, and other network conditions. When the packets reach their destination, they are reassembled in the proper order. Another alternative is *broadcasting*, in which data is sent out (typically in packets) to all nodes on a network and is retrieved only by the intended recipient. Broadcasting is used primarily with LANs.

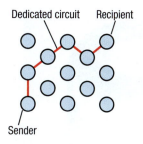

**Dedicated circuit**   **Recipient**

**Sender**

**CIRCUIT-SWITCHED NETWORKS**
Data uses a dedicated path from the sender to the recipient.

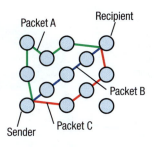

**Packet A**   **Recipient**

**Packet B**

**Packet C**

**Sender**

**PACKET-SWITCHED NETWORKS**
Data is sent as individual packets, which are assembled at the recipient's destination.

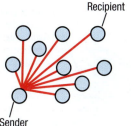

**Recipient**

**Sender**

**BROADCAST NETWORKS**
Data is broadcast to all nodes within range; the designated recipient retrieves the data.

**FIGURE 7-17**
Circuit-switched, packet-switched, and broadcast networks.

# NETWORKING MEDIA

To connect the devices in a network, either *wired media* (physical cables) or *wireless media* (typically radio signals) can be used. The most common wired and wireless networking media are discussed next.

> **TIP**
>
> Many networks use both wired and wireless networking media; the type of media used typically depends on the devices being connected.

## Wired Networking Media

The most common types of wired networking media are twisted-pair, coaxial, and fiber-optic cable.

### Twisted-Pair Cable

A **twisted-pair cable** is made up of pairs of thin strands of insulated wire twisted together (see Figure 7-18). Twisted-pair is the least expensive type of networking cable and has been in use the longest. In fact, it is the same type of cabling used inside most homes for telephone communications. Twisted-pair cabling can be used with both analog and digital data transmission and is commonly used for LANs. Twisted-pair cable is rated by *category*, which indicates the type of data, speed, distance, and other factors that the cable supports. *Category 3 (Cat 3)* twisted-pair cabling is regular telephone cable; higher speed and quality cabling—such as *Category 5 (Cat 5)*, *Category 6 (Cat 6)*, and *Category 7 (Cat 7)*—is frequently used in home or business networks. The pairs of wires in twisted-pair cabling are twisted together to reduce interference and improve performance. To further improve performance, twisted-pair cabling can be *shielded* with a metal lining. Twisted-pair cables used for networks have different connectors than those used for telephones. Networking connectors are typically *RJ-45* connectors, which look similar to, but are larger than, *RJ-11* telephone connectors.

### Coaxial Cable

**Coaxial cable** (also known as *coax cable*) was originally developed to carry a large number of high-speed video transmissions at one time, such as to deliver cable TV service. A coaxial cable (see Figure 7-18) consists of a relatively thick center wire surrounded by insulation and then covered with a shield of braided wire to block electromagnetic signals from entering the cable. Coaxial cable is commonly used today in computer networks, for

>**Twisted-pair cable.** A networking cable consisting of wire strands twisted in sets of two and bound into a cable. >**Coaxial cable.** A networking cable consisting of a center wire inside a grounded, cylindrical shield, capable of sending data at high speeds.

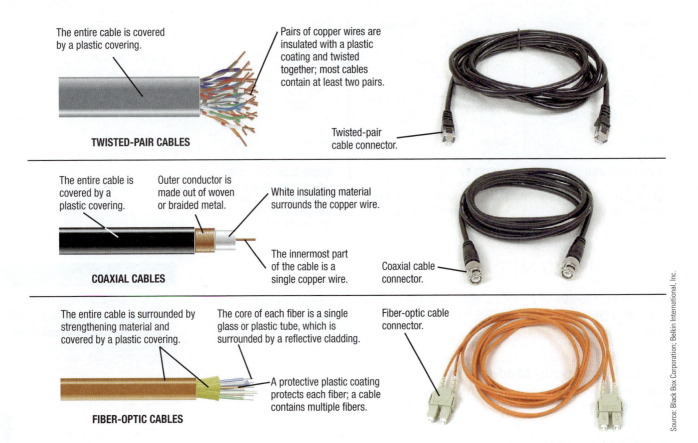

The entire cable is covered by a plastic covering.

Pairs of copper wires are insulated with a plastic coating and twisted together; most cables contain at least two pairs.

**TWISTED-PAIR CABLES**

Twisted-pair cable connector.

The entire cable is covered by a plastic covering.

Outer conductor is made out of woven or braided metal.

White insulating material surrounds the copper wire.

The innermost part of the cable is a single copper wire.

**COAXIAL CABLES**

Coaxial cable connector.

The entire cable is surrounded by strengthening material and covered by a plastic covering.

The core of each fiber is a single glass or plastic tube, which is surrounded by a reflective cladding.

Fiber-optic cable connector.

A protective plastic coating protects each fiber; a cable contains multiple fibers.

**FIBER-OPTIC CABLES**

Source: Black Box Corporation; Belkin International, Inc.

⚠ **FIGURE 7-18**
Wired network transmission media.

short-run telephone transmissions outside of the home, and for cable television delivery. Although more expensive than twisted-pair cabling, it is much less susceptible to interference and can carry more data more quickly. While not used extensively for networking home computers at the moment, that may change with the relatively new option of networking via the existing coax in a home. Coax is also used with home multimedia networks. The most common types of connectors used with coaxial cable are the slotted *BNC connectors* that are turned once to lock or unlock them into place (and are on the cable shown in Figure 7-18) and the threaded *F connectors* frequently used with cable TV and antenna applications.

### Fiber-Optic Cable

**Fiber-optic cable** is the newest and fastest of these three types of wired transmission media. It contains multiple (sometimes several hundred) clear glass or plastic fibers, each about the thickness of a human hair (refer again to Figure 7-18). Each fiber has the capacity to carry data for several television stations or thousands of voice conversations, but each fiber can only send data in one direction. Data sent over a fiber-optic cable is represented by light pulses and is sent at speeds of up to trillions of bits per second.

Fiber-optic cable is commonly used for the high-speed backbone lines of a network, such as to connect networks housed in separate buildings or for the Internet infrastructure. It is also used for telephone backbone lines and, increasingly, is being installed by telephone companies all the way to the home or business to provide super-fast connections directly to the end user. The biggest advantage of fiber-optic cabling is speed; the main

>**Fiber-optic cable.** A networking cable that utilizes hundreds of thin transparent fibers over which lasers transmit data as light.

disadvantage of fiber-optic cabling is the initial expense of both the cable and the installation. Fiber-optic connectors are less standardized than connectors for other types of wired media, so it is important to use cables with the connectors that match the hardware with which the cable will be used. Common connectors include the push-pull *SC connector* (shown in Figure 7-18) and the tabbed *SC* and slotted *ST connectors*.

## Wireless Networking Media

Wireless networks usually use *radio signals* to send data through the airwaves. Depending on the networking application, radio signals can be short range (such as when used to connect a wireless keyboard or mouse to a computer), medium range (such as when used to connect a computer to a wireless LAN or public hotspot), or long range (such as when used to provide Internet access or cell phone coverage to a relatively large geographic area or to broadcast TV or radio shows). The radio signals used in wireless networks and the types of technologies used to transmit them are discussed next.

### The Electromagnetic and Wireless Spectrums

All wireless applications in the United States—such as wireless networks, mobile phones, radio and TV broadcasts, sonar and radar applications, and GPS systems—use specific *frequencies* as assigned by the *Federal Communications Commission (FCC)*. Frequencies are measured in *hertz (Hz)* and the frequencies that make up the *electromagnetic spectrum*—the range of common *electromagnetic radiation* (energy)—are shown in Figure 7-19. Different parts of the spectrum have different properties (including the distance a signal can travel, the amount of data a signal can transmit in a given period of time, and the types of objects a signal can pass through), which make certain frequencies more appropriate for certain applications. As illustrated in this figure, most wireless networking applications use frequencies located in the *radio frequency (RF) band* at the low end (up to 300 GHz) of the electromagnetic spectrum—this range is sometimes referred to as the *wireless spectrum*.

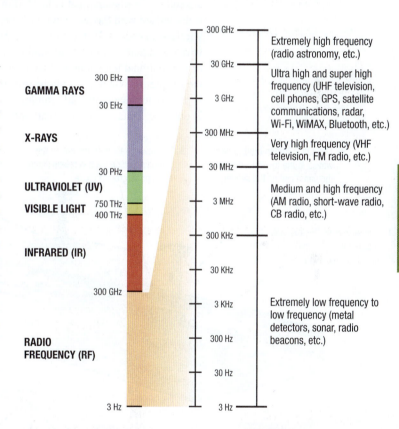

The frequencies assigned to an application, such as FM radio or cell phone service, typically consist of a range of frequencies to be used as needed for that application. For instance, FM radio stations broadcast on frequencies from 88 MHz to 108 MHz and each radio station in a particular geographic area is assigned its own frequency. Most radio frequencies in the United States are licensed by the FCC and can only be used for that specific application by the licensed individuals in their specified geographic areas. However, frequencies within an unlicensed part of the spectrum can be used by any product or individual. For example, cordless landline phones typically use frequencies in the 900 MHz band, and wireless networking often uses frequencies in the 2.4 GHz and 5 GHz bands. A frequency range can be further broken down into multiple *channels*, each of which can be used simultaneously by different users. There are also ways to combine multiple signals to send them over a transmission medium at one time to allow more users than would otherwise be possible.

Because the number of wireless applications is growing all the time and there is a limited amount of the parts of the spectrum appropriate for today's wireless networking

**FIGURE 7-19**

**The electromagnetic spectrum.** Each type of communication is assigned specific frequencies within which to operate.

**NET**

applications, the wireless spectrum is crowded and frequencies are in high demand. One benefit of the 2009 switch from analog to digital television broadcasts is that it freed up some of the VHF and UHF frequencies for other applications. As a new part of the spectrum becomes available, it is either assigned a function by the FCC or auctioned off to wireless providers, such as wireless telephone providers and TV broadcasters. The next auction—in the 600 MHz band of the broadcast TV spectrum—is scheduled for 2016. The FCC is continually working to free up spectrum for mobile broadband and other rapidly growing wireless applications.

## Cellular Radio Transmissions

**Cellular radio** transmissions are radio signals sent to and from cell phones via *cellular (cell) towers*—tall metal towers with antennas on top. Cellular service areas are divided into overlapping honeycomb-shaped zones called *cells*; each cell contains one cell tower (see Figure 7-20). When a cell phone user begins to make a call, it is picked up by the appropriate cell tower (the one that is located in the cell in which the cell phone is located and that is associated with the user's wireless provider). That cell tower then forwards the call to the wireless provider's *Mobile Telephone Switching Office (MTSO)*, which routes the call via a wireless signal or an underground cable to the recipient's telephone via his or her mobile or conventional telephone service provider (depending on the type of phone being used by the recipient). When a cell phone user moves out of the current cell into a new cell, the call is passed automatically and seamlessly to the appropriate cell tower in the cell that the user is entering. Data (such as e-mail and Web pages) sent via cell phones works in a similar

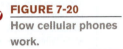

**FIGURE 7-20**

**How cellular phones work.**

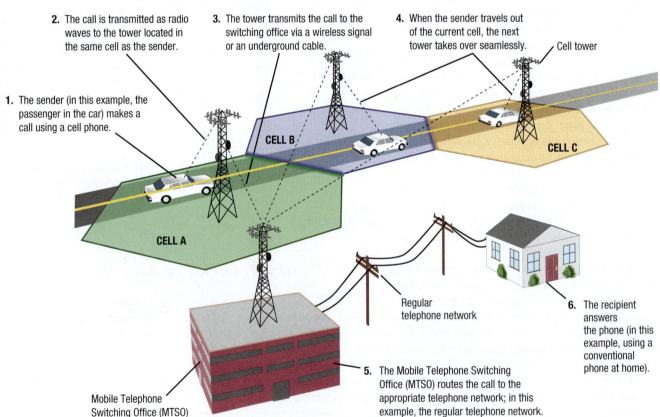

**2.** The call is transmitted as radio waves to the tower located in the same cell as the sender.

**3.** The tower transmits the call to the switching office via a wireless signal or an underground cable.

**4.** When the sender travels out of the current cell, the next tower takes over seamlessly.

Cell tower

**1.** The sender (in this example, the passenger in the car) makes a call using a cell phone.

CELL B

CELL C

CELL A

Regular telephone network

**6.** The recipient answers the phone (in this example, using a conventional phone at home).

Mobile Telephone Switching Office (MTSO)

**5.** The Mobile Telephone Switching Office (MTSO) routes the call to the appropriate telephone network; in this example, the regular telephone network.

> **Cellular radio.** A form of broadcast radio sent to and from cellular telephones via cell towers.

manner. The speed of cellular radio transmissions depends on the type of *cellular standard* being used, as discussed later in this chapter.

## Microwave and Satellite Transmissions

*Microwaves* are high-frequency radio signals that can send large quantities of data at high speeds over long distances. Microwave signals can be sent or received using microwave stations or communications satellites, but they must travel in a straight line from one station or satellite to another without encountering any obstacles because microwave signals are *line of sight*. **Microwave stations** are earth-based stations that can transmit microwave signals directly to each other over distances of up to about 30 miles. To avoid buildings, mountains, and the curvature of the earth obstructing the signal, microwave stations are usually placed on tall buildings, towers, and mountaintops. Microwave stations typically contain both a dish-shaped *microwave antenna* and a transceiver. When one station receives a transmission from another, it amplifies it and passes it on to the next station. Microwave stations can exchange data transmissions with communications satellites, discussed next, as well as with other microwave stations. Microwave stations designed specifically to communicate with satellites (such as those used to provide satellite TV and satellite Internet services) are typically called *satellite dishes*. Satellite dishes are usually installed permanently where they are needed, but they can also be mounted on trucks, boats, RVs, and other types of transportation devices when portable transmission capabilities are necessary or desirable, such as when used for military or recreational applications.

**Communications satellites** are space-based devices launched into orbit around the earth to receive and transmit microwave signals to and from earth (see the satellite Internet example in Figure 7-21). Communications satellites were originally used to facilitate microwave transmission in places where microwave stations were not economically viable (such as over large, sparsely populated areas) or were physically impractical (such as over large bodies of water), and they were used primarily by the military and communications companies (such as for remote television news broadcasts). Today, communications satellites are used to send and receive transmissions to and from a variety of other devices, such as personal satellite dishes used for satellite television and Internet service, GPS receivers, satellite radio receivers, and satellite phones. They are also used for *earth observation* (*EO*) applications, including weather observation, mapping, and government surveillance.

**FIGURE 7-21**
**How satellite Internet works.**

3. An orbiting satellite receives the request and sends it down to the satellite dish at the ISP's operations center.

2. The request is sent up to a satellite from the individual's satellite dish.

1. Data, such as a Web page request, is sent from the individual's computer to the satellite dish via a satellite modem.

4. The ISP's operations center receives the request (via its satellite dish) and transfers it to the Internet.

**THE INTERNET**

5. The request travels over the Internet as usual. The requested information takes a reverse route back to the individual.

tatniz/Shutterstock.com; Hughes Network Systems LLC; Google Inc.

> **Microwave station.** An earth-based device that sends and receives high-frequency, high-speed radio signals. > **Communications satellite.** An earth-orbiting device that relays communications signals over long distances.

Traditional communications satellites maintain a *geosynchronous* orbit 22,300 miles above the earth and, because they travel at a speed and direction that keeps pace with the earth's rotation, they appear (from the earth) to remain stationary over any given spot. Because these satellites are so far above the surface of the earth, there is a slight delay while the signals travel from the earth, to the satellite, and back to the earth again. This delay—less than one half-second—is not normally noticed by most users (such as individuals who receive Internet or TV service via satellite) but it does make geosynchronous satellite transmissions less practical for voice, gaming, and other real-time communications. Because of this delay factor, *low earth orbit* (*LEO*) satellite systems were developed for use with satellite telephone systems. LEO satellites typically are located anywhere from 100 to 1,000 miles above the earth and, consequently, provide faster transmission than traditional satellites. *Medium earth orbit* (*MEO*) systems typically use satellites located about 1,000 to 12,000 miles above the earth and are used most often for GPS.

### Infrared (IR) Transmissions

One type of wireless networking that does not use signals in the RF band of the electromagnetic spectrum is **infrared (IR) transmission**, which sends data as infrared light rays over relatively short distances. Like an infrared television remote control, infrared technology requires line-of-sight transmission. Because of this limitation, many formerly infrared devices (such as wireless mice and keyboards) now use RF radio signals instead. Infrared transmissions are still used with some remote controls. They are also sometimes used to transmit data between mobile devices, as well as between gaming consoles, handheld gaming devices, and other home entertainment devices.

## COMMUNICATIONS PROTOCOLS AND NETWORKING STANDARDS

A *protocol* is a set of rules to be followed in a specific situation; in networking, for instance, there are *communications protocols* that determine how devices on a network communicate. The term *standard* refers to a set of criteria or requirements that has been approved by a recognized standards organization (such as the *American National Standards Institute* (*ANSI*), which guides the development of business standards, or *IEEE*, which develops technology standards) or is accepted as a de facto standard by the industry. Standards are extremely important in the computer industry because they help hardware and software manufacturers ensure that the products they develop can work with other computing products. *Networking standards* typically address both how the devices in a network physically connect (such as the types of cabling that can be used) and how the devices communicate (such as the communications protocols that can be used). Communications protocols and the most common wired and wireless networking standards are discussed in the next several sections.

**TIP**

Examples of the networking adapters used with the various networking standards are included later in this chapter.

### TCP/IP and Other Communications Protocols

The most widely used communications protocol today is **TCP/IP**. TCP/IP is the protocol used for transferring data over the Internet and actually consists of two protocols: *Transmission Control Protocol* (*TCP*), which is responsible for the delivery of data, and *Internet Protocol* (*IP*), which provides addresses and routing information. TCP/IP uses packet switching to transmit data; when the packets reach their destination, they are reassembled in the proper order (see Figure 7-22). Support for TCP/IP is built into operating systems, and IP addresses

---

>**Infrared (IR) transmission.** A wireless networking medium that sends data as infrared light rays. >**TCP/IP.** A networking protocol that uses packet switching to facilitate the transmission of messages; the protocol used with the Internet.

are commonly used to identify the various devices on computer networks.

The first widely used version of IP was *Internet Protocol Version 4* (*IPv4*), which was standardized in the early 1980s. IPv4 uses 32-bit addresses and so allows for $2^{32}$ (4.3 billion) unique addresses. While still in use today, IPv4 was never designed to be used with the vast number of devices that access the Internet today and IPv4 addresses are running out. Consequently, a newer version of IP (*IPv6*) was developed and is in the process of being implemented. IPv6 uses 128-bit addresses (and so allows for $2^{128}$ unique addresses). This provides enough unique addresses so that all smart devices in a home or business can be accessible on the Internet

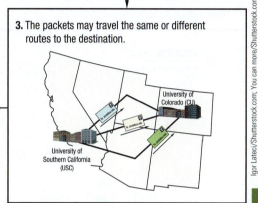

**1.** Each message is split into packets.

SUE'S PC

**2.** The packets are addressed to the same destination.

From: SueG@usc.edu    0¢
To: JimS@cu.edu

From: SueG@usc.edu    0¢
To: JimS@cu.edu

From: SueG@usc.edu    0¢
To: JimS@cu.edu

**4.** The packets are reassembled into the message at the destination.

JIM'S PC

**3.** The packets may travel the same or different routes to the destination.

University of Colorado (CU)

University of Southern California (USC)

Igor Latec//Shutterstock.com; You can more//Shutterstock.com

directly via their unique IP address, instead of being identified by the IP address of the router to which they are connected, as in IPv4. Consequently, the use of IPv6 addressing will make home automation and other applications involving smart devices easier to implement. It is expected that external systems (such as company Web sites) will switch over to IPv6 first and that IPv4 and IPv6 will coexist for several years. However, in some countries (such as China) where IPv4 addresses are scarce, end users are expected to switch over faster. In the United States, the government has mandated that all federal agencies be capable of switching to IPv6 and to purchase only IPv6-compatible new hardware and software. Experts suggest that businesses perform a network audit to determine what hardware and software changes will be needed to switch to IPv6 so that the business is prepared when the change is necessary.

While TCP/IP is used to connect to and communicate with the Internet, other protocols are used for specific Internet applications. For instance, as discussed in Chapter 1, *HTTP* (*Hypertext Transfer Protocol*) and *HTTPS* (*Secure Hypertext Transfer Protocol*) are protocols used to display Web pages, and *FTP* (*File Transfer Protocol*) and *SFTP* (*Secure File Transfer Protocol*) are protocols used to transfer files over the Internet. Protocols used to send and receive e-mail over the Internet include *SMTP* (*Simple Mail Transfer Protocol*) and *POP3* (*Post Office Protocol*), respectively.

## Ethernet (802.3)

**Ethernet (802.3)** is the most widely used standard for wired networks. It is typically used with LANs that have a star topology (though it can also be used with WANs and MANs) and can be used in conjunction with twisted-pair, coaxial, or fiber-optic cabling. Ethernet

**FIGURE 7-22**
**How TCP/IP works.**
TCP/IP networks (like the Internet) use packet switching.

NET

**TIP**

The ongoing development of faster Ethernet standards is necessary because Internet traffic is expected to quadruple in the next five years and networks need to be able to handle the increased traffic.

>**Ethernet (802.3).** The most widely used wired LAN networking standard.

| STANDARD | MAXIMUM SPEED |
|---|---|
| 10BASE-T | 10 Mbps |
| Fast Ethernet (100BASE-T or 100BASE-TX) | 100 Mbps |
| Gigabit Ethernet (1000BASE-T) | 1,000 Mbps (1 Gbps) |
| 10 Gigabit Ethernet (10GBASE-T) | 10 Gbps |
| 40 Gigabit Ethernet | 40 Gbps |
| 100 Gigabit Ethernet | 100 Gbps |
| 400 Gigabit Ethernet* | 400 Gbps |
| Terabit Ethernet* | 1,000 Gbps (1 Tbps) |

*Under consideration for development

**FIGURE 7-23**
Ethernet standards.

was invented in the mid-1970s and has continued to evolve over the years; about every three years the new approved amendments are incorporated into the existing IEEE 802.3 Ethernet standard to keep it up to date. Figure 7-23 summarizes the various Ethernet standards; of these, the most common today are *Fast Ethernet*, *Gigabit Ethernet*, and *10 Gigabit Ethernet*. The *40 Gigabit Ethernet* and *100 Gigabit Ethernet* standards were ratified in 2010. Development of the even faster *400 Gigabit Ethernet* and *Terabit Ethernet* standards are currently being explored; if ratified, they are expected to be used for connections between servers, as well as for delivering video, digital X-rays and other digital medical images, and other high-speed, bandwidth-intensive networking applications.

Devices connected to an Ethernet network need to have an Ethernet port either built in or added using an expansion card. Ethernet networks can contain devices using multiple Ethernet speeds, but the slower devices will only operate at their respective speeds.

A relatively new Ethernet development is *Power over Ethernet* (*PoE*), which allows electrical power, in addition to data, to be sent over the cables in an Ethernet network (often referred to as *Ethernet cables*), as shown in Figure 7-24. Consequently, PoE devices are not plugged into an electrical outlet, as long as they are connected to an Ethernet port that supports PoE. If the device (such as the wireless access point in Figure 7-24) is connected to a non-PoE port, a *PoE injector* is used to send power to the device over an Ethernet cable. PoE is most often used in business networks with remote devices (such as outdoor networking hardware, security cameras, and other devices) that are often not located near a power outlet. It can also be used to place networked devices near ceilings or other locations where a nearby power outlet may not be available, and in homes to connect wired devices (such as security cameras) to a home network without running new electrical wiring.

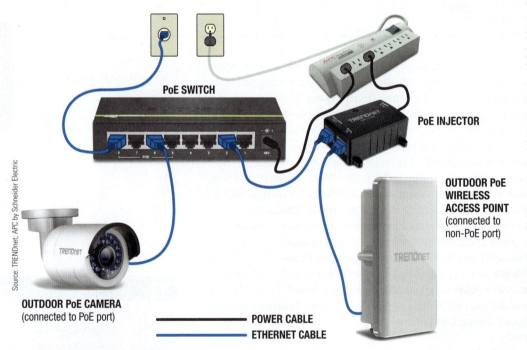

Source: TRENDnet; APC by Schneider Electric

PoE SWITCH

PoE INJECTOR

OUTDOOR PoE WIRELESS ACCESS POINT (connected to non-PoE port)

OUTDOOR PoE CAMERA (connected to PoE port)

━━━ POWER CABLE
━━━ ETHERNET CABLE

**FIGURE 7-24**
With Power over Ethernet (PoE), devices are powered through Ethernet cables.

## Powerline and G.hn

*Powerline* (also called *Power Line Communications* or *PLC*) *networking* allows network data to be transmitted over existing electrical wiring. One example is *broadband over powerline* (*BPL*), which can deliver broadband Internet to homes and businesses via the existing outdoor power lines. While currently available only in very limited areas in the United States through power companies, BPL has potential for delivering broadband Internet access to remote locations, although momentum for BPL appears to be slowing. One Powerline alternative to the Ethernet standard for wired home networks is the *HomePlug* Powerline standard, which allows computers to be networked over existing power lines within a home using conventional electrical outlets. HomePlug Powerline networks are quick and easy to set up (see Figure 7-25) and are relatively fast (up to 1 Gbps for the newest *HomePlug AV2* standard). In addition to networking computers, HomePlug AV can be used to network home entertainment devices and it is fast enough to support streaming HD video. HomePlug can also be used to extend Wi-Fi networks to locations (such as basements) that are otherwise hard to reach.

The *G.hn* standard was developed as a unified worldwide standard for creating home networks over any existing home wiring, including phone lines, power lines, and coaxial cable. While it will coexist with the HomePlug standard for the near future, G.hn supporters view it as the future standard for wired home networking. G.hn products are just beginning to become available.

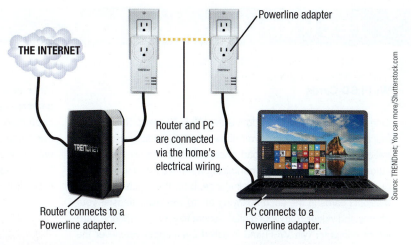

Powerline adapter

THE INTERNET

Router and PC are connected via the home's electrical wiring.

Router connects to a Powerline adapter.

PC connects to a Powerline adapter.

Source: TRENDnet; You can more/Shutterstock.com

**FIGURE 7-25**
**HomePlug Powerline networks.** Enable you to network devices over existing power lines.

## Wi-Fi (802.11)

One of the most common networking standards used with wireless LANs is **Wi-Fi (802.11)**—a family of wireless networking standards that use the IEEE 802.11 standard. Wi-Fi (sometimes called *wireless Ethernet* because it is designed to easily connect to a wired Ethernet network) is the current standard for wireless networks in the home or office, as well as for public Wi-Fi hotspots. Wi-Fi hardware is built into virtually all portable computers and most mobile devices today. Wi-Fi capabilities are also becoming increasingly integrated into everyday products, such as printers, digital cameras, portable digital media players, external hard drives, baby monitors, gaming consoles, home medical monitors, home audio systems, televisions, Blu-ray Disc players, and home appliances (see Figure 7-26), to allow those devices to connect with other devices or to access the Internet wirelessly. For a look at a Wi-Fi-enabled consumer product you can use to automatically upload digital photos to your favorite photo-sharing sites—Wi-Fi flash memory cards—see the Technology and You box.

The speed of a Wi-Fi network and the area it can cover depend on a variety of factors, including the *Wi-Fi standard* and hardware being used, the number of solid objects (such as walls, trees, or buildings) between the access point and the computer or other device being used, and the amount of interference from cordless phones, baby monitors, microwave ovens, and other devices that also operate on the same radio frequencies as some Wi-Fi devices. In general, Wi-Fi is designed for medium-range data transfers—typically between 100 and 300 feet indoors and 300 to 900 feet outdoors. Usually both signal speed and distance degrade with interference. The distance of a Wi-Fi network can be extended using additional antennas and other hardware designed for that purpose, as discussed shortly.

A summary of different Wi-Fi standards is shown in Figure 7-27; of these, the most widely used today are *802.11n* and *802.11ac*. Beginning with the 802.11n standard, *MIMO (multiple in, multiple out) antennas* are used to transfer multiple streams of data at one time. As a result of this and

**FIGURE 7-26**
**Smart appliances.** This coffeemaker is controlled by a smartphone via the home's Wi-Fi network.

Source: Belkin International, Inc.

NET

>**Wi-Fi (802.11).** A widely used networking standard for medium-range wireless networks.

# TECHNOLOGY AND YOU

### Wi-Fi SD Cards

One relatively new Wi-Fi product is the *Wi-Fi SD card*. These cards (such as the *Eyefi Mobi cards* shown in the accompanying illustration) are designed to upload photos and videos wirelessly and automatically from a camera containing a Mobi card to a computer or mobile device via Wi-Fi. For instance, both the regular and professional cards in the accompanying photo wirelessly transfer your photos and videos from your digital camera to your smartphone, tablet, or computer (via Wi-Fi and installed Eyefi apps) whenever the devices are within range of each other. You can then immediately view, organize, edit, and share your photos and videos on all your connected devices. *Eyefi Mobi Pro* cards also can transfer files over your home Wi-Fi network, as well as upload the *RAW* files often used by professional photographers. Both types of cards automatically sync photos and videos to the user's Eyefi Cloud account (a starter subscription is included with the purchase of a card and then an annual subscription can be added if desired).

In addition to allowing you to share your photos immediately with others (while on a vacation or at a special event, for example), using a Wi-Fi SD card for your digital photos can also give you the peace of mind that your photos are backed up on your other devices and/or online. This is especially beneficial if your camera is stolen or the card becomes damaged. In fact, using an Eyefi card enabled one woman to catch the individual who stole her camera gear while she was on vacation—her photos, along with images of the thief with the camera gear, were uploaded to her computer and the police were able to apprehend the thief and recover the stolen gear.

Source: Eye-Fi, Inc.

**FIGURE 7-27**
Wi-Fi standards.

other improvements, 802.11n allows for data transmissions typically about five times as fast as 802.11g and about twice the range. The newer 802.11ac standard supports speeds up to about 1.3 Gbps—about three times as fast as 802.11n—to better support high-speed file transfers and HD video streaming.

Typically, products using the various types of Wi-Fi can be used on the same network as long as they operate on the same frequencies. Wi-Fi products are backward compatible (so 802.11g devices can be used on 802.11n networks, for example, but they will only connect at 802.11g speeds, and 802.11n devices can be used on an 802.11ac network, but the 802.11n devices will work at 802.11n speeds). Updates, called *extensions*, to the 802.11 standard are developed on a regular basis. These updates are usually to increase speed, distance, or security. One emerging Wi-Fi standard is *802.11af*, sometimes called *White-Fi*. This standard addresses the use of Wi-Fi devices in lower frequencies, such as 600 MHz, currently associated with the unused TV spectrum known as white space. If

| WI-FI STANDARD | DESCRIPTION |
|---|---|
| 802.11b | An early Wi-Fi standard; supports data transfer rates of 11 Mbps. |
| 802.11g | An older Wi-Fi standard; supports data transfer rates of 54 Mbps and uses the same 2.4 GHz frequency as 802.11b, so their products are compatible. |
| 802.11a | An older Wi-Fi standard; supports data transfer rates of 54 Mbps, but uses a different radio frequency (5 GHz) than 802.11b/g (2.4 GHz), making the standards incompatible. |
| 802.11n | A current Wi-Fi standard; supports speeds up to about 450 Mbps and has twice the range of 802.11g. It can use either the 2.4 GHz or 5 GHz frequency. |
| 802.11ac | The newest Wi-Fi standard; supports speed up to about three times faster than 802.11n and uses the 5 GHz frequency (though most 802.11ac routers are *dual band* to also support 2.4 GHz devices for backward compatibility). |
| 802.11ax* | A proposed Wi-Fi standard; expected to support speeds of more than 2 Gbps. |

* Expected by 2018

the FCC approves the use of some of this frequency for unlicensed devices, the lower frequency would enable 802.11af devices to communicate better through walls, trees, and other obstacles and over longer distances. To ensure that Wi-Fi hardware from various vendors will work together, consumers can look for products that are *Wi-Fi CERTIFIED* by the *Wi-Fi Alliance* (see Figure 7-28).

While Wi-Fi is very widely used today, it does have some limitations—particularly its relatively limited range. For instance, an individual using a Wi-Fi hotspot inside a Starbucks coffeehouse will lose that Internet connection when he or she moves out of range of that network and will need to locate another hotspot at his or her next location. In addition, many businesses may be physically too large for a Wi-Fi network to span the entire organization. While hardware can be used to extend a Wi-Fi network, larger wireless networks may use WiMAX or a cellular standard instead.

Source: Wi-Fi Alliance.

**FIGURE 7-28**
Wi-Fi CERTIFIED logo.

## WiMAX (802.16)

**WiMAX (802.16)** is a series of standards designed for longer range wireless networking connections, typically MANs. Similar to Wi-Fi, *fixed WiMAX* (also known as *802.16a*) is designed to provide Internet access to fixed locations (sometimes called *hotzones*), but the coverage is significantly larger (a typical hotzone radius is between 2 and 6 miles. With fixed WiMAX, it is feasible to provide coverage to an entire city or other geographical area by using multiple WiMAX towers and overlapping hotzones (see Figure 7-29), similar to the way cell phone cells overlap to provide continuous cell phone service. WiMAX can use licensed radio frequencies, in addition to unlicensed frequencies like Wi-Fi, to avoid interference issues. *Mobile WiMAX* (*802.16e*) is the mobile version of the WiMAX wireless networking standard. It is designed to deliver broadband wireless networking to mobile users via a smartphone, portable computer, or other WiMAX-enabled device. Mobile WiMAX is capable of speeds of approximately 70 Mbps, but speeds of 1 to 6 Mbps are more typical.

In the United States, WiMAX is most often used in rural areas. However, many mobile WiMAX services (such as from the original leading supporter, Sprint) are moving to cellular standards (such as LTE) instead.

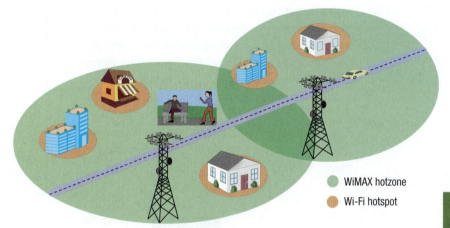

● WiMAX hotzone
● Wi-Fi hotspot

**FIGURE 7-29**
WiMAX vs. Wi-Fi.
A WiMAX hotzone is larger than a Wi-Fi hotspot and so has a greater range; it can provide service to anyone in the hotzone, including mobile users.

## Cellular Standards

*Cellular standards* have evolved over the years to better fulfill the demand for mobile Internet, mobile multimedia delivery, and other relatively recent mobile trends. The original *first-generation cell phones* were analog and designed for voice data only. Starting with *second-generation (2G) cell phones*, cell phones were digital, supported both data and voice, and were faster than earlier cell phones. Common *2G wireless standards* included *GSM* (*Global System for Mobile communications*) and *CDMA* (*Code Division Multiple Access*), which supported speeds up to 14.4 Kbps and were not compatible with each other.

The current standards for cellular networks today in the United States and many other countries are *3G* (*third generation*) and *4G* (*fourth generation*). 3G and 4G networks use packet-switching (like TCP/IP) instead of circuit-switching (like conventional telephones

>**WiMAX (802.16).** A wireless networking standard that is faster and has a greater range than Wi-Fi.

## ASK THE EXPERT

**Frank Ellermeyer,** Vice President and Chief Technology Officer, McDonald's Corporation

### How has the widespread use of Wi-Fi and smartphones affected companies such as McDonald's?

Because our customers always come first, McDonald's is committed to Wi-Fi being free, fast, and always available. Wi-Fi and the enablement of mobile capabilities have become the cornerstone of providing a relevant customer service experience. We are building brand ambassadors through our customer loyalty programs and we will keep innovating digital solutions. Internal to our company, mobile first is our strategic approach to every product and service that we deliver. Wi-Fi has forever changed the way we think and it would be challenging to function without it. Therefore, everything we do for our customers will be mobile enabled.

and earlier mobile phones). Typically, 3G speeds in the United States are between 1 and 3 Mbps; 4G speeds typically range from about 3 to 10 Mbps. While the original specification for 4G called for speeds of 100 Mbps, the term *4G* is currently being used to describe cellular phone service that is significantly faster than 3G service. Many cell phones today can switch between 3G and 4G, such as to use a 3G network in a location where a 4G network is not within range or to use 3G if 4G usage exceeds the individual's monthly 4G limit. Because 3G and 4G speeds are equivalent to the speeds many home broadband Internet users experience, Internet access via a 3G or 4G network is often referred to as *mobile broadband*. Today, 4G capabilities are integrated into some portable computers, tablets, and other devices to enable users to connect to the Internet via their wireless provider when needed (see Figure 7-30). Devices without built-in 4G can connect to a cellular network via a mobile hotspot, as discussed later in this chapter.

Cellular standards for 3G networks depend on the type of cellular network being used. For instance, GSM mobile networks (like AT&T Wireless and T-Mobile) typically use the *HSDPA* (*High Speed Downlink Packet Access*)/*UMTS* (*Universal Mobile Telecommunications System*) 3G standard; CDMA networks (like Verizon Wireless and Cricket Wireless) typically use the *EV-DO* (*Evolution Data Optimized*) 3G standard instead. The primary standard for 4G networks today is *Long Term Evolution* (*LTE*), although some companies may use mobile WiMAX instead. Currently, LTE-Advanced is the fastest cellular standard, though new standards are always in the works. For example, the next 4G development is expected to be *LTE-Unlicensed* (*LTE-U*), also referred to as *Licensed-Assisted Access* (*LAA*), which uses both the regular licensed cellular frequencies and part of the 5 GHz band of unlicensed spectrum in order to enable wireless providers to offer better coverage and faster speeds.

**FIGURE 7-30**
Connecting to a 4G cellular network with a notebook.

The next generation of cellular technology, called *5G*, is a long way from reality, but companies in the wireless industry are already working to define what it will be. The 5G standard is expected to be both significantly faster and smarter than the current 4G standard. For example, 5G networks may be able to understand situations and respond accordingly, such as providing a connection with a faster response time to a smart car while providing a slower, less responsive connection to a smart thermostat. In addition, 5G is expected to open up new possibilities, such as road sensors communicating with smart cars to adjust car speed in response to upcoming road or traffic conditions. It is expected that 5G will operate on higher frequencies than 4G; if so, new infrastructure will be required because higher frequency signals do not travel as far as lower frequency signals. The speed of 5G connections may reach 10 Gbps—fast enough to download an HD movie in mere seconds. And companies are getting close already. For example, Nokia Networks has demonstrated speeds of up to 10 Gbps in 5G tests, while Samsung recently achieved 7.5 Gbps.

## Bluetooth and Other Short-Range Wireless Standards

There are several wireless networking standards in existence or being developed that are designed for short-range wireless networking connections. Most of these are used to facilitate PANs or very small, special-purpose home networks, such as connecting home entertainment devices or appliances within a home. The most common of these standards are discussed next.

### Bluetooth, Wi-Fi Direct, WiGig, and Wireless HD

**Bluetooth** is a wireless standard that was originally designed for very short-range (10 meters, approximately 33 feet, or less) connections, though there is no maximum range and some industrial products have a range of 300 feet. Bluetooth is designed to replace cables between devices, such as to connect a wireless keyboard or mouse to a desktop computer (see Figure 7-31), to send print jobs wirelessly from a portable computer to a printer, or to connect a smartphone to a wireless headset. Bluetooth devices automatically recognize and network with each other when they get within transmission range. For instance, Bluetooth enables a wireless keyboard and mouse to be connected to a computer automatically as soon as the computer is powered up. Bluetooth signals can transmit through clothing and other nonmetallic objects, so a smartphone or other device in a pocket or briefcase can connect with Bluetooth hardware (such as a headset) without having to be removed from the pocket or briefcase. One of the key enhancements in the newest Bluetooth specification (*Bluetooth 4.0*, also called *Bluetooth Smart*) is energy efficiency, which enables small devices to run for years on a single button-sized battery. Consequently, Bluetooth is increasingly being used with consumer devices, such as to connect a smartphone to a smart watch or portable speaker, or to connect a pedometer, heart rate monitor, or other health and fitness device together or to a smartphone. For example, the smart tennis racket shown in Figure 7-32 includes Bluetooth capabilities to transfer data about swing speed, ball speed, and more to a connected device via an app, also shown in Figure 7-32.

Bluetooth works using radio signals in the frequency band of 2.4 GHz, the same as some Wi-Fi devices and it supports transfers up to 26 Mbps. Once two Bluetooth-enabled devices come within range of each other, their software identifies each other (using their unique identification numbers) and establishes a link. Because there may be many Bluetooth devices within range, up to 10 individual Bluetooth networks (called *piconets*) can be in place within the same physical area at one time. Each piconet can connect up to eight devices, for a maximum of 80 devices within any 10-meter radius. To facilitate this, Bluetooth divides its allocated radio spectrum into multiple channels of 1 MHz each. Each Bluetooth device can use the entire range of frequencies, jumping randomly (in unison with the other devices in that piconet) on a regular basis to minimize interference between piconets, as well as from other devices (such as garage-door openers, Wi-Fi

The desktop computer, keyboard, and mouse form a piconet to communicate with each other.

**FIGURE 7-31**

**Bluetooth.** Bluetooth is designed for short-range wireless communications.

**FIGURE 7-32**

**Bluetooth tennis racket.**

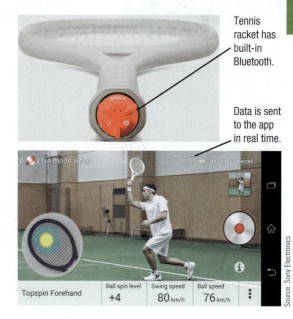

Tennis racket has built-in Bluetooth.

Data is sent to the app in real time.

Source: Sony Electronics

NET

---

> **Bluetooth.** A networking standard for very short-range wireless connections; the devices are automatically connected once they get within the allowable range.

Creating a hotspot via a Wi-Fi Direct phone.

The Wi-Fi Direct hotspot now appears on the list of Wi-Fi hotspots.

Courtesy Nick Morley

networks, and some cordless phones and baby monitors) that use the same frequencies. Because Bluetooth transmitters change frequencies 1,600 times every second automatically, it is unlikely that any two transmitting devices will be on the same frequency at the same time.

Other standards that are designed to connect nearby peripheral devices but that transfer data more quickly are Wi-Fi Direct, WiGig, and Wireless HD. **Wi-Fi Direct** enables Wi-Fi devices (such as computers, smartphones, printers, and gaming devices) to connect directly to each other using Wi-Fi signals without needing a router or an access point. A compatible app is required for many tasks, though a Wi-Fi Direct smartphone can often create a Wi-Fi hotspot for other Wi-Fi devices just by using the smartphone's Wi-Fi settings to *tether* those devices to the smartphone's Internet connection (see Figure 7-33). Wi-Fi Direct is not designed to replace traditional Wi-Fi networks, but it is considered a competitor to Bluetooth because it has the advantage of faster speeds (up to 250 Mbps) and a greater range (up to 600 feet).

**WiGig (802.11ad)** and **WirelessHD (WiHD)** are most often used to wirelessly connect computers and home entertainment devices together, such as to stream video from a computer or Blu-ray player to an HDTV. Both WiGig and WiHD operate in the 60 GHz frequency band, which allows for faster speeds (up to about 7 Gbps and 28 Gbps, respectively) within a single room. Wireless HD also incorporates a smart antenna system that allows the system to steer the transmission, allowing for non-line-of-sight communications.

**FIGURE 7-33**

**Wi-Fi Direct.** Allows Wi-Fi devices to connect directly to one another.

✓ **TIP**

If your computer doesn't have Bluetooth capability built in, you can add it via a USB *Bluetooth adapter*.

### ZigBee, Z-Wave, and Low-Power Wi-Fi (802.11ah)

One networking standard designed for inexpensive and simple short-range networking (particularly sensor networks) is *ZigBee* (*802.15*). ZigBee is intended for applications that require low data transfer rates and several years of battery life. For instance, ZigBee can be used for home and commercial automation systems to connect a wide variety of devices (such as appliances and lighting, heating, and security systems). ZigBee is also used in industrial manufacturing, personal home healthcare, device tracking, telecommunications, and wireless sensor networks. ZigBee is designed to accommodate more than 65,000 devices on a single network and supports speeds up to 250 Kbps, depending on the frequency being used (several different frequencies are available for ZigBee networks). ZigBee networks have a range of 10 to 50 meters (about 33 to 164 feet) between devices, depending on power output and environmental characteristics.

A wireless networking standard designed primarily for home automation is *Z-Wave*. Devices with built-in Z-Wave capabilities or an attached Z-Wave module can communicate with each other and be controlled via home control modules, as well as remotely via a computer or smartphone. There can be up to 232 devices on a single Z-Wave network and each device (a lamp, thermostat, television set, garage door opener, or pool control, for instance) has its own unique code. Devices can control each other (such as having your garage door opener programmed to turn on your house lights when you arrive home) and sequences of actions can be programmed to be performed with a single button (such as turning off the house lights, activating the security system, locking the doors, and programming the coffeemaker to brew morning coffee when a single button programmed to perform those tasks is pressed at bedtime). Z-Wave signals have a range of about 90 feet indoors.

# TREND

## Smart Homes

Home automation is taking off. For example, systems using Z-Wave technology are available that enable you to control your lights and door locks, as well as be notified of door/window/motion sensor activation, via your smartphone. There are also a variety of Wi-Fi-based home automation products, such as smart thermostats and lights that you can control with your smartphone.

Another home automation option is using your smartphone as your door key. For example, *Kevo* (a system made by Kwikset using technology developed by UniKey—see the accompanying illustration) uses proximity sensors and Bluetooth 4.0 in conjunction with an iPhone app to allow you to unlock your door by just touching the lock, provided your phone is within range of your door. If you misplace your phone, you can use a key fob instead of your iPhone, or the actual door key. However, using your iPhone has additional advantages—including the ability to send virtual keys to others (permanent keys to friends and family members and temporary keys to others who need access to your home on

a certain date and time, for instance) so they can use their phones as a key, as well as the ability to check the status of your locks and virtual keys online. And, because the system uses battery power and Bluetooth, it functions even if your power or Internet connection is out. In addition, you can have multiple keys stored in your phone, which means no more fumbling with keys on a keyring!

Source: UniKey Technologies, Inc.

There is also a Wi-Fi standard under development that is designed to network sensors and other devices in home automation networks. *Low Power Wi-Fi (802.11ah)* operates in the 900 MHz band and is expected to have speeds of around 150 Kbps. Whether it will replace other standards with similar purposes (such as ZigBee and Z-Wave) remains to be seen.

For a look at how short-range wireless networking is changing home automation, see the Trend box. For a summary of the wireless networking standards just discussed, see Figure 7-34.

**NET**

**FIGURE 7-34**

**Examples of wireless networking standards.**

| CATEGORY | WIRELESS STANDARD | APPLICATION | APPROXIMATE RANGE |
|---|---|---|---|
| Short range | Bluetooth<br>WiGig | To connect peripheral devices to a computer or mobile device or to connect devices together. | 33 feet |
| | WiGig<br>WirelessHD (WiHD) | To connect and transfer multimedia content between home consumer electronic devices (computers, TVs, DVD players, printers, etc.). | 33 feet |
| | ZigBee<br>Z-Wave<br>Low Power Wi-Fi (802.11ah) | To connect a variety of home, personal, and automation devices. | 33 feet–164 feet |
| Medium range | Wi-Fi (802.11) | To connect computers and other devices to a local area network. | 100–300 feet indoors;<br>300–900 feet outdoors |
| | Wi-Fi Direct | To connect computers and other devices directly together. | 600 feet |
| Long range | WiMAX<br>Mobile WiMAX | To provide Internet access to a large geographic area for fixed and/or mobile users. | 6 miles non-line of sight;<br>30 miles line of sight |
| | Cellular standards (3G, 4G, 5G) | To connect mobile phones and other devices to a cellular network for telephone and Internet service. | 10 miles |

**TIP**

You can often update the *firmware*—embedded instructions—for a router and other networking hardware to improve performance or obtain new capabilities. Firmware updates are usually downloaded from the manufacturer's site; often router updates need to be installed with a computer connected to the device via a wired, not wireless, connection.

# NETWORKING HARDWARE

Various types of hardware are necessary to create a computer network, to connect multiple networks together, or to connect a computer or network to the Internet. The most common types of networking hardware used in home and small office networks are discussed next.

## Network Adapters and Modems

A **network adapter**, also called a **network interface card** (**NIC**) when it is in the form of an expansion card, is used to connect a computer to a network (such as a home or business network). A **modem** (derived from the terms *modulate* and *demodulate*) is used to connect a computer to a network over telephone lines. Technically, to be called a *modem*, a device must convert digital signals (such as those used by a computer) to modulated analog signals (such as those used by conventional telephone lines) and vice versa. However, in everyday use, the term *modem* is also used to refer to any device that connects a computer to a broadband Internet connection, such as a *cable modem* used for cable Internet service. In addition, the term *modem* is often used interchangeably with the term *network adapter* when describing devices used to obtain Internet access via certain networks, such as cellular networks.

Most computers and mobile devices today come with a network adapter and/or modem built into the device, typically as a network interface card, as a chip included on the motherboard, or as circuitry built directly into the CPU. The type of network adapter and modem used depends on the type of network (such as Ethernet, Wi-Fi, or cellular) and Internet access being used. For instance, to connect a computer to an Ethernet network, an Ethernet network adapter is used. To connect a computer to a cable Internet connection, typically both a cable modem (such as the one shown in Figure 7-35) and an Ethernet

**⌄ FIGURE 7-35**
Network adapters and modems.

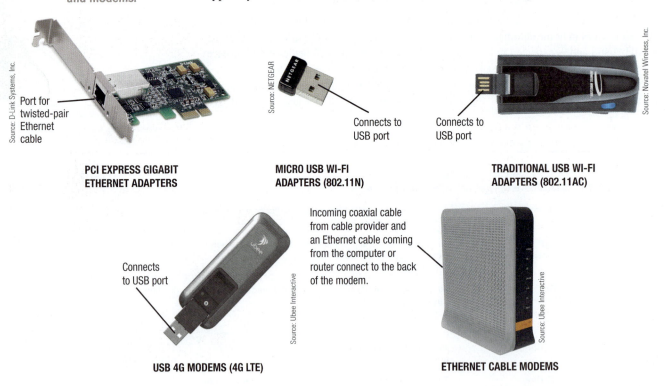

Source: D-Link Systems, Inc.

Port for twisted-pair Ethernet cable

**PCI EXPRESS GIGABIT ETHERNET ADAPTERS**

Source: NETGEAR

Connects to USB port

**MICRO USB WI-FI ADAPTERS (802.11N)**

Connects to USB port

Source: Novatel Wireless, Inc.

**TRADITIONAL USB WI-FI ADAPTERS (802.11AC)**

Connects to USB port

Source: Ubee Interactive

**USB 4G MODEMS (4G LTE)**

Incoming coaxial cable from cable provider and an Ethernet cable coming from the computer or router connect to the back of the modem.

Source: Ubee Interactive

**ETHERNET CABLE MODEMS**

> **Network adapter.** A network interface, such as a network interface card or an external network adapter. > **Network interface card (NIC).** An expansion card through which a computer can connect to a network. > **Modem.** Technically, a device that enables a computer to communicate over analog networking media, such as to connect that computer to the Internet via telephone lines, but also commonly refers to any network device that connects a computer to a broadband Internet connection.

network adapter are used. To connect a computer to a cellular or Wi-Fi network, a cellular or Wi-Fi network adapter, respectively, is used. Some examples of network adapters and modems are shown in Figure 7-35.

When a new type of networking connectivity is needed (such as wanting to use a newer Wi-Fi standard, wanting to add 4G capabilities, or switching to a different type of Internet connection), an external adapter or modem can be obtained. The network adapter or modem needs to be for the appropriate type of network, as well as support the type of networking media (such as twisted-pair cabling, coaxial cabling, or wireless signal) being used.

## Switches, Routers, and Other Hardware for Connecting Devices and Networks

A variety of networking hardware are used to connect the devices on a network, as well as to connect multiple networks together. For instance, as mentioned earlier in this chapter, networks using the star topology need a central device to connect all of the devices on the network. In a wired network, this device was originally a *hub*. A hub transmits all data received to all network devices connected to the hub, regardless of which device the data is being sent to, so the bandwidth of the network is shared and the network is not very efficient. Today, the central device in a wired network is usually a **switch**. A switch contains ports to which the devices on the network connect (typically via networking cables) and facilitates communications between the devices, similar to a hub. But, unlike a hub, a switch identifies which device connected to the switch is the one the data is intended for and sends the data only to that device, rather than sending data out to all connected devices. Consequently, switches are more efficient than hubs. An emerging trend is *software defined networking* (*SDN*) in which outside software is used to control network traffic, instead of the software built into the networking hardware (such as hubs and switches).

To connect multiple networks (such as two LANs, two WANs, or a LAN and the Internet), a **router** is used. Routers pass data on to the intended recipient only and can plan a path through the network to ensure the data reaches its destination in the most efficient manner possible, and they are used to route traffic over the Internet.

A **wireless access point** is a device that allows wireless devices to connect to a network. In home and small business networks, typically a single **wireless router** device—a router with a built-in wireless access point and, typically, a switch—is used to connect both wireless (via Wi-Fi) and wired (via Ethernet cables) devices to a network, as well as to connect that network to an Internet connection via the appropriate broadband modem (see Figure 7-36). Some broadband modems today include wireless router capabilities, which you can use to create a wireless network and obtain Internet access using a single piece of hardware. There are also *travel wireless routers* you can use while on the go (refer again to Figure 7-36). To connect just two LANs together, a **bridge** can be used. The most common use for a bridge in a home network is to wirelessly connect a group of wired devices (such as a home entertainment system consisting of a TV, Blu-ray player, and gaming console) to a home network.

▼ **FIGURE 7-36**
**Wireless routers.**
Provide wireless users access to each other and an Internet connection.

Both 802.11ac and 802.11n devices connect wirelessly.

USB devices (such as a printer or external hard drive) can connect here.

Wired devices can connect here.

Broadband modem providing Internet access connects here.

**CONVENTIONAL WIRELESS ROUTERS**
This 802.11ac router also includes a switch and wireless access point.

A wired Internet connection connects here.

**TRAVEL WIRELESS ROUTERS**
This 802.11a/b/g/n router enables multiple devices to share a single wired Internet connection.

Up to 10 devices can connect to the hotspot via Wi-Fi.

**MOBILE BROADBAND ROUTERS**
This 3G/4G router creates a mobile hotspot, which enables multiple devices to share a mobile broadband connection.

Source: TRENDnet; Belkin International, Inc.; T-Mobile USA, Inc.

NET

> **Switch.** A device used to connect multiple devices on a single (typically wired) network; forwards packets to only the intended recipient.
> **Router.** A device that connects multiple networks together; routes packets to their next location in order to efficiently reach their destination.
> **Wireless access point.** A device that connects wireless devices to a network. > **Wireless router.** A router with a built-in wireless access point; most often used to connect wireless devices to a network and an Internet connection and often contains a built-in switch. > **Bridge.** A device used to bridge or connect two LANs; most often used to connect wired devices wirelessly to a network.

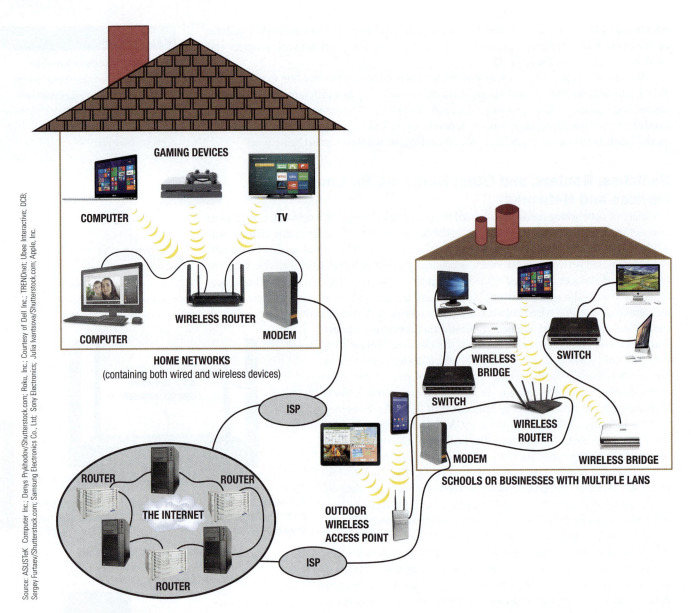

Source: ASUSTeK Computer Inc.; Denys Prykhodov/Shutterstock.com; Roku, Inc.; Courtesy of Dell Inc.; TRENDnet; Ubee Interactive; DCB; Sergey Furtaev/Shutterstock.com; Samsung Electronics Co., Ltd.; Sony Electronics; Julia Ivantsova/Shutterstock.com; Apple, Inc.

**GAMING DEVICES**

COMPUTER — TV

WIRELESS ROUTER

COMPUTER — MODEM

**HOME NETWORKS**
(containing both wired and wireless devices)

ISP

ROUTER — ROUTER

**THE INTERNET**

ROUTER

ISP

OUTDOOR WIRELESS ACCESS POINT

WIRELESS BRIDGE — SWITCH

SWITCH

WIRELESS ROUTER

MODEM — WIRELESS BRIDGE

**SCHOOLS OR BUSINESSES WITH MULTIPLE LANS**

**FIGURE 7-37**
**Networking hardware.** As shown in this example, many different types of hardware are used to connect networking devices.

**TIP**

When using any type of wireless router, it is very important to secure it against unauthorized access. This and other security precautions are discussed in Chapter 9.

There are also routers and other devices used to connect multiple devices to a cellular network. For instance, *mobile broadband routers* are used to share a mobile wireless Internet connection with multiple devices (such as a smartphone, personal computer, and handheld gaming device)—essentially creating a Wi-Fi hotspot that connects to your 3G or 4G Internet connection. Small mobile broadband routers (such as the one shown in Figure 7-36) are designed to enable you to easily create a *mobile hotspot* when you are on the go.

Figure 7-37 provides an example of how the devices discussed in this section, as well as the other networking hardware discussed in the next section, might be used in a network.

## Other Networking Hardware
Additional networking hardware is often needed to extend the range of a network and to share networking media, as discussed next.

## Repeaters, Range Extenders, and Antennas

**Repeaters** are devices that amplify signals along a network. They are necessary whenever signals have to travel farther than would be otherwise possible over the networking medium being used. Repeaters are available for both wired and wireless networks; repeaters for a wireless network are often called **range extenders**. Range extenders usually connect wirelessly to the network and repeat the wireless signal to extend coverage of that network outside or to an additional floor of a building, or to eliminate *dead spots*—areas within the normal network range that don't have coverage. Some *WDS* (*Wireless Distribution System*) wireless access points can be used as range extenders by extending the network coverage from one access point to another.

Another alternative for increasing the range of a Wi-Fi network is using a *higher-gain* (stronger) **antenna**. The MIMO antennas used by many 802.11n and 802.11ac routers allow for faster connections and a greater range than older wireless networks, but sometimes this still isn't enough. Using a network adapter designed for the router being used typically helps the network range to some extent; so does replacing the antenna on the router with a higher-gain antenna or adding an *external antenna* to a networking adapter, if the adapter contains an antenna connector.

Antennas come in a variety of formats and are classified as either *directional antennas* (antennas that concentrate the signal in a particular area) or *omnidirectional antennas* (antennas that are equally effective in all directions). Directional antennas have a greater range than omnidirectional antennas, but they have a more limited delivery area. The strength of an antenna is measured in *decibels* (*dB*). For applications where a large Wi-Fi coverage area is needed (such as in a large business or a hotel), high-gain outdoor antennas can be used (in conjunction with outdoor range extenders and access points, if needed) to enable the network to span a larger area than the hardware would normally allow.

Antennas are also increasingly being used to deliver fixed wireless Internet access (discussed in more detail in Chapter 8) via Wi-Fi using high-gain antennas. For Internet delivery, one base station typically broadcasts to many recipients (called a *point-to-multi-point* (*PMP* or *P2MP*) connection). Private antenna systems may have just one recipient; if so, it is called a *point-to-point* (*PP* or *P2P*) connection instead. An antenna that is designed for long-range Wi-Fi signal transmission is shown in Figure 7-38.

## Multiplexers

High-speed communications lines are expensive and almost always have far greater capacity than a single device can use. Because of this, signals from multiple devices are often combined and sent together to share a single communications medium. A *multiplexer* combines the transmissions from several different devices and sends them as one message. For instance, multiple analog signals can be sent at one time by using multiple frequencies, and multiple optical signals can be sent at one time by using multiple wavelengths. Regardless of how the signals are sent, when the combined signal reaches its destination, the individual messages are separated from one another. Multiplexing is frequently used with fiber-optic cables and other high-capacity media to increase data throughput. For instance, if eight signals are multiplexed and sent together over each fiber in one fiber-optic cable, then the throughput of that cable is increased by a factor of eight.

Source: Ubiquiti Networks, Inc.

**NET**

**FIGURE 7-38**
A long-range Wi-Fi antenna.

---

> **Repeater.** A device on a network that amplifies signals. > **Range extender.** A repeater for a wireless network. > **Antenna.** A device used for receiving or sending radio signals; often used to increase the range of a network.

# SUMMARY

## WHAT IS A NETWORK?

*Communications* refers to data being sent from one device to another over a distance—such as over long-distance phone lines, via privately owned cables, or by satellite. A **computer network** is a collection of computers and other hardware devices that are connected together to share hardware, software, and data, as well as to facilitate electronic communications. Computer networks include home networks, business networks, and the Internet.

## NETWORKING APPLICATIONS

Some of the oldest networking applications are conventional telephone service and television and radio broadcasting. Many of today's networking applications take place via the Internet. There are, however, a variety of other important business and personal applications that utilize networks. For making phone calls while on the go, **mobile phones**—namely, **cellular (cell)** and **satellite phones**—are used; **dual-mode phones** can utilize more than one network, such as to place calls via both a cellular and Wi-Fi network. There are a variety of **global positioning system (GPS)** and monitoring system applications used by individuals and businesses; many homes today also have a *multimedia network*. To communicate and work with others remotely, **videoconferencing**, *collaborative computing*, and **telecommuting** applications are used; **telesurgery** and other **telemedicine** applications can be used to provide remote medical care.

## NETWORK CHARACTERISTICS

Networks can be either **wired networks** (where devices are physically connected) or **wireless networks** (where devices are connected with wireless signals). Wired networks are found in businesses and some homes; wireless networks are becoming very common in both businesses and homes, and are frequently found in public locations to provide a wireless connection or **hotspot** to the Internet. Networks can be classified in terms of their *topology* or physical arrangement (such as a **star network**, **bus network**, or **mesh network**). They can also be classified according to their *architecture* (such as *client-server* networks, which consist of *server* devices that provide network services to *client* computers, or *peer-to-peer* (*P2P*) networks, in which the users' computers and the shared peripherals in the network communicate directly with one another instead of through a server). With *Internet peer-to-peer* (*P2P*) *computing*, files are exchanged directly with other peers via the Internet.

Networks can also be classified by size. **Personal area networks (PANs)** connect the devices immediately around an individual; **local area networks (LANs)** connect geographically close devices, such as within a single building; **metropolitan area networks (MANs)** provide Internet access to cities; and **wide area networks (WANs)** span relatively wide geographical areas. Networks classified as **intranets** are private networks that implement the infrastructure and standards of the Internet and the World Wide Web, **extranets** are private networks accessible to authorized outsiders, and **virtual private networks (VPNs)** are used to transfer private information over a public communications system.

## DATA TRANSMISSION CHARACTERISTICS

Data that travels over a network can use **analog signals** (where data is sent as continuous waves) or **digital signals** (where data is coded as 0s and 1s). Data transmissions can also be characterized by their bandwidth (the amount of data that can be transferred at one time), whether it uses **serial transmission** or **parallel transmission**, how serial transmissions are timed (namely, *synchronous*, *asynchronous*, or *isochronous transmission*), and whether it transmits in *simplex*, *half-duplex*, or *full-duplex* directions. Data can also be transferred using *circuit switching*, *packet switching*, or *broadcasting*.

## NETWORKING MEDIA

Networking media used with wired networks include **twisted-pair**, **coaxial**, and **fiber-optic cable**. Wireless networks typically send messages through the air in the form of *radio signals* and typically use the frequencies in the *radio frequency* (*RF*) band of the *electromagnetic spectrum*. Wireless signals can be sent using **cellular radio** transmissions (which send and receive data via *cell towers* located within designated areas or *cells*), using **microwave stations** and/or **communications satellites** (which send and receive data to and from microwave stations and satellites), or using **infrared** (**IR**) **transmissions** (which send data over short distances as infrared light rays).

**Chapter Objective 5:**
Name specific types of wired and wireless networking media and explain how they transmit data.

## COMMUNICATIONS PROTOCOLS AND NETWORKING STANDARDS

A *communications protocol* determines how the devices on a network communicate; a networking standard typically addresses both how the devices connect and the communications protocols used. The most common communications protocol is **TCP/IP**—the protocol used with the Internet. The most common networking standard for wired networks is **Ethernet** (**802.3**), which is available in a variety of speeds, as well as the *Power over Ethernet* (*PoE*) standard, which allows both power and data to be transferred via an Ethernet network. Alternatives for wired networks increasingly being used within the home include the *Powerline* standard and the emerging universal *G.hn* standard. *Broadband over powerline* (*BPL*) can be used to deliver Internet via the existing power pole infrastructure.

The most common networking standard for home and business wireless LANs is **Wi-Fi** (**802.11**). Wi-Fi is designed for medium-range wireless transmissions, and there are various versions of the standard that support different speeds and distances. When a network with a greater range is needed, **WiMAX** (**802.16**) can be used. **Wi-Fi Direct** enables Wi-Fi devices to be connected directly, without additional hardware. There are a variety of *cellular standards* used with mobile phones; the current standards are *3G* and *4G*. For very short-range applications (such as to connect a keyboard to a computer), **Bluetooth** can be used. Other standards used to connect devices wirelessly include **WiGig** (**802.11ad**) and **WirelessHD** (**WiHD**), which are most often used to connect home electronic devices, and *ZigBee* (*802.15*), *Z-Wave*, and the emerging *Low-Power Wi-Fi* (*802.11ah*), which are most often used for sensor networks and home automation.

**Chapter Objective 6:**
Identify the most common communications protocols and networking standards used with networks today.

## NETWORKING HARDWARE

Computer networks require a variety of hardware. Computers usually connect to a network through either a **network adapter** (called a **network interface card** (**NIC**) when it is in the form of an expansion card); a **modem** is used to connect to a network via telephone lines, though many devices that connect a computer to the Internet today are commonly referred to as modems. The type of network adapter or modem used depends on the type of computer, connection, and networking media being used.

A **switch** is used to connect multiple (typically wired) devices to a network. **Routers** connect multiple devices together; **wireless routers** typically include a router, switch, and **wireless access point** to connect both wireless and wired devices to a network and the Internet. A **bridge** can be used to connect two LANs or a wired device to a wireless network. **Repeaters**, **range extenders**, and **antennas** can be used to extend the range of a network; *multiplexers* are most commonly used with larger networks.

**Chapter Objective 7:**
List several types of networking hardware and explain the purpose of each.

NET
(((o)))

# REVIEW ACTIVITIES

## KEY TERM MATCHING

a. antenna

b. Bluetooth

c. computer network

d. digital signal

e. Ethernet (802.3)

f. global positioning system (GPS)

g. mesh network

h. switch

i. TCP/IP

j. WirelessHD (WiHD)

**Instructions:** Match each key term on the left with the definition on the right that best describes it.

1. _____ A collection of computers and other hardware devices that are connected together to share hardware, software, and data, as well as to communicate electronically with one another.

2. _____ A device used for receiving or sending radio signals; often used to increase the range of a network.

3. _____ A device used to connect multiple devices on a single (typically wired) network; forwards packets to only the intended recipient.

4. _____ A networking standard for very short-range wireless connections; the devices are automatically connected once they get within the allowable range.

5. _____ A network in which there are multiple connections between the devices on the network so that messages can take any of several possible paths.

6. _____ A wireless networking standard designed for very fast transfers between home electronic devices.

7. _____ A networking protocol that uses packet switching to facilitate the transmission of messages; the protocol used with the Internet.

8. _____ A system that uses satellites and a receiver to determine the exact geographic location of the receiver.

9. _____ A type of signal where the data is represented by 0s and 1s.

10. _____ The most widely used wired LAN networking standard.

## SELF-QUIZ

**Instructions:** Circle **T** if the statement is true, **F** if the statement is false, or write the best answer in the space provided. **Answers for the self-quiz are located in the References and Resources Guide at the end of the book.**

1. **T  F**  GPS systems are used only by the government.

2. **T  F**  With serial transmissions, each bit of data is sent individually.

3. **T  F**  The Internet is an example of a LAN.

4. **T  F**  The type of cable used inside most homes for telephone service is twisted-pair wire.

5. **T  F**  A router is a type of modem.

6. With a(n) _____ network topology, all devices are connected in a line to a central cable.

7. A(n) _____ phone can be used with more than one communications network, such as when used with both a cellular and Wi-Fi network.

8. A small network designed to connect the personal devices for an individual (such as via Bluetooth) is called a(n) _____.

9. A(n) _____ is a network that transfers private information securely over the Internet or other public network.

10. Match each description to its networking application, and write the corresponding number in the blank to the left of the description.

    **a.** _____ To diagnose a patient from a distance.

    **b.** _____ To work for a company in New York when you live in California.

    **c.** _____ To watch a video in the living room that is stored on your computer.

    **d.** _____ To receive telephone calls while you are out shopping.

    **e.** _____ To determine your physical location while hiking in the mountains.

1. Multimedia networking
2. GPS
3. Telemedicine
4. Telecommuting
5. Cellular phone

**EXERCISES**

1. Match each description to its networking hardware, and write the corresponding number in the blank to the left of each description.

    **a.** _____ A device used to connect multiple devices on a wired network.

    **b.** _____ A device that enables a computer to communicate over telephone lines.

    **c.** _____ A device used to connect wireless devices to a network.

    **d.** _____ A device used to amplify signals on a network.

1. Repeater
2. Modem
3. Switch
4. Wireless access point

2. Match each description to the networking standard most suited for this purpose, and write the corresponding number in the blank to the left of each description.

    **a.** _____ To connect a portable computer to a wireless hotspot.

    **b.** _____ To connect a wireless keyboard to a computer.

    **c.** _____ To create a wired home or business network.

    **d.** _____ To wirelessly connect home entertainment devices.

1. Bluetooth
2. Wi-Fi
3. WiGig
4. Ethernet

3. If you need to transfer a 35 MB file from one computer to another over a Fast Ethernet network that supports data transfer rates of 100 Mbps, how long should it take to download the file? What real-world conditions might affect this download time?

4. What is the most common use of the TCP/IP networking standard?

5. Explain the difference between Wi-Fi and Bluetooth, including speed, range, and the purpose of each networking standard.

**NET**

**DISCUSSION QUESTIONS**

1. As discussed in the chapter, Internet peer-to-peer (P2P) networking involves sharing files and other resources directly with other computers via the Internet. While some content is legally exchanged via an Internet P2P network, some content (such as movies and music) is exchanged illegally. Should Internet P2P networks be regulated to ensure they are used for only legal activities? Why or why not? If a P2P network set up for legitimate use is used for illegal purposes, should the organization or person who set up the P2P network be responsible? Would you want to use an Internet P2P network?

2. Interference with wireless devices is happening much more often than in the past. For instance, unlicensed walkie-talkies used on TV sets have interfered with police radios, and British air traffic control transmissions have been interrupted by transmissions from nearby baby monitors. If devices that use unlicensed radio frequencies interfere with each other, whose fault is it? The individual for buying multiple products that use the same radio frequency? The manufacturers for not ensuring their products can switch channels as needed to use a free channel? The government for allowing unregulated airwaves? Is there a solution to this problem? Who, if anyone, should be responsible for fixing this problem?

# PROJECTS

**HOT TOPICS**

1. **Wireless Power** As discussed in the How It Works, box, wireless charging is now available to charge smartphones and other devices via wireless charging surfaces.

   For this project, research wireless charging to determine the current status. Select a device, such as a smartphone or tablet that you own or would like to own, and research the wireless power options. Does it have built-in wireless charging capabilities? If not, can they be added with an adapter? What wireless charging standard does the device use? Where would you be able to charge this device wirelessly? How does the price and convenience of wireless charging compare with traditional charging methods? Which would you prefer to use? Why? At the conclusion of your research, prepare a one-page summary of your findings and opinions and submit it to your instructor.

**SHORT ANSWER/ RESEARCH**

2. **Unwired** As discussed in the chapter, home networks—particularly wireless home networks—are becoming very common today to connect computers, printers, and other devices together, as well as to provide Internet access to computers, smartphones, smart TVs, and other devices.

   For this project, suppose that you have a home desktop computer and you are planning to buy a notebook computer to use at home, as well as on the go. You would like to network the two computers wirelessly. Determine the hardware you will need to accomplish this. Create a labeled sketch of the network and a list of the hardware you would need to acquire. Next, research the approximate cost of the hardware to determine the overall cost of the network. Does the cost seem reasonable for the benefits? Would you want to network your home computers in this manner? If you also wanted to use a printer with both computers, would you need any additional hardware? Why or why not? At the conclusion of your research, prepare a one-page summary of your findings and submit it to your instructor, along with your sketch and list of hardware.

**HANDS ON**

3. **Geocaching** Geocaching is a GPS application that is essentially a form of high-tech hide and seek—someone hides a water-tight container filled with a "treasure" (usually toys or cheap collectors' goodies) and posts the location of the cache (in GPS coordinates) on a geocaching Web site. Other individuals use their GPS equipment to find the cache and then sign a log (if one is included in the cache), take an item from the cache, and put another object into the cache as a replacement.

   For this project, find out how to geocache, including the required equipment and any "rules" or courtesies common among geocachers regarding listing or finding a cache, by searching online or visiting a geocaching Web site (such as **www.geocaching.com**). Next, use a geocaching site to find information about a cache currently hidden close to your city and determine what you would need to do in order to find it. At the conclusion of your research, prepare a one-page summary of your findings and submit it to your instructor.

4. **Net Neutrality and Your ISP** The term *net neutrality* refers to the equality of data as it is transferred over the Internet. For instance, the data from an individual and the data from Microsoft are treated the same. A recent controversy surrounding the cable giant Comcast brought up the possibility of ISPs interfering with the delivery of Internet data. According to complaints by customers, Comcast has been blocking the use of P2P sites like BitTorrent to download movies, music, and other large files. Comcast, like most ISPs, includes a statement in its terms of service that allows it to use tools to "efficiently manage its networks," in order to prevent those customers using a higher than normal level of bandwidth from interfering with the access of other customers. However, the Comcast issue was considered by many to be a blatant net neutrality issue—blocking access to multimedia from sources other than its own cable sources. Do you think the actions taken by Comcast were ethical? Does an ISP have a right to block selected Internet traffic? Why or why not? Was there a more ethical way Comcast could have handled the problem of some users consuming a higher than normal level of bandwidth?

For this project, form an opinion about the ethical ramifications of ISPs blocking selected Internet traffic and be prepared to discuss your position (in class, via an online class forum, or via a class blog, depending on your instructor's directions). You may also be asked to write a short paper expressing your opinion.

**ETHICS IN ACTION**

5. **Wired Home Network** If you have two or more computers at home and want to share files, an Internet connection, or a printer, you will need to set up a home network. Although a wireless network is an option, wired networks still exist and new options for wired networks are emerging.

For this project, suppose that you want to set up a wired home network. Create a scenario (real or fictitious) that describes the number of computers and other devices involved, where each item is located, and the tasks for which the network will be used. Select a wired networking option (such as Ethernet or Powerline) and determine the steps and equipment necessary to implement that network for your scenario. Be sure to include the cost of the necessary hardware and how the network would be physically installed. Share your findings (including a diagram of your proposed network) with your class in the form of a presentation. The presentation should not exceed 10 minutes and should make use of one or more presentation aids, such as a whiteboard, handouts, or a computer-based slide presentation (your instructor may provide additional requirements). You may also be asked to submit a summary of the presentation to your instructor.

**PRESENTATION/
DEMONSTRATION**

6. **Is It Ever Ethical to Wi-Fi Piggyback?** Wi-Fi piggybacking refers to using an unsecured Wi-Fi network to access the Internet without authorization. Some people piggyback on a stranger's Wi-Fi network for a quick Google search or e-mail check; others use a neighbor's Wi-Fi connection on a regular basis. According to a recent poll, about one-third of individuals have Wi-Fi piggybacked at one time or another. The legality of Wi-Fi piggybacking varies from location to location and it is illegal in the United Kingdom and in some states in the United States. Individuals have been arrested and prosecuted for Wi-Fi piggybacking—typically for using the network for illegal activities, such as downloading child pornography. Does the appropriateness of Wi-Fi piggybacking change based on the type of network being used (business or home, for instance)? What about the type or amount of use, such as checking e-mail or viewing a map while traveling versus using your neighbor's Internet connection on a daily basis? When a Wi-Fi network is left unsecured, does that mean that outside use is invited? Or, similar to an unlocked front door, is it ethical to enter only with their permission? What if the piggybacking results in an individual's Internet service being canceled as a result of violating their Internet provider's terms of use—would that impact your opinion? How would you feel if someone piggybacked on your Wi-Fi network?

Pick a side on this issue, form an opinion and gather supporting evidence, and be prepared to discuss and defend your position in a classroom debate or in a one- to two-page paper, depending on your instructor's directions.

**BALANCING ACT**

**NET**

# chapter 8

# The Internet

**After completing this chapter, you will be able to do the following:**

1. Discuss how the Internet evolved and what it is like today.

2. Identify the various types of individuals, companies, and organizations involved in the Internet community and explain their purposes.

3. Describe device and connection options for connecting to the Internet, as well as some considerations to keep in mind when selecting an ISP.

4. Understand how to search effectively for information on the Internet and how to cite Internet resources properly.

5. List several ways to communicate over the Internet, in addition to e-mail.

6. List several useful activities that can be performed via the Web.

7. Discuss censorship and privacy and how they are related to Internet use.

## outline

**Overview**

**Evolution of the Internet**
From ARPANET to Internet2
The Internet Community Today
Myths About the Internet

**Getting Set Up to Use the Internet**
Type of Device
Type of Connection and Internet Access
Selecting an ISP and Setting Up Your Devices

**Searching the Internet**
Search Sites
Search Strategies
Evaluating Search Results
Citing Internet Resources

**Beyond Browsing, Searching, and E-Mail**
Other Types of Online Communications
Social Networking/Social Media
E-Commerce
Online Entertainment
Online News, Reference, and Information
Online Education and Writing

**Censorship and Privacy Issues**
Censorship
Web Browsing Privacy
E-Mail Privacy

## OVERVIEW

**W**ith the prominence of the Internet in our personal and professional lives today, it is hard to believe that there was a time not too long ago when few people had even heard of the Internet, let alone used it. But technology is continually evolving and, in fact, it is only relatively recently that it has evolved enough to allow the use of online multimedia applications—such as downloading music and movies, watching TV and videos, and playing multimedia interactive games—to become everyday activities. Today, the Internet and the World Wide Web are household words, and, in many ways, they have redefined how people think about computers, communications, and the availability of news and information.

Despite the popularity of the Internet, however, many users cannot answer some important basic questions about it. What makes up the Internet? Is it the same thing as the World Wide Web? How did the Internet begin, and where is it heading? What is the most effective way to use the Internet to find specific information? This chapter addresses these types of questions and more.

Chapter 8 begins with a discussion of the evolution of the Internet, followed by a look at the many individuals, companies, and organizations that make up the Internet community. Next, the chapter covers different options for connecting to the Internet, including the types of devices, Internet connections, and ISPs that are available today. Then, one of the most important Internet skills you should acquire— efficient Internet searching—is discussed. To help you appreciate the wide spectrum of resources and activities available over the Internet, we also take a brief look at some of the most common applications available via the Internet. The chapter closes with a discussion of a few of the important societal issues that apply to Internet use. ■

## EVOLUTION OF THE INTERNET

The **Internet** is a worldwide collection of separate, but interconnected, networks accessed daily by billions of people using a variety of devices to obtain information, disseminate information, access entertainment, or communicate with others. While the term *Internet* has become a household word only during the past two decades or so, the Internet has actually operated in one form or another for much longer than that.

### From ARPANET to Internet2

The roots of the Internet began with an experimental project called ARPANET. The Internet we know today is the result of the evolution of ARPANET and the creation of the World Wide Web (Web).

>**Internet.** The largest and most well-known computer network, linking billions of devices all over the world.

## ARPANET

The U.S. Department of Defense *Advanced Research Projects Agency* (*ARPA*) created **ARPANET** in 1969. One objective of the ARPANET project was to create a computer network that would allow researchers located in different places to communicate with each other. Another objective was to build a computer network capable of sending or receiving data over a variety of paths to ensure that network communications could continue even if part of the network was destroyed, such as in a nuclear attack or by a natural disaster.

Initially, ARPANET connected four supercomputers and enabled researchers at a few dozen academic institutions to communicate with each other and with government agencies. As the project grew during the next decade, students were granted access to ARPANET as hundreds of college and university networks were connected to it. These networks consisted of a mixture of different computers so, over the years, protocols were developed for tying this mix of computers and networks together, for transferring data over the network, and for ensuring that data was transferred intact. Additional networks soon connected to ARPANET, and this *internet*—or network of networks—eventually evolved into the present day Internet.

The Internet infrastructure today is used for a variety of purposes, such as researching topics of interest; exchanging e-mail and other messages; participating in videoconferences and making telephone calls; downloading software, music, and movies; purchasing goods and services; watching TV and video online; accessing computers remotely; and sharing files with others. Most of these activities are available through the primary Internet resource—the World Wide Web (Web).

## The World Wide Web

In its early years, the Internet was used primarily by the government, scientists, and educational institutions. Despite its popularity in academia and with government researchers, the Internet went virtually unnoticed by the public and the business community for over two decades because 1) it required a computer and 2) it was hard to use (see the left image in Figure 8-1). As always, however, computer and networking technology improved and new applications quickly followed. Then, in 1989, a researcher named *Tim Berners-Lee* proposed the idea of the **World Wide Web** (**Web**). He envisioned the World Wide Web as a way to organize information in the form of pages linked together through selectable text or images (which are today's hyperlinks) on the screen. Although the introduction of Web pages did not replace all other Internet resources (such as e-mail and collections of downloadable files), it became a popular way for researchers to provide written information to others.

In 1993, a group of professors and their students at the University of Illinois *National Center for Supercomputing Applications* (*NCSA*) released the *Mosaic* Web browser. Soon

**▼ FIGURE 8-1**

**Using the Internet: Back in the "old days" versus now.**

ericleifrancais/Shutterstock.com

Source: CBS Interactive; Boris Shevchuk/Shutterstock.com

**EARLY 1990s**
Even at the beginning of the 1990s, using the Internet for most people meant learning how to work with a cryptic sequence of commands. Virtually all information was text-based.

**TODAY**
Today's Web organizes much of the Internet's content into easy-to-read pages that can contain text, graphics, animation, video, and interactive content that users access via hyperlinks.

> **ARPANET.** The predecessor to the Internet, named after the Advanced Research Projects Agency (ARPA), which sponsored its development.
> **World Wide Web (Web).** The collection of Web pages available through the Internet.

after, use of the World Wide Web began to increase dramatically because Mosaic's graphical user interface (GUI) and its ability to display images on Web pages made using the World Wide Web both easier and more fun than in the past. Today's Web pages are a true multimedia, interactive experience (see the *Big Brother* Web site shown in Figure 8-1). They can contain text, graphics, animation, sound, video, and three-dimensional virtual reality objects.

A growing number of today's Web-based applications and services are referred to as *Web 2.0* applications. Although there is no precise definition, Web 2.0 generally refers to applications and services that use the Web as a platform to deliver rich applications that enable people to collaborate, socialize, and share information online. Some Web 2.0 applications (such as cloud computing) have been discussed in previous chapters; others (such as social media, RSS feeds, podcasts, blogs, and wikis) are covered later in this chapter.

Although the Web is only part of the Internet, it is by far the most widely used part. Today, most companies regard their use of the Internet and their World Wide Web presence as indispensable competitive business tools, and many individuals view the Internet—and especially the Web—as a vital research, communications, and entertainment medium.

One remarkable characteristic of both the Internet and World Wide Web is that they are not owned by any person or business, and no single person, business, or organization is in charge. Web pages are developed by individuals and

## ASK THE EXPERT

**Frank Liberio,** Senior Vice President, Chief Information Officer, McDonald's Corporation

**How important is it for a business to have a Web site today if it doesn't sell products and services online?**

McDonald's serves more than 60 million people around the world every day and our Web sites allow us to connect with them on the topics that are important to them and in the way that they want to connect. It's all about customer convenience. Whether browsing on a smartphone, desktop, or laptop, customers have easy access to all things McDonald's.

For example, nutritional data lets them make informed food and beverage choices. *Our food. Your questions.* webisodes allow customers to proactively address questions and concerns about our food. Customers can find in-depth information about our sustainability efforts, financial performance, career opportunities, and franchising. Our Web sites also provide a forum for customers to ask questions and provide feedback that is critical to our continued improvement.

In some markets, Web commerce meets the whenever-wherever digital desires of customers. For McDonald's, it is an evolving platform for enabling services like promotional offers, online ordering, and payment.

organizations, and are hosted on Web servers owned by individuals, schools, businesses, or other entities. Each network connected to the Internet is privately owned and managed individually by that network's administrator, and the primary infrastructure that makes up the *Internet backbone* is typically owned by communications companies, such as telephone and cable companies. In addition, the computers and other devices used to access the Internet belong to individuals or organizations. So, while individual components of the Internet are owned by individuals and organizations, the Internet as a whole has no owner or network administrator. The closest the Internet comes to having a governing body is a group of organizations that are involved with issues such as establishing the protocols used on the Internet, making recommendations for changes, and encouraging cooperation between and coordinating communications among the networks connected to the Internet.

### Internet2

*Internet2* is a consortium of researchers, educators, and technology leaders from industry, government, and the international community that is dedicated to the development of revolutionary Internet technologies. Internet2 uses high-performance networks linking about 500 member institutions to deploy and test new network applications and technologies. Internet2 is designed as a research and development tool to help develop technologies that ensure the Internet in the future can handle tomorrow's applications, and it is now being used to deploy advanced applications and technologies that might not be possible otherwise with today's Internet. Much of Internet2 research is focused on speed. In fact, the Internet2 backbone network was recently upgraded to support 8.8 Tbps. This network is the first national network to use 100 Gigabit Ethernet over its entire footprint; it will be used to support high bandwidth applications, such as telemedicine and distance learning, to schools, libraries, hospitals, and other organizations.

## The Internet Community Today

The Internet community today consists of individuals, businesses, and a variety of organizations located throughout the world. Virtually anyone with a computer or other Internet-enabled device can be part of the Internet, either as a user or as a supplier of information or services. Most members of the Internet community fall into one or more of the following groups.

### Users

*Users* are people who use the Internet to retrieve content or perform online activities, such as to look up a telephone number, read the day's news headlines or top stories, browse through an online catalog, make an online purchase, download a music file, watch an online video, make a phone call, or send an e-mail message. According to the Pew Internet & American Life Project, about 87% of U.S. adults (and 97% of individuals between the ages of 18 and 29) are Internet users, using the Internet at work, home, school, or another location. The availability of low-cost computers, low-cost or free Internet access (such as at libraries, schools, and other public locations), smartphones, and bundled pricing for obtaining Internet service in conjunction with telephone and/or television service has helped Internet use begin to approach the popularity and widespread use of telephones and TVs.

### Internet Service Providers (ISPs)

**Internet service providers** (**ISPs**) are businesses or other organizations (see some examples in Figure 8-2) that provide Internet access to others, typically for a fee. ISPs (sometimes called *wireless ISPs* or *WISPs* when referring to ISPs that offer service via a wireless network) include most communications and media companies, such as conventional and wireless phone providers, cable providers, and satellite providers. Some ISPs (such as cable and cellular phone companies) offer Internet service over their private networks; other ISPs provide Internet service over the regular telephone lines or the airwaves. While many ISPs (such as AT&T and EarthLink) provide service nationwide, others provide service to a more limited geographical area. Regardless of their delivery method and geographical coverage, ISPs are the onramp to the Internet, providing their subscribers with access to the World Wide Web, e-mail, and other Internet resources. In addition to Internet access, some ISPs provide proprietary online services available only to their subscribers. A later section of this chapter covers ISPs in more detail, including factors to consider when selecting an ISP.

### Internet Content Providers

**Internet content providers** supply the information that is available through the Internet. Internet content providers can be commercial businesses, nonprofit organizations, educational institutions, individuals, and more. Some examples of Internet content providers are listed next.

➤ A photographer who posts samples of her best work on a Web page.

➤ A musician who posts his music video on YouTube.

**FIGURE 8-2**

Companies that provide Internet access today include telephone, cable, and satellite companies.

Source: AT&T; Verizon Communications; Comcast; T-Mobile USA, Inc.; EarthLink, Inc.; ViaSat, Inc.

---

> A software company that creates a Web site to provide product information and software downloads.

> A national news organization that maintains an online site to provide up-to-the-minute news, feature stories, and video clips.

> A television network that develops a site for its TV shows, including episode summaries, cast information, and links to watch past episodes online.

## Application Service Providers (ASPs) and Web Services

**Application service providers** (**ASPs**) are companies that manage and distribute Web-based software services to customers over the Internet. Instead of providing access to the Internet like ISPs do, ASPs provide access to software applications via the Internet. In essence, ASPs rent access to software programs to companies or individuals—typically, customers pay a monthly or yearly fee to use each application. As discussed in Chapter 6, this software can be called cloud software, Web-based software, Software as a Service (SaaS), and cloudware. Common ASP applications for businesses include office suites, graphics suites, collaboration and communications software, accounting programs, and e-commerce software.

One type of self-contained business application designed to work over the Internet or a company network is a **Web service**. A Web service can be added to Web pages to provide standardized Web-based applications that share business logic, data, and processes (such as to include mapping information or to enable Web-site sign on). For example, Web developers for secure Web sites (such as Zappos.com, shown in Figure 8-3) can use an Amazon Web service to allow their customers to log onto those secure Web sites by using their Amazon account logon information; similar Web services are available that use Facebook or Google account information. A Web service can also be used to provide a service via a user's computer and the Internet. For instance, the *FedEx QuickShip* Web service allows users to create a shipment to any Microsoft Outlook contact from within Microsoft Outlook. It is important to realize that Web services are not stand-alone applications—instead, they are simply a standardized way of allowing Web-based applications to share data and work together. A company that provides Web services is sometimes referred to as a *Web services provider*.

**▽ FIGURE 8-3**

**Web services.** This Web service enables Web developers to use Amazon's authentication system for users.

Clicking this button logs a Zappos.com customer in via an Amazon Web service and the customer's Amazon account.

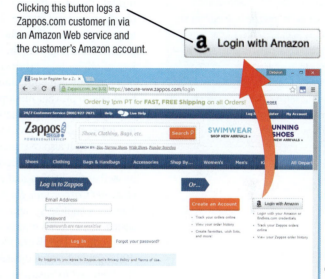

Source: Zappos.com

## Infrastructure Companies

*Infrastructure companies* are the enterprises that own or operate the paths or "roadways" along which Internet data travels, such as the Internet backbone and the communications networks connected to it. Examples of infrastructure companies include conventional and mobile phone companies, cable companies, and satellite Internet providers.

## Hardware and Software Companies

A wide variety of hardware and software companies make and distribute the products used with the Internet and Internet activities. For example, companies that create or sell the software used in conjunction with the Internet (such as Web browsers, e-mail programs, e-commerce and multimedia software, and Web development tools) fall into this category. So, too, do the companies that make the hardware (network adapters, modems, cables, routers, servers, computers, and smartphones, for instance) that is used with the Internet.

## The Government and Other Organizations

Many organizations influence the Internet and its uses. Governments have the most visible impact; their laws can impact both the information made available via Web servers located in a particular country and the access individuals residing in that country have to the Internet. For example, in France, it is illegal to sell items or post online content related to racist groups or activities; in China there are tight controls imposed on what information is published on Web servers located in China, as well as on the information available to its citizens. And in the United States, anything illegal offline is also illegal online.

Legal rulings also can have a large impact on the communications industry in general. In the United States, for example, the 1968 *Carterfone Decision* allowed companies other than AT&T to utilize the AT&T infrastructure and the 1996 *Telecommunications Act* deregulated the entire communications industry so that telephone companies, cable TV providers, and satellite operators were free to enter each other's markets. In addition to making these types of decisions, the Federal Communications Commission (FCC) also greatly influences the communications industry through its ability to allocate radio frequencies (as discussed in Chapter 7) and to implement policies and regulations, such as those that impact *net neutrality*—the basic concept that all content on the Internet is equal; that is, all packets traveling over the Internet are delivered on a first-come, first-served basis regardless of where they originated. The ability of the government to approve or block potential mergers between communications companies and to break apart companies based on antitrust law to prevent monopolies also impacts the Internet and communications industry.

Key Internet organizations are responsible for many aspects of the Internet. For example, the *Internet Society* provides leadership in addressing issues that may impact the future of the Internet. It also oversees the groups responsible for Internet infrastructure standards, such as determining the protocols that can be used and how Internet addresses are constructed, as well as facilitating and coordinating Internet-related initiatives around the world. *ICANN* (*Internet Corporation for Assigned Names and Numbers*) coordinates activities related to the Internet's naming system, such as IP address allocation and domain name management. For instance, it reviews nominations for new top-level domains and determines which new TLDs to introduce. The *World Wide Web Consortium* (*W3C*) is an international community of over 400 organizations dedicated to developing new protocols and specifications to be used with the Web and to ensure its interoperability. In addition, many colleges and universities support Internet research and manage blocks of the Internet's resources.

## Myths About the Internet

Because the Internet is so unique in the history of the world—and its content and applications keep evolving—several widespread myths about it have surfaced.

### Myth 1: The Internet Is Free

This myth stems from the fact that there has traditionally been no cost associated with accessing online content—such as news and product information—or with e-mail exchange, other than what the Internet users pay their ISPs for Internet access. And many people—such as students, employees, and consumers who opt for free Internet service or use free access available at public libraries or other public locations—pay nothing for Internet access. Yet it should also be obvious that someone, somewhere, has to pay to keep the Internet up and running.

Businesses, schools, public libraries, and most home users pay Internet service providers flat monthly fees to connect to the Internet. In addition, businesses, schools, libraries, and other large organizations might have to lease high-capacity communications lines (such as from a telephone company) to support their high level of Internet traffic.

> **TIP**
>
> A recent FCC decision reclassified broadband ISPs as *common carriers*, which means they are treated as public utilities. The FCC also defined "Open Internet," which prohibits broadband providers from blocking access to legal Internet content, slowing down any legal Internet content, or favoring some Internet traffic over others in exchange for money or other considerations.

Mobile users that want Internet access while on the go typically pay hotspot providers or wireless providers for this access. ISPs, phone companies, cable companies, and other organizations that own part of the Internet infrastructure pay to keep their parts of the Internet running smoothly. ISPs also pay software and hardware companies for the resources they need to support their subscribers. Eventually, most of these costs are passed along to end users through ISP fees. ISPs that offer free Internet access typically obtain revenue by selling on-screen ads that display on the screen when the service is being used.

Another reason the idea that the Internet is free is a myth is the growing trend of subscription or per-use fees to access Web-based resources. For instance, fee-based streaming music and movies are very common today (see Figure 8-4) and some journal or newspaper articles require a fee to view them online. In fact, many newspapers and magazines have moved entirely online and most charge a subscription fee to view the level of content that was previously published in a print version. In lieu of a mandatory fee, some Web sites request a donation for use of the site. Many experts expect the use of fee-based Internet content to continue to grow at a rapid pace.

**FIGURE 8-4**
**Fee-based Web content.** The use of fee-based Web content, such as streaming movies via Netflix as shown here, is growing.

Source: Netflix

## Myth 2: Someone Controls the Internet

As already discussed, no single group or organization controls the Internet. Governments in each country have the power to regulate the content and use of the Internet within their borders, as allowed by their laws. However, legislators often face serious obstacles getting legislation passed into law—let alone getting it enforced. Making governmental control even harder is the "bombproof" design of the Internet itself. If a government tries to block access to or from a specific country or Web site, for example, users can use a third party (such as an individual located in another country or a different Web site) or software (such as a virtual private network) to circumvent the block. This recently occurred in Turkey when the government blocked access to social networking sites in response to government unrest—a vast number of Turkish citizens were able to send Facebook and Twitter updates via VPN services routed through other countries.

## Myth 3: The Internet and the World Wide Web Are Identical

Because you can now use a Web browser to access most of the Internet's resources, many people think the Internet and the Web are the same thing. Even though in everyday use many people use the terms *Internet* and *Web* interchangeably, they are not the same thing. Technically, the Internet is the physical network, and the Web is the collection of Web pages accessible over the Internet. A majority of Internet activities today take place via Web pages, but there are Internet resources other than the Web that are not accessed via a Web browser. For instance, files can be uploaded and downloaded using an FTP (File Transfer Protocol) program and conventional e-mail can be accessed using an e-mail program.

# GETTING SET UP TO USE THE INTERNET

Getting set up to use the Internet typically involves three decisions—determining the types of devices you will use to access the Internet, deciding which type of connection is desired, and selecting the Internet service provider to be used. Once these determinations have been made, you can set up your Internet access and your devices.

## Type of Device

The Internet today can be accessed using a variety of devices. The types of devices used depend on a combination of factors, such as the devices available to you, if you need

**TIP**

Many people use multiple devices to access the Internet; if so, the connection type and ISP for each device needs to be determined.

# TECHNOLOGY AND YOU

### Mobile Data Caps

As a result of individuals streaming TV and videos from the Internet, downloading music and movies, playing online multiplayer games, participating in video phone calls, and otherwise performing high-bandwidth activities using their smartphones and tablets, mobile data use has increased tremendously. This has created the issue of wireless carriers potentially running out of bandwidth available for customers, resulting in outages or delays. In response, many wireless carriers have implemented *data caps* and have eliminated unlimited data plans (though many plans still have unlimited talk and text). With a data cap, customers have a download limit for data (such as 3 GB per month) and either temporarily lose high-speed Internet access (such as being slowed down from 4G to 3G speeds—called *data throttling*) or are charged an additional fee if they exceed that limit.

One explanation for the increased data usage is speed—4G data speeds are significantly faster than 3G service and the results (such as faster Web pages and smoother streaming videos) make it easier for users to go through a large amount of bandwidth in a relatively short period of time.

So how do you avoid the expensive or annoying ramifications associated with going over your data cap? The best way is to not go over your limit in the first place. To help with this, use Wi-Fi instead of your cellular connection whenever possible. It is also prudent to monitor your data usage to make sure you stay under your data cap (you can also use this information to decide if you need to consider upgrading to a higher plan if your usage is typical but still over your data cap). Some smartphones have an option for viewing your total data usage for the current and past billing periods, as well as usage per app or Web site to help you see where you are using the most data. Some also allow you to view this data separately for Wi-Fi and cell to see which apps are using the most cellular data.

Another useful tool is third-party apps designed to help you monitor your bandwidth usage. One such app is *Onavo Extend*, shown in the accompanying illustration. It gives you a breakdown of consumption by app, so you know your worst bandwidth offenders. As a bonus, it compresses your incoming data by up to 500% so you can do up to five times more with your data plan before going over your limit.

Source: Onavo Mobile Ltd.

---

access just at home or while on the go, and what types of Internet content you want to access. Some possible devices are shown in Figure 8-5 and discussed next.

## Personal Computers

Most users who have access to a personal computer (such as a desktop or notebook computer) at home, work, or school will use it to access the Internet. One advantage of using personal computers for Internet access is that they have relatively large screens for viewing Internet content and keyboards for easier data entry. They can also be used to view or otherwise access virtually any Web page content, such as graphics, animation, music, games, and videos. In addition, they typically have a large hard drive and are connected to a printer so Web pages, e-mail messages, and downloaded files can be saved and/or printed easily.

## Smartphones, Tablets, and Other Mobile Devices

Smartphones and other mobile devices are also often used to view Web page content, exchange e-mail and other messages, and download music and other online content. In fact, mobile Web use—or *wireless Web*, as it is sometimes called—is one of the fastest growing uses of the Internet today (nearly two-thirds of American adults now own a smartphone).

✔ **TIP**

According to a recent Nielsen report, people now use smartphones more than personal computers to access the Internet.

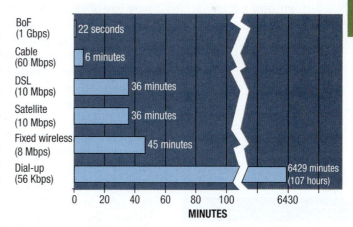

**PERSONAL COMPUTERS**  **SMARTPHONES**  **SMART TVS**

While smartphones are convenient to use on the go, they typically have a relatively small display screen; tablets typically have a larger screen size for easier viewing. Some mobile devices include a built-in or sliding keyboard for easier data entry; others utilize pen, voice, or touch input instead.

### Gaming Devices and Televisions

Another option is using a gaming device (such as a gaming console or handheld gaming device) to access Web content, in addition to using that device to play games. For instance, the Sony PlayStation, Sony PSP, Nintendo Wii U, and Nintendo 3DS all have Web browsers that can be used to access Web content. Smart TVs (one example is shown in Figure 8-5) can connect to the Internet in order to display Web content (the type of Web content available depends on the smart TV being used and the apps installed on that TV). It is estimated that the number of smart TVs will exceed 750 million (over one-quarter of all TV sets worldwide) by 2018.

### Type of Connection and Internet Access

In order to use the Internet, you need to connect a computer or other device to it. Typically, this occurs by connecting the device you are using to a computer or a network (usually belonging to your ISP, school, or employer) that is connected continually to the Internet. As discussed in Chapter 7, there are a variety of wired and wireless ways to connect to another device. Most types of connections today are *broadband* or high-speed connections. Although broadband is defined by the FCC as 25 Mbps or faster, many home Internet connections considered broadband connections today are significantly slower than 25 Mbps. As applications requiring high-speed connections continue to grow in popularity, access to broadband Internet speeds is needed in order to take full advantage of these applications. For instance, high-definition video, video chat, video-on-demand (VOD), and other multimedia applications all require broadband connections (see Figure 8-6). For a look at an issue related to the increased use of multimedia Internet content—mobile data caps—see the Technology and You box.

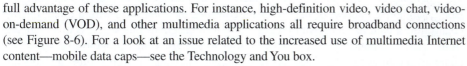

| | |
|---|---|
| BoF (1 Gbps) | 22 seconds |
| Cable (60 Mbps) | 6 minutes |
| DSL (10 Mbps) | 36 minutes |
| Satellite (10 Mbps) | 36 minutes |
| Fixed wireless (8 Mbps) | 45 minutes |
| Dial-up (56 Kbps) | 6429 minutes (107 hours) |

0  20  40  60  80  100  6430
**MINUTES**

The difference between dial-up and direct Internet connections is discussed next, followed by an overview of the most common types of Internet connections used for personal use today; these types of Internet connections are also summarized in Figure 8-7. Many providers today offer bundles (such as cable TV, telephone, and Internet service) to lower an individual's overall total cost for the services. Similar to the mobile data caps discussed in the Technology and You box, some home broadband Internet services have data caps (you typically either are throttled down significantly or are charged an additional fee when you go

| TYPE OF INTERNET CONNECTION | AVAILABILITY | APPROXIMATE MAXIMUM SPEED* | APPROXIMATE MONTHLY PRICE |
|---|---|---|---|
| Conventional dial-up | Anywhere there is telephone service | 56 Kbps | Free–$30 |
| Cable | Virtually anywhere cable TV service is available | 6–200 Mbps | $30–110 |
| DSL | Within 3 miles of a switching station that supports DSL | 3–15 Mbps | $30–40 |
| Satellite | Anywhere there is a clear view of the southern sky and where a satellite dish can be mounted and receive a signal; most often in rural or mountainous areas | 5–15 Mbps | $40–80 |
| Fixed wireless | Selected areas where service is available; most often in rural areas | 2–12 Mbps | $60–250 |
| Broadband over fiber (BoF) | Anywhere fiber has been installed to the building; most often in urban areas | 5 Mbps–1 Gbps | $30–70 |
| Mobile wireless (4G) | Virtually anywhere cellular phone service is available | 3–100 Mbps | Varies greatly depending on data plan |

* Download speed; most connections have slower upload speeds.

**FIGURE 8-7**
Typical home Internet connection options.

**TIP**

If you have a direct Internet connection, leave your e-mail program open on your computer to retrieve your e-mail on a continual basis.

over your limit), while others offer unlimited Internet access.

## Dial-Up vs. Direct Connections

**Dial-up connections** (in which your computer dials up and connects to your ISP's computer only when an Internet connection is needed) work over standard telephone lines. To connect to the Internet, your computer dials its modem and then connects to a modem attached to a computer belonging to your ISP via the telephone lines. While you are connected to your ISP, your computer can access Internet resources. To end your Internet session, you disconnect from your ISP. One advantage of a dial-up connection is security. Because you are not continually connected to the Internet, it is much less likely that anyone (such as a hacker, as discussed in Chapter 9) will gain access to your computer via the Internet, either to access the data located on your computer or, more commonly, to use your computer in some type of illegal or unethical manner. However, dial-up connections are significantly slower than other types of connections; they are also inconvenient because you have to instruct your computer to dial up your ISP every time you want to connect to the Internet. Also, your telephone line will be tied up while you are accessing the Internet, unless you have a second phone line. The most common type of dial-up Internet service is conventional dial-up.

Most Internet connections today are **direct connections**, which keep your devices continually connected to your provider and, therefore, continually connected to the Internet. With a direct connection (such as cable, DSL, satellite, or fixed wireless), you access the Internet simply by opening a Web browser, such as Edge, Internet Explorer, Chrome, Safari, or Firefox. Direct Internet connections are broadband connections, are often available in different *tiers* (which means you have a choice of speeds and the price varies accordingly), are commonly used in homes and businesses, and are often connected to a LAN to share the Internet connection with multiple devices within the home or business. Because direct connections keep your computer connected to the Internet at all times (as long as your computer is powered up), it is important to protect your computer from unauthorized access or hackers. Consequently, all computers with a direct Internet connection should use a firewall program. Firewall programs block access to a computer from outside computers and enable each user to specify which programs on his or her computer are allowed to have access to the Internet. Firewalls, as well as other network and Internet security precautions, are discussed in more detail in Chapter 9.

> **Dial-up connection.** A type of Internet connection in which the computer or other device must dial up and connect to a service provider's computer via telephone lines before being connected to the Internet. > **Direct connection.** A type of Internet connection in which the computer or other device is connected to the Internet continually.

## Conventional Dial-Up

**Conventional dial-up Internet access** uses a conventional dial-up modem connected to a standard telephone jack with regular twisted-pair telephone cabling. Conventional dial-up Internet access is most often used with the home desktop computers of users who don't need, or do not want to pay for, broadband Internet service. Advantages include inexpensive hardware, ease of setup and use, widespread availability (including remote areas), and increased security. The primary disadvantage is slow connection speed—a maximum of 56 Kbps.

## Cable

**Cable Internet access** uses a direct connection and is one of the most widely used types of home broadband connections. Cable Internet access is very fast (typically around 25 Mbps) and is available wherever cable TV access is available, provided the local cable provider supports Internet access. Consequently, cable Internet access is not widely available in rural areas. Cable Internet access requires a cable modem.

## DSL

**DSL (Digital Subscriber Line) Internet access** is a type of direct connection that transmits via standard telephone lines, but it does not tie up your telephone line. DSL Internet access requires a DSL modem and is available only to users who are relatively close (within three miles) to a telephone switching station and who have telephone lines capable of handling DSL Internet access. DSL speeds are slower than cable speeds and the speed of the connection degrades as the distance between the modem and the switching station gets closer to the three-mile limit. Consequently, DSL Internet access is usually only available in urban areas. Download speeds can be up to about 25 Mbps, but they are more typically around 10 Mbps.

## Satellite

**Satellite Internet access** also uses a direct connection and has speeds similar to DSL Internet access, but it is more expensive than both DSL and cable Internet access and it almost always has a data cap. However, it is often the only broadband option for rural areas. In addition to a satellite modem, it requires a *transceiver* satellite dish mounted outside the home or building to receive and transmit data to and from the satellites being used. Installation requires an unobstructed view of the southern sky (to have a clear line of sight between the transceiver and appropriate satellite), and performance might degrade or stop altogether during very heavy rain or snowstorms.

## Fixed Wireless

**Fixed wireless Internet access** uses a direct connection and is similar to satellite Internet access in that it uses wireless signals, but it uses radio transmission towers (either stand-alone towers like the one shown in Figure 8-8 or transmitters placed on existing cell phone towers) instead of satellites. Fixed wireless Internet access requires a modem and, often, an outside-mounted transceiver. Fixed wireless companies typically use Wi-Fi or WiMAX technology to broadcast the wireless signals to customers. Speeds are typically between 2 and 10 Mbps, though the speed depends somewhat on the distance

**NET**

**FIGURE 8-8**
**Fixed wireless towers.** This WiMAX tower is installed at the peak of Whistler Mountain in British Columbia.

Source: Tranzeo Wireless USA

>**Conventional dial-up Internet access.** Dial-up Internet access via standard telephone lines. >**Cable Internet access.** Fast, direct Internet access via cable TV lines. >**DSL (Digital Subscriber Line) Internet access.** Fast, direct Internet access via standard telephone lines. >**Satellite Internet access.** Fast, direct Internet access via the airwaves and a satellite dish. >**Fixed wireless Internet access.** Fast, direct Internet access available in some areas via the airwaves.

between the tower and the customer, the types and number of obstacles in the path, and the type and speed of the connection between the wireless transmitter and the Internet.

### Broadband over Fiber (BoF)

A relatively new type of very fast direct connection available to homes and businesses in areas where there is fiber-optic cabling available all the way to the building is generically called **broadband over fiber** (**BoF**) or **fiber-to-the-premises** (**FTTP**) **Internet access**, with other names being used by individual providers, such as Verizon's *Fios* and *Google Fiber*. These fiber-optic networks are often used to deliver telephone and TV service in addition to Internet service. Where available, BoF service is very fast—up to 1 Gbps. BoF requires a special networking terminal installed at the building to convert the optical signals into electrical signals that can be sent to a computer or over a LAN.

### Mobile Wireless

**Mobile wireless Internet access** is the type of direct connection most commonly used with smartphones and tablets to keep them connected to the Internet via a cellular network, even as they are carried from place to place. Some mobile wireless services can be used with computers as well as with mobile devices. To add Internet access to a mobile device, typically a *data plan* is needed. As discussed in Chapter 7, the speed of mobile wireless depends on the cellular standard and specific network being used, but 4G networks are often between 3 and 15 Mbps, with speeds up to 100 Mbps available in some areas. Costs for mobile wireless Internet access vary widely. Many plans available today from wireless providers offer unlimited voice and text but have a data cap and so charge by the amount of data used or included in the plan. A growing trend is *prepaid* and *pay as you go plans*, in which you purchase service month to month (or day to day), instead of committing to a lengthy contract.

### Wi-Fi Hotspots

While not typically used for primary home Internet access, another option for Internet access is a **Wi-Fi hotspot**—a location with a direct Internet connection and a wireless access point that allows users to connect wirelessly (via Wi-Fi) to the hotspot in order to use its Internet connection (see Figure 8-9). Public Wi-Fi hotpots are widely available today, including at many coffeehouses and restaurants; at hotels, airports, and other locations frequented by business travelers; and

> **FIGURE 8-9**
> **Wi-Fi hotspots.**
> Hotspots are used to wirelessly connect to the Internet via the Internet connection belonging to a business, city, school, or other organization.

**COFFEEHOUSES AND OTHER PUBLIC LOCATIONS**
Often fee-based, though some are available for free.

**HOTELS AND CONFERENCE CENTERS**
Often free for guests.

**HOSPITALS, BUSINESSES, AND OTHER ORGANIZATIONS**
Usually designed for employees but are sometimes also available free to visitors.

**COLLEGE CAMPUSES**
Usually designed for students and faculty; sometimes used directly in class, as shown here.

---

> **Broadband over fiber (BoF) Internet access.** Very fast, direct Internet access via fiber-optic networks; also referred to as **fiber-to-the-premises (FTTP) Internet access**. > **Mobile wireless Internet access.** Internet access via a mobile phone network. > **Wi-Fi hotspot.** A location that provides wireless Internet access to the public.

in or near public areas such as libraries, subway stations, and parks. Some public Wi-Fi hotspots are free; others charge per hour, per day, or on a subscription basis. College campuses also typically have Wi-Fi hotspots to provide Internet access to students; many businesses and other organizations have Wi-Fi hotspots for use by employees in their offices, as well as by employees and guests in conference rooms, waiting rooms, lunchrooms, and other on-site locations.

## Selecting an ISP and Setting Up Your Devices

Once the type of Internet access to be used is determined, the final steps to getting connected to the Internet are selecting an ISP and setting up your devices. While this discussion is geared primarily toward a home Internet connection used with a personal computer, some of the concepts apply to business or mobile users as well.

### Selecting an ISP

The type of device used (such as a personal computer or smartphone), the type of Internet connection and service desired (such as cable Internet access or mobile wireless Internet access), and your geographical location (such as metropolitan or rural) will likely determine your ISP options. The pricing and services available often vary within a single ISP, as well as from one ISP to the next. The questions listed in Figure 8-10 can help you narrow your ISP choices and determine the questions you want answered before you decide on an ISP and a service package. A growing trend is for ISPs to offer a number of *tiers*; that is, different combinations of speeds and/or data caps for different prices so users requiring faster service or a more generous data plan can get it but at a higher price.

 **FIGURE 8-10**

**Choosing an ISP.**
Some questions to ask before making your final selection.

NET

### Setting Up Your Internet Connection and Devices

The specific steps for setting up your Internet connection depend on the type of device, the type of connection, and the ISP you have chosen to use. Some types of Internet connections, such as satellite and broadband over fiber, require professional installation; with other types, you can install the necessary hardware (typically a modem that connects to your computer or wireless router via an Ethernet cable) yourself. Mobile device setup usually doesn't require any additional hardware. You may be asked to select a username and password at some point during the ordering or setup process; this information may be used to log on to the Internet connection or log on to a Web site to access your billing information, usage data, and so forth once your service is set up.

During the process of setting up your Internet connection, you may need to add additional hardware to connect other computers and devices that you want to be able to access the Internet. For instance, to share a broadband connection, you can connect other devices

| AREA | QUESTIONS TO ASK |
|------|------------------|
| Services | Is the service compatible with my device? |
| | Is there a monthly data cap? If so, do I have a choice of tiers? |
| | How many e-mail addresses can I have? |
| | What is the size limit on incoming and outgoing e-mail messages and attachments? |
| | Do I have a choice between conventional and Web-based e-mail? |
| | Are there any special member features or benefits? |
| | Does the service include Web site hosting, Wi-Fi hotspots, or other benefits? |
| Speed | How fast are the maximum and usual download (ISP to my device) speeds? |
| | How fast are the maximum and usual upload (my device to ISP) speeds? |
| | How much does the service slow down under adverse conditions, such as high traffic or poor weather? |
| Support | Is telephone-based technical support available? |
| | Is Web-based technical support (such as via e-mail or live chat) available? |
| | Is there ever a charge for technical support? |
| Cost | What is the monthly cost for the service? Is it lower if I prepay a few months in advance? Are different tiers available? |
| | Is there a setup fee? If so, can it be waived with a long-term agreement? |
| | What is the cost of any additional hardware needed, such as modem or transceiver? Can the fee be waived with a long-term service agreement? |
| | Are there any other services (telephone service or TV, for instance) available from this provider that can be combined with Internet access for a lower total cost? |

directly to the modem (via an Ethernet cable or a Wi-Fi connection) if the modem contains a built-in switch or wireless router, respectively. If the modem does not include wireless routing capabilities, you will need to connect the modem to a wireless router (typically via an Ethernet cable) in order to share the Internet connection with your wireless devices via Wi-Fi.

# SEARCHING THE INTERNET

Most people who use the Internet turn to it to find specific information. For instance, you might want to find out the lowest price of the latest *Star Trek* Blu-ray movie, the flights available from Los Angeles to New York on a particular day, a recipe for clam chowder, the weather forecast for the upcoming weekend, a video of the last presidential inaugural address, or a map of hiking trails in the Grand Tetons. The Internet provides access to a vast array of interesting and useful information, but that information is useless if you cannot find it when you need it. Consequently, one of the most important skills an Internet user can acquire today is how to search for and locate information on the Internet successfully. Basic Internet searching was introduced in Chapter 1, but understanding the various types of search sites available and how they work, as well as some key searching strategies, can help you perform more successful and efficient Internet searches. These topics are discussed next.

## Search Sites

**Search sites** (such as *Google* and *Bing*) are Web sites designed specifically to help you find information on the Web. Most search sites use a **search engine**—a software program—in conjunction with a huge database of information about Web pages to help visitors find Web pages that contain the information they are seeking. Search site databases are updated on a regular basis. Typically, this occurs using small, automated programs (often called *spiders* or *web crawlers*) that use the hyperlinks located on Web pages to *crawl* (jump continually) from page to page. At each Web page, the spider program records important data about the page into the search site's database, such as the page's URL, its title, the words that appear frequently on the page, and the keywords and descriptive information added to the page's code by the Web page author at the time the page was created. Spider programs can be tremendously fast, visiting millions of pages per day. In addition to spider programs, search site databases also obtain information from Web page authors who submit Web page URLs and keywords associated with their Web sites to the search site, or who embed *metatags* (such as those that list keywords for the Web page or a description of the Web page for search sites) into their Web pages. The size of the database used varies with each particular search site, but it typically includes information collected from billions of Web pages.

To begin a search using a search site, type the URL for the desired search site in the Address bar of your browser (alternately, many Web browsers allow you to type search terms in the Address bar instead of a URL and the search will be performed using whichever search site is specified as the default search site). Most search sites today are designed for keyword searches; some sites allow directory searches as well. These two types of searches are discussed next. In addition, as the ability to search becomes more and more important, new types of searching are being developed. For example, *ChaCha Search* uses human guides that you can chat with via the ChaCha Search page or via

>**Search site.** A Web site designed to help users search for Web pages that match specified keywords or selected categories. >**Search engine.** A software program used by a search site to retrieve matching Web pages from a search database.

text message if you can't find the information you are looking for (you need a free account to view the responses).

## Keyword Search

The most common type of Internet search is the **keyword search**—that is, when you type appropriate **keywords** (one or more key terms) describing what you are looking for into a search box. The site's search engine then uses those keywords to return a list of Web pages (called *hits*) that match your search criteria; you can view any one of these Web pages by clicking its corresponding hyperlink (see Figure 8-11). Search sites differ in determining how close a match must be between the specified search criteria and a Web page before a link to that page is displayed, so the number of hits returned typically varies from one search site to another. To reduce the number of hits displayed, good search strategies (discussed shortly) can be used. Search sites also differ with respect to the order in which the hits are displayed. Some sites list the most relevant sites or most popular sites (usually judged by the number of Web pages that link to it) first; others list Web pages belonging to organizations that pay a fee to receive a higher rank (typically called *sponsored links*) first.

The keyword search is the most commonly used search type. It is used not only on conventional search sites like the Google search site shown in Figure 8-11 but also on many other Web sites. For instance, many types of Web pages include a keyword search box like the one shown in Figure 8-12 so visitors can search that Web site to find information (such as items for sale via the site or specific documents or Web pages located on that site). These Web site searches are typically powered by search engine technology, such as by *Google Site Search* or the open source *Apache Lucene* search application.

## Directory Search

An alternate type of Internet search available on some search sites is the **directory search**, which uses lists of categories instead of a search box. To perform a directory search, click the category that best matches what you are looking for in order to display a list of more specific subcategories within the main category. You can then click specific subcategories to display more specific topics until you see hyperlinks to Web pages matching the information you are looking for.

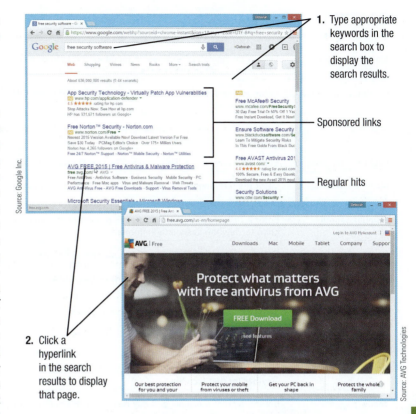

1. Type appropriate keywords in the search box to display the search results.

Sponsored links

Regular hits

2. Click a hyperlink in the search results to display that page.

**FIGURE 8-11**
Using a search site.

**FIGURE 8-12**
Web page keyword searches.

Search box

---

> **Keyword search.** A type of Internet search where keywords are typed in a search box to locate information on the Internet. > **Keyword.** A word typed in a search box on a search site or other Web page to locate information related to that keyword. > **Directory search.** A type of Internet search where categories are selected to locate information on the Internet.

| FUNCTION | EXPLANATION |
|---|---|
| Calculator | Enter a mathematical expression (such as *65\*150*) or a conversion (such as *18 inches in cm*) to see the result. |
| Currency converter | Enter an amount and currency types (such as *10 Euro in USD*) to see the corresponding value. |
| Dictionary | Enter the term *define* followed by a term to view definitions for that term from online sources. |
| Flight information | Enter an airline and a flight number to see status information. |
| Movie showtimes | Enter the term *movie* followed by a ZIP Code to view movies showing in that area. |
| Number search | Enter a UPS, FedEx, or USPS tracking number; an area code; or a UPC code to view the associated information. |
| Sports scores | Enter a team or league name to see scores, schedules, and more. |
| Sunrise/sunset | Enter the term *sunrise* or *sunset* followed by a city name to see the time of the sunrise or sunset in that city. |
| Street maps | Enter an address to find a map to that location. |
| Time | Enter the term *time* followed by a city name to see the current time in that city. |
| Weather | Enter the term *weather* followed by a city name or ZIP Code to view the weather for that location. |
| Yellow pages | Enter a type of business and city name or ZIP Code to view businesses in that local area. |

**EXAMPLES:**

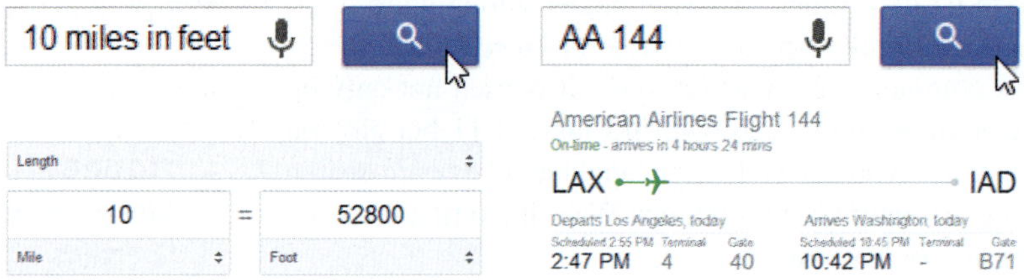

10 miles in feet

| Length | |
|---|---|
| 10 | = 52800 |
| Mile | Foot |

AA 144

American Airlines Flight 144
On-time - arrives in 4 hours 24 mins
LAX ●→ → ● IAD
Departs Los Angeles, today — Arrives Washington, today
Scheduled 2:55 PM  Terminal — Gate     Scheduled 10:45 PM  Terminal — Gate
2:47 PM     4     40          10:42 PM     -     B71

Source: Google Inc.

**FIGURE 8-13**
Google search tools.

## Search Site Tools

Many search sites contain a variety of tools that can be used to find specific types of information. For instance, many search sites include links next to the search box that allow you to search for items other than Web pages, such as music files, videos, images, maps, news articles, products for sale—even files on your computer. Google is one of the most versatile search sites at the present time and is continually adding new search options. In addition to the options just listed, Google allows a variety of special searches to be conducted by typing specific search criteria in its search box to find other useful information, such as to quickly track a shipped package, look up a telephone number or definition, check on the status of an airline flight, determine the current weather or time for a specific location, or make a calculation or conversion. Some examples of search tools that can be performed using the Google search box are listed in Figure 8-13.

## Search Strategies

There are a variety of strategies that can be used to help whittle down a list of hits to a more manageable number (some searches can return billions of Web pages). Some search strategies can be employed regardless of the search site being used; others are available only on certain sites. Some of the most useful search strategies are discussed next.

## Using Phrases

One of the most straightforward ways to improve the quality of the hits returned is to use *phrase searching*—essentially typing more than one keyword in a keyword search. Most search engines automatically list the hits that include all the keywords first, followed by hits matching most of the keywords, continuing down to hits that fit only one of the keywords. To force this type of sorting, virtually all search engines allow you to use some type of character—often quotation marks—to indicate that you want to search for the entire phrase together. Because search options vary from site to site, it is best to look for a search tips link on the search site you are using; the search tips should explain all of the search options available for that site. Examples of the results based on different search phrases to find Web pages about hand signals used with dogs and conducted at two search sites are listed in Figure 8-14. Notice that while the last two search phrases shown in Figure 8-14

| SEARCH PHRASE USED | SEARCH SITE | NUMBER OF PAGES FOUND | TITLE OF FIRST TWO NONSPONSORED PAGES FOUND* |
|---|---|---|---|
| dogs | Google | 750,000,000 | Dog – Wikipedia, the free encyclopedia<br>Dog Breeds \| Browse 151 Dog Breeds \| Petfinder |
| | Bing | 35,100,000 | Dog – Wikipedia, the free encyclopedia<br>Dog Breeds, A-Z List of Small to Large Dog Breeds |
| hand signals | Google | 15,300,000 | Using Turn or Hand Signals - DriversEd.com<br>Hand Signals – Wikipedia, the free encyclopedia |
| | Bing | 12,000,000 | List of gestures - Wikipedia, the free encyclopedia<br>Hand Signals – Wikipedia, the free encyclopedia |
| dog hand signals | Google | 1,870,000 | Dog Training Hand Signals – A picture instructional guide<br>Essential Hand Signals for Dogs \| POPSUGAR Pets |
| | Bing | 2,990,000 | Dog Training Hand Signals – A picture instructional guide<br>Utilize Dog Hand Signals In Your Training |
| "dog hand signals" | Google | 5,460 | Dog Training Hand Signals – A picture instructional guide<br>Dog Training with Hand Signals - Purina® Dog Chow® |
| | Bing | 16,900 | Dog Training Hand Signals – A picture instructional guide<br>Utilize Dog Hand Signals In Your Training |

* Highlighted entries indicate Web pages about dog hand signals.

**FIGURE 8-14**

**Examples of phrase searching.** Using different search phrases and different search sites can significantly change the search results.

both returned relevant (and similar) Web pages, the number of Web pages found varied dramatically (thousands of pages versus millions).

## Using Search Operators

To further specify exactly what you want a search engine to find, *search operators* can often be used in keyword searches. For example, putting your search phrase in quotation marks returns only pages with the same words in the same order as you specified, and putting a hyphen (or minus sign) before a word excludes that key term from the search. For instance, if you want a search engine to find all documents that contain recipes for seafood appetizers, you can use the search phrase *seafood appetizer recipes* or "*seafood appetizer recipes*". If you want to exclude recipes that contain crab, you can use the search phrase *seafood appetizer recipes -crab*. The rules for search operators can vary from search site to search site, so be sure to check the search tips for the search site that you are using to see what operators can be used on that site. Some search sites also include an *Advanced Search* option that helps you specify search operators and other advanced search techniques using a fill-in-the-blank form.

## Using Multiple Search Sites

Most users have a favorite search site that they are most comfortable using. However, as illustrated in Figure 8-14, different search sites can return different results. It is important to realize that sometimes a different search site might perform better than the one you use regularly. If you are searching for something and are not making any progress with one search site, then try another search site.

**TIP**

When searching, be efficient—if an appropriate Web page is not included among the first page or two of hits, redo the search using more specific criteria, a different search site, or a different search strategy.

## Using Appropriate Keywords, Synonyms, Variant Word Forms, and Wildcards

When choosing the keywords to be used with a search site, it is important to select words that represent the key concept you are searching for. For example, if you want to find out about bed and breakfasts located in the town of Leavenworth, Washington, a keyword phrase (such as *Leavenworth Washington bed and breakfast*) should return appropriate results. If your initial search does not produce the results you are hoping for, you can try *synonyms*—words that have meanings similar to other words. For example, you could replace *bed and breakfast* with *hotel* or *lodging*. To search for a search term and its

NET

| FIELD TYPE | EXAMPLE | EXPLANATION |
|---|---|---|
| Title | title: "tax tips" | Searches for Web pages containing the words "tax tips" in the page title. |
| Text | text: "tax tips" | Searches for Web pages containing "tax tips" in the text of the page. |
| Site | forms site:irs.gov | Searches for Web pages associated with the keyword "forms" that are located only on the irs.gov Web site. |
| Domain | tax tips site:*.gov | Searches for Web pages associated with the keywords "tax tips" that are located on government Web sites (they can have anything for the first part of the domain name, but must have a .gov TLD). |

 **FIGURE 8-15**

**Field searching.**

Field searches limit search results to just those pages that match specific field criteria, in addition to any specified search criteria.

synonyms at the same time in Google, type the tilde symbol (~) immediately in front of your search term, such as *~bed and breakfast* to have Google search for *bed and breakfast*, as well as automatically also search for *hotels*, *motels*, and other synonymous terms.

*Variant*—or alternate—word forms are another possibility. Try to think of a different spelling or form of your keywords if your search still does not work as desired. For example, *bed and breakfast* could be replaced or supplemented with the variants *bed & breakfast* and *B&B*, and the *hand signals* keywords used in Figure 8-14 could be replaced with the variants *hand signal* and *hand signaling*. Using alternative spellings is a form of this strategy, as well. Another strategy that is sometimes used with keywords is the *wildcard* approach. A wildcard is a special symbol that is used in conjunction with a part of a word to specify the pattern of the terms you want to search for. For instance, the asterisk wildcard (*) is used to represent one or more letters at the asterisk location, so on many sites searching for *hand sign** would search for *hand sign*, *hand signal*, *hand signals*, *hand signaling*, and any other keywords that fit this specific pattern.

## Using Field Searches

Another strategy that can be used when basic searching is not producing the desired results is *field searching*. A field search limits the search to a particular search characteristic (or *field*), such as the page title, URL, page text, top-level domain, or Web site (see Figure 8-15). When a field search is performed, only the hits associated with the Web pages that match the specified criteria in the specified field are displayed. You can also use field searching in conjunction with regular search terms, such as to search for a particular keyword on just Web sites that use a specific domain. Many, but not all, search engines support some type of field searching. Check the search tips for the particular search site you are using to see if it has that option.

## Evaluating Search Results

Once a list of Web sites is returned as the result of a search, it is time to evaluate the sites to determine their quality and potential for meeting your needs. Two questions to ask yourself before clicking a link in the search results are as follows:

> Does the title and listed description sound appropriate for the information you are seeking?

> Is the URL from an appropriate company or organization? For example, if you want technical specifications about a particular product, you might want to start with information on the manufacturer's Web site. If you are looking for government publications, stick with government Web sites.

After an appropriate Web page is found, the evaluation process is still not complete. To determine if the information can be trusted, you should evaluate both the author and the source to decide if the information can be considered reliable and whether or not it is biased. Be sure to also check for a date to see how up to date the information is—many online articles are years old. If you will be using the information in a report, paper, or other document in which accuracy is important, try to verify the information with a second source.

| TYPE OF RESOURCE | CITATION EXAMPLE* |
|---|---|
| Online magazine article | Kedmey, Dan. "Why Thieves Love the Apple Watch." *Time*. Time, 14 May 2015. Web. 30 March 2016. <http://time.com/3858762/apple-watch-theft/>. |
| Online journal article | Nix, Maria. "Legislation Claiming to Protect Workers Would Hurt RNs." American Journal of Nursing 115.7 (2015): 14. Web. 21 Apr. 2016. <http://journals.lww.com/ajnonline/Fulltext/2015/07000/Legislation_Claiming_to_Protect_Workers_Would_Hurt.7.aspx>. |
| Online news article | Wagstaff, Keith. "Amazon Unveils Flight Plan for Its Prime Air Delivery Drones." NBC News. 28 July 2015. Web. 26 May 2016. <http://www.nbcnews.com/tech/innovation/amazon-drones-n399771>. |
| Web page content (not an article) | "Spear Phishing: Scam, Not Sport." *Norton*. Web. 25 Mar. 2016. <http://us.norton.com/spear-phishing-scam-not-sport/article>. |
| E-mail | Rodriquez, M. "Re: Solar Powered Cars." Message to the author. 2 May 2016. E-mail. |

* MLA does not require the use of a URL but it is acceptable to include the URL in your citation.

## Citing Internet Resources

According to the online version of the Merriam-Webster Dictionary, the term *plagiarize* means "to steal and pass off the ideas or words of another as one's own" or to "use another's production without crediting the source." To avoid plagiarizing Web page content, you need to credit Web page sources—as well as any other Internet resources—when you use them in papers, on Web pages, or in other documents.

The guidelines for citing Web page content are similar to those for written sources. In general, the author, date of publication, and article or Web page title are listed along with the date the article was retrieved from the Internet and the URL of the Web page used to retrieve the article if desired or required. If in doubt when preparing a research paper, check with your instructor as to the style format (such as *American Psychological Association* (*APA*), *Modern Language Association* (*MLA*), or *Chicago Manual of Style*) he or she prefers you to follow and refer to that guide for direction. Some citation examples using the MLA format are shown in Figure 8-16.

**FIGURE 8-16**

**Citing Web sources.**
These examples follow the Modern Language Association (MLA) format.

**NET**

# BEYOND BROWSING, SEARCHING, AND E-MAIL

In addition to basic browsing and e-mail (discussed in Chapter 1) and the search techniques just discussed, there are a host of other activities that can take place via the Internet. Some of the most common are discussed next.

**FIGURE 8-17**

**Skype.** This app can be used for a variety of online communications.

## Other Types of Online Communications

Many types of online communications methods exist. E-mail is one of the most common; other types of online communications are discussed in the next few sections. While in the past, online communications programs were dedicated to a single task, today's programs can typically be used for a variety of online communications. For instance, the *Skype* program shown in Figure 8-17 can be used to exchange instant messages (IMs), make voice and video calls, and work with your Microsoft Outlook contacts; the Gmail Web mail service can be used to exchange instant messages and make voice and video calls, in addition to sending and receiving e-mail messages. This online communications convergence trend is found in both personal and business applications; in business, it is referred to as *unified communications* (*UC*).

Call control buttons.

Click to start a video or voice call to this contact.

The messages from both you and your contact appear here.

This is currently a video call.

Type a new message here.

Source: Microsoft Corporation

Source: WhatsApp Inc.

🔺 **FIGURE 8-18**

**Group messaging.** Works the same as traditional IM, just with more people.

With UC, all of a business's communications (such as e-mail, instant messaging, videoconferencing, customer service center communications, and telephone calls via both in-office landlines and smartphones) are tied together and work with a single unified mailbox and interface—often via a cloud UC provider.

## Instant Messaging and Text Messaging

**Instant messaging**, also commonly referred to as **chat**, allows you to exchange real-time typed messages with people on your *contact list* or *buddy list*—a list of individuals (such as family, friends, and business associates) that you specify or with whom you have already exchanged messages. Instant messages (IMs) can be sent via computers and smartphones via *messaging programs* (such as *AIM*, *Yahoo! Messenger*, the Skype program shown in Figure 8-17, or the *WhatsApp* mobile app shown in Figure 8-18). They are also frequently sent via social networking sites like Facebook and Google+ (referred to as *social messaging*). For a look at how you can now send funds via social messaging, see the How It Works box. Originally a popular communications method among friends, IM has also become a valuable business tool.

In order to send an IM, you must be signed in to your messaging service. You can then select a contact and send a message, which then appears immediately on your contact's device. You can also typically engage in other types of activities with your contact via the messaging program, such as sending a photo or file, starting a voice or video conversation, or starting a *group call* or *conversation* (refer again to Figure 8-18). Instant messaging capabilities are also often integrated into Web pages, such as to ask questions of a customer service representative.

Because messaging applications typically display the status of your buddies (such as if they are online or if they have set their status to "Busy" or "In a meeting"), instant messaging is an example of an application that uses *presence technology*—technology that enables one computing device to identify the current status of another device. Presence technology is increasingly being integrated into devices and applications.

**Text messaging** is a form of messaging frequently used by mobile phone users. Also called *Short Message Service* or *SMS*, text messaging is used to send short (less than 160 character) text-based messages via a cellular network. If the messages also include photos, audio, or video, *Multimedia Messaging Service* or *MMS* is used instead. In either case, the messages are typically sent to the recipient via his or her mobile phone number and are delivered to the recipient's mobile phone immediately. While some smartphones can text over Wi-Fi, most texts are sent via a cellular network and so text or data charges may apply.

While e-mail is still important for business online communications, messaging is beginning to replace e-mail for personal communications—particularly with teenagers and other individuals who carry a smartphone with them at all times. According to the director of engineering at Facebook, "The future of messaging is more real time, more conversational, and more casual."

## Twittering and Social Networking Updates

**Twittering** refers to posting short (up to 140 character) updates (called *tweets*) about what you are doing or thinking about at any moment to the *Twitter* social network. The updates can be sent via text message, the Twitter mobile app, or the Twitter Web site. Individuals see the tweets of people they *follow* on their Twitter home page; they can view other tweets by searching Twitter via Twitter usernames (that are unique and preceded by the symbol @) or

---

> **Instant messaging.** A way of exchanging real-time typed messages with other individuals; also called **chat**. > **Text messaging.** A way of exchanging real-time typed messages with other individuals via a cellular network and, typically, cell phones. > **Twittering.** Sending short status updates via the Twitter service.

# HOW IT WORKS

## Social Commerce

*Social commerce* is the use of social networks to perform financial transactions. One of the earliest social commerce activities was the ability to buy gifts within Facebook for your friends. One of the most recent options is the ability to send funds via social messaging.

Two of the first social media apps to incorporate free money transfers between individuals into messaging services are Snapchat (via *Snapcash*) and Facebook (via *Facebook Messenger*). Both services require participants to be at least 18 years old and funds to be sent and received via debit cards issued by a U.S. bank.

For example, to send money to one of your Facebook friends, start or open a Messenger conversation with that friend. Tap the *Send Money* button containing the dollar sign at the bottom of the window (see the accompanying illustration) and then enter the amount you want to send. After tapping the *Send* button, you will be asked to supply your debit card information if needed. Click *Pay* and the funds will be sent.

To receive money from a friend, open the conversation that contains the money sent to you by your friend. Tap the *Add Card* link in the message to add your debit card information (if you have not already added a debit card) in order to receive the money.

Snapcash works in a similar manner except that you type a dollar sign and the amount you want to send (such as *$15*) and

a green Snapcash button will appear to execute the transaction. To receive funds, tap the funds notification button that appears when you have been sent money.

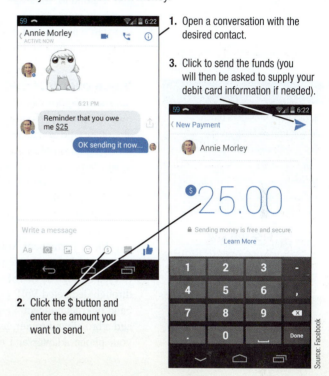

1. Open a conversation with the desired contact.

3. Click to send the funds (you will then be asked to supply your debit card information if needed).

2. Click the $ button and enter the amount you want to send.

Source: Facebook

---

*hashtags* (key terms that are preceded by the symbol #), as shown in Figure 8-19. You can also send *direct messages* to one of your followers, which are then seen only by you and the recipient.

Features similar to Twitter tweets (generally referred to as *status updates*) are available on some social networking sites (most notably, Facebook) to keep your friends up to date on your current activities, as discussed shortly. The use of Twitter and status updates is changing the way some people communicate online. Twitter is used today to get updates on the weather, to ask for assistance with problems or to conduct information searches—even for personal safety purposes. For instance, as shown in Figure 8-19, the U.S. State Department uses Twitter to issue traveling advisories. Increasingly, people turn to Twitter to comment on newsworthy events—such as terrorist attacks, natural disasters, and breaking news—as they occur.

**FIGURE 8-19**
Twitter.

Click to see the tweets of the people you follow.

Type a hashtag or username here to display tweets corresponding to that hashtag or username.

Hashtag; click to view related tweets.

Click to follow State Dept. tweets.

Source: Twitter

## Forums

For asking questions of, making comments to, or initiating discussions with a large group of individuals, **forums** (also called *discussion groups* and *message boards*) can be used. Forums are Web pages designed to facilitate written discussions on specific subjects, such as TV shows, computers, movies, investing, gardening, music, photography, or politics. They typically have a *moderator* who monitors the forum to remove inappropriate posts. When a participant posts a message, it is displayed for anyone accessing the forum to read and respond to. Messages are usually organized by topics (called *threads*); participants can post new messages in response to an existing message and stay within that thread, or they can start a new thread. Forum participants do not have to be online at the same time so participants can post and respond to messages at their convenience.

## Voice over Internet Protocol (VoIP)

*Internet telephony* is the original industry term for the process of placing telephone calls over the Internet. Today, the standard term for placing telephone calls over the Internet or any other type of data network is **Voice over Internet Protocol** (**VoIP**) and it can take many forms. At its simplest level, VoIP calls can take place from one device to another device, such as by starting a voice conversation with an online contact using a messaging program such as Skype (shown previously in Figure 8-17) or a smartphone app such as *Hangouts Dialer* or *FaceTime*. Device to device calls placed over the Internet are generally free. Often calls can be received from or made to conventional or mobile phone numbers for a small fee, such as 2 cents per minute or $2.99 per month for unlimited calling for domestic calls.

More permanent VoIP setups (sometimes referred to as *digital voice* or *broadband phone*) are designed to replace conventional landline phones in homes and businesses. VoIP is offered through some ISPs, such as cable, telephone, and wireless providers; it is also offered through dedicated VoIP providers, such as *Vonage*. Permanent VoIP setups require a broadband Internet connection and a *VoIP phone adapter* that goes between a conventional phone and a broadband router, as shown in Figure 8-20. Once your phone calls are routed through your phone adapter and router to the Internet, they travel to the recipient's phone, which can be another VoIP phone, a mobile phone, or a landline phone. VoIP phone adapters are typically designed for a specific VoIP provider. With these more permanent VoIP setups, most users switching from landline phone service can keep their existing telephone number.

The biggest advantage of VoIP is cost savings, such as unlimited local and long-distance calls for about $25 per month, or Internet and VoIP services bundled together for about $50 per month. One of the biggest disadvantages of VoIP is that it does not function during a power outage or if your Internet connection (such as your cable connection for cable Internet users) goes down, though some VoIP services are able to forward calls to a landline or mobile phone during outages.

## Web Conferences and Webinars

As discussed in Chapter 7, the term *videoconferencing* refers to the use of computers or mobile devices, video cameras, microphones, and other communications

**▽ FIGURE 8-20**

**Voice over IP (VoIP).**
Permanent VoIP setups allow telephone calls to be placed via a broadband Internet connection using a conventional telephone.

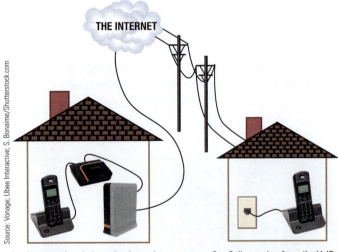

THE INTERNET

Source: Vonage; Ubee Interactive; S. Bonaime/Shutterstock.com

1.  A conventional phone is plugged into a VoIP adapter, which is connected to a broadband modem.

2.  Calls coming from the VoIP phone travel over the Internet to the recipient's phone.

---

> **Forum.** A Web page that enables individuals to post messages on a particular topic for others to read and respond to; also called a discussion group or message board. > **Voice over Internet Protocol (VoIP).** The process of placing telephone calls via the Internet.

technologies to conduct real-time, face-to-face meetings between people in different locations. Videoconferencing that takes place via the Internet is often called *Web conferencing* or *online conferencing*. **Web conferences** typically take place via a personal computer or mobile device (see Figure 8-21) and are used by businesses and individuals. As previously discussed, many free messaging programs or mobile apps support video phone calls. While some of these programs or apps can support multiple participants, business Web conferences that require multiple participants or other communications tools (such as a shared whiteboard or the ability for attendees to share the content displayed on their computer screens) may need to use a *Web conferencing service* (such as *WebEx*) or a premium service from Skype or another messaging service instead. Business Web conferencing is often used for meetings between individuals located in different geographical locations, as well as for employee training, sales presentations, customer support, and other business applications.

Source: Polycom, Inc.

**FIGURE 8-21**
**Web conferencing.**
Allows individuals to talk with and see each other in real time.

   **Webinars** (Web seminars) are similar to Web conferences, but typically have a designated presenter and an audience. Although interaction with the audience is usually included (such as question-and-answer sessions), a Webinar is typically more one-way communication than a Web conference. A completely one-way presentation (such as a recorded Webinar played back on demand) is sometimes referred to as a *Webcast*.

## Social Networking/Social Media

A **social networking site** can be loosely defined as any site that enables individuals to connect and interact with other individuals, such as by following each other's activities or posting messages. The collection of social networking sites and other online platforms used to transmit or share information with a broad audience is referred to as **social media**. Some examples of social networking sites are Facebook and Google+ (which allow users to post information about themselves for others to read) and *Meetup* (which connects people in specific geographic areas with common hobbies and interests). In addition to social networking sites, social media includes *media-sharing sites* like *YouTube* and *Flickr*, *micro-blogging* sites like Twitter, and *social curation sites* like *Digg*, *Reddit*, and *Pinterest* (which allow individuals to share Web content with others). Social media activities can be performed via personal computers, though the use of *mobile social networking*—social networks accessed with a smartphone or other mobile device—is more common today, making social networking a real-time, on-the-go activity. Some reasons for this are that most individuals carry a smartphone with them all the time, many individuals

## ASK THE EXPERT

Courtesy Throw the Fight

**Ryan Baustert,** Guitarist, Throw the Fight

**What impact does the Internet and social media have on the music industry today?**

The Internet has had a major impact on us. The best marketing is when the distance between artist and audience is short and direct. Due to sites like Facebook, Twitter, and Instagram, we are able to stay better connected and interact with our fans on a more personal level. We can also gauge how our music is received by peoples' reactions and comments online.

   It's much easier to promote shows, tours, and album releases, as well. More recently, with the explosion of Twitter and Instagram, we can go one step further and give fans more insight into what is going on in our lives behind the scenes. This, in turn, helps us build brand loyalty.

---

**>Web conference.** A face-to-face meeting taking place via the Web; typically uses video cameras and microphones to enable participants to see and hear each other. **>Webinar.** A seminar presented via the Web. **>Social networking site.** A site that enables individuals to connect and interact with other individuals. **>Social media.** The collection of social networking sites and other communications channels used to transmit or share information with a broad audience.

**SHARE**
Share Web content via online communications or social networks.

**LOG IN**
Log in to a Web site using social network credentials.

⚠ **FIGURE 8-22**
**Social networks are integrated into many Web sites.**

▼ **FIGURE 8-23**
**Social networking sites.** Facebook is shown here.

like to communicate with others via the Web while they are on the go, and smartphones enable location applications to be integrated into the social media experience.

Social media is also increasingly being integrated with other online activities. For instance, you can exchange messages or have video calls with your friends from within Google+ or Facebook; you can share YouTube videos via an e-mail message, a video call, or one of your social networking pages from a YouTube video page (see Figure 8-22); and you can view your friends' Facebook updates in Skype. In addition, many Web sites include links on their site to allow a visitor to access the business's Facebook page, *Like* content (such as a video) on the business's Web site, or log in to the site using the visitor's logon credentials from Facebook or another social network (refer again to Figure 8-22).

Social networking sites are used most often to communicate with existing friends. Facebook, for instance, allows you to post photos, videos, music, status updates, and other content for your *Facebook friends* (individuals you have chosen to communicate with via Facebook) to view. You can also chat with your Facebook friends who are currently online, and Like or comment on the posts shown on your friends' Facebook pages or in the *news feed* on your Facebook page. For privacy purposes, you can limit access to your Facebook page to the individuals you identify (such as just to your Facebook friends).

In addition to being used to communicate with existing friends, social media is also used to learn about individuals you currently don't know. For instance, college-bound students can use social media to meet other incoming freshmen before the school year starts, look up the profiles of their dorm roommates, find fellow students with common interests, and more—all before actually setting foot on campus. They are also used to share information during natural disasters, such as New Yorkers sharing transportation updates and gas station availability via Twitter during the power outages following Hurricane Sandy.

In addition to being used for personal use, social media today is also viewed as a business marketing tool. For instance, Twitter, Facebook, and YouTube are often used by businesses, political candidates, emerging musicians, and other professionals or professional organizations to increase their online presence (see Figure 8-23). There are also business social networking sites designed for business networking. Some of these sites (such as *LinkedIn*) are used for recruiting new employees, finding new jobs, building professional contacts, and other business activities. Others (such as *StartupNation*) are designed to help entrepreneurs connect with business owners and resources, and exchange ideas. Other specialized social networking sites include sites designed for children (which usually work in a manner similar to Facebook but that have safeguards in place to prevent personal information from being posted, to monitor language, and so forth) and families (which are used to exchange messages, view online tasks lists, and access a shared family calendar).

When using a social networking site, adults and children should be cautious about revealing too much personal information via these sites, both for personal safety reasons and to prevent the information from being used in personalized, targeted spear phishing attacks, discussed in Chapter 9. In addition, social networking content is increasingly being monitored by colleges (to find inappropriate behavior by students and to research college applicants) and employers (to find unprofessional behavior by current employees and to research potential job candidates). Because of this, all individuals should be careful about the types of photos and other content they post online. There have been numerous cases over the past few years of students being disciplined or not admitted to a college, and individuals being fired or not hired, due to content posted to a social networking site. Consequently, it is a good idea for individuals to take a close look at their online posts and photos and remove anything that might be potentially embarrassing if viewed by current or future employers, a future partner, or other people important to them now or in the future.

Another emerging issue is what happens to social media content when someone dies unexpectedly; because family members and heirs cannot access the sites without logon information or access to the deceased's e-mail for password recovery purposes, they cannot edit the content or delete the account. In response, some special services have emerged to help individuals store information about their online assets (such as logon information) and to designate a beneficiary—the person designated to receive that information or to whom the account ownership will be transferred upon the individual's death. An alternative is for individuals to leave the necessary online contact and access information, as well as instructions regarding how to notify online friends and sites, with a trusted friend or relative who is instructed to use the information only in the event of the individual's death.

## E-Commerce

Online shopping and online investing are examples of **e-commerce**—performing financial transactions online. E-commerce offers numerous advantages for customers, including the convenience of shopping from home any time of the day or night, easier comparison shopping, a higher degree of selection, potential cost savings, and the ability to customize products easily. Advantages for businesses include reduced costs, increased customer satisfaction, a broader customer base, and potentially higher sales. However, because online fraud, credit card fraud, and identity theft (a situation in which someone gains enough personal information to pose as another person) are continuing to grow at a rapid pace, it is important to be cautious when participating in online financial activities. To protect yourself, use a credit card or *online payment service* such as *PayPal* (which charges your credit card, deducts funds from your bank account, or transfers money from your online account balance to pay for items) whenever possible when purchasing goods or services online so that any fraudulent activities can be disputed. Also, be sure to enter your payment information only on a secure Web page and don't perform any financial transactions via a public Wi-Fi hotspot. Online financial accounts should also be protected with strong user passwords that are changed frequently. Internet security and strong passwords are discussed in detail in Chapter 9.

### Online Shopping and Online Auctions

**Online shopping** is commonly used to purchase both physical products (such as clothing, books, DVDs, shoes, furniture, and more) and downloadable products (such as software, movies, music, and e-books) via Web pages. Typically, shoppers locate the items they

> **TIP**
>
> Social media today is also used by law enforcement. For instance, investigators hunting for the second bomber in the 2013 Boston Marathon attack used the suspects' social networking sites, as well as posts and videos uploaded by witnesses, in the search.

> **TIP**
>
> E-commerce sites can be classified by the type of entity buying and selling the goods and services, such as *business-to-consumer* (*B2C*), *business-to-business* (*B2B*), or *consumer-to-consumer* (*C2C*) Web sites.

NET

---

>**E-commerce.** Financial transactions performed over the Internet. >**Online shopping.** Buying products or services over the Internet.

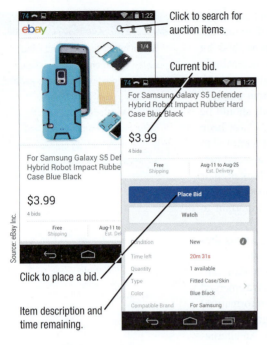

Click to search for auction items.

Current bid.

Click to place a bid.

Item description and time remaining.

**FIGURE 8-24**
Online auctions.

Source: eBay Inc.

would like to purchase using an online shopping site (typically set up by an online retailer or a manufacturer), and then they add those items to their online *shopping carts* or *shopping bags*. The site's *checkout* process—including supplying the necessary billing and shipping information—is then used to complete the sale. After the payment is processed, the item is either shipped to the customer (if it is a physical product), or the customer is given instructions on how to download it (if it is a downloadable product). According to a recent estimate, U.S. online sales will exceed $500 billion by 2020. For a look at the various payment options available for online stores, see the Inside the Industry box.

**Online auctions** are one of the most common ways to purchase items online from other individuals. Sellers list items for sale on an auction site (such as *eBay*, shown in Figure 8-24) and pay a small listing fee if required, and then pay a commission to the auction site when the item is sold. Individuals can visit the auction site and enter bids on auction items until the end of the auction. At that time, the person with the highest bid is declared the successful bidder (provided the minimum selling price, if one was established, was met) and arranges payment for and delivery of the item directly with the seller. *Buy It Now* auctions have a set price instead that a bidder can agree to in order to purchase the item. Another common way to purchase items from other individuals is via online classified ads, such as those posted on the popular *Craigslist* site.

## Online Banking and Online Investing

Many banks today offer **online banking** as a free service to their customers to enable customers to check balances on all their accounts (such as checking, credit card, mortgage, and investment accounts), view cashed checks and other transactions, deposit checks remotely, pay bills electronically, and perform other activities related to their bank accounts. Online banking is continually growing and can be performed via a computer or smartphone. Online banking is typically performed via the bank's Web site or mobile app (such as the Bank of America mobile app shown in Figure 8-25), though some activities at some banks can be carried out via text messages.

Buying and selling stocks, bonds, mutual funds, and other types of securities is referred to as **online investing**. Although stock quotes are available on many search and news sites, trading stocks and other securities requires an *online broker*. The biggest advantages of online investing include lower transaction fees and the ability to quickly buy or sell stock when desired, without having to make a phone call—a convenience for those investors who do a lot of trading. Common online investing services include the ability to order sales and make purchases; access performance histories, corporate news, and other useful investment information; and set up an *online portfolio* that displays the status of the stocks you specify. On some Web sites, stock price data is delayed 20 minutes; on other sites, real-time quotes are available. Like other Web page data, stock price data is current at the time it is retrieved via a Web page, but it may not be updated (and you will not see current quotes, for instance) until you reload the Web page using your browser's Refresh or Reload toolbar button.

**FIGURE 8-25**
Mobile banking.

Source: Bank of America Corporation; Chardchanin/Shutterstock.com

---

>**Online auction.** An online activity where bids are placed for items, and the highest bidder purchases the item. >**Online banking.** Performing banking activities via the Web. >**Online investing.** Buying and selling stocks or other types of investments via the Web.

# INSIDE THE INDUSTRY

### E-Commerce Payment Options

Successfully performing electronic financial transactions is the cornerstone of any e-commerce site. Therefore, a business should give careful thought to which payment options it will offer and how it will process payments securely and accurately. The payment options used with an e-commerce site vary but are typically displayed on the checkout page (see the Overstock.com checkout page in the accompanying illustration).

The most common payment options for sites that sell to consumers are credit and debit cards. Many e-commerce sites also accept payments from *online payment services*, such as PayPal, which transfer money from the buyer's online payment account to the seller's account to complete the transaction. To pay for an e-commerce purchase via PayPal or to collect PayPal funds, you must have a PayPal account (opening an account is free). Purchases can be deducted from the buyer's PayPal account cash balance or set up to charge payments to a credit card or transfer the appropriate amount of funds from the buyer's bank account as purchases are made. Some e-commerce sites also accept other forms of digital payment, such as via the *Bill Me Later* service (which pays the online store and then

bills the shopper separately), *Bitcoins* (which is a form of virtual currency that can be exchanged for government-issued currency as needed), and *digital gift cards* and *promo codes* (which reduce the purchase price after the gift card or code information is supplied on the checkout page).

Source: Overstock.com

**Options for online payments include credit/debit cards, PayPal, Bitcoins, and gift cards/promo codes.**

## Online Entertainment

There are an ever-growing number of ways to use the Web for entertainment purposes, such as listening to music, watching TV and videos, and playing online games. In addition, for individuals who find reading relaxing, there is also a wide variety of online books and magazines that can be downloaded and read via a personal computer, tablet, or mobile device. Some online entertainment applications can be accessed with virtually any type of Internet connection; others are only practical with a broadband connection. Some online entertainment applications require the use of a *media player program* or *plug-in* (such as *QuickTime Player* or *Silverlight*) to deliver multimedia content.

> **TIP**
>
> To view streaming video without it appearing choppy, Internet service that delivers a minimum download speed of 1.5 Mbps is recommended.

## Online Music

There are a number of options available today for **online music**, such as listening to *Internet radio stations* like *Pandora* and *iHeartRadio.com* (see Figure 8-26 on the next page), watching music videos on YouTube or *Yahoo! Music*, or downloading music from *online music stores*, such as the *iTunes Music Store* or *Amazon Digital Music*. Music can be listened to or downloaded via a computer or mobile device. Downloaded music can be played directly from that device; it can also be copied to a CD to create a custom music CD or transferred to a portable digital media player or smartphone provided the download agreement does not preclude it.

> **Online music.** Music played or obtained via the Web.

**ONLINE RADIO**

**ONLINE TV AND MOVIES**

**FIGURE 8-26**

TV, videos, and movies are commonly watched online.

> **TIP**
>
> According to a recent Sandvine report, more than 36% of peak download Internet traffic in the United States is attributed to Netflix.

> **TIP**
>
> An emerging trend is *gamification*; that is, using gaming elements (like the ability to earn points or rewards) in a non-entertainment context, such as for customer and employee engagement.

## Online TV, Videos, and Movies

Watching TV shows, videos, and movies online is another very popular type of online entertainment (refer again to Figure 8-26). **Online videos** (such as news videos and movie trailers, videos posted to Web sites belonging to businesses and other organizations, personal videos posted to blogs and social networking pages, and videos shared via YouTube) are widely available.

Another option is **online TV** and **online movies**. Both are available from wireless providers, TV networks, and third-party Web sites. Some content can be watched *live*, which means it is available at the time it is being aired (such as news broadcasts and sporting events), but most content is streamed upon demand at the user's convenience (with streaming video, the video plays from the server when it is requested so you need an Internet connection in order to view the video). For example, you can watch episodes of your favorite network shows via Web sites for ABC, CBS, FOX, and other TV networks; you can also watch TV shows and movies via third-party streaming services such as *Amazon Instant Video*, *Netflix*, and *Hulu Plus* (shown in Figure 8-26). These services may include some free content; other content is typically available via a monthly subscription or a fee for each TV episode or movie watched. The process of selecting movies or TV shows that are delivered to your device at your request is called **video-on-demand** (**VOD**).

While most VOD is streamed to a computer or smart TV, some can be downloaded to a smartphone or tablet, or a DVR or other device (such as a digital media player, a Blu-ray player, or a gaming console) that is connected to your TV. Rented movies can usually be viewed only for a limited time; purchased movies are theoretically viewable forever. One of the most popular VOD options is Netflix, which offers unlimited video streaming to a TV, gaming console, computer, or mobile device for about $8 per month. A new trend is the development of TV shows that are only available online (such as *Alpha House* on Amazon and *Arrested Development* and *House of Cards* on Netflix); these are sometimes called *webisodes*.

## Online Gaming

**Online gaming** refers to games played over the Internet. Many sites—especially children's Web sites—include games for visitors to play. There are also sites whose sole purpose is hosting games that can be played online. Some of the games are designed to be played alone or with just one other person. Others, called *online multiplayer games*, are designed to be played online against many other online gamers. Online multiplayer games (such as *Doom*, *EverQuest*, *Final Fantasy*, and *City of Heroes*) are especially popular in countries, such as South Korea, that have readily available high-speed Internet connections and high levels of Internet use in general. Gaming consoles and portable gaming devices that have built-in Internet connectivity can also be used for multiplayer online gaming. Online gaming is also associated quite often with *Internet addiction*—the inability to stop using the Internet or to prevent extensive use of the Internet from interfering with other aspects of one's life. Internet addiction is a growing concern and is discussed in more detail in Chapter 13.

---

> **Online video.** Video watched or downloaded via the Web. > **Online TV.** Live or recorded TV shows available via the Web. > **Online movie.** A feature film available via the Web. > **Video-on-demand (VOD).** The process of downloading movies and television shows, on demand, via the Web. > **Online gaming.** Playing games via the Web.

## Online News, Reference, and Information

There is an abundance of news and other important information available through the Internet. The following sections discuss some of the most widely used news, reference, and information resources.

### News and Reference Information

News organizations, such as television networks, newspapers, and magazines, nearly always have Web sites that are updated on a continual basis to provide access to current local and world news, as well as sports, entertainment, health, travel, politics, weather, and other news topics (see the *NBC News* Web site in Figure 8-27). Many news sites also have searchable archives to look for past articles, although some require a fee to view back articles. Once articles are displayed, they can typically be saved, printed, or sent to other individuals via e-mail. A growing trend is for newspapers and magazines to abandon print subscriptions and to provide Web-only service—primarily for cost reasons. Although some subscribers miss the print versions, there are some advantages to digital versions, such as the ability to easily search through content in some digital publications. Other online news resources include news radio programs that are broadcast over the Internet, as well as the wide variety of news video clips available through many Web sites.

*Reference sites* are designed to provide users access to specific types of useful information. For example, reference sites can be used to generate maps (see the *MapQuest* Web site in Figure 8-27), check the weather forecast, look up the value of a home, or provide access to encyclopedias, dictionaries, ZIP Code directories, and telephone directories. One potential downside to the increased availability of online reference sites is use by criminals. For instance, one California lawmaker has introduced a bill requiring mapping sites to blur out details of schools, churches, and government buildings after being informed that some terrorists have used these maps to plan bombings and other attacks.

**FIGURE 8-27**

Online news and reference Web sites.

**NET**

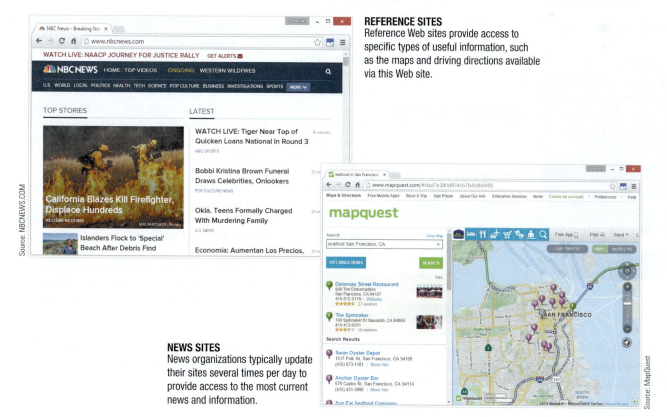

**REFERENCE SITES**
Reference Web sites provide access to specific types of useful information, such as the maps and driving directions available via this Web site.

**NEWS SITES**
News organizations typically update their sites several times per day to provide access to the most current news and information.

Source: NBCNEWS.COM

Source: MapQuest

Source: feedly

**FIGURE 8-28**

**RSS readers.** RSS feeds (right) can often be organized into categories (left).

**FIGURE 8-29**

**Podcasts.**

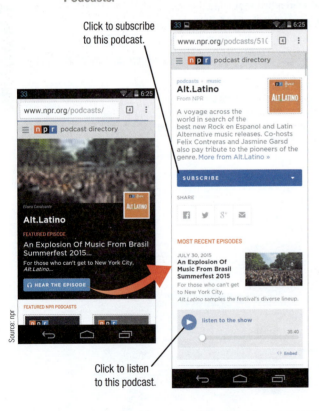

Click to subscribe to this podcast.

Click to listen to this podcast.

Source: npr

## RSS Feeds and Podcasts

**RSS** (**Really Simple Syndication**) is an online tool designed for delivering news articles, blogs (discussed shortly), and other content regularly published to a Web site. Provided the content has an associated *RSS feed*, individuals can *subscribe* (usually for free) to that feed and then the content will be delivered as it becomes available. You can subscribe to an RSS feed by clicking a *subscribe* link on the associated Web page to add the feed content to your browser *feed list*; if you are using an *RSS reader* (such as *Feedly* shown in Figure 8-28), you can typically search for new feeds using that program. RSS readers often allow you to organize your feed into categories, as shown in Figure 8-28. As new content for the subscribed feed becomes available, it will be accessible via the feed links.

Another Web resource that can provide you with useful information is a **podcast**—a recorded audio or video file that can be downloaded via the Internet. The term *podcast* is derived from the iPod portable digital media player (the first widely used device for playing digital audio files), although podcasts today can also be listened to using a computer or smartphone.

*Podcasting* (creating and publishing a podcast) enables individuals to create self-published, inexpensive Internet radio broadcasts in order to share their knowledge, express their opinions on particular subjects, or share original poems, songs, or short stories with interested individuals. Originally created and distributed by individuals, podcasts are now also being created and distributed by businesses. For instance, some commercial radio stations are making portions of their broadcasts available via podcasts (see Figure 8-29), and a growing number of news sites and corporate sites now publish podcasts regularly. Podcasts are also used for educational purposes. Podcasts are typically uploaded to the Web on a regular basis, and RSS feeds can be used to notify subscribers when a new podcast is available.

## Product, Corporate, Government, and Other Information

The Web is a very useful tool for locating product and corporate information. Manufacturer and retailer Web sites often include product specifications, instruction manuals, and other information that is useful to consumers before or after they purchase a product and consumer reviews are widely available online to help purchasers evaluate their options before buying a product online or in a physical store. For investors, a variety of corporate information is available online, from both company Web sites and sites (such as *Hoovers.com*) that offer free or fee-based corporate information. For a look at an emerging Internet trend that is beginning to impact both business and individuals—the Internet of Things (IoT)—see the Trend box.

Government information is also widely available on the Internet. Most state and federal agencies have Web sites to provide information to citizens, such as government publications, archived documents, forms, and legislative bills. You can also perform a variety of

> **RSS (Really Simple Syndication).** A tool used to deliver selected Web content to subscribers as the content is published to a Web site.
> **Podcast.** A recorded audio or video file that can be played or downloaded via the Web.

tasks, such as downloading tax forms and filing your tax returns online. In addition, many cities, counties, and states allow you to pay your car registration fees, register to vote, view property tax information, or make an appointment to renew your driver's license online.

There is also a wide variety of information available from nonprofit organizations, conservation groups, and political parties. For instance, there are numerous online resources for learning the positions of political candidates and other information important to voters, such as the nonpartisan *FactCheck.org* Web site shown in Figure 8-30.

## Online Education and Writing

*Online education*—using the Internet to facilitate learning—is a rapidly growing Internet application. The Internet can be used to deliver part or all of any educational class or program; it can also be used to supplement or support traditional education. In addition, many high school and college courses use Web content—such as online syllabi, schedules, discussion boards, podcasts, and tutorials—as required or suggested supplements. There are also Web-based *learning management systems* (such as *Blackboard*, shown in Figure 8-31) that are often used to deliver course content, manage assignments and grades, and more; and the use of *student response systems*—where students use a special device or their smartphone to respond to surveys or review questions during in-class lectures is growing. The next few sections take a look at some of the most widely used online education applications.

**FIGURE 8-30**
FactCheck.org.

### Web-Based Training and Distance Learning

The term **Web-based training (WBT)** refers to any instruction delivered via the Web. It is commonly used for employee training, as well as for delivering instruction in an educational setting. **Distance learning** occurs whenever students take classes from a location that is different from the one where the delivery of instruction takes place. Distance learning typically includes Web-based training and is available through many high schools, colleges, and universities, as well as organizations that provide professional certifications. Distance learning can be used to learn just one task or new skill; it can also be used to complete an *online course* or an entire degree online via an accredited college or university. Typically the majority of distance learning coursework is completed over the Internet, although schools

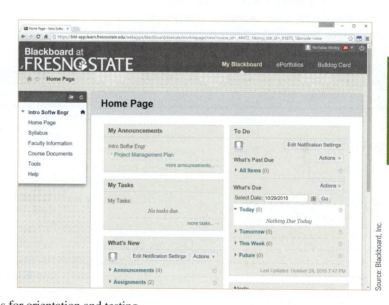

might require some in-person contact, such as sessions for orientation and testing.

The biggest advantage of Web-based training and distance learning is that they are usually experienced individually and at the user's own pace. In addition, content can be updated as needed and online content and activities typically provide immediate feedback to the student. One disadvantage is the possibility of technological problems—because students need a working device and an Internet connection to access the material, they cannot participate if their device, their Internet connection, or the Web server hosting the material goes down. Another concern among educators is the lack of face-to-face contact; to help with this, some distance learning classes today use *synchronous* or *live online learning*,

**FIGURE 8-31**
**Blackboard.** Can be used to view and complete assignments, view grades and announcements, and more.

---

# TREND

### The Internet of Things (IoT)

One of the hottest Internet topics today is the *Internet of Things* (*IoT*). The Internet of Things refers to a world where everyday physical objects are connected to, and uniquely identifiable on, the Internet so they can communicate with other devices. Also called *Machine-to-Machine* (*M2M*) because it involves primarily machines talking directly to one another, the IoT is expected to greatly impact our lives and the way we get information and control objects. Devices included in the Internet of Things can range from sensors in your shoes, to smart fitness devices, to healthcare monitors, to home automation systems (see the accompanying illustration), to smart farm equipment, to smart freeways and traffic lights. While still in the early stages, some aspects of the Internet of Things, such as smart homes and fitness PANs, exist today. As the Internet of Things matures, the connected smart devices will continue to make our lives more convenient, save us money, and provide us with other advantages. Businesses will benefit from getting feedback from equipment (being notified when a machine in the field needs service or refilling, for instance, without an employee having to physically monitor it), being able to automate more processes,

and getting faster and more accurate feedback about point-of-sale purchases.

One concern about the Internet of Things is how best to protect the security and privacy of individuals from hackers and data leaks. That concern will likely need to be addressed before the Internet of Things becomes mainstream.

Source: AT&T

where students and instructors are online at the same time, which encourages interaction, questions and answers, and other types of instant feedback. In addition, there are a number of security issues surrounding distance learning—such as the difficulty in ensuring that the appropriate student is completing assignments or taking exams. Some possible solutions for this latter concern are discussed in the next section.

## Online Testing

In both distance learning and traditional classes, *online testing*—which allows students to take tests via the Internet—is a growing trend. Objective tests (such as those containing multiple choice or true/false questions), performance-based exams (such as those given in computer classes to test student mastery of software applications), and essay exams can all be administered and taken online. Typically objective and performance-based online tests are graded automatically, providing fast feedback to the students, as well as freeing up the instructor's time for other activities. One recent debate focuses on the use of computers to automatically grade essay tests, as discussed in the Balancing Act project at the end of Chapter 6.

One challenge for online testing is ensuring that an online test is taken by the appropriate individual and in an authorized manner in order to avoid cheating. Some distance learning programs require students to go physically to a testing center to take the test or to find an acceptable test proctor (such as an educator at a nearby school or a commanding officer for military personnel). Other options are using smart cards, fingerprint scans, and other means to authenticate students taking an online exam from a remote location. *Online proctoring* services are also available. One service, *ProctorU*, uses human proctors that authenticate test takers using their student ID card and a webcam and then watch the students via the webcam to ensure they follow the exam rules. Other proctoring services are software based and can authenticate students via a face scan or photo ID scan, capture audio and video for the instructor to view if needed, flag suspicious movements (such as a person entering or leaving the testing area), and lock down the student's device so that no other programs or Web sites can be opened during the exam.

## Blogs, Wikis, and Other Types of Online Writing

Some types of online writing, such as e-mail, instant and text messaging, and social networking updates, were discussed earlier in this chapter. A few additional types of online writing are discussed next.

A **blog**—derived from the words *Web* and *log*—is a Web page that contains short, frequently updated entries in chronological order, typically as a means of expression or communication (see the food blog shown in Figure 8-32). In essence, a blog is an online personal journal accessible to the public that is usually created and updated by one individual. Blogs are written by a wide variety of individuals—including ordinary people, as well as celebrities, writers, students, and experts on particular subjects—and can be used to post personal commentary, research updates, comments on current events, political opinions, celebrity gossip, travel diaries, television show recaps, and more.

Blogs are most often created via blogging sites such as *Blogger* and *WordPress*. Blogs are also frequently published on school, business, and personal Web sites. Blogs often contain text, photos, and video clips; are usually updated frequently; and can be posted via computers, e-mail, and smartphones. With their increased use and audiences, bloggers and the *blogosphere* (the complete collection of blogs on the Internet) are beginning to have increasing influence on businesses, politicians, and individuals today.

Another form of online writing is the **wiki**. Wikis, named for the Hawaiian phrase *wiki wiki* meaning *quick*, are a way of creating and editing collaborative Web pages quickly and easily. Similar to a blog, the content on a wiki page can be edited and republished to the Web just by pressing a Save or Submit button. However, wikis are intended to be modified by others and so are especially appropriate for collaboration, such as for class Web pages or group projects. To protect the content of a wiki from sabotage, the entire wiki or editing privileges for a wiki can be password protected.

**FIGURE 8-32**
**Blogs.** Allow individuals to post entries to an online personal journal.

---

>**Blog.** A Web page that contains short, frequently updated entries in chronological order, typically by just one individual. >**Wiki.** A collaborative Web page that is designed to be edited and republished by a variety of individuals.

**FIGURE 8-33**
**Wikis.** Can be edited by any authorized individual.

One of the largest wikis is *Wikipedia* (shown in Figure 8-33), a free online encyclopedia that is updated by volunteer contributors from all over the world. While most Wikipedia contributors edit articles in a responsible manner, there are instances of erroneous information being added to Wikipedia pages intentionally. As with any resource, visitors should carefully evaluate the content of a Wikipedia article before referencing it in a report, Web page, or other document, as discussed earlier in this chapter.

An **e-portfolio**, also called an *electronic portfolio* or *digital portfolio*, is a collection of an individual's work accessible through a Web site. Today's e-portfolios are typically linked to a collection of student-related information, such as résumés, papers, projects, and other original works. Some e-portfolios are used for a single course; others are designed to be used and updated throughout a student's educational career, culminating in a comprehensive collection of information that can be used as a job-hunting tool.

## CENSORSHIP AND PRIVACY ISSUES

There are many important societal issues related to the Internet. Network and Internet security is covered in Chapter 9. Two other important issues—censorship and privacy—are discussed next, in the context of Internet use. Other societal issues—including ethics, health, and the environment—related to computer use are discussed in further detail in Chapter 13.

### Censorship

The issue of Internet censorship affects all countries that have Internet access. In some countries, Internet content is filtered by the government, typically to hinder the spread of information from political opposition groups, to filter out subjects deemed offensive, or to block information from sites that could endanger national security. Some countries also block information (such as blogs and personal Web pages) from leaving the country, and have occasionally completely shut down Internet access to and from the country during political protests to stop the flow of information in and out of that country.

In the United States, the First Amendment to the U.S. Constitution guarantees a citizen's right to free speech. This protection allows people to say things to others without fear of arrest. But how does the right to free speech relate to potentially offensive or indecent materials available over the Internet where they might be observed by children or by people who do not wish to see them? There have been some attempts in the United States to regulate Internet content—what some would view as *censorship*—over the years. For example, the *Communications Decency Act*, which was signed into law in 1996, made it a criminal offense to distribute patently indecent or offensive material online in order to protect children from being exposed to inappropriate Web

> **E-portfolio.** A collection of an individual's work accessible via the Web.

content. In 1997, however, the Supreme Court overturned the portion of this law pertaining to indecent material on the basis of free speech, making this content legal to distribute via the Internet and protecting Web sites that host third-party content from being liable for that content.

Another example of legislation designed to protect children from inappropriate Web content is the *Children's Internet Protection Act* (*CIPA*). CIPA requires public libraries and schools to implement Internet safety policies and technologies to block children's access to inappropriate Web content in order to receive certain public funds. This law was fought strenuously by free speech advocacy groups and some library associations on the basis that limiting access to some Internet content violates an individual's First Amendment rights to free speech. While CIPA was eventually upheld by the Supreme Court, the Court modified the law to require a library to remove the blocking technologies for an adult library patron at the patron's request.

Source: ContentWatch, Inc.

**FIGURE 8-34**
Internet filtering.

One technology commonly used to conform to CIPA regulations is **Internet filtering**— the act of blocking access to particular Web pages or types of Web pages. It can also be used by individuals to protect themselves from material they would view as offensive, by parents to protect their children from material they feel is inappropriate, by employers to keep employees from accessing non-work-related sites, by some ISPs and search sites to block access to potentially objectionable materials, and by schools and libraries to control the Web content that children are able to view in order to be in compliance with CIPA. Internet filtering typically restricts access to Web pages that contain offensive language, sex/pornography, racism, drugs, or violence. It can also be used to block access to specific sites (such as social networking sites, YouTube, or eBay), as well as to restrict the total number of hours or the time of day that the Internet can be used.

Most browsers include some Internet filtering options. For instance, Google's *SafeSearch* option blocks Web sites containing sexually explicit content from Google Search results. More comprehensive Internet filtering can be obtained with stand-alone filtering programs, such as *NetNanny* (shown in Figure 8-34).

## Web Browsing Privacy

Privacy, as it relates to the Internet, encompasses what information about individuals is available, how it is used, and by whom. As more and more transactions and daily activities are being performed online, there is the potential for vast amounts of private information to be collected and distributed without the individual's knowledge or permission. Therefore, it is understandable that public concern regarding privacy and the Internet is on the rise. Although privacy is discussed in more detail in Chapter 9, a few issues that are of special concern to Internet users regarding Web browsing privacy and e-mail privacy are discussed in the next few sections.

---

**>Internet filtering.** Using a software program or browser option to block access to particular Web pages or types of Web pages.

**NET** (⦿)

Click to view
cookie settings.

Click to delete
stored cookies.

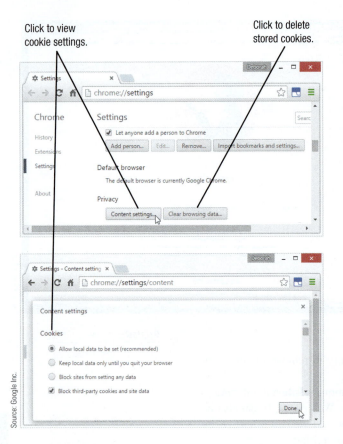

Source: Google Inc.

▲ **FIGURE 8-35**
**Blocking third-party cookies in Chrome.**

## Cookies

Many Web pages today use **cookies**—small text files that are stored on your hard drive by a Web server—to identify return visitors and their preferences. Cookies can be *session based cookies* (which are erased when you close your browser) or *persistent cookies* (which are stored on your hard drive). About one-half of persistent cookies are *first-party cookies*, which are cookies that belong to the Web site you are visiting and are only read by that site. These cookies can provide some benefits to consumers, such as saving a shopping cart or remembering personalized settings. *Third-party cookies* (cookies placed on your hard drive by a company other than the one associated with the Web page that you are viewing—typically a Web advertising company) are usually viewed as a higher privacy risk. Many of these are *tracking cookies*, which can track your activities across multiple Web sites. For example, tracking cookies can be used to display Web page ads based on your browsing activities or to send information to Facebook each time you visit a Web page with a Like button on that page if you have a Facebook cookie on your hard drive.

The information stored in a cookie file typically includes the name of the cookie, its expiration date, and the domain that the cookie belongs to. In addition, a cookie contains either personal information that you have entered while visiting the Web site or an ID number assigned by the Web site that allows the Web site's server to retrieve your personal information from its database. Such a database can contain two types of information: *personally identifiable information* (*PII*) and *non-personally identifiable information* (*Non-PII*). Personally identifiable information is connected with a specific user's identity—such as his or her name and address—and is typically given during the process of ordering goods or services. Non-personally identifiable information is anonymous data—such as which product pages were viewed or which advertisements located on the site were clicked—that is not directly associated with the visitor's name or another personally identifiable characteristic.

To notify you about cookie use, many sites display a notification on your first visit so you can choose not to use the site if you object to its use of cookies. To control overall cookie use, you can use your browser's privacy settings to delete all cookies stored on your hard drive, as well as to block third-party cookies (see Figure 8-35). In addition, security software typically scans for tracking cookies and will quarantine those cookie files at your request.

Another alternative is the *private browsing* option available with many Web browsers, including Internet Explorer, Edge, Chrome, and Safari. As discussed more in Chapter 9, this option allows you to browse the Web without leaving any history of the sites you visited (including browsing history, form data, cookies, usernames, and passwords) on the computer you are using. Private browsing is useful for individuals using school, library, or other public computers to visit password-protected sites, research medical information, or perform other tasks that the user may prefer to keep private. Individuals using a computer to shop for gifts or other surprises for family members who share the same computer may find the feature useful, as well.

> **Cookie.** A small file stored on a user's hard drive by a Web server; commonly used to identify personal preferences and settings for that user.

Another Web privacy issue is the privacy of social media data. The best preventative measure is to not post anything online that you would not want the general public to view. But you can also use the privacy settings for each social network that you utilize to specify who can see what in your profile. For instance, Facebook allows you to specify what content can be seen by the "Public" (anyone) and what can only be seen by "Friends" (your Facebook friends).

**CAUTION CAUTION CAUTION CAUTION CAUTION CAUTION CAUT**

If your security software includes tracking cookie protection, be sure it is enabled to avoid these cookies from being stored on your computer. Setting your browser's privacy settings to block third-party cookies can offer you some additional protection against tracking cookies.

## Spyware and Adware

**Spyware** is the term used for any software program that is installed without the user's knowledge and that secretly gathers information about the user and transmits it through his or her Internet connection. Spyware is sometimes used to provide advertisers with information used for marketing purposes, such as to help select advertisements to display on each person's computer. The information gathered by the spyware software is usually not associated with a person's identity. But spyware is a concern for privacy advocates because it is typically installed without a user's direct knowledge (such as at the same time another program is installed, often when a program is downloaded from a Web site or a P2P service) and conveys information about a user's Internet activities. Spyware can also be used by criminals to retrieve personal data stored on your computer for use in criminal activities, as discussed in more detail in Chapter 9.

A related type of software is *adware*, which is free or low-cost software that is supported by on-screen advertising. Many free programs that can be downloaded from the Internet include some type of adware, which results in on-screen advertising. The difference between spyware and adware is that adware typically does not gather information and relay it to others via the Internet (although it can), and it is not installed without the user's consent. Adware might, however, be installed without the user's direct knowledge because many users do not read licensing agreements before clicking OK to install a new program. When this occurs with a program that contains adware, the adware components are installed without the user's direct knowledge.

## E-Mail Privacy

Many people mistakenly believe that the e-mail they send and receive is private and will never be read by anyone other than the intended recipient. Because it is transmitted over public media, however, only encrypted (electronically scrambled) e-mail can be transmitted safely, as discussed in Chapter 9. Although unlikely to happen to your personal e-mail, nonencrypted e-mail can be intercepted and read by someone else. Consequently, from a privacy standpoint, a nonencrypted e-mail message should be viewed more like a postcard than a letter (see Figure 8-36). In addition, businesses and ISPs typically archive (keep copies of) e-mail messages that travel through their servers and are required to comply with subpoenas from law enforcement agencies for archived e-mail messages.

**FIGURE 8-36**
You cannot assume e-mail messages are private, unless they are encrypted.

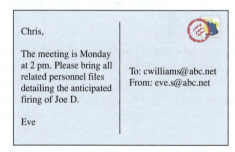

Chris,

The meeting is Monday at 2 pm. Please bring all related personnel files detailing the anticipated firing of Joe D.

Eve

To: cwilliams@abc.net
From: eve.s@abc.net

**REGULAR (NONENCRYPTED E-MAIL) = POSTCARD**

From: eve.s@abc.net

To: cwilliams@abc.net

CONFIDENTIAL

**ENCRYPTED E-MAIL = SEALED LETTER**

>**Spyware.** A software program that is installed without the user's permission and that secretly gathers information to be sent to others.

# SUMMARY

## EVOLUTION OF THE INTERNET

**Chapter Objective 1:**

Discuss how the Internet evolved and what it is like today.

The origin of the **Internet**—a worldwide collection of interconnected networks that is accessed by millions of people daily—dates back to the late 1960s. At its start and throughout its early years, the Internet was called **ARPANET**. It was not until the development of the **World Wide Web** (**Web**) that public interest in the Internet began to soar. Most companies have Web sites today and consider the Web to be an indispensable business tool. While the Web is a very important and widely used Internet resource, it is not the only one. Over the years, *protocols* have been developed to download files, send e-mail messages, and perform other tasks, in addition to using Web pages. Today, the term *Internet* has become a household word and, in many ways, has redefined how people think about computers and communications. The next significant improvement to the Internet infrastructure may be the result of projects such as *Internet2*.

**Chapter Objective 2:**

Identify the various types of individuals, companies, and organizations involved in the Internet community and explain their purposes.

The Internet community is made up of individual *users*; companies, such as **Internet service providers** (**ISPs**), **Internet content providers**, **application service providers** (**ASPs**), *infrastructure companies*, and a variety of software and hardware companies; the government; and other organizations. Virtually anyone with a device with communications capability can be part of the Internet, either as a user or supplier of information or services. **Web services** are self-contained business functions that operate over the Internet.

Because the Internet is so unique in the history of the world—and it remains a relatively new and ever-changing phenomenon—several widespread myths about it have surfaced. Three such myths are that the Internet is free, that it is controlled by some central body, and that it is synonymous with the World Wide Web.

## GETTING SET UP TO USE THE INTERNET

**Chapter Objective 3:**

Describe device and connection options for connecting to the Internet, as well as some considerations to keep in mind when selecting an ISP.

Most Internet connections today are **direct connections** (always connected to the Internet), though some are **dial-up connections** (which need to dial up and connect to the Internet to provide access). Dial-up connections are typically **conventional dial-up Internet access**; common types of direct Internet connections include **cable**, **DSL** (**Digital Subscriber Line**), **satellite**, **fixed wireless**, **mobile wireless**, and **broadband over fiber** (**BoF**)—also called **fiber-to-the-premises** (**FTTP**)—**Internet access**. Individuals can also connect to the Internet via a **Wi-Fi hotspot**. When preparing to become connected to the Internet, you need to decide which type of device (personal computer or smartphone, for instance), which type of Internet connection, and which specific Internet service provider to use. Once all these decisions are made, you can acquire the proper hardware and software and set up your system for Internet access.

## SEARCHING THE INTERNET

**Chapter Objective 4:**

Understand how to search effectively for information on the Internet and how to cite Internet resources properly.

**Search sites** are Web sites that enable users to search for and find information on the Internet. They typically locate pages using a **keyword search** (in which the user specifies **keywords** for the desired information)—a **search engine** retrieves the list of matching Web pages from a database. A **directory search** (in which the user selects categories corresponding to the desired information) is another possibility. Search site databases are generally maintained by automated *spider* programs.

There are a variety of search strategies that can be used, including typing phrases instead of single keywords; using *search operators*; trying the search at multiple search sites; and using *synonyms*, *variant word forms*, *wildcards*, and *field searches*. Once a list of links to Web pages matching the search criteria is displayed, the hits need to be evaluated for their relevancy. If the information found on a Web page is used in a paper, report, or other original document, the source should be credited appropriately.

## BEYOND BROWSING, SEARCHING, AND E-MAIL

The Internet can be used for many different types of activities in addition to basic Web browsing and e-mail exchange. Common types of online communications include **instant messaging** or **IM** (also commonly referred to as **chat**) and **text messaging** (sending real-time typed messages via a computer or mobile phone, respectively), **Twittering** (sending short status updates via Twitter), **forums** (online locations where people post messages on a particular topic for others to read and respond to), **Web conferences** (real-time meetings taking place via the Web that typically use video cameras and microphones to enable participants to see and hear each other), and **Webinars** (seminars presented over the Web). **Social networking sites** (part of the collection of **social media** available today) also allow the members of an online community to communicate and exchange information. **Voice over Internet Protocol** (**VoIP**) refers to making voice telephone calls over the Internet.

Common Web activities for individuals include a variety of consumer **e-commerce** activities, such as **online shopping**, **online auctions**, **online banking**, and **online investing**. When performing any type of financial transaction over the Internet, it is very important to use only secure Web pages.

Online entertainment applications include **online gaming**, downloading music files and other types of **online music**, **online TV**, **online movies**, and other types of **online video**. Selecting and receiving TV shows and movies via the Web is called **video-on-demand** (**VOD**). A wide variety of news, reference, government, product, and corporate information is available via the Web as well. **RSS** (**Really Simple Syndication**) feeds can be used to deliver current news, **podcasts**, and other Web content to individuals as it becomes available.

Online education options include **Web-based training** (**WBT**) and **distance learning**. *Online testing* can be used for both objective and performance-based exams and can be secured by a variety of means. Online writing includes **blogs** (Web pages that contain frequently updated entries by individuals), **wikis** (Web pages designed to be created and edited by multiple individuals), and **e-portfolios** (collections of an individual's work).

## CENSORSHIP AND PRIVACY ISSUES

Among the most important societal issues relating to the Internet are *censorship* and *privacy*. Web content is not censored as a whole, but **Internet filtering** can be used by parents, employers, educators, and anyone wishing to prevent access to sites they deem objectionable on computers for which they have control. Privacy is a big concern for individuals, particularly as it relates to their Web activity. **Cookies** are typically used by Web sites to save customized settings for that site and can also be used for advertising purposes. Another item of possible concern is **spyware** (software installed without the user's permission that sends information to others). Unless an e-mail message is encrypted, it should not be assumed to be completely private.

**Chapter Objective 5:**
List several ways to communicate over the Internet, in addition to e-mail.

**Chapter Objective 6:**
List several useful activities that can be performed via the Web.

**Chapter Objective 7:**
Discuss censorship and privacy and how they are related to Internet use.

NET

# REVIEW ACTIVITIES

## KEY TERM MATCHING

a. cookie

b. dial-up connection

c. direct connection

d. distance learning

e. Internet

f. keyword

g. podcast

h. search engine

i. social media

j. World Wide Web (Web)

**Instructions:** Match each key term on the left with the definition on the right that best describes it.

1. _____ A learning environment in which the student is physically located away from the instructor and other students; commonly, instruction and communications take place via the Web.

2. _____ A type of Internet connection in which the computer or other device is connected to the Internet continually.

3. _____ A small file stored on a user's hard drive by a Web server; commonly used to identify personal preferences and settings for that user.

4. _____ A software program used by a search site to retrieve matching Web pages from a search database.

5. _____ A type of Internet connection in which the computer or other device must dial up and connect to a service provider's computer via telephone lines before being connected to the Internet.

6. _____ A recorded audio or video file that can be played or downloaded via the Web.

7. _____ A word typed in a search box on a search site to locate information on the Internet.

8. _____ The collection of social networking sites and other communications channels used to transmit or share information with a broad audience.

9. _____ The collection of Web pages available through the Internet.

10. _____ The largest and most well-known computer network, linking billions of devices all over the world.

## SELF-QUIZ

**Instructions:** Circle **T** if the statement is true, **F** if the statement is false, or write the best answer in the space provided. **Answers for the self-quiz are located in the References and Resources Guide at the end of the book**.

1. **T F** When the Internet was first developed, it was called Mosaic.

2. **T F** On the Internet, an *access provider* and a *content provider* are essentially the same thing.

3. **T F** With a direct connection, you need only open your browser to start your Internet session.

4. **T F** A Wi-Fi hotspot is used to provide Internet access to individuals via a wireless connection.

5. **T F** A Webinar is a Web site designed to allow individuals to easily create and publish blogs.

6. _____ is a type of always-on broadband Internet service that transmits data over standard telephone lines but does not tie up your phone line.

7. With a(n) _____ search, keywords are typed into the search box; with a(n) _____ search, users select categories to find matching Web pages.

8. Performing financial transactions over the Internet is called _____.

9. With a(n) _____ , people bid on products over the Internet, and the highest bidder purchases the item.

10. Match each Internet application to its possible situation, and write the corresponding number in the blank to the left of each situation.

   a. _____ To communicate with a friend in a different state.

   b. _____ To post a question about a product that you hope other individuals will answer.

   c. _____ To pay a bill without writing a check.

   d. _____ To find Web pages containing information about growing your own Bonsai trees.

1. Online banking

2. E-mail

3. Internet searching

4. Forum

---

## EXERCISES

1. Match each type of Internet access to its description, and write the corresponding number in the blank to the left of each description.

   a. _____ A common type of home broadband connection; does not use standard phone lines.

   b. _____ Provides access to the Internet via a very fast fiber-optic network.

   c. _____ Accesses the Internet via standard phone lines and ties up your phone; the maximum speed is 56 Kbps.

1. Conventional dial-up

2. BoF

3. Cable

2. What would each of the following searches look for?

   a. mustang -car _____

   b. snorkel* _____

   c. text: "Internet privacy" domain:*.gov _____

3. List three different sets of keywords that could be used to search for information on how to maintain a trumpet.

4. Explain the difference between a blog, a wiki, and a podcast.

5. List one advantage and one disadvantage of the use of Web site cookies.

## NET

---

## DISCUSSION QUESTIONS

1. Twittering became virtually an overnight sensation, but some question its usefulness. Do you want to know the routine activities your friends (or other individuals you choose to follow) are doing during the day? Is it useful information to tweet that your bus is stuck in traffic or that you are having a bad day? Do you follow anyone on Twitter or do you tweet regularly? Why or why not? Because Twitter updates have to be very short, some may think that twittering on the job does not take up enough time to be a concern, but what about the distraction factor? Should employers allow employees to use Twitter, Facebook, and other popular online activities during work hours? Why or why not?

2. Some courtrooms today are becoming high-tech, such as using videoconferencing systems to allow defendants and witnesses to participate in proceedings from remote locations. Allowing defendants to participate remotely from the jail facility saves travel time and expense, as well as eliminates any risk of flight. Remote testimony from witnesses can save both time and money. But, could having defendants and witnesses participate remotely affect the jury's perspective? If the videoconference takes place via the Internet, can it be assured that proceedings are confidential? Do you think the benefits of these systems outweigh any potential disadvantages?

# PROJECTS

HOT TOPICS

**1. Social Commerce** As discussed in the How It Works box, social commerce is an emerging option for sending funds to other individuals.

For this project, research social commerce. How common is it? Select one type of social media and investigate the social commerce options available via that site. Can you make purchases or send money to others? What funding options are accepted? Have you ever used the social commerce options available on this site? Why or why not? With the wide use of social media today, do you think the integration of social commerce is a good idea or a risky idea? At the conclusion of your research, prepare a one-page summary of your findings and opinions and submit it to your instructor.

SHORT ANSWER/
RESEARCH

**2. Online Travel Planning** Planning and booking travel arrangements online is a very popular Internet activity today and there are a number of sites that can be used.

For this project, review two popular travel sites, such as Expedia.com and Travelocity.com, to see what services they offer and how easy it is to locate the information needed to plan and book a flight via those sites. Select a destination and use one of the sites to obtain a quote for a particular flight on a particular day. Next, go to the Web site for the airline of the flight and use the site to obtain a quote for the same flight. Is there a difference in price or flight availability? Could you make a reservation online through both sites? Would you feel comfortable booking an entire vacation yourself online, or are there services that a travel agent could provide that you feel would be beneficial? Do you think these sites are most appropriate for making business travel plans or vacation plans, or are they suited to both? At the conclusion of your research, prepare a one-page summary of your findings and submit it to your instructor.

HANDS ON

**3. Web Searching** Search sites can be used to find Web pages containing specific information, and there are strategies that can be used to make Web searching an efficient and useful experience.

For this project, go to the Google search site and perform the following searches, then submit your results and printouts to your instructor. (Note: Some of the answers will vary from student to student.)

**a.** Search for *rules*. How many pages were found? What is the name of the first page in the list of hits? Next, search for *backgammon rules*. How many pages were found? Use the hits to find a picture of how a backgammon board is initially set up, then, print that page.

**b.** Search to find a recipe for Buffalo Chicken Wings; a map of where your house, apartment, or dorm is located; and the ZIP Code for 200 N. Elm Street, Hinsdale, IL and print the pages containing this information.

**c.** Go to the Advanced Search option. Use the form fields to perform a search for Web pages that contain all of the words *hiking trails Sierras*, do not contain the word *horse*, and have the domain *.gov*. After the hits are displayed, record the actual search phrase that is listed in the search box along with the name and URL of the first page displayed in the list of hits.

4. **Paid Bloggers** Blogs are traditionally online personal journals where the blogger expresses his or her opinion on desired topics. Unlike professional journalists, bloggers typically post because they want to, not because they have been hired to do so. However, as discussed in the chapter, bloggers are increasingly being paid or "sponsored" to blog. Is this ethical? If a blogger is paid to post his or her honest opinion about a product or service, does that lessen the credibility of that post? Does it change your opinion if the blogger reveals that it is a sponsored blog? If you based a purchase on a review posted in a blog that you later found out was sponsored, would you feel misled? How, if at all, do sponsored posts affect the blogosphere as a whole?

   For this project, form an opinion about the ethical ramifications of paid blogging and be prepared to discuss your position (in class, via an online class forum, or via a class blog, depending on your instructor's directions). You may also be asked to write a short paper expressing your opinion.

**ETHICS IN ACTION**

5. **Advanced Search** Most search sites today include advanced features to help you more efficiently find the information you are searching for.

   For this project, select one search site (such as Google or Bing) and research the advanced search options the site supports. How does the advanced search work—do you have to type special symbols or is there a form that can be used? What operators does the site support? Are you able to search for only pages that were recently updated? Are you able to find pages that link to a specified Web page? Can you search for specified file types, such as images or videos? Do you find the advanced search options for your selected site useful? Share your findings and opinions with the class in the form of a short presentation. The presentation should not exceed 10 minutes and should make use of one or more presentation aids, such as a whiteboard, handouts, or a computer-based slide presentation (your instructor may provide additional requirements). You may also be asked to submit a summary of the presentation to your instructor.

**PRESENTATION/ DEMONSTRATION**

**((o)) NET**

6. **In a Cyber War, Is it Ethical to Kill Enemy Hackers?** Cyber wars are heating up. Foreign governments (particularly China) are continually being accused of trying to hack into the computer systems of both the U.S. government and high-tech companies. Cybersecurity is a very important issue today and is a source of ongoing discussion between countries such as the United States and China. For instance, hackers allegedly working for the Chinese government recently breached a federal government network and information about four million current and former federal employees was compromised. While China's government denies any involvement and the countries are not officially at war, how do actual wars and cyber wars differ? Is a country hacking into another country's computer systems an act of war? If so, should those hackers be fair targets for retaliation? Just as the military is permitted to kill enemy soldiers attacking its country or its citizens, should they also kill enemy hackers? Is cyber warfare any less of an actual conflict than ground or air-based physical combat? What about computer programmers that control the drones and missles used in combat—are they fair targets?

   Pick a side on this issue, form an opinion and gather supporting evidence, and be prepared to discuss and defend your position in a classroom debate or in a one- to two-page paper, depending on your instructor's directions.

**BALANCING ACT**

# chapter 9

# Security and Privacy

**After completing this chapter, you will be able to do the following:**

1. Explain why computer users should be concerned about security and privacy as they relate to computing devices, networks, and the Internet.

2. Identify some risks associated with hardware loss, hardware damage, and system failure, and understand ways to safeguard a computing device against these risks.

3. List several examples of unauthorized access and unauthorized use and explain several ways to protect against them.

4. Provide several examples of computer sabotage and explain how individuals and businesses can protect against it.

5. Discuss online theft, identity theft, spoofing, phishing, and other types of dot cons and detail steps an individual can take to protect against these threats.

6. Identify some personal safety risks associated with Internet use and list steps individuals can take to protect themselves.

7. Describe some privacy concerns regarding databases, electronic profiling, spam, and telemarketing, and identify ways individuals can protect their privacy.

8. Discuss several types of electronic surveillance and monitoring, and list ways individuals can protect their privacy.

9. Discuss the current state of network and Internet security and privacy legislation.

## OVERVIEW

As previously discussed, computing devices, networks, and the Internet provide many benefits, such as helping us be more efficient and effective workers and adding convenience and enjoyment to our personal lives. However, there are downsides as well. The widespread use of computers, networks, and the Internet increases the risk of hardware theft, unauthorized computer access, fraud, and other types of computer crime. In addition, the vast amount of business and personal data stored on computers accessible via company networks and the Internet increases the chances of data loss and privacy breaches due to crime or employee errors. Some online activities can even put our personal safety at risk, if we are not careful.

This chapter first looks at a variety of security concerns stemming from the use of computers, networks, and the Internet in our society, including hardware and information theft, unauthorized access and use, computer viruses and other types of sabotage, and online fraud. Safeguards for each of these concerns are also covered, with an explanation of precautions that can be taken to reduce the chance that these security problems will happen to you. We then turn to privacy concerns, including the possible risks to personal privacy and precautions that can be taken to safeguard one's privacy. The chapter closes with a summary of legislation related to network and Internet security and privacy. ■

## WHY BE CONCERNED ABOUT COMPUTER, NETWORK, AND INTERNET SECURITY AND PRIVACY?

From losing a term paper because your computer is stolen or damaged, to a hacker using your personal information to make fraudulent purchases, to someone harassing you online in a discussion group, a variety of *security concerns* related to computers, networks, and the Internet exist. Many security concerns today can be categorized as computer crimes. **Computer crime**—sometimes referred to as *cybercrime*—includes any illegal act involving a computer. Cybercrime is a multibillion-dollar business that is often performed by seasoned criminals. In fact, according to the FBI, organized crime organizations in many countries are increasingly turning to computer crime to more easily target millions of potential victims.

*Privacy concerns* related to computers, networks, and the Internet also impact our lives. For example, **information privacy** refers to the rights of individuals and companies to control how information about them is collected and used. Some information privacy concerns include the privacy of Web site activities and e-mail messages, as well as the high number of security breaches on systems that contain personal information. Businesses need to be concerned with protecting the privacy of the personal information they store because data breaches violate the privacy of their customers. In addition, data breaches are costly, and they can result in lawsuits and damaged reputations.

**NET**

---

>**Computer crime.** Any illegal act involving a computer. >**Information privacy.** The rights of individuals and companies to control how information about them is collected and used.

With the growing use of wireless networks, social media, cloud computing, mobile computing, and individuals accessing company networks remotely—paired with the vast amount of sensitive information stored in databases accessible via the Internet today—security and privacy have never been more important. Consequently, all computer users should be aware of the security and privacy concerns surrounding the use of computing devices, networks, and the Internet, and they should take appropriate precautions, as discussed throughout this chapter.

# HARDWARE LOSS, HARDWARE DAMAGE, AND SYSTEM FAILURE

*Hardware loss* can occur when a personal computer, USB flash drive, smartphone, or other piece of hardware is stolen or is lost by the owner. Hardware loss can also result from hardware damage (both intentional and accidental) and from system failure. All of these instances are both security and privacy concerns.

## Hardware Loss and Damage

One of the most obvious types of hardware loss is **hardware theft**, which occurs when hardware (such as a computer, printer, or smartphone) is stolen from an individual or from a business, school, or other organization. Although security experts stress that the vast majority of hardware theft is done for the value of the hardware itself, corporate executives and government employees may be targeted for computer theft for the information contained on their computers. And even if the data on a device is not the primary reason for a theft, any unencrypted sensitive data stored on the stolen device is at risk of being exposed or used for fraudulent purposes.

Hardware loss also occurs when an individual misplaces or otherwise loses a piece of hardware. In addition to the inconvenience and expense of having to replace lost hardware, individuals risk identity theft and other fraudulent activities (as discussed shortly) if the lost hardware contains sensitive data. Businesses storing sensitive data have to deal with the numerous issues and potential consequences if that data is breached, such as notifying customers that their personal information was exposed (as required by nearly all of the states in the United States), responding to potential lawsuits, and trying to repair damage to the company's reputation.

Computer hardware can also be damaged by power fluctuations, heat, dust, static electricity, water, and abuse. For instance, fans clogged by dust can cause a computer to overheat, dropping a device will often break it, and spilling a drink on a keyboard or leaving a smartphone in the pocket of your jeans while they go through the wash will likely damage or ruin it. In addition to accidental damage, computers and other hardware can also be intentionally damaged by burglars, vandals, disgruntled employees, and other individuals who have access to the hardware. Just like lost hardware, damaged hardware results in data loss, unless the data contained on the damaged device is backed up.

## System Failure and Other Disasters

Although many of us may prefer not to think about it, **system failure**—the complete malfunction of a computer system—and other types of computer-related disasters do happen. From accidentally deleting a file to having your computer just stop working, computer problems can be a huge inconvenience, as well as cost you a great deal of time and money.

>**Hardware theft.** The theft of computer hardware. >**System failure.** The complete malfunction of a computer system.

When the system contains your personal documents and data, it is a problem; when it contains the only copy of your company records or controls a vital system—such as a nuclear power plant—it can be a disaster.

System failure can occur because of a hardware problem, a software problem, or computer sabotage. It can also occur because of a natural disaster or a terrorist attack. The terrorist attack on the New York City World Trade Center (WTC) Twin Towers on September 11, 2001, illustrated this all too clearly. When the Twin Towers collapsed, nearly 3,000 people were killed and hundreds of offices—over 13 million square feet of office space—were completely destroyed; another 7 million square feet of office space was damaged. In addition to the devastating human loss, the offices located in the WTC lost their computer systems—including all the equipment, records, and data stored at that location. The ramifications of these system failures and the corresponding data loss were felt around the world by all the businesses and people connected directly or indirectly to these organizations.

## ASK THE EXPERT

Courtesy SONIC

**Craig Miller,** Chief Information Officer, Sonic, America's Drive-In

**If the computers or software supporting the order entry system in one of your restaurants fails, can the restaurant still process orders?**

Even in this age of dependency on technology, SONIC drive-in locations can continue to run should our point-of-sales (POS) system not function. Each drive-in is equipped with a crash kit that includes guest tickets for order taking, menus for pricing reference, and a "tax chart" so that crew members can manually take orders. SONIC crew members also have specific steps that our Operations team has set out for them to follow. Our main focus is to ensure guest satisfaction remains high, even if our system goes down.

## Protecting Against Hardware Loss, Hardware Damage, and System Failure

To protect against hardware loss, hardware damage, and system failure, a number of precautions can be taken, as discussed next.

### Door and Computer Equipment Locks

Locked doors and other access control methods can be simple deterrents to hardware theft. For instance, doors to facilities should be secured with door locks, alarm systems, and whatever other access control methods are needed to make it difficult to gain access to hardware that might be stolen. In addition, employees should be trained regarding the proper procedures for ensuring visitors only have access to the parts of the facility that they are authorized to access.

To secure computers and other hardware to a table or other object that is difficult to move, *cable locks* (see Figure 9-1) can be used. Cable locks are often used to permanently secure hardware in schools and businesses. They are also used by college students, business travelers, and other individuals while on the go to temporarily secure their portable devices when they are not being used. To facilitate using a computer lock, most portable computers today come with a *security slot*—a small opening built into the system unit case designed for computer locks; other devices may be used with a *security case* instead (refer again to Figure 9-1). Computer locks are available in key and number or letter combination versions.

**TIP**

iPad security cases are increasingly being used with iPads in retail environments so they can be securely used by employees and/or customers, such as to place orders and take payments via the *Square* payment processing service.

**FIGURE 9-1**
Cable locks secure computers and other hardware.

**NOTEBOOK LOCKS**
This combination cable lock connects to the security slot built into the notebook computer.

Source: Kensington Computer Products Group

**SECURITY CASES**
This iPad security case/stand encloses the iPad and secures it via a keyed cable lock.

As an additional precaution with portable computers, *laptop alarm software* that emits a very loud alarm noise if the computer is unplugged, if USB devices are removed, or if the computer is shut down without the owner's permission can be used. With smartphones, *wireless tether* systems that tie the smartphone to a key fob in order to sound an alarm and lock the smartphone if the phone and key fob become further away than the specified allowable distance can be used.

In addition to physically securing devices, it is also extremely important for businesses to ensure that employees follow security protocols related to portable storage media, such as signing in and out portable hard drives, USB flash drives, and other storage media if required, and keeping those devices locked up when they are not in use.

**FIGURE 9-2**

**Encrypted devices.**

The data on this encrypted USB flash drive cannot be accessed until the user enters the appropriate PIN.

## Encryption and Self-Encrypting Hard Drives

**Encryption** is a way of temporarily making data unreadable in order to protect that data from being viewed by unauthorized individuals. It can be used to protect the data on a device from being readable if the device is lost or stolen. **Full disk encryption (FDE)** provides an easy way to protect data because it automatically encrypts everything stored on a drive so users don't have to remember to encrypt sensitive documents. A hard drive that uses FDE (often referred to as a **self-encrypting hard drive**) cannot be accessed without providing the appropriate username and password, biometric characteristic, or other authentication control, as discussed shortly.

Encryption can also be used to protect the data stored on removable media, such as a USB flash drive; a strong password, a biometric feature, or a PIN number (such as is used with the device shown in Figure 9-2) provides access to the data on the drive. Many encrypted devices allow multiple users to be registered as authorized users (such as by assigning each individual a password or registering his or her fingerprint image); some allow a portion of the device to be designated as unencrypted for nonsensitive documents, if desired. Many businesses today are requiring that all portable computers, portable storage devices, tablets, and smartphones issued to employees be encrypted in order to protect against a data breach if the device is lost or stolen.

## Device Tracking Software and Antitheft Tools

Some software tools are designed for recovery, instead of prevention; that is, they are designed to locate lost or stolen hardware. One example is *device tracking software*. When a device with tracking software installed is reported lost or stolen, the tracking software sends information about the location of the device (typically determined by GPS or the nearest Wi-Fi network) to the tracking software company on a regular basis so that the information can be provided to law enforcement agencies to help them recover the device. Some tracking software can even take video or photos with the device's camera to help identify and prosecute the thief.

**FIGURE 9-3**

**Remote locking.**

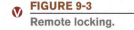

Your device has been remotely locked as a security measure. Enter your BullGuard Mobile Security password to unlock your device

Enter your password

Most tracking software can survive operating system reinstallations and hard drive reformats. Some can also display a message on the screen when the device is reported lost or stolen, such as a plea to return the device for a reward or a simple statement like "THIS DEVICE IS STOLEN" on the desktop or lock screen to call attention to the fact that the device is stolen. Another common option is the ability to *remotely lock* the device and display a message that the device is locked and won't function without the appropriate password (see Figure 9-3). A feature included in many device tracking programs is a kill switch—a technology that causes the device to self-destruct, as discussed in the Trend box.

> **Encryption.** A method of scrambling electronic content in order to make it unreadable if an unauthorized user intercepts it.
> **Full disk encryption (FDE).** A technology that encrypts everything stored on a storage medium automatically, without any user interaction.
> **Self-encrypting hard drive.** A hard drive that uses full disk encryption.

## Proper Hardware Care

Proper care of hardware can help to prevent serious damage to devices. An obvious precaution is to not harm your hardware physically, such as by dropping a device or knocking a piece of hardware off a desk. *Protective cases* (see Figure 9-4) can be used to help protect portable devices against minor abuse. These cases are usually padded or made from protective material to prevent damage due to occasional bumps and bangs; they typically also have a thin protective layer over the device's display to protect against scratches. Some protective cases are water resistant to protect the device from rain or dust damage. There are also neoprene *laptop sleeves* available to protect portable computers from scratches and other damage when they are carried in a conventional briefcase or bag.

For users who need more protection than a protective case can provide, **ruggedized devices** (such as the ones shown in Figure 9-5) that are designed to withstand much more physical abuse than conventional devices can be used. Ruggedized devices range from *semirugged* (such as devices that can withstand being dropped or submerged into water) to *ultrarugged* (such as devices that can withstand drops onto concrete, extreme temperature variations, and use while being bounced around over rough terrain in a vehicle). Ultrarugged devices are used most often by individuals who work out of an office, such as field workers, construction workers, outdoor technicians, military personnel, police officers, and firefighters.

To protect hardware from damage due to power fluctuations, it is important for all users to use a **surge suppressor**—a device that goes between a power outlet and the devices to be plugged into that outlet—with a computer whenever it is plugged into a power outlet. When electrical power spikes occur, the surge suppressor prevents them from harming your devices. For the best protection, surge suppressors should also be used with all the powered components that have a wired connection to the computer (such as a monitor or printer). There are small surge suppressors designed for use while on the go, and more powerful surge suppressors designed for business and industrial use.

To keep a desktop computer or a server powered up when the electricity goes off in addition to protecting against power fluctuations, an **uninterruptible power supply (UPS)**, which contains a built-in battery, can be used. The length of time that a UPS can power a system depends on the type and number of devices connected to the UPS, the power capacity of the UPS device, and the age of the battery. For extended power outages, *generators* are needed.

Dust, heat, static electricity, and moisture can also be

Source: Griffin Technology

**FIGURE 9-4**
Protective cases.

**TIP**

Use surge suppressors to also protect your televisions and other sensitive electronics from power fluctuations.

**FIGURE 9-5**
Ruggedized devices.

Source: Sony Electronics

**SEMIRUGGED (WATERPROOF) SMARTPHONES**

Source: Xplore Technologies Corp.

**RUGGED TABLETS**

> **Ruggedized device.** A computing device that is designed to withstand much more physical abuse than a conventional computing device. > **Surge suppressor.** A device that protects hardware from damage due to electrical fluctuations. > **Uninterruptible power supply (UPS).** A device containing a built-in battery that provides continuous power to a computer and other connected components when the electricity goes out.

# TREND

### Kill Switches

Due to the rising number of violent thefts of smartphones in major U.S. cities, *kill switches*—software that enables owners to render stolen devices inoperable–have been getting increased attention. In fact, Michigan and California recently passed laws requiring that all smartphones sold in those states include a kill switch.

Some features of kill switches are included in many device tracking apps. For example, the *Android Device Manager* shown in the accompanying illustration displays the current location of a selected device after a user logs on to his or her account. It also has the ability to ring the device, lock the device and display a message on the lock screen, or erase the device. Some stand-alone kill switches go one step further and actually destroy the device. For example, some encrypted hard drives automatically delete the encryption key after a specific number of unsuccessful password entry attempts, which leaves the device inaccessible. Kill switches are typically activated by the customer or by the tracking company upon customer request when the device is determined to be lost or stolen. Users of some cloud services can also use those services to remotely wipe their mobile devices when needed.

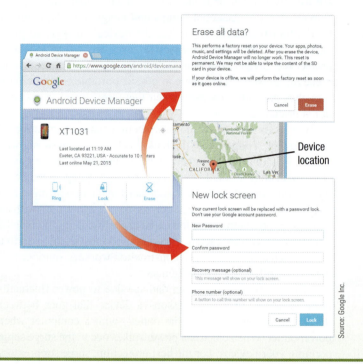

Device location

Source: Google Inc.

---

dangerous to hardware, so do not place your devices in direct sunlight or in a dusty area. You can periodically use a small handheld vacuum made for electrical equipment to remove the dust from the keyboard, from inside the system unit of a computer, and from the fan vents, but be very careful when vacuuming inside the system unit. Also, be sure the system unit has plenty of ventilation, especially around the fan vents, and avoid placing a portable computer on a soft surface, such as a couch or a bed, to help prevent overheating. Unless your computer is ruggedized, do not get it wet or otherwise expose it to adverse conditions. Be especially careful with smartphones and other mobile devices when you are near water (such as a swimming pool, lake, or large puddle) so you do not drop them into the water.

Both internal and external magnetic hard drives also need to be protected against jostling or other excess motion that can result in a head crash. Unless your portable computer contains a solid-state drive instead of a magnetic hard drive, it is a good idea to turn off the computer or hibernate it before moving it. In addition, don't remove a USB storage device (such as a USB flash drive or USB hard drive) when it is being accessed; instead, use the *Safely Remove Hardware and Eject Media* icon in the system tray on a Windows computer first. Be sure to also keep DVDs in their protective *jewel cases* and handle them carefully to prevent fingerprints and scratches.

### Backups and Disaster Recovery Plans

As discussed and illustrated in Chapter 5, creating a backup means making a duplicate copy of important files so you can restore those files if needed. Businesses should make backups of at least all new data on a regular basis (at least once per day) and include data located on both company computers and employer-issued smartphones, unless those

> **TIP**
>
> Be sure backup generators and servers are located in an appropriate location; for example, they should not be in a basement or in any locations prone to flooding. As an extra precaution, consider moving primary servers to or using backup servers or cloud backup services in regions of the country that don't have the same risk factors as the company's location.

devices are synched to the cloud. Individuals should make backups of important documents as they are created and back up the rest of their data periodically. Businesses and individuals that utilize cloud computing should also back up important data stored online. Backup media needs to be secured (such as in a fire-resistant safe, online, or off site) and sensitive data should be encrypted.

For an even higher level of security than a scheduled backup, *continuous data protection* (*CDP*) can be used. A CDP backup system backs up data in real time as it changes so that data can be recovered from any point in time with no data loss. Although expensive when used with large quantities of data, it is one of the best ways to ensure that company data is protected.

To supplement backup procedures, businesses and other organizations should have a **disaster recovery plan** (also called a *business continuity plan*)—a plan that spells out what the organization will do to prepare for and recover from a disruptive event, such as a fire, natural disaster, terrorist attack, or computer failure. Disaster recovery plans should include information about who will be in charge immediately after the disaster has occurred, what alternate facilities and equipment can be used, where backup media is located, the priority of getting each operation back online, disaster insurance coverage information, emergency communications methods, and so forth. Traditionally, alternate locations (called *hot sites*) equipped with the computers, cabling, desks, and other equipment necessary to keep a business's operations going were used so businesses could resume business operations immediately after a disaster. Today, alternate office space (sometimes called *cold sites*) that can be used following a disaster but that require the business to provide the needed computers and other necessary equipment are often used instead of hot sites to provide disaster recovery at a lower cost. In either case, *cloud data recovery services* are often used to provide the alternative location with copies of backed up data when a disaster occurs. Regardless of the type of alternative site, the location and resources to be used should be set up ahead of time and coordinated with the backup service if one is being used, and location and access information should be included in the disaster recovery plan. Businesses that host their e-mail on site should also consider making arrangements with an *emergency mail system provider* to act as a temporary mail server if the company mail server is not functioning. Copies of the disaster recovery plan should be located off site.

## ASK THE EXPERT

*Courtesy DriveSavers Data Recovery*

**Mike Cobb,** Director of Engineering, DriveSavers Data Recovery

**Of the hard drives sent to you for recovery, what is the most common type of problem you see and is there a way that problem can be prevented?**

We often receive hard drives that have severe media damage. That means that the read/write heads have come in contact with the platters and scraped off portions of the surface and data. This often occurs because the hard drive was left powered on after the problem occurred. The platters inside a drive spin at high speed, so a great deal of damage can occur in a very short period of time as the heads bounce around and create more debris. Eventually the damage becomes too great for even a professional data recovery company to overcome.

The best rule of thumb to prevent the loss of critical data is to back up religiously and to verify that the backup is really backing up the critical files. In addition, if a hard drive exhibits any sign of failure including unusual noises (such as repetitive clicking or grinding) and if the data is irreplaceable and has not been backed up recently, the best solution is to immediately shut down the computer and then seek the assistance of a professional data recovery company like DriveSavers.

**(o) NET**

**TIP** ✓

Be sure to also back up important nonelectronic documents in your life, such as birth certificates, tax returns, passports, and so forth, by making copies of them and storing the copies in a safe place.

> **Disaster recovery plan.** A written plan that describes the steps a company will take following the occurrence of a disaster.

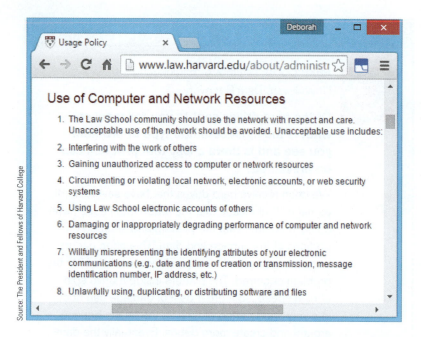

Source: The President and Fellows of Harvard College

**Use of Computer and Network Resources**

1. The Law School community should use the network with respect and care. Unacceptable use of the network should be avoided. Unacceptable use includes:

2. Interfering with the work of others

3. Gaining unauthorized access to computer or network resources

4. Circumventing or violating local network, electronic accounts, or web security systems

5. Using Law School electronic accounts of others

6. Damaging or inappropriately degrading performance of computer and network resources

7. Willfully misrepresenting the identifying attributes of your electronic communications (e.g., date and time of creation or transmission, message identification number, IP address, etc.)

8. Unlawfully using, duplicating, or distributing software and files

**FIGURE 9-6**
A sample code of conduct.

**TIP**

According to a recent IBM report, the total cost per data breach in the United States is $6.5 million—the highest of any country.

# UNAUTHORIZED ACCESS AND UNAUTHORIZED USE

**Unauthorized access** occurs whenever an individual gains access to a computer, network, file, or other computing resource without permission. **Unauthorized use** involves using a computing resource for unauthorized activities, even if the user is authorized to access that resource. For example, while a student may be authorized to access the Internet via a campus computer lab, some use—such as viewing pornography—would likely be deemed off-limits and, consequently, viewed as unauthorized use. For some companies, employees checking personal e-mail or visiting personal Facebook pages using work resources might be classified as unauthorized use.

Unauthorized access and many types of unauthorized use are criminal offenses in the United States and many other countries. They can be committed by both *insiders* (people who work for the company whose computers are being accessed) and *outsiders* (people who do not work for that company). To explain acceptable computer use to their employees, students, or other users, many organizations and educational institutions publish guidelines for behavior, often called *codes of conduct* or *acceptable use policies* (see the Harvard Law School example in Figure 9-6).

## Hacking

**Hacking** refers to the act of breaking into a computer or network. It can be performed in person if the *hacker* has physical access to the computer or network being hacked, but it is more often performed via the Internet or another network.

Typically, the motivation for hacking is to steal data, sabotage a computer system, or perform some other type of illegal act. In particular, the theft of consumer data (such as credit card numbers) has increased dramatically over the past several years. Some of the most notable recent breaches include the Target data breach in which 40 million debit and credit card numbers were stolen, the Goodwill data breach in which nearly 900,000 credit and debit cards were compromised, and two separate Home Depot data breaches where 56 million credit and debit cards and 53 million e-mail addresses, respectively, were stolen. Hackers are also increasingly aiming attacks at very specific individuals, such as product designers and other individuals who have access to valuable corporate data.

In addition to being a threat to individuals and businesses, hacking is also considered a very serious threat to national security in the United States. The increased number of systems that are controlled by computers and are connected to the Internet, along with the continually improving abilities of hackers, has led to an increased risk of *cyberterrorism*—where terrorists launch attacks via the Internet. Current concerns include attacks by individual terrorists, as well as by other countries, against the computers controlling vital systems (such as the nation's power grids, banks, and water filtration facilities), as well as computers related to national defense, the airlines, and the stock market.

>**Unauthorized access.** Gaining access to a computer, network, file, or other computing resource without permission. >**Unauthorized use.** Using a computing resource for unapproved activities. >**Hacking.** Using a computer to break into a computing resource.

Hackers often gain access via a wireless network because wireless networks are widely used and they are easier to hack into than wired networks. As discussed in Chapter 7, it is possible to gain access to a wireless network just by being within range of a wireless access point, unless the access point is sufficiently protected. Although security features are built into wireless routers and other networking hardware, they are typically not enabled by default. As a result, many wireless networks belonging to businesses and individuals are left unsecured. Securing a Wi-Fi network is discussed shortly.

## War Driving and Wi-Fi Piggybacking

Some Wi-Fi hotspots are intended to be used by the public. To help locate public Wi-Fi hotspots, a number of services are available, such as browser-based mapping applications and smartphone apps that identify free and fee-based hotspots for a specific geographical location (see the *Wi-Fi Finder* app in Figure 9-7). Mobile apps have the advantage of automatically determining your geographical location to display information about hotspots in your current geographical area.

Using a private but unsecured Wi-Fi network without authorization, however, is called **war driving** or **Wi-Fi piggybacking**, depending on the location of the hacker at the time (driving in a car or from the hacker's current location, respectively). Both war driving and Wi-Fi piggybacking are ethically—if not legally—questionable acts. In some countries, such as the UK, the laws are clear that unauthorized access of a Wi-Fi connection is illegal. In the United States, federal law is not as clear, although some states (such as Michigan) have made using a Wi-Fi connection without permission illegal. War driving and Wi-Fi piggybacking can also lead to illegal behavior, such as individuals deciding to use credit card numbers or other data they uncover for fraudulent purposes.

Advocates of war driving and Wi-Fi piggybacking state that, unless individuals or businesses protect their access points, they are welcoming others to use them. Critics compare that logic to that of an unlocked front door—you cannot legally enter a home just because the front door is unlocked.

## Interception of Communications

Instead of hacking into a computer or network, some criminals gain unauthorized access to data, files, messages, and other content as it is being sent over the Internet. For instance, unencrypted messages, files, logon information, and more sent over a wireless network (such as while using a public Wi-Fi hotspot or over an unsecured home or business Wi-Fi network) can be captured and read by anyone within range using software designed for that purpose. In addition, the data on mobile devices with Bluetooth capabilities enabled can be accessed by other Bluetooth devices that are within range and any sensitive data stored on a smartphone can be accessed by a hacker if the phone is connected to an unsecured Wi-Fi network. With an increasing number of smartphone owners storing sensitive data (such as passwords for online banking and social media, and credit card account numbers) on their devices, the risk of that data being intercepted is increasing.

Another way criminals can intercept credit and debit card information is during the card verification process; that is, intercepting the data from a card in real time as a purchase is being authorized. Often, this occurs via *packet sniffing* software installed by hackers at payment terminals (such as restaurant cash registers or gas station credit/debit card readers)—the packet sniffing software gathers credit card data during transactions and then sends it to the hacker.

**NET**

**A FIGURE 9-7**

**Wi-Fi finders.** Online mapping services and smartphone apps can show you the available Wi-Fi hotspots for a particular geographic area.

---

>**War driving.** Driving around an area with a Wi-Fi-enabled device to find a Wi-Fi network in order to access and use it without authorization.
>**Wi-Fi piggybacking.** Accessing an unsecured Wi-Fi network from your current location without authorization.

**TIP**

To prevent a hacker from obtaining your logon information from an unused online account during a data breach, delete your old accounts if you are no longer using them.

## Protecting Against Unauthorized Access and Unauthorized Use

To protect against unauthorized access and unauthorized use of a computer system, the first step is to control access to an organization's facilities and computer networks in order to ensure that only authorized individuals are granted access. In addition, steps need to be taken to ensure that authorized individuals access only the resources that they are supposed to access.

### Access Control Systems

*Access control systems* are used to control access to facilities, devices, computer networks, company databases, Web site accounts, and other assets. They can be *identification systems*, which verify that the person trying to access the facility or system is listed as an authorized user, and/or *authentication systems*, which determine whether or not the person attempting access is actually who he or she claims to be. In businesses, access control systems are often integrated into a comprehensive *identity management (IDM) system* designed to manage users' access to enterprise systems, such as to grant them secure and appropriate access to the systems they are allowed to access in as convenient a manner as possible. The most common types of access control systems are discussed next.

#### Possessed Knowledge Access Systems

A **possessed knowledge access system** is an identification system that requires the individual requesting access to provide information that only the authorized user is supposed to know. **Passwords**, the most common type of possessed knowledge, are secret words or character combinations associated with an individual. They are typically used in conjunction with a *username* (often a variation of the person's first and/or last names or the individual's e-mail address). Username/password combinations are often used to restrict access to networks, computers, Web sites, routers, and other computing resources—the user is granted access only after supplying the correct information. Passwords are sometimes also called *passphrases*; numeric passwords are often called *PINs* (*personal identification numbers*) or *passcodes*. One of the biggest disadvantages of password-based systems is that any individual possessing the proper password will be granted access to the system because the system recognizes the password. Another disadvantage is that passwords can be guessed or deciphered by a hacker or a hacker's computer easily unless *strong password* strategies are used. Figure 9-8 shows some tips for creating strong passwords.

**FIGURE 9-8** Strategies for creating strong passwords.

| PASSWORD STRATEGIES |
| --- |
| Make the password at least eight characters and include both uppercase and lowercase letters, as well as numbers and special symbols. |
| Choose passwords that are not in a dictionary—for instance, mix numbers and special characters with abbreviations or unusual words you will remember but that do not conform to a pattern a computer can readily figure out. |
| Do not use your name, your kids' or pets' names, your address, your birthdate, or any other public information as your password. |
| Determine a *passphrase* that you can remember and use corresponding letters and symbols (such as the first letter of each word) for your password. For instance, the passphrase "My son John is five years older than my daughter Abby" could be used to remember the corresponding strong password "Msji5yotMd@". |
| Develop a system using a basic password for all Web sites plus site-specific information (such as the first two letters of the site and a number you will remember) to create a different password for each site, but still ones you can easily remember. For instance, you can combine your dog's name with the site initials followed by a number that is significant to you to form a password such as "RoverAM27" for Amazon.com. |
| Do not keep a written copy of the password in your desk or taped to your monitor. If you need to write down your password, create a password-protected file on your computer that contains all your passwords or use a password manager program. |
| Use a different password for your highly sensitive activities (such as online banking or stock trading) than for other Web sites. If a hacker determines your password on a low-security site (which is easier to break into), he or she can use it on an account containing sensitive data if you use the same password on both accounts. |
| Change your passwords frequently—at least every 6 months. |

>**Possessed knowledge access system.** An access control system that uses information only an individual should know to identify that individual.
>**Password.** A secret combination of characters used to gain access to a computing device, network, Web site, or other resource.

When selecting answers to the personal questions used for password recovery on Web sites, don't supply answers that a hacker may be able to guess based on information found on your Facebook page or other online source. Instead, supply answers that you can remember but that also follow strong password rules. For instance, if your birthplace is San Carlos, you could enter *$@n_C@rl0$* as the answer to that question.

**FIGURE 9-9**
**Possessed objects.**
Can grant access to both facilities and computing resources.

Source: HID Global Corporation

## Possessed Object Access Systems

**Possessed object access systems** use physical objects for identification purposes and are frequently used to control access to facilities and computer systems. Common types of possessed objects are smart cards, RFID-encoded badges, magnetic cards, *USB security tokens*, and smartphones that are swiped through or placed close to a reader to be read (see Figure 9-9). One disadvantage of using possessed objects is that they can be lost or, like passwords, can be used by an unauthorized individual if that individual has possession of the object.

## Biometric Access Systems

**Biometric access systems** identify users by a particular *biometric* characteristic—a measurable, unique physical characteristic. Most biometric systems use the individual's fingerprint, hand, face, or iris, although other personal characteristics (such as the individual's voice, signature, or gait) can also be used. Because the means of access (usually a part of the body) cannot typically be used by anyone other than the authorized individual, biometric access systems can perform both identification and authentication. They are often used to control access to secure facilities (such as corporate headquarters and prisons); to log users on to computers, networks, and secure Web sites (by using a reader or camera connected to or built into the device being accessed); to punch employees in and out of work; and to confirm individuals' identities at ATM machines, government agencies, and law enforcement or military checkpoints. Biometric readers are also often built into smartphones so they can be used to unlock the smartphone, as well as to authorize transactions.

**FIGURE 9-10**
**Biometric access and identification systems.**

To identify and authenticate an individual, biometric access systems typically use a *biometric reader* (such as a *fingerprint reader* or a *hand geometry reader*) or a digital camera, depending on the biometric characteristic being measured, in conjunction with software and a database. The system matches the supplied biometric data with the biometric data that was stored in the database when the individual was enrolled in the system and authenticates the individual if the data matches. To speed up the process, many biometric access systems require users to identify themselves first (such as by entering a username or swiping a smart card), and then the system uses that identifying information to verify that the supplied biometric data matches the identified person. Examples of biometric access systems are shown in Figure 9-10.

Source: HID Global Corporation

**FINGERPRINT READERS**
Typically used to protect access to work facilities or computers, to log on to secure Web sites, for law enforcement identification, and to pay for products or services.

Source: Sensible Vision, Inc.;
Roman Samokhin/Shutterstock.com

**FACE RECOGNITION SYSTEMS**
Typically used to control access to highly secure areas, to identify individuals for law enforcement purposes, and to log on to devices or apps, as shown here.

> **Possessed object access system.** An access control system that uses a physical object an individual has in his or her possession to identify that individual. > **Biometric access system.** An access control system that uses one unique physical characteristic of an individual (such as a fingerprint, a face, veins, or a voice) to identify and authenticate that individual.

**1.** When you log on from an unrecognized device, an OTP is sent to your smartphone.

**2.** Enter that code here to log on.

Source: Facebook

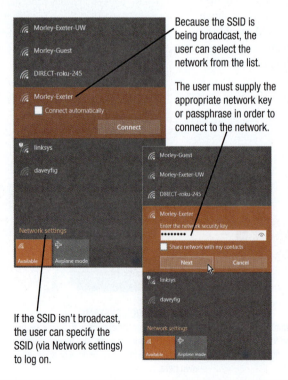

⚠ **FIGURE 9-11**
Facebook two-factor authentication.

⚠ **FIGURE 9-12**
Accessing a Wi-Fi network.

Because the SSID is being broadcast, the user can select the network from the list.

The user must supply the appropriate network key or passphrase in order to connect to the network.

If the SSID isn't broadcast, the user can specify the SSID (via Network settings) to log on.

One advantage of using a biometric access system is its very high accuracy (even identical twins who have the same DNA structure have different fingerprints and irises). In addition, biometric characteristics cannot be forgotten (like a password), cannot be lost and do not have to be pulled out of a briefcase or pocket (like an access card or other type of possessed object), and cannot be used by a hacker. The primary disadvantages of biometric access systems are that the hardware and software required are more expensive than for other types of access systems and that the data used for authentication (such as a fingerprint or an iris image) cannot be reset if it is compromised.

### Two-Factor Authentication

For increased security, **two-factor authentication** (using two different methods to authenticate a user) can be used. Two-factor authentication adds an additional level of security to an access control system because hackers are much less likely to be able to gain access to two different required factors. Two-factor authentication often uses a conventional username/password combination in conjunction with a possessed object or biometric characteristic. Often the possessed object is something you already carry with you (such as a smartphone or credit card) that generates a *one-time password* (*OTP*) via a mobile app, text message, or by pressing a button on a credit card. The OTP must be entered in conjunction with your username/password in order to log on to the account.

The use of two-factor authentication systems is growing. For instance, many banks offer two-factor authentication for online and mobile banking, and it is an option for Google, Twitter, and Facebook users. In Facebook, for example, once two-factor authentication (called *Login Approvals*) is enabled, you will see the security code screen shown in Figure 9-11 whenever you log in with your Facebook logon information using a new browser or device; you will need to enter the OTP sent to your smartphone before you will be logged into your Facebook account.

### Controlling Access to Wireless Networks

It is also important to protect against unauthorized access of wireless networks. The most important precaution is to secure network routers. Wi-Fi security standards include *WEP* (*Wired Equivalent Privacy*), which is now considered an inadequate level of security, and the more secure *WPA* (*Wi-Fi Protected Access*) and *WPA2* standards. To protect against unauthorized access, Wi-Fi network owners should secure their networks using WPA or WPA2. At the time the network is secured, a *network security key* or passphrase is specified; that network security key or passphrase must be supplied in order to access the network (see Figure 9-12). In addition, the name of the network (called the *SSID*) can be hidden from view by switching off the SSID broadcast feature so that neighbors or casual war drivers will not see the network. Once a network is secured, users who want to connect to that network need to either select or supply the network SSID name (depending on whether or not the SSID is being broadcast) and then enter the network security key or passphrase assigned to that network (refer again to Figure 9-12). The steps for securing a wireless router are discussed in more detail in the How It Works box.

> **Two-factor authentication.** Using two different methods to authenticate a user.

## Firewalls

A **firewall** is a security system that essentially creates a barrier between a computer or a network and the Internet in order to protect against unauthorized access. Firewalls are typically two-way, so they check all incoming (from the Internet) and outgoing (to the Internet) traffic and allow only authorized traffic to pass through the firewall. *Personal firewalls* are software programs designed to protect personal computers from hackers attempting to access those computers through their Internet connections. Personal firewalls can be stand-alone programs (such as the free *Comodo Firewall* program shown in Figure 9-13); they are also built into many operating systems (such as the *Windows Firewall* program). Many routers, modems, and other pieces of networking hardware also include built-in firewall capabilities to help secure the networks these devices are used with.

**FIREWALL ALERTS**
You are notified when a new program requests access.

**FIREWALL SETTINGS**
You can specify settings for individual programs if desired.

Source: Comodo Group, Inc.

**FIGURE 9-13**
**A personal firewall.**

Firewalls designed to protect business networks can be software-based, hardware-based, or a combination of the two, and they can be used to prevent network access by hackers and other outsiders, as well as to control employee Internet access.

Firewalls work by closing down all external communications to unauthorized computers and programs. While business firewalls are set up by the network administrator and those settings typically cannot be changed by end users, individuals may choose to change the settings for their personal firewall. For example, you can choose to be notified when any application program on the computer is trying to access the Internet, to specify the programs that are allowed to access the Internet, or to block all incoming connections temporarily. In addition to protecting your computer from outside access, firewall programs also protect against any spyware or other malicious programs located on your computer that are designed to send data from your computer to a hacker at the hacker's request.

A related type of security system increasingly being used by businesses today and included in many security suites is an *intrusion prevention system* (*IPS*). Whereas a firewall tries to block unauthorized traffic, an IPS continuously monitors and analyzes incoming and outgoing traffic to try to detect possible attacks as they are occurring. If an attack is in progress, IPS software can immediately block it.

> **TIP**
>
> If a legitimate application installed on your computer needs to access the Internet but cannot, check your firewall settings—you may need to unblock that program.

## Encryption

As previously discussed, encryption is used to make data unreadable to unauthorized individuals. Encryption temporarily converts data into a form, known as a cipher, which is unreadable until it is *decrypted* (unscrambled). Encryption is used with secure Wi-Fi networks and VPNs (discussed in Chapter 7) to secure data that is transferred over those networks. Encryption is also used with secure Web pages and can be used to secure files. The most common security protocol used with **secure Web pages** is *Transport Layer Security* (*TLS*), though this protocol is still commonly referred to by the name of its predecessor *Secure Sockets Layer* (*SSL*). The URL for Web pages using TPS/SSL begins with *https:* instead of *http:*.

As previously discussed, self-encrypting hard drives automatically encrypt all content stored on those drives. Encryption can also be added to individual files stored on a hard drive or other storage medium so those files will be unreadable if opened by an

> **TIP**
>
> The U.S. government has mandated that all public government Web sites use secure Web pages by the end of 2016 in order to protect the data sent back and forth via government sites.

> **Firewall.** A collection of hardware and/or software intended to protect a computer or computer network from unauthorized access.
> **Secure Web page.** A Web page that uses encryption in order to protect information transmitted via that Web page.

# HOW IT WORKS

## Securing a Wireless Home Router

Securing a home wireless network prevents unauthorized individuals from using it. Security settings are specified on the router's configuration screen, such as the one shown here. To open this screen, type the IP address assigned to your router (such as 192.168.0.1—check your router's documentation for its default IP address and username) in your browser's Address bar. Use the default password to log on the first time, and then, using the configuration screen, change the password to prevent unauthorized individuals from changing your router settings. To secure the router, enter the network name (SSID) you want to have associated with the router, select the appropriate security mode (such as WPA or WPA2) to be used, and then type a secure passphrase to be used in order to log on to the network.

For additional security, you can disable SSID broadcast to hide your router name from view or use *MAC* (*Media Access Control*) *address filtering* to specify only the devices (via their MAC addresses) that are allowed to access the network. Other precautions include designating specific times (such as when you are away from home) that the router will deny access to any device and reducing the strength of the wireless signal if its current strength reaches farther than you need.

Use the router's IP address to display the router's configuration screen.

Use this tab to enable MAC address filtering.

Use this tab to change the administrator password used to access this configuration screen.

Type your desired SSID here.

Disable SSID broadcast here.

Select the desired security mode here.

Type your desired network key here.

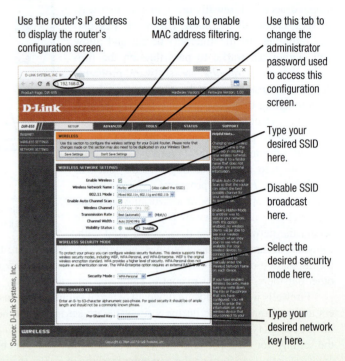

Source: D-Link Systems, Inc.

**Configuring a home router.**

---

unauthorized person. In addition, encryption can be added manually to a file or an e-mail message before it is sent over the Internet to ensure that the content is unreadable if the file or message is intercepted during transit. The two most common types of encryption in use today are private key encryption (most often used to encrypt files or the content of a hard drive or other device) and public key encryption (often used with content being transmitted over the Internet, such as via secure Web pages and encrypted e-mail).

**Private key encryption**, also called *symmetric key encryption*, uses a single secret *private key* (essentially a password) to both encrypt and decrypt the file or message. Consequently, if private key encryption is used to send files securely to others, the recipients must know the private key. Private key encryption is supported by a variety of programs today, including Microsoft Office and Adobe Acrobat; it is also used by some *Web-based encrypted e-mail services* (such as the free *Lockbin* service).

**Public key encryption**, also called *asymmetric key encryption*, utilizes a pair of encryption keys (one private key and one *public key*) obtained through a *Certificate Authority*, such as Verisign or Thawte, to encrypt and decrypt documents. These two keys are related mathematically to each other and are assigned to a particular individual. An individual's public key is not secret and is available for anyone to use, but the corresponding private key is secret and is used only by the individual to whom it was assigned. The recipient's public key is used to

---

> **Private key encryption.** A type of encryption that uses a single key to encrypt and decrypt the file or message. > **Public key encryption.** A type of encryption that uses key pairs to encrypt and decrypt the file or message.

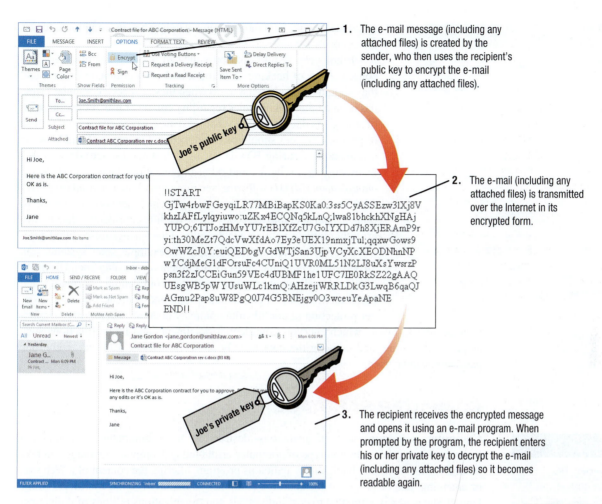

1. The e-mail message (including any attached files) is created by the sender, who then uses the recipient's public key to encrypt the e-mail (including any attached files).

2. The e-mail (including any attached files) is transmitted over the Internet in its encrypted form.

3. The recipient receives the encrypted message and opens it using an e-mail program. When prompted by the program, the recipient enters his or her private key to decrypt the e-mail (including any attached files) so it becomes readable again.

**FIGURE 9-14**
Using public key encryption to secure an e-mail message in Microsoft Outlook.

encrypt a file or an email message; the recipient's private key is used to decrypt the encrypted contents (see Figure 9-14 for an example of sending an encrypted email).

There are various strengths of encryption available; the stronger the encryption, the more difficult it is to crack. Older 40-bit encryption (which can only use keys that are 40 bits or 5 characters long) is considered *weak encryption* and is no longer supported by Windows and other applications. Stronger encryption includes *strong 128-bit encryption* (which uses 16-character keys) and *military-strength 2,048-bit encryption* (which uses 256-character keys), although not without some objections from law enforcement agencies and the government because they state that terrorists routinely use encryption methods to communicate.

## Additional Precautions

Additional precautions can be used to avoid data (both on devices and sent over the Internet) from being compromised while using a public Wi-Fi hotspot. For example, in addition to using a firewall, VPN, and encryption, individuals should turn off automatic Wi-Fi connections to prevent being automatically connected to a hotspot, pay attention to the names of the available hotspots displayed to make sure they connect to a legitimate access point (not an *evil twin* masquerading as a legitimate hotspot), disable *ad hoc* connections to prevent another device from connecting to their device, and turn off file sharing and Bluetooth.

Employers should also take additional precautions to avoid intentional and accidental security breaches by employees. To begin with, the background of all potential employees should be investigated to verify qualifications and experience and to uncover any criminal activity. Access for each employee should be limited to only the resources needed for his or her job (referred to as the *Principle of Least Privilege*) and the company should monitor for any attempts to access off-limit resources. In addition, all access to the system for an

Source: Airwatch

**FIGURE 9-15**
**Mobile device management (MDM) software.** Secures and manages the mobile devices used in an organization.

✓ **TIP**

According to a recent IDC survey, more than 90% of U.S.-based companies had employee-owned devices that were accessing corporate data.

individual should be removed immediately when that employee leaves the company for any reason.

Employees should also be educated about the seriousness and consequences of hacking, data theft, and other computer crimes, and they should be taught what to do when they suspect a computer crime has been committed. Policies regarding computer use, proper disposal of storage media containing sensitive data, encryption use, and the use of personal devices should be developed and enforced. To address the challenge of securing BYOD (Bring Your Own Device) devices that many business, schools, and other organizations face, *mobile device management (MDM) software* (see Figure 9-15) can be used to specify what personal devices can be used with which network resources. To protect against employees copying or sending confidential data to others either intentionally or accidentally, *data-leakage* (also called *data-loss*) *prevention systems* can be used. For example, some systems scan all outgoing communications for documents containing Social Security numbers, intellectual property, and other confidential information and block them if they might contain prohibited content. For even stronger protection of confidential company documents, *enterprise rights-management software*, which encrypts confidential documents and limits functions such as printing, editing, and copying the data to only authorized users with the appropriate password, can be used.

## COMPUTER SABOTAGE

**Computer sabotage**—acts of malicious destruction to a computer or computing resource—is another common type of computer crime today. Computer sabotage can take several forms, including launching a malicious program, altering the content of a Web site, or changing data or programs located on a computer. Computer sabotage is illegal in the United States and is estimated to cost individuals and organizations billions of dollars per year, primarily for labor costs related to correcting the problems caused by the sabotage, lost productivity, and lost sales.

### Botnets

A computer that is controlled by a hacker or other computer criminal is referred to as a **bot**; a group of bots that are controlled by one individual and can work together in a coordinated fashion is called a **botnet**. Today, millions of U.S. computers are unknowingly part of a botnet. Criminals (called *botherders*) create botnets to perform computer sabotage, as well as to steal personal data to be used in an illegal manner.

### Computer Viruses and Other Types of Malware

**Malware** is a generic term that refers to any type of malicious software. Malware programs are intentionally written to perform destructive acts, such as damaging programs, deleting files, erasing hard drives, or slowing down the performance of computers. This damage can take place immediately after a device is *infected* (that is, the malware software is installed) or it can begin when a particular condition is met. A malware program that activates when it detects a certain condition, such as when a particular keystroke is pressed or an employee's name is deleted from an employee file, is called a *logic bomb*. A logic bomb that is triggered by a particular date or time is called a *time bomb*. Malware can infect any device—including personal computers, smartphones, tablets, and printers—that contain computer hardware and software.

Writing malware or even posting malware code on the Internet is not illegal, but it is considered highly unethical and irresponsible behavior. Distributing malware, on the other hand, is illegal, and virus writers who release their malware are being vigorously prosecuted. Malware can be very costly in terms of the labor costs associated with removing the viruses and correcting any resulting damage, as well as the cost of lost productivity of employees. One type of malware often used by computer criminals to send sensitive data secretly from infected computers to the criminal—spyware—was discussed in Chapter 8. The most common other types of malware are discussed next.

## Computer Viruses

A **computer virus** is a software program that is installed without the permission or knowledge of the computer user, is designed to alter the way a computer operates, and can replicate itself to infect any new media it has access to. Computer viruses are often embedded into program or data files (such as software, games, videos, and music files downloaded from Web pages or shared via a P2P service). They are spread whenever the infected file is downloaded, is transferred to a new device via an infected removable storage medium, or is e-mailed to another device (see Figure 9-16). Viruses can also be installed when a recipient clicks a link in a message or loads a Web page that contains a malicious advertisement that

**FIGURE 9-16**
How a computer virus or other type of malicious software might spread.

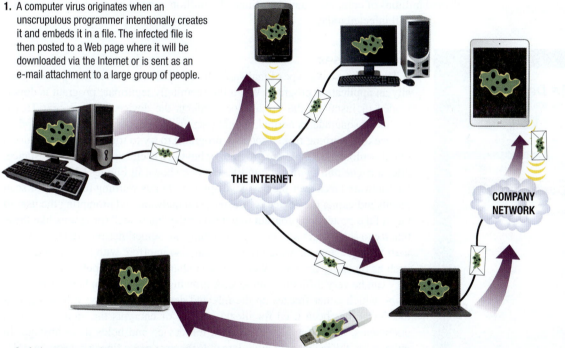

1. A computer virus originates when an unscrupulous programmer intentionally creates it and embeds it in a file. The infected file is then posted to a Web page where it will be downloaded via the Internet or is sent as an e-mail attachment to a large group of people.

3. A virus can spread very quickly because every device that comes in contact with the virus—whether through an infected removable storage medium, infected downloaded file, or infected e-mail attachment—becomes infected, unless antivirus software is used to prevent it.

2. When the infected file is opened, the virus copies itself to that device's hard drive and the device is infected. The virus may then e-mail itself to people in the newly infected device's e-mail address book or copy itself to any removable storage medium inserted into that device.

THE INTERNET

COMPANY NETWORK

>**Computer virus.** A software program installed without the user's knowledge and designed to alter the way a computer operates or to cause harm to the computer system.

installs malware. Viruses have even been found embedded in photos of bogus Craigslist items sent to potential buyers. Regardless of how it is obtained, once a copy of the infected file reaches a new device, the virus embeds itself into program, data, or system files on the new device and remains there, affecting that device according to its programmed instructions, until it is discovered and removed.

## Computer Worms

A **computer worm** is another common form of malware. A worm is designed to cause damage by creating copies of its code and sending those copies to other devices via a network. Although worms can be sent via an e-mail attachment and launched when the attachment is open, typically worms do not require any user action to infect the user's device. Instead, a worm scans the Internet looking for computers and other devices that are vulnerable to that particular worm and sends a copy of itself to those devices to infect them. Some worms are specifically written to take advantage of newly discovered *security holes* (vulnerabilities) in operating systems and e-mail programs before the *security patch* to correct that vulnerability is available; these types of attacks are called *zero-day attacks*. Unfortunately, the use of zero-day attacks is growing rapidly and the time required to release security patches to correct security holes is increasing. For example, a record 24 zero-day attacks were discovered in 2014 and it took 204 days, 22 days, and 53 days, respectively, to provide patches for the three most exploited vulnerabilities.

Because of its distribution method, a worm can spread very rapidly and be very persistent. For example, the *Conficker* worm (which was originally released in 2008) quickly infected millions of computers and an estimated 1 million computers around the world are still infected today.

## Trojan Horses

A **Trojan horse** is a type of malware that masquerades as something else—usually an application program. When the seemingly legitimate program is downloaded or installed, the Trojan horse infects the device. Many recent Trojan horses masquerade as normal ongoing activities (such as the Windows Update service or a warning from a security program) to try to trick unsuspecting users into downloading a malware program or buying a useless program. For instance, after a *rogue anti-malware app* like the one shown in Figure 9-17 is installed, the malware takes over the device, displaying bogus warning messages or scan results indicating the device is infected with malware and prompting the user to buy a fake protection program to get rid of the "malware" (programs like these that try to scare users into buying something are sometimes referred to as *scareware*). Rogue anti-malware programs can also interfere with normal activities, such as blocking access to Web sites and changing the computer settings, and they can be very difficult to remove. A growing type of Trojan horse is *ransomware*, which either freezes up the infected device and displays a message that the device has been used for illegal activity or encrypts the victim's photos, documents, and other files located on the device and holds them hostage. In either case, the malware creator demands the user pay a fine or ransom in order to unlock the device or decrypt the files. Still other Trojan horses are spyware designed to find sensitive information about an individual or a company located on infected computers and then send that information to the malware creator.

Unlike viruses and worms, Trojan horses cannot replicate themselves. Trojan horses are usually spread by being downloaded from the Internet, though

**FIGURE 9-17**

**Rogue anti-malware apps.** Try to trick victims into purchasing subscriptions to remove nonexistent malware supposedly installed on their devices.

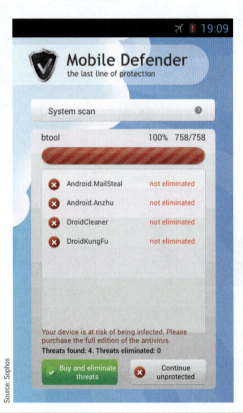

Source: Sophos

>**Computer worm.** A malicious program designed to spread rapidly to a large number of computers by sending copies of itself to other computers.
>**Trojan horse.** A malicious program that masquerades as something else.

they may also be sent as an e-mail attachment, either from the Trojan horse author or from individuals who forward it, not realizing the program is a Trojan horse.

## Mobile Malware

Malware is increasingly targeting mobile devices, such as smartphones and tablets. In fact, Symantec Corporation recently found that about 17% of all Android apps (nearly one million total) were actually malware in disguise. The primary goal of the majority of mobile malware is to try to obtain the mobile banking credentials stored on or entered via a mobile device.

## Denial of Service (DoS) Attacks

A **denial of service (DoS) attack** is an act of sabotage that attempts to flood a network server or Web server with so many requests for action that it shuts down or simply can no longer handle requests, causing legitimate users to be denied service. If enough useless traffic is generated, the server has no resources left to deal with legitimate requests, as illustrated in Figure 9-18).

DoS attacks today are often directed toward popular or controversial sites and are typically carried out via multiple computers (referred to as a *distributed denial of service attack* or *DDoS attack*). DDoS attacks are typically performed by botnets created by hackers; the computers in the botnet participate in the attacks without the owners' knowledge. Denial of service attacks can be very costly in terms of business lost (such as when an e-commerce site is shut down), as well as the time and expense required to bring the site back online.

### ASK THE EXPERT

**James Nguyen,** Norton by Symantec

**Does a smartphone need virus protection?**

Contrary to popular belief, smartphones are prone to attacks and have OS flaws. Because of this, attackers have developed strategies to steal or compromise the personal data stored on smart devices. Consequently, it is increasingly important to use mobile security software to secure your smartphone against malware, phishing scams, and intrusive ads, as well as to prevent you from downloading unsafe apps or clicking on dangerous links. In addition, you should set up a screen lock passcode and enable tracking software so a lost or stolen device can be locked and located.

### TIP
The largest DDoS attack so far generated a staggering 400 Gbps of traffic.

**FIGURE 9-18**
**How a denial of service (DoS) attack might work.**

1. Hacker's computer sends several simultaneous requests; each request asks to establish a connection to the server but supplies false return information. In a distributed DoS attack, multiple computers send multiple requests at one time.
**Hello? I'd like some info...**

2. The server tries to respond to each request but can't locate the computer because false return information was provided. The server waits for a short period of time before closing the connection, which ties up the server and keeps others from connecting.
**I can't find you, I'll wait and try again...**

3. The hacker's computer continues to send new requests so, as a connection is closed by the server, a new request is waiting. This cycle continues, which ties up the server indefinitely.
**Hello? I'd like some info...**

**Hello? I'd like some info...**

**I'm busy, I can't help you right now.**

4. The server becomes so overwhelmed that legitimate requests cannot get through and, eventually, the server usually crashes.

**HACKER'S COMPUTER**

**WEB SERVER**

**LEGITIMATE COMPUTER**

> **Denial of service (DoS) attack.** An act of sabotage that attempts to flood a network server or a Web server with so much activity that it is unable to function.

## Data, Program, or Web Site Alteration

Another type of computer sabotage occurs when a hacker breaches a computer system in order to delete data, change data, modify programs, or otherwise alter the data and programs located there. For example, a student might try to hack into a school database to change his or her grade or a hacker might change a program located on a company server in order to steal money or information.

Data on Web sites can also be altered by hackers. For instance, social media accounts are increasingly being targeted by hackers. In 2013, for instance, the Associated Press Twitter account was hacked and used to tweet that the president had been injured by explosions at the White House—the stock market tumbled in response. It is also becoming more common for hackers to compromise legitimate Web sites and then use those sites to perform malware attacks. For example, a hacker may alter a legitimate site to display an official-looking message that informs the user that a particular software program must be downloaded, or a hacker may post a rogue banner ad on a legitimate site that redirects the user to a malware site instead of the site for the product featured in the banner ad. According to a report by security company Websense, more than half of the Web sites classified as malicious are actually legitimate Web sites that have been compromised.

## Protecting Against Computer Sabotage

One of the most important protections against computer sabotage is using up-to-date security software. This and other precautions are discussed next.

### Security Software

**Security software** protects devices against malware and other threats. It typically includes a variety of security features, such as a firewall; protection against viruses, spyware, and bots; and protection against some types of online fraud, which is discussed shortly. Security software helps prevent malware from being installed on your devices because it deletes or *quarantines* (safely isolates) any suspicious content as it arrives; regular full system scans can detect and remove any threats that find their way onto your device.

One of the most important components of security software is **antivirus software**, which protects against computer viruses, computer worms, Trojan horses, and other types of malware (see Figure 9-19). Like most security software components, antivirus software typically runs continuously to monitor the device,

**ANTIVIRUS SOFTWARE**

**ANTISPYWARE SOFTWARE**

**MOBILE SECURITY APPS**

---

>**Security software.** Software, typically a suite of programs, used to protect a device against a variety of threats. >**Antivirus software.** Software used to detect and eliminate computer viruses and other types of malware.

as well as incoming messages, Web page content, and downloaded files, in order to prevent malicious software from executing. Many antivirus programs also automatically scan devices when they are connected to a USB port to ensure those devices are not infected. *Antispyware software* (such as the *SUPERAntiSpyware* program shown in Figure 9-19) can detect and remove spyware. *Mobile security software* is used to protect smartphones and other mobile devices.

To prevent personal devices from infecting a school or business network, schools and businesses should ensure that students and employees are using up-to-date security software. Some colleges now require new students to go through a *quarantine process*, in which students are not granted access to the college network until they complete a security process that checks their devices for security threats, updates their operating system, and installs security software. Some additional virus prevention strategies are listed in Figure 9-20.

| VIRUS PREVENTION STRATEGIES |
| --- |
| Use antivirus software to check incoming e-mail messages and files, and download updated virus definitions on a regular basis. |
| Limit the sharing of flash memory cards, USB flash drives, and other removable storage media with others. |
| Only download files from reputable sites. |
| Only open e-mail attachments that come from people you know and that do not have an executable file extension (such as .exe, .com, .bat, or .vbs); double-check with the sender before opening an unexpected, but seemingly legitimate, attachment. |
| For any downloaded file you are unsure of, upload it to a Web site (such as VirusTotal.com) that tests files for viruses before you open them. |
| Keep the preview window of your e-mail program closed so you will not view messages until you determine that they are safe to view. |
| Regularly download and install the latest security patches available for your operating system, browser, Java and other plug-ins, and e-mail programs. |
| Avoid downloading files from P2P sites. |

**FIGURE 9-20**

Sensible precautions can help protect against computer virus infections.

## Other Precautions Against Computer Sabotage

Individuals and businesses can protect against some types of computer sabotage (such as program, data, or Web site alteration) by controlling access to their devices and networks, as discussed earlier in this chapter. Intrusion protection systems can help businesses detect and protect against denial of service (DoS) attacks; some personal security software includes intrusion protection as well. In addition, most Web browsers have security settings that can be used to help prevent programs from being installed on a computer without the user's permission, such as prompting the user for permission whenever a download is initiated. Enabling these security settings is a wise additional precaution.

# ONLINE THEFT, ONLINE FRAUD, AND OTHER DOT CONS

A booming area of computer crime involves online fraud, theft, scams, and related activities designed to steal money or other resources from individuals or businesses—these are collectively referred to as **dot cons**. Some of the most common types of dot cons are discussed next.

## Theft of Data, Information, and Other Resources

*Data theft* or *information theft* is the theft of data or information located on or being sent from a computer or other device. It can be committed by stealing a device and then accessing the data on that device; it can also take place by hacking into a device and stealing data or intercepting data as it is being transmitted over the Internet or a network. Common types of data and information stolen via the Internet or another network include customer data (such as Web site passwords or credit card information) and proprietary corporate information.

>**Dot con.** A fraud or scam carried out through the Internet.

Money is another resource that can be stolen via a computer. Company insiders sometimes steal money by altering company programs to transfer small amounts of money—for example, a few cents of interest from a large number of bank accounts—to an account controlled by the thieves. This type of crime is sometimes called *salami shaving*. The amount taken from each victim is small enough that it often goes unnoticed but, added together, the amount can be substantial. Another example of monetary theft performed via computers involves hackers electronically transferring money illegally from online bank accounts, traditional bank accounts, credit card accounts, or accounts at online payment services such as PayPal to their accounts.

## Identity Theft, Phishing, Social Media Hacking, and Pharming

A growing dot con trend is obtaining enough information about an individual to perform fraudulent financial transactions, often in conjunction with identity theft. Techniques frequently used to obtain the necessary personal information to commit identity theft are phishing, spear phishing, social media hacking, and pharming.

### Identity Theft

**Identity theft** occurs when someone obtains enough information about a person to be able to masquerade as that person—usually to buy products or services in that person's name (see Figure 9-21). Typically, identity theft begins when a thief obtains a person's name, address, and Social Security number, often from a discarded or stolen document (such as a preapproved credit card application that was sent in the mail), from information obtained via the Internet (such as from a résumé posted online), or from information located on a device (such as information located on a stolen computer or hacked server, or information sent from a device via a computer virus or spyware program installed on that device). The thief may then order a copy of the individual's birth certificate, obtain a "replacement" driver's license, make purchases and charge them to the victim, and/or open credit or bank accounts in the victim's name. Assuming the thief requests a change of address for these new accounts after they are opened, it may take quite some time—often not until a company or collections agency contacts the victim about overdue bills—for the victim to become aware that his or her identity has been stolen.

**FIGURE 9-21**
**How identity theft works.**

1. The thief obtains information about an individual from discarded mail, employee records, credit card transactions, Web server files, or some other method.

2. The thief makes purchases, opens new credit card accounts, and more in the victim's name. Often, the thief changes the address on the account to delay discovery.

3. The victim usually finds out by being denied credit or by being contacted about overdue bills generated by the thief. Clearing one's name after identity theft is time consuming and can be very difficult and frustrating for the victim.

> **Identity theft.** Using someone else's identity to purchase goods or services or otherwise illegally masquerade as that individual.

# INSIDE THE INDUSTRY

### Skimming and EMV

Skimming is a common technique for stealing identifying information from a credit or debit card. It often occurs at ATM machines that have been compromised with hidden electronics that capture the personal data stored in the magnetic stripe on the card, as well as the PIN number used with the card. Criminals are then able to manufacture counterfeit credit or debit cards using the stolen information.

One change on the horizon is the shift to *EMV cards*. EMV is the newest standard for payment cards (it is named after Europay, MasterCard, and Visa—the companies that developed the standard) and it is used to authenticate credit and debit card transactions made with EMV cards. Instead of storing data in a magnetic stripe, EMV cards are embedded with a chip that encrypts personal data so that it cannot be easily stolen. In addition, the chip generates a unique transaction code every time the card is used to make purchases so, even if that code is intercepted, it can't be used again and so cannot be used in a counterfeit card. Consequently, EMV is much more secure than traditional card processing. To use an EMV card, it is inserted into an EMV-compliant payment terminal and remains there until the transaction is completed (see the accompanying photo).

Most developed countries around the world have already transitioned to EMV. The United States, however, has lagged behind. Approximately 70% of U.S. credit cards and 40% of debit cards will be EMV-enabled by the end of 2015, but many merchants have not yet acquired the new payment terminals and certification required to accept EMV cards. Consequently, many EMV cards issued in the United States still have a magnetic stripe on the card in addition to the chip, making the cards as insecure as traditional cards when used with a traditional terminal. One incentive to transition quickly is the recent shift of liability for fraud from the credit card company to the party—either the issuing financial institution or the merchant—that has not adopted chip technology.

**EMV cards protect against skimming and fraudulent transactions.**

---

Although identity theft often takes place via a computer today, information used in identity theft can also be gathered from trash dumpsters, mailboxes, and other locations. Other commonly used techniques are skimming and social engineering. *Skimming* involves stealing credit card or debit card numbers by using an illegal device attached to a credit card reader or an ATM machine that reads and stores the card numbers (a hidden camera is sometimes used to capture ATM PIN numbers); the thief retrieves the skimming devices at a later time to obtain the stolen numbers. (For a closer look at skimming and how the emerging EMV cards will help reduce fraud in the future, see the Inside the Industry box.) *Social engineering* involves pretending—typically via phone or e-mail—to be a bank officer, potential employer, IT employee, or other trusted individual in order to get the potential victim to supply personal information. Today, social engineering schemes often use social media to obtain the information needed to gain the trust of a victim.

Unfortunately, identity theft is a very real danger to individuals today. According to recent statistics, there is a new identity theft victim in the United States every two seconds. Identity theft can be extremely distressing for victims, can take years to straighten out, and can be very expensive. Some identity theft victims, such as Michelle Brown, believe that they will always be dealing with their "alter reality" to some extent. For a year and a half, an identity thief used Brown's identity to buy over $50,000 in goods and services, to rent properties—even to engage in drug trafficking. Although the culprit was eventually arrested and convicted for other criminal acts, she continued to use Brown's identity and was even booked into jail using Brown's stolen identity. As a final insult after the culprit was in prison, U.S. customs agents detained

> **TIP**
>
> To help prevent identity theft, do not include your Social Security number on your résumé or any other document posted online.

the real Michelle Brown when she was returning from a trip to Mexico because of the criminal record of the identity thief. Brown states that she has not traveled out of the country since, fearing an arrest or other serious problem resulting from the theft of her identity, and estimates she has spent over 500 hours trying to correct all the problems related to the identity theft.

## Phishing and Spear Phishing

**Phishing** (pronounced "fishing") is the use of a *spoofed* communication (typically an e-mail message appearing to come from a well-known legitimate organization but that is actually sent from a *phisher*) to trick the recipient into revealing sensitive personal information (such as Web site logon information or credit card numbers). Once obtained, this information is used in identity theft and other fraudulent activities. A phishing e-mail typically looks legitimate and contains links in the e-mail that appear to go to the Web site of the legitimate business, but the links go to the phisher's Web site that is set up to look like the legitimate site instead—an act called *Web site spoofing*. Phishing e-mails are typically sent to a wide group of individuals and usually include an urgent message stating that the individual's credit card or account information needs to be updated and instructing the individual to click the link provided in the e-mail in order to keep the account active. If the victim clicks the link and supplies the requested information via the spoofed site, however, the criminal gains access to all information provided by the victim, such as account numbers, credit card numbers, and Web site passwords. In addition to e-mail, phishing attempts can occur today via instant messages, text messages, fake messages sent via eBay or Facebook, Twitter tweets, pop-up security alert windows, and even links in YouTube videos. Phishers also frequently utilize spyware—clicking the link in the phishing e-mail installs the spyware on the victim's computer, and it will remain there (transmitting passwords and other sensitive data to a phisher) until it is detected and removed.

To trick victims into using the spoofed Web site, phishing e-mails and the spoofed Web sites often look legitimate (see Figure 9-22), using copies of the spoofed organization's logo and other Web site content from the legitimate Web site, a secure connection between the victim and the criminal's server, and the domain name of the legitimate company (such as *ebay* for an eBay phishing page) as part of the URL of the spoofed Web site. Other phishing schemes use *typosquatting*, which is setting up spoofed Web sites with URLs slightly different from legitimate sites (such as www.amazom.com) to catch individuals who make a typo when trying to reach the legitimate site in hopes they will not notice the slightly different URL and supply logon information via the spoofed site.

**FIGURE 9-22**
**Phishing.** Phishing schemes typically use legitimate-looking e-mails to trick users into providing private information.

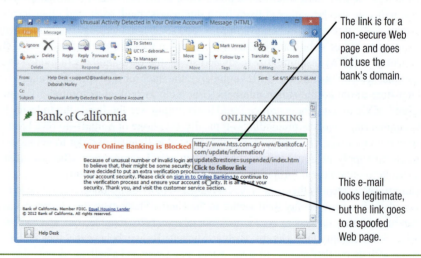

The link is for a non-secure Web page and does not use the bank's domain.

This e-mail looks legitimate, but the link goes to a spoofed Web page.

> **Phishing.** The use of spoofed electronic communications (typically e-mail messages) to obtain credit card numbers and other personal data to be used for fraudulent purposes.

**Spear phishing** is the use of phishing e-mails that are targeted to a specific individual and typically appear to come from an organization or person that the targeted individual has an association with. These e-mails often include personalized information (such as the potential victim's name, employer, and other information frequently found on social media and other public resources) to make them seem even more legitimate. Some attacks use spoofed logon pages for social networking sites to obtain an individual's logon information and password, which can then be used to try to log onto other Web sites (such as e-commerce and online banking sites) in hopes the individual uses the same logon information for these sites.

Spear phishers also frequently target employees of selected organizations by posing as someone within the company, such as a human resource or technical support employee. These spear phishing e-mails often request confidential information (such as logon IDs and passwords) or direct the employee to click a link to supposedly reset his or her password. The goal for corporate spear phishing attacks is usually to steal intellectual property, such as software source code, design documents, or schematics.

## Social Media Hacking

A more recent trend is **social media hacking**, in which a hacker obtains access to a victim's social media account in order to post comments or send messages as that individual. The messages typically contain phishing links and are sent to the victim's friends, who are much more likely to click on the links because they appear to come from a friend. In addition to individuals' social media accounts being hacked, business accounts have been recent targets as well. While hacking into a business's social media account and hijacking it temporarily is often a public embarrassment, sometimes the consequences of business social media hacking are more severe (like when the stock market dipped after the AP Twitter hack that there was an explosion at the White House).

## Pharming

**Pharming** is a scam that redirects traffic intended for a commonly used Web site to a spoofed Web site set up by the pharmer in an effort to obtain users' personal information. Sometimes pharming takes place via malicious code sent to a computer or other device via an e-mail or other message. More often, however, it takes place via changes made to a *DNS server*— a computer that translates URLs into the appropriate IP addresses needed to display Web pages. Pharming can take place via one of the 13 *root DNS servers* (the DNS servers used in conjunction with the Internet), but it more often takes place via a *company DNS server* (the DNS server that routes Web page requests corresponding to company URLs)—typically for a commonly used Web site. After hacking into a company DNS server, the pharmer changes the IP addresses used in conjunction with a particular company URL (called *DNS poisoning*) so that any Web page requests made via the legitimate company URL are routed (via the company's poisoned DNS server) to a spoofed Web page located on the pharmer's Web server. Consequently, even though a user types the proper URL to display the legitimate company Web page in his or her browser, the spoofed page is displayed instead.

Because spoofed sites are set up to look like the legitimate sites, the user typically does not notice any difference, and passwords or any other information sent via that site are captured by the pharmer. To avoid suspicion, some pharming schemes capture the user's account name and password as it is entered the first time on the spoofed site, and then display a password error message. The spoofed site then redirects the user back to the legitimate site where he or she is able to log on to the legitimate site, leaving the user to think that he or she must have just mistyped the password the first time, but, by then, the pharmer has already captured the victim's logon information and can use it to gain access to the victim's account.

**TIP**

Spear phishing attacks often increase after the occurrence of large data breaches (such as the Epsilon data breach) that expose names and e-mail addresses of individuals, along with the businesses that these individuals patronize.

**TIP**

With *drive-by pharming*, the pharmer changes the victim's DNS server (specified in the victim's router settings) to the pharmer's DNS server in order to direct the victim to spoofed versions of legitimate Web sites when the victim enters the URLs for those sites.

>**Spear phishing.** A personalized phishing scheme targeted at an individual. >**Social media hacking.** The act of accessing someone else's social media account to make changes to the content or to perform an activity as that individual, often for phishing purposes. >**Pharming.** The use of spoofed domain names to obtain personal information in order to use that information in fraudulent activities.

## Online Auction Fraud and Other Internet Scams

**Online auction fraud** occurs when an online auction buyer pays for merchandise that is never delivered, or that is delivered but is not as represented. It can also occur when an online buyer receives the proper items but falsely claims that they never arrived. Similar to many types of Internet cons, prosecution is difficult for online auction fraud because multiple jurisdictions are usually involved. Although most online auction sites have policies that suspend sellers with a certain number of complaints lodged against them, it is very easy for those sellers to come back using a new e-mail address and identity.

Other scams that can occur via Web sites or unsolicited e-mails include loan scams, work-at-home cons, pyramid schemes, bogus credit card offers and prize promotions, and fraudulent business opportunities. These offers typically try to sell potential victims nonexistent services or worthless information, or they try to convince potential victims to voluntarily supply their credit card details and other personal information. Some scammers hack into a system to obtain e-mail addresses to use as targets for a scam that is based on something those individuals have in common in order to increase the odds of a potential victim falling for the scam. Others send messages to a potential victim impersonating a distant friend, a grandchild, or an old classmate (typically found via social media) and requesting money (such as by saying they are traveling out of the country and were robbed). A new *online romance scam* involves criminals who pose as U.S. soldiers and who strike up an online romance with individuals before requesting money from the victims.

One persistent Internet scam is the *Nigerian letter fraud* scheme. This scheme involves an e-mail message that appears to come from the Nigerian government and that promises the potential victim a share of a substantial amount of money in exchange for the use of the victim's bank account. Supposedly, the victim's bank account information is needed to facilitate a wire transfer (but the victim's account is emptied instead) or up-front cash is needed to pay for nonexistent fees (but that is kept by the con artist). The scams often change to fit current events or a recent natural disaster; however, they always involve a so-called fortune that is inaccessible to the con artist without the potential victims' help (see Figure 9-23), and the victims always lose any money they provide.

Other scams involve con artists who solicit donations for charitable organizations after disasters and other tragic events but who keep the donations instead, or who post fake job listings on job search sites to elicit personal information (such as Social Security numbers) from job seekers.

**FIGURE 9-23**
A Nigerian letter fraud e-mail.

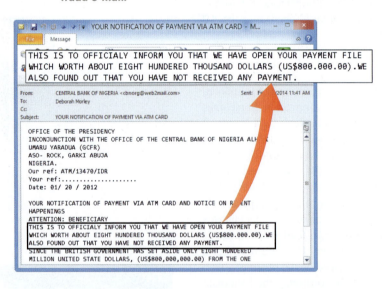

## Protecting Against Online Theft, Online Fraud, and Other Dot Cons

The best protection against many dot cons is protecting your identity; that is, protecting any identifying information about you that could be used in fraudulent activities. Another protection is common sense. Be extremely cautious of any unsolicited e-mail messages you receive and realize that if an offer sounds too good to be true, it probably is. Some general precautions that apply to a variety of dot cons are discussed next, followed by an explanation of antiphishing tools and digital IDs.

> **Online auction fraud.** When an item purchased through an online auction is never delivered after payment, or the item is not as specified by the seller.

## General Precautions to Protect Against Identity Theft, Phishing, and Other Dot Cons

To protect your sensitive information, send it only via secure Web servers and do not disclose personal information—especially a Social Security number or a mother's maiden name—unless it is absolutely necessary and you know how the information will be used and that it will not be shared with others. In addition, never give out sensitive personal information to anyone who requests it over the phone or by e-mail—businesses that legitimately need personal information will not request it via phone or e-mail. Encrypting computers and other hardware containing sensitive information so that it will not be readable if the hardware is lost or stolen, as well as using security software (and keeping it up to date) to guard against malware that can send information from your device or about your activities (the Web site passwords that you type, for example) to a criminal, are other important precautions. In addition, be sure to shred preapproved credit card offers and other documents containing personal information before disposing of them and don't place outgoing mail containing sensitive information in your mailbox—mail it at the post office instead.

Keeping a close eye on your credit card bills and credit history is also important to make sure you catch any fraudulent charges or accounts opened by an identity thief as soon as possible. Make sure your bills come in every month (some thieves will change your mailing address to delay detection), and read credit card statements carefully to look for unauthorized charges. Be sure to follow up on any calls you get from creditors, instead of assuming it is just a mistake. Most security experts also recommend ordering a full credit history on yourself a few times a year to check for accounts listed in your name that you did not open and any other problems. The *Fair and Accurate Credit Transactions Act* (*FACTA*) enables all Americans to get a free copy of their credit report, upon request, each year from the three major consumer credit bureaus (*Equifax*, *Experian*, and *TransUnion*). Ideally, you should request a report from one of these bureaus every four months to monitor your credit on a regular basis. Some additional tips for minimizing your risk of identity theft are listed in Figure 9-24.

To avoid phishing schemes, never click a link in an e-mail message to go to a secure Web site; instead, always type the URL for that site in your browser (which is not necessarily the URL shown in an e-mail message). Some tips for spotting a phishing e-mail are listed in Figure 9-25. Remember that spear phishing schemes may include personalized information (such as your name)—do not let that fool you into thinking the phishing e-mail is legitimate. To prevent a drive-by pharming attack, all businesses and individuals should change the administrator password for routers, access points, and other networking hardware from the default password to a strong password. Individuals can also change the DNS server for their router to one (such as *OpenDNS*) that uses filtering to block malicious sites and protect against pharming attempts.

### TIPS FOR AVOIDING IDENTITY THEFT

Protect your Social Security number—give it out only when necessary.

Be careful with your physical mail and trash—shred all documents containing sensitive data.

Secure your computer—update your operating system and use up-to-date security (antivirus, antispyware, firewall, etc.) software.

Be cautious—never click on a link in an e-mail message or respond to a too-good-to-be-true offer.

Use strong passwords for your computer and online accounts.

Verify sources before sharing sensitive information—never respond to e-mail or phone requests for sensitive information.

Be vigilant while on the go—safeguard your wallet, smartphone, and portable computer.

Watch your bills and monitor your credit reports—react immediately if you suspect fraudulent activity.

**FIGURE 9-24**
Tips to reduce your risk of identity theft.

**TIP**

You can order your free credit reports online quickly and easily via the *AnnualCreditReport.com* Web site, which is sponsored by and supported by all three major credit bureaus.

**FIGURE 9-25**
Tips for identifying phishing e-mail messages.

### A PHISHING E-MAIL OFTEN . . .

Tries to scare you by stating that your account will be closed or that you are a victim of fraud.

Asks you to provide personal information, such as your bank account number, account password, credit card number, PIN number, mother's maiden name, or Social Security number.

Contains a bogus link (point to a hyperlink in the message to view the URL for that link—a phisher would have to use a URL like microsoft.phisher.com, not microsoft.com).

Uses legitimate logos from the company the phisher is posing as.

Appears to come from a known organization, but one you do not have an association with.

Contains spelling or grammatical errors.

When dealing with individuals online through auctions and other person-to-person activities, it pays to be cautious. Before bidding on an auction item, check out the feedback rating of the seller to see comments written by other auction sellers and buyers as well as the sellers' return policy. Always pay for auctions and other online purchases using a credit card or an online payment service (such as PayPal) that accepts credit card payments so you can dispute the transaction through your credit card company, if needed. In addition, some auction sites and online payment services offer free buyer protection against undelivered items or auction items that are significantly different from their description. To protect buyers of expensive items, PayPal also temporarily holds payments to ensure that the merchandise is as specified before the payment is released to the seller.

With any dot con, it is important to act quickly if you think you have been a victim. For instance, you should work with your local law enforcement agency, credit card companies, and the three major consumer credit bureaus to close any accessed or fraudulent accounts, place fraud alerts on your credit report, and take other actions to prevent additional fraudulent activity while the fraud is being investigated.

### Antiphishing Tools

In addition to the precautions just discussed, there are *antiphishing tools* built into many e-mail programs and Web browsers designed to help notify users of possible phishing Web sites. For instance, some e-mail programs will disable links in e-mail messages identified as questionable, unless the user overrides them; most recent browsers warn users when a Web page associated with a possible phishing URL is requested (see Figure 9-26); and antiphishing capabilities are included in many recent security suites.

Some secure Web sites also use additional security layers to protect against identity thieves. For example, some online banking sites analyze users' habits to look for patterns that vary from the norm, such as accessing accounts online or making purchases at an hour or from a location unusual for that individual, or a higher than normal level of online purchases. If a bank suspects the account may be compromised, it contacts the owner for verification. Some financial institutions have also added an additional step in their logon process—displaying an image or word preselected by the user and stored on the bank's server in order to prove to the user that the site being viewed is the legitimate (not a phishing) site. On many secure sites, if the system does not recognize the device that the user is using to log on to the system, the user is required to go through an authentication process (typically by correctly answering *cognitive authentication questions*) before being allowed to access the system via that device. The questions used are specifically designed to be "out of wallet" questions—easy for the individual to answer but difficult for hackers to guess the correct answer or find in a stolen wallet. For additional protection, some banks also offer customers the option of adding the use of one-time passwords (typically sent via text message) to their online banking logon procedure.

Warning: Dangerous Site

**Whoa!**
Are you sure you want to go there?

http://go.spktrk.com/aff_r?offer_id=1160&aff_i... may be risky to visit.

**Why were you redirected to this page?**
When we visited this site, we found it exhibited one or more risky behaviors.

« Back    Visit anyway

Source: McAfee, Inc.

**FIGURE 9-26**
**Unsafe Web site alerts.**

### Digital IDs

Another tool that can be used to authenticate the identity of an individual or Web site is a **digital ID** (also called a **digital certificate**). Digital certificates are granted by Certificate Authorities and contain the name of the person, organization, or Web site being certified along with a certificate serial number and an expiration date.

> **Digital ID.** A group of electronic data that can be used to verify the identity of a person or organization; includes a key pair that can be used for encryption and digital signatures; also called a **digital certificate**.

Digital certificates used with secure Web pages guarantee the Web pages are secure and actually belong to the stated organization in order to protect against phishing and other online scams that use spoofed sites. Secure Web sites can obtain either a normal *SSL/TLS digital certificate* or a more secure *Extended Validation* (*EV*) *SSL digital certificate* that is intended to provide consumers with a higher level of trust while online. While both digital certificates require an application process, the verification process to obtain an EV SSL digital certificate is more thorough, requiring the Certificate Authority to verify the legal identity and physical location of the Web site owner, as well as verify that the Web site owner has exclusive control over the domain name. With both types of certificates, individuals can click the secure Web page icon in their browser window to view that site's digital certificate in order to ensure that the certificate is valid and issued to the company associated with the Web site being viewed (see Figure 9-27).

A digital certificate also includes a public/private key pair. In addition to being used to encrypt files (as previously discussed), these keys can be used to digitally sign an e-mail message or other document in order to authenticate that document. The sender's private key is used to digitally sign the document and that key, along with the contents of the document, generates a unique **digital signature**. When a digitally signed document is received, the recipient's device uses the sender's public key to verify the digital signature. Because the digital signature will be deemed invalid if the content of the signed document is changed, digital signatures guarantee that the document was sent by a specific individual and that it was not altered after it was signed.

Individuals can obtain a free digital certificate for personal use from several Certificate Authorities (such as the *Comodo Group*). Once you have a digital certificate, you need to install it on your device and then you can use the digital signature option in your e-mail program to sign all or just selected messages. At this time, most Web mail programs (such as Gmail) do not support the use of digital signatures.

Click to view certificate information.

Green indicates a valid EV SSL digital certificate.

Source: Comodo Group, Inc.

**FIGURE 9-27**
**EV SSL certificates.** The browser's Address bar reflects information about the digital certificate being used.

**NET**

**TIP**

Windows users can install a digital certificate on their Windows computer by typing *certmgr.msc* in the Windows search box.

**TIP**

The goal of the *Let's Encrypt* project (sponsored by organizations such as Mozilla, Cisco, and the Internet Society) is to increase the use of secure Web sites by giving away free SSL/TLS certificates.

# PERSONAL SAFETY ISSUES

In addition to being expensive and inconvenient for both businesses and individuals, cyber-crime can also be physically dangerous. Although most of us may not ordinarily view using the Internet as a potentially dangerous activity, cases of physical harm due to Internet activity do happen. For example, children and teenagers have become the victims of pedophiles who arranged face-to-face meetings by using information gathered via e-mail, online games, social media, or other online sources. In addition, children and teens are threatened by classmates via e-mail, social media posts, or text messages. Adults may fall victim to unscrupulous or dangerous individuals who misrepresent themselves online, and the availability of personal information online has made it more difficult for individuals to hide from people who may want to do them harm, such as abused women trying to hide from their abusive husbands.

## Cyberbullying and Cyberstalking

Two of the most common ways individuals are harassed online are cyberbullying and cyberstalking. **Cyberbullying** is bullying others via the Internet, such as through e-mail, social media, or another online communications method. Cyberbullying can take place

> **Digital signature.** A unique digital code that is attached to a file or an e-mail message to verify the identity of the sender and guarantee the file or message has not been changed since it was signed. > **Cyberbullying.** The use of online communications to bully another person.

**FIGURE 9-28**

An anti-cyberbullying Web banner.

openly, but often it occurs anonymously, such as a bully sending messages via a hacked social media or e-mail account, or a bully hacking a victim's social media account and changing the content. Unfortunately, cyberbullying is common, and is especially prevalent among teens—more than one-third of all U.S. teenagers have been cyberbullied, according to a recent report. Some of the victims have even committed suicide because of it. Consequently, antibullying policies and campaigns have been initiated by many school districts, as well as by government organizations (see Figure 9-28), and many states have introduced new laws or amended existing harassment laws to address cyberbullying.

Repeated threats or other malicious behavior that poses a credible threat of harm carried out online is referred to as **cyberstalking**. Cyberstalkers sometimes find their victims online; for instance, someone who posts a comment that the cyberstalker does not like on social media or bloggers who are harassed and threatened because of their blogging activities. Other times the attack is more personal, such as employers who are stalked online by ex-employees who were fired or otherwise left their position under adverse conditions and celebrities who are stalked online by fans. Cyberstalking typically begins with online harassment and can lead to offline stalking and possibly physical harm to, and sometimes even the death of, the victim.

Although there are as yet no specific federal laws against cyberstalking, all states have made it illegal, and some federal laws do apply if the online actions include computer fraud or another type of computer crime, suggest a threat of personal injury, or involve sending obscene e-mail messages.

## Sexting and Sextortion

*Sexting* is the act of sending sexually explicit photos or messages (*sexts*) to others. It is growing rapidly among both teens and adults and is a risky behavior, due to the fact that, once sent, the sender of a compromising photo or message loses control of it and it can live on the Internet forever. While individuals may believe that a sext they send will only be viewed by the intended recipient, nearly 25% are also seen by other people, according to a recent study. For teens, this often happens when a relationship ends and the recipient sends the photo or message to others or posts a photo online for revenge, which can lead to depression, anxiety, cyberbullying, and other harmful issues. For adults, it can lead to embarrassment and potential career implications. Sexting can also lead to *sextortion*—where someone who sees a sext threatens to expose it unless the individual sends more explicit photos.

## Online Pornography

A variety of controversial and potentially objectionable material is available on the Internet. Although there have been attempts to ban this type of material from the Internet, they have not been successful due to free speech and constitutional challenges. For example, the *Communications Decency Act*, signed into law in 1996—which made it a criminal offense to distribute patently indecent or offensive material online—was ruled unconstitutional in 1997 by the U.S. Supreme Court. However, like its printed counterpart, online pornography involving minors is illegal. Because of the strong link experts believe exists between child pornography and child molestation, many experts are very concerned about the amount of child pornography that can be found and distributed via the Internet. They also believe that the Internet makes it easier for sexual predators to act out, such as by striking up "friendships" with children online and convincing these children to meet them in real life.

A new online pornography issue involves teens and sexting. If a sext sent from a teen under the age of 18 is viewed by authorities, the teen can be charged with distributing child pornography and recipients can be charged with possessing child pornography. If a teen is convicted of either charge, he or she will have to register as a sex offender, although some states have lesser charges for a minor's first offense.

## Protecting Against Cyberbullying, Cyberstalking, and Other Personal Safety Concerns

The growing amount of attention paid to cyberbullying and cyberstalking is leading to more efforts to improve safeguards. For example, many social networking sites have privacy features that can be used to protect the private information of their members. In addition, numerous states in the United States have implemented cyberbullying and cyberstalking laws. Although no surefire way exists to completely protect against cyberbullying, cyberstalking, and other online dangers, the common-sense precautions listed in Figure 9-29 can help reduce the chance of a serious personal safety problem occurring due to online activities.

# DATABASES, ELECTRONIC PROFILING, SPAM, AND OTHER MARKETING ACTIVITIES

There are marketing activities that can be considered privacy risks or, at least, a potential invasion of privacy. These include databases, electronic profiling, and spam.

## Databases and Electronic Profiling

Information about individuals can be located in many different databases. For example, educational institutions have databases containing student information, organizations use databases to hold employee information, and physicians and health insurance providers maintain databases containing individuals' medical information. If these databases are adequately protected from hackers and other unauthorized individuals and if the data is not transported on a portable computer or other device that may be vulnerable to loss or theft, then these databases do not pose a significant privacy concern to consumers because the information can rarely be shared without the individuals' permission. However, the data stored in these types of databases is not always sufficiently protected and has been breached quite often in the past. Consequently, these databases, along with marketing databases and government databases that are typically associated with a higher risk of personal privacy violations and are discussed next, are of growing concern to privacy advocates.

**Marketing databases** contain marketing and demographic data about people, such as where they live and what products they buy. This information is used for marketing purposes, such as sending print or e-mail advertisements that fit each individual's interests or trying to sign people up over the phone for some type of service. Virtually anytime you provide information about yourself online or offline—for example, when you subscribe to a magazine, fill out a sweepstakes entry or product registration card, or order a product or service—there is a good chance that the information will find its way into a marketing database.

Marketing databases are also used in conjunction with Web activities, such as social media activity and Web searches. For instance, the data stored on Facebook, Google+, and

### ONLINE SAFETY TIPS

Be cautious and discrete online; use gender-neutral, nonprovocative identifying names, such as jsmith, instead of janesmith or iamcute.

Be careful about the types of photos you post of yourself online and do not reveal personal information (such as your real name, address, or telephone number) to people you meet online.

Do not respond to any insults or other harassing comments you may receive online.

Do not include personal information on social media that could be used by an online stalker.

Do not send sexts to others.

Be sure to monitor childrens' computer and smartphone activities.

Be sure to give children and teens computer use guidelines, including which types of online activities are allowed and which ones are not allowed, to never reveal personal information about themselves online, and to always tell an adult if an online individual requests personal information, a meeting, or issues a threat.

**FIGURE 9-29**
Some tips to keep you safe online.

**NET**

**TIP**

Search for yourself using search sites and online telephone books to see what personal information is available about you on the Internet.

---

>**Marketing database.** A collection of data about people that is stored in a large database and used for marketing purposes.

**TIP**

To download a copy of your data stored within Google products, use the *Google Takeout* service.

other social networking sites can be gathered and used for advertising purposes by marketing companies, and the activities of users of personalized search services (where users log in to use the service) can be tracked and that data can be used for marketing purposes. And companies with services that collect a wide variety of data, such as Google with its Chrome, Gmail, Calendar, Hangouts, Checkout, and Google+ services, worry some privacy advocates.

Information about individuals is also available in **government databases**. Some information (such as Social Security earnings and income tax returns) is confidential and can legally be seen only by authorized individuals. Other information (such as birth records, marriage certificates, and divorce information, as well as property purchases, assessments, liens, and tax values) is available to the public, including to the marketing companies that specialize in creating marketing databases.

In the past, the data about any one individual was stored in a variety of separate locations, such as at different government agencies, individual retail stores, and the person's bank and credit card companies. Because it would be extremely time consuming to locate all the information about one person from all these different places, there was a fairly high level of information privacy. Today, however, most of an individual's data is stored on computers that can communicate with each other, and some *database search services* are available online for free or for a fee (see some examples in Figure 9-30). Although often the ability to search online databases is an advantage—such as checking the background of a potential employee or looking up a misplaced phone number—it does raise privacy concerns. In response to the increased occurrence of identity theft, some local governments have removed birth and death information from their available online database records.

Collecting in-depth information about an individual is known as **electronic profiling**. Electronic profiles are generally designed to provide specific information and can include an individual's name, current and previous addresses, telephone number, marital status, number and age of children, spending habits, and product preferences. The information retrieved from electronic profiles is then sold to companies upon request to be used for marketing purposes. For example, one company might request a list of all individuals in a particular state whose street addresses are considered to be in an affluent area and who buy baby products. Another company

**FIGURE 9-30**

**A variety of searchable databases are available via the Internet.**

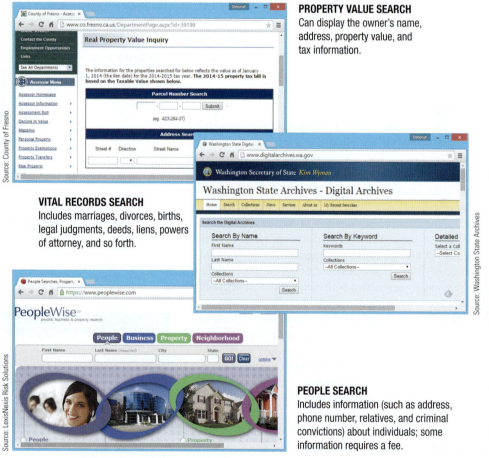

**PROPERTY VALUE SEARCH**
Can display the owner's name, address, property value, and tax information.

**VITAL RECORDS SEARCH**
Includes marriages, divorces, births, legal judgments, deeds, liens, powers of attorney, and so forth.

**PEOPLE SEARCH**
Includes information (such as address, phone number, relatives, and criminal convictions) about individuals; some information requires a fee.

Source: County of Fresno

Source: Washington State Archives

Source: LexisNexis Risk Solutions

>**Government database.** A collection of data about people that is collected and maintained by the government. >**Electronic profiling.** Using electronic means to collect a variety of in-depth information about an individual, such as name, address, income, and buying habits.

might request a list of all SUV owners in a particular city who have not purchased a car in five years.

Most businesses and Web sites that collect personal information have a **privacy policy** that discloses how the personal information you provide will be used. As long as their actions do not violate their privacy policy, it is legal for businesses to sell the personal data that they collect. However, some privacy policies are difficult to decipher, and most people do not take the time to read them before using a site. In addition, many businesses periodically change their privacy policies without warning, requiring consumers to reread privacy policies frequently or risk their personal information being used in a manner that they did not agree to when the information was initially provided.

## Spam and Other Marketing Activities

**Spam** refers to unsolicited e-mail sent to a large group of individuals at one time. The electronic equivalent of junk mail (see Figure 9-31), spam is most often used to sell products or services to individuals. Spam is also used in phishing schemes and other dot cons and is frequently sent via botnets. A great deal of spam involves health-related products, counterfeit products, pornography, and new—and often fraudulent—business opportunities and stock deals. Kapersky Labs recently estimated that 66% of all e-mail messages are spam.

At best, spam is an annoyance to recipients and can slow down a mail server's delivery of important messages. At worst, spam can disable a mail network completely, or it can cause recipients to miss or lose important e-mail messages because those messages were caught in a spam filter or were accidentally deleted by the recipient while he or she was deleting a large number of spam e-mail messages. Most Internet users spend several minutes each day dealing with spam, making spam very expensive for businesses in terms of lost productivity, consumption of communications bandwidth, and drain of technical support. Spam sent to a smartphone (either via text message or e-mail) is also expensive for end users that have a limited data or text message allowance.

One of the most common ways of getting on a spam mailing list is by having your e-mail address entered into a marketing database, which can happen when you sign up for a free online service or use your e-mail address to register a product or make an online purchase. Spammers also use software to gather e-mail addresses from Web pages, forum posts, and social media. Many individuals view spam as an invasion of privacy because it arrives on computers without permission and costs them time and other resources (bandwidth, mailbox space, and hard

**FIGURE 9-31**
**Examples of spam.**

**E-MAIL SPAM**

**TEXT MESSAGE SPAM**

Source: Google Inc.

---

> **Privacy policy.** A policy, commonly posted on a company's Web site, that explains how personal information provided to that company will be used. > **Spam.** Unsolicited, bulk e-mail sent over the Internet.

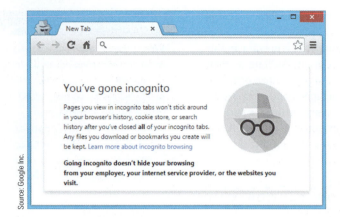

**FIGURE 9-32**

Private browsing can protect your Web-surfing privacy at public computers.

**FIGURE 9-33**

How to safeguard your personal information.

### TIPS FOR PROTECTING PERSONAL INFORMATION

Read a Web site's privacy policy before providing any personal information to see if the Web site reserves the right to share your information with others—if so, do not use the site if that is unacceptable to you.

Avoid putting too many personal details on your Web site or a social media site.

Avoid using location-based services that share your location information with strangers, and check the privacy options for the sites you use to limit who can see the content that you post.

Use your throw-away e-mail address when you sign up for free trials or other services that may result in spam.

Consider using privacy software, such as *Privacy Guardian*, to hide your personal information as you browse the Web so it is not revealed and your activities cannot be tracked by marketers.

Supply only the required information when you are completing an online form; if you are asked for more personal information than you are comfortable providing, don't use the site.

Unless you are using private browsing, use browser options to delete any personal information and settings stored on a public computer at the end of your session, and be sure to log out of any Web sites you were using before leaving the computer.

drive space, for instance). While most spam is legal, there are requirements that must be adhered to in order for it to be legal. For instance, the *CAN-SPAM Act of 2003* established requirements (such as using truthful subject lines and honoring remove requests) for commercial e-mailers, as well as specified penalties for companies and individuals that break the law.

## Protecting the Privacy of Personal Information

There are a number of precautions that individuals can take to protect the privacy of their personal information. For example, using the *private browsing* mode offered by some browsers (see Figure 9-32) can prevent personal information from being left on a public computer. Businesses also need to take adequate measures to protect the privacy of information stored on their servers and storage media. These precautions are discussed next.

### Safeguard Your E-Mail Address

Protecting your e-mail address is one of the best ways to avoid spam. One way to accomplish this is to use one private e-mail address for family, friends, colleagues, and other trusted sources and to use a **throw-away e-mail address**—such as a second address obtained from your ISP or a free e-mail address from Outlook.com or Gmail—for online shopping, signing up for free offers, product registration, and other activities that typically lead to junk e-mail that you can check as needed. Another advantage of using a throw-away e-mail address for only non-critical applications is that you can quit using it and obtain a new one if spam begins to get overwhelming or too annoying.

To comply with truth-in-advertising laws, an *unsubscribe e-mail address* included in an unsolicited e-mail must be a working address. If you receive a marketing e-mail from a reputable source, you may be able to unsubscribe by clicking the supplied link or otherwise following the unsubscribe instructions. Because spam from less-legitimate sources often has unsubscribe links that do not work or that are present only to verify that your e-mail address is genuine—a very valuable piece of information for future use—many privacy experts recommend never replying to or trying to unsubscribe from any spam.

### Be Cautious about Revealing Personal Information

In addition to protecting your e-mail address, protecting your personal information is a critical step toward safeguarding your privacy. Consequently, it makes sense to be cautious about revealing your private information to anyone. Some tips for safeguarding personal information are listed in Figure 9-33.

> **Throw-away e-mail address.** An e-mail address used only for nonessential purposes and activities that may result in spam; the address can be disposed of and replaced if spam becomes a problem.

## Use Filters and Opt Out

To avoid seeing and having to deal with the spam that arrives in your Inbox, various tools can be used. For example, some ISPs automatically block all e-mail messages originating from known or suspected spammers, as well as block messages containing possible viruses, so those e-mail messages never reach the individuals' mailboxes. Other ISPs flag suspicious e-mail messages as possible spam or malicious e-mails, based on their content or subject lines, in order to warn individuals. To deal with spam that does make it to your device, you can use an **e-mail filter**—a tool for automatically sorting your incoming e-mail messages. E-mail filters used to capture spam are called **spam filters**.

Many e-mail programs and services have built-in spam filters that identify possible spam and either flag it or move it to a *Spam folder* or *Junk E-mail folder*. In addition, you can create custom e-mail filters to route messages automatically to particular folders based on stated criteria. For example, you can specify that e-mail messages with keywords frequently used in spam subject lines (such as *free, porn, opportunity, last chance, weight, pharmacy,* and similar terms) be routed into a folder named *Possible Spam*, and you can specify that all e-mail messages from your boss's e-mail address be routed into an *Urgent* folder. Filtering can help you find important messages in your Inbox by preventing it from becoming cluttered with spam. However, be sure to check your Spam folders periodically to locate any e-mail messages mistakenly filed there—especially before you permanently delete those messages.

Another way to reduce the amount of spam you receive is to *opt out*. Opting out refers to following a predesignated procedure to remove yourself from marketing lists, or otherwise preventing your personal information from being obtained by or shared with others. By opting out, you instruct companies you do business with not to share your personal information with third parties. You can also opt out of being contacted by direct and online marketing companies.

To opt out from a particular company or direct marketing association, you can contact them directly—many organizations include opt-out instructions in the privacy policies posted on their Web sites. For Web sites that use registered accounts, opt-out options are sometimes included in your personal settings. However, opt-out procedures can be confusing and time consuming, and they do not always work well. Consequently, some privacy groups are pushing to change to an opt-in process, in which individuals would need to *opt in* (request participation in) to a particular marketing activity before companies can collect or share any personal data (as is the case in the European Union). At this time, the general practice in the U.S. business community is to use your information as allowed for by each privacy policy unless you specifically opt out.

## Secure Servers and Otherwise Protect Personal Information

Any business that stores personal information about employees, customers, or other individuals must take adequate security measures to protect the privacy of that information. Secure servers and encryption can protect the data stored on a server; firewalls and access systems can protect against unauthorized access. To prevent personal information from being sent intentionally or inadvertently via e-mail, organizations can use e-mail encryption systems that automatically encrypt or block e-mail messages containing certain keywords. For instance, some hospitals use encryption systems that scan all outgoing e-mail messages and automatically encrypt or block all messages that appear to contain patient-identifiable information, such as a Social Security number, medical record number, patient name, or medical term like "cancer." The recipient of an encrypted e-mail message typically receives a link to a secure Web site to log in and view the encrypted e-mail message.

**TIP**

If your e-mail program mistakenly files an e-mail into your Spam folder, look for an option such as a *Not Spam* button to instruct the filter to not treat future messages from that individual as spam—many spam filters can "learn" what you view as spam based on your feedback.

**TIP**

Register both your landline and smartphone numbers with the *National Do Not Call Registry* at www.donotcall.gov to prevent telemarketing calls from companies you do not have a business relationship with.

**TIP**

Don't forget that once you post content on a Web site or send it via e-mail, you cannot control how long it will "live" in digital form. Be very careful about the personal information you post and send to avoid the possibility of that information creating problems for you in the future.

> **E-mail filter.** A tool that automatically sorts your incoming e-mail messages based on specific criteria. > **Spam filter.** An e-mail filter used to redirect spam from a user's Inbox.

**BEFORE SHREDDING**          **AFTER SHREDDING**

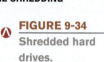

**FIGURE 9-34**

Shredded hard
drives.

Source: Data Killers

## Properly Dispose of Hardware Containing Data

Both individuals and businesses need to be very careful with
papers, portable hard drives, and other media that contain
personal data. For instance, many recent data breaches have
occurred because of carelessness, such as papers containing
personal information being found in dumpsters, lost in transit, or faxed to the wrong individual. Papers, CDs, DVDs, and
other media that contain sensitive data and need to be disposed
of should be shredded, and the hard drives of devices to be
disposed of should be *wiped*—overwritten several times using
special *disk-wiping* or *disk-erasing* software—before they are
sold or recycled. Unlike the data on a drive that has merely
been erased or even reformatted, data on a properly wiped
drive is very difficult or impossible to recover.

Wiping is typically viewed as an acceptable precaution
for deleting sensitive data (such as Web site passwords and tax
returns) from hard drives and other storage media belonging
to individuals, as well as for storage media to be reused within an organization. However,
before disposing of storage media containing sensitive data, businesses should consider
physically destroying the media, such as by shredding or melting the hardware. To help with
this process, a *data destruction service* is often used. Once a hard drive has been shredded
(see Figure 9-34), it is virtually impossible for any data to be recovered from the pieces.

## ELECTRONIC SURVEILLANCE AND MONITORING

**FIGURE 9-35**

Computer
monitoring
software. Can be
used to monitor
employee computer
activity, as shown here.

There are many ways electronic tools can be used to watch individuals, listen in on their
conversations, or monitor their activities. Some of these tools—such as devices used by
individuals to eavesdrop on wireless telephone conversations—are not legal for individuals
to use. Other products and technologies, such as the GPS devices that are built into some
cars so they can be located if they are stolen or the ankle bracelets used for monitoring
offenders sentenced to house arrest, are used for law enforcement purposes. Some common types of electronic surveillance and monitoring
are discussed next.

The current tab shows the top
Web sites visited by employees.

Click to view screenshots
of employee activities.

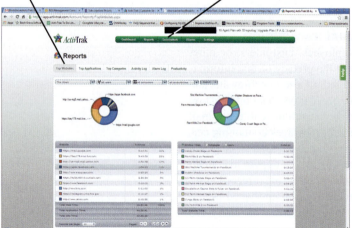

Source: ActivTrak.com

### Computer Monitoring Software

**Computer monitoring software** is used specifically for the purpose of recording keystrokes, logging the programs or Web sites accessed, or otherwise
monitoring someone's computer activity. Computer-
monitoring programs are typically marketed toward
parents, spouses, law enforcement agencies, or
employers. Computer monitoring programs can keep
a log of all computer keystrokes performed on a computer, record the amount of time spent on each app and
Web site, take screenshots at specified intervals, and
provide reports summarizing the computer activity
(see Figure 9-35). In addition, some computer monitoring software can block specific Web sites, as well as

>**Computer monitoring software.** Software that records an individual's computer usage, such as capturing images of the screen, recording the
actual keystrokes used, or creating a summary of Web sites and programs accessed.

notify a designated party (such as the parent or computer administrator) if the individual using the computer being monitored uses specified keywords (such as inappropriate language for children or terms referring to company secrets for employees) or visits a Web site deemed inappropriate.

In addition to computer monitoring products designed for individuals and businesses, there are also computer monitoring programs available for use only by law enforcement and other government agencies. With proper authorization and with cooperation from a suspect's ISP, law enforcement agencies can use computer monitoring software to intercept files and e-mail messages sent to or from a suspect's computer. If the documents are encrypted, *keystroke logging software* (software that records all keystrokes made on the device onto which it is installed) can be used to record e-mail messages and documents before they are encrypted, as well as to record the private keys used to encrypt messages and files.

## Video Surveillance

**Video surveillance**—the use of video cameras to monitor activities—is routinely used at retail stores, banks, office buildings, and other privately owned facilities that are open to the public to monitor activities taking place at those facilities for security purposes. It is also used for law enforcement purposes in public locations, such as streets, parks, airports, sporting arenas, and subway systems. These cameras are typically located outside and attached to or built into fixtures, such as lamp posts (see Figure 9-36), or attached to buildings. Video surveillance cameras are also commonly installed in schools in the United States and other countries to enable administrators to monitor both teacher and student activities and to have a record of incidents as they occur; home video surveillance systems are also available.

Public video surveillance systems are often used in conjunction with *face recognition* technology to try to identify known terrorists and other criminals, to identify criminals when their crimes are caught on tape, and to prevent crimes from occurring. Some public video surveillance systems are also beginning to be used in conjunction with software to try to identify suspicious behavior (such as a person leaving a bag unattended in a public location) and alert authorities to these possible threats before they do any damage.

Many privacy advocates object to the use of video surveillance and face recognition technology in public locations; their concerns are primarily based on how the video captured by these systems will be used. However, law enforcement agencies view this technology as just one more tool to be used to protect the public, similar to scanning luggage at the airport.

A related privacy concern is the inclusion of imaging capabilities in many mobile devices today, such as smartphones and tablets. Although digital cameras in mobile devices are often used to help law enforcement (such as when citizens take photos of crimes as they are being committed), some fear that the ubiquitous nature of mobile devices will lead to increased privacy violations. To protect the privacy of their members while working out and in the dressing rooms, some athletic clubs and other recreational facilities have banned mobile phones. Mobile phones and other devices that contain a camera are also being banned by some schools to prevent cheating, by many courthouses to prevent witness or jury intimidation, and by many research and production facilities to prevent corporate espionage. For a look at some privacy issues surrounding the growing use of wearable devices, see the Technology and You box.

Leonard Zhukovsky/Shutterstock.com

**FIGURE 9-36**
**Public video surveillance is common in metropolitan areas.**

**NET**

---

>**Video surveillance.** The use of video cameras to monitor activities of individuals, typically for work-related or crime-prevention purposes.

# TECHNOLOGY AND YOU

### Wearables and Privacy

The demand for wearables is huge and growing every day, but, similar to when mobile phones with cameras first became available, there are privacy concerns. One privacy concern is the ability of some wearable devices to discreetly gather data about individuals. For example, people wearing Google Glass can take photos or record video of others, and people with audio recording devices like *Kapture* (shown in the accompanying illustration) can record the conversations of others. Because the recording capabilities of wearable devices can be activated much less conspicuously than they can on a smartphone, wearable devices make it more possible to record data about an individual without his or her knowledge.

Another privacy concern is what is being done with the vast amount of data your wearables gather about you. While many devices have privacy settings that can control how data is shared, they often enable sharing by default. Consequently, data about your health, location, and activities could inadvertently be shared with others, opening up the risk of stalking, burglary, extortion, or employment or health insurance ramifications.

The ethical and legal use of wearables will likely be debated for some time. In the meantime, the legal system must apply current laws to wearables and other new technology as it is introduced and businesses may determine policies that are appropriate for that business. For example, similar to smartphones being banned from some locker rooms and other sensitive public locations for privacy reasons, some restaurants and bars have banned Google Glass on the basis that it may make some customers uncomfortable.

Source: Kapture

## Employee Monitoring

**Employee monitoring** is the act of recording or observing the actions of employees while on the job. Common employee monitoring activities include screening telephone calls, reviewing e-mail, and tracking computer and Internet usage using computer monitoring software, as previously discussed. The primary reason is to monitor Internet usage for legal liability, but monitoring employee productivity is another motivating factor. Although many employees feel that being watched at work is an invasion of their personal privacy, it is legal and very common in many countries, including the United States.

For monitoring the physical locations of employees, video cameras are often used, but another possibility is the use of smart or RFID-enabled ID cards (sometimes called *proximity cards*). While these cards are most often used for access control—such as to facilitate access to a building or computer network, to automatically lock an employee's computer when he or she gets a certain distance away from it, and to automatically unlock the computer when the employee returns—they can also be used to track the physical location of employees. Other types of employee monitoring systems designed for tracking an employee's location include GPS systems that track an employee via his or her smartphone and those that notify the employer if the employee's company vehicle exits a prescribed work area.

Comprehensive employee monitoring systems can be expensive; however, many companies view the cost as insignificant when compared with the risk of a potential multimillion-dollar lawsuit (such as from employees when offensive e-mail messages are circulated within the office or when an employee includes statements that defame another business

> **Employee monitoring.** Observing or reviewing employees' actions while they are on the job.

or reveal private information in a company blog). It is becoming increasingly common for U.S. firms to face sexual harassment and/or racial discrimination claims stemming from employee e-mail and Internet use and lawsuits can be costly—for example, Chevron was once ordered to pay female employees $2.2 million to settle a sexual harassment lawsuit stemming from inappropriate e-mails sent by male employees.

## Presence Technology

**Presence technology** is the ability of one computing device (such as a computer or smartphone) to identify another device on the same network (such as the Internet) and determine its status. It can be used to tell when someone is using his or her computer or smartphone, as well as the individual's availability for communications, such as whether or not the individual is able and willing to take a voice or video call. Presence capabilities are integrated into many messaging programs; for example, they let you see when your Facebook friends are online. Presence capabilities are also used in some business communications programs (see Figure 9-37). While some aspects of presence technology are useful and intriguing, such as being able to tell that a loved one's flight arrived safely when you notice that his or her smartphone is on again, knowing if a friend or colleague is available for a phone call before dialing the number, or identifying the location of your children at any point in time, privacy advocates are concerned about the use of this technology. They are concerned about presence technology being used to target ads and information to individuals based on their current physical location (such as close to a particular restaurant at lunchtime) and other activities that they view as potential privacy violations. In addition, there are concerns about location data being archived and how that archived data may be used.

Online
In a meeting
Offline
Away
Urgent interruptions only

Source: Modality Systems Ltd /Ignition Industries Inc.

⚠ **FIGURE 9-37**
**Presence technology.** Presence icons indicate the status of individual contacts.

## Protecting Personal and Workplace Privacy

There are not many options for protecting yourself against computer monitoring by your employer or the government or against video surveillance systems. However, you can protect against monitoring or surveillance by malicious software by securing your personal devices. To prevent location data associated with your smartphone from being available to strangers, change the privacy settings of the services you use to limit location data to specific friends, if that option is available. If you don't use location-based services frequently, turn off the GPS feature on your smartphone until you need it. As an additional bonus, turning off GPS and location-based services on your smartphone will also extend your phone's battery life.

## The Employer's Responsibilities

To protect the personal privacy of their employees and customers, businesses and organizations have a responsibility to keep private information about their employees, the company, and their customers safe. Strong security measures, such as firewalls, security software, and access prevention methods for both computer data and facilities, can help to protect against unauthorized access by hackers and unauthorized monitoring of employee activities. Businesses and organizations should take precautions against both intentional and accidental breaches of privacy by employees. In addition, businesses and organizations

**TIP**

Ensuring that the private data stored by a business is adequately protected is increasingly the responsibility of a *chief privacy officer* (*CPO*)—a rapidly growing new position in business today.

> **Presence technology.** Technology that enables one computing device to locate and identify the current status of another device via the Internet or other network.

have the responsibility to monitor their employees' activities to ensure workers are productive. In general, businesses must maintain a safe and productive workplace environment and protect the privacy of their customers and employees, while at the same time ensure the company is not vulnerable to lawsuits. They should also include an explanation of the types of employee monitoring used in the company employee policy.

### The Employees' Responsibilities

Employees have the responsibility to read the company's employee policy when initially hired and then review it periodically to ensure that they understand the policy and do not violate any company rules while working for that organization. In addition, because at-work activities may legally be monitored by an employer, it is wise—from a privacy standpoint—to avoid personal activities at work. From reading the organization's employee policy, an employee can determine if any personal activities are allowed at all (such as checking personal e-mail during the lunch hour), but it is safer to perform personal activities at home, regardless. Be especially careful with any activity, such as sending a joke via e-mail to a coworker, that might be interpreted as harassment. For personal phone calls, employees should use their smartphones during their lunch hour or rest break.

# NETWORK AND INTERNET SECURITY AND PRIVACY LEGISLATION

The high level of concern regarding computer security, Internet security, and personal privacy has led state and federal legislators to pass a variety of laws since the 1970s. Internet security and privacy are viewed as two of the top policy issues facing Congress today, and numerous bills have been proposed in the last several years regarding spam, telemarketing, spyware, online profiling, smart and self-driving cars, cybersecurity, location privacy, and other security and privacy issues. One controversial bill under consideration is *CISA* (*Cyber Intelligence Sharing Act*), which would allow for voluntary information sharing between private companies and the government to prevent and respond to cybersecurity threats.

Despite a renewed interest in security and privacy legislation, due at least in part to the relatively recent leak of National Security Agency (NSA) surveillance operations, Congress has had difficulty passing new legislation related to network and Internet security and privacy. One reason for this is jurisdictional issues because many computer crimes affect businesses and individuals located in geographic areas other than the one in which the computer criminal is located and hackers can make it appear that activity is coming from a different location than it really is. Another reason is that the speed at which technology changes makes it difficult for the legal system to keep up. In addition, privacy is difficult to define and there is a struggle to balance protection with freedom of speech and other civil liberties. However, Congress regularly amends existing laws to better address current cybersecurity and privacy concerns.

Another issue that impacts new security and privacy legislation is weighing the need to implement legislation versus the use of voluntary methods to protect computer security and personal privacy. For instance, the *Child Online Protection Act* (*COPA*) has been controversial since it was passed in 1998, and, in fact, it has never been implemented. This legislation prohibited making pornography or any other content deemed harmful to minors available to minors via the Internet. This law was blocked by the U.S. Supreme Court several times, based on the likelihood that it violates the First Amendment and that less-restrictive alternatives (such as Internet filtering) can be used instead to prevent the access of inappropriate materials by minors. A list of selected federal laws related to computer and Internet security and privacy are shown in Figure 9-38.

| DATE | LAW AND DESCRIPTION |
|---|---|
| 2009 | **American Recovery and Reinvestment Act**<br>Requires HIPAA covered entities to notify patients when protected health information has been compromised. |
| 2006 | **U.S. SAFE WEB Act of 2006**<br>Grants additional authority to the FTC to help protect consumers from spam, spyware, and Internet fraud and deception. |
| 2005 | **Real ID Act**<br>Establishes national standards for state-issued driver's licenses and identification cards. |
| 2004 | **Identity Theft Penalty Enhancement Act**<br>Adds extra years to prison sentences for criminals who use identity theft (including the use of stolen credit card numbers) to commit other crimes. |
| 2003 | **CAN-SPAM Act**<br>Implements regulations for unsolicited e-mail messages and lays the groundwork for a federal Do Not E-Mail Registry. |
| 2003 | **Do Not Call Implementation Act**<br>Amends the Telephone Consumer Protection Act to implement the National Do Not Call Registry. |
| 2003 | **Health Insurance Portability and Accountability Act (HIPAA)**<br>Includes a Security Rule that sets minimum security standards to protect health information stored electronically. |
| 2003 | **PROTECT Act**<br>Includes provisions to prohibit virtual child pornography. |
| 2002 | **Sarbanes-Oxley Act**<br>Requires archiving a variety of electronic records and protecting the integrity of corporate financial data. |
| 2001 | **USA PATRIOT Act**<br>Grants federal authorities expanded surveillance and intelligence-gathering powers, such as broadening the ability of federal agents to obtain the real identity of Internet users and to intercept e-mail and other types of Internet communications. |
| 2000 | **Children's Internet Protection Act (CIPA)**<br>Requires schools and libraries that receive discounts through the E-rate program to enact Internet safety policies, including filtering for obscene content. |
| 1998 | **Identity Theft and Assumption Deterrence Act of 1998**<br>Makes it a federal crime to knowingly use someone else's means of identification, such as name, Social Security number, or credit card, to commit any unlawful activity. |
| 1998 | **Child Online Protection Act (COPA)**<br>Prohibits online pornography and other content deemed harmful to minors; has been blocked by the Supreme Court. |
| 1998 | **Children's Online Privacy Protection Act (COPPA)**<br>Regulates how Web sites can collect information from minors and communicate with them. |
| 1998 | **Telephone Anti-Spamming Amendments Act**<br>Applies restrictions to unsolicited, bulk commercial e-mail. |
| 1986 | **Electronic Communications Privacy Act**<br>Extends traditional privacy protections governing postal delivery and telephone services to include e-mail, mobile phones, and voice mail. |
| 1984 | **Computer Fraud and Abuse Act of 1984**<br>Makes it a crime to break into computers owned by the federal government. This act has been regularly amended over the years as technology has changed. |
| 1974 | **Education Privacy Act**<br>Stipulates that, in both public and private schools that receive any federal funding, individuals have the right to keep the schools from releasing information such as grades and evaluations of behavior. |
| 1974 | **Privacy Act**<br>Stipulates that the collection of data by federal agencies must have a legitimate purpose. |
| 1970 | **Fair Credit Reporting Act**<br>Prevents private organizations from unfairly denying credit and provides individuals the right to inspect their credit records. |
| 1970 | **Freedom of Information Act**<br>Gives individuals the right to inspect data concerning them that is stored by the federal government. |

NET

**FIGURE 9-38**
Computer and
Internet security and
privacy legislation.

# SUMMARY

## WHY BE CONCERNED ABOUT COMPUTER, NETWORK, AND INTERNET SECURITY AND PRIVACY?

**Chapter Objective 1:**
Explain why computer users should be concerned about security and privacy as they relate to computing devices, networks, and the Internet.

There are a number of important security concerns related to computers and the Internet. Many of these are **computer crimes**. Because computers and networks are so widespread and many opportunities for criminals exist, all computer users should be aware of the risks so they can take appropriate precautions. There are also a number of important privacy concerns related to computers and the Internet. For instance, **information privacy** refers to the rights of individuals and companies to control how information about them is collected and used. Other common concerns include the privacy of Web site activities and e-mail messages, as well as data breaches that reveal personal information.

## HARDWARE LOSS, HARDWARE DAMAGE, AND SYSTEM FAILURE

**Chapter Objective 2:**
Identify some risks associated with hardware loss, hardware damage, and system failure, and understand ways to safeguard a computing device against these risks.

Hardware loss (such as from **hardware theft**), hardware damage (both intentional and unintentional), and **system failure** are important concerns. To protect against hardware theft, door and equipment locks can be used. To protect against accidental hardware damage, **surge suppressors**, **uninterruptible power supplies (UPSs)**, proper storage media care, and precautions against excess dust, heat, and static electricity are important. **Ruggedized devices** can be used when necessary. **Encryption** can be used to protect individual files and the content of data stored on a storage medium by using **full disk encryption (FDE)** and **self-encrypting hard drives**. Most businesses should develop a **disaster recovery plan** for natural and man-made disasters.

## UNAUTHORIZED ACCESS AND UNAUTHORIZED USE

**Chapter Objective 3:**
List several examples of unauthorized access and unauthorized use and explain several ways to protect against them.

Two risks related to networks and the Internet are **unauthorized access** and **unauthorized use**. **Hacking** is electronically breaking into a computer or network. **War driving** and **Wi-Fi piggybacking** refer to the unauthorized use of an unsecured Wi-Fi network. Data can be intercepted as it is transmitted over the Internet or a wireless network. Protection against unauthorized access and use include **possessed knowledge access systems** that use **passwords** or other types of possessed knowledge; **possessed object access systems** that use physical objects; and **biometric access systems** that identify users by a particular unique biological characteristic, such as a fingerprint. **Two-factor authentication** systems are more effective than single-factor systems.

To protect wireless networks, they should be secured; **firewalls** protect against unauthorized access. Sensitive transactions should be performed only on **secure Web pages**; sensitive files and e-mails should be secured with encryption. **Public key encryption** uses a private key and matching public key; **private key encryption** uses only a private key. Employers should take appropriate precautions with current and former employees to limit the risk of unauthorized access and use, as well as accidental exposure of sensitive information.

## COMPUTER SABOTAGE

**Chapter Objective 4:**
Provide several examples of computer sabotage and explain how individuals and businesses can protect against it.

**Computer sabotage** includes **malware** (**computer viruses**, **computer worms**, and **Trojan horses** designed to cause harm to computer systems), **denial of service (DoS) attacks** (designed to shut down a Web server), and data and program alteration. Computer sabotage is often performed via the **bots** in a **botnet**. Protection against computer sabotage includes using appropriate access control systems to keep unauthorized individuals from accessing computers and networks, as well as using **security software**, such as **antivirus software**.

## ONLINE THEFT, ONLINE FRAUD, AND OTHER DOT CONS

There are a variety of types of theft, fraud, and scams related to the Internet—collectively referred to as **dot cons**. Data, information, or money can be stolen from individuals and businesses. A common crime today is **identity theft**, in which an individual poses as another individual, such as to make purchases posing as the victim. The information used in identity theft is often gathered via **phishing**, **spear phishing**, **social media hacking**, and **pharming**. **Online auction fraud** is another common dot con.

To protect against identity theft, individuals should guard their personal information carefully. To avoid other dot cons, individuals should steer clear of offers that seem too good to be true and never click a link in an unsolicited e-mail message. To verify a Web site, a **digital ID** (also called a **digital certificate**) can be used; a **digital signature** can be used to verify the sender of a document. Digital certificates include key pairs that can be used to both digitally sign documents and to encrypt files.

## PERSONAL SAFETY ISSUES

There are also personal safety risks for both adults and children stemming from Internet use, such as **cyberbullying** and **cyberstalking**. The growing *sexting* and *sextortion* trends, along with online pornography, are other risks. To protect their personal safety, adults and children should be cautious in online communications, and children should be taught never to reveal personal information to others online without a parent's consent.

## DATABASES, ELECTRONIC PROFILING, SPAM, AND OTHER MARKETING ACTIVITIES

The extensive use of **marketing databases**, **government databases**, and **electronic profiling** creates privacy concerns and often results in **spam** (unsolicited bulk e-mail). An organization's **privacy policy** addresses how any personal information submitted to that company will be used. To protect personal information, use a **throw-away e-mail address** for activities that may result in spam, provide only the required data on Web sites, and do not provide personal details online. **E-mail filters** can be used to manage your e-mail; **spam filters** can identify and isolate possible spam. Individuals and businesses should be cautious when disposing of old hardware.

## ELECTRONIC SURVEILLANCE AND MONITORING

**Computer monitoring software** that can record an individual's computer use is viewed as a privacy violation by some, as is the increased use of **video surveillance** in public locations. Although it is allowed by law, some employees view **employee monitoring** as an invasion of their privacy. **Presence technology** allows individuals to determine the availability of other individuals before contacting them.

To protect the privacy of employees and customers, businesses have a responsibility to use firewalls, password-protected files, encryption, and other methods to keep private information about their employees, the company, and their customers safe. Businesses also have the responsibility to monitor employee activities in order to ensure that employees are performing their jobs correctly and are not putting the company at risk. For the highest level of privacy while at the workplace, employees should perform only work-related activities on the job

## NETWORK AND INTERNET SECURITY AND PRIVACY LEGISLATION

Although network and Internet security and privacy are viewed as extremely important issues today, legislating these issues is difficult due to ongoing changes in technology, jurisdictional issues, and varying opinions. Some legislation has been enacted; new legislation is being considered on a regular basis.

**Chapter Objective 5:**
Discuss online theft, identity theft, spoofing, phishing, and other types of dot cons and detail steps an individual can take to protect against these threats.

**Chapter Objective 6:**
Identify some personal safety risks associated with Internet use and list steps individuals can take to protect themselves.

**Chapter Objective 7:**
Describe some privacy concerns regarding databases, electronic profiling, spam, and telemarketing, and identify ways individuals can protect their privacy.

**NET**

**Chapter Objective 8:**
Discuss several types of electronic surveillance and monitoring, and list ways individuals can protect their privacy.

**Chapter Objective 9:**
Discuss the current state of network and Internet security and privacy legislation.

# REVIEW ACTIVITIES

## KEY TERM MATCHING

a. computer virus

b. denial of service (DoS) attack

c. dot con

d. encryption

e. firewall

f. hacking

g. identity theft

h. phishing

i. Trojan horse

j. uninterruptible power supply (UPS)

**Instructions:** Match each key term on the left with the definition on the right that best describes it.

1. _____ A collection of hardware and/or software intended to protect a computer or computer network from unauthorized access.

2. _____ A fraud or scam carried out through the Internet.

3. _____ A malicious program that masquerades as something else.

4. _____ A method of scrambling electronic content to make it unreadable if it is intercepted by an unauthorized user.

5. _____ A device containing a built-in battery that provides continuous power to a computer and other connected components when the electricity goes out.

6. _____ A software program installed without the user's knowledge and designed to alter the way a computer operates or to cause harm to the computer system.

7. _____ An act of sabotage that attempts to flood a network server or a Web server with so much activity that it is unable to function.

8. _____ The use of spoofed electronic communications (typically e-mail messages) to obtain credit card numbers and other personal data to be used for fraudulent purposes.

9. _____ Using a computer to break into a computing resource.

10. _____ Using someone else's identity to purchase goods or services or otherwise illegally masquerade as that individual.

## SELF-QUIZ

**Instructions:** Circle **T** if the statement is true, **F** if the statement is false, or write the best answer in the space provided. **Answers for the self-quiz are located in the References and Resources Guide at the end of the book.**

1. T F A computer virus can only be transferred to another computer via a storage medium.

2. T F An access control system that uses passwords is a possessed knowledge access system.

3. T F Using a password that is two characters long is an example of two-factor authentication.

4. T F Electronic profiling is the act of using electronic means to collect a variety of in-depth information about an individual, such as name, address, income, and buying habits.

5. T F Cyberstalking is the use of spoofed e-mail messages to gain credit card numbers and other personal data to be used for fraudulent purposes.

6. Driving around looking for a Wi-Fi network to access is referred to as _____.

7. _____ access control systems use some type of unique physical characteristic of a person to authenticate that individual.

8. A(n) _____ plan can help a business get operational again following a fire, an act of sabotage, or a similar disaster.

9. A(n) _____ can be added to a file or an e-mail message to verify the identity of the sender and guarantee the file or message has not been changed.

10. Match each computer crime to its description, and write the corresponding number in the blank to the left of the description.

   a. _____ A person working for the Motor Vehicle Division deletes a friend's speeding ticket from a database.

   b. _____ An individual does not like someone's comment on a message board and begins to send that individual harassing e-mail messages.

   c. _____ An individual sells the same item to 10 individuals via an online auction site.

   d. _____ A person accesses a computer belonging to the IRS without authorization.

1. Online auction fraud

2. Hacking

3. Data or program alteration

4. Cyberstalking

---

**EXERCISES**

1. Write the appropriate letter in the blank to the left of each term to indicate whether it is related to unauthorized access (U) or computer sabotage (C).

   a. _____ Time bomb     c. _____ Malware     e. _____ War driving

   b. _____ DoS attack     d. _____ Wi-Fi piggybacking

2. Match each privacy risk with its related phrase, and write the corresponding number in the blank to the left of each phrase.

   a. _____ Throw-away e-mail address     1. Employee monitoring

   b. _____ Computer monitoring software     2. Video surveillance

   c. _____ Riding public transportation     3. Spam

3. Supply the missing words to complete the following statements regarding public/private key pairs.

   a. With an encrypted e-mail message, the recipient's _____ key is used to encrypt the message, and the recipient's _____ key is used to decrypt the message.

   b. With a digital signature, the sender's _____ key is used to sign the document, and the sender's _____ key is used to validate the signature.

4. To secure files on your computer so they are unreadable to a hacker who might gain access to your computer, what type of encryption (public key or private key) would be the most appropriate? Explain.

5. List two precautions you can take to protect against someone hacking your social media accounts.

---

**DISCUSSION QUESTIONS**

1. The term *hacktivism* is sometimes used to refer to the act of hacking into a computer system for a politically or socially motivated purpose. While some view hacktivists no differently than they view other hackers, hacktivists contend that they break into systems in order to bring attention to political or social causes. Is hacktivism a valid method of bringing attention to specific causes? Why or why not? Should hacktivists be treated differently from other types of hackers when caught?

2. Spam is increasingly being filtered by ISPs and e-mail programs, and pop-up blockers can block many Web page advertisements. If this trend continues and these activities are no longer viable marketing activities, what will the long-term effect be? Will free Web content begin to disappear? Is paying Internet users to receive spam or view Web ads a viable option? Just as with television, some amount of advertising is typically necessary in order to support free content. What do you think is the optimal balance for the Web?

NET

# PROJECTS

1. **EMV Cards** As discussed in the Inside the Industry box, credit and debit cards are being replaced with the more secure EMV cards.

   For this project, research the current status of EMV cards in the United States. Are financial institution and stores now liable for fraud if they do not have EMV-capable payment terminals? Do EMV cards today also contain magnetic stripes? If not, have there been any cases of an EMV card being used for fraudulent transactions? If so, how was the fraud carried out? How does the security of EMV cards at retail stores compare with mobile payment options such as Apple Pay? Which do you prefer to use and why? At the conclusion of your research, prepare a one-page summary of your findings and opinions and submit it to your instructor.

2. **E-Voting** E-voting—casting ballots online or via an electronic e-voting machine—has been surrounded by controversy. Concerns include the accuracy and security of e-voting machines, the ability of online voting systems to prevent someone from voting as another individual and to protect the privacy of votes cast electronically, and the ability to perform an accurate recount.

   For this project, research the current status of e-voting. Is e-voting being used in the United States? If so, have universal standards been developed for all e-voting machines used in the United States or is that decision made on a state-by-state basis? What security measures have been developed to ensure e-voting systems cannot be hacked and that only the registered voter is permitted to cast his or her vote? Form an opinion about the use of e-voting machines and online voting. Would you be comfortable casting your vote via an e-voting machine? How about online? At some point, do you think online voting will become the norm? If so, how would you suggest handling individuals who have no Internet access available to them on Election Day? At the conclusion of your research, prepare a one-page summary of your findings and submit it to your instructor.

3. **Virus Check** There are several Web sites that include a free virus check, as well as other types of diagnostic software.

   For this project, locate a free virus check (such as one available from Microsoft or from a company that makes antivirus software) and run the free virus check. NOTE: If you are on a school computer, only run online checks (do not download programs without permission from your instructor). If the check takes more than 10 minutes and there is an option to limit the check to a particular drive and folder, redo the check but scan only part of the hard drive (such as the Documents folder) to save time. After the virus scan is completed, print the page displaying the result. Did the program find any viruses or other security threats? At the conclusion of this task, submit your printout with any additional comments about your experience to your instructor.

4.  **Teaching Computer Viruses** Some college computer classes include instruction on writing computer viruses. At one university, precautions for containing code created during this course include allowing only fourth-year students to take the course, not having a network connection in the classroom, and prohibiting the removal of storage media from the classroom. Do you think these precautions are sufficient? Should writing virus code be allowed as part of a computer degree curriculum? Some believe that students need to know how viruses work in order to be able to develop antivirus software; however, the antivirus industry disagrees, and most antivirus professionals were never virus writers. Is it ethical for colleges to teach computer virus writing? Is it ethical for students to take such a course? Will teaching illegal and unethical acts (such as writing virus code) in college classes help to legitimize the behavior in society? Would you feel comfortable taking such a course? Why or why not?

    For this project, form an opinion about the ethical implications of writing virus code in college classes and be prepared to discuss your position (in class, via an online class forum, or via a class blog, depending on your instructor's directions). You may also be asked to write a short paper expressing your opinion.

5.  **Virus Hoaxes** In addition to the valid reports about new viruses found in the news and on antivirus software Web sites, reports of viruses that turn out to be hoaxes abound on the Internet. In addition to being an annoyance, virus hoaxes waste time and computing resources. In addition, they may eventually lead some users to routinely ignore all virus warning messages, leaving them vulnerable to a genuine, destructive virus.

    For this project, visit at least two Web sites that identify virus hoaxes, such as the Symantec or McAfee Web sites and Snopes.com. Explore the sites to find information about recent virus hoaxes, as well as general guidelines for identifying virus hoaxes and other types of online hoaxes. Share your findings with the class in the form of a short presentation. The presentation should not exceed 10 minutes and should make use of one or more presentation aids, such as a whiteboard, handouts, or a computer-based slide presentation (your instructor may provide additional requirements). You may also be asked to submit a summary of the presentation to your instructor.

6.  **Is Mobile Banking More Secure than Online Banking?** You likely have used your smartphone to pay a bill or deposit a check. While common today, it is still newer than traditional online banking performed via a computer and so does not have as long of a track record. While banks are continually upgrading their security systems in response to new threats and technologies, is the security of online and mobile banking equal? Some consider traditional online banking safer because it has been tested longer, is used with computers that may have better security software installed, and can be performed via home computers that are not as likely to be lost or misplaced as mobile devices. Others view mobile banking as safer because individuals tend to have their smartphones with them at all times and so can be notified more quickly of security breaches, GPS information can be used to identify transactions that occur in a different physical location from the registered location of the phone (and therefore might be fraudulent), and mobile banking accounts are often associated with a single smartphone. Mobile banking can be performed via a Web app, mobile Web site, or text messaging. Is one method safer than the other? How do the risks associated with mobile banking compare with the risks associated wtih traditional online banking? Would you feel safer using one or the other? Why?

    Pick a side on this issue, form an opinion and gather supporting evidence, and be prepared to discuss and defend your position in a classroom debate or in a one- to two-page paper, depending on your instructor's directions.

# Networks and the Internet

Courtesy Intel Corporation

**Shishir Singh is the Vice President and General Manager of the Network Security Business Unit at Intel Security Group. Before joining Intel Security, he served as the Vice President of Engineering, Network Security, at McAfee and the Senior Vice President of Engineering at Cyphort Inc. Shishir holds Master's degrees in Computer Science and Electrical Engineering, has presented and published multiple academic papers for IEEE, and has multiple patents pending in the area of behavior-based modeling for malware analysis.**

## A conversation with SHISHIR SINGH

**Vice President and General Manager, Network Security Business Unit, Intel Security Group**

*". . . protect your identity and your online reputation—it will keep you and your data safe and will improve your career prospects."*

### My Background . . .

I am the Vice President and General Manager of the Network Security Business Unit at Intel Security Group. I lead the engineering, product management, marketing, and sales functions that drive worldwide growth for this area of the business. I began my career as a scientist at the Defense Research and Development Organization (DRDO) in Bangalore, India. After that, I held several engineering leadership positions at technology companies including Cisco Systems and McAfee, Inc. I joined the Intel organization when Intel acquired McAfee. Over the years, my area of expertise has become security technologies and I am continually working to develop the next generation of security technology products. In addition to my technical expertise, organizational and people skills are also very important in my current position because I manage a global team spread across multiple locations on three continents.

### It's Important to Know . . .

**How the Internet and other networks work.** Because the Internet is so integrated into our society today, it is important for people to understand the basic functions of the Internet—how it connects devices and resources, how people access it, how data is stored, and what the cloud is—so that they may understand how best to use and secure this resource in both their personal and professional lives.

**Protecting your identity is essential.** Online theft, identity theft, and other privacy and security risks impact what we call our "identity." Protecting identities is a unique area of security that is important because it touches each of us personally—as employees, as students, and as individuals. In the digital world, you are your digital identity. What is associated with your digital identity becomes associated with you—and that could impact your finances, your legal standing, and your career.

**Passwords alone are not an adequate security control.** Today, most of our digital identities are protected by passwords. Unfortunately, a simple username and password is easy to break. What's worse, many of us use the same username and password over and over again so once one account—say, an online e-mail account—is breached, all other accounts (such as your bank account) using that same combination are then directly accessible. To make matters worse, the password policies often implemented to help prevent this (such as using a unique strong password for every account, changing them every few months, and telling people not to save them anywhere) increases these habits. Implementing better controls, such as two-factor and biometric authentication (e.g. voice and facial recognition used with our McAfee LiveSafe cloud storage product), is both safer and easier!

### How I Use this Technology . . .

Because my job involves collecting requirements for Internet Security software and appliances, I use this knowledge and these solutions daily in my professional life. But I also use them in my personal life. For example, I use antivirus protection for all of my devices and I use two-factor or strong authentication to protect my financial and personal e-mail accounts.

## What the Future Holds . . .

Today in our connected society, our identity is our most valuable and our most vulnerable link. And our society will continue to become more connected. The Internet of Things (IoT) is moving beyond mobile devices and networked cars to wearable devices, household items, medical devices, and other items we use in our daily lives. In the near future, we will be connected in ways we're just beginning to imagine. As this happens, it will become increasingly important that we—as individuals, students, and a business community—continue to watch the trends around identity protection; how trust relationships are established between people, systems, data and applications; and the laws and governance for personal privacy.

*" . . . a simple username and password is easy to break "*

Already, the most vulnerable link in our networks today is our identity, and it will become more vulnerable in the even more connected future. And, as the consumerization of IT increases the pressure to move business tools and applications to the cloud, businesses will be more challenged than ever to securely grant remote, mobile, and highly social business users and their identities easy access while not compromising their security—especially as the lines between the personal and professional continue to blur. To address these challenges, Intel Security and other companies are actively developing solutions like McAfee LiveSafe and True Key by Intel Security that use technologies such as multi-factor authentication, which combines passwords with other methods like biometrics, smartphones, chips in our devices, or other physical objects.

In the future, we can expect to see accelerated movement toward these solutions and technologies as we leave our weak and difficult to keep track of passwords behind.

## My Advice to Students . . .

Protect yourself by implementing multi-factor authentication and strong passwords—today. And all of us, particularly students, should be careful of what we publish in social media. You can expose yourself to risk by sharing too much data about where you live, who you know, and what you are doing. If you share too much information, it can also impact your online reputation. Employers are increasing their scrutiny of social presence when considering job applicants and you don't want something you say or post online to hurt your job prospects in the future. So, protect your identity and your online reputation—it will keep you and your data safe, and will improve your career prospects.

## Discussion Question

Shishir Singh stresses the importance of protecting your digital identity. Think about the systems that contain personal data about you. How would you feel if those systems were breached and your information was stolen? Does your viewpoint change if the information was monetary (such as credit card information) versus private information (such as grades or health information)? What security precautions, if any, do you think should be imposed by laws? Are organizations that hold your personal data morally responsible for going beyond the minimum requirements? Be prepared to discuss your position (in class, via an online class forum, or via a class blog, depending on your instructor's directions). You may also be asked to write a short paper expressing your opinion.

> **For more information about McAfee products or other Intel Security products, visit www.intelsecurity.com. For information about specific security issues and solutions, visit www.mcafee.com/identity and blogs.mcafee.com.**

# module

# Systems

The hardware and software discussed in earlier chapters in this book, along with data, people, and procedures, all work together to form a variety of systems. These systems are the topic of this module.

Chapter 10 focuses on information systems. It first discusses the types of information systems found in organizations, and then looks at the activities performed during the system development process. Chapter 11 covers the program development process—one important step in the system development process—and the various tools and programming languages developers may choose from when creating new programs. Database management systems are the subject of Chapter 12. This chapter discusses database concepts in much more detail than in previous chapters, including more specific database vocabulary, wider coverage of possible database models, and how databases are used in conjunction with the World Wide Web.

wavebreakmedia/Shutterstock.com

# in this module

*"System capabilities have made enormous increases in efficiency possible, and have also opened up new types of business and social activities . . ."*

For more comments from Guest Expert **Stuart Feldman** of ACM (Association for Computing Machinery) and Google, see the **Expert Insight on . . . Systems** feature at the end of the module.

# chapter 10

# Information Systems and System Development

**After completing this chapter, you will be able to do the following:**

1. Understand what information systems are and why they are needed.

2. Discuss who uses information systems in a typical organization.

3. Identify several types of information systems commonly found in organizations and describe the purpose of each.

4. Explain the individuals responsible for system development.

5. Identify and describe the different steps of the system development life cycle (SDLC).

6. Discuss several approaches used to develop systems.

# OVERVIEW

So far in this textbook we have looked at a wide variety of hardware and software. In this chapter, we turn to the process of putting these elements together with people, procedures, and data to form complete systems.

There are a number of systems in place to facilitate our national security, the power grid, and other important aspects of our daily lives. A variety of systems are also found in all organizations, including systems to facilitate accounting activities, such as issuing bills and processing payrolls; systems to provide information to help managers make decisions; systems to enable the sale and delivery of products; and systems to enable workers to exchange information and collaborate on projects. Systems typically require considerable effort to design, build, and maintain and, while no two system development projects are exactly alike, there is a set of general principles and procedures that can be used during system development to enhance the likelihood of the project's success. Those principles and procedures are the primary subject of this chapter.

The chapter opens with a discussion of information systems—systems that support the information needs of companies. We discuss how information systems are used by different levels of employees in an organization, and we look at the most common types of information systems. From there we turn to the process of system development, beginning with the computer professionals who develop systems and their primary responsibilities. We then look at the system development life cycle—the activities that are typically followed when developing a new system. The chapter closes with a discussion of the different system development approaches that can be taken. ∎

## WHAT IS AN INFORMATION SYSTEM?

A **system** is a collection of *elements* and *procedures* that interact to accomplish a goal. A football game, for example, is played according to a system. It consists of elements (two teams, a playing field, referees, and so on) and procedures (the rules of the game) that interact to determine which team is the winner. A transit system is a collection of elements and procedures (people, buses or trains, fares, and schedules, for instance) designed to get people from one place to another. An **information system (IS)** is a collection of elements (people, hardware, software, and data) and procedures that interact to generate information needed by the users in an organization (see Figure 10-1). Information systems manage and process data from the time it is generated (such as data resulting from orders, documents, and other business transactions) through its conversion into information. Typically, information systems are computerized, although they don't have to be. The information that information systems provide is used to support a wide variety of activities, from day-to-day transactions to long-term strategic planning.

**▽ FIGURE 10-1**
**Components of an information system.**

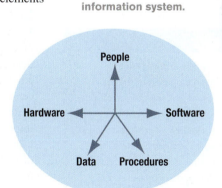

---

>**System.** A collection of elements and procedures that interact to accomplish a goal. >**Information system (IS).** A system used to generate information to support users in an organization.

Although the majority of information systems within organizations serve employees, some information systems need to be accessed by customers and suppliers, as well as by employees while on the go. Consequently, information systems are increasingly being designed for remote access, such as via the Internet and via mobile devices.

An emerging type of system is the **digital ecosystem**, which is the collection of people, products, services, and business processes related to a digital element. For instance, the *Apple digital ecosystem* consists of Apple hardware, software, and online services.

## The Need for System Development

Businesses typically use a variety of information systems. These systems are created and modified in response to changing needs within an organization and shifting conditions within its surrounding environment. When problems arise in an existing system or when a new system is needed, system development comes into play. In general terms, **system development** is the process of analyzing a work environment, designing a new system or modifying the exisiting system to fit current needs, acquiring any needed hardware and software, training users, and getting the new or modified system to work.

System development may be required for many reasons. For instance, new laws may call for the collection of new types of data or require specific reports regarding financial data, or may implement new security or privacy procedures (such as those required in the United States by the *Sarbanes-Oxley Act* and the *Health Insurance Portability and Accountability Act (HIPAA) Privacy Rule*, respectively). A government may also change the legal requirements for retaining business data. In addition, new technology may prompt the revision of a system. For instance, it is common today for a business to provide customers and suppliers with access to some information systems via the Internet, and the growing use of RFID, NFC, EMV credit cards, smartphones, and other technologies may require changes to some systems to accommodate that technology. An organization may also make a change to its information systems to gain a competitive edge.

In the early days of commercial computing, businesses used computers almost exclusively to perform routine processing tasks related to business transactions, such as to process orders and payments. As time passed, however, it became apparent that computers could do much more than just *transaction processing*—they could also provide a variety of information to assist employees with decision making. In addition, computers could be used to better understand the structure and operations of a company in order to make better strategic decisions. Two general concepts related to systems—enterprise architecture and business intelligence (BI)—are discussed next, followed by a look at the users of information systems.

## Enterprise Architecture

**Enterprise architecture** is a conceptual blueprint that defines the structure and operations of an *enterprise* (a business, organization, government agency, or other entity). It provides a detailed picture of an organization, its functions, and its systems, as well as the relationships among these items. The goal of enterprise architecture is to determine how an organization can most effectively achieve its current and future objectives. With the complexity of today's systems, enterprise architecture allows managers to better organize and maximize the use of information technology (IT) resources, as well as make informed decisions with fewer mistakes. Experts agree that developing an enterprise architecture is not easy and requires a great deal of time and effort. The first step is usually to examine the existing systems and functions to identify gaps, overlaps, and other possible issues. Enterprise architecture development is usually viewed as a long-term process, but, after it is in place, it is a valuable tool.

> **Digital ecosystem.** The collection of people, goods, services, and business processes related to a digital element. > **System development.** The process of designing and implementing a new or modified system. > **Enterprise architecture.** A comprehensive framework used to describe and manage an organization's business functions and systems.

## Business Intelligence (BI)

While enterprise architecture provides an overall picture of an organization, **business intelligence** (**BI**) is the process of gathering, storing, accessing, and analyzing data about a company in order to make better business decisions. For instance, BI can help a business identify its most profitable customers and offer them products at the right prices to increase sales, or BI can be used to optimize inventory systems in order to decrease costs while ensuring products are available as needed. Typically, information systems are used to support BI, often in conjunction with sophisticated analysis and modeling tools to analyze data—a process referred to as **business analytics** (**BA**). While in the past BA tools were difficult to work with, today's BA tools—such as *digital dashboards* that display information from a variety of sources in one location—are more user-friendly (see Figure 10-2). Many of the information systems discussed in the next few sections can be classified as *business intelligence systems*.

Business intelligence systems are often used in conjunction with data stored in a **data warehouse**, which stores data for an entire enterprise (a *data mart* stores data that is similar to the data stored in a data warehouse, but it is usually smaller and stores data related to a particular subject or department). Data warehouses and data marts typically contain data from a variety of sources, including data from product sales and other business transactions, activities performed via the company Web site (called *clickstream* data), customer surveys, marketing data, and so on. **Data mining**—the use of intelligent software to find subtle patterns that may not be evident otherwise—is often used with data warehouses and data marts to identify patterns and relationships among data. Data mining can be used to identify processes that need improvement; it can also be used for *customer profiling*—a useful sales and marketing tool to help companies match customers with products they would be likely to purchase. Walmart is one company that uses extensive data mining in order to market specific types of merchandise in its local stores based on the characteristics of the people who live in that geographical area. Data mining used in conjunction with Web site data is referred to as *Web mining*; the analysis of text-based data (such as online forms, e-mails, and call-center notes) is referred to as *text mining*. Mining and analyzing data from blogs and social media Web sites (such as monitoring customer sentiments and analyzing comments about company products and competitive products) is called *social media analytics*. The various forms of data mining can be used to generate information useful for decision making that would otherwise be too time consuming and expensive, or even impossible, to generate manually.

The massive amounts of data (transaction data, e-mail messages, social media posts, and so forth) generated today is collectively referred to as **big data** and, according to IBM, amounts to 2.5 quintillion bytes of data per day. Big data is difficult to process using traditional techniques due to its size; consequently, *big data analytics* has emerged and is evolving to meet current needs. One rapidly growing area is *predictive analytics*, which uses analytical tools to predict future outcomes. For a look at how big data and analytics are now being used in a variety of industries, see the How It Works box.

Source: IBM Corporation

**⚠ FIGURE 10-2**
**Business analytics (BA).**

**TIP** ✓

In response to the growing need for, and predicted shortage of, analytical experts for the vast amount of business data collected today, many colleges and universities are now offering graduate programs in business analytics.

**TIP** ✓

Twitter users send between one and five billion Tweets per month.

## Users of Information Systems

Some information systems are very specialized and are used by just one individual or department in an organization; others are more general purpose and may be used by nearly all employees. Systems that are used by an entire enterprise are referred to as **enterprise systems**.

---

> **Business intelligence (BI).** The process of gathering, storing, accessing, and analyzing data in order to make better business decisions. > **Business analytics (BA).** The process of analyzing data to evaluate a company's operations. > **Data warehouse.** A comprehensive collection of data about a company and its customers. > **Data mining.** The process of using intelligent software to analyze data warehouses for patterns and relationships. > **Big data.** The vast amount of business data generated today. > **Enterprise system.** A system that is used throughout an entire enterprise.

# HOW IT WORKS

## Big Data . . . For Everything

Big data is big. It is generated by everything around us, such as by every digital transaction and social media exchange, as well as by sensors and other IoT components. The trick to big data is extracting meaningful value from it. From professional sports to casinos to retail stores to airlines to medical centers to museums and aquariums, data is being gathered with the hopes that analytics can generate both descriptive and predictive information that can be used to make better decisions.

Sports teams, both professional and collegiate, are early adopters of this technology. Analytics are used with players (such as to determine which players to choose in drafts, to develop customized training programs geared toward individual players' identified strengths and weaknesses, and to determine which plays and players to use during games based on real-time data gathered during that game); they are also used for marketing purposes. For example, teams use analytics to better understand what services fans want (including products at stadium concession stands and team stores, ticket promotions, and mobile services during games) to increase fan loyalty and sales.

Point Defiance Zoo & Aquarium in Washington State (see the accompanying photo) is a more recent adopter. It collects millions of data records each day about visitor exhibit and event preferences, visitor participation in conservation initiatives, visitor feedback posted on Facebook and other social media channels, popularity of exhibits (based on check-ins at exhibits with mobile devices), and more. The zoo is using an IBM Big Data analytics system to uncover the patterns and trends in its data to help drive ticket sales, enhance visitor experiences, and increase visitor participation in raising awareness of wildlife conservation. And it's working—the zoo's online sales program grew by more than 700 percent in the first two years of the system and membership renewals doubled by using targeted discount renewal offers to individuals with memberships about to expire. The system also includes external data (such as weather) to make decisions regarding staffing and animal enrichment times.

Successful analytics requires both quality data from the appropriate sources and the proper system to analyze it. The complexity of today's analytics typically requires more than just a statistician or marketer—it requires specialists like data scientists, data engineers, and analytics managers to develop and maintain the appropriate system that meets each individual situation. This is good news for the IT job market—according to recent estimates, there will be a shortfall of 190,000 data scientists by 2018.

Source: Point Defiance Zoo & Aquarium

---

Systems that link and are used by multiple enterprises—such as a business and its suppliers and other business partners—are often called *inter-enterprise systems*.

While some information systems may be used by all levels of employees, others are designed for management decision making. Information systems can provide managers with efficient access to the information they need when making decisions. However, in order to do this, information systems must be set up to deliver the correct information to the manager at the right time.

Managers are usually classified into three categories (*executive, middle,* and *operational*), based on the job functions they perform and the types of decisions they make. These positions are often pictured as a *management pyramid* (see Figure 10-3) to illustrate their usual ratio and hierarchical ranking—executive managers are fewer in number and at the top of the pyramid, and operational managers are greater in number and near the bottom of the pyramid. Figure 10-3 also includes the other users of information systems—namely, nonmanagement workers and *external users*, such as customers, suppliers, and strategic partners.

Managers most often manage the employees who are one level below them on the pyramid. For example, executive managers are typically in charge of middle managers, and operational managers supervise nonmanagement workers. Each group of users and the types of decisions those users typically make are summarized next.

➤ *Executive managers*—include the highest management positions in an organization, such as the president and chief executive officer (CEO); they use information systems to make relatively unstructured, long-term strategic decisions.

➤ *Middle managers*—include managers who fall between executive managers and operational managers; they use information systems to make moderately structured, tactical decisions.

➤ *Operational managers*—include supervisors, office managers, foremen, and other managers who supervise nonmanagement workers; they use information systems to make highly structured, operational decisions geared toward meeting short-term objectives.

➤ *Nonmanagement workers*—include office workers, accountants, engineers, and other workers; they use information systems to make the on-the-job decisions necessary to perform their jobs.

➤ *External users*—include individuals outside an organization, such as customers, suppliers, and other types of strategic partners; they use the organization's information systems to obtain the information needed in the context of their relationship with that organization.

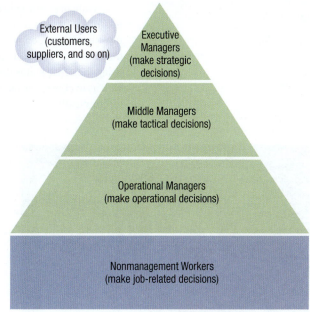

**FIGURE 10-3**
**Information system users.** Include managers, nonmanagement employees, and external users.

**FIGURE 10-4**
**Types of information systems.**

# TYPES OF INFORMATION SYSTEMS

There are many different types of information systems in use today. While some information systems are unique and others vary somewhat from company to company, they can usually be grouped by their basic functions into one of six categories summarized in Figure 10-4 and discussed next.

## Office and User Productivity Support Systems

Computers are widely used to increase productivity and facilitate communications in the office. The combination of hardware, software, and other resources used for this purpose is collectively referred to as an **office system** or an *office information system*. Office systems are used by virtually all employees. Some examples of office systems are described next.

### Document Processing Systems

The cornerstone of most organizations is the document—memos, letters, reports, manuals, forms, invoices, and so forth. Consequently, a major focus of office systems relates to the electronic creation, distribution, and storage

| TYPE OF SYSTEM | DESCRIPTION |
|---|---|
| Office and user productivity systems | Facilitate communications and enhance productivity in office tasks |
| Transaction processing systems | Process and record business transactions |
| Decision making support systems | Provide needed information to decision makers |
| Integrated enterprise systems | Integrate activities throughout an entire enterprise |
| Design and manufacturing systems | Help with the design and/or manufacturing of products |
| Artificial intelligence systems | Perform actions based on characteristics of human intelligence |

> **Office system.** A type of system in which hardware, software, and other resources are used to facilitate communications and enhance productivity.

of documents—sometimes referred to as *document processing*. Although the predicted *paperless office* has yet to materialize and some in the industry are not sure it will anytime soon, most business documents today are stored digitally. **Document processing systems** include the hardware and software needed to create electronic documents (such as the ones created using the office suites discussed in Chapter 6 and the digital forms discussed in Chapter 4), as well as to convert printed documents into electronic form so they can be processed or archived electronically.

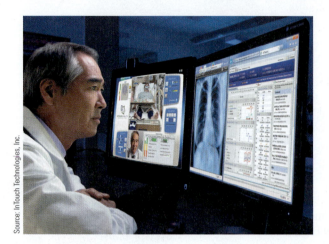

**FIGURE 10-5**

**Digital data.** Many types of medical data are now being created and stored in digital form.

**TIP**

The average person will generate more than one million gigabytes of health-related data alone in his or her lifetime, according to an IBM estimate.

## Document Management Systems (DMSs) and Content Management Systems (CMSs)

To help store, organize, and retrieve documents once they have been created in or converted to digital form, a **document management system** (DMS) can be used. A DMS can store documents that may be needed on a regular basis, as well as documents stored for archival purposes. Document management systems that can include images, multimedia files, and other content in addition to conventional documents are typically called **content management systems** (CMSs). For instance, a DMS can be used for normal office documents (such as letters, forms, reports, and spreadsheets), while a CMS can be used for the vast amounts of electronic data (such as patient data, test and lab results, and digital X-rays) medical offices and hospitals need to store and access today (see Figure 10-5). Using digital versions of documents has many advantages, including increased efficiency, better service, and a reduction of errors. For instance, hospital information systems can enable physicians to remotely access patient records and X-rays; they can also reduce medication errors because medication bottles and patient wristbands can be scanned to confirm a drug and its dosage match that patient before the drug is administered. The use of these *e-health* systems, including the use of *electronic health records* (*EHRs*), is becoming the norm. In fact, healthcare information technology is considered one of the fastest-growing industries in the United States.

## Communications Systems

The various types of **communications systems** in place in many organizations include e-mail, messaging, videoconferencing, collaborative (workgroup) computing, and telecommuting. These systems, discussed in detail in Chapter 7, allow employees to communicate with each other, as well as with business partners and customers.

## Transaction Processing Systems (TPSs)

Virtually every organization carries out a number of routine, structured business transactions, most of which involve some form of tedious recordkeeping. These operations, such as payroll and accounts receivable, inspired some of the earliest commercial applications for computers. Because these systems involve processing business transactions—paying employees and recording customer purchases and payments, for instance—they are called **transaction processing systems** (TPSs). TPS transactions are typically processed in *real time*; that is, data in the system is updated as the transactions are entered. This contrasts with *batch processing*, in which a set (or *batch*) of transactions are collected over a period

---

> **Document processing system.** A type of system used to create electronic documents. > **Document management system (DMS).** A type of system used to store, organize, and retrieve documents once they have been created in or converted to digital form. > **Content management system (CMS).** A document management system that includes images, multimedia files, and other content in addition to conventional documents. > **Communications system.** A system that allows employees to communicate with each other, as well as with business partners and customers. > **Transaction processing system (TPS).** A type of information system that processes and records data created by an organization's business transactions.

of time and then processed all together (such as each evening) without any interaction with the user. While batch processing is still sometimes used for large routine tasks, such as printing payroll checks and invoices, most TPSs today use real-time processing.

Some of the most common types of transaction processing systems are discussed next. In addition to these normal business transaction processing systems, there are also specialty transaction processing systems used by law enforcement, the military, financial institutions, and other organizations. For instance, city, state, and federal governments need systems to process tax payments, fines, and other transactions, and law enforcement and judicial organizations need systems to issue citations and judgments. Like other transaction processing systems, these systems are increasingly being automated.

## Order Entry Systems

Whether by phone, by mail, via the Internet, or in person, many organizations handle some type of order processing on a daily basis. The systems used to help employees record order data are called **order entry systems**. Two specific types of order entry systems are *e-commerce systems* (used for financial transactions performed over the Internet) and *point-of-sale (POS) systems* (used for purchases that occur in person, such as at a brick-and-mortar store checkout counter or in a restaurant—see Figure 10-6).

## Payroll Systems

**Payroll systems** compute employee taxes, deductions, and pay, and then use this information to issue paychecks. These systems also typically prepare payroll reports for management and for tax purposes for federal, state, and local governments.

Courtesy Speedline Solutions Inc.

## Accounting Systems

**Accounting systems** refer to the variety of systems in place to record the details of a company's financial transactions (such as payments and purchases) for accounting purposes. For instance, *accounts receivable systems* keep track of customers' purchases, payments, and account balances and produce invoices and monthly account statements; *accounts payable systems* keep track of purchases made and bills to be paid, and then issue checks when needed. Many accounting systems feed into a *general ledger system*, which keeps track of all financial transactions and produces income statements, balance sheets, and other accounting documents.

**⚠ FIGURE 10-6**
POS order entry systems.

## Decision Making Support Systems

Many information systems are designed to help individuals make decisions. Some of these systems assist with routine operating decisions; others are designed for less-structured decisions. Three of the most common types of decision support systems are discussed next.

### Management Information Systems (MISs)

A **management information system** (**MIS**) is an information system that provides decision makers with regular, routine, and timely information that is used to make decisions. In other words, the goal of an MIS is to provide managers and other decision makers with the information they need to perform their jobs. Often, the data used by an MIS is obtained

---

>**Order entry system.** A type of transaction system that records and manages order processing. >**Payroll system.** A type of transaction system that generates employee payroll amounts and reports. >**Accounting system.** A type of transaction system that deals with the financial transactions and financial recordkeeping for an organization. >**Management information system (MIS).** A type of information system that provides decision makers with preselected information that can be used to make middle-management decisions.

Source: IBM Corporation

during transaction processing. For example, a sales manager might receive reports on a regular basis detailing the sales orders received during a certain time period, an inventory supervisor might receive reports summarizing the current status of inventory, and a manager in the accounts receivable department might receive a report on a regular basis that lists customers with overdue balances. These three types of reports are called *detailed, summary*, and *exception reports*, respectively, and are the three primary types of reports that an MIS generates either on paper or via a dashboard. The information generated from an MIS is most frequently used to make moderately structured, middle-management decisions that often focus on the efficiency of the company. A dashboard showing information to be used by retail buyers to make decisions is shown in Figure 10-7.

⚠ **FIGURE 10-7**
A sales MIS.

## Decision Support Systems (DSSs)

A **decision support system** (**DSS**) is an information system that is also used to help make decisions. Unlike the more structured transaction processing and management information systems, however, decision support systems are most often used by middle and executive managers for unstructured decisions. Unstructured decisions often need to be based on unpredictable events or incomplete knowledge, as well as qualitative instead of quantitative data. DSSs may incorporate data from internal (within a particular enterprise) and external (outside of that enterprise) sources. External data used in a DSS might include interest rates, current construction costs, consumer confidence index numbers, the Dow Jones Industrial Average, and other economic indicators. A DSS specifically targeted to upper management is called an *executive information system* (*EIS*).

▽ **FIGURE 10-8**
A car-buying DSS.

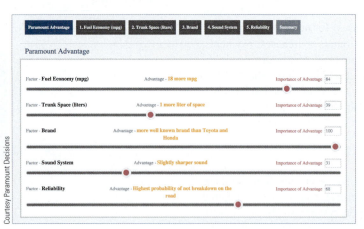

Courtesy Paramount Decisions

Decision support systems are used for a variety of applications in a diverse group of industries, including making business management decisions; making agricultural production decisions; scheduling and modifying routes for trucks, planes, and other transportation vehicles to react to real-time changing events (such as new pickups or deliveries for a delivery vehicle); and assisting healthcare providers with clinical decisions such as diagnosis and treatment. A decision support system designed for determining which car to purchase based on the user's requirements and perceived advantages is shown in Figure 10-8.

## Geographic Information Systems (GISs)

A **geographic information system** (**GIS**) is an information system that combines geographic information (such as maps and terrain data) with other types of data (such as information about customers, sales, population, income, and so forth) in order to provide a better understanding of the relationships among the data. GIS output is typically in the form of data superimposed on maps, which allows decision makers to see relationships, patterns, or trends that they may not see otherwise. GISs are commonly used to make a variety of decisions that involve locations, such as finding the best location for a new store, analyzing the flood or tornado risk for a particular home or neighborhood, developing regional marketing plans, or detecting crime patterns for specific geographic locations. For example, visualizing potential locations for a new store on a map, along with data representing other factors—such as traffic, population, weather, housing prices, household income, crime statistics, and possible environmental concerns like wetlands or protected species that might hamper construction—can help a manager select the optimal location.

GISs are also an essential component of emergency response and disaster relief systems (see the Esri GIS for the 2015 Nepal earthquake in Figure 10-9). They are used to build search maps for rescue workers, to translate street addresses of survivors requiring helicopter rescues into map coordinates for the helicopter pilots, and to create maps illustrating various issues, such as where electrical power has and has not been restored. The process of gathering, processing, and interpreting geographical information is referred to as *geomatics*; an emerging college major is *geomatics engineering*.

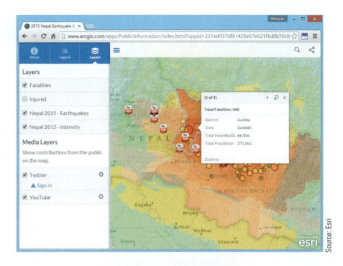

Source: Esri

**FIGURE 10-9**

**Geographic information systems (GISs).** This GIS illustrates the severity of the 2015 Nepal earthquake, as well as fatalities, injuries, and social media activity, by geographical region.

## Integrated Enterprise Systems

Some types of systems in a business or other enterprise are designed to be *integrated systems*; that is, separate systems that are designed to work in conjunction with other systems. Some specific examples are discussed next.

### Electronic Data Interchange (EDI)

**Electronic data interchange** (**EDI**) refers to the transfer of data electronically between companies using networks, such as the Internet. With EDI, the computers located at one company are linked to the computers of key customers or suppliers so that business data and information (such as purchase orders and invoices) can be exchanged electronically as needed. EDI can speed up *business processes* (sets of tasks and activities used to accomplish a specific organizational goal) tremendously, such as by enabling a company to order the appropriate materials automatically from the appropriate supplier when the stocks of those materials have reached the designated reorder point.

### Enterprise Resource Planning (ERP)

**Enterprise resource planning** (**ERP**) is a special type of large, integrated system that ties together all types of a company's activities, such as planning, manufacturing, sales, marketing, distribution, customer service, and finance. Instead of each department having its own separate system, as in the past, an ERP system combines them all into a single, integrated application. Data is usually stored in a central database and the ERP system provides a standard access medium to all employees who need to access that data. For example, when an order is placed, the employee who takes the order from a customer

## ASK THE EXPERT

**David Tron,** Vice President, IT Development, McDonald's Corporation

### What role does technology play in the day-to-day operations at McDonald's?

Technology plays a role in virtually every part of McDonald's operations with the primary goal of providing an optimum customer experience. It also reduces the complexity of day-to-day operations. At the front-counter, digital menu boards deliver a modern and streamlined view of our products while simplifying content management. The Point of Sale (POS) system simplifies the order-entry process. Orders are quickly assembled and served based on information displayed on monitors throughout the kitchen and service areas. In the drive-thru, technology increases order accuracy by displaying orders to customers during the ordering process. Increasingly, mobile technology allows customers to receive customized offers, place orders, and pay via smartphones.

Technology also plays a key role in the back office—scheduling labor, tracking and ordering inventory, and providing real-time reports and alerts that are essential to smooth operations. Centrally managed menu information is sent to the restaurants each day and Learning Management Systems provide up-to-date training for managers and crew.

has all the information necessary to complete the order (such as the customer's credit information and shipping address, the company's inventory levels, and the shipping schedule). Throughout the order fulfillment and billing process, everyone in the company who deals with the order has access to the same information related to that customer's order, without having to reenter the data. When one department finishes with the order, the ERP system may automatically route it to the next department. At any point in the process, the order status can be determined by anyone in the company authorized to access the system.

Today's ERP applications are commonly Web-based so authorized users both inside and outside the company can get easy access to ERP-generated data. When information from an ERP or other type of internal system is exchanged between different applications (either within an organization or between organizations), it is called *enterprise application integration* (*EAI*).

### Inventory and Product Management Systems

**Inventory management systems** (sometimes called *inventory control systems*) are systems designed to help track and manage inventory (see Figure 10-10). They can help optimize ordering to reduce costs and manage inventory in real time during the manufacturing or order fulfillment process. Many are Web-based so they can be accessed using any device from anywhere and can integrate inventory with sales from multiple channels, such as for businesses that sell products via multiple online storefronts as well as via direct sales. The process of overseeing materials, as well as the information and finances related to those materials, as they move through the entire *supply chain* (from the original supplier to the consumer) is often referred to as *supply chain management* (*SCM*). The goal of SCM is to reduce operating and inventory costs while meeting delivery objectives and

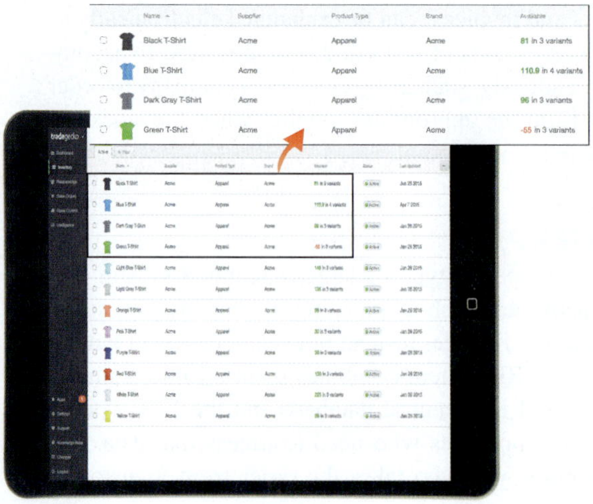

**FIGURE 10-10**
Inventory management systems.

>**Inventory management system.** A system used to track and manage inventory.

increasing profits; that is, to be able to deliver the right product to the right place, at the right time, and at the right price. One ordering strategy sometimes used in manufacturing to eliminate wasted resources (such as materials, money, and warehouse space) is *just-in-time* (*JIT*). With a JIT system, inventory, production resources, and finished products are limited to the right number at the right time as required to fill orders. Some inventory management systems go beyond just managing inventory to acting as a complete distribution system (including inventory, order, shipping, and transportation management among other features)—this type of system is often referred to as a *warehouse management system* (*WMS*). Increasingly, inventory management and warehouse management systems use RFID technology, in addition to barcodes, to track inventory.

**Product lifecycle management** (**PLM**) **systems** are designed to manage a product as it moves through the various stages of its life cycle, from design to manufacturing to retirement. PLM systems organize and correlate all information about a product (such as specifications, quality history, customer feedback, research and testing results, and sales history) to help companies improve products, create and manage the production of products more efficiently, get more products on the market faster, and increase product profitability.

Both inventory and product lifecycle management systems are often designed to work together with other systems, such as a company's ERP system.

## Design and Manufacturing Systems

The systems used to improve productivity at the product design stage and at the manufacturing stage are typically referred to as *design and manufacturing systems*. Two of the most common design and manufacturing systems are discussed next.

### Computer-Aided Design (CAD)

The purpose of **computer-aided design** (**CAD**) is to reduce the time designers spend developing products. CAD software, such as *AutoCAD*, is available to help design buildings, bridges, and other structures; design new products; design mechanical and electrical systems; create landscape and interior designs; design 3D renderings of items to be printed using a 3D printer (see Figure 10-11); and so forth. Advantages of using CAD include the ability to make modifications to a design more easily and quickly, as well as to test it under simulated conditions (such as testing the design of a new building for earthquake stability to determine if the design is compliant with current regulations or if it needs revision). In addition, the ability of most CAD programs today to create realistic 3D renderings of designs allows individuals to more easily picture what a finished product will look like, including "walking through" a new building or landscape design virtually. These features allow accurate decisions to be made early in the design process to save both time and money.

**FIGURE 10-11**

**Computer-aided design (CAD).** CAD programs can be used for a wide variety of design applications.

### Computer-Aided Manufacturing (CAM)

**Computer-aided manufacturing** (**CAM**) is used to help manage manufacturing operations and control the machinery used in those processes. For instance, computers can open and shut valves as directed by their programs, shape and assemble parts to create products, and control the robots (discussed shortly) used to carry out many manufacturing processes. CAM is widely used today to build cars, ships, and other products; monitor power plants;

# INSIDE THE INDUSTRY

### The Turing Test and the Loebner Prize

According to John McCarthy, who coined the term *artificial intelligence* (*AI*) in 1956 and is considered by many to be one of its fathers, AI is "the science and engineering of making intelligent machines." In other words, AI researchers are working to create intelligent devices controlled by intelligent software programs; in essence, machines that think and act like people. In 1950, Alan Turing—one of the first AI researchers—argued that if a machine could successfully appear to be human to a knowledgeable observer, then it should be considered intelligent. To illustrate this idea, Turing developed a test—later called the *Turing Test*—in which one observer interacts electronically with both a computer and a person. During the test, the observer submits written questions electronically to both the computer and the person, evaluates the typed responses, and tries to identify which answers came from the computer and which came from the person. Turing argued that if the computer could repeatedly fool the observer into thinking it was human, then it should be viewed as intelligent. Many Turing Test contests have been held over the years.

In 1990, Dr. Hugh Loebner initiated the *Loebner Prize*, pledging a grand prize of $100,000 and a solid gold medal (see the accompanying photo) for the first computer whose responses to a Turing Test were indistinguishable from a human being's responses. A contest is held every year, awarding a prize of $4,000 and a bronze medal to the most humanlike computer, but so far, the gold medal has not been awarded. However, some experts believe that a computer will pass the Turing Test within the next 20 years.

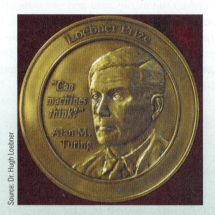

Source: Dr. Hugh Loebner

**The Loebner Prize gold medal.**

manufacture food and chemicals; and perform a number of other functions. Advantages of using CAM include consistency, human safety, and reduced manufacturing time. CAD and CAM are commonly used in conjunction with each other (referred to as *CAD/CAM systems*) to speed up both the design and manufacturing of products. For instance, the introduction of a CAD/CAM system used to design and produce custom-made sockets used in prosthetic limbs for injured U.S. soldiers has greatly reduced the time needed to fit the soldiers with new limbs. Using this system, a mold for the socket can be created in 20 minutes or less, which is significantly faster than a plaster cast mold that might take a day or two to create. Because soldiers require new sockets as their limbs heal (up to eight before leaving the hospital), this system is a significant improvement in the treatment of this type of injury. In addition, the recent explosion of 3D printers has led to CAD/CAM systems consisting of software to design objects to be printed, as well as software to control the 3D printer.

## Artificial Intelligence Systems

Although they cannot yet think completely on their own, computers and software programs have become more sophisticated, and computers are being programmed to act in an increasingly intelligent manner. When computer systems perform in ways that would be considered intelligent if observed in human beings, it is referred to as *artificial intelligence* (*AI*). For a look at two activities related to AI—the Turing Test and the Loebner Prize—see the Inside the Industry box.

Some of the initial advances in AI were made in the area of game playing—namely, chess. Early chess-playing programs were easily defeated by amateur chess players. But, as computers became more powerful and AI software became more sophisticated, chess-playing programs improved significantly. In 1996, IBM's Deep Blue computer won two of six games in a chess match against then world chess champion Garry Kasparov. A landmark moment in AI history occurred in 1997 when Deep Blue beat Kasparov in a rematch, winning the match 3½ to 2½ (three of the six games ended in a draw). And in late 2006, world chess champion Vladimir Kramnik lost a match to the chess program *Deep Fritz*—the beginning of the end of human beings being able to beat chess programs, in the opinion of some AI researchers. One reason for this is that, once the human player makes a mistake, there is no hope (as there would be with a human opponent) that the computer opponent will make its own mistake at a later time to level the playing field in that game.

A more recent development in the area of AI and game-playing is IBM's Watson supercomputer that has the ability to analyze complex questions and form answers well enough to compete with human beings on the *Jeopardy!* game show and win (see Figure 10-12). Watson is designed to mirror the same cognitive learning process that humans have. It gathers data from a wide variety of sources at unprecedented speeds and then interprets and evaluates that data in order to find and disclose patterns and offer answers that humans may not have discerned, much faster than any person or group of people ever could. With the increase in big data applications, expanding this ability to teach computers to find and classify desired patterns in massive quantities of data (called *deep learning*) is growing in importance. Watson, for example, is used in a wide variety of industries, including healthcare, finance, government, retail—even sports (see the Fantasy Football application in Figure 10-13). Some recent advances include teaching Watson how to "see" and analyze medical images, as well as teaching it how to communicate in languages other than English, including Spanish, Portuguese, and Japanese. Another recent AI development is the new Qualcomm smartphone processor that includes AI, which it uses to detect and adapt to security and privacy threats.

While today's AI applications contain some aspect of artificial intelligence, they still tend to mimic human intelligence rather than display pure intelligence. Technological advances will undoubtedly help AI applications continue to evolve and become more intelligent and sophisticated in the future. However, just as the debate about what constitutes intelligence in nonhumans will continue, so will the debate about how far we as a society should delve into the area of artificial intelligence.

Systems that use artificial intelligence are called **artificial intelligence (AI) systems**. Some examples of AI systems are discussed next.

## Intelligent Agents

**Intelligent agents** (also called *virtual assistants* and *smart assistants*) are programs that perform specific tasks to help make a user's work environment more efficient or entertaining. Typically, the agent program runs in the background until it is time for the agent to perform a task, and it usually modifies its behavior based on the user's actions or instructions. Intelligent agents are found on Web sites, as well as incorporated into software programs and mobile operating systems. Some specific types of intelligent agents include the following:

> *Application assistants*—provide help or assistance for a particular application program. Some can detect when the user might be having trouble with the program and automatically offer appropriate advice. Others add speech capabilities to common programs, such as instant messaging programs.

> *Chatterbots*—carry on written "conversations" with people in a *natural language* (such as English, Spanish, French, or Japanese). Chatterbots are often represented by an animated character and typically respond both verbally and with appropriate facial expressions to appear more lifelike. Chatterbots are most often used on Web sites to answer questions from visitors.

Source: IBM Corporation

**⬥ FIGURE 10-12**

**IBM Watson.** Easily beat two *Jeopardy!* champions in 2011.

We've partnered with IBM Watson™

IBM Watson helps us look at analysts across the board and surface news based on their optimism, how they feel about a player, and how their historic behavior might deviate.

Tom has been trending positively with analysts lately

NFL power rankings, Week 13: Patriots in command, Cardinals fall - SBNation.com
www.sbnation.com

Source: IBM Corporation

**⬥ FIGURE 10-13**

**IBM Watson's analysis of quarterback Tom Brady.**

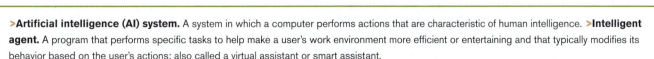

>**Artificial intelligence (AI) system.** A system in which a computer performs actions that are characteristic of human intelligence. >**Intelligent agent.** A program that performs specific tasks to help make a user's work environment more efficient or entertaining and that typically modifies its behavior based on the user's actions; also called a virtual assistant or smart assistant.

Source: Microsoft Corporation

> *Personal assistants*—answer natural language questions and give you reminders based on the time and your current location (such as weather alerts, traffic warnings, and appointment reminders); usually are mobile apps, such as *Siri* for Apple devices, *Google Now* for Android devices, and *Cortana* for Windows 10 devices (see Figure 10-14). A virtual assistant under development is Facebook Messenger's *M*, which currently uses humans to approve or correct answers—the trainers' activities are recorded to gather data to help develop a more advanced automated system.

> *Shopping bots*—search online stores to find the best prices for specified products.

> *Entertainment bots*—provide entertainment, such as a virtual pet to take care of or an animated character to play games with.

Intelligent agents are expected to be an important part of the *Semantic Web*—a predicted evolution of the current Web in which all Web content is stored in a manner similar to data in a database so that it can be retrieved easily when needed to fulfill user requests. To accomplish this, the *semantics* (structure) of the data is defined in a standard manner (using tags and other identifying data), similar to the way XML is used to mark documents and data today in a universal manner. Whether or not the Semantic Web—viewed as part of the next generation *Web 3.0* by some—actually arrives, and arrives in the format in which it is now envisioned, remains to be seen.

**◬ FIGURE 10-14**
Windows 10
Cortana.

**Ⓥ FIGURE 10-15**
An expert system
at work.

## Expert Systems

**Expert systems** are software programs that can make decisions and draw conclusions, similar to a human expert. Expert systems have two main components: a *knowledge base* (a database that contains facts provided by a human expert and rules that the expert system should use to make decisions based on those facts) and an *inference engine* (a software program that applies the rules to the data stored in the knowledge base in order to reach decisions). For instance, as shown in Figure 10-15, an expert system used to authorize credit card purchases would have a knowledge base with facts about customers and rules about credit authorization, such as "Do not automatically authorize purchase if the customer has exceeded his or her credit limit."

Expert systems are widely used for tasks such as diagnosing illnesses, making financial forecasts, scheduling routes for delivery vehicles, diagnosing mechanical problems, and performing credit authorizations. Some expert systems are designed to take the place of human experts, while others are designed to assist them. For instance, medical expert systems are often used to assist

**QUERY:** Should we approve a $700 purchase for Mr. Jones?

**RESPONSE:** Yes

INFERENCE ENGINE

The inference engine is the computer program that runs the expert system. It processes queries by checking rules in the knowledge base against the customer database.

**KNOWLEDGE BASE**

**RULES**

Authorize purchase only if the customer has an active account.

Authorize purchase only if the customer has not exceeded his or her credit limit.

Authorize purchase automatically if the customer has made less than three purchases today.

**CUSTOMER DATABASE**

Jones is customer account 0000-9999.

Jones has a $5,000 credit limit.

Jones has spent $1,529 in the current period.

Jones has made two transactions today.

Andrey_Popov/Shutterstock.com

> **Expert system.** A computer system that provides the type of advice that would be expected from a human expert.

physicians with patient diagnoses, suggesting possible diagnoses based on the patient's symptoms and other data supplied to the expert system. Because it has access to an extensive knowledge base, the expert system may provide more possible diagnoses to the attending physician than he or she may have thought of otherwise.

When using an expert system, it is important to realize that its conclusions are based on the data and rules stored in its knowledge base, as well as the information provided by the users. If the expert knowledge is correct, the inference engine program is written correctly, and the user supplies accurate information in response to the questions posed by the expert system, the system will draw correct conclusions; if the knowledge base is wrong, the inference engine is faulty, or the user provides inaccurate input, the system will not work correctly.

## Neural Networks

Artificial intelligence systems that attempt to imitate the way a human brain works are called **neural networks**. Neural networks (also called *neural nets*) are networks of processors that are connected together in a manner similar to the way the neurons in a human brain are connected. They are designed to emulate the brain's pattern-recognition process in order to recognize patterns in data and make more progressive leaps in associations and predictions than conventional computer systems. Neural networks are used in areas such as handwriting, speech, and image recognition; medical imaging; crime analysis; credit card fraud detection; biometric identification (see Figure 10-16); and *vision systems* that use cameras to inspect objects and make determinations—for example, the systems that check products for defects at manufacturing plants or that recognize stamps during postal processing. Neural network technology is also starting to be applied to computer chips. These chips—called *neuromorphic chips*—use interconnected neuron-like components to be configured more like brains than traditional chips and are expected to help computers and other devices anticipate and learn, as well as to speed up processing.

Source: Crossmatch

**FIGURE 10-16**
**Neural network systems.** Are often used in biometric identification systems, such as to analyze fingerprints.

## Robotics

**Robotics** is the field devoted to the study of **robots**—devices, controlled by a person or a computer, that can move and react to sensory input. Robots are widely used by the military and businesses to perform high-precision but monotonous jobs, as well as to perform tasks that are dangerous or impossible for people to perform. There are also robots designed to perform personal tasks for individuals. The appearance of robots varies depending on their purpose, such as robotic arms permanently connected to an assembly line, robots built on sturdy mobile platforms designed to travel over rough terrain, robots with fins for water tasks, robots

### ASK THE EXPERT

Courtesy iRobot Corporation

**iRobot** **Mario Munich,** Senior Vice President of Technology, iRobot

**How will robots impact our daily lives in the next few years?**

Robotics is one of the most promising areas for scientific innovation and economic growth in America. Decreasing costs, technological advancements, and increasing adoption mean the robots of the future will help us accomplish an even greater variety of tasks in the home, in the field, in hospitals, in the workplace, and beyond. In order to deliver on the promise of robots, it is very important that the industry remain focused on building practical solutions—robots that solve real world problems and provide value. Today, robots can assist us with daily tasks such as cleaning the floors and pool. Looking ahead, robots also have tremendous potential for extending the independence of a growing elder population, allowing people to stay in their homes longer and have increased access to care.

SYS

---

>**Neural network.** An expert system in which the human brain's pattern-recognition process is emulated by the computer system. >**Robotics.** The study of robot technology. >**Robot.** A device, controlled by a human operator or a computer, that can move and react to sensory input.

Source: iRobot Corporation

**PACKBOT ROBOT**
Designed to investigate dangerous, hostile, or inaccessible areas prior to human entry.

U.S. Air Force photo/Staff Sgt. Whitney Amstutz

**REMOTE PILOTED AIRCRAFT (RPA)**
Designed to perform reconnaissance, surveillance, airstrikes, and other tasks.

**FIGURE 10-17**
Military robots.

shaped like animals (such as snakes or spiders) to give them special climbing abilities, and robots that resemble pets or human beings for consumer applications. Some examples of how robots are used in the military, in business, and for personal use are discussed next.

### Military Robots

Robots are used extensively by the U.S. military (see Figure 10-17). For instance, they are used in areas of conflict to investigate caves, buildings, trails, and other locations before soldiers enter them to make sure the locations are safe, and they are used to help soldiers locate and dispose of bombs, landmines, and other explosive devices. In addition to land-based robots, there are also military robots designed for underwater use (such as to detect mines or perform underwater surveillance and reconnaissance), as well as *Remote Piloted Aircraft* (*RPA*), also called *Unmanned Aerial Systems* (*UASs*) or *drones* (such as the one shown in Figure 10-17, which is about to launch at Kandahar Airfield in Afghanistan). Currently, military robots are controlled remotely by soldiers, though researchers are working on more *autonomous robots* that can navigate on their own, perceiving obstacles and determining their course without continuous directions from a human operator, to accompany soldiers into combat. According to national security expert John Pike, autonomous armed robotic soldiers may become a reality as soon as 2020.

Another military robotic application is the *exoskeleton suit*, whose name refers to a hard protective or supportive outer structure. Currently being researched and developed in the United States by several organizations under grants from the Defense Advanced Research Projects Agency (DARPA), exoskeleton suits are wearable battery-operated robotic systems designed to give an individual additional physical capabilities and protection. For instance, an exoskeleton suit can give a soldier the ability to run faster and carry heavier items than he or she could without the suit—up to 200 pounds at a top speed of 10 mph for one prototype. One recent new military exoskeleton application is a system that senses and corrects even slight arm tremors in order to increase shooting accuracy. Exoskeleton suits in the future may include additional capabilities, such as being made of bulletproof material that is able to solidify on demand to form a shield or turn into a medical cast if a soldier is injured. Other possible features of an exoskeleton suit include changing its color automatically for camouflage purposes; relaying information via sensors about a soldier's health, injuries, and location to field headquarters; and administering painkillers or applying pressure to a wound when directed by a physician. DARPA is also involved with the development of robotic prosthetic arms that feel, look, and perform like natural arms—these robotic arms will be used by military personnel who are injured in the line of duty.

### Business and Industrial Robots

Robots are used in business for a variety of purposes, such as for looking for intruders, gas leaks, and other hazards, as well as working on factory assembly lines and other monotonous tasks (see Figure 10-18). Robots are also used for mining coal, repairing oil rigs, locating survivors in collapsed mines and buildings, and other dangerous tasks. They are also used

**FIGURE 10-18**
Business robots.

Courtesy Rethink Robotics, Inc.

**ASSEMBLY LINE ROBOTS**

Source: iRobot Corporation

**REMOTE PRESENCE ROBOTS**

# TREND

### Robot Butlers and Orderlies

Robots are appearing everywhere and hotels are not the exception. A new trend in hotel guest relations is the use of *robot butlers* to fulfill guest requests, such as extra towels or room service orders. Now being introduced in some hotels in the Silicon Valley, these robots (see the accompanying photos), are three feet tall and weigh 100 pounds. They can carry up to 10 pounds of items to deliver and have an integrated tablet screen in order to interact with guests and staff. When a guest orders items to be delivered to the room, those items are loaded into the robot butler's enclosed compartment and then the robot independently navigates to the guest's room. It has a 4G and Wi-Fi connection so it can call the hotel elevator to change floors and it can call the guest when it arrives at the guest's door. The guest removes the items from the enclosed compartment on the top of the robot and then the robot returns to its charging station.

Service robots are also beginning to appear in hospitals. Like robot butlers, these *robot orderlies* are autonomous, meaning they can navigate on their own as directed by their program, using onboard maps and integrated sensors. They can also communicate with elevators, as well as with automatic doors, via Wi-Fi. At the new UCSF Medical Center at Mission Bay in San Francisco, for example, 25 robot orderlies called *Tugs* comprise the largest fleet of free-roaming hospital robots in the world. Tugs are used to transport blood samples, food, medication, linens, waste, and supplies around the huge facility. Traveling an average of 12 miles per day each, Tugs free up hospital staff for more important tasks and save on workplace injuries. For security purposes, sensitive items are transported in locked drawers or cabinets that require either a PIN or fingerprint to unlock, depending on the item being transported.

Robot butler independently navigates to the guest's room.

Guest removes items from the enclosed hatch.

Source: Savioke

to facilitate videoconferencing and other *remote presence* applications by sitting in for a remote participant and relaying video and audio images to and from that participant. For instance, the remote presence robot shown in Figure 10-18 is designed to enable remote individuals (such as team members, supervisors, consultants, etc.) to more actively participate in meetings and other face-to-face encounters from their remote locations. In addition, robots are used for robot-assisted surgery (as discussed in Chapter 7) and for service tasks such as search and rescue missions and fighting fires. For a look at how autonomous robots are now being used in some hotels and hospitals, see the Trend box.

**CAUTION  CAUTION  CAUTION  CAUTION  CAUTION  CAUTION  CAUT**

While some robots are designed to be durable and used in adverse conditions, remember that robotic devices are electronic. To avoid the risk of electric shock and damage to robotic devices, do not use them in the water or in other adverse conditions unless the instructions specifically state that the action is safe.

### Personal Robots

There are also a number of *personal robots* (sometimes called *service robots*) available or in development to assist with personal tasks. Some personal robots are primarily entertainment robots and are designed to interact with people (such as by reciting phrases, delivering messages, taking photos or video, or singing and dancing). Others are designed to be toys or companions for children. Still other personal robots are designed for household tasks, such as to mow the lawn, vacuum the floors (see Figure 10-19), wash windows, or clean the pool. Some personal robots can act autonomously once they are assigned a program; others

Source: iRobot Corporation

**HELPER ROBOTS**
Perform household tasks; this robot automatically vacuums the carpets and floors in a home.

Source: 3D Systems, Inc.

**PERSONAL EXOSKELETON SUITS**
Enable disabled individuals to walk.

**FIGURE 10-19**
Personal robots.

**TIP**

The personal exoskeleton market is expected to exceed $2 billion by 2021, according to a recent forecast.

are designed to be controlled remotely—increasingly via smartphones. Another personal robotic application is the development of personal exoskeleton suits, which are becoming available to enhance individuals' abilities (such as to help elderly or disabled individuals walk or lift things more easily), as well as to enable active individuals to be even more physical. For example, the exoskeleton suit shown in Figure 10-19 was designed using a 3D scanner and printed using a 3D printer in order to be custom-fitted; it enabled the wheelchair-bound recipient to walk for the first time in over 20 years.

Household robots that can assist individuals with more complex tasks, such as putting away the dishes or picking up toys before vacuuming the living room, are a little further in the future—after robot technology improves to allow for better navigation and improved physical manipulation, and after prices come down. In fact, it has been reported that the South Korean government expects to have at least one robot in every South Korean household by 2020. Robots of the future are expected to have a more *humanoid* form than the household robots currently on the market.

### Societal Implications of Robots

Many would agree that the use of robots has numerous benefits to society—such as adding convenience to our lives, replacing human beings for dangerous tasks, and monitoring and assisting the disabled and the elderly. But some individuals are concerned that, as true artificial intelligence becomes closer to reality, a class of robots with the potential for great harm could be created. For instance, some individuals believe that extensive use of military robots will lower the barriers to warfare because they can stage attacks with little immediate risk to human soldiers. In response, several organizations—including the South Korean government and the European Robotics Research Network (EURON), as well as OSHA (Occupational Safety & Health Administration) in the United States—are developing standards for robots, users, and manufacturers concerning the appropriate use and development of robots. The U.S. military is also studying ways to ensure robotic soldiers can be programmed to recognize and obey international laws of war and the U.S. military's rules of engagement in order to prevent them from performing acts such as firing on a hospital or crowd of civilians, even if enemy forces are nearby. Regardless of the progress made in implementing controls on robots, the roles robots should take in our society are likely to be debated for quite some time.

## RESPONSIBILITY FOR SYSTEM DEVELOPMENT

As mentioned earlier, system development is the process that includes planning, building, and maintaining systems. When a need arises for a new system or a system no longer meets the needs of the organization and needs to be modified, the job of system development begins. System development can take place in-house (usually by the organization's information systems (IS) department) or it can be outsourced to external companies.

## The Information Systems (IS) Department

The **information systems (IS) department**—also called the **information technology (IT) department**—is responsible for developing, running, and maintaining the computing devices and information systems in an organization, as well as processing the vast amount of data that passes through the organization to keep its critical systems (such as transaction processing systems) running smoothly. The IS department varies in structure from one company to another, but includes most, if not all, of the technology personnel for that organization. For instance, an IS department may include the people who design and implement information systems, the people who provide support services to computer users, the people who create and manage networks and databases, and the people who secure the company systems and networks from unauthorized access.

The IT person most involved with system development is the **systems analyst**. When a new system or a system modification is needed, the systems analyst manages the necessary activities related to designing and implementing the new or modified system throughout all stages of the system development process. Another individual critical to system development is the *business analyst*, who is charged with making sure that new systems meet the business requirements of the organization. Other key individuals include the *application programmers* (who code computer programs to perform the tasks specified in the design specifications), the *operations personnel* (who manage day-to-day processing once a system has become operational), and the *security specialist* (who is responsible for securing the organization's hardware, software, and data). In some organizations, the systems analyst takes on the roles of some of these other individuals, in addition to the traditional systems analyst responsibilities.

As new technologies (such as 3D printing, the IoT, autonomous robots, and drones) become mainstream or new types of security risks appear, demand for new IT-related positions are created. For example, one IT specialty area with high demand is cybersecurity. U.S. corporations, as well as government agencies, are recruiting *cybersecurity specialists* to protect networks against hackers and other criminals. An emerging new tech-related position is the *Chief Data Officer* or *Chief IoT Officer*, who is charged with managing IoT-generated data and coordinating the development of connected products. Figure 10-20 lists some of the most typical IT jobs.

## Outsourcing

When an organization hires an outside firm to perform specific tasks, it is referred to as **outsourcing**. System development can be outsourced, but it is typically just specific development tasks (such as creating a new software program or Web application) that are outsourced, not the entire system development process. Many companies also outsource a variety of ongoing system tasks, such as customer service, technical support, credit card processing, and payroll accounting. Much of outsourcing today is *offshore*; that is, outsourced to another country. In the United States, business tasks are often sent to India, China, and the Philippines. The use of *nearshoring* (outsourcing to nearby countries, such as Canada and Latin America for U.S. companies) is also growing—Latin America is especially attractive to many U.S. companies today for customer service and other tasks that involve direct communications with customers because of America's large Hispanic market.

> **TIP**
>
> The titles for IS/IT jobs vary from company to company and by the focus of a particular position. When job-hunting, be sure to look for jobs with similar titles, such as *information systems security manager* and *security specialist* for security-related positions.

> **TIP**
>
> The increased use of drones has also created a demand for drone pilots and crew—especially in the U.S. military.

> **TIP**
>
> The annual U.S. outsourcing market for IS tasks alone currently exceeds $100 billion.

> **Information systems (IS) department.** The department in an organization responsible for that organization's computers, systems, and other technology; also called the **information technology (IT) department**. > **Systems analyst.** A person who studies systems in an organization in order to determine what work needs to be done and how this work may best be achieved. > **Outsourcing.** Turning over specific business tasks to an outside vendor; increasingly, the vendor is located in a different country with lower labor costs.

**Application programmer/software developer**
Codes application software; often identified by the language or platform being used, such as **C# developer**, **JavaScript developer**, or **.NET developer**.

**Business analyst**
Identifies the business needs of a system and makes sure systems meet those needs.

**Chief information officer (CIO)**
Oversees routine transaction processing and information systems activities, as well as other computer-related areas. Also known as the **vice president of information systems**.

**Cloud architect**
Evaluates a company's computing needs and deploys appropriate cloud solutions to meet them.

**Cloud engineer**
Plans and conducts technical tasks associated with the implementation and maintenance of virtualized or cloud systems.

**Cloud product manager**
Plans the concepts, strategies, positions, and sales used with cloud-based products.

**Cloud services developer**
Designs and builds the end-user interfaces and tools used with cloud services.

**Communications analyst**
Analyzes, maintains, and troubleshoots data communications networks and assists with connectivity.

**Computer operations manager**
Oversees the computer operations staff and facility.

**Database administrator**
Responsible for setting up and managing large databases within an organization.

**Database analyst**
Responsible for designing and developing an organization's data flow models and database architecture.

**Data center architect**
Manages the whole data center environment, including servers, virtualization, power, cooling, security, and so on.

**Data entry operator**
Responsible for keying data into a computer system.

**Digital marketing manager/social media manager**
Promotes a company and attracts customers via digital platforms, such as social media, e-mail, and blogs.

**Help desk technician/specialist**
Assists users in solving software and hardware problems.

**Information engineer**
Analyzes an organization's data to locate trends, problems, and other useful information for management.

**Knowledge engineer**
Responsible for setting up and maintaining the expert knowledge base used in expert system applications.

**Multimedia developer**
Develops multimedia content for Web sites and applications.

**Network/computer systems administrator**
Responsible for planning and implementing the networks and/or computers within an organization.

**Network engineer**
Responsible for the overall implementation, maintenance, and optimization of network hardware, software, and communications; called a **cloud network engineer** when the infrastructure is cloud based.

**Network operator/troubleshooter**
Responsible for overseeing the day-to-day activities for a network and performing necessary duties to keep the network operating smoothly.

**Network systems and data communications analyst**
Manages the networks in an organization and determines what changes, if any, are needed. Also known as a **network architect**.

**Network technician**
Installs, maintains, and upgrades networking hardware and software.

**Security specialist/information systems security manager**
Responsible for seeing that an organization's hardware, software, and data are protected from hackers, malware, natural disasters, accidents, and the like. Also known as the **chief security officer (CSO)**.

**Software/application software/systems software engineer**
Designs and builds complex software applications; called a **cloud software engineer** when the software is cloud based.

**Systems administrator**
Responsible for maintaining a large, multiuser system; called a **cloud systems administrator** when the system is cloud based.

**Systems analyst**
Studies systems in an organization to determine what changes need to be made and how to best accomplish these changes.

**Systems engineer**
Oversees and coordinates the various engineering tasks performed during systems development.

**Systems programmer**
Codes system software, fine-tunes operating system performance, and performs other system software-related tasks.

**Trainer**
Trains users about a particular program, system, or technology.

**Web analytics developer**
Measures user interactions with company Web sites and uses that data to optimize the sites.

**Web designer/developer**
Designs and develops Web sites.

**Web programmer**
Writes the program code necessary for a Web site, such as to provide animation and database connectivity.

**Webmaster**
Responsible for all technical aspects of a Web site.

**FIGURE 10-20**

Examples of IS/IT jobs.

# TECHNOLOGY AND YOU

### Digital Badges

*Digital badges* consist of icons that represent academic achievements or acquired skills. They are increasingly being offered by educational institutions, Web sites, individual companies, and other learning sources. For example, digital badges are offered by the University of Notre Dame, Purdue University, NASA, the Smithsonian Institution, New York City high schools, and professional certification companies like the HR Certification Institute. Standard badges (ones that are the same for everyone who is awarded that badge) can be earned by online activities (such as by completing an online course or by creating a Web site); some universities also allow instructors to create custom badges to recognize and validate other skills and experiences obtained by students (such as for service projects, military service, or work experience). Badges typically include information about the issuer, how and when the badge was earned, links to evidence of work completed, and authentication information.

The idea behind digital badges is that learning today happens everywhere, often outside a formal setting, and it should be recognized. A *digital badge system* can accomplish this. Badges can be shown to potential employers and educational institutions as evidence of skill sets acquired and other accomplishments; they

can also be used to award privileges, such as only allowing an individual access to a resource after a badge representing the proper preparation (such as a "Digital Safety" badge for students beginning to use a computer lab) is earned. Digital badges can be displayed using a *badge management system*, such as *Mozilla Backpack*, the *Passport* system (see the accompanying photo) used by Purdue University, or a *Credly* account. Digital badges can typically be shared online, such as via your Facebook or LinkedIn page, your Twitter feed, your blog, your digital portfolio, or your online résumé.

*Courtesy Purdue University*

---

Many outsourcing firms have a fixed location from which workers operate, but a growing trend is *homesourcing* (also called *homeshoring*); that is, outsourcing work to home-based workers. Originally, *call-center* type work (such as customer service) was the most common type of work homesourced, but today homesourcing has evolved to include professionals such as architects, accountants, educators, editors, and more. The home-based workers can be employees of the company who telecommute from home, but are more often temporary workers (either self-employed individuals or individuals working for a homesourcing company). In either case, advantages for the worker include convenience and no commuting time or expense; employers benefit because they may be able to get more experienced and qualified workers (such as experienced retired workers or educated stay-at-home moms).

Another sourcing option is *crowdsourcing*; that is, outsourcing a task to a large—typically undefined—group of people. Crowdsourcing takes place via the Internet and is sometimes used by businesses to solicit free feedback on a product or service (often via social media channels today); it is also used to locate individuals who will be paid to perform a service. For instance, the *crowdSPRING* crowdsourcing marketplace (see Figure 10-21) allows individuals and businesses to post specifications and pricing for design and other creative projects. Designers submit entries and revise them based on feedback, and then the winning design is selected. For a look at one tool that you can use to promote your education, training, and skills—digital badges—see the Technology and You box.

One of the primary reasons companies outsource is cost. Because the pay rate is much lower in other countries, the cost savings for

> **TIP** ✔
>
> Raising funds from a large number of people via the Web (such as for a cause or to fund a project via *Kickstarter*) is called *crowdfunding*.

▼ **FIGURE 10-21**
**Crowdsourcing is a growing trend.**

*Source: crowdSPRING, LLC*

offshore outsourcing can be enormous. Outsourcing also allows companies to be flexible with their staffing, using additional workers only when they are needed and hiring the best employees regardless of their physical locations. In fact, the terms *global sourcing* and *strategic sourcing* are now being used in some companies instead of outsourcing to describe the process of hiring employees as needed, regardless of where they are located or if they are employees of the company. Some companies are also committed to practicing *socially responsible outsourcing*—looking at factors such as how an outsourcing company treats its employees, interacts with its community, adheres to high ethical standards, and minimizes its impact on the environment when selecting an outsourcing company. This new focus on socially responsible outsourcing stems from a variety of factors, including the emergence of outsourcing as a critical process at many companies, the increased attention on ethical standards within a company's own operations, and the recent concerns about poor treatment or working conditions of employees at outsourcing companies.

While outsourcing has its advantages, it is not without drawbacks. Personnel changes at the outsourcing company, conflicts between in-house and outsourcing personnel, communications problems, and cultural differences may all create issues. In addition, quality control and security are very important factors—especially in countries such as China and Russia that have known government-run *cyberespionage* programs targeting U.S. companies. Some outsourcing companies try to reassure their clients by utilizing very strict security measures, such as conducting employee searches, providing no opportunities for employees to copy files, allowing no outside phone access, and so forth. At other outsourcing companies, however, security measures are lax. And when a problem—such as the theft of data or proprietary information—occurs, prosecution and data recovery are much more complicated because they must be pursued via law enforcement agencies in the outsourcing company's country. Another concern is the possibility of offshore outsourcing being used to sabotage software or otherwise launch a cyberattack on the United States or U.S. companies. To minimize these risks, some companies are creating *captive offshoring sites* in countries where it is less expensive to do business; that is, organizing their own facilities and hiring employees in a foreign country instead of using a third-party outsourcing company. Although more expensive than conventional outsourcing, captive offshoring does give a company much more control over the employees and procedures used than with conventional outsourcing.

# THE SYSTEM DEVELOPMENT LIFE CYCLE (SDLC)

There are many specific tasks involved with system development. Although the arrangement and order of these tasks may vary from organization to organization and project to project, system development typically involves six steps or phases, which make up the **system development life cycle** (**SDLC**), as illustrated in Figure 10-22. The SDLC describes the development of a system from the time it is first studied until the time it is updated or replaced. As shown in Figure 10-22, each step results in some type of *documentation* that carries forward to the next step in the cycle. The activities that may occur during each step of the SDLC are discussed next.

## Preliminary Investigation

When a proposal for a new system or system modification is submitted, one of the first steps is to conduct a **preliminary investigation**. The purpose of this investigation is to define and evaluate the situation relatively quickly, to see if it is worthy of further study. The preliminary investigation typically examines the nature of the problem, possible solutions, and

---

>**System development life cycle (SDLC).** The process consisting of the six phases of system development: preliminary investigation, system analysis, system design, system acquisition, system implementation, and system maintenance. >**Preliminary investigation.** The phase of the system development life cycle in which a brief feasibility study is performed to assess whether or not a full-scale project should be undertaken.

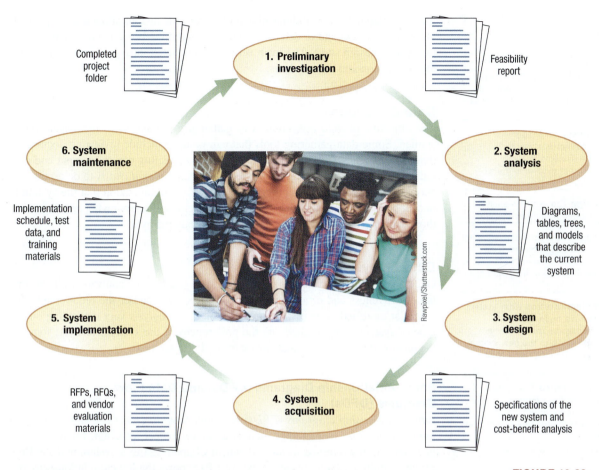

Completed project folder

1. Preliminary investigation

Feasibility report

6. System maintenance

2. System analysis

Implementation schedule, test data, and training materials

Diagrams, tables, trees, and models that describe the current system

Rawpixel/Shutterstock.com

5. System implementation

3. System design

RFPs, RFQs, and vendor evaluation materials

4. System acquisition

Specifications of the new system and cost-benefit analysis

**FIGURE 10-22**

**The system development life cycle (SDLC).** Each phase of the system development life cycle produces some type of documentation to pass on to the next phase.

the approximate costs and benefits of each proposed solution. In this phase, like all of the phases of the SDLC, the systems analyst plays an important role—see Figure 10-23 on the next page for a summary of the duties of the systems analyst.

## Documentation: Feasibility Report

The main output of the preliminary investigation is the *feasibility report*, which includes the systems analyst's findings on the status of the existing system, as well as the benefits and feasibility of changing to a new system. Feasibility is commonly measured using a few different perspectives, such as whether the organization has (or can acquire) the hardware, software, and personnel needed to implement the new system; whether the new system would fit well with the other systems in the organization; and whether the estimated benefits of the new system outweigh the estimated costs. The feasibility report also contains the systems analyst's recommendations about whether or not the project should move on to the next stage in the SDLC: system analysis.

## System Analysis

**System analysis** is the phase of system development in which the current system and identified problems are studied in depth and the needs of system users are assessed. The principal purpose of this stage is to help the systems analyst study the current system and

> **System analysis.** The phase of the system development life cycle in which the current system and identified problems are thoroughly examined to determine what should be done.

then organize his or her findings in order to draw conclusions about the adequacy of the current system and to determine whether or not the project should move on to the system design stage. The main activities conducted during system analysis are data collection and data analysis.

**DUTIES OF THE SYSTEMS ANALYST**

**Preliminary investigation** During this phase, the systems analyst studies the problem briefly and suggests solutions to management.

**System analysis** If management decides that further analysis is warranted, the systems analyst studies the current system and user needs in depth.

**System design** The systems analyst develops a model of the new system.

**System acquisition** Upon management approval of the design, the systems analyst decides which vendors to use and acquires the needed hardware and software.

**System implementation** After system components have been acquired, the systems analyst supervises the process of changing to the new system, converting data, training users, and so forth.

**System maintenance** The systems analyst evaluates the system on an ongoing basis to determine any corrections or modifications that should be considered.

**FIGURE 10-23**
The role of the systems analyst in the six phases of system development.

## Data Collection

The objective of *data collection* is to gather useful data about the system being studied. Some data-gathering tools that can be used include reviewing documents that show how the system is intended to work, collecting copies of input and output screens and available reports, reviewing *organizational charts* to determine the people and areas of responsibility in the part of the organization that the system is or will be located, sending questionnaires to users, and interviewing and observing those who use the system or the information produced by it.

## Data Analysis

Once data about the system is gathered, it then needs to be analyzed to determine the effectiveness and efficiency of the current system and/or the requirements for a new or modified system. The tools used in *data analysis* vary depending on the type of system being studied and the preferences of the systems analyst; some of the most widely used data analysis tools are discussed next.

### Entity-Relationship Diagrams (ERDs) and Data Flow Diagrams (DFDs)

*Entity-relationship diagrams* (*ERDs*) and *data flow diagrams* (*DFDs*) are used to model the *entities* (something, such as a person, object, or event, for which data is collected, as discussed in more detail in Chapter 12) in a system and the flow of data within a system, respectively. An ERD shows the logical relationships and interaction among system entities, such as customers, employees, and orders. A DFD illustrates the activities that are part of a system, as well as the data or information flowing into and out of each activity. In essence, it provides a visual representation of data movement in an organization. Figure 10-24 shows a data flow diagram for the order processing operation of an e-commerce company.

### Decision Tables and Decision Trees

*Decision tables* are useful for identifying procedures and summarizing the decision making process for one step of a system. For example, the decision table in Figure 10-24 summarizes the "Verify order is valid" decision process of the data flow diagram in that same figure along with the correct action to take based on all possible conditions. For instance, according to the information in the first column in the decision table shown in Figure 10-24, a new customer with incomplete information will result in an invalid order. The process of creating the table helps to ensure that all possible conditions have been considered. When the data in a decision table is expressed in a tree format, it is called a *decision tree*.

### Business Process Modeling Notation (BPMN)

*Business Process Modeling Notation* (*BPMN*) is a graphical, standardized notation used to model a business process. It is often used to model the business processes used within systems and is designed to be readily understood by all individuals (including executives, managers, system developers, and end users) involved in analyzing, designing, managing, or using a system. BPMN expresses business processes graphically using *Business Process Diagrams* (*BPDs*)—which look similar to the flowcharts used to illustrate programs, as discussed in detail in Chapter 11.

| RULES | POSSIBLE ORDER SCENARIOS | | | | | | | |
|---|---|---|---|---|---|---|---|---|
| **CONDITIONS** New customer? | Y | Y | Y | Y | N | N | N | N |
| New customer information complete? | N | Y | Y | Y | – | – | – | – |
| 30+ day balance>0? | – | – | – | – | N | Y | N | N |
| Valid quantity and product number? | – | Y | N | Y | Y | – | N | Y |
| Quantity in stock? | – | Y | – | N | Y | – | – | N |
| **ACTIONS** Valid order—proceed to assembly stage | | X | | | X | | | |
| Valid backorder—send backorder notices to customer and assembly stage | | | | X | | | | X |
| Invalid order | X | | X | | | X | X | |

**DECISION TABLES**
This decision table describes the actions taking place in the "Verify order is valid" process. Each column represents one scenario; N = No, Y = Yes, and X indicates the resulting action for each scenario. The rules in this decision table determine whether or not an order moves on to the order assembly stage (according to company policy, orders are not accepted for customers with overdue balances).

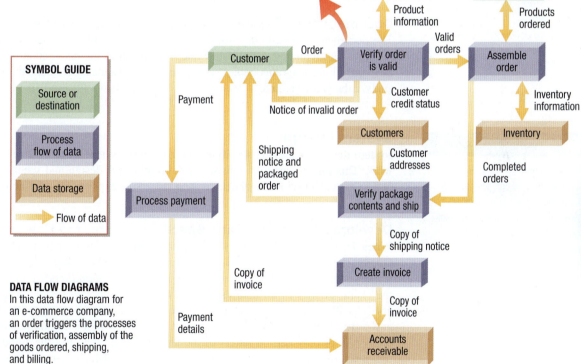

**SYMBOL GUIDE**

- Source or destination
- Process flow of data
- Data storage
- → Flow of data

**DATA FLOW DIAGRAMS**
In this data flow diagram for an e-commerce company, an order triggers the processes of verification, assembly of the goods ordered, shipping, and billing.

**FIGURE 10-24**

**Data flow diagrams and decision tables.** These tools are frequently used to analyze a system during the system analysis phase of the SDLC.

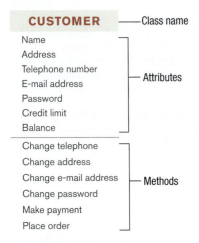

**CLASS DIAGRAM**
Lists the attributes and methods that all instances in the class (in this case, the Customer class) possess.

**USE CASE DIAGRAM**
Lists a user of the system (in this case, a real customer) and its use cases (the actions the user may take).

 **FIGURE 10-25**

**Class and use case diagrams.** These tools are frequently used to model object-oriented systems.

### Class Diagrams and Use Case Diagrams

*Class diagrams* and *use case diagrams* are used to illustrate systems that are based on the concept of *objects*. Unlike more traditional systems that treat processes and data as separate components, object-oriented systems contain objects consisting of data (called *attributes* or *variables*) that describe the object and the processes (called *methods*) that can be used with that data. A group of objects that share some common properties is called a *class*; an object *inherits*—or automatically possesses—all characteristics of the class to which it belongs. Many programs and databases today are object oriented. As shown in Figure 10-25, class diagrams are used to describe the types of objects in a system (specifically, the attributes and methods used with a particular class) and use case diagrams are used to illustrate the users (people or other systems) who interact with the system. Objects and object-oriented programming are discussed in more detail in Chapter 11; object-oriented databases are discussed in Chapter 12.

### Documentation: Diagrams, Tables, Trees, and Models

The documentation resulting from the system analysis phase includes any instruments (such as questionnaires or interview questions) used in the data-gathering stage, as well as the resulting diagrams, tables, trees, models, and other tools used to summarize and analyze the gathered data.

### System Design

**System design** focuses on specifying what the new system will look like and how it will work. This phase primarily consists of developing the design and specifications for the new system and performing a detailed analysis of the expected benefits and costs.

### Developing the Design and Specifications for the New System

When designing a system, the systems analyst must take into account a variety of factors. One important factor is input. The systems analyst needs to determine the data that will be input into the new system and then usually creates a *data dictionary* (which describes the characteristics of all data used in a system) for the new system. The data dictionary typically includes the type of each piece of data in a system and its allowable size, any restrictions on its format (such as having to be within a certain numerical range or consisting of only certain letters of the alphabet), and who has the authority to update that piece of data. Data dictionaries and designing a database are discussed in detail in Chapter 12.

In addition to a data dictionary, the systems analyst will also create the diagrams (such as data flow diagrams (DFDs), class diagrams, Business Process Diagrams (BPDs), and so forth) necessary to illustrate the new system. *User interface (UI) designs* (see

> **System design.** The phase of the system development life cycle in which a model of the new system and how it will work is formally established.

Figure 10-26) are also typically created to illustrate the input screens, output screens, Web pages, and other items that users will use to interact with the new system; these designs should be compatible with all of the devices that will be used to enter data into the system (such as computers, tablets, smartphones, and so forth).

Other factors to be considered when designing a new system include the devices, processing power, and cloud services that will be required to host and use the system; the other systems the new system must interact with; and the type and format of information that will be output. In addition, the system design should address the security features that will be needed to ensure that data is input accurately and secured against data loss. Other security considerations include restricting physical access to the computers used in the system, adequately securing the networks used with the new system, and the necessary backup and disaster recovery procedures. Security issues and precautions were discussed in Chapter 9.

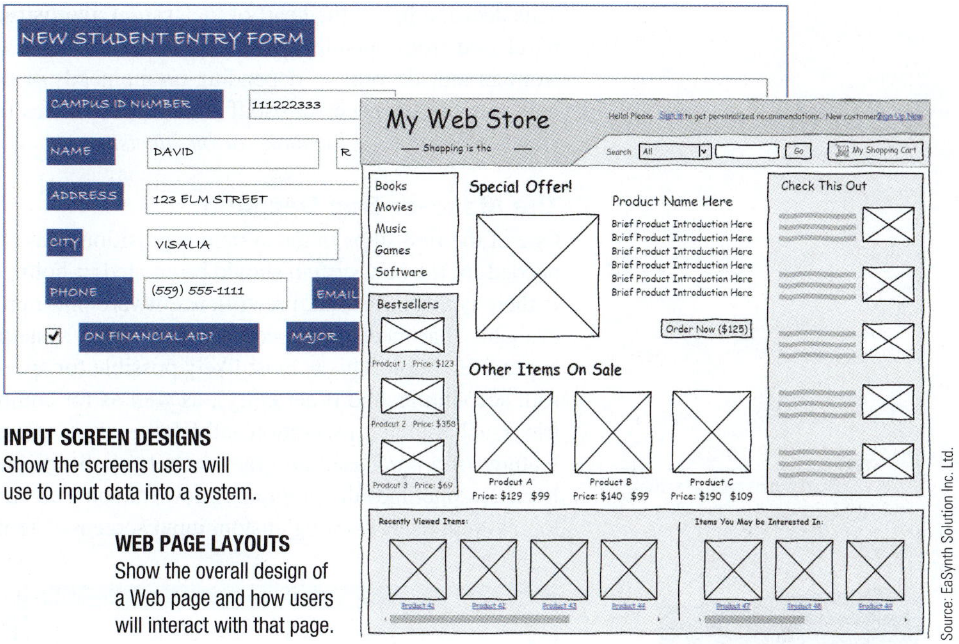

**INPUT SCREEN DESIGNS**
Show the screens users will use to input data into a system.

**WEB PAGE LAYOUTS**
Show the overall design of a Web page and how users will interact with that page.

Source: EaSynth Solution Inc. Ltd.

**FIGURE 10-26**
User interface (UI) designs are created during the system design phase.

## Cost-Benefit Analysis

Once the new system has been designed, most organizations will perform a *cost-benefit analysis* to help determine whether the expected benefits of implementing the new system are worth its expected cost in order to determine if the design for the new system should be implemented. The cost of a new system includes the initial investment in hardware, software, and training, as well as ongoing expenses, such as for new personnel, cloud services, and maintenance. Some benefits can be computed relatively easily by calculating the amount of labor the new system will save, the reduction in paperwork it will allow, and so on. These gains are called *tangible benefits* because they represent quantifiable dollar amounts. Other benefits, such as improvements in customer service or better information supplied to decision makers, are called *intangible benefits* and are significantly more difficult to express as dollar amounts. While the existence of intangible benefits complicates the cost-benefit decision, they are sometimes more important than tangible benefits and so need to be considered. For instance, management must consider both tangible and intangible benefits to evaluate questions such as "Are the new services that we can offer to customers worth the $3 million these services will cost us?"

## Documentation: System Design/Specifications

The system design and specifications developed during the system design phase consist of all the documentation necessary to illustrate the new system, including the data dictionary; DFDs, class diagrams, and other diagrams; input and output designs; necessary security controls; and so forth.

## System Acquisition

Once a system has been designed and the required types of hardware and software have been specified, the systems analyst must decide where to obtain the necessary components.

**TIP**

Refer to the appropriate documentation when creating a UI for a mobile platform, such as Apple's *iOS Human Interface Guidelines* and the user interface information located on the Android Developers Web site.

**TIP**

Be sure to give adequate thought to your UI design—it is a key component to creating a good overall *user experience* or *UX*.

This decision lies at the heart of the **system acquisition** phase. While hardware is usually purchased from outside vendors, software can be developed either in-house or obtained from an outside vendor, depending on the needs of the company and whether or not the company has the necessary staff and other resources for in-house development. This decision is referred to as the *make-or-buy decision*.

## The Make-or-Buy Decision

One of the first steps in the system acquisition phase is determining whether the software needed for the new system should be created in-house or acquired from a software vendor. If there is a commercial, prewritten software program (either installed or cloud software) available that meets the specifications for the system, that is often the fastest and least expensive option. This is most likely possible for specific, but general, tasks (such as payroll, accounting, and order entry), as well as for common systems used in specific industries (such as hotel reservation and construction management systems). Although the basic features of a purchased program cannot usually be altered without violating the software license, sometimes the programs allow for some customization, such as adding a company logo to reports or creating custom input screens. The most time-consuming and expensive "buy" option is having the necessary software developed from a company that specializes in creating custom systems.

Three options for acquiring a hotel reservation system are shown in Figure 10-27. While two of the options shown (installed software and cloud software) allow for some customization (changing the labels on the input screens, adding the company logo and photographs of the hotel, changing the number and type of rooms, and so forth), they likely would not meet system specifications quite as closely as custom software would. Consequently, some compromises might be necessary in order to use these first two alternatives. However, if installed software or cloud software adequately meets the needs for the new system, it is a significantly less-expensive option compared with purchasing a custom software program.

If an organization decides to develop its own custom application software instead of acquiring software from an outside vendor, it moves into the program

**FIGURE 10-27**
Software acquisition options.

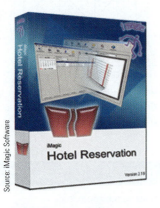

Source: iMagic Software

**INSTALLED SOFTWARE**
Installed on the hotel computers; typically allows for a small amount of customization.

Source: Custom Soft - Offshore Outsourcing and Software Outsourcing Company India

**CUSTOM SOFTWARE**
Can be created to meet all the specifications for the new system, as time and funding permit.

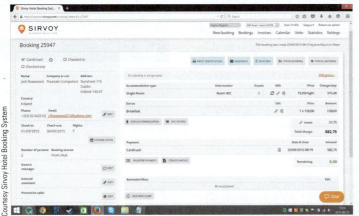

Courtesy Sirvoy Hotel Booking System

**CLOUD SOFTWARE**
Accessed via the Internet; typically allows for a small amount of customization.

> **System acquisition.** The phase of the system development life cycle in which hardware, software, and other necessary system components are acquired.

development process, described in detail in Chapter 11. This process uses the system specifications generated in the system design phase of the SDLC and continues through writing, testing, and maintenance of the program. Once the program development life cycle (PDLC) has been completed, the system development life cycle continues, just as it would if the software had been purchased.

## RFPs and RFQs

Once it has been determined which specific types of hardware and/or software must be obtained for the new system, some organizations may go directly to a strategic partner to purchase the necessary items. Other organizations may choose to or may be required (as is the case with items over a particular dollar amount that will be purchased with public funds) to prepare a *request for proposal* (*RFP*). This document contains a list of technical specifications for the equipment, software, and services needed for the new system, as determined during the system design phase, and requests that vendors propose products that meet those specifications. If the organization already knows exactly which hardware, software, and services it needs from vendors and is interested only in a quote on that specific list of items, a *request for quotation* (*RFQ*)—that names the desired items and asks only for a quote—may be used instead. In either case, the RFP or RFQ document is made available to potential vendors (such as by being mailed to a list of vendors who have participated in the past or by being advertised in a posted document or newspaper notice). Each interested vendor then sends a response (called a *bid*) back to the initiating organization, indicating its recommended solution and price (for an RFP) or just the price (for an RFQ).

## Evaluating Bids

Once vendors have submitted their bids in response to an RFP or RFQ, the acquiring organization must decide which one to accept. Organizations typically have procedures in place to evaluate bids fairly in order to identify the bid with the lowest price that meets the necessary criteria. Part of the evaluation may include the use of a **benchmark test** (which is a systematic process for evaluating hardware and software, as discussed in Chapter 2) to evaluate the components proposed by one or more vendors. Benchmark test results for some existing products (such as computers and commercial software programs) are available through independent testing organizations and trade magazines. An organization may also choose to have a benchmark test performed at the vendor's testing center to determine how well the chosen hardware/software configuration will work. If the hardware to be used in the new system is already in place in the organization, another alternative is installing a demo or trial version of the proposed software on that hardware to see how the software performs. Although benchmark tests for the products under consideration may be difficult to find or perform, the results of these tests (when available) can be helpful in evaluating bids for proposed products.

## Documentation: RFPs, RFQs, and Vendor Evaluation Materials

The documentation gathered during the system acquisition stage includes the RFP or RFQ sent to potential vendors, the proposals received, and any documentation produced during the evaluation of the bids (such as bid rankings and benchmark test results).

## System Implementation

Once the required new hardware has been purchased and the required software has been purchased or developed, the **system implementation** phase can begin. This phase includes

---

>**Benchmark test.** A test used to measure computer system performance under typical usage conditions prior to purchase. >**System implementation.** The phase of the system development life cycle that encompasses activities related to making the system operational.

the tasks necessary to make the system operational, including getting existing data ready to move to the new system (called *data migration*) and installing the new hardware and software. Before data is transferred to the new system, however, the system should be thoroughly tested to ensure it is working properly. Often individual components of the system are tested alone first, and then the complete system is tested. *Test data* that is realistic and includes incorrect data that might accidentally occur during actual use (such as inputting a negative order quantity or leaving a required address field blank) should be developed and used during the preliminary testing process to ensure that input errors are detected by the new system.

Once the system has passed the testing stage, the system conversion process can begin. Typically, system conversion takes place using one or more of the strategies shown in Figure 10-28. With *direct conversion*, the old system is completely deactivated and the new system is immediately implemented—a fast, but extremely risky, strategy. With *parallel conversion*, both systems are operated in tandem until it is determined that the new system is working correctly, and then the old system is deactivated. With *phased conversion*, the system is implemented by module, with each module being implemented with either a direct or a parallel conversion. With *pilot conversion*, the new system is used at only one

**FIGURE 10-28**

**System conversion.**
Converting from an old system to the new one often follows one of these four approaches.

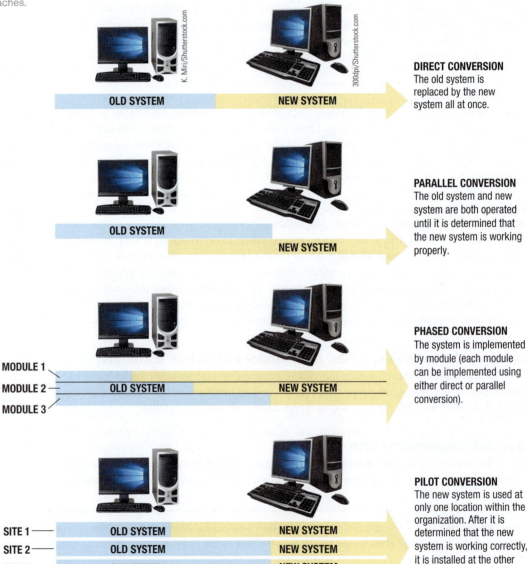

**DIRECT CONVERSION**
The old system is replaced by the new system all at once.

**PARALLEL CONVERSION**
The old system and new system are both operated until it is determined that the new system is working properly.

**PHASED CONVERSION**
The system is implemented by module (each module can be implemented using either direct or parallel conversion).

**PILOT CONVERSION**
The new system is used at only one location within the organization. After it is determined that the new system is working correctly, it is installed at the other locations.

location within the organization. After it is determined that the new system is working correctly, it is installed at the other locations.

After the system is working properly, the final step of the system implementation process is training the end users. The necessary users' manuals and other training materials should be developed and supplied to the users. The training can then take place on the actual system, ideally with a variety of realistic sample data so that users will be exposed to the various situations they will encounter. Training usually occurs in one-on-one or group sessions led by a trainer familiar with the system, although self-paced Web-based training may also be used, if available and appropriate.

### Documentation: Implementation Schedule, Test Data and Results, and Training Materials

The implementation schedule, test data and results, and any documentation regarding the type of implementation used should all be saved for future reference. The test data may be needed at a later time; for instance, if modifications are made to the system and it needs to be retested. The data and corresponding results are also useful if a problem occurs in the future in order to determine if the problem is the result of a situation that was not taken into consideration during the system design process or if there is another reason for the new problem. Users' manuals and other training materials should also be saved for future use.

## System Maintenance

**System maintenance** is usually viewed as an ongoing process, beginning when the system is fully implemented and continuing on until the end of the system's life. One of the first activities that often takes place after the system has been implemented is a *post-implementation review*. This is basically a follow-up evaluation that is used to evaluate the new system, including determining whether or not it is meeting its intended goals and identifying any glitches in the new system that need to be corrected.

Common ongoing system maintenance activities include modifying existing software and adding additional software and hardware to the system, as needed, either to update what is already in place or to add new features. It also includes correcting any problems or situations that have arisen since the system was implemented, and ensuring the security of the system remains intact. Maintenance can be costly to an organization, and it is not unusual to spend several dollars in maintenance over time for every dollar that was originally put into developing the system.

A well-designed system should be flexible enough to accommodate changes over a reasonable period of time with minimal disruption. However, if a major change eventually becomes necessary, the organization should consider developing another system to replace the current one. At this point, the system development life cycle—beginning with the preliminary investigation—begins again.

### Documentation: Completed Project Folder

After the post-implementation review has been completed, its results are added to the documentation accumulated from the other stages of the SDLC. Because the system is fully implemented at this point, it is a good time to ensure that all documentation has been gathered and organized in some manner, such as inside a *project folder*. This documentation is useful for auditors who may need to assess that proper procedures were followed during

>**System maintenance.** The phase of the system development life cycle in which minor adjustments are made to the finished system to keep it operational until the end of the system's life or until the time that the system needs to be redesigned.

the system development process, as well as for systems analysts if the system needs to be modified in the future.

# APPROACHES TO SYSTEM DEVELOPMENT

While most system development projects include the six basic SDLC phases, the exact sequence and tasks performed during each phase, and the names and number of the phases, may vary depending on the organization and the type of system being developed. For instance, smaller systems in smaller companies may follow a less formal process of development, such as skipping or condensing some activities. Other development projects may go back and repeat a previous step to refine the process before moving on. Compare this process with an example from everyday life—vacation planning. People do not always design their entire vacation plan as the first step and then execute it, without modification, as the second step. They might design a plan ahead of time, but when the first day of the vacation is over, they might use that day's experiences as a basis for modifying the plan for the second day. Many systems are designed this way as well.

Regardless of the name or order of the phases used during system development, the tasks performed are typically the ones included in the SDLC. Some of the most common approaches to system development are discussed next.

## The Traditional Approach

In **traditional system development**, the phases of system development are carried out in a preset order: 1) preliminary investigation, 2) system analysis, 3) system design, 4) system acquisition, 5) system implementation, and 6) system maintenance. Each phase begins only when the one before it has been completed, which is why this approach is sometimes referred to as the *waterfall model* (see Figure 10-29). Although the strict waterfall design has no interactivity between the phases, in practice the adjacent phases often interact, as shown by the dotted lines in Figure 10-29. So, for instance, if a problem is discovered during the system design phase, the systems analyst may decide to go back to the system analysis phase for further study, before returning to the system design phase.

With traditional system development, the entire system is planned and built before anyone gets to test it or use it. As each phase of development is completed, users "sign off" on the recommendations presented to them by the systems analyst, indicating their acceptance. Although this approach allows the system development process to proceed in a logical order, it often is viewed as being too time consuming. For instance, by the time the new system finally becomes operational, important new needs that were not part of the original plan may have already arisen. Also, the system developed may turn out to be the wrong one because some managers and other users of information systems have difficulty expressing their information needs and it may not be until they begin to use the new system that they discover that it is not really what they need.

These problems notwithstanding, the traditional system development approach is useful when the system being developed is one with which there is a great deal of experience, where user requirements are easy to determine in advance, and where management wants the system completely spelled out before giving its approval. Often, the traditional system development approach is reserved for the development of large transaction processing systems.

> **Traditional system development.** An approach to system development whereby the six phases of the system development life cycle are carried out in a predetermined sequence.

## The Iterative Approach

The newer *iterative* (repetitive) *approach* to system development allows the system to be developed incrementally, with a series of development steps being repeated until the system is finalized. This approach allows the developer to take advantage of what was learned during the development of earlier versions of the system. One example of this approach is **prototyping**, in which the focus is on initially developing a small model, or **prototype**, of the system or a portion of the system. The prototype is then tested by users and that feedback is used to modify or redesign the system as needed (refer again to Figure 10-29). As soon as a prototype is refined to the point where management feels confident that a larger version of the system will succeed, either the prototype can be expanded into the final system or the organization can move ahead with the remaining steps of the system development process, using the prototype as a model.

Prototyping and the traditional system development approach sometimes are combined when building new systems—for instance, by following the traditional approach but using prototyping during the analysis and design phases to clarify user needs.

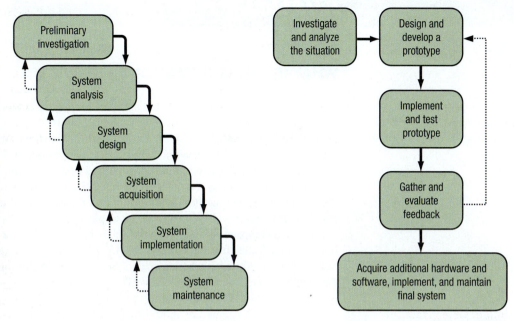

**WATERFALL METHOD (TRADITIONAL APPROACH)**
Each step in the SDLC is carried out in order, although some interaction typically occurs.

**PROTOTYPING (ITERATIVE APPROACH)**
An iterative process in which a prototype is designed, developed, and tested, and then an improved prototype is developed and tested, and the process is repeated until the final version is reached.

**FIGURE 10-29**
Two different approaches to system development.

## The End-User Development Approach

With the *end-user development approach*, the user is primarily responsible for the development of the system. This is in contrast to the other types of development discussed here, in which a qualified computer professional (usually the systems analyst) takes charge of the system development process. End-user development is most feasible when the system being developed is relatively small and inexpensive. For instance, an end user might develop a small marketing system designed to send a group of form letters or e-mails to one or more mailing lists. In developing the system, the user might follow a prototyping approach or a condensed version of the traditional system development approach. When end-user development is used in an organization, it is important that measures are taken to ensure that the system is compatible with existing systems and that no new problems are introduced (such as security risks or a system developed that cannot be effectively supported). Nonetheless, when computer professionals within an organization are too overloaded to build small but important systems that users need quickly, end-user development may be the only alternative.

> **Prototyping.** A system development alternative whereby a small model of the system is built initially and then refined as needed.
> **Prototype.** A model, such as one used to represent a system.

# SUMMARY

## WHAT IS AN INFORMATION SYSTEM?

A **system** is a collection of elements and procedures that interact to accomplish a goal; a **digital ecosystem** is the collection of people, goods, services, and business processes related to a digital element. An **information system** (**IS**) is a system used to generate information to support users in an organization. **System development** is the process that consists of all activities needed to put a new or modified system into place. System development may be required for many reasons. A comprehensive framework used to describe and manage an organization's business functions and systems is called **enterprise architecture**. **Business intelligence** (**BI**) is the process of gathering, storing, accessing, and analyzing data about a company in order to make better business decisions; the process of analyzing the data is called **business analytics** (**BA**). Data about a company and its customers is often stored in a **data warehouse** or *data mart*, and **data mining** can be used to analyze that data for patterns and relationships. The vast amount of business data generated today is often referred to as **big data**.

Information systems are most often used by decision makers—typically, managers, such as operational, middle, and executive managers. Managers usually manage the employees who are one level below them on the management pyramid. Managers, non-management workers, and external individuals may all need access to some information systems to make decisions. Information systems used throughout an entire enterprise are called **enterprise systems**.

## TYPES OF INFORMATION SYSTEMS

Typically, many types of information systems are used in businesses and other organizations. Systems used to increase productivity and facilitate communications in the office include **office systems**, **document processing systems**, **document management systems** (**DMSs**), **content management systems** (**CMSs**), and **communications systems**. **Transaction processing systems** (**TPSs**) perform tasks that generally involve the tedious recordkeeping that organizations handle regularly; common TPSs include **order entry**, **payroll**, and **accounting systems**. These types of systems are most commonly used by operational managers.

**Management information systems** (**MISs**) provide decision makers—primarily middle managers—with preselected types of information. A **decision support system** (**DSS**) helps middle and executive managers organize and analyze decision making information, typically to make unstructured decisions. *Executive information systems* (*EISs*) are decision support systems customized to meet the special needs of executive managers. A **geographic information system** (**GIS**) is an information system that combines geographic information with other types of data in order to provide a better understanding of the relationships among the data.

Enterprise-wide systems include **electronic data interchange** (**EDI**), **enterprise resource planning** (**ERP**), **inventory management systems**, and **product lifecycle management** (**PLM**) **systems**.

Computers are widely used in industry to improve productivity at both the design stage—via **computer-aided design** (**CAD**)—and the manufacturing stage—via **computer-aided manufacturing** (**CAM**). The ability of some computer systems to perform in ways that would be considered intelligent if observed in human beings is referred to as *artificial intelligence* (*AI*). Currently, the four main types of **artificial intelligence** (**AI**) **systems** are **intelligent agents**, **expert systems**, **neural networks**, and **robotics**—the study of **robot** technology. Robots for military, business, and personal use are available today.

# RESPONSIBILITY FOR SYSTEM DEVELOPMENT

Developing, running, and maintaining the computers and information systems in an organization is usually the responsibility of the **information systems (IS) department**—also called **information technology (IT) department**. There are many IS jobs; **systems analysts** are the people involved most closely with the development of systems. Other IS personnel include *business analysts*, *application programmers*, *operations personnel*, and *security specialists*. When a company lacks the in-house expertise, time, or money to do its own system development, it often turns to **outsourcing**.

**Chapter Objective 4:**
Explain the individuals responsible for system development.

# THE SYSTEM DEVELOPMENT LIFE CYCLE (SDLC)

System development usually proceeds through six phases, which are often referred to collectively as the **system development life cycle** (**SDLC**). The first step is to conduct a **preliminary investigation**. This investigation addresses the nature of the problem under study, the potential scope of the system development effort, the possible solutions, and the costs and benefits of these solutions. By the end of this phase, a *feasibility report* discussing the findings of the preliminary investigation is prepared.

During the **system analysis** phase, the main objectives are to study the application in depth to assess the needs of users and to prepare a list of specific requirements that the new system must meet. These objectives are accomplished through *data collection* and *data analysis*. A number of tools can help with analysis, including *entity-relationship diagrams* (*ERDs*), *data flow diagrams* (*DFDs*), *decision tables, decision trees, class diagrams, use case diagrams*, and *Business Process Modeling Notation* (*BPMN*).

The **system design** phase consists of developing a model of the new system and performing a detailed analysis of benefits and costs. Various tools, such as a *data dictionary* and *input/output diagrams*, can be helpful during this phase. Security procedures to be used with the new system should be included in the system design. Once a system has been designed and the required types of software and hardware have been specified, the **system acquisition** phase begins. The *make-or-buy decision* determines whether the necessary components will be developed in-house or purchased. Many organizations that elect to buy system components use a *request for proposal* (*RFP*) or a *request for quotation* (*RFQ*) to obtain input and *bids* from vendors. Vendors submitting bids are commonly evaluated through a *vendor rating system* and then, possibly, a **benchmark test**.

Once arrangements have been made with one or more vendors for delivery of the necessary hardware and software, the **system implementation** phase begins. This phase includes all the remaining tasks that are necessary to make the system operational, including conversion of data, preparing any equipment to work in the new systems environment, and training. **System maintenance** is an ongoing process that begins when the system is fully implemented and continues until the end of the system's life.

**Chapter Objective 5:**
Identify and describe the different steps of the system development life cycle (SDLC).

# APPROACHES TO SYSTEM DEVELOPMENT

In **traditional system development**, the phases of the SDLC are carried out in the traditional order, sometimes called the *waterfall model*. One example of the *iterative approach* is **prototyping**, which focuses on developing small models, or **prototypes**, of the target system. *End-user development* is a system development approach in which the user is primarily responsible for building the system. This is in contrast to other types of development, in which a qualified computer professional, such as a systems analyst, takes charge of the system development process.

**Chapter Objective 6:**
Discuss several approaches used to develop systems.

# REVIEW ACTIVITIES

## KEY TERM MATCHING

a. business analytics (BA)

b. computer-aided design (CAD)

c. data warehouse

d. geographic information system (GIS)

e. management information system (MIS)

f. neural network

g. robot

h. system development life cycle (SDLC)

i. systems analyst

j. transaction processing system (TPS)

**Instructions:** Match each key term on the left with the definition on the right that best describes it.

1. _____ A comprehensive collection of data about a company and its customers.

2. _____ A device, controlled by a human operator or a computer, that can move and react to sensory input.

3. _____ A general term applied to the use of computer technology to automate design functions.

4. _____ An expert system in which the human brain's pattern-recognition process is emulated by the computer system.

5. _____ An information system that combines geographic information with other types of data (such as information about customers, sales, and so forth) in order to provide a better understanding of the relationships among the data.

6. _____ A person who studies systems in an organization in order to determine what work needs to be done and how this work may best be achieved.

7. _____ A type of information system that processes and records data created by an organization's business transactions.

8. _____ A type of information system that provides decision makers with preselected information that can be used to make middle-management decisions.

9. _____ The process consisting of the six phases of system development: preliminary investigation, system analysis, system design, system acquisition, system implementation, and system maintenance.

10. _____ The process of analyzing data to evaluate a company's operations.

## SELF-QUIZ

**Instructions:** Circle **T** if the statement is true, **F** if the statement is false, or write the best answer in the space provided. **Answers for the self-quiz are located in the References and Resources Guide at the end of the book.**

1. **T  F**  Executive managers tend to make highly unstructured decisions.

2. **T  F**  A decision support system would most likely be used by a nonmanagement worker.

3. **T  F**  An expert system is an example of an office system.

4. **T  F**  Assigning business tasks to an external company is referred to as outsourcing.

5. **T  F**  Users are only involved in the system development life cycle if the end-user approach is being used.

6. The software program used in an expert system in conjunction with the knowledge base to reach decisions is called the _____.

7. A(n) _____ is the computer professional who is most involved in the system development process.

8. Benefits that are easy to quantify in dollars are called _____ benefits.

9. A(n) _____ is a model of a system that is built during systems development.

10. Match each term with its description, and write the corresponding number in the blank to the left of each description.

   a. _____ Used to store, organize, and retrieve electronic documents.

   b. _____ The process of gathering, storing, accessing, and analyzing data in order to make better business decisions.

   c. _____ Used to provide upper managers with the information they need to make decisions.

1. DSS
2. DMS
3. BI

---

1. Match each SDLC phase with its description, and write the corresponding number in the blank to the left of each description.

   a. _____ The final phase of the SDLC.

   b. _____ The phase that involves studying the existing system in depth.

   c. _____ The phase in which the old system is converted to the new system.

   d. _____ The phase that involves RFP or RFQ preparation and benchmark tests.

   e. _____ The phase in which a feasibility study is performed.

   f. _____ The phase that generates system specifications and a cost-benefit analysis.

1. design
2. preliminary investigation
3. maintenance
4. implementation
5. analysis
6. acquisition

2. Match each activity with its type of information system, and write the corresponding number in the blank to the left of each activity.

   a. _____ A robot painting cars in a factory.

   b. _____ A manager receiving the same type of report every month.

   c. _____ A person buying a software package online.

   d. _____ An architect using a computer system to plan the layout of an office building.

1. TPS
2. CAD
3. MIS
4. AI

3. Indicate what category of employees are managed by operational managers and what type of information systems those employees would most commonly use.

4. Explain the difference between a request for proposal (RFP) and a request for quotation (RFQ).

5. Assume that a company is ready to install a new system at a single location. If it has a reasonable amount of time in which to implement the new system, select the two most appropriate conversion methods for the company to consider and explain under what circumstances it might want to select one method over the other.

---

1. Some employers today are using a variety of *soft benefits* (such as free or low-cost on-site childcare, gyms, massages, and restaurants) to recruit and keep talented employees. For instance, Google employees get free lunch and dinner, among other benefits. What are the advantages and disadvantages to both employers and employees of these types of employee benefits? Would these soft benefits make you more inclined to work at that company? Why or why not? What about *gamification*—the use of awarded points, rewards, and other game-type incentives?

2. Many everyday objects (such as amusement park rides, cars, elevators, and ovens) that you might not normally associate with a computer or information system, in fact, are today. There are obvious benefits, but are there risks as well? For instance, would you feel more or less comfortable riding on a roller coaster that was computer controlled? Do the benefits of computerizing an increasing number of everyday objects outweigh the potential risks? Why or why not?

# PROJECTS

1. **Today's Robots** As discussed in the Trend box, robots can be used today for a variety of activities in businesses and the military, as well as in the home.

   For this project, select one type of robot device on the market today—for instance, a robot toy, vacuum cleaner, or lawn mower; a security or manufacturing robot; a robot used by the military or NASA; a robot used by law enforcement agencies; or a service robot—and research it. Find out what the robot does, how much it costs, how it is powered and controlled, and if it can be reprogrammed. Does the robot replace a non-robotic product or an employee position? If so, what product or employee position does it replace and what are the advantages of the robotics part of the product? Do you think this is a worthwhile or beneficial product? If the product is one you could encounter in everyday life, would you feel comfortable using it? At the conclusion of your research, prepare a one-page summary of your findings and opinions and submit it to your instructor.

2. **Digital Badges** As discussed in the Technology and You box, digital badges are increasingly being offered by schools and other organizations to represent academic achievements or acquired skills.

   For this project, research digital badges and locate a possible badge that you could earn through your college or a Web site. Determine what activities you would need to perform or what knowledge you would need to demonstrate to earn the badge. What badge system would you need to use in order to display this badge? Could you share the badge on social media, your digital portfolio, or your résumé? Do you think digital badges give individuals an advantage when applying to college or a job? Explain. At the conclusion of your research, prepare a one-page summary of your experience and submit it to your instructor.

3. **Your Decision** As discussed in the chapter, the construction of a decision table or decision tree can be beneficial during the system development process. However, decision tables can also be used to illustrate the options involved with personal decisions, such as for your education or your future career plans.

   For this project, select a particular job you may want to pursue upon graduation and construct a "Career Options" decision table that includes various conditions and rules and that could be used to determine if you have completed the necessary actions to obtain that job. On the table, mark your current status for each specified condition and the decision that results from this input in the appropriate location at the bottom of the table. Prepare a short summary of what conditions in your table you have already accomplished and which ones are still to come, and submit your summary to your instructor along with your marked-up decision table.

4. **Smart Robots** Robotics research is continuing to make smarter and more capable robots. For instance, NASA researchers have developed a way to make a crew of robots work together to grasp, lift, and move heavy loads across rough, varied terrain. The software allows the robots to "share a brain" so that each robot knows what the rest are doing and they can work together, such as to determine how to maneuver around a rock or other obstacle. But can robots get too smart? Is it ethical to continue to replace human laborers with robots? Does it make a difference if the jobs are dangerous? What steps should our society take to ensure that robots cannot become physically dangerous or otherwise pose a risk to human beings? If robotics technology evolves to the point where robots can look and act like human beings, is it ethical to create robots that might be mistaken for human beings?

For this project, form an opinion about the ethical ramifications of making smarter and more capable robots and be prepared to discuss your position (in class, via an online class forum, or via a class blog, depending on your instructor's directions). You may also be asked to write a short paper expressing your opinion.

**ETHICS IN ACTION**

5. **Computer Certification** There are a number of certification programs available for computer professionals in a variety of areas, such as application software, computer networking, programming, and system security. Four of the companies or organizations offering the most respected and widely used certification programs are Microsoft, Novell, Cisco Systems, and the Institute for Certification of Computing Professionals (ICCP).

For this project, select one of the companies or organizations listed in the previous paragraph and research the computer certification programs it currently offers. Select one specific program and determine who the certificate is targeted to, what type of training or testing is required, if you have to have on-the-job work experience to qualify, and what fees and other additional requirements are necessary. Is it an on-site program, or can you complete the program online? Do you think this certification would be useful when looking for a job? Does the program offer digital badges as well? Share your findings and opinions with the class in the form of a short presentation. The presentation should not exceed 10 minutes and should make use of one or more presentation aids, such as a whiteboard, handouts, or a computer-based slide presentation (your instructor may provide additional requirements). You may also be asked to submit a summary of the presentation to your instructor.

**PRESENTATION/ DEMONSTRATION**

6. **Should Unlicensed Drivers Be Allowed to Use Self-Driving Cars?** Self-driving cars are getting closer to becoming a reality for consumers. While currently in the testing stage, self-driving cars could be on the market soon. In anticipation, states are beginning to determine regulations for these vehicles. One of the biggest questions is whether or not a licensed driver will be required to be in the vehicle. One could argue that a human driver isn't necessary once self-driving cars are declared safe and legal and not requiring one would create one new benefit—the ability of unlicensed drivers (such as visually-impaired individuals and underage children) to be safely and legally transported without the use of a licensed driver. But should these individuals be allowed to use self-driving cars? Will we ever be certain enough that autonomous cars are safe to eliminate the need for a human being to be available to take control of the car if needed? Is it discrimination if unlicensed individuals aren't allowed to use these cars? If a licensed driver is required, what if that individual is intoxicated or under the influence of drugs—should that be illegal even if the car is driving? Should autonomous cars be allowed to run errands alone, such as picking up a pizza or parking the car after the passengers get out? Would you feel comfortable being driven by an autonomous car? Why or why not?

Pick a side on this issue, form an opinion and gather supporting evidence, and be prepared to discuss and defend your position in a classroom debate or in a one- to two-page paper, depending on your instructor's directions.

**BALANCING ACT**

SYS

# chapter 11

# Program Development and Programming Languages

**After completing this chapter, you will be able to do the following:**

1. Understand the differences between structured programming, object-oriented programming (OOP), aspect-oriented programming (AOP), and adaptive software development.

2. Identify and describe the activities involved in the program development life cycle (PDLC).

3. Understand what constitutes good program design and list several tools that can be used by computer professionals when designing a program.

4. Explain the three basic control structures and how they can be used to control program flow during execution.

5. Discuss some of the activities involved with debugging a program and otherwise ensuring it is designed and written properly.

6. List some tools that can be used to speed up or otherwise facilitate program development.

7. Describe several languages used for application development today and explain their key features.

# OVERVIEW

If you want to build a house, you would probably begin with some research and planning. You might research current trends and regulations related to home design, draw up some floor plans, estimate the cost of construction, and so on. In other words, you would not start digging a hole and pouring concrete on the first day. Creating successful application programs works the same way—you need to do considerable planning before you jump into coding the application.

When computer professionals need to develop new applications, they use a programming language—a set of rules used to write computer programs. In Chapter 10, we discussed developing complete systems. In this chapter, we look specifically at practices and tools for developing the application programs used within these systems.

The chapter opens with a discussion of the most common approaches to program design and development, followed by a look at the program development life cycle; that is, the phases that occur when a new program needs to be created or an existing program needs to be modified. In this section, topics—such as tools that can be used to design a program, good program design techniques, and types of program errors—are discussed. Next, we turn our attention to tools that can facilitate program development. The chapter closes with a look at some of the most popular programming languages, as well as the markup and scripting languages that are used to create Web applications. ∎

# APPROACHES TO PROGRAM DESIGN AND DEVELOPMENT

There have been various approaches to program development over the years. Two of the most significant approaches are procedural programming and object-oriented programming (OOP). Newer approaches include aspect-oriented programming (AOP) and agile software development (ASD).

## Procedural Programming

**Procedural programming** focuses on the step-by-step instructions that tell the computer what to do to solve a problem. It is based on the concept of the *procedure call*—locating specific tasks in *procedures* (small sections of program code also called *modules* or *subprograms*) that are called by the main program code when those tasks need to be performed. After a procedure finishes, program control returns to the main program. This approach allows each procedure to be performed as many times as needed and at the appropriate time without requiring multiple copies of the same code, so the overall

> **TIP**
>
> Although this chapter focuses on program development, many of the techniques and principles discussed can also be applied to Web application development.

> **>Procedural programming.** An approach to program design in which a program is separated into small modules that are called by the main program or another module when needed.

program is smaller and the main program is easier to understand. Reusing code in this manner also allows for faster development time and reduced maintenance costs.

Prior to procedural programming, programs were written as one large set of instructions containing statements that sent control to different parts of the program as needed to perform actions in the proper order. To accomplish this, these programs used statements that jumped from one part of the program code to another, such as a "GOTO 100" statement to send program control to line 100 of the code to execute commands from that point in the program code on, until another GOTO statement was reached. This jumping around continued until the program ended. This type of code is sometimes referred to as *spaghetti code* because it is a disorganized and intertwined jumble of statements, which makes following the logic of the program as difficult as tracing the path of a single strand of spaghetti in a plate of spaghetti. Procedural programming eliminates this problem by sending control out to a module that performs a specific task whenever it is necessary to perform that task, and then returning to the main program when the task is complete.

*Structured programming* goes one step further, breaking the program into very small modules of code that perform a single task and prohibiting the use of the GOTO statement. Structured programming embodies a *top-down design* philosophy, in which the overall general tasks that need to be performed by the program are first defined at the highest levels of the hierarchy and then are broken down further at the lower levels until they are represented by the very specific tasks that need to be carried out (see Figure 11-1). Although structured programming is technically a subset of procedural programming, sometimes the terms "structured programming" and "procedural programming" are used interchangeably.

In a computer program, **variables** are named memory locations that are defined for that particular program and are used to store the current value of data items used in the program. In a procedural program, variables can be accessed and their values changed from any module in the program, as appropriate. For instance, a *GrossPay* variable containing an employee's gross pay would be needed in several modules (such as in the *Gross Pay, Deductions, Net Pay*, and *Output* modules in the program represented in Figure 11-1). A *StateTaxAmount* variable containing an employee's state tax amount would be needed in several modules, such as to be assigned the appropriate value in the *Compute state taxes* module and then used to compute and

**◉ FIGURE 11-1**
**Structured programming.**

A structured program is divided into individual modules; each module represents a very specific processing task.

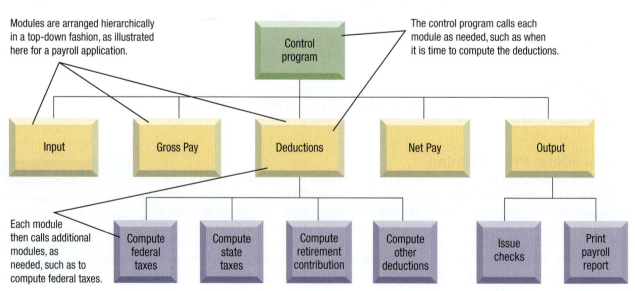

Modules are arranged hierarchically in a top-down fashion, as illustrated here for a payroll application.

The control program calls each module as needed, such as when it is time to compute the deductions.

Control program

Input | Gross Pay | Deductions | Net Pay | Output

Each module then calls additional modules, as needed, such as to compute federal taxes.

Compute federal taxes | Compute state taxes | Compute retirement contribution | Compute other deductions | Issue checks | Print payroll report

>**Variable.** A named memory location defined in a computer program that is used to store the current value of a data item used in that program.

output an employee's pay in the *Net Pay* and *Output* modules. In a computer program, variables are usually designated as *integers* (numeric values that do not have a decimal portion), *real numbers* (numeric values that may have a decimal portion), *character* or *string values* (non-numeric values consisting of the characters on the keyboard), or *Boolean values* (values that represent one of two states—yes (true) or no (false)). Once a variable has been *declared*—that is, given a name and assigned a particular data type—it can be used in program statements, such as to store a value in that variable or to use that variable in a formula. When referring to a variable in a program, its assigned name is used; the exact coding of program statements for variable definition and other programming commands varies depending on the programming language being used, as illustrated later in this chapter.

## Object-Oriented Programming (OOP)

Instead of focusing on the specific steps and tasks a program must take to solve a problem, **object-oriented programming** (**OOP**) focuses on the things (or *objects*) that make up a program. As described in Chapter 10, an object contains data (usually referred to as *attributes*) that describe the object, as well as the processes (called *methods*) that can be used with that object (see Figure 11-2). A group of objects that share some common properties (attributes and methods) form a *class*; classes may be further divided into *subclasses*. Each specific object in a class (referred to as an *instance*) *inherits*—or automatically possesses— all of the attributes and methods of the class to which it belongs. Just like the variables used in procedural programming, attributes are defined as a particular type of data and the value of each attribute may vary from instance to instance.

The methods used in OOP are similar to the modules used in procedural programming in that they include specific operations that can be performed on an object. For example, the class of objects representing buttons displayed on the screen for a particular program might include one attribute for the color of the button, one attribute for the size of the button as displayed on the screen, one attribute for the button's location on the screen, and one attribute for the text to appear on the button (refer again to Figure 11-2). The button class would also include methods for any actions that might be taken with the button objects, such as to display, hide, or dim them. When a button object receives a *message* asking it to perform a particular method, the button object executes the specific actions contained in that method. For instance, a button object receiving a message to invoke the *Display* method might result in the button being displayed on the screen; if that button later received a message to invoke the *Hide* method, the button would then be hidden from view.

It is important to realize that each individual object (instance) in a class has the attributes and methods associated with that class, but the values of the attributes may vary from instance to instance. For example, one object in the button class may have a value of *red* for the button color attribute and another may have a value of *blue* for that same attribute. Objects may also have additional attributes and methods that are not common to all members of the class.

An object's attributes can be in a variety of formats, such as numeric, text, image, video, audio, and so forth. This characteristic of OOP, combined with the ability to manipulate different types of objects with the same methods, leads to new applications that are difficult, or impossible, to create with procedural programming languages. For example, the statement

$$c = a + b$$

is a typical statement in most programming languages and is most often used to combine (add) two numbers. In an OOP language, however, the same statement could be used to

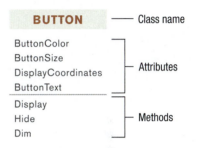

**FIGURE 11-2**

**Button class.**

This class diagram illustrates that each object (instance) in the Button class has four attributes to hold data about the current state of the button and three methods to perform actions when messages are received.

> **Object-oriented programming (OOP).** An approach to program design in which a program consists of objects that contain data (attributes) and processes (methods) to be used with those objects.

combine two strings of data (contained in the attributes a and b) to display a first and last name next to each other. The same statement could also be used to combine two audio clips, or one video clip and one soundtrack, in order to play them at the same time.

Another advantage of OOP is that objects can be accessed by multiple programs. The program being used to access an object determines which of the object's methods are available to that program. Therefore, objects can be reused without having to alter the code associated with each object, which shortens program development time. For convenience, many *object-oriented programming languages* have built-in *class libraries* that contain ready-to-use, predefined classes for common tasks, such as creating a form (for a user interface) or adding a text box or button to a form, used with object-oriented programs. When needed, new objects and classes can be created.

## Aspect-Oriented Programming (AOP)

**Aspect-oriented programming** (**AOP**) is a software development approach that continues the programming trend of breaking a software program into small and more manageable pieces that overlap in functionality as little as possible. Specifically, AOP more clearly separates different functions so that program components can be developed and modified independently from one another and the components can be reused easily. Although both procedural programming and object-oriented programming focus on separating components (by using modules and classes, for example), some common tasks or *programming policies* cannot be separated easily using procedural programming or OOP. Because of this, important programming policies (such as running a security check, performing error-handling procedures, and opening a database connection) may end up being located in hundreds or thousands of places scattered throughout a program's code, making it very difficult to update them when needed. AOP can encapsulate these policies or functions into *aspects*—code segments that can be used as needed without having to repeat the code throughout the program; this helps to reduce redundancy, improve software quality, and lower IT development and maintenance costs. According to IBM, AOP has yielded significant benefits in the quality of the code and the speed with which programmers can write programs. AOP and OOP are currently considered to be complementary, not competing, technologies, although some AOP advocates view AOP as the next evolution in programming.

## Adaptive and Agile Software Development

Program development methodologies that are designed to make program development faster or more efficient and that focus on adapting the program as it is being written are referred to as *adaptive software development*. Adaptive software development typically features *iterative development* (a cyclical approach that allows the repetition of steps and tasks as needed) and/or *incremental development* (developing one piece at a time). One of the most recent adaptive software development approaches is **agile software development** (**ASD**). Like earlier adaptive software development approaches—such as *rapid application development* (*RAD*) and *extreme programming* (*XP*)—the goal of ASD is to create software quickly. However, ASD focuses on building and delivering small functional pieces of applications as the project progresses, instead of delivering one large application at the end of the project. Each piece is typically treated like a separate miniature software project of its own, and the development process is repeated for each piece. ASD emphasizes teams of people (programmers, managers, business experts, customers, and so forth)

> **Aspect-oriented programming (AOP).** An approach to program design in which different functions are clearly separated so program components can be developed and modified independently from one another, and the components can be easily reused with separate, nonrelated objects. > **Agile software development (ASD).** An approach to program design that uses short development cycles in order to produce small functional pieces of a program on an ongoing basis.

working closely together, which provides for continuous learning and adaptation as the project is developed—end-user input throughout the development process is considered especially important. With mobile apps, many developers are going a step further with *continuous mobile innovation*—viewing the mobile development process as rapid and ongoing, deploying a product as soon as possible and then releasing updates on a continual basis.

## THE PROGRAM DEVELOPMENT LIFE CYCLE (PDLC)

Creating application programs is referred to as *application software development* or **program development**. Program development traditionally takes place during the system acquisition phase of the system development life cycle (SDLC), discussed in Chapter 10, and uses the system specifications that were developed during the system design phase of the SDLC. Once program development has been completed, the SDLC continues. The phases involved in program development are referred to as the **program development life cycle** (**PDLC**) and are illustrated in Figure 11-3.

The activities that take place during each phase of the program development life cycle (PDLC) are discussed in the next few sections. As each development activity takes place, documentation is generated. The types of documentation generated, which consist of details about what the program does and how it works, are summarized in Figure 11-3.

### Problem Analysis

As discussed in detail in Chapter 10, the systems analyst develops a set of specifications during the system design phase of the SDLC that indicates exactly what the new system should do and how it should work. These specifications (data flow diagrams, class diagrams, input and output designs, database designs, data dictionary, and so forth) are used during **problem analysis**—the first phase of the PDLC. During this phase, these specifications are reviewed by the systems analyst and the **programmer**—the person who will use a programming language

> FIGURE 11-3

**The program development life cycle (PDLC).** Each phase of the program development life cycle produces some type of documentation to pass on to the next phase.

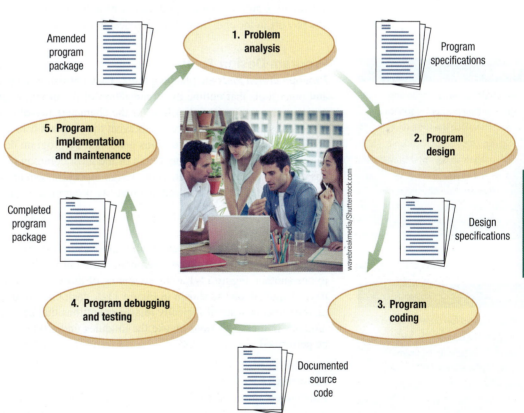

Amended program package

Program specifications

1. Problem analysis

5. Program implementation and maintenance

2. Program design

Completed program package

Design specifications

4. Program debugging and testing

3. Program coding

Documented source code

wavebreakmedia/Shutterstock.com

SYS

---

to code the software program according to these specifications. They will determine the programming language to be used, how the new program will need to interact with other programs in the organization, and other important considerations. The systems analyst and the programmer may also meet with the users of the new system to fully understand what features the software program they are creating for the new system must include. Only when the problem is completely understood should the systems analyst and the programmer move on to the next phase of the PDLC—program design.

### Documentation: Program Specifications

The main result of this first phase in the PDLC is a set of program specifications outlining what the program must do. Typically, there will also be a schedule or a timetable for completing, testing, and implementing the program.

## Program Design

In the **program design** phase of the PDLC, the specifications developed during the problem analysis phase are used to develop an *algorithm* for the program; that is, the set of steps that are needed in order for the program to perform all the tasks that it is supposed to do. Only when the program design is complete and tested does the next phase—the actual program coding—begin.

Good program design helps the development process go more smoothly and makes revisions to the software program easier to do when changes to the program are needed in the future. Careful planning and design of a computer program are extremely important and pay off in the end. Some program design tools and guidelines are discussed next.

### Program Design Tools

*Program design tools* are planning tools. They consist of diagrams, charts, tables, models, and other tools that outline the organization of the program tasks, the steps the program or program component will follow, or the characteristics of objects used by the program. These tools are used to define exactly what the program is to do; once a program has been coded and implemented, the designs generated by program design tools can also provide useful program documentation. Some of the most common program design tools are discussed next. In general, the program design models shown in this textbook are very basic; the program design models used in a real-life program are much more complex.

### Structure Charts

*Structure charts* (sometimes called *hierarchy charts*) depict the overall organization of a structured program. They show the modules used in a program and how the modules relate to one another. Figure 11-1 at the beginning of this chapter contains a structure chart for a payroll application. As shown in Figure 11-1, each box on the chart represents a program module; that is, a set of logically related operations that perform a well-defined task. The modules in the upper rows invoke the modules under them whenever those tasks need to be performed.

### Flowcharts

**Flowcharts** are used to illustrate the step-by-step logic that is to take place within a program, module, or method. The steps in a flowchart are arranged in the same logical

>**Program design.** The phase of the program development life cycle in which the program specifications are expanded into a complete design of the new program. >**Flowchart.** A program design tool that graphically shows step-by-step the actions a computer program will take.

sequence as their corresponding program statements in the program. As shown in Figure 11-4, flowcharts use graphical symbols (such as the *decision symbol* to indicate two paths that can be taken depending on whether the result of the condition stated in the decision is true or false) and *relational operators* (such as < for *less than* and = for *equal to*) to portray the sequence of steps needed to fulfill the logic in that program, module, or method. Flowcharts can be drawn by hand, but *flowcharting software* can make it easier to create and modify flowcharts.

The program illustrated by the flowchart in Figure 11-4 will test all entries in an employee file to determine the employees who have computer experience and at least five years of company service, print the names of the employees who meet these two conditions as they are identified, and then print the total number of employees meeting the criteria when the end of the employee file is reached. To accomplish this, a *looping* operation is needed to repeat some of the steps in the program until the end of the employee file is reached, and a *counter* variable is incremented as needed to keep track of the number of employees meeting both criteria. After the last employee record is read and processed, the value of the counter is printed to complete the printed report, and then the program ends.

**Wireframes**

A **wireframe** is a visual representation of the overall design of an application, often a mobile app. Traditionally, wireframes focused on the visual functional elements used (such as the location of headers, footers, navigation bars, content text, buttons,

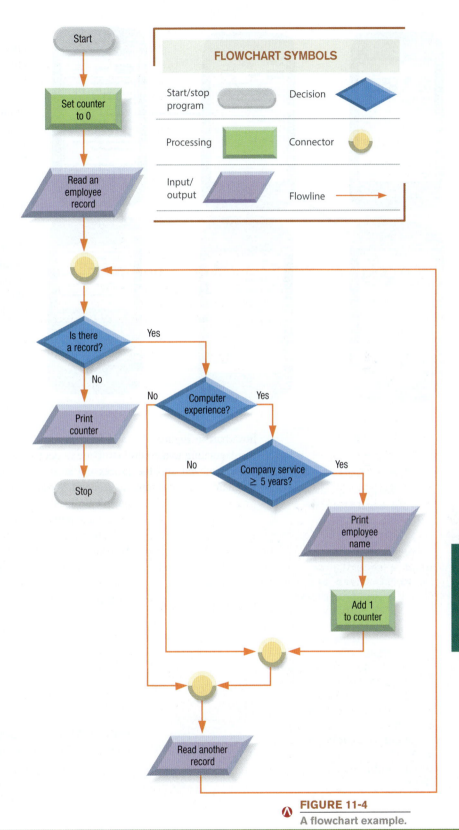

**FIGURE 11-4**
A flowchart example.

> **Wireframe.** A visual representation of the overall design and logic of an application.

and so forth) and, consequently, were more of a user interface (UI) design tool. However, they are increasingly being used to visually describe the logic and flow of the various screens used in a mobile app, in addition to the appearance of those screens (see Figure 11-5). *Wireframe software* can also be used to create prototypes of mobile apps that can be used to present design ideas to end users or clients in order to finalize the appearance and functions of an app before it is developed.

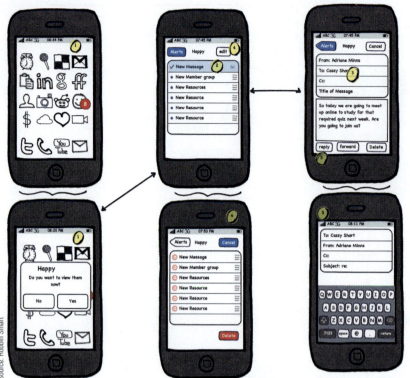

Source: Robbin Smart

**⋀ FIGURE 11-5**
Wireframes.

**⋁ FIGURE 11-6**
**Pseudocode.** For the flowchart logic shown in Figure 11-4.

### Pseudocode

**Pseudocode** also expresses the steps in a program, module, or method, but it uses English-like statements in place of the flowchart's graphical symbols (see Figure 11-6). No formal set of standard rules exists for writing pseudocode; however, the closer the words and phrases used in pseudocode are to the basic computer operations that will occur in the program, the easier it is to move from pseudocode to actual program code. Figure 11-6 shows the pseudocode for the program shown in the flowchart in Figure 11-4 and follows some commonly used conventions. For instance, all words relating to a control structure (a decision or loop, as discussed in more detail shortly) are capitalized and the processing steps contained within those structures are indented. Standard words for input and output (*Read* for reading from a file and *Print* for output on paper) are used, variables (such as *counter* and *employee_name*) have meaningful names, the actions the computer will take are written in descriptive natural language, and the keywords *Start* and *Stop* are used to begin and end the pseudocode.

Although it takes longer to model a program or program component using pseudocode, translating a program from pseudocode to a programming language is much faster and more straightforward than from a flowchart to a programming language. Flowcharts, however, are sometimes better than pseudocode for visualizing the logic of a program, and they are usually faster to create. Sometimes a flowchart is first developed to identify the logic of a program or program component, and then the steps of the program are expressed in more detail using pseudocode.

### Unified Modeling Language (UML) Models

**Unified Modeling Language** (UML) is a set of standard notations that is widely used for modeling object-oriented programs. The UML standards are developed by the *Object Management Group* (*OMG*). The most current version (*UML 2.5*)

```
Start
counter = 0
Read a record
DO WHILE there are records to process
    IF computer_experience
        IF company_service ≥ 5 years
            Print employee_name
            Increment counter
        ELSE
            Next statement
        END IF
    ELSE
        Next statement
    END IF
    Read another record
END DO
Print counter
Stop
```

includes a variety of diagrams for modeling basic structures (like the class diagrams shown in Figure 11-7 and in Figure 10-25 in Chapter 10) and diagrams for modeling behavior (such as the use case diagram shown in Figure 10-25 in Chapter 10). Similar to flowcharts, UML diagrams can be drawn by hand, though using a software program designed for that purpose makes creating and editing the diagrams easier.

The class diagram shown in Figure 11-7 illustrates the attributes and methods for objects in a Bicycles class, such as might be used in an OOP program to model bicycles controlled by users in a simulation or game. A similar model (without the attributes for current gear and speed and with different methods) could be used in an inventory or order entry program for a sporting goods store. As shown in the figure, the Bicycles class specifies the attributes and methods that all objects in the Bicycles class have in common. Each individual object (instance) in the Bicycles class has a value for each attribute to indicate the overall characteristics of that particular bike (such as type, category, size, color, and number of gears), as well as the current gear and current speed being used. Note that while each instance inherits the attributes and methods of the class, the values for the attributes may or may not be the same for all instances in that class. For example, while the two bike instances shown in Figure 11-7 have the same value (0) for *CurrentSpeed*, the values for all the other attributes are different. The methods included in the Bicycles class express the actions the Bicycles objects can take, such as to change gears and speed, accelerate and brake, stop, and turn.

**CLASS**
A group of objects that share the same basic properties. A class diagram defines the attributes and methods that all instances in the class possess.

**INSTANCES**
The specific objects in a class, such as Bike1 and Bike2 in this example.

**INHERITANCE**
All instances of a class inherit all attributes and methods of the class. The values of the attributes for each instance may be different from other instances.

**FIGURE 11-7**
**Class diagrams.**
This example shows one class and two instances of that class.

## Control Structures

A **control structure** is used to illustrate when, how, and in what order the statements in a computer program, module, or method are performed. The three fundamental control structures are sequence, selection, and repetition; these control structures are illustrated in Figure 11-8 on the next page and discussed next.

### The Sequence Control Structure

A **sequence control structure** is simply a series of statements that follow one another. After the first statement has been carried out completely, the program control moves to the next statement, and so forth.

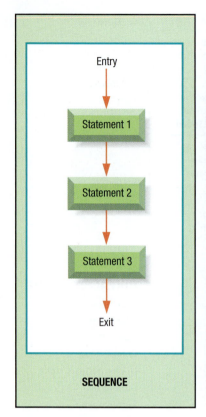

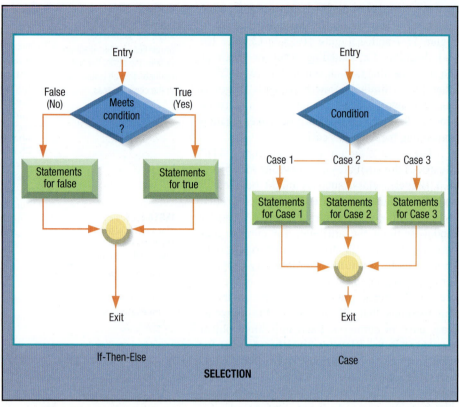

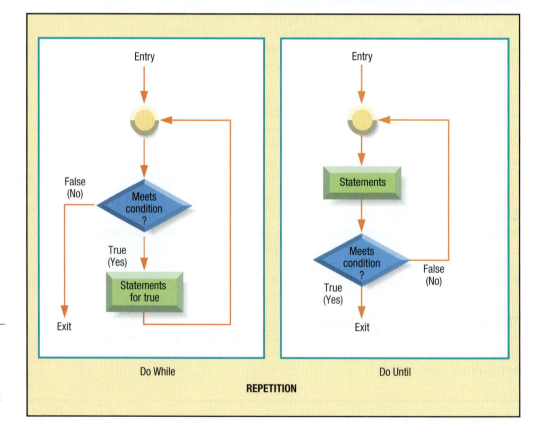

**FIGURE 11-8**
**The three fundamental control structures.** Note that each structure example has only one entry point and only one exit point.

## The Selection Control Structure

With a **selection control structure**, the direction that the program control takes depends on the results of a certain condition. The basic selection control structure is the *if-then-else structure* shown in Figure 11-8, in which the condition can only result in two possibilities—true or false. *If* a certain condition is true, *then* the program follows one path and executes the statements on that path; *else*, if false, the program follows a different path.

An alternate selection control structure can be used when there are more than two possibilities. This structure—known as the *case control structure* and shown in Figure 11-8—allows for as many possible results of the specified condition as needed. For example, the flowchart in Figure 11-4 uses two *nested* if-then-else statements (one statement located inside another) to test for the two conditions "Computer experience?" and "Company service ≥ 5 years?". Because the second condition is only tested if the first condition is true, these two conditions together result in the following three possibilities, or *cases*:

> ➤ Case 1: No computer experience

> ➤ Case 2: Computer experience, company service < 5 years

> ➤ Case 3: Computer experience, company service ≥ 5 years

The case control structure with these three choices could be used in the flowchart in Figure 11-4 instead of the two nested if-then-else statements. The statements for printing the employee's name and incrementing the counter would be listed under Case 3 (the other cases would result in no action being taken within the case structure), and the next action after exiting the case structure would be to read another record (refer to the bottom of the flowchart in Figure 11-4).

## The Repetition Control Structure

The **repetition control structure** (also called the *iteration control structure*) is used when one or more statements are to be repeated in a *loop* until a particular condition is reached. There are two forms of this control structure: The *do while structure*, in which the statements in the loop are repeated as long as a certain condition is true ("do *while* true"), and the *do until structure*, in which the statements in the loop are repeated as long as a certain condition is false ("do *until* true"). It is important to realize that if the condition is not true when the program first reaches a do while loop, the statements within the loop will never be executed because the decision test is located at the top of the loop (refer again to Figure 11-8). With a do until loop, the statements in the loop are always executed at least one time, because the decision test is located at the bottom of the loop (refer again to Figure 11-8).

## Good Program Design

Good program design is essential. If a program is not well planned before the coding process begins, it usually results in a more time-consuming and, potentially, lower-quality result than if the design process had been carried out properly. In general, time spent planning is time well spent. A few principles that should be kept in mind to help facilitate good program design are discussed next.

**TIP**

The idea of *if-then* is beginning to be applied to the Web; services (called *channels*) that use the *IFTTT* (*If this, then that*) approach perform actions based on specified triggers, such as saving e-mail attachments to your Dropbox account whenever one is received or copying photos you are tagged in to your Flickr account whenever they are posted on Facebook.

> **Selection control structure.** A series of statements in which the results of a decision determine the direction the program takes. > **Repetition control structure.** A series of statements in a loop that are repeated until a particular condition is met.

| DIRECTIONS FOR PERSON | DIRECTIONS FOR COMPUTER |
|---|---|
| 1. Please make a piece of toast with margarine for me. | 1. Take one slice of bread out of the bag of bread, then close the bag. |
| | 2. Put the bread into the slot on the toaster, narrow edge first with the widest part of the bread fitting into the widest part of the slot. |
| | 3. Push the start lever on the toaster down. |
| | 4. When the toast pops up, remove the toast from the toaster. |
| | 5. Place the toast on a plate. |
| | 6. Open the silverware drawer, take out a knife, then close the silverware drawer. |
| | 7. Open the refrigerator, remove the margarine, then shut the refrigerator. |
| | 8. Take the lid off the margarine. |
| | 9. Scoop out one teaspoon of margarine with the knife. |
| | 10. Spread the margarine on the top side of the toast, evenly covering that surface of the toast. |
| | 11. Place the lid back on the margarine. |
| | 12. Open the refrigerator, replace the margarine, then shut the refrigerator. |

Les Scholz/Shutterstock.com

**FIGURE 11-9**

**Writing instructions for a computer versus a person.**

A computer requires step-by-step instructions.

**Be Specific**

When illustrating the instructions that a computer will follow, *all* things that the computer must do or consider must be specified. Although the instruction "Please make a piece of toast with margarine for me" would be a request that another person could follow easily, it is not specific enough for a computer to follow.

To instruct a computer properly, every step the computer must perform and every decision the computer must make has to be stated precisely (see Figure 11-9).

### Follow the One-Entry-Point/One-Exit-Point Rule

An important characteristic of the control structures just discussed is that each permits only one entry point into and one exit point out of any structure (refer again to Figure 11-8). This property is sometimes called the *one-entry-point/one-exit-point rule*. Programs that adhere to this rule are much more readable, their logic is easier to follow, and they are easier to modify in the future.

### No Infinite Loops or Logic Errors

An *infinite loop* is a set of instructions that repeats forever. An infinite loop occurs when the condition to exit a loop never occurs, such as when a do while condition never becomes false or a do until condition never becomes true. This can happen when the statement to increment a counter is forgotten, when the wrong operators are used—such as less than (<) instead of greater than (>)—or when a similar error in logic is made. To test for infinite loops and other *logic errors*, it is a good idea to test your finished program design, as discussed next.

### Program Design Testing

Once the algorithm for a program or program component has been completed, the design should be tested to locate any errors in the logic of the program. One of the most common ways to test a design is to perform a *desk check*. In a desk check, the programmer "walks" through the program design (such as by following the steps of a finished flowchart), keeping track of the values of any loop counters and other variables in a *tracing table* to ensure the program does what it is intended to do. At the end of the program, the output should be the expected values, based on the test data used. If the output is incorrect, there is an error in the design that needs to be located and corrected before the program moves on to the coding stage. Examples of desk checking a flowchart representing the steps needed to input two numbers and compute their sum (one correct flowchart and one flowchart containing an error) are shown in Figure 11-10.

### Documentation: Design Specifications

The documentation resulting from the design phase of the PDLC is a set of design specifications that illustrates the program needed to fulfill the program requirements. The design specifications can be expressed using one or more design tools, such as structure charts, flowcharts, wireframes, pseudocode, UML models, and any modified UI designs. The test data and results from desk checking should be included as well.

**✓ TIP**

The wireframe or other representation of the UI design should also be tested to make sure it is intuitive and easy to use; if the tester has a hard time finding an option on the screen or using an app feature, the design should be rethought.

## DESK CHECK RESULTS FOR CORRECT FLOWCHART

| Flowchart Stage | Counter | Decision Test Results (Counter < 2) | Number | Sum |
|---|---|---|---|---|
| Initialization | 0 | – | – | 0 |
| First decision test | 0 | T (enters loop) | – | 0 |
| After first loop | 1 | – | 6 | 6 |
| Second decision test | 1 | T (enters loop) | 6 | 6 |
| After second loop | 2 | – | 3 | 9 |
| Third decision test | 2 | F (exits loop) | 3 | 9 |

Test data: 6, 3; Expected results: Sum = 9; Actual results: Sum = 9

## DESK CHECK RESULTS FOR INCORRECT FLOWCHART

| Flowchart Stage | Counter | Decision Test Results (Counter < 2) | Number | Sum |
|---|---|---|---|---|
| Initialization | 1 | – | – | 0 |
| First decision test | 1 | T (enters loop) | – | 0 |
| After first loop | 2 | – | 6 | 6 |
| Second decision test | 2 | F (exits loop) | 6 | 6 |

Test data: 6, 3; Expected results: Sum = 9; Actual results: Sum = 6

**ADDING TWO NUMBERS**
**(correct design)**

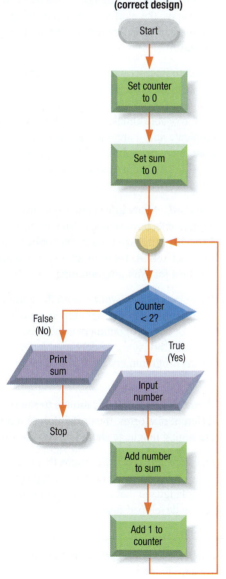

**ADDING TWO NUMBERS**
**(incorrect design)**

Error in flowchart (Because counter is initially set to 1, the loop is performed once and only one number is input before the sum is printed.)

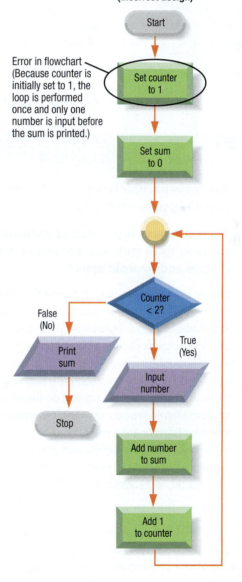

**FIGURE 11-10**

Desk checking a flowchart.

## Program Coding

Once the program design is complete, the next phase is **program coding**—the process of **coding** or writing the actual program steps in the proper format for a particular programming language. Each programming language has its own *syntax*, or rules, regarding how programs can be written, so choosing the programming language to be used is typically the first step. To help produce code rapidly while, at the same time, creating programs that are both easy to maintain and as error free as possible, many organizations use consistent coding standards and reusable code. These topics are discussed next.

### Choosing a Programming Language

There are a number of different programming languages to choose from when coding a program. These languages are discussed in detail later in this chapter, but several factors that may affect the programming language used are listed next.

> **TIP**
>
> Markup and scripting languages that are often used to create Web apps and Web sites are discussed toward the end of this chapter.

> *Suitability*. Some programming languages are more suited for some applications than others. For instance, an OOP language (such as C# or Python) would be used with an object-oriented program and a Web programming language (such as Java) is often used with Web programs. For mobile apps, the platform the app is being designed for determines the language used. For example, Apple apps are built using Objective C and Android apps typically use Java.

> *Integration*. If the application is going to need to interact with existing programs, it may need to be coded in the same language as those other programs. Tools—such as Microsoft's *.NET Framework*, which is designed for building integrated applications from reusable chunks of code that can communicate and share data, and which is often used to create mobile and Web apps—help to bridge different platforms and programming languages.

> *Standards*. Many information systems departments have standards that dictate using a specific language for a given application—such as COBOL for transaction processing and Java for Web programming.

> *Programmer availability*. Both the abilities of current in-house programmers and the skills of new programmers need to be considered. Choosing a widely used language means programmers can be hired more easily.

> *Portability*. If the application is to run on different platforms, the portability of a programming language should be considered.

> *Development speed*. Programs that reuse large chunks of code or that use a programming language that is easier to code and test can be developed faster.

## ASK THE EXPERT

*Courtesy WillowTree Apps*

WILLOWTREE **Kevin Snead, iOS Team Lead/Senior Software Engineer, WillowTree, Inc.**

**What software skills does an individual need today to write mobile applications, such as iPhone and Android apps?**

Mobile development is no different than traditional software development—it requires an understanding of application architecture, data structures, and efficient algorithms. It is also important to realize that, although your software is displayed on a smaller screen, it is not any less complex, and apps should be written to always be waiting on the user, prepared to immediately provide relevant information. This need for performance requires an understanding of networking, cellular radios, and graphics rendering. In addition, the ability to learn and apply new technologies quickly is essential for an effective developer.

> **Program coding.** The phase of the program development life cycle in which the program code is written using a programming language.
>
> **Coding.** The process of writing the programming language statements to create a computer program.

# TECHNOLOGY AND YOU

### Programming Contests

Think you're an awesome programmer? There are a number of contests available in which programmers can show off their stuff. One example is the *TopCoder Open*, in which college students and professionals compete for bragging rights and their share of the $300,000 prize purse. Individuals select from six competitions (Algorithm, UI Design, Development, Marathon, Informational Architecture, and Prototype) and then compete online in qualification rounds to advance in the competition. For instance, the Algorithm Competition begins with timed online Qualification Rounds consisting of three phases. In the Coding Phase, contestants have 75 minutes to code solutions for three problems. Solutions must be each contestant's original work and can be coded in Java, C++, C#, or Python. During the Challenge Phase, contestants have 15 minutes to challenge the functionality of other competitors' code. Contestants gain or lose points depending on the outcome of the challenges they make and the challenges made against them. During the System Testing Phase, an automated tester applies a set of inputs to each submitted solution and tests the code to see if the output is correct. Contestants with code deemed to be flawed lose all points previously earned for that code. Ultimately, 12 semifinalists compete on site at the contest (some TopCoder Open competitors are shown in the accompanying photograph).

In addition to the TopCoder Open, TopCoder offers competitions online in software design, development, assembly, and testing—including some contests specifically for high school students. Companies and government agencies also sponsor TopCoder competitions to crowdsource the development of software solutions. Winning a programming contest is good for your reputation and résumé, and it can also net you some pretty decent bucks.

**TopCoder Open competitors.**

*Source: TopCoder*

## The Coding Process

To code a program, the programmer creates it in the selected programming language. Usually this is done by launching the desired programming language application, and then selecting on-screen options and typing code using the proper syntax for the language being used to create the program. Once the program is created, it is saved as a file. This version of the program is called the **source code**. For a look at some programming contests available for both professional and amateur coders alike, see the Technology and You box.

## Coding Standards

In the early days of computers, programmers were largely left to code programs in their own styles. The result was often a confusing collection of statements that, while producing correct results, were difficult for anyone except the original programmer to understand.

> **Source code.** A computer program before it is compiled.

**COMMENTS**

Comments are usually preceded by a specific symbol (such as `*`, `C`, `'`, `#`, or `/**`); the symbol used depends on the programming language being used. Comment lines are ignored by the computer.

Comments at the top of a program should identify the name and author of the program, date written and last modified, purpose of the program, and variables used in the program.

Comments in the main part of a program should indicate what each section of the program is doing. Blank comment lines can also be used to space out the lines of code, as needed for readability.

Lines not marked as comments are executable code.

```
****************************************************************
* This program inputs two numbers, computes their sum,        *
* and displays the sum.                                       *
*                                                             *
* Written by: Deborah Morley  3/12/16                         *
****************************************************************
* Variable list                                              *
* SUM: Running sum                                           *
* CNTR: Counter                                              *
* NUM: Number inputted                                       *
*                                                            *
       REAL SUM, CNTR, NUM
****************************************************************
*
* INITIALIZE VARIABLES
     SUM = 0
     CNTR= 0
*
* INPUT NUMBER, ADD IT TO THE SUM, INCREMENT COUNTER, AND THEN
* REPEAT UNTIL TWO NUMBERS HAVE BEEN ENTERED
     DO 10 CNTR = 1, 2
```

**FIGURE 11-11**

Program comments.

**TIP**

It is more accurate and more efficient to write comments—particularly comments explaining the logic of a program—at the time the program is coded, instead of trying to add the comments at the end of a project.

To avoid this problem, many organizations today follow a set of *coding standards*—a list of rules designed to standardize programming styles. These coding standards help make programs more universally readable and easier to maintain.

The proper use of *comments* or *remarks* is one of the most important, but often one of the least adhered to, coding standards in organizations. Comments are notes within the actual program code that identify key features and steps of the program but that are written in such a way that the computer knows to ignore them when the program is executed (see Figure 11-11). Usually there is a comment section at the top of the program that identifies the author, the date the program was written or last modified, and the names and descriptions of the variables used in the program. Comments also typically appear at the beginning of each main section of the program to describe the function of that section, such as "Initialize variables," "Compute taxes," and "Calculate net amount due." Comments are also called *internal documentation*—that is, documentation located within the program—and they are especially useful when a program needs to be modified.

## Reusable Code

Different programs often perform some of the same basic tasks, such as computing sales tax or displaying product or employee information. If the code for these general tasks is treated as *reusable code*, it enables whole portions of new programs to be created with chunks of pretested, error-free code segments, which greatly reduces development time. Some programming approaches are specifically designed to have reusable components, such as the class libraries that can be used with object-oriented programming.

## Documentation: Documented Source Code

The program coding phase results in finished source code; that is, the program written in the desired programming language. The source code should implement the logic illustrated by the program design specifications and include enough internal documentation (comments) to make the source code understandable and easy to update.

# INSIDE THE INDUSTRY

**The Original Program "Bug"**

A program *bug* is an error that causes a program to malfunction. The first official recorded use of the word *bug* in the context of computing is associated with the temporary failure of the Mark II computer, which was in service at the Naval Weapons Center in Dahlgren, Virginia, on September 9, 1945. The problem was traced to a short circuit caused by a moth caught between two contacts in one of the computer's relays. The offending moth was taped into the log book with the notation, "First actual case of bug being found" (see the accompanying photograph).

Legend has it that *Grace Hopper*, a naval officer and mathematician who is often referred to as the *mother of computing*, actually discovered the moth. Hopper, who became the first woman to achieve the rank of rear admiral in the U.S. Navy, led the committee that invented COBOL and is credited with developing the first compiler.

Although some say the wording implies that the term *bug* was already in existence at the time and that this was the first instance of an actual bug being found in a computer, many prefer to believe that this was the origin of the term. Regardless, it is certainly the most widely known "bug" story, and it will likely be repeated for decades to come.

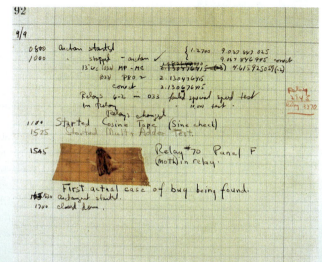

**The dead moth that caused the temporary failure of the Mark II computer in 1945, thought to be the origin for the computer term *bug,* was taped into the actual log book for that computer.**

Source: U.S. Navy

## Program Debugging and Testing
The **program debugging and testing** phase of the PDLC involves testing the program to ensure is it correct and works as intended. It starts with **debugging**—the process of ensuring that a program is free of errors, or *bugs* (for a look at a popular story regarding the origin of the term *bug*, see the Inside the Industry box). Debugging is usually a lengthy process, sometimes amounting to more than 50% of a program's development time. The more careful you are when you are designing a program, testing the logic of the program's design, and writing the actual code, then the less time you will typically need to debug the program.

## Translating Coded Programs into Executable Code
Before a program can be run—and, therefore, before it can be debugged—it needs to be translated from the source code that a programmer writes into **object code** (a binary or machine language version of the program) that the computer can execute. Code is converted from source code to object code using a **language translator**. Typically, a programming application program includes the appropriate language translator so the

> **TIP**  ✓
>
> Rewards for discovering bugs on Google Web sites, services, or apps range from $100 to $20,000 depending on the seriousness of the bug discovered.

---

> **Program debugging and testing.** The phase of the program development life cycle that ensures a program is correct and works as intended.
> **Debugging.** The process of ensuring a program is free of errors. **Object code.** The machine language version of a computer program generated when the program's source code is compiled. **Language translator.** A software program that converts source code to object code.

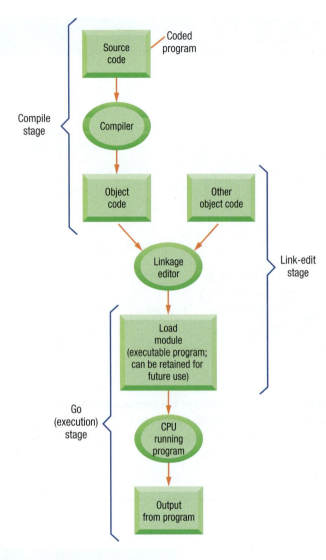

Compile stage

Go (execution) stage

Link-edit stage

**FIGURE 11-12**

**Compiler and linkage editor.** A compiler and a linkage editor convert source code into executable code.

program can be coded, translated, and executed using the same software program. The three most common types of language translators are discussed next.

### Compilers

A **compiler** is designed for a specific programming language (such as Java or Python) and translates programs written in that language into machine language so they can be executed. For instance, a program written in the Java programming language needs a Java compiler; Java source code cannot be converted into object code using a Python compiler.

A typical compiling process is shown in Figure 11-12. First, the source code for a program is translated into object code (the *compile stage*), then it is combined with any other modules of object code (either previously written by the programmer or stored in a common library) that the computer needs in order to run the program (the *link-edit stage*). This produces an executable program called a *load module*, which typically has an *.exe* file extension. At this point, the compiling process has reached the *Go (execution) stage* and the executable load module can be executed, as well as retained for later use.

### Interpreters

**Interpreters** are also language-specific, but they translate source code differently than compilers. Rather than creating object code and an executable program, an interpreter reads, translates, and executes the source code one line at a time as the program is run, every time the program is run. One advantage of using interpreters is that they are relatively easy to use and they help programmers discover program errors more easily because the execution usually stops at the point where an error is encountered. Consequently, interpreters are useful for beginning programmers.

The major disadvantage associated with interpreters is that they work less efficiently than compilers do because they translate each program statement into machine language just before executing it each time the program is run. As a result, interpreted programs run more slowly. This is especially true when the program must repeatedly execute the same statements thousands of times, reinterpreting each one every time. In contrast, a compiler translates each program statement only once—when the object code is created. Compiled programs need to be recompiled only when the source code is modified, such as if an error is discovered and corrected, or the program is updated.

### Assemblers

The third type of language translator, an *assembler*, converts assembly language statements into machine language. Assembly language, discussed later in this chapter, is used almost exclusively by professional programmers to write efficient code and is associated with a specific computer architecture, such as specific Windows computers, specific Apple computers, a particular type of mainframe, a specific supercomputer, or a specific type of mobile device. An assembler works like a compiler, producing object code. However, instead of being associated with a specific programming language, it is used with a specific assembly language and, consequently, with a specific computer architecture.

## Preliminary Debugging

The debugging process begins after the source code is complete and it is ready to be compiled or interpreted. With most programs, compiling or interpreting a program for the first time will result in errors—the preliminary debugging process consists of locating and correcting these errors. The first goal is to eliminate syntax errors and other errors that prevent the program from executing; then, any run time errors or logic errors can be identified and corrected, as discussed next.

## Compiler and Syntax Errors

Errors that occur as the program is being interpreted or compiled (often called *compiler errors* because most programs are compiled) prevent the program from running and so need to be corrected before the logic of the program can be tested. These errors are typically **syntax errors**, which occur when the programmer has not followed the proper *syntax* (rules) of the programming language being used. For example, a computer is not able to understand what you are trying to do if you misspell PRINT as PRNT, if you type END OF IF STATEMENT instead of the correct phrase END IF, if you put a required comma or semicolon in the wrong place, or if you try to use the wrong property with an object. As shown in Figure 11-13, when the program is being compiled and a syntax error is reached, an error message is typically displayed. Often this error message indicates the approximate location of the error in the program code (such as by underlining the error with a wavy line as in Figure 11-13) to help the programmer locate and correct it.

**FIGURE 11-13**

**Syntax errors.** Occur when the syntax (grammar rules) for a program is not followed precisely; they become obvious when compiling a program.

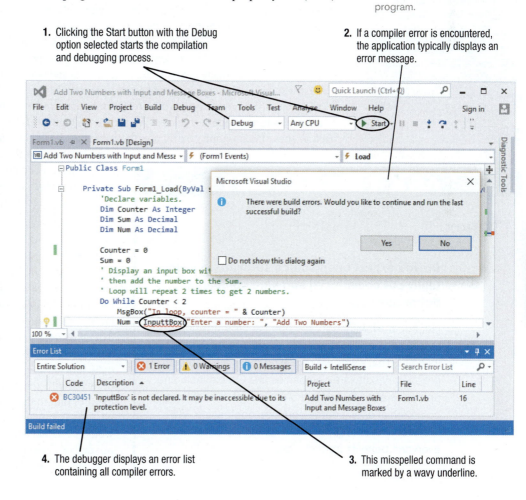

1. Clicking the Start button with the Debug option selected starts the compilation and debugging process.

2. If a compiler error is encountered, the application typically displays an error message.

3. This misspelled command is marked by a wavy underline.

4. The debugger displays an error list containing all compiler errors.

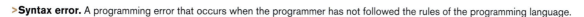

> **Syntax error.** A programming error that occurs when the programmer has not followed the rules of the programming language.

## Run Time and Logic Errors

*Run time errors* are errors that occur while the program is running and, consequently, are typically debugged after all syntax errors have been corrected. Sometimes run time errors occur because the program tries to do something that isn't possible, such as dividing a numeric value by zero. With this type of error, the program typically stops executing and an error message is displayed. However, many run time errors are due to **logic errors**; that is, errors in the logic of the program. Programs containing logic errors typically run—they just produce incorrect results. For instance, logic errors occur when a formula is written incorrectly, when a mistake is made with a decision condition (such as using the wrong relational operator or initializing a counter variable to the wrong value), or when the wrong variable name is used. After a logic error is identified, the programmer corrects it and runs the program again to see if all errors have been removed. This "execute, check, and correct" process is repeated until the program is free of bugs. If a logic error is serious enough, it may involve going back to the program design phase—a costly mistake that emphasizes the importance of good program design.

Most logic errors should be located and corrected during the program design stage if a good desk check procedure is used. However, when logic errors occur during preliminary debugging, *dummy print statements*—statements that are temporarily inserted into the code to display status information on the screen—can be used to help locate the error. Dummy print statements can be inserted at various locations within the program's code to show how a program is branching (such as printing the text *"Inside loop, counter = "* followed by the current value of the counter variable) and to output the values of key variables at specific places in the program. Knowing the values of key variables and where program control is branching can help the programmer figure out what the logic error is and where it is located.

For example, running a program to add two numbers based on the logic in the incorrect flowchart in Figure 11-10 would result in an incorrect sum because only one number is input before the loop terminates. As shown in Figure 11-14, dummy print statements used to show the program control and the values of the counter and sum variables at specific locations in the program reveal that only one number is being input when the program runs; this information can help the programmer determine more quickly that the counter is incorrectly being initialized to 1, instead of to 0.

## Testing

At the end of the preliminary debugging process, the program will appear to be correct. At this time, the original programmer—or, preferably, someone else—runs the program with extensive *test data* to try to find any additional errors remaining in the program. Good test data reflects the same type of data that will be used with the finished program to subject the program to the conditions it will encounter when it is implemented. Ideally, the test data would be actual data but, in order to protect the privacy of personal information during testing, test data is usually created that has the same

> **Logic error.** A programming error that occurs when running a program produces incorrect results.

1. With logic errors, such as initializing a counter to the wrong number as shown here, the program will run but the output will be wrong.

2. Adding dummy print statements to display the values of key variables and key locations in the program can help to determine the error.

3. The dummy print statements, as well as the regular input and output messages belonging to the program, are displayed at the appropriate times when the program is executed.

4. The dummy print statements, which reveal that the loop is performed only once before the sum is displayed here, help the programmer locate the counter initialization error.

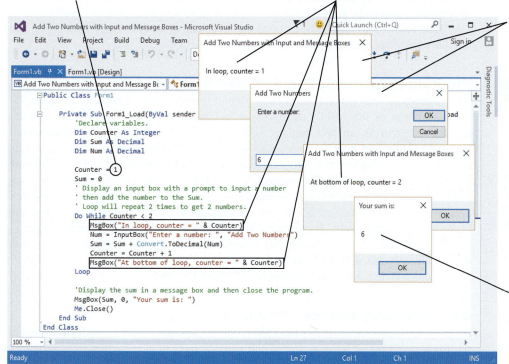

**FIGURE 11-14**

**Logic errors.** Are more difficult to identify; dummy print statements can help determine the error.

structure as actual data but does not contain any personally identifiable information. The test data should also check for nonstandard situations or possible input errors to make sure the proper corresponding actions are included in the program. For example, will the program issue a check if the amount is $0.00 or will it allow a product quantity of less than 0? Although rigorous testing significantly decreases the chance of an unnoticed error revealing itself after the program is implemented, there is no foolproof guarantee that the completed program will be bug free. However, proper debugging and testing is vital because an error that costs only a few dollars to fix at this stage in the development process may cost many thousands of dollars to correct after the program is implemented.

Programs created for mass distribution often have two additional stages of testing: an internal on-site test (sometimes called an *alpha test*) and one or more rounds of outside tests (called *beta tests*). For instance, companies creating new versions of commercial software programs, such as when Microsoft develops a new version of Microsoft Office, enlist a large number of beta testers to test the versions for bugs and compatibility problems, as well as to provide suggestions for improvement, while the programs are in development. *Beta versions* of freeware and open source software are also often available to the public for testing. Beta testing allows the programs to be tested by a wide variety of individuals using a wide variety of hardware and so is a much more thorough test for programs that are to be distributed out of house than just alpha testing would be.

**TIP**

Good design and testing can put you ahead of the curve because, according to one recent study, only 6.4% of large development projects (those with labor costs of $10 million or more) were completely successful—close to half were abandoned or started over.

## Documentation: Completed Program Package

When the program debugging and testing phase is finished, a copy of the test data, test results, finished program code, and other documentation generated during this phase should be added to the program package. The test data is useful for future program modifications, as well as to see under what conditions the program was tested if a problem develops in the future.

So far, virtually all the documents in the collected program documentation could be referred to as *developer documentation*—tools that may be useful when a programmer needs to look at or modify the program code in the future. To finish the *program package*, the necessary *user documentation* should also be developed. User documentation normally consists of a user's manual containing instructions for running the program, a description of software commands, and so forth. It can be integrated into the program itself (such as via a Help feature); it can also be external user documentation that is used for training and reference purposes, particularly for new systems.

## Program Implementation and Maintenance

After a program has finished the debugging and testing phase, it is ready to be implemented as part of the SDLC, as discussed in Chapter 10. Once the system containing the program is up and running, the *implementation process* of the **program implementation and maintenance** phase is complete. However, virtually every program requires ongoing maintenance. *Program maintenance* is the process of updating software so it continues to be useful. For instance, if new types of data are added to a company database, program maintenance is necessary so that existing programs can use the new data. Software revisions, new equipment announcements, new legislative mandates, and changes in the way business is conducted also commonly trigger program maintenance.

Program maintenance is costly for organizations. It has been estimated that many organizations spend well over one-half—some estimates put it closer to 75%—of their programming time maintaining existing application programs.

### Documentation: Amended Program Package

As program maintenance takes place, the program package should be updated to reflect what new problems or issues occurred and what changes to the program were necessary because of them. If a problem is too serious for routine program maintenance, the program development cycle should begin again.

## TOOLS FOR FACILITATING PROGRAM DEVELOPMENT

If you ask most IT managers when they need programs to be finished, you will usually get an answer like "yesterday." The sad truth in business today is that programmers are typically under tremendous time pressure to get programs finished as quickly as possible. In extreme cases, getting product into the user's hands is not just a priority—it is *the* priority. To help programmers create quality systems and programs in a timely manner, many types of *program development tools* are available, as discussed next. The tools can be used in both traditional and adaptive software development approaches.

### Application Lifecycle Management (ALM) Tools

**Application lifecycle management** (**ALM**) is a broad term to describe creating and managing an application throughout its entire life cycle—from design through coding and testing, to maintenance, and, eventually, to retirement. ALM software typically has several integrated components that work together for a variety of tasks, such as those that take place during the system design and program development process, and are designed to automate, manage, and simplify the program development process. For instance, many ALM programs include program design tools—such as those used to create data flow diagrams, structure charts, and the other tools discussed earlier in this chapter and in Chapter 10—and the ability to generate the program code from the finished design to create the application. In a nutshell,

---

> **Program implementation and maintenance.** The phase of the program development life cycle in which the program is implemented and then maintained, as needed, to remain useful. > **Application lifecycle management (ALM).** A broad term to describe complete systems that can be used to create and manage an application throughout its entire life cycle—from design through retirement.

an ALM system can help software developers define a solid model of a program first, and then implement that model in whatever programming language is needed—and in as many programming languages as needed—with no additional effort because the ALM program's *code generator* generates much of the code automatically upon demand. Consequently, this saves programming time, as well as enables companies without a large programming staff to develop applications in-house without having to outsource the coding portion of the program development process. Additional tools that can be included in ALM programs are requirements management, configuration management, and issue tracking, as discussed next.

*Requirements management* refers to keeping track of and managing program requirements as they are defined and then modified throughout the program development process. It is important for software requirements to be defined accurately and completely at the beginning of a project because poorly written or inconsistent requirements can lead to costly reworks or even failure of a project. Once the requirements have been defined, the requirements management process continues throughout the program development process to manage the requirements as they evolve. Because the requirements for a program often change during development—due to technological improvements, competitive pressures, or budget changes, for instance—requirements management software facilitates real-time collaboration among the individuals working on a project to ensure that everyone sees and works with the same version of the current requirements. The overall goal of requirements management is to ensure that the delivered solution actually meets the needs of the business.

*Configuration management* refers to keeping track of the progress of a program development project, such as documenting revisions, storing each version of the program so it can be recreated if needed, and keeping track of all components used in the final program. Software that supports configuration management may also include security and control features, such as preventing unauthorized access to project files or alerting the appropriate individual whenever a project file is altered.

*Issue tracking* (see Figure 11-15) involves recording issues (such as bugs or other problems that arise during program development and testing or issues that arise after the system is in place) as they become known, assigning them to a team member, and tracking their status. Software that supports issue tracking can be used during program development, as well as after the system has been implemented.

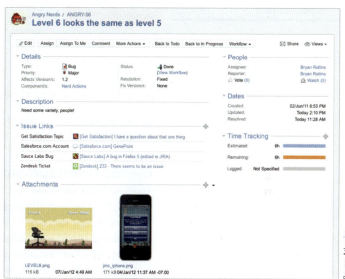

Source: Atlassian

**FIGURE 11-15**

**Issue tracking software.** Allows you to track issues during the development and life of an application, such as the game app shown here.

## Application Generators

An *application generator* is a software program that helps programmers develop software. Some application generators (such as the ones included in some ALM programs, as previously discussed) generate source code. Others may generate program components (such as macros, reports, or forms) to be used by the end user.

## Macros

A *macro* is a sequence of saved actions (such as keystrokes, mouse clicks, and menu selections) that can be replayed whenever needed within the application program in which it was created. Macros are most often used to automate repeated or difficult tasks. Programmers can create predefined macros to be included with a finished program; many programs also allow the end user to create custom macros as needed. For example, the user could create a macro in a word processing program to type a standard closing to a letter or to create a table of a specified size with a certain formatting applied, whenever he or she presses a specific key combination (such as [Ctrl]+[Y]).

Programmers typically write macros using a *macro programming language* (such as *Visual Basic for Applications* (*VBA*) for Microsoft Office macros), though some programs have *macro recorders* so the programmer or end user can record macros instead of having to code them (you start the macro recorder and then perform the desired keystrokes and mouse clicks). After the recorder is turned off and the macro is saved and assigned a name or keystroke combination, the code generated by the macro recorder can typically be edited to make minor modifications, as needed, and the macro can be executed.

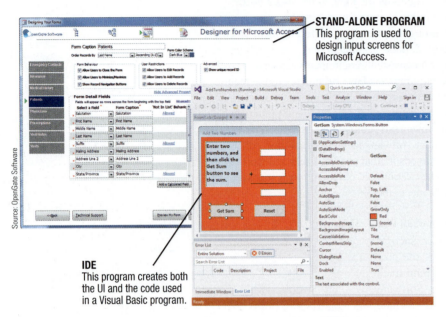

**STAND-ALONE PROGRAM**
This program is used to design input screens for Microsoft Access.

**IDE**
This program creates both the UI and the code used in a Visual Basic program.

🅐 **FIGURE 11-16**
User interface (UI) builders.

*Source: OpenGate Software*

## Report Generators and User Interface (UI) Builders

A *report generator* is a tool that prepares reports to be used with a software program quickly and easily. For instance, report generators for database management systems allow reports to be created simply by declaring which data fields are to be represented as report columns and how the data should be sorted; once defined, a report can be edited as needed, and then generated on demand. *User interface (UI) builders* create the menus, forms, and input screens used with a program or database (one example of a UI builder for Microsoft Access is shown in Figure 11-16). UI builders can be stand-alone programs or included in an integrated development enviroment (IDE), discussed shortly. Creating reports and forms for databases is discussed in more detail in Chapter 12.

## Device Development Tools

Tools to help facilitate the development of software used with computers and mobile devices have been available for quite some time. However, tools for developing programs for devices that use embedded software (such as cars, ATM machines, robots, and other consumer devices)—called *device software development tools*—have not been available until recently. One example is *Wind River Workbench*, which is designed to accelerate the development of devices that use either Wind River's *VxWorks* operating system or Wind River's version of Linux.

## Software Development Kits (SDKs), Application Program Interfaces (APIs), and Integrated Development Environments (IDEs)

To help with the more rapid development of traditional programs and mobile apps, a number of tools are available. A **software development kit** (**SDK**) is a set of development tools that enables programmers to develop applications for a particular platform (such as iOS or Android devices) or a particular programming language (such as Dart) more quickly and easily. SDKs are often released by hardware or software companies to assist developers in creating new applications for existing products. For instance, the

>**Software development kit (SDK).** A programming package designed for a particular platform that enables programmers to develop applications for that platform more quickly and easily.

*iOS SDK* allows third parties to develop applications for the iPhone and iPad, the *Android SDK* is used to create Android apps, and the *Dart SDK* is used to create Dart programs. SDKs typically contain programming tools, documentation, sample code, and at least one **application program interface** (**API**) designed to help applications interface with a particular operating system and the resources available for particular devices, such as cameras and geolocation information. APIs are also used in conjunction with Web sites; for example, Google's *Maps API* and Google's *OpenSocial API* allow developers to add Google Maps or social networking applications easily to Web sites, respectively.

To help create applications more quickly, **integrated development environments** (**IDEs**) include a variety of tools (such as a UI builder, source code editor, debugger, and compiler) for one or more programming languages (such as C# or Java) and are used to create applications for one or more platforms (such as Windows, iOS, and Android). They typically include SDKs and APIs to help you create an application and then the IDE creates multiple versions of that application to run on your desired platforms. For example, the *Xamarin Studio* IDE shown in Figure 11-17 is used to create mobile apps for a variety of platforms much more quickly than creating each app individually. After the user creates an application coded in C# or F# and designs the Android and iOS UI using the UI builder, the IDE creates versions of the app for the platforms the user specifies, such as Android and iOS smartphones and smart watches. Other common IDEs include *Visual Studio* and *Eclipse*. For a look at some tips for creating a useful user experience (UX) for mobile apps today, see the Trend box.

**FIGURE 11-17**
**Xamarin Studio IDE.**

Courtesy Xamarin Inc.

---

**CAUTION   CAUTION   CAUTION   CAUTION   CAUTION   CAUTION   CAUT**

Before running code written in any programming language, be sure you know how to interrupt program execution in case you have a logic error and the program becomes stuck in an endless loop. For instance, to stop the debugging process in Visual Basic, press [Ctrl] +[Break].

## LANGUAGES USED FOR APPLICATION DEVELOPMENT

As discussed earlier, deciding which language will be used is an important program development decision. There are a vast number of programming, markup, and scripting languages to choose from; however, often the type of application being developed will dictate the type of language that should be used.

### Types of Languages

A **programming language** is a set of rules, words, symbols, and codes used to write computer programs. To write a computer program, you need an appropriate software program for the programming language you will be using—this software allows you to code the program and convert the finished source code into object code. It may also include a variety of tools that make it easier to develop, debug, edit, maintain, and manage programs.

> **TIP**
>
> There are free open source editors, compilers, and IDEs available online for many of the programming languages discussed in this section, such as the free *Java Development Kit* (*JDK*) available from the Oracle Technology Network Web site.

---

> **Application program interface (API).** A set of commands, functions, and protocols used to help applications interface with a specific operating system, Web site, or device. > **Integrated development environment (IDE).** A collection of application development tools that have a common user interface and are used to develop and test software programs. > **Programming language.** A set of rules, words, symbols, and codes used to write computer programs.

# TREND

**Mobile UX**

When designing applications (either mobile apps or Web sites) for smartphones and other mobile devices, it is important to create a good *user experience* (*UX*). Some basic guidelines include the following:

> Determine the primary objectives of the application and who your targeted audience is before designing the application.
> Keep the design of the application simple, clean, efficient, and task-oriented.
> Make the application fast and responsive and be sure updates to mobile apps are useful and have been thoroughly tested.
> Don't require users to sign in to use the Web site or app unless absolutely necessary.

Some emerging trends in mobile applications include the following:

> Using *flat designs* (instead of drop shadows, embossing, beveling and other effects).
> Using larger and more unique typefaces to set the application apart from competitive applications.
> Using physically larger (but still quick-to-load) images on retail sites.
> Including product videos on Web sites and social media to market products.

> Providing easy to use discounts on retail applications and placing the discounts where they entice visitors to make purchases.
> Using software to track visitors' behaviors and preferences to provide a targeted experience.
> Developing both a mobile app and a Web site and making it easy for visitors to download your app from your site (see the Web site in the accompanying illustration) because apps often provide mobile users with a better experience than Web sites.

Easy to download mobile app.

Flat design and interesting typeface.

Large, but quick-to-load, images.

Clean and task-oriented design.

Source: hats.com

**Markup languages** are most often used to create Web pages and Web applications. They are coding systems that define the structure, layout, and general appearance of the content located on a Web page. Markup languages use *markup tags* that are inserted around content to identify where those elements are to be displayed on the Web page and how they should look.

**Scripting languages** are programming languages that are interpreted instead of compiled, so they are executed one command at a time and at the time they are run. They are most often used to add *dynamic content* (content that will be changed based on user actions, such as pointing to or selecting a Web page object) to a Web page or to integrate a Web page with a database, as discussed more in Chapter 12. With a scripting language, the program instructions—called *scripts*—are built directly into a Web page's code. Specific programming, markup, and scripting languages are discussed next.

## Categories of Programming Languages

Programming languages can be classified by the types of programs they are designed to create, such as procedural (also called *imperative*) languages for programs using the procedural approach or object-oriented languages for programs using the object-oriented approach. However, they are also often categorized by their level or generation; that is, how evolved the programming language is.

> **Markup language.** A type of language that uses symbols or tags to describe what a document should look like. > **Scripting language.** A programming language that is interpreted at run-time instead of being compiled.

## Low-Level Languages

The earliest programming languages are referred to as **low-level languages**. This name refers to the fact that programmers used these languages to write instructions at a very low level (such as just using 0s and 1s) so that the computer's hardware could easily and quickly understand them. In a low-level language, each line of code corresponds to a single action by the computer system and the code is *machine dependent*, which means that it is written for one specific type of computer. For example, a program written in a low-level language for a particular mainframe at one organization cannot be used on a different type of mainframe or on one of the organization's personal computers.

One example of a low-level language is **machine language**. Machine language programs consist solely of 0s and 1s; consequently, they are the only programs whose source code is understandable to the computer without being translated first. While virtually no one programs in machine language anymore, all programs are converted into machine language by a language translator before they can be executed, as discussed earlier in this chapter.

**Assembly language** is a low-level language that was developed to replace some of the 0s and 1s of machine language with names and other symbols that are easier for programmers to understand and remember. Assembly language programs take longer to write and maintain than programs written in higher-level languages, but their big advantage is executional efficiency. Consequently, a program may occasionally be written in assembly language to make it especially efficient.

An example of a program for adding two numbers (the program illustrated by the correct flowchart shown in Figure 11-10) written in assembly language for one type of computer system is shown in Figure 11-18. Also included in that figure are some machine language statements that correspond to the assembly language statements in the program.

## ASK THE EXPERT

Courtesy ACM

**Kathleen Fisher,** Tufts University, Past Chair of ACM Special Interest Group on Programming Languages

### What is the most important programming language for a college computer student to learn today?

There is no one programming language that is the most important to learn. Rather, it is important for students to understand how programming languages allow people to express precisely what they want computers to do. Each language provides its own way of accomplishing this task by providing a model of computation. As a result, different languages are best suited to different tasks. For example, low-level systems coding is easiest in a language like C, whose model is close to the underlying machine. In contrast, compilers are particularly easy to write in functional languages like ML, Haskell, and Scheme because such languages facilitate tree transformations, the lifeblood of compilers.

When faced with a programming task, astute programmers select the most appropriate language for the task, taking into consideration the characteristics of the candidate languages and their available libraries and tools. As with natural languages, each programming language that a student learns makes learning the next one easier.

## High-Level Languages

**High-level languages** are closer to natural languages than low-level languages and therefore, make programs easier to write. They are also typically *machine independent*, which makes programs written in these languages much more flexible because they can be used with more than one computer without alteration. Although a program is normally written for a specific operating system, with a machine-independent program the programmer does not need to know the specific details about the hardware that will be used to run the program. Included in this class of languages are what have come to be known as *third-generation programming languages (3GLs)*. Most programming languages used today are 3GLs. Some examples of

> **Low-level language.** A class of programming languages that is highly detailed and machine-dependent. > **Machine language.** A binary-based programming language, consisting only of 0s and 1s, that a computer can execute directly. > **Assembly language.** A low-level programming language that uses names and other symbols to replace some of the 0s and 1s in machine language. > **High-level language.** A class of programming languages that is closer to natural language and easier to work with than a low-level language.

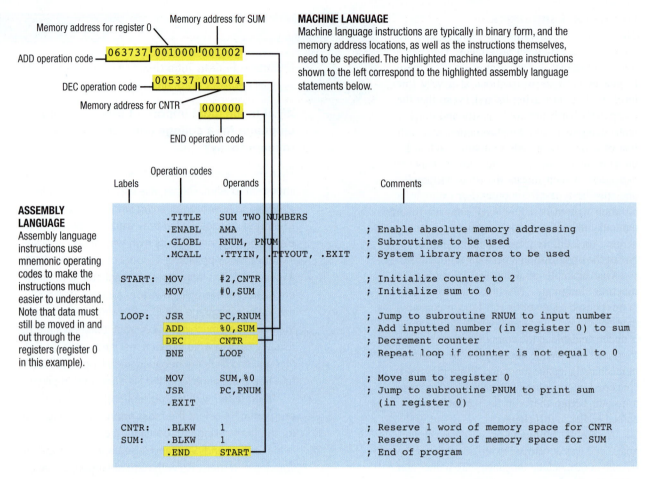

Memory address for register 0

Memory address for SUM

ADD operation code — 063737 | 001000 | 001002

DEC operation code — 005337 | 001004

Memory address for CNTR

000000

END operation code

**MACHINE LANGUAGE**

Machine language instructions are typically in binary form, and the memory address locations, as well as the instructions themselves, need to be specified. The highlighted machine language instructions shown to the left correspond to the highlighted assembly language statements below.

Labels   Operation codes   Operands   Comments

**ASSEMBLY LANGUAGE**

Assembly language instructions use mnemonic operating codes to make the instructions much easier to understand. Note that data must still be moved in and out through the registers (register 0 in this example).

```
          .TITLE  SUM TWO NUMBERS
          .ENABL  AMA                        ; Enable absolute memory addressing
          .GLOBL  RNUM, PNUM                 ; Subroutines to be used
          .MCALL  .TTYIN, .TTYOUT, .EXIT     ; System library macros to be used

START:    MOV     #2,CNTR                    ; Initialize counter to 2
          MOV     #0,SUM                     ; Initialize sum to 0

LOOP:     JSR     PC,RNUM                    ; Jump to subroutine RNUM to input number
          ADD     %0,SUM                     ; Add inputted number (in register 0) to sum
          DEC     CNTR                       ; Decrement counter
          BNE     LOOP                       ; Repeat loop if counter is not equal to 0

          MOV     SUM,%0                     ; Move sum to register 0
          JSR     PC,PNUM                    ; Jump to subroutine PNUM to print sum
          .EXIT                              ;   (in register 0)

CNTR:     .BLKW   1                          ; Reserve 1 word of memory space for CNTR
SUM:      .BLKW   1                          ; Reserve 1 word of memory space for SUM
          .END    START                      ; End of program
```

**FIGURE 11-18**

Assembly and machine language.

**FIGURE 11-19**

Scratch.

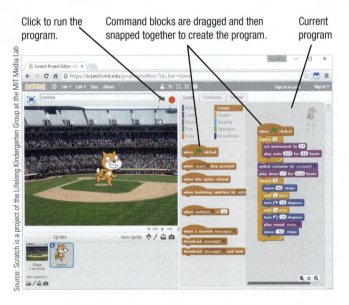

Click to run the program.

Command blocks are dragged and then snapped together to create the program.

Current program

procedural 3GLs are Fortran, COBOL, Pascal, BASIC, and C. High-level object-oriented programming languages include C++, C#, Java, Dart, and Python. These languages are all discussed shortly.

Some 3GLs incorporate visual elements to assist in program development—these programs are referred to as *visual programming environments* (*VPEs*). VPEs allow programmers to create the user interface graphically and to create a substantial amount of code simply by dragging and dropping objects and then defining their appearance and behavior. And, when code is typed, the program often assists in creating the code by listing options (such as appropriate methods that may be used with an object), by properly indenting and color-coding the code, and so forth. There are visual environments available for many programming languages.

A programing language that creates programs entirely using graphical elements is called a *visual programming language* (*VPL*). For instance, the free *Scratch* programming language shown in Figure 11-19 is a graphical programming language designed for educational purposes. Scratch enables children to create interactive, animated programs quickly and easily by snapping graphical blocks of commands together. Even though creating complex programs and animations using Scratch is easy because of this building block approach, this program still allows beginning programmers to experiment with and learn basic programming concepts, such as variables and loops.

### Fourth-Generation Languages (4GLs)

**Fourth-generation languages** (**4GLs**) are also sometimes called *very-high-level languages*. Although there is no precise definition of 4GLs, they are even further from machine language than third-generation languages, and, therefore, are much easier to use. One property that makes 4GLs easier to use is that they are *declarative*, rather than procedural like third-generation languages. This means that when you program using a 4GL, you tell the computer *what* to do without telling it *how* to do it. Consequently, when using a *declarative programming language*, the computer figures out how to do what you want it to do. Because 4GLs often allow programmers to create programs while writing very little code, if any, using 4GLs also results in increased productivity. A disadvantage to using 4GLs is that they can result in less-efficient object code when they are compiled into machine language.

Fourth-generation languages are commonly used today to access databases. For example, structured query language (SQL) is a 4GL commonly used to write queries to retrieve information from a database, as discussed in more detail in Chapter 12. Some of the app builders and other tools discussed earlier that are used to help facilitate program development are also sometimes considered fourth-generation languages.

## Common Programming Languages

There have been a number of programming languages developed over the years. Some earlier languages, such as *PL/1* (a structured programming language used for business and scientific applications) and *SmallTalk* (one of the first object-oriented programming languages), are not widely used today. Others, such as Fortran, are in the process of being phased out in many organizations. A few of the most significant traditional programming languages are discussed and illustrated next, followed by a brief look at some of the newer languages in use today.

### Fortran

**Fortran**, originally called **FORTRAN** (*FORmula TRANslator*), dates back to 1954 and is the oldest high-level programming language. It was designed by scientists and is oriented toward manipulating formulas for scientific, mathematical, and engineering applications. Fortran is a very efficient language for these types of applications and is still used for high-performance computing tasks, such as forecasting the weather. A related programming language developed by Oracle is *Fortress*. Similar to Fortran, Fortress is designed for high-performance computing, and so it is designed to take advantage of multi-core processors and computers with multiple processors. Fortress is now available as an open source program, but it is no longer being updated.

A Fortran program to add two numbers (as illustrated in the correct flowchart in Figure 11-10) is shown in Figure 11-20. Note the short comments above each main section in the program.

> ▼ **FIGURE 11-20**
> The adding-two-numbers program written in Fortran.

Comments are preceded by an asterisk or a C.

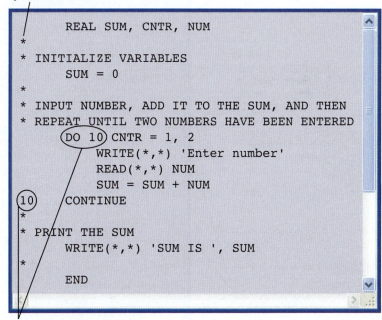

```fortran
      REAL SUM, CNTR, NUM
*
*  INITIALIZE VARIABLES
      SUM = 0
*
*  INPUT NUMBER, ADD IT TO THE SUM, AND THEN
*  REPEAT UNTIL TWO NUMBERS HAVE BEEN ENTERED
      DO 10 CNTR = 1, 2
          WRITE(*,*) 'Enter number'
          READ(*,*) NUM
          SUM = SUM + NUM
  10  CONTINUE
*
*  PRINT THE SUM
      WRITE(*,*) 'SUM IS ', SUM
*
      END
```

Program statements can be numbered in order to control loops and other types of branching.

---

> **Fourth-generation language (4GL).** A class of programming languages that is closer to natural language and easier to work with than high-level languages. > **Fortran.** A high-level programming language used for mathematical, scientific, and engineering applications; originally called **FORTRAN**.

## COBOL

**COBOL** (*COmmon Business-Oriented Language*) is a structured programming language designed for business transaction processing. COBOL programs are typically made up of a collection of modules, as shown in the adding-two-numbers program in Figure 11-21. Its strengths lie in batch processing and its stability—two reasons why so many COBOL programs still exist today, even though some consider the language to be outdated. However, COBOL programs are lengthy and take a long time to write and maintain, and many businesses are migrating from it gradually. To avoid the expense of rewriting all the COBOL code in an organization, as well as possible problems that may arise if the business processes included in those programs are inadvertently altered during translation, some companies are leaving most of their *back-end software* (server software that is not accessed by end users) in COBOL and just moving *front-end software* (the software accessed by end users) and new applications to other languages.

While COBOL is not inherently suited to developing interactive applications or cloud software, new versions of COBOL are evolving to support new applications. For instance, COBOL now supports the creation of object-oriented COBOL programs and existing COBOL applications can be converted to *COBOL.NET* so they can better integrate with other .NET applications. However, with a large percentage of business applications still written in COBOL and many original COBOL programmers reaching retirement age, programmers who can program in the conventional COBOL programming language are still needed.

**FIGURE 11-21**

The adding-two-numbers program written in COBOL.

Comments are preceded by an asterisk.

Most COBOL programs use a number of modules to break the program into manageable pieces. These submodules are called from the main control module using these statements.

Three submodules are used in this program.

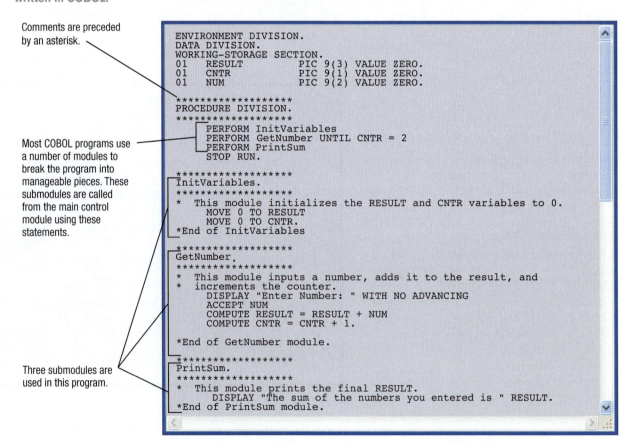

```
ENVIRONMENT DIVISION.
DATA DIVISION.
WORKING-STORAGE SECTION.
01    RESULT         PIC 9(3) VALUE ZERO.
01    CNTR           PIC 9(1) VALUE ZERO.
01    NUM            PIC 9(2) VALUE ZERO.

*******************
PROCEDURE DIVISION.
*******************
      PERFORM InitVariables
      PERFORM GetNumber UNTIL CNTR = 2
      PERFORM PrintSum
      STOP RUN.

*******************
InitVariables.
*******************
*   This module initializes the RESULT and CNTR variables to 0.
      MOVE 0 TO RESULT
      MOVE 0 TO CNTR.
*End of InitVariables

*******************
GetNumber.
*******************
*   This module inputs a number, adds it to the result, and
*   increments the counter.
      DISPLAY "Enter Number: " WITH NO ADVANCING
      ACCEPT NUM
      COMPUTE RESULT = RESULT + NUM
      COMPUTE CNTR = CNTR + 1.

*End of GetNumber module.

*******************
PrintSum.
*******************
*   This module prints the final RESULT.
      DISPLAY "The sum of the numbers you entered is " RESULT.
*End of PrintSum module.
```

> **COBOL.** A high-level programming language developed for transaction processing applications.

## Pascal

**Pascal**, named after the mathematician Blaise Pascal, was created to fill the need for a teaching tool to encourage structured programming. Pascal typically uses control structures extensively to manipulate program modules in a systematic fashion. Pascal also supports an abundance of data types and is especially appropriate for math and science applications.

## BASIC and Visual Basic

**BASIC** (*Beginner's All-purpose Symbolic Instruction Code*) was designed as an easy-to-learn beginner's language. It was traditionally one of the most widely used instructional languages for beginners because it was easy to learn and use and because it worked well on almost all computers. BASIC is often used for interactive programs, where the program pauses for user input. After the action is taken, the program continues.

**Visual Basic** is a version of BASIC that uses a visual programming environment to help programmers quickly and easily create programs. It is part of the *Visual Studio* suite of programming products. Recent versions of Visual Studio include support for parallel processing, application lifecycle management, and cloud development, as well as the ability to integrate with more databases than previous versions of Visual Studio. Visual Basic code written for the .NET Framework is referred to as *VB.NET* code.

## C, C++, C#, Objective-C, and F#

**C** is much closer to assembly language than other high-level languages. This allows for very efficient code, but it can also make programming in C more difficult. However, C has proven to be a powerful and flexible language that is used for a variety of applications.

**C++** is a newer object-oriented version of C. It includes the basic features of C, making all C++ programs understandable to C compilers, but it has additional OOP features. One C++ IDE is *Microsoft Visual C++*. The adding-two-numbers program written in C++ is shown in Figure 11-22.

The newest version of C is **C#** (pronounced "C sharp"). A hybrid of C and C++, C# is most often used to create Web and Windows applications. A version of C used to write programs for Apple devices is *Objective-C*, but it may eventually be replaced by the emerging *Swift* language. *F#* was developed for the .NET platform as an improvement to C# and a language more suitable for calculations and data manipulations.

**V FIGURE 11-22**
The adding-two-numbers program written in C++.

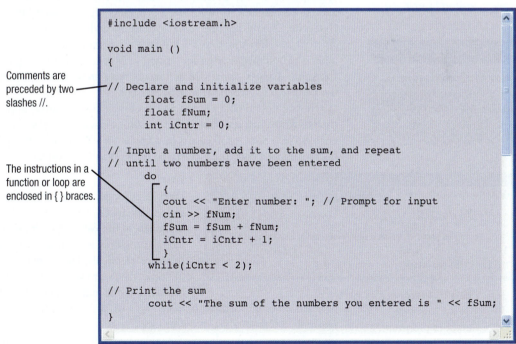

Comments are preceded by two slashes //.

The instructions in a function or loop are enclosed in { } braces.

```cpp
#include <iostream.h>

void main ()
{

// Declare and initialize variables
    float fSum = 0;
    float fNum;
    int iCntr = 0;

// Input a number, add it to the sum, and repeat
// until two numbers have been entered
    do
        {
        cout << "Enter number: "; // Prompt for input
        cin >> fNum;
        fSum = fSum + fNum;
        iCntr = iCntr + 1;
        }
    while(iCntr < 2);

// Print the sum
    cout << "The sum of the numbers you entered is " << fSum;
}
```

**SYS**

---

>**Pascal.** A structured, high-level programming language often used to teach structured programming, especially appropriate for use in math and science applications. >**BASIC.** An easy-to-learn, high-level programming language that was developed to be used by beginning programmers. >**Visual Basic.** A version of the BASIC programming language that uses a visual programming environment. >**C.** A high-level structured programming language that has the execution efficiency of an assembly language. >**C++.** A newer, object-oriented version of the C programming language. >**C#.** The newest, object-oriented version of the C programming language.

The java.io package will handle the user input; * indicates all classes will be available.

```
import java.io.*;
   public class AddTwo {
        public static void main(String[] args) throws IOException {
           BufferedReader stdin =
              new BufferedReader ( new InputStreamReader( System.in ) );
           String inData;
           int iSum = 0;
           int iNum = 0;
           int iCntr = 0;
// Input a number, add it to the sum, and repeat
// until two numbers have been entered
   do
   {
   System.out.println("Enter number: ");
   inData = stdin.readLine();              // get number in character form
   iNum = Integer.parseInt( inData );      // convert inData to integer
   iSum = iSum + iNum;
   iCntr = iCntr + 1;
   }
   while (iCntr < 2);

// Print the sum
      System.out.println("The sum of the numbers you entered is " + iSum);
         }
      }
```

Comments within the code are preceded by two slashes //.

The *out* attribute and *println* method in the System class of the java.io package are used to output the results.

⚠ **FIGURE 11-23**
The adding-two-numbers program written in Java.

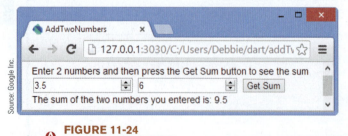

Source: Google Inc.

⚠ **FIGURE 11-24**
The adding-two-numbers program running in Dartium.

## Java

**Java** is an object-oriented programming language that is commonly used to write Web applications. It was developed by Sun Microsystems (which is now owned by Oracle) and is open source software. Java programs are compiled into a format called *bytecode*. Bytecode usually has the *.class* extension and can run on any computer that includes *Java Virtual Machine* (*Java VM*)—the program required to run bytecode programs. The adding-two-numbers program written in Java is shown in Figure 11-23. Java is also used for Android apps—for a look at how to create an Android app using the Android SDK and the Eclipse IDE, see the How It Works box.

In addition to being used to write complete stand-alone applications, Java can also be used to write *Java applets*—small programs inserted into Web pages and run using a Java-enabled Web browser. To use a Java applet on a Web page, the applet's .class files containing the applet's code must be stored in the Web site's folder.

## Dart

**Dart** is an open source, object-oriented programming language developed by Google and designed as a JavaScript replacement for Web apps. Unlike JavaScript (in which each element requires a separate instruction, even if the instructions are identical), Dart supports *SIMD* (single instruction, multiple data) processing to enable similar multiple data elements to be manipulated together. Consequently, Dart is much more efficient with some types of Web elements. Dart apps can run directly in *Dartium*, a Dart-enabled browser (see Figure 11-24). To run in other browsers, Dart programs are compiled to JavaScript code. JavaScript is discussed in more detail shortly.

>**Java.** A high-level, object-oriented programming language frequently used for Web applications. >**Dart.** A high-level, open source, object-oriented programming language developed by Google and designed to replace JavaScript in Web applications.

# HOW IT WORKS

## Creating Apps Using the Android SDK and Eclipse

An Android *project* contains all of the app files; *activities* are the screens that the user interacts with; and the *onCreate()* method launches the designated activity object. Once you have designed an app and have installed the *ADT Bundle* from the Android Web site, you are ready to launch the *Eclipse IDE* and create your Android project. Creating a simple app to add two numbers is shown in the accompanying figure; an overview of the steps is described next.

1. Create a new project and use the displayed screens to give the app a name, assign a custom launcher icon to the app, and create a *Blank Activity* (the first screen that the user will see).

2. Modify the blank activity XML file using objects in the *View* class (drag *widgets* from the *Palette* and then change their

properties as needed). The elements used in the app below are *<TextView>* and *<EditView>*, which display text or an input box, respectively, and *<Button>*, which adds a button that contains the designated text and can perform the actions assigned to it in the Java file (such as adding two numbers and displaying the sum) when clicked. Edit the XML file as needed to complete your desired UI.

3. Modify the Java code, if needed, to perform the necessary actions (such as adding the two numbers and displaying the sum when the Get Sum button is clicked).

4. Run the app using the *Android Emulator* with the device you want to emulate. Edit the XML or Java files and rerun as needed until the app is complete and working properly.

**1.** Create a new project.

App name and launcher icon.

**2.** Add elements to the initial activity to create the UI.

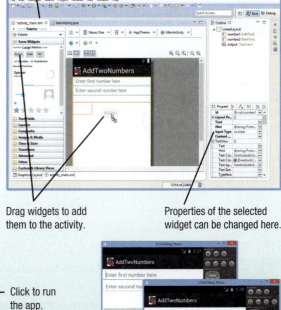

Drag widgets to add them to the activity.

Properties of the selected widget can be changed here.

XML file     Java file

**3.** Edit the .xml and .java files as needed.

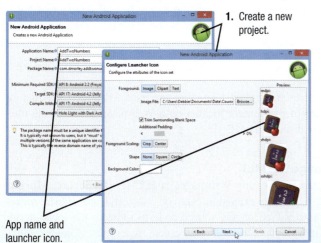

First input box code.

Click to select an emulator.

Click to run the app.

Compute sum code.

**4.** Launch the app in the desired emulator.

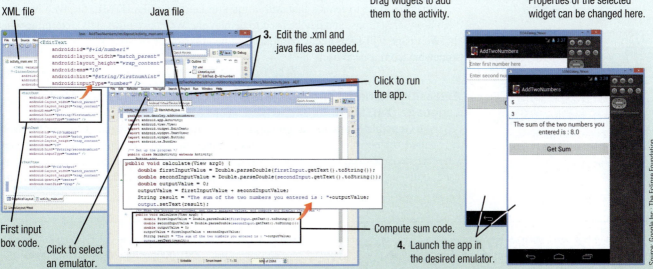

The sum of the two numbers you entered is : 8.0

Get Sum

```
# Initialize variable
total = 0.0

# Input a number, add it to the total, and repeat
# until two numbers have been entered
for iteration in range(2):
    text = raw_input("Enter number: ")
    total = total + float(text)

# Print the sum
print "The sum of the numbers you entered is", total
```

Comments are preceded by a pound symbol #.

The indented statements in this for statement will be executed two times.

**FIGURE 11-25**
The adding-two-numbers program written in Python.

### Python

**Python** is an open source, dynamic, object-oriented programming language that can be used to develop a variety of applications, including gaming, scientific, database, and Web applications. Python programs run on computers using the Windows, Linux, UNIX, OS X, or OS/2 operating systems, as well as on some mobile devices. One advantage of Python is code readability. Python is widely used today by many large organizations, and some colleges—such as MIT—are replacing other languages with Python for some programming courses. See Figure 11-25 for the Python version of the adding-two-numbers program.

## Common Markup and Scripting Languages

While markup and scripting languages were originally used for Web pages, they are also used today for Web applications, mobile apps, and other applications. Consequently, programming, markup, and scripting languages are beginning to be collectively referred to as *application development languages* or just *languages*. Some of the most common markup and scripting languages are discussed next.

### Markup Languages

As mentioned earlier in this chapter, markup languages are used to define the structure, layout, and general appearance of the content located on a Web page. Some of the most common markup languages are discussed next.

#### Hypertext Markup Language (HTML)

The markup language designed for creating Web pages is **HTML (Hypertext Markup Language)**. HTML files have the file extension *.htm* or *.html* and use *HTML tags*—text-based codes embedded into a Web page's source code to indicate the location and appearance of content on that Web page, as well as to create hyperlinks. Some examples of HTML tags are shown in Figure 11-26. As shown in this figure, some HTML tags are *paired tags*, which surround the content to be associated with that HTML tag.

It is important to realize that with a markup language like HTML, the Web browser, Web browser settings, and device used to display the Web page ultimately determine what the Web page will look like. Consequently, the appearance of your Web pages may vary somewhat from user to user.

#### Extensible Markup Language (XML) and Extensible Hypertext Markup Language (XHTML)

**XML (Extensible Markup Language)** is a set of rules for exchanging data over the Web. It is called "extensible" because the data contained in XML documents can be extracted when needed and used in a variety of ways, such as combined to create new documents or used to display a single Web page in a format appropriate for the device being used. This

> **Python.** A high-level, open source, dynamic, object-oriented programming language that can be used to develop a wide variety of applications.
> **HTML (Hypertext Markup Language).** A markup language widely used for creating Web pages. **>XML (Extensible Markup Language).**
A set of rules used for exchanging data over the Web; addresses only the content, not the formatting of the data, and the content displays in an appropriate format based on the device being used.

is possible because XML focuses on identifying the data itself—not the format of that data. To accomplish this, *XML tags* are assigned to pieces of data (such as surrounding the name of a client or an employee with the tag pair <name> </name>). There are no standard XML tags; instead, each organization using XML determines the XML tags to be used with that organization's documents. Once the data is tagged, it can be used with any XML document created for that organization. XML is increasingly being used with ordinary business documents and company databases to allow easy retrieval and updating of data by applications.

**XHTML (Extensible Hypertext Markup Language)** is a version of HTML that is based on XML. Like HTML, XHTML is used to create Web pages but it also supports XML, so XML-tagged data can be incorporated easily into XHTML Web pages. When this occurs, XML controls what content is displayed, and XHTML controls the appearance and format of that content. XHTML tags are similar to HTML tags, but there are stricter rules about how the markup tags are written. For instance, XHTML is case sensitive, so all tags must be written in lowercase; all tags must be *closed* (have an ending tag); and the tags must be in the proper order around elements. For example, the statement

    <b><i>This text should be bold and italic.</i></b>

must be used instead of

    <b><i>This text should be bold and italic.</b></i>

While the latter sequence will work in HTML, it will not work properly in XHTML. As long as the stricter rules are followed, however, basic HTML tags—such as the ones shown in Figure 11-26—can be used in XHTML Web pages.

| TAG | PURPOSE |
|---|---|
| <html></html> | Marks the beginning and end of an HTML document. |
| <head></head> | Marks the head section, which contains the page title and meta tags. |
| <title></title> | Marks the title of the Web page. |
| <body></body> | Contains all the content of the Web page, including text, hyperlinks, and images. |
| <h1></h1> to <h6></h6> | Formats headings larger or smaller than the regular (non-heading) text in the document; H1 is the largest text. |
| <img> | Indicates an image file to be inserted; attributes included within this tag specify the image filename, display size, alternative text, title, border, etc. |
| <a></a> | Defines a hyperlink using the specified URL; can include an image filename, hyperlink text, and other attributes. |
| <b></b> | Bolds text. |
| <!-- --> | Indicates a comment that won't display when the Web page is viewed. |
| <hr> | Inserts a horizontal rule. |
| <p> | Inserts a paragraph break (starts a new paragraph). |

**FIGURE 11-26**
Sample HTML tags.

> **TIP**
>
> HTML tags are also used to identify keywords and other Web page meta tags that are used by search sites to classify Web pages.

## HTML5

The specifications for HTML and XHTML are developed by the World Wide Web Consortium (W3C) and are continually evolving. The current version of HTML is **HTML5** and is designed to replace the previous versions of both HTML and XHTML. In addition to supporting previous versions of HTML (although some older tags and attributes have been deleted or replaced), HTML5 is designed to support the creation of more complex and dynamic Web pages and applications, such as to add interactivity and the ability to play multimedia regardless of the device being used and without a plug-in. A simple example of an HTML5 Web page is shown in Figure 11-27 on the next page. This example shows some new HTML5 tags (such as video and nav bar, discussed shortly). It also illustrates the following three main sections of an HTML5 Web page:

> ➤ A *declaration* statement at the top of the page indicating that HTML is being used (the only option with HTML5, as opposed to the various *doctypes* used with XHTML pages). Notice the opening <html> tag following the declaration is closed at the end of the Web page using the </html> tag.

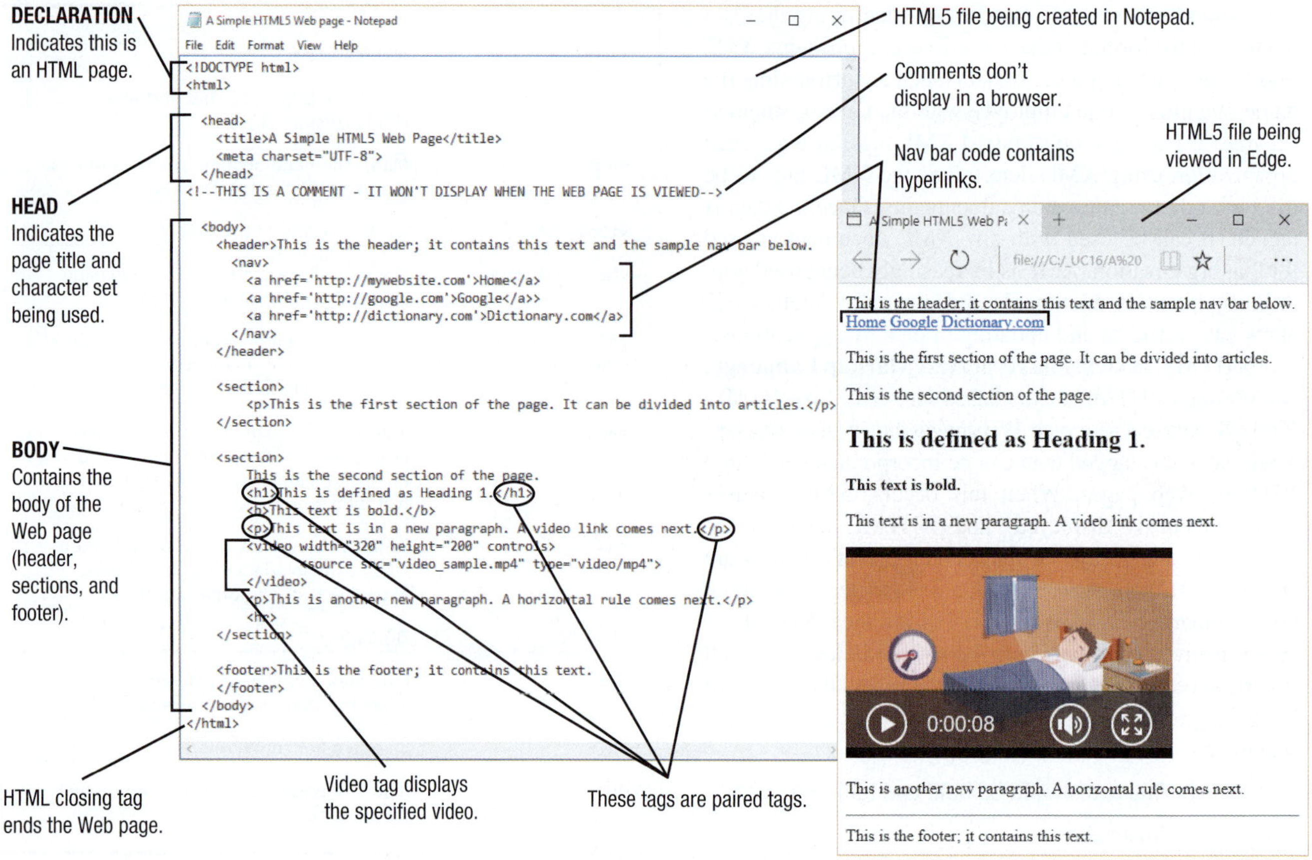

DECLARATION
Indicates this is
an HTML page.

HEAD
Indicates the
page title and
character set
being used.

BODY
Contains the
body of the
Web page
(header,
sections, and
footer).

HTML closing tag
ends the Web page.

Video tag displays
the specified video.

These tags are paired tags.

HTML5 file being created in Notepad.

Comments don't
display in a browser.

Nav bar code contains
hyperlinks.

HTML5 file being
viewed in Edge.

**FIGURE 11-27**
An example of
HTML5 source
code and its
corresponding Web
page.

> A *head* statement that contains the title to be displayed on the browser's tab when the Web page is viewed and any desired meta tags (such as to indicate the *character set* being used, as in Figure 11-27, or the keywords to be associated with the Web page.

> The *body* (content) of the Web page; it can contain a header, footer, and navigation bar, as well as be divided into sections and articles.

Some of the most interesting new features in HTML5 include new *<video>* and *<audio>* tags for media playback and control directly from within the browser; tags (such as *<header>*, *<footer>*, *<article>*, *<section>*, and *<nav>*) used to better identify the parts of a Web page (which is important for search engines); and the *<canvas>* tag that creates a bitmapped surface to work with, such as to build charts and graphs. HTML5 also gives Web apps the opportunity to store information offline to allow the apps to load more quickly. An advantage of using HTML5, in conjunction with other non-proprietary tools like JavaScript, is that they are open standards. Consequently, no proprietary software is required (Web pages can be created using just a text editor) and the features are already supported by most current Web browsers, so no plug-ins are required.

### Scripting Languages

As mentioned previously, scripting languages are often used to add dynamic content to a Web page and are embedded (via scripts) into a Web page's code. They are also used as middleware to tie a Web site to a database. Middleware and cloud databases are discussed in detail in Chapter 12. Web page scripts can be run by the Web browser being used to view the Web page (referred to as a client-side script) or by the Web server hosting the Web page being viewed (referred to as a server-side script).

**TIP**

Google recently converted all Flash-based advertisements that play in Chrome to use HTML5 instead.

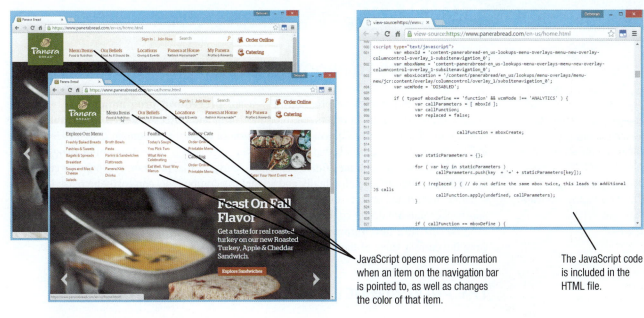

JavaScript opens more information when an item on the navigation bar is pointed to, as well as changes the color of that item.

The JavaScript code is included in the HTML file.

### JavaScript

**JavaScript** was developed to enable Web authors to implement interactive content on Web sites, such as to animate an item or pop up a window or text when that item is pointed to (see the Panera Bread Web site in Figure 11-28). JavaScript code is executed by the Web browser (on the client side), so it can function after the Web page loads without having to communicate with the Web server. JavaScript is included in the Web page source code, either as commands included directly in the file or as a link to an external JavaScript file. (JavaScript files have a *.js* extension.)

### VBScript

**VBScript** (*Visual Basic Scripting Edition*) is a scripting language developed by Microsoft that is based on the Visual Basic programming language. VBScript is used for purposes similar to what JavaScript is used for—it enables Web developers to include interactive elements, such as pop-up content, on their Web pages. Individuals who are already familiar with Visual Basic can easily incorporate VBScript content into their Web pages. VBScript can be used to write both client-side and server-side scripts.

### PHP

*PHP* (also called *PHP: Hypertext Preprocessor*) is commonly used to create dynamic Web pages. PHP scripts are enclosed within *PHP tags* and are executed on the server so the user cannot view the PHP code.

### Perl

Short for *Practical Extraction and Report Language, Perl* was originally developed as a programming language designed for processing text. Because of its strong text-processing abilities, Perl has become one of the most popular languages for writing *CGI scripts*—scripts that can accept data from and return data to a Web server. CGI scripts are often used to enable Web servers to interact dynamically with users, such as to process data entered into Web page forms.

**FIGURE 11-28**
JavaScript is commonly used on Web pages.

**TIP**

*Cascading Style Sheets (CSSs)* specify the appearance of the different elements on a Web site and can be used to provide a consistent appearance for that site.

>**JavaScript.** A scripting language often used to add animation and interactivity to Web pages and Web applications.

# SUMMARY

## APPROACHES TO PROGRAM DESIGN AND DEVELOPMENT

Two common approaches to program design are **procedural programming**, in which programs are written in an organized, modular form, and **object-oriented programming** (**OOP**), in which programs consist of a collection of *objects* that contain data (*attributes*) and *methods* to be used with that data. A newer approach is **aspect-oriented programming** (**AOP**), which separates functions more clearly so that program components can be developed and modified individually and so that the components can easily be reused with separate, nonrelated objects. Other possible approaches are *adaptive software development* approaches that are designed to make program development faster or more efficient, such as **agile software development** (**ASD**). **Variables** (called *attributes* in OOP) are used to store the current value of the data items used in a program.

## THE PROGRAM DEVELOPMENT LIFE CYCLE (PDLC)

Creating application programs is referred to as **program development**. The phases involved with program development are called the **program development life cycle** (**PDLC**). The PDLC begins with **problem analysis**, in which the system specifications are reviewed by the systems analyst and **programmer** to understand what the proposed system—and corresponding new program—must do. In the next phase—**program design**—the program specifications from phase one are refined and expanded into a complete set of design specifications that express the *algorithm* for the program. In the **program coding** phase, the program is written using a programming language. The **program debugging and testing** phase ensures the program works correctly. During the **program implementation and maintenance** phase, the program is put into use and maintained as needed.

Good program design is essential. Some key design principles include being very specific, using only one *entry point* into and one *exit point* out of any structure, and ensuring that there are no *infinite loops* in your programs. Many *program design tools* are available to help programmers as they design programs. *Structure charts* depict the overall hierarchical organization of program modules. Program **flowcharts** use graphical symbols and relational operators to provide a graphic display of the sequence of steps involved in a program or program component. **Wireframes** are often used with mobile apps to illustrate the logic and the flow from screen to screen, as well as the UI design. **Pseudocode** is a structured technique that uses English-like statements in place of the graphic symbols of the flowchart. **Unified Modeling Language** (**UML**) is a set of standard notations often used when modeling object-oriented programs.

There are three fundamental **control structures** typically found in programs. A **sequence control structure** is simply a series of procedures that follow one another. The **selection** (or *if-then-else*) **control structure** involves a choice: *If* a certain condition is true, *then* follow one procedure; *else*, if false, follow another. When more than two conditions exist, the *case control structure* can be used. A **repetition control structure** repeats the statements in a loop until a certain condition is met. A loop can take one of two forms: *do while* or *do until*.

Once the program design for an application is finished and the logic is tested (such as by performing a *desk check*), the next phase is **program coding**. **Coding**, which is the job of programmers, is the process of writing a program in a particular *programming language* based on a set of design specifications. Among the techniques that have been developed to increase programmer productivity are coding standards and *reusable code*.

The next phase is **program debugging and testing**. **Debugging** is the process of making sure that a program is free of errors, or "bugs." Before a program can be run—and, therefore, before it can be debugged—it needs to be translated from the code a programmer writes to the code a computer can execute. A **language translator** converts the application program's **source code** into *machine language* or **object code**. A **compiler** translates the entire program into machine language before executing it. An **interpreter** translates and executes program statements one line at a time. An *assembler* is used to convert an assembly language program into machine language.

Most bugs can be classified as being either **syntax errors** or **logic errors**. While programs with syntax errors will not run, programs with logic errors will run but with erroneous results. Once preliminary debugging is complete, programs will also have to be thoroughly *tested*. Commercial software programs are also often *beta tested*. After the testing process is complete, the last phase of the PDLC (**program implementation and maintenance**) begins and involves first getting the program up and running in the new system, and then updating the software, as needed, so that it continues to be useful.

**Chapter Objective 5:**
Discuss some of the activities involved with debugging a program and otherwise ensuring it is designed and written properly.

## TOOLS FOR FACILITATING PROGRAM DEVELOPMENT

*Program development tools* can be used to facilitate the program development process. **Application lifecycle management** (**ALM**) tools can be used to create and manage an application throughout its entire life cycle—from design through testing; many include *code generators* to help programmers by generating code based on the design already created with another component of the program. *Application generators*, such as *macros* and *report generators*, enable programmers and end users to code new applications quickly. **Integrated development environments** (**IDEs**) consist of a collection of development tools that have a common interface in order to help create applications more quickly. **Software development kits** (**SDKs**) are programming packages designed for a particular platform (such as iOS or Android) or a particular programming language (such as Dart) that enable programmers to develop applications more quickly and easily; **application program interfaces** (**APIs**) allow software to interface with a particular operating system, Web site, or device.

**Chapter Objective 6:**
List some tools that can be used to speed up or otherwise facilitate program development.

## LANGUAGES USED FOR APPLICATION DEVELOPMENT

**Programming languages** include **low-level languages** (such as **machine language** and **assembly language**) and **high-level languages** (such as **Fortran** or **FORTRAN**, **COBOL**, **Pascal**, **BASIC**, **C**, **C++**, **C#**, and **Java**. **Fourth-generation languages** (**4GLs**), are predominantly *declarative languages*, whereas high-level languages are typically *procedural* or *object-oriented programming languages*. Programming languages can also use a *visual programming environment* (*VPE*) like **Visual Basic**. Different programming languages are designed for different purposes. Newer open source object-oriented programming languages include **Dart** and **Python**.

Web sites are often created with a **markup language**, which use *markup tags* to define the structure, layout, and general appearance of the content located on Web pages. The markup language typically used to create Web pages is **HTML** (**Hypertext Markup Language**)—the current version is **HTML5**. The **XML** (**Extensible Markup Language**) version of HTML is **XHTML** (**Extensible Hypertext Markup Language**). **Scripting languages**, such as **JavaScript**, *VBScript*, *PHP*, and *Perl* can be used to add interactive elements to Web pages and Web applications, as well as to connect a database to a Web application.

**Chapter Objective 7:**
Describe several languages used for application development today and explain their key features.

SYS

# REVIEW ACTIVITIES

## KEY TERM MATCHING

**a.** coding

**b.** compiler

**c.** debugging

**d.** flowchart

**e.** markup language

**f.** object code

**g.** object-oriented programming (OOP)

**h.** software development kit (SDK)

**i.** source code

**j.** syntax error

**Instructions:** Match each key term on the left with the definition on the right that best describes it.

**1.** _____ A computer program before it is compiled.

**2.** _____ A language translator that converts an entire program into machine language before executing it.

**3.** _____ An approach to program design in which a program consists of objects that contain data (attributes) and processes (methods) to be used with those objects.

**4.** _____ A programming package designed for a particular platform that enables programmers to develop applications for that platform more quickly and easily.

**5.** _____ A type of language that uses symbols or tags to describe what a document should look like.

**6.** _____ A programming error that occurs when the programmer has not followed the rules of the programming language.

**7.** _____ A program design tool that graphically shows step-by-step how a computer program will process data.

**8.** _____ The machine language version of a computer program generated when the program's source code is compiled.

**9.** _____ The process of ensuring a program is free of errors.

**10.** _____ The process of writing the programming language statements to create a computer program.

## SELF-QUIZ

**Instructions:** Circle **T** if the statement is true, **F** if the statement is false, or write the best answer in the space provided. **Answers for the self-quiz are located in the References and Resources Guide at the end of the book.**

**1.  T  F**  A systems analyst is an individual who writes the code for a computer program.

**2.  T  F**  The terms *class* and *inheritance* are associated with the object-oriented programming approach.

**3.  T  F**  With a *do until* structure, the program statements in the loop are always executed at least once.

**4.  T  F**  BASIC is an example of an object-oriented programming language.

**5.  T  F**  A *wireframe* is another name for a flowchart.

**6.** A(n) _____ (called an *attribute* in an OOP) in a computer program holds the current value of a data item in that program.

**7.** A(n) _____ converts the source code of an application program into executable object code (machine language) one line at a time.

**8.** Using an incorrect formula is an example of a(n) _____ error.

**9.** _____ software development is an approach that uses short development cycles in order to produce small functional pieces of a program on an ongoing basis.

**10.** Indicate the proper order of the phases in the program development life cycle (PDLC) by writing the numbers from 1 to 5 in the blanks to the left of the phases.

**a.** _____ program coding

**b.** _____ program design

**c.** _____ program implementation and maintenance

**d.** _____ program debugging and testing

**e.** _____ problem analysis

---

**1.** List at least three types of information that should be included in a program's internal documentation (comments).

**2.** Match each description with the most appropriate language, and write the corresponding number in the blank to the left of each description.

**a.** _____ A high-level programming language used to write Web applications and applets.

**b.** _____ A low-level programming language.

**c.** _____ A markup language used to create Web pages and Web applications.

**d.** _____ A high-level programming language that can be used to develop a wide variety of applications.

1. assembly language
2. Java
3. Python
4. HTML5

**3.** Draw a flowchart for the following situation: Input a person's age. If the person is less than 21 years old, the message "You are under 21." should be displayed. For individuals 21 or older, display the message "You are 21 or older." Be sure to test your flowchart to make sure it illustrates the proper logic.

**4.** Write pseudocode for the problem described in Exercise 3 above.

**5.** Trace through the flowchart shown to the right that illustrates the logic of a program that computes the sum of two numbers. Create a tracing table as you go to see if the flowchart does what is intended (use any numbers for your input). If it does not do what it is supposed to do, identify the problem and state how it could be corrected.

---

**1.** When human beings and computers are both involved in accomplishing a task and something goes wrong, we tend to blame the computer. There is little question about the existence of software bugs, but can all real-world problems involving computers (such as erroneous bank transactions, military training incidents, or privacy breaches) be attributed to errors in the software program? Today, do you think it is more likely that a computer or a human being would be responsible for a serious system problem? Why?

**2.** There is a trend in programming to make coding easier and more automatic. Some welcome this trend, but others are concerned about future programmers not learning necessary programming fundamentals if programming is no longer required. For instance, without understanding how looping and variable initializations work, how easily would an individual be able to find a logic error in a looping process? Do you think programmers of the future should still learn programming fundamentals, even if coding is no longer required? Why or why not?

# PROJECTS

1. **Mobile UX** As discussed in the Trend box, it is important to develop a good user experience (UX) when developing applications. The UX for a Web site often varies with the device being used.

   For this project, load a Web page you are familiar with on a PC and on a smartphone or tablet. Compare the content and appearance of both versions of the site. How are they similar? How are they different? Navigate through the site on both versions—is it comfortable using the site on the smartphone or tablet? What could be changed on the Web site to make a more enjoyable or usable mobile UX? At the conclusion of your research, prepare a one-page summary of your findings and opinions and submit it to your instructor.

2. **New Languages** New languages are developed regularly, such as to meet new needs or to make programming easier for beginners.

   For this project, identify and research one new or emerging programming, markup, or scripting language. Determine why the program was developed, who it is geared for, the cost to use it (if any), and what applications it is designed for. Check online to see if there is a demonstration or a free version available; if so, view the demo or try out the programming language, if possible. Does the program require a separate compiler or interpreter? Can it be used for stand-alone programs and for Web applications? Do you think this new program fulfills a need? Why or why not? At the conclusion of your research, prepare a short summary of what you learned and submit it to your instructor.

3. **Pass or Fail** Flowcharts can be used to model any sequence of actions, in addition to being used to design programs. For example, any scenario that has a sequence of steps with different paths depending on predetermined factors (such as passing or failing a course based on the grades you earn on various assignments and tests) can be illustrated using a flowchart.

   For this project, draw a flowchart that depicts the sequence of steps involved in passing the course for which you are using this textbook. To simplify the diagram, you may assume that you will either pass or fail this class (no grade will be issued) and that there are only three graded components (midterm, final, and projects). The flowchart should print the names of all students on the instructor's roster who have passed the course by achieving a score of at least 70% on each graded component. In addition, you should print the total number of students on the roster, as well as the number that passed the class. Be sure to trace the flowchart to verify your logic, and then write a pseudocode version of this situation. When you have completed this task, submit a copy of the flowchart and pseudocode to your instructor.

4. **Consumer Hacks** There have been many instances where individuals have hacked into consumer products—such as toys, mobile phones, gaming consoles, DVRs, and more—to alter their functionality. Some of these hacks (such as ones that required the hacker to break the encryption built into a robot in order to reprogram it to perform other activities) violate the *Digital Millennium Copyright Act*, which prohibits breaking technological controls placed on any copyrighted work. Do you think hacking into a product you own is ethical? Have you ever considered hacking into a product you own? If so, for what purpose? Do you think consumer hacks should be illegal if the hack requires breaking the product's encryption? If so, should the law apply to those individuals who break through a copy protection scheme for their own use only, or should the law apply just to those individuals who share the circumvention process with others? What about those individuals who try to break a copy protection or security technology just to prove it can be done? Should they be prosecuted, sued, or congratulated for exposing a weakness in the existing technology?

For this project, form an opinion about the ethical ramifications of consumer hacks and be prepared to discuss your position (in class, via an online class forum, or via a class blog, depending on your instructor's directions). You may also be asked to write a short paper expressing your opinion.

**ETHICS IN ACTION**

5. **Bug Hunters** Many security freelance programmers in the software industry (sometimes referred to as *bug hunters*) like to search for security flaws in their spare time and make this information public. The goal is to make unsuspecting users aware of the possible security problems that currently exist and encourage the producer of the software to write security patches to fix these problems.

For this project, research one recent major security flaw discovered in a widely used software program and present a summary about who found the flaw, how the information was made public, what the security problem was, and how the problem was resolved (or is being resolved). Share your findings and opinions with the class in the form of a short presentation. The presentation should not exceed 10 minutes and should make use of one or more presentation aids, such as a whiteboard, handouts, or a computer-based slide presentation (your instructor may provide additional requirements). You may also be asked to submit a summary of the presentation to your instructor.

**PRESENTATION/
DEMONSTRATION**

6. **Are We Too Dependent on Our Smartphones?** If you can name it, there is probably an app for it. While certainly useful, our smartphones are used for an ever-growing collection of tasks. But do we rely on them too much? Is being able to Google the answer to every question that arises a benefit of improved technology or is it decreasing our ability for independent thinking and problem solving? Is the amount of time children spend playing games on their phones and text messaging their friends impacting their ability to interact with others face to face? Most children today can type rapidly on a smartphone keyboard and use the GPS feature on their phone to find any destination they may wish to go to but many schools are no longer teaching handwriting and some children have never even seen a paper map, let alone used one—will this put today's children at a disadvantage when they become adults? What tasks do you use your mobile phone or smartphone for? Would you be able to perform those tasks without your phone? Are we becoming so dependent on our smartphones that we will be unable to function without them? Why or why not?

Pick a side on this issue, form an opinion and gather supporting evidence, and be prepared to discuss and defend your position in a classroom debate or in a one- to two-page paper, depending on your instructor's directions.

**BALANCING ACT**

# chapter 12

# Databases and Database Management Systems

After completing this chapter, you will be able to do the following:

1. Explain what a database is, including common database terminology, and list some of the advantages and disadvantages of using databases.

2. Discuss some basic concepts and characteristics of data, such as data hierarchy, entity relationships, and data definition.

3. Describe the importance of data integrity, security, and privacy and how they affect database design.

4. Identify some basic database classifications and discuss their differences.

5. List the most common database models and discuss how they are used today.

6. Understand how a relational database is designed, created, used, and maintained.

7. Describe some ways databases are used on the Web.

# OVERVIEW

**P**eople often need to sort through a large amount of data rapidly to retrieve one piece of information. To do this quickly and easily, a database is often used. Databases can be a variety of sizes, from an address book created and used by an individual, to a company-wide database consisting of customer data used by company employees, to a product database used in conjunction with an e-commerce site to enable online shoppers to place real-time orders, to a search engine database consisting of data about billions of Web pages and accessed by individuals around the world.

This chapter focuses on databases and the software used to create, maintain, and use them. The chapter opens with a look at what a database is, the individuals who use databases, and how databases evolved. We then look at some important database concepts and vocabulary, followed by an explanation of database classifications and models, with an extended discussion of the most widely used database model: the relational database. The chapter closes with a discussion of how databases are used on the Web. ∎

## WHAT IS A DATABASE?

As discussed in Chapter 6, a **database** is a collection of related data that is stored and organized in a manner that enables information to be retrieved as needed. *Database software*—more formally called a **database management system** (**DBMS**)—is used to create, maintain, and access a database. A DBMS also controls the organization of the data and protects the integrity and security of the data so it is entered accurately into the database and then protected against both intentional and accidental damage. While batch processing can be used with databases, most database applications today occur in real time.

A key component of a DBMS is the *database engine*—the part of the program that actually stores and retrieves data. In addition to a database engine, most DBMSs come bundled with a set of tools to perform a variety of necessary tasks, such as creating forms (used to input data) and reports (used to output data), and interfacing with query languages and programming languages for complex applications. Programming languages typically used with databases today include Python, Java, and C#, although some older legacy database systems still use COBOL.

A database typically consists of interrelated **tables** that contain fields and records. As discussed in Chapter 6, a **field** (also called a **column**) holds a single category of data (such as customer names or employee phone numbers) that will be stored in a database. A **record** (also called a **row**) is a collection of related fields. The technical difference between the terms *row* and *record* in database terminology is that a row is contained within a single database table, but a record is a collection of fields, which can be either

**SYS**

>**Database.** A collection of related data that is stored in a manner enabling information to be retrieved as needed; in a relational database, a collection of related tables. >**Database management system (DBMS).** A type of software program used to create, maintain, and access databases. >**Table.** In a relational database, a collection of related records. >**Field.** A single category of data to be stored in a database, such as a person's last name or phone number; also called a **column**. >**Record.** A collection of related fields in a database; also called a **row**.

a specific row from a single table or a collection of related fields from multiple tables, such as the records shown in the results of the Order Request screen in Figure 12-1 and discussed next. However, in this chapter, as in common usage, the two terms are used interchangeably.

To illustrate these concepts, a simplified example of a possible *relational database*—the type of database most widely used at the present time—is shown in Figure 12-1 and discussed next.

## A Simple Relational Database Example

Figure 12-1 illustrates an inventory system for a ski equipment retailer. The tables shown in this figure contain data related to the retailer's products: the Product table (for product descriptions and selling prices), the Inventory table (for current stock levels of products), and the Inventory on Order table (for future shipments of products that have been ordered from suppliers). Each table consists of several fields (columns) and records (rows). The Product table, for example, contains four fields—Product Number, Product Name, Supplier, and Price—and five records—one each for Skis, Boots, Poles, Bindings, and Wax. Each record in the Product table contains data for each of the four fields. The Inventory table contains three fields and five records, and the Inventory on Order table contains four fields and six records. To keep this example simple, the tables containing data about customers and their orders (Customer table and Order table, respectively) are not shown and the skis, boots, and poles are not itemized by size. Real-world databases typically consist of many more tables than are used in this example, each containing thousands of records.

For this example, imagine that you are the sales manager of this company and a customer calls on the phone and wants to order 160 pairs of ski boots. First, you need to find out if the

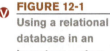

**FIGURE 12-1**

Using a relational database in an inventory system.

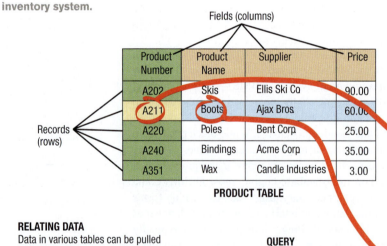

**Fields (columns)**

### PRODUCT TABLE

| Product Number | Product Name | Supplier | Price |
|---|---|---|---|
| A202 | Skis | Ellis Ski Co | 90.00 |
| A211 | Boots | Ajax Bros | 60.00 |
| A220 | Poles | Bent Corp | 25.00 |
| A240 | Bindings | Acme Corp | 35.00 |
| A351 | Wax | Candle Industries | 3.00 |

**Records (rows)**

### INVENTORY TABLE

| Product Number | Current Stock | On Order? |
|---|---|---|
| A202 | 15 | Yes |
| A211 | 90 | Yes |
| A220 | 30 | Yes |
| A240 | 25 | Yes |
| A351 | 8 | No |

**RELATING DATA**
Data in various tables can be pulled together by their common field (Product Number).

### INVENTORY ON ORDER TABLE

| Order Number | Product Number | Shipment Date | Quantity |
|---|---|---|---|
| 1001 | A202 | 1/8 | 30 |
| 1002 | A240 | 1/8 | 15 |
| 1003 | A211 | 1/9 | 50 |
| 1004 | A202 | 1/9 | 40 |
| 1005 | A220 | 1/10 | 35 |
| 1006 | A211 | 1/12 | 60 |

**QUERY**
When the user supplies a product number and order size, all other relevant information needed to complete an Order Request screen is gathered and displayed automatically.

**ORDER REQUEST SCREEN**

Date : 1/8  ORDER REQUEST
Productnumber A211
Order size  160

Productname is  Boots
Projected fill date for order is : 1/12

| Date | Deliveries | Projected Stock |
|---|---|---|
| today | 0 | 90 |
| 1/9 | 50 | 140 |
| 1/12 | 60 | 200 |

Igor Shikov/Shutterstock.com

order can be filled from stock currently in inventory. If it cannot, you need to know how long it will be before enough stock is available to fill the order. Using your computer, you execute the appropriate command to display an Order Request screen and enter the product number "A211" and the order size "160" as shown in Figure 12-1. The DBMS then displays the name of the product (Boots, in this example), the current level of stock in inventory (90), and as many upcoming shipments of this product (50 and 60) as needed to fill the order. It also provides an estimate as to when the order can be filled: January 12. Within seconds, right in front of you, you have the information you need to respond to the customer's request and close the order.

In a relational database, data from several tables is tied together (*related*) using fields that the tables have in common so that information can be extracted from multiple tables as needed. For instance, in Figure 12-1, data from all three tables was pulled together through a common Product Number field (the green shaded columns) to complete the Order Request screen shown in that figure. Specifically, the Product table was first accessed to locate and display the product name; next, the Inventory table was used to determine and display the number of boots currently in stock; and finally, the Inventory on Order table was used to look up and display the quantities and delivery dates for as many incoming shipments as needed to get a total of at least 160 boots. The end user is typically not aware that multiple tables are being used or of the relationships between tables; instead the user knows only that the information is "somewhere in the database system" and it is retrieved and displayed when requested.

The field in a table that is used to relate that table to other tables is called the **primary key**. A primary key must uniquely identify each record in that table, which means that no two records within a table can have the same value in the primary key field. To ensure the uniqueness of the primary key, it usually consists of an identifying number, such as a student ID number, customer number, or product number. For example, in Figure 12-1, the Product Number field is the primary key field for the Product and Inventory tables and the Order Number field is the primary key field for the Inventory on Order table. When selecting a primary key field, it is important to pick a field that contains unique data that is not likely to change. Consequently, fields containing names, phone numbers, and addresses are poor choices for a primary key (see Figure 12-2). Although phone numbers and complete addresses are unique, they may change and will not necessarily always be associated with the original individual.

While most complex database systems will have multiple interrelated tables, you can create a database that does not interrelate tables, or you can create a database that has only a single table, if that's appropriate for your application. DBMSs available for use on personal computers include *Microsoft Access, OpenOffice Base,* and *Corel Paradox* (part of the Microsoft Office, Apache OpenOffice, and WordPerfect Office software suites, respectively). Of these, Access is the most widely used. For more comprehensive enterprise databases, *Oracle Database*, *IBM DB2*, *Microsoft SQL Server*, *MySQL*, or another more robust DBMS may be used instead.

**TIP**

Primary keys can be a combination of two key fields (called *composite primary keys*), but single primary keys are more typical in simple databases; only single primary keys are used in the examples in this chapter.

The yellow fields will always contain unique data and so are good to use as primary keys.

The blue fields will not always contain unique data and so are not good to use as primary keys.

| | | | |
|---|---|---|---|
| Product Number | Product Name | Supplier | Price |
| Student ID Number | Student Name | Address | Phone |
| Customer Number | Address | Phone | Balance |

**FIGURE 12-2**
**Primary key fields.**
A primary key field must contain unique data so it can be used to identify each record in the table.



## Individuals Involved with a Database Management System

To be effective, data in a DBMS must be initially entered into the database, updated as necessary to stay current, and then retrieved in the form of information. Consequently, virtually all DBMSs include a user interface for easy data input, modification, and retrieval. There must also be a way for the database to be backed up and protected against unauthorized access. The individuals most often involved with creating, using, managing, and protecting a DBMS are described next.

>**Primary key.** A specific field in a database table that uniquely identifies the records in that table.

### Database Designers

As the name suggests, a *database designer* is the individual responsible for designing a database. Because data and databases are so critical in business today, it is essential for databases to be designed appropriately so they can efficiently fulfill the needs of a business. Database designers work with systems analysts and other individuals involved in the system development life cycle (SDLC) to identify the types of data to be collected, the relationships among the data, the types of output required, and other factors that affect the design of the database, and then they design the database accordingly. These individuals are also sometimes called *data architects*, *database engineers*, and *database analysts*.

### Database Developers and Programmers

*Database developers* create the actual database based on the design generated by the database designer and get it ready for data entry. This process includes setting up the database structure and creating the user interface, typically using the tools included with the DBMS. Many databases also require custom programs used to access the database or to tie the database to other applications, such as to a Web site for an e-commerce application. Creating these programs, when needed, is the job of the *database programmer*. Sometimes the user interface is also built using a programming language when very specific requirements exist. In some organizations, one individual may be both the database developer and database programmer; he or she may function as the database designer, as well.

### Database Administrators

*Database administrators* (*DBAs*) are the people responsible for managing the databases within an organization. They perform regular maintenance, assign and monitor user access to the database, monitor the performance of the database system, perform backups, and carry out other necessary maintenance and security duties. Database administrators also work closely with database designers, developers, and programmers to ensure that the integrity and security of the data will remain intact when a new system is designed or changes are made to an existing system. The DBA also periodically runs reports and checks the data in the database to confirm that the structural integrity of the data is intact. Database integrity and security are discussed later in this chapter.

### Users

The *users* are the individuals who enter data, update data, and retrieve information from the database when necessary; that is, the individuals who use the database. Typically, users have no knowledge of how the underlying database is structured, how data is organized, or how data is retrieved. Instead, they interact with the database via a user interface consisting of menus, buttons, and fill-in-the-blank forms (such as the Order Request screen shown in Figure 12-1).

---

## ASK THE EXPERT

*i*nfodatix   **Robert Terry,** Principal Consultant, Infodatix

**What skills are essential for a database developer or database programmer today?**

Database technology is always changing. New trends that a database expert should be aware of include Big Data, NoSQL, and Hadoop. A database developer should be an expert in SQL (structured query language), which is the foundation for all database programming languages. But the most important skill and knowledge a database expert should have is in traditional relational database theory. The two most popular database programs today are Microsoft SQL and MySQL. A person interested in learning databases can find free versions of these to download and install, and then get started by building practice databases or by following tutorials found on the Web. Databases are the foundation for most software and Web/smartphone applications. Anyone interested in any kind of software programming would be well-advised to gain a strong foundation in database design and development.

| MODEL | FLAT FILES | HIERARCHICAL | NETWORK | RELATIONAL | OBJECT-ORIENTED | MULTI-DIMENSIONAL |
|---|---|---|---|---|---|---|
| **YEAR BEGAN** | 1940s | 1960s | 1960s | 1970s | 1980s | 1990s |
| **DATA ORGANIZATION** | Flat files | Trees | Trees | Tables and relations | Objects | Data cubes, tables and relations, or a combination |
| **DATA ACCESS** | Low-level access | Low-level access with a standard navigational language | Low-level access with a standard navigational language | High-level, nonprocedural languages | High-level, nonprocedural, object-oriented languages | OLAP (Online Analytical Processing) tools or programming languages |
| **SKILL LEVEL REQUIRED TO ACCESS DATA** | Programmer | Programmer | Programmer | User | User | User |
| **ENTITY RELATIONSHIPS SUPPORTED** | One-to-one | One-to-one, one-to-many | One-to-one, one-to-many, many-to-many | One-to-one, one-to-many, many-to-many | One-to-one, one-to-many, many-to-many | One-to-one, one-to-many, many-to-many |
| **DATA AND PROGRAM INDEPENDENCE** | No | No | No | Yes | Yes | Yes |

**FIGURE 12-3**

**The evolution of databases.** Databases have evolved over the years, becoming more flexible, more capable, and easier to use.

## The Evolution of Databases

Databases have evolved dramatically since the early 1960s. This evolution has occurred in response to our increased reliance on information systems; advances in programming languages; the need to store and retrieve a variety of complex data, such as multimedia objects (digital images, video files, audio files, and so forth); and the vast use of databases on the Web. The most significant advances in databases can be summarized primarily in terms of their organization of data and access to data. The organization of data has evolved from a collection of independent flat files with tree or branching structures and high levels of data redundancy, to a collection of tables and objects that support multimedia objects with a minimum of data redundancy, to databases that can be viewed from a variety of perspectives or *dimensions*. A summary of this evolution is shown in Figure 12-3; the models and relationships listed in the figure are discussed in more detail later in this chapter. For a look at how file management systems used with flat files differ from database management systems, see the Inside the Industry box.

## Advantages and Disadvantages of the DBMS Approach

Because a DBMS can pull data out of more than one table at a time (compared with a file management system that can only work with one table at a time, as discussed in the Inside the Industry box), there is a very low level of redundancy in the tables in a DBMS database. In fact, often only a single field (the primary key) appears in more than one file. This low level of redundancy has several advantages. For instance, a DBMS database typically has a faster response time and lower storage requirements than a file management system, and it is easier to secure. In addition, data accuracy is increased because updates (such as an address change for a customer) are only made to a single table, cutting down on the possibility of data errors and inconsistencies that can occur when the same update has to be made manually to multiple tables (such as when using a file management system).

One of the most significant disadvantages of the DBMS approach is increased vulnerability. Because the data in the database is highly integrated, the potential for data loss (for example, if records or tables are accidentally deleted, the system fails, or the database is

# INSIDE THE INDUSTRY

## File Management Systems

A *file management system* is a program that allows the creation of individual database tables (often referred to as *flat files*). Each table is stored in its own physical file and is not related to any other file. Consequently, file management systems can work with only one table at a time, and each table has to contain all the data that may need to be accessed or retrieved at one time. As a result, file management systems have a much higher level of redundancy than database management systems. For example, in the accompanying illustration, in addition to the single green-shaded column (Product Number), the Product Name, Supplier, and Price data (the blue-shaded columns) must be entered and stored in all three tables. This redundancy can lead to data entry errors in the database, as well as storage issues because the files contain more data than they would if a DBMS was used. It also requires additional work. For example, the task illustrated

in Figure 12-1 would require the sales manager to perform the following steps using a file management system:

1. Use the product number to look up the product name in the Product table.
2. Use the product number to check the Inventory table to see if the company can fill the order from current stock.
3. If current stock is inadequate, check the Inventory on Order table (using the product number) to see when enough stock will be available to fill the order.
4. Use the Inventory on Order table to determine the date on which the order can be filled.

Because using a file management system with flat files is much slower than using a database management system with related tables, both service to customers and efficiency suffer. As a result, file management systems are rarely used today. They are useful, however, in appreciating the advantages of a DBMS and some of the advances the industry has made over the years.

| PRODUCT NUMBER | PRODUCT NAME | SUPPLIER | PRICE |
|---|---|---|---|
| A202 | Skis | Ellis Ski Co. | 90.00 |
| A211 | Boots | Ajax Bros. | 60.00 |
| A220 | Poles | Bent Corp. | 25.00 |
| A240 | Bindings | Acme Corp. | 35.00 |
| A351 | Wax | Candle Industries | 3.00 |

**PRODUCT TABLE**

| PRODUCT NUMBER | PRODUCT NAME | SUPPLIER | PRICE | CURRENT STOCK | ON ORDER? |
|---|---|---|---|---|---|
| A202 | Skis | Ellis Ski Co. | 90.00 | 15 | Yes |
| A211 | Boots | Ajax Bros. | 60.00 | 90 | Yes |
| A220 | Poles | Bent Corp. | 25.00 | 30 | Yes |
| A240 | Bindings | Acme Corp. | 35.00 | 25 | Yes |
| A351 | Wax | Candle Industries | 3.00 | 8 | No |

**INVENTORY TABLE**

| ORDER NUMBER | PRODUCT NUMBER | SHIPMENT DATE | PRODUCT NAME | SUPPLIER | PRICE | QUANTITY |
|---|---|---|---|---|---|---|
| 1001 | A202 | 1/8 | Skis | Ellis Ski Co. | 90.00 | 30 |
| 1002 | A240 | 1/8 | Bindings | Acme Corp. | 35.00 | 15 |
| 1003 | A211 | 1/9 | Boots | Ajax Bros. | 60.00 | 50 |
| 1004 | A202 | 1/9 | Skis | Ellis Ski Co. | 90.00 | 40 |
| 1005 | A220 | 1/10 | Poles | Bent Corp. | 25.00 | 35 |
| 1006 | A211 | 1/12 | Boots | Ajax Bros. | 60.00 | 60 |

**INVENTORY ON ORDER TABLE**

**REDUNDANT FIELDS**
Instead of just having one key field duplicated like in the databases created using a DBMS (green shaded columns), flat files created using file management systems require many more fields to be duplicated (green and blue shaded columns). Notice that the blue shaded columns shown here appear only in the Product table in Figure 12-1; when using a DBMS, these fields are not included in the Inventory and Inventory on Order tables.

**Because file management systems cannot retrieve data from more than one table at a time, there is a much higher level of redundancy.**

breached) is much greater. Consequently, security and backup procedures are an extremely important part of using a DBMS, as discussed in more detail shortly.

# DATA CONCEPTS AND CHARACTERISTICS

Data is frequently considered to be one of an organization's most valuable assets. Without it, businesses would find it impossible to perform some of their most basic activities. Data is also the heart of a database. Consequently, its concepts and characteristics need to be understood in order to successfully design, create, and use a database. Some of the most important concepts and characteristics are discussed in the following sections.

## Data Hierarchy

Data in a database has a definite hierarchy. At the lowest level, characters are entered into database fields (columns), which hold single pieces of data in the database, such as product names or quantities (refer again to Figure 12-1). At the next level are records (rows)— groups of related fields (such as all the fields for a particular product). At the next level are tables, which are made up of related records. At the top of the hierarchy is the database, which consists of a group of related tables.

## Entities and Entity Relationships

An **entity** is something (such as a person, object, or event) of importance to the business or organization. When an entity is something that a business or an organization wants to store data about in a database system, it typically becomes a database table. The characteristics of an entity are called **attributes**. For instance, if a business collects data about customers, then Customer is an entity. Possible Customer attributes are last name, first name, phone number, address, and so forth. Attributes typically become fields in the entity's database table.

A *relationship* describes an association between two or more entities. The three basic *entity relationships* are discussed next.

### One-to-One Entity Relationships

*One-to-one* (*1:1*) *entity relationships* exist when one entity is related to only one other entity of a particular type. For example, if a business has multiple store locations and each store has a single manager, the relationship between Store and Manager is a 1:1 relationship. For each store location, you can determine the appropriate manager; for each manager, you can identify his or her store. In this type of relationship, each record in the table belonging to the first entity can have only one matching record in the table belonging to the second entity. This type of relationship is not common, however, because all the data would typically be located in a single table instead of creating a separate table (such as one table for stores and one for managers, in this example) for each entity.

### One-to-Many Entity Relationships

*One-to-many* (*O:M*) *entity relationships* are the most common and exist when one entity can be related to more than one other entity. For example, if a supplier supplies more than one product to the company, the relationship between Supplier and Products is an O:M relationship and the supplier would have a single entry in the Supplier table but would appear multiple times in the Product table. Consequently, if a specific product number is

---

> **Entity.** Something (such as a person, an object, or an event) that is important to a business or an organization; typically becomes a database table in a database system for that business or organization. > **Attribute.** A characteristic of an entity.

known, its supplier can be determined easily, but if a supplier is known, a single product number cannot be identified.

## Many-to-Many Entity Relationships

*Many-to-many (M:M) entity relationships* exist when one entity can be related to more than one other entity, and those entities can be related to multiple entities of the same type as the original entity. For example, if an order can contain multiple products and one product can appear on many orders, the relationship between Orders and Products is an M:M relationship. If an order number is known, a single corresponding product number cannot be identified, and if a product number is known, a single corresponding order cannot be identified. Consequently, this type of relationship requires a third table—such as an Order Details table used in conjunction with an Orders table and a Products table—to tie the two tables together.

## Data Definition

**Data definition** involves describing the properties of the data that go into each database table, specifically the fields that make up the database. During the data definition process, the following are supplied for each field:

> *Name* (must be unique within the table).

> *Data type* (such as *Short Text*, *Long Text*, *Number*, *Currency*, *Yes/No*, *Hyperlink*, or *Date/Time*); indicates the type of data that will be entered into the field.

> *Description* (an optional description of the field).

> *Properties* (such as the *field size* and *format* of the field, any allowable range or required format for the data that will be entered into the field, whether or not the field is required, and any initial value to appear in that field when a new record is added).

The properties that can be set for a field depend on the data type being used for that field. For instance, for fields using the Short Text data type, the field size indicates the number of characters that may be entered for that field. For Number fields, the field size typically indicates how much storage space (in bytes) can be used for each entry and if decimal places are allowed. For instance, the field size *Integer* for Number fields in Microsoft Access can hold any number from -32,768 to 32,767; the *Long Integer* field size can be used for Number fields that will store longer integers. If a field needs to store decimal places, the *Double* or *Decimal* field sizes can be used instead.

The finished specifications for a table (including the fields and the properties for those fields) are commonly referred to as the *table structure*. For example, the structure of the Inventory table from Figure 12-1 (shown being created in Microsoft Access in Figure 12-4) consists of three main fields: Product Number, Current Stock, and On Order?. The Product Number field contains text (character-based) data so the Short Text field type is assigned to the Product Number field. A field size of 4 is specified in this field's properties because product numbers for this business consist of four characters (one letter followed by three numbers). The Current Stock field contains numeric data that must be integers (have no decimal places) because stock is counted in product units; consequently, the Number data type and the Long Integer field size are assigned to this field. The On Order? field in this table is specified as a *Yes/No* field. Fields using this data type contain a value representing

---

> **Data definition.** The process of describing the properties of data that are to be included in a database table.

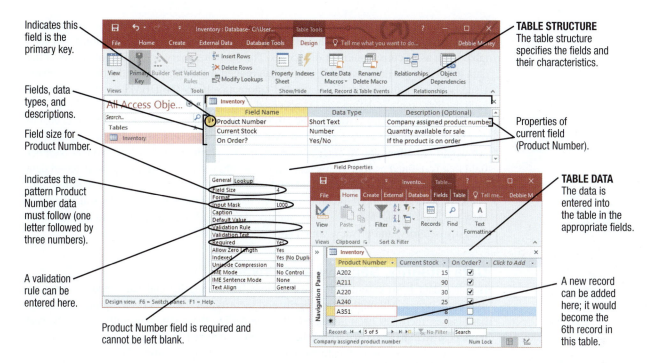

Indicates this field is the primary key.

Fields, data types, and descriptions.

Field size for Product Number.

Indicates the pattern Product Number data must follow (one letter followed by three numbers).

A validation rule can be entered here.

Product Number field is required and cannot be left blank.

**TABLE STRUCTURE**
The table structure specifies the fields and their characteristics.

Properties of current field (Product Number).

**TABLE DATA**
The data is entered into the table in the appropriate fields.

A new record can be added here; it would become the 6th record in this table.

 **FIGURE 12-4**

**Data definition.** Each field in a database has a defined data type and properties that can be assigned to that field.

*true* (typically entered by the user as a *T* for *true*, *Y* for *yes*, or a checked box, depending on the program being used), or a value representing *false* (typically entered by the user as an *F* for *false*, *N* for *no*, or an unchecked box). In the Inventory table, a product that is on order is given the value *true*; a product not on order has the value *false*.

Other properties that can be assigned to a field include an *input mask* to specify the format (such as letters, numbers, or symbols) that must be entered into a field, whether or not the field is *required* (if so, it cannot be left blank), and any *validation rules* (specific allowable values for the field, such as a certain range of numeric values for a numeric field or a particular date range for a date field) needed to ensure only valid data is entered into the field. If data typed into a field does not match the data type or the input mask for the field, violates a validation rule, or is blank when the field is required, that record will not be added to the table until the error is corrected, as discussed shortly. The additional properties assigned to the Product Number field in the Inventory table shown in Figure 12-4 include an input mask of *L000* to ensure that only product numbers that fit this pattern (one letter followed by three numbers) are entered in the Product Number field, and the field is specified as required.

DBMSs designed for use with large computer systems usually include a special language component dedicated to the data definition process. Such languages have generically come to be known as *data definition languages* (*DDLs*). In addition to simply defining data, a major function of the DDL in these large packages is security—protecting the database from unauthorized use. Data security is discussed in more detail shortly.

**TIP**

Some database programs—such as Microsoft Access—allow you to create a table by just entering data and the program will create the table structure based on the data entered. The table structure and field properties can then be modified, if needed.

## The Data Dictionary
The **data dictionary** contains all data definitions for a database, including table structures (containing the names, types, and properties of each field in a table), security information

---

>**Data dictionary.** The repository of all data definitions in a database.

(such as the password needed to view or edit a table), relationships between the tables in the database, and so on. Also included in the data dictionary is basic information about each table, such as its current number of records. The data dictionary does not contain any of the data located *in* the database tables, only data (called **metadata**) *about* the database tables. Usually the data dictionary file is created automatically by the DBMS as the structure of each database table is defined and is accessed only by the DBMS, not by the end user.

The data dictionary is used by the DBMS as data is being entered into a table to ensure that the data does not violate any of its assigned properties. For example, the data dictionary would not allow you to enter a seven-character product number in a Product Number field that is defined as four characters long, it would not allow you to type text-based data into a field defined as a Number field, and it would not allow you to leave a required field blank. In addition, without the proper password, the data dictionary would not allow you to view password-protected data. Consequently, these measures can be used to increase data integrity, security, and privacy, which are discussed next.

## Data Integrity, Security, and Privacy

Because data is so essential to organizations, data integrity and data security are very important issues. Although data integrity and security have always been high-priority database issues, there has been increased attention paid to these issues recently due to the vast number of database security breaches that have occurred in the past few years, as well as the ongoing creation of national databases containing sensitive data, such as health-care information. The total destruction of the computer containing a crucial database, as well as the threat of unauthorized access and data alteration of a vital database system, is being viewed as a much more real possibility than just a few years ago. There are also increasing regulations for database security, such as the updated *Payment Card Industry Data Security Standards* (*PCI DSS*) that require security checks on all databases containing credit card data, as well as require companies to ensure that any third parties that they deal with (such as Web hosting providers) have proper controls in place for securing credit card data. Consequently, many businesses and government organizations are evaluating their data integrity and security methods and improving them, if needed. Database privacy is also of increasing concern to businesses and many individuals, as database breaches are becoming more frequent and as governments are increasingly implementing new data privacy legislation and regulations.

### Data Integrity

**Data integrity** refers to the accuracy of data. The long-standing computer saying *garbage in, garbage out* is very appropriate for database systems. The quality of the information generated from a database is only as good as the accuracy of the data contained in the database. Although it is possible to generate poor information from quality data (such as by making poor assumptions or using poor data analysis), it is virtually impossible to generate quality information from inaccurate data. Because so many important decisions are based on information generated by information systems (which almost always use some type of database), data integrity is a vital concern for organizations. Responsible, reliable employees at the data entry level, teamed with good data validation methods, can increase the accuracy of the data in a database.

**Data validation** refers to the process of ensuring that the data entered into a database is valid; that is, it matches the specified data type, format, and allowable value for each field. As previously discussed and shown in Figure 12-4, input masks and validation

---

>**Metadata.** Data about data, such as the data contained in a data dictionary. >**Data integrity.** The accuracy of data. >**Data validation.** The process of ensuring that data entered into a database is valid (matches the data definition).

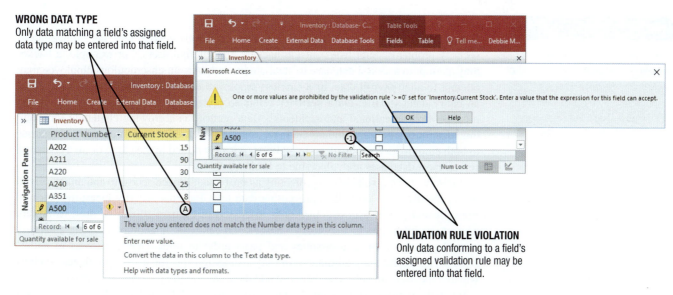

**WRONG DATA TYPE**
Only data matching a field's assigned data type may be entered into that field.

**VALIDATION RULE VIOLATION**
Only data conforming to a field's assigned validation rule may be entered into that field.

> **FIGURE 12-5**
>
> **Data validation.**
> Using appropriate data properties can prevent invalid data from being entered into a database table.

rules can be assigned to a field to ensure that data is entered in the specified format and meets the specified criteria. *Record validation rules* can also be assigned to a table, when appropriate; these rules are checked after all fields in a record are completed but before the record is saved. Record validation rules are used when the value of one field in the record needs to be checked against another field in that same record to be sure it is valid, such as to ensure a ship date isn't earlier than the order date. As previously discussed, the data dictionary is responsible for comparing all data entered into a table with the designated requirements and only allows data to be entered into the database table if it follows the specified rules. If invalid data is supplied (such as text in a number field or a negative number in a field with a validation rule of >=0, as in Figure 12-5), a message will usually be displayed on the screen, and the record is not entered into the database table until all fields contain valid data.

In some systems, data integrity is enforced on a *per transaction* basis. This means that if invalid data is supplied and not corrected at some point during the steps necessary to enter a complete transaction into the system, then the entire transaction will fail, not just that one step of the transaction. This ensures that a complete, valid transaction is always entered into the system at one time and that the database is never left with just one piece of a transaction completed. Even if multiple tables will be affected by the transaction, users will not be able to see the changes made due to that transaction until the transaction is *committed*; that is, until all steps in the transaction are deemed valid and the appropriate changes are made to all the affected tables. Once a transaction has been committed, all changes pertaining to the transaction become visible in all corresponding tables at the same time.

Because different users and applications may be trying to change the same data at the same time, it is important that a database be able to temporarily "lock" data that is being accessed so that no other changes can be made to the data until the first user or application is finished. For example, going back to the inventory database scenario shown in Figure 12-1, assume that while the sales manager is working on the order for the 160 boots, using information pulled from the Inventory and Inventory on Order tables, another person in the sales department gets a request for 75 of the same boots. If the database does not lock the pertinent tables while they are being accessed, both of these employees could sell the same 75 in-stock boots to different customers at the same time. This potential problem can be avoided if *database locking* is used. Databases often support various types of locking, such as *row-level locking* (in which an entire table row is locked when any part of that record is being modified), and *column-level locking* (in which the table column involved in the changes is locked until the changes to that field have been completed).

## Data Security

Because large databases are typically used by numerous people, they are vulnerable to security problems, both from outside hackers and internal users. For example, a hacker may attempt to access a database to steal credit card data, an unscrupulous employee may attempt to alter payroll data, or a careless employee may accidentally delete a record or an entire database file. **Data security** refers to protecting data against destruction and misuse—both intentional and accidental. Data security is a growing challenge for many organizations as they are finding the need to grant increased access to company databases to both employees and outsiders. In addition, whether hosted in the cloud or on a company server, most databases are vulnerable to hackers.

Data security involves both protecting against unauthorized access to and unauthorized use of the database, as well as preventing data loss. External security measures (such as firewalls and proper access controls, as discussed in Chapter 9) can be used to protect against outside access to a company network and database. In addition to using an access control system (such as usernames and passwords) to limit database access to authorized users, the database administrator may also assign specific access privileges (such as whether the user can only read data, can add data, can modify data, and so forth) to specific individuals or groups of individuals. Similarly, sensitive data, such as salaries, can be hidden from view so that only certain users of the database are able to retrieve it or modify it. These privileges are usually incorporated into the data dictionary and are enforced by the DBMS to ensure only authorized individuals are permitted to view and change data.

One emerging data security risk is the exploitation of known but unpatched vulnerabilities by hackers; that is, hackers breaching a not-yet-patched system through a vulnerability that has been made public via the release of a new database patch. Because many organizations do not install patches immediately—in fact, a 90-day patch cycle is not uncommon—and because code specifically written to exploit a newly discovered vulnerability is often posted to the Web by hackers within hours of when a database patch designed to fix that vulnerability is released, there is often ample time for a criminal to access a database via a known vulnerability before that database is patched. In addition to installing patches as soon as they become available, actively monitoring databases for unusual activity and unauthorized access, as well as adequately locking down data at the database level, can help avoid these types of database breaches. Database vulnerability assessment tools can also be used to detect security weaknesses (such as unpatched vulnerabilities and weak passwords) that an attacker can exploit. For instance, the *database activity monitoring (DAM) program* shown in Figure 12-6 monitors a

**FIGURE 12-6**

**Database security tools.** This program secures databases and displays alerts for vulnerabilities and attacks.

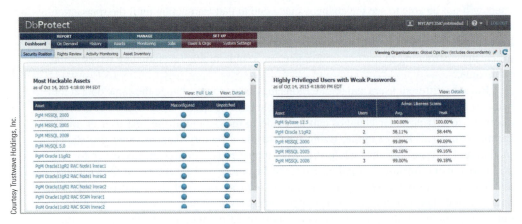

Courtesy Trustwave Holdings, Inc.

---

>**Data security.** Protecting the data located in a database against destruction and misuse.

database continually to detect and report possible intrusions, vulnerabilities, and other threats in real time; it also updates its knowledge base of known database security threats automatically to protect against new threats as they become known. To avoid security problems at the application level, some companies use scanning tools during software development to locate and plug security holes in application software while it is being developed, instead of after it has been deployed. Stronger database encryption tools are also being integrated into DBMSs, as well as being integrated into stand-alone *database encryption software*.

To protect against data loss caused by a database failure, an accidental deletion, or another problem that renders the main copy of a database unusable, stringent backup procedures should be implemented. To protect against data loss due to disasters (such as hard drive failure or the total destruction of the facility due to a fire, flood, or other disaster), appropriate disaster-recovery procedures should be used. Possible precautions include keeping a redundant copy of the database on a mirrored drive, backing up the data at very frequent intervals to an off-site location, and having a comprehensive disaster-recovery plan, as discussed in Chapter 9.

## ASK THE EXPERT

Courtesy Trustwave

**Trustwave** **Mark Trinidad,** Senior Product Manager, Trustwave

**What is the most important thing a business should do today to secure its data?**

Nearly all of the confidential and highly regulated data that businesses store is stored in databases and remains in those databases 99% of the time. The most important step organizations can take to secure their data is to secure their databases. First, you should apply the latest security patches from the database vendors, starting with your most critical systems. Next, eliminate default and weak passwords, and implement controls to lock accounts automatically in case of a password attack. Regularly perform a thorough review of user rights and access controls, using the *principle of least privilege* to control database access rights on a strictly as-needed basis. Finally, implement database activity monitoring and intrusion detection so that if someone does try to break into your system, you will know it and can stop the attack before serious damage can be done. If you have more than a handful of databases to protect, consider automation via a database security, risk, and compliance scanning solution.

## Data Privacy

A company that stores data about individuals is responsible for protecting the privacy of that data. **Data privacy** is a growing concern because of the vast amounts of personal data stored in databases today and the many data privacy breaches that are occurring. Because nearly every state requires businesses to notify individuals when their personal data has been lost or exposed to outsiders, data breaches can be costly. In addition to potential loss of customers, costs include printing and postage for notification letters, legal counsel, offers to appease customers (such as free credit monitoring for a period of time), and potential lawsuit settlements. A recent estimate of the cost of a data breach in the United States is more than $200 per compromised record for an average total cost of $6.5 million per data breach. To protect the privacy of collected data, companies should first make sure that all the data they are collecting and storing is, in fact, necessary, and then they need to evaluate their data security measures to ensure that the data is adequately protected. Additional data privacy issues were discussed in Chapter 9.

> **Data privacy.** Protecting the privacy of the data located in a database.

## Data Organization

Virtually all databases are organized in some manner to facilitate the retrieval of information. Arranging data for efficient retrieval is called *data organization*. Most methods of data organization use a primary key to identify the locations of records so they can be retrieved when needed. The use of a primary key and a data organization method allows a specific record to be efficiently located, regardless of the actual order the records are stored in the table. The two most common types of data organization used today—indexed and direct—are discussed next. Both are frequently used with real-time transaction processing, in which records are accessed and updated as transactions occur. An older type of data organization is *sequenced organization*, in which the order of the records is physically based on the content of the key field. Sequenced organization is designed for use with batch processing using a sequential access medium (such as magnetic tape) and so is not frequently used today. For a look at an emerging database organization option increasingly being used for big data applications—column databases—see the How It Works box.

### Indexed Organization

With **indexed organization**, an **index** is used to keep track of where data is stored in a database. An index is a small table consisting only of the primary key field and the location information for each record (see Figure 12-7). For example, the Customer table shown in Figure 12-7 uses the Customer Number field as the primary key, so the index for

**FIGURE 12-7**

Indexed organization is often used for real-time transaction processing.

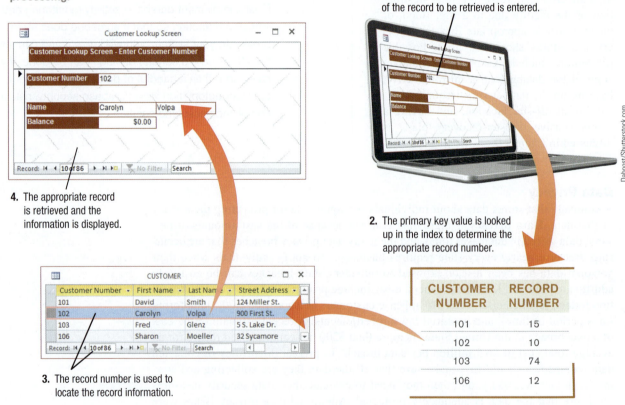

1. Primary key (Customer Number) of the record to be retrieved is entered.

4. The appropriate record is retrieved and the information is displayed.

2. The primary key value is looked up in the index to determine the appropriate record number.

3. The record number is used to locate the record information.

**CUSTOMER TABLE**

**INDEX FOR CUSTOMER TABLE**

| CUSTOMER NUMBER | RECORD NUMBER |
|---|---|
| 101 | 15 |
| 102 | 10 |
| 103 | 74 |
| 106 | 12 |

Daboost/Shutterstock.com

---

>**Indexed organization.** A method for organizing data on a storage medium or in a database that uses an index to specify the exact storage location. >**Index.** A small table containing a primary key and the location of the record belonging to that key; used to locate records in a database.

# HOW IT WORKS

## Column Databases

To increase database performance (particularly with data warehouses and other big data applications that are used to retrieve information, such as analytic queries as opposed to transactional applications), *column databases* that store related data vertically in table columns instead of in rows can be used. While the database tables in a column database appear to the user to be organized into rows and columns like a conventional row-oriented database, the way the data is physically stored on the storage medium (by columns instead of by rows) is different from the way it is stored in row-oriented databases (by rows)—see the accompanying illustration. Because of this physical organization, column database organization minimizes the time needed to read the storage medium, which greatly improves performance. Column orientation also allows for a higher level of data compression because there are often many similar, if not identical, entries in a single column.

| Emp_no | Dept | Emp_last | Emp_first | Hire_date |
|---|---|---|---|---|
| 1 | Acct | Smith | Janice | 01/15/2011 |
| 2 | IT | Lee | Tim | 05/16/2009 |
| 3 | Acct | McNeil | Patrick | 04/01/2013 |
| 4 | Sales | Wilson | Sammy | 08/11/2015 |
| 5 | IT | Morales | Jack | 11/16/2014 |

**Row-Oriented Database**

| 1 | Acct | Smith | Janice | 01/15/2011 |
| 2 | IT | Lee | Tim | 05/16/2009 |
| 3 | Acct | McNeil | Patrick | 04/01/2013 |

**Column-Oriented Database**

| 1 | Acct | Smith | Janice | 01/15/2011 |
| 2 | IT | Lee | Tim | 05/16/2009 |
| 3 | Acct | McNeil | Patrick | 04/01/2013 |

Database needs to read all columns (because data is read by rows) to access the requested data.

Database needs to read only three columns to access the requested data.

**Example of retrieving the names of all IT employees using a row vs. a column database.**

the Customer table (also shown in that figure) includes the Customer Number field, plus the current record number for each record in the Customer table. As shown in the figure, indexes are sorted in order by the primary key field (Customer Number, in this example), so records can be looked up in the index by the primary key field very quickly; the record number is then used to quickly retrieve the requested record from the database. In addition to a record number index, as in Figure 12-7, there can also be indexes to determine the physical location of the record on a storage medium, such as a track or a cylinder number. Indexes are usually viewed only by the program, not by the end user.

## Direct Organization

Although indexed files are suitable for many applications, it is potentially more time consuming than is appropriate for some real-time applications. **Direct organization** was developed to provide faster access. With direct organization, the computer uses each record's primary key field and a mathematical formula called a *hashing algorithm* to determine a unique address that identifies where the record is physically stored in the database file. Several hashing algorithms have been developed. One of the simplest involves dividing the primary key field by a particular prime number. The prime number is determined by the number of records to be stored or the number of storage areas to be used. The *remainder* of this division procedure (see Figure 12-8) becomes the address at which the record is physically stored.

Hashing procedures are difficult to develop, and they pose certain problems. For example, hashing procedures usually result in two or more records being assigned the same storage address, an event known as a

**FIGURE 12-8**
Direct organization is frequently used for faster real-time processing.

**HASHING PROCEDURE**

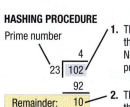

Prime number

4
23 ) 102
    92
Remainder: 10

1. The primary key value (in this case the Customer Number) is divided by a prime number.

2. The remainder indicates the location to be used for that record (in this case, 10).

---

>**Direct organization.** A method of arranging data on a storage medium that uses hashing to specify the exact storage location.

*collision*. When this occurs, one record is placed in the computed address location and assigned a "pointer" that chains it to the other record, which is typically placed in an available location closest to the hashed address. Good hashing procedures result in an acceptable number of collisions for the table size used—usually a larger table requires the possibility of a larger number of collisions in order to have sufficient speed.

Some systems use a combination of both indexed and direct organization—the key field indicates where the record is located within the table, and a hashing procedure is used to determine where the record is physically stored on the storage medium.

# DATABASE CLASSIFICATIONS

A database system can be classified in a variety of ways, including the number of users it supports, the number of tiers it has, where the database is located, and so forth. These distinctions are discussed next.

## Single-User vs. Multiuser Database Systems

**Single-user database systems** are located on a single computer and are designed to be accessed by one user. Single-user database systems are widely used for personal applications and very small businesses. Most business database systems today are designed for multiple users, and the database is accessed via a network. Because two or more users in a **multiuser database system** may try to access and modify the same data at the same time, some type of database locking must be used to prevent users from making conflicting changes to the same data at the same time.

## Client-Server and N-Tier Database Systems

Multiuser database systems are typically **client-server database systems**. As discussed in Chapter 7, client-server networks consist of servers that supply resources to other computers (such as personal computers), which function as client devices. Similarly, a *client-server database system* is a database system that has both clients and at least one server. In a typical client-server database application, the client is called the *front end*, and the database server is called the *back end*. The back-end server contains a DBMS and the database itself, and it processes the commands coming from the front-end client computers. A typical client-server database system scenario is illustrated in Figure 12-9.

While some client-server database systems just have two parts (the clients and the server), others have at least one middle component or *tier* between the client and the server; these systems are referred to as *n-tier database systems*. The additional tiers—such as the middle

**Ⓥ FIGURE 12-9**
Client-server
database systems.

**FRONT END (CLIENT COMPUTERS)**
The client computers typically utilize a graphical user interface to access the database located on the back-end server.

**BACK END (SERVER)**
The server contains the database used to fulfill the requests of the client computers.

Daboost/Shutterstock.com

300dpi/Shutterstock.com

> **Single-user database system.** A database located on a single computer and designed to be accessed by a single user. > **Multiuser database system.** A database designed to be accessed by multiple users. > **Client-server database system.** A database system where the database is located on a server and accessed by client devices.

tier in a *three-tier database system*, shown in Figure 12-10—typically contain software referred to as middleware. Middleware usually includes the programs used with the database and the programs needed to connect the client and server components of the database system, as discussed later in this chapter.

One advantage of the n-tier architecture is that it allows the program code used to access the database to be separate from the database, and the code can be divided into any number of logical components. The programs contained in each tier in an n-tier database system can be written in programming languages different from the programming languages used in the other tiers. Tiers can also use different platforms and can be changed or relocated without affecting the other tiers. Consequently, n-tier database systems provide a great deal of flexibility and scalability, allowing the system to be modified as new needs and opportunities arise. N-tier database systems are most commonly found in e-commerce database applications, as discussed toward the end of this chapter.

## Centralized vs. Distributed Database Systems

With a **centralized database system**, the databases used by the system are all located on a single computer, such as a server or mainframe computer (see Figure 12-11). With a **distributed database system**, the data is separated into several databases, each of which is stored on a different computer that may be in different physical locations from one another but that are connected via a network; for instance, there might be one database stored on a server located at the company headquarters and additional databases stored on computers located at each retail store belonging to that company. With a distributed database system, the database system is logically set up to act as a single database and appears that way to the user. Consequently, the entire database system can be accessed through the network by any authorized user, regardless of which computer the requested data is physically stored on. For example, basic customer data (such as addresses and phone numbers) may be stored at the corporate headquarters while customer credit histories may be stored in the

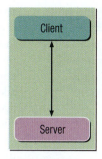 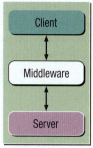

**2-TIER MODEL**
Has just two parts: a client and a server.

**N-TIER MODEL**
Includes middleware, which contains additional programs used to connect the client and server tiers.

**FIGURE 12-10**
A 2-tier vs. an n-tier database model.

**FIGURE 12-11**
Centralized vs. distributed databases.

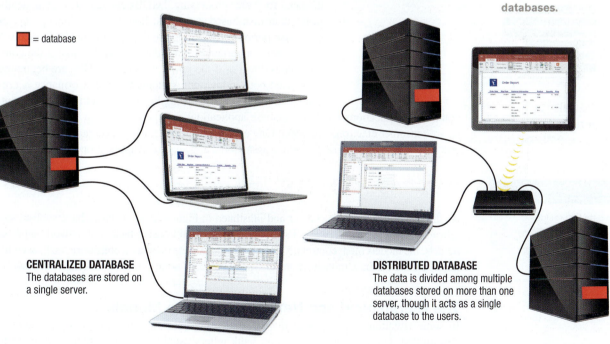

= database

**CENTRALIZED DATABASE**
The databases are stored on a single server.

**DISTRIBUTED DATABASE**
The data is divided among multiple databases stored on more than one server, though it acts as a single database to the users.

Gravi/Shutterstock.com; Daboost/Shutterstock.com; Courtesy D-Link Systems, Inc.; Natalia Siverina/ com; Mr. Aesthetics/Shutterstock.com

>**Centralized database system.** A database system in which all of the data used by the system is located on a single computer. >**Distributed database system.** A database system in which the data used by the system is located on multiple computers that are connected via a network.

credit department located in another office across town. However, employees in the credit department can access both the basic customer data and the credit history data as if it were located in a single database stored in a single location.

In determining where to store specific data in a distributed DBMS, factors such as communications cost, response time, storage cost, and security are key considerations. In addition, data is often stored at the site where it is needed most frequently and is best managed, or at the location that makes data retrieval most efficient. For instance, the Digg Web site reportedly uses about 20 database servers to store its news stories and its database is broken into pieces, with each piece stored on a different database server. This configuration improves performance by isolating heavy workloads—a practice coined as *sharding* by Google developers. The goal of distributing the database in this manner is to get the vast majority of the database system to work very fast. When the user requests information from a distributed DBMS, the user is typically not aware of the steps performed by the DBMS to display the requested information, nor where that data was retrieved from.

Distributed databases that support cloud computing are referred to as cloud databases and are becoming more common. For instance, Amazon's *SimpleDB* Web service works with other Amazon cloud services to store, process, and query cloud-based data. Cloud databases are discussed in more detail later in this chapter.

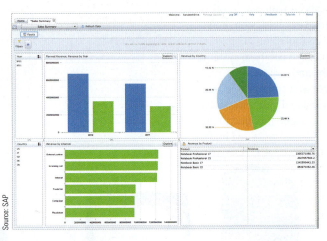

**FIGURE 12-12**
In-memory data-bases (IMDBs).

## Disk-Based vs. In-Memory Database Systems

While most databases are stored on hard drives (located on personal computers, servers, or mainframes, for instance), **in-memory databases** (**IMDBs**), also called *main memory databases* (*MMDBs*), are designed to hold all data in the main memory of the computer, rather than on disk. The use of in-memory databases is growing because of the lower cost of RAM today and the need for faster processing. IMDBs can perform dramatically faster than disk-based databases; however, backing up data or otherwise periodically storing the data on a nonvolatile medium is extremely important because data in RAM is lost if the computer goes down or if the power goes out. IMDBs are beginning to be used both in high-end systems where performance is crucial (such as in e-commerce applications) and in small-footprint, embedded applications (such as database applications installed on set-top boxes and other smart consumer electronic devices). One emerging option is using a single IMDB, like the one shown in Figure 12-12, for both transactional and analytical applications.

## DATABASE MODELS

As discussed earlier in this chapter and illustrated in Figure 12-3, databases have evolved significantly since the early 1960s. Two older models are the hierarchical and network database models; the models more commonly used today include the relational, object-oriented, and multidimensional database models. A newer type of database is the hybrid XML-relational model.

### The Hierarchical and Network Database Models

In some situations, the types of queries that users need to make are highly predictable and limited. For example, in banking, bank tellers usually only need facts pertaining to

> **In-memory database (IMDB).** A database that stores all data in memory instead of on a storage medium; also called a main memory database (MMDB).

current customer account balances, deposits, and withdrawals. In such transaction processing environments, *hierarchical* and *network database models*—which are designed more for speed and security than flexibility—are sometimes used. A *hierarchical database management system* organizes data in a tree structure (like an organization chart or structure chart). Typically, a one-to-many relationship exists between data entities, so all entries in the second row of the hierarchy are listed under only one top-row entry. If a second-row entry needs to be associated with more than one top-row entry, however, a *network database management system* (which allows both one-to-many and many-to-many relationships) can be used.

Most databases created today do not use the hierarchical or network models, but these models, which are generally used with legacy mainframe systems, are still operational and so must be maintained.

## The Relational Database Model

The **relational database management system** (**RDBMS**) is the most widely used database model today. As discussed earlier in this chapter, relational databases organize data using tables. Tables are independent, but data can be retrieved from related tables via primary key fields when needed.

Before a relational database can be created, it should be properly designed. Next, the structures for the tables in the database can be created, and then the initial data can be entered into each table. Finally, the database can be used (such as adding, modifying, or deleting records or retrieving information from the database)—called *data manipulation*—and maintained on an ongoing basis. These topics are discussed in the next few sections.

### Designing a Relational Database

The steps involved with designing a relational database are summarized in Figure 12-13. As shown in this figure, the first step in designing a relational database is to identify the purpose of the database and the activities that it will be used for (such as to keep track of rental properties, student grades, or customer orders). Then the data (fields) that needs to be included in the database can be determined and the fields can be organized into tables. To determine which fields go in which table, you should group fields that logically belong together—each group of fields will form one table.

After initially placing the necessary fields into tables, it is important to evaluate the proposed table structure to ensure that all fields are represented and in the proper table, and to select the primary key field for each table. If needed, the tables can be restructured to reduce the redundancy of the data. To keep redundancy to a minimum, fields should be included in only one table whenever possible; they should not be placed in multiple tables unless they are needed to relate one table to another. Another consideration when designing and evaluating the basic structure of each table is ensuring the fields are constructed in a manner consistent with the type of information that will need to be extracted from the database. For example, if you want to be able to generate a list of people by just their last name, two separate fields (such as *Last Name* and *First Name*) should be used instead of just a single field called *Name*.

> **TIP**
>
> When you are beginning to design a new database, sketching a diagram of the reports and other desired database output can be helpful in identifying the fields that need to be included in the database.

 **FIGURE 12-13**
Database design steps.

**BASIC DATABASE DESIGN PROCEDURES**

1. Identify the purpose of the database.

2. Determine the tables and fields to include in the database.

3. Assign the fields to the appropriate table and restructure as needed to minimize redundancy (normalization).

4. Finalize the structure of each table by listing each field's name, type, size, and so on and then by selecting a primary key (data definition).

SYS

>**Relational database management system (RDBMS).** A type of database system in which data is stored in tables related by common fields; the most widely used database model today.

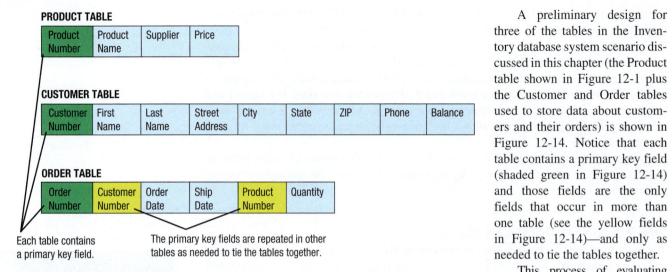

**PRODUCT TABLE**

| Product Number | Product Name | Supplier | Price |
|---|---|---|---|

**CUSTOMER TABLE**

| Customer Number | First Name | Last Name | Street Address | City | State | ZIP | Phone | Balance |
|---|---|---|---|---|---|---|---|---|

**ORDER TABLE**

| Order Number | Customer Number | Order Date | Ship Date | Product Number | Quantity |
|---|---|---|---|---|---|

Each table contains a primary key field.

The primary key fields are repeated in other tables as needed to tie the tables together.

**FIGURE 12-14**

**A preliminary design for three tables in the Inventory database.**

A preliminary design for three of the tables in the Inventory database system scenario discussed in this chapter (the Product table shown in Figure 12-1 plus the Customer and Order tables used to store data about customers and their orders) is shown in Figure 12-14. Notice that each table contains a primary key field (shaded green in Figure 12-14) and those fields are the only fields that occur in more than one table (see the yellow fields in Figure 12-14)—and only as needed to tie the tables together.

This process of evaluating and correcting the structures of the tables in a database to minimize data redundancy is called **normalization**. Normalization is usually viewed as a multistep process, adjusting the fields in the tables as needed to move the table structures from *zero normal form* (*ZNF*) to usually *third normal form* (*3NF*), although procedures exist to reach *fifth normal form* (*5NF*). The overall objective of the normalization process is to ensure that redundant fields from table to table are kept to a minimum. A non-normalized table structure is considered to be zero normal form (ZNF). The next three normal forms can be summarized as follows:

> *First normal form* (*1NF*)—the table has unique fields (no *repeating groups*; that is, groups of related entries that belong to one unique person or thing, such as a customer, an order, and so forth) and all fields are dependent on the primary key. Any repeating groups have been placed in a second table and related to the original table via a primary key field (such as Customer Number or Order Number). For instance, at this point, the fields relating to the contact information for a customer would only appear in one table, such as a Customer table, and would be related to the other tables by a unique primary key field, such as a Customer Number field.

> *Second normal form* (*2NF*)—the table is in 1NF with no *partial dependencies*; that is, fields in a table that are dependent on part of the primary key (if the table has a composite primary key made up of multiple key fields), and all fields are dependent on a single primary key or on all of the fields in a composite primary key. Any partial dependencies have been removed and these dependent fields (such as those containing product information in an Order table) are placed in a separate table and related to the original table via a primary key field (such as a Product Number field occurring in both tables).

> *Third normal form* (*3NF*)—the table is in 2NF with no *transitive dependencies*; that is, two fields that are not primary keys and are dependent on one another, such as the Supplier Name and Supplier Number fields in a Product table. These dependent fields are placed in a separate table and related to the original table via a primary key field (such as a Supplier Number field occurring in both tables).

Once the fields for each table have been identified, the name, data type, and other necessary properties should be determined for each field. These properties include field size, any input masks or validation rules that should be used to check data as it is entered into the table, and

>**Normalization.** The process of evaluating and correcting the structure of a database table to minimize data redundancy.

whether or not a field is a required field, as discussed in the Data Definition section earlier in this chapter. Once the design is complete, the database is ready to be created, as discussed next.

## Creating a Relational Database

To create a relational database, a new database file (that will contain all tables and other objects included in the database) is first created and named. Next, each table in the database is created, using the table structure developed during the database design process. Once the table structure is complete, data can be entered into the tables and the tables can be related as needed.

### Creating the Tables

In Microsoft Access, tables can be created in either *Design view* or *Datasheet view*, as illustrated in Figure 6-21 in Chapter 6 and reviewed in Figure 12-15. To create a table in Design view, you enter each field name and specify the data type and other properties as needed, and then save the table using an appropriate table name. To create a table in Datasheet view, you typically enter the first record of data into the table to initially create the fields for that table, and then you can change the field names and other properties as needed using the *Table Tools Fields* tab on the Ribbon in recent versions of Microsoft Access. You then need to save the table using an appropriate table name. However, only very basic properties (such as the field name, data type, and whether or not the field is required) can be specified using the table's Datasheet view, so the table's Design view is often still needed to finalize the table structure (such as to change the primary key or add a validation rule or an input mask).

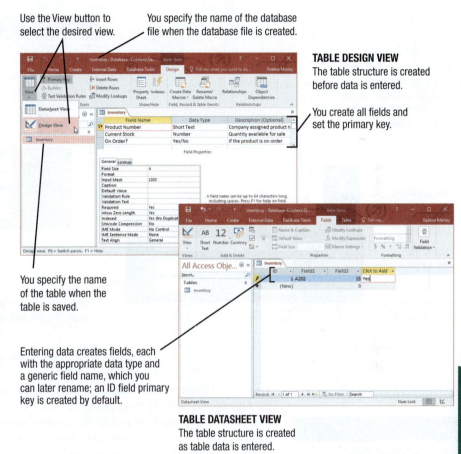

Use the View button to select the desired view.

You specify the name of the database file when the database file is created.

**TABLE DESIGN VIEW**
The table structure is created before data is entered.

You create all fields and set the primary key.

You specify the name of the table when the table is saved.

Entering data creates fields, each with the appropriate data type and a generic field name, which you can later rename; an ID field primary key is created by default.

**TABLE DATASHEET VIEW**
The table structure is created as table data is entered.

**FIGURE 12-15**
Tables can be created using Design view or Datasheet view.

### Entering and Editing Data

If a new database is to be used with existing data, the data needs to be transferred from the old files to the new system—a process called *data migration*. If new data is to be used, it is entered into the appropriate database table. A table's Datasheet view can be used to enter data into that table as previously described; however, a **form** can be used instead for easier data entry and a more professional appearance. Each form is associated with a specific table; when a form is created, it automatically includes all of the fields in that table. Once created, you can edit the form using the form's Design view, such as to change the form color or the font size used, delete fields, rearrange the placement of the fields on the form, or add a company logo. Creating and using a form is shown in Figure 12-16.

---

>**Form.** A formatted way of viewing and editing a table in a database.

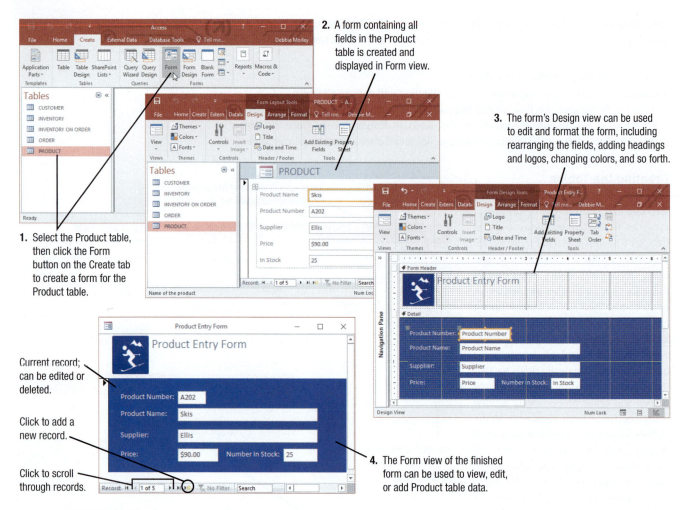

**2.** A form containing all fields in the Product table is created and displayed in Form view.

**3.** The form's Design view can be used to edit and format the form, including rearranging the fields, adding headings and logos, changing colors, and so forth.

**1.** Select the Product table, then click the Form button on the Create tab to create a form for the Product table.

Current record; can be edited or deleted.

Click to add a new record.

Click to scroll through records.

**4.** The Form view of the finished form can be used to view, edit, or add Product table data.

**FIGURE 12-16**

**Forms.** Forms can be used to view, edit, and add table data.

**TIP**

When you initially create a new object, such as a form or report, it is associated with the current table—be sure the appropriate table is selected before using the Create tab on the Ribbon to create the new object.

**TIP**

To separate a group of form fields in a form's Design view so the fields can be moved independently, right-click and select *Remove Layout* from the *Layout* option.

Either a table's Datasheet view or the *Form view* for a form can be used to input, view, and edit data for a table. In either case, records can be added to the table (click the *New (blank) record* button at the bottom of the table or form to display a new blank record), deleted from the table (use the Home tab on the Ribbon (or the Delete key on the keyboard) to delete the current record), or edited (display the appropriate record and then click the field to be edited). Regardless of whether the table's Datasheet view or a form's Form view is used to edit the table data, it is the same data that is being edited. So if a new record is added using a form's Form view, for example, the new record will be visible when the table is viewed using that table's Datasheet view and, if an address is edited in the table's Datasheet view, the updated address will be visible when the record is viewed using a form.

### Relating Tables

After all the tables in a database application have been created and their primary keys designated, the tables can be *related* to one another via their primary keys so that a primary key for one table can be used to extract data from other tables as needed. For instance, once a Customer table (containing customer data) and an Order table (containing order data) are related via the Customer table's Customer Number primary key field, then that field can be used to extract information from both of these tables, such as to generate an order report or an invoice containing data from the Customer table and the Order table. The process of relating tables in the Inventory database discussed throughout this chapter is shown in Figure 12-17. This figure also illustrates how, once the tables are related, the related data located in other tables can be viewed from inside a single table.

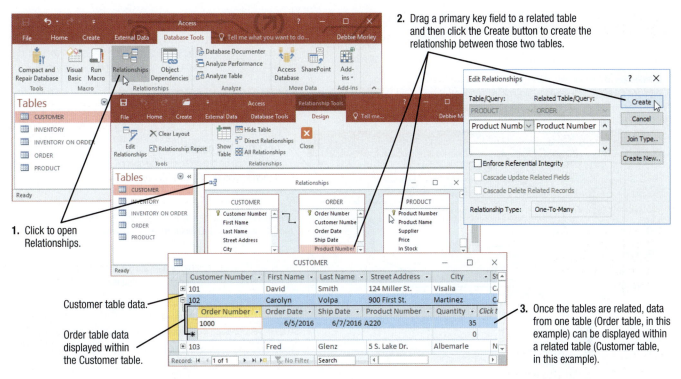

**2.** Drag a primary key field to a related table and then click the Create button to create the relationship between those two tables.

**1.** Click to open Relationships.

Customer table data.

Order table data displayed within the Customer table.

**3.** Once the tables are related, data from one table (Order table, in this example) can be displayed within a related table (Customer table, in this example).

⚠ **FIGURE 12-17**
**Relating tables.**

## Retrieving Information from a Relational Database

Database information retrieval can be performed by looking up and then displaying a single record that contains the desired information about that entity (such as looking up a customer's phone number or current balance by displaying the appropriate record in the Customer table). However, more often information is retrieved from a database using a query or a report.

A **query** extracts specific information from a database by specifying particular conditions (called *criteria*) about the data you would like to retrieve, such as retrieving all names of customers who live in Tennessee or all products whose inventory level is below 100 units. Every DBMS provides tools users can use to query the database for information. One possibility is using a *query language*, such as **structured query language** (**SQL**)— the standard query language for relational databases. To create a query, users can either type a query using SQL or, more commonly, use the query tools built into the DBMS (such as a *query design screen* or *query wizard*) to create a query object. In either case, the query can then be used to extract the data from the table associated with the query that meets the query conditions. An example of creating a query for the Product table using the query design screen in Microsoft Access (along with the SQL version of that query that can be viewed and edited if desired by selecting the *SQL View* option from the View menu) is shown in Figure 12-18 on the next page. As shown in this figure, the query is created, named, and saved as an object in the database file. Each time this query is run (by opening the appropriate query object), only the records in the Product table meeting the criteria are displayed. In addition to retrieving information from a single table, queries can retrieve information from multiple tables, if the tables are related.

Queries need to be designed to extract the requested information as efficiently as possible. Poorly written queries can impact the overall performance of the system, especially if they are executed frequently—in some systems, queries may be enacted several times

**TIP**

An example of an open-source relational DBMS based on SQL is *MySQL*.

> **Query.** A request to see information from a database that matches specific criteria. > **Structured query language (SQL).** A popular query language standard for information retrieval in relational databases.

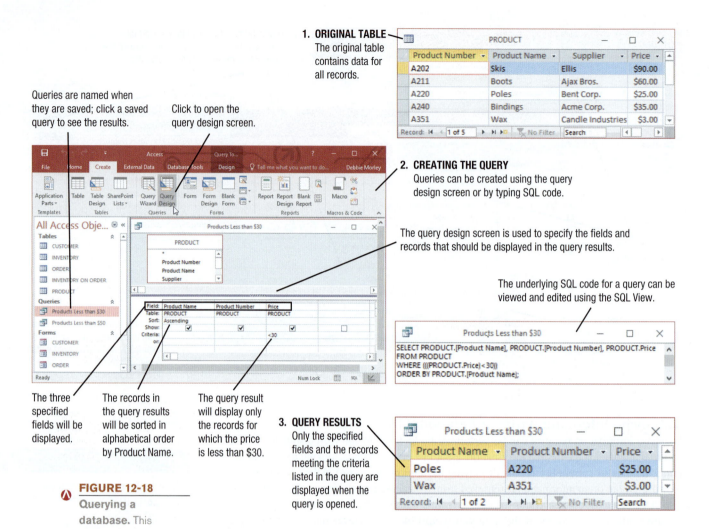

**1. ORIGINAL TABLE**
The original table contains data for all records.

Queries are named when they are saved; click a saved query to see the results.

Click to open the query design screen.

**2. CREATING THE QUERY**
Queries can be created using the query design screen or by typing SQL code.

The query design screen is used to specify the fields and records that should be displayed in the query results.

The underlying SQL code for a query can be viewed and edited using the SQL View.

The three specified fields will be displayed.

The records in the query results will be sorted in alphabetical order by Product Name.

The query result will display only the records for which the price is less than $30.

**3. QUERY RESULTS**
Only the specified fields and the records meeting the criteria listed in the query are displayed when the query is opened.

⚠ **FIGURE 12-18**
**Querying a database.** This example pulls information from the Product table in the Inventory database.

✓ **TIP**

Companies must ensure their databases are protected against *SQL injection*—an attack in which hackers enter SQL commands into a database's form fields (instead of the expected data) in order to gain access to the data stored in that database.

per second. Even a marginal improvement in performance of frequently used queries can significantly improve the overall performance of the system. Consequently, it is the job of the database administrator to identify regularly used queries that need improvement and to suggest ways in which to make them perform better. Common techniques include alterations to the query itself to improve its performance, adding "hints" to the query to tell the database which tables should be accessed first to speed up performance, and adding additional indexes to heavily used tables.

When more formal or attractive output is needed, a **report** can be used. In essence, a report is a formatted way of looking at some or all of the data contained in a database. The fields to be included in a report are specified when the report is created. A report can be designed to include all the records located in its associated table, or it can be designed to include just the results of a query. Like queries, reports in Microsoft Access are saved as objects in the database file, they can pull information from more than one table at a time if the tables are related, and they display the specified data from the appropriate tables at the time the report is run. Reports are often created initially using a report wizard (such as the Microsoft Access *Report Wizard* shown in Figure 12-19) and then their appearance can be modified using Design view, similar to the way a form can be modified.

> **Report.** A formatted way of looking at information retrieved from a database table or the results of a query.

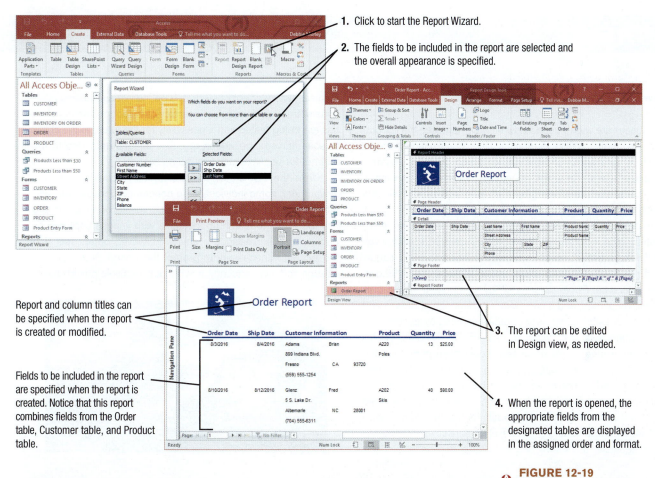

1. Click to start the Report Wizard.

2. The fields to be included in the report are selected and the overall appearance is specified.

Report and column titles can be specified when the report is created or modified.

Fields to be included in the report are specified when the report is created. Notice that this report combines fields from the Order table, Customer table, and Product table.

3. The report can be edited in Design view, as needed.

4. When the report is opened, the appropriate fields from the designated tables are displayed in the assigned order and format.

⚠ **FIGURE 12-19**

**Reports.** Display table information with a more formal, businesslike appearance.

## Maintaining a Relational Database

Although small, personal databases may need little or no maintenance, large enterprise databases frequently require regular maintenance. Maintenance activities are usually performed by the database administrator and include the following tasks:

➤ Upgrading the database software as needed and installing security patches as they become available.

➤ Repairing or restoring data that has become corrupt, such as the result of a storage media error or a computer virus.

➤ Modifying the table structure to add new fields or to accommodate values that turned out to be different from those anticipated when the database was designed, such as a customer last name that is longer than the field size specified for the Last Name field.

➤ Adding new indexes, which can be used to speed up queries.

➤ Deleting obsolete data, such as for customers who no longer exist or who have not placed orders for a specified period of time.

➤ Continually evaluating and improving the security measures used with the database.

**SYS**

## ASK THE EXPERT

Courtesy Dice

**Shravan Goli,** President, Dice

### What is the hottest IT-oriented job today and what do you expect it to be in the future?

The tech market is constantly changing, with certain positions gaining popularity as companies adapt their hiring needs. In spite of the ever evolving nature of the marketplace, there are some positions that continue to top the list and will remain a priority for companies in the years to come. For example, "Big Data" and "cloud" positions are and will continue to be in high demand as companies need to process and leverage data in order to analyze overall business trends and performance.

# TREND

## Law Enforcement Databases

Databases are widely used in law enforcement (see the accompanying photo). While databases have been used for years to store data about criminal cases, stolen property, firearms, organized crime networks, counterfeit documents, and more, new databases are emerging that hold non-traditional data (such as photos, videos, DNA profiles, and biometric data). One example is the FBI's *Next Generation Identification* (*NGI*) system. NGI includes the *Advanced Fingerprint Identification Technology* (*AFIT*) component, which has improved fingerprint-matching accuracy from about 92% to over 99.6%. The *Interstate Photo System (IPS)* component holds over 23 million photos, and it can search through the photos to find and rank possible matches to photos submitted by law enforcement agencies. The *National Palm Print System (NPPS)* component stores millions of searchable palm prints and the *Repository for Individuals of Special Concern* (*RISC*) component provides mobile access for law enforcement officers nationwide to rapidly search through a repository of wanted criminals, terrorists, and sex offenders for matches to a submitted fingerprint. In addition, the *Rap Back* service enables authorized agencies to receive ongoing status notifications of any criminal history or activity reported on individuals holding positions of trust, such as school teachers. Iris-recognition capabilities are being tested and a possibility for the future is the ability to scan surveillance videos or public images uploaded to the Internet for possible matches during searches.

While the FBI states that the system complies with the *Privacy Act*, some individuals are concerned because the system includes individuals who are not criminals or suspects and has the ability to match up identities with images captured by public video surveillance systems. However, others feel that the system is necessary to protect the United States and its citizens and, consequently, is worth any possible privacy risks.

Courtesy iKey, Ltd.

CAUTION CAUTION CAUTION CAUTION CAUTION CAUTION CAUT

Because database tables are saved automatically, you cannot undo or undelete deleted rows or columns. Before clicking the Yes button to verify a deletion, make sure the proper row or column is being deleted, and back up your databases regularly so you can restore any data deleted in error.

## The Object-Oriented Database Model

Traditionally, database software has dealt with *structured* types of data; that is, primarily text-based data that can be organized neatly into columns (fields) and rows (records). Structured data is the type you have mostly been reading about in this chapter and probably the type you have been working with on your computer. However, evolving user needs and technologies have changed the types of data in use today. In addition to handling conventional record data (such as text, numbers, and dates), many of today's database applications now need to store a wide variety of types of data, such as documents, photographs, videos, RFID data, and so on. (For a look at a new law enforcement database, see the Trend box.) An **object-oriented database management system** (**OODBMS**) is often able to store and

> **Object-oriented database management system (OODBMS).** A type of database system in which multiple types of data are stored as objects along with their related code.

retrieve complex, unstructured data better than a relational database management system. Unlike a relational database in which each record has a similar format, little similarity may exist among the data elements that form the objects. An object-oriented database is also a better choice for database applications in which the structure may change frequently.

Similar to object-oriented programming applications (discussed in Chapter 11), an OODBMS stores data in objects. An object contains data along with the methods (actions) that can be taken with that data. Objects in an OODBMS can contain virtually any type of data—a video clip, a photograph with a narrative, text with music, and so on—along with the methods to be used with that data. Objects stored in an OODBMS can be retrieved using queries, such as with queries written in *object query language* (*OQL*)—an object-oriented version of SQL. The objects can also be reused in other applications to develop new applications very quickly. The key characteristics for an OODBMS (including objects, attributes, methods, classes, and inheritance) are similar to the OOP principles discussed in Chapter 11. In fact, OOP languages, such as Java or C#, are often used to manipulate data stored in an object-oriented database. OODBMSs are becoming more common on databases accessed via the Internet. For instance, a Web-based OODBMS containing images and information from the *Sloan Digital Sky Survey* (an astronomical survey that is mapping one-quarter of the entire sky in detail, including 1 billion celestial objects) is shown in Figure 12-20.

## Hybrid Database Models

Some databases are *hybrid databases*; that is, a combination of two or more database types or models. For instance, a database that combines object and relational database technology can be referred to as an *object-relational database management system* (*ORDBMS*). One emerging type of hybrid database is the **hybrid XML/relational database**—a type of database that can store and retrieve both XML data and relational data. Several vendors have implemented XML data management capabilities into their relational database management systems, but IBM's *DB2* program goes one step further. DB2 contains a *hybrid XML/relational database server*, which allows XML data to be entered into a database while preserving its structure (the XML data and its properties). This means that nonrelational business data (such as Excel spreadsheets or word processing documents) can be combined with traditional relational data in the same database easily and efficiently. Keeping the XML data structure intact allows queries and other data operations to be much more efficient. Both the relational and XML data stored in the database can be accessed via queries and otherwise manipulated, and they can work together in a single application as needed (see Figure 12-21).

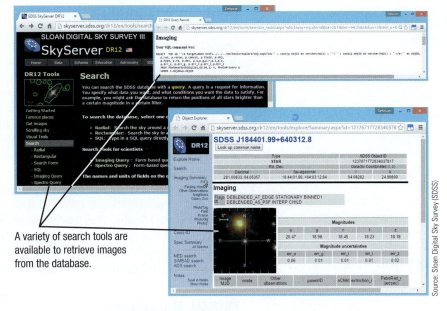

A variety of search tools are available to retrieve images from the database.

Source: Sloan Digital Sky Survey (SDSS)

**FIGURE 12-20**
**The Sloan Digital Sky Survey object-oriented database.**

**FIGURE 12-21**
**Hybrid XML/relational databases.**

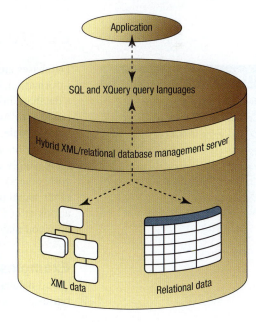

SYS

---

>**Hybrid XML/relational database.** A type of database system that can store and retrieve both XML data and relational data.

### Multidimensional Databases

The growth and importance of data warehousing (discussed in Chapter 10) has led to another type of database model—the **multidimensional database** (**MDDB**), a type of database optimized for data warehouse applications. Whereas relational databases are appropriate for transactional applications in which data is retrieved or updated typically by rows and object-oriented databases are appropriate when a variety of types of objects need to be stored and retrieved, multidimensional databases are designed to store a collection of summarized data for quick and easy data analysis. The data is typically collected from a variety of enterprise-wide activities (often from existing relational databases) and is then summarized and restructured to enable it to be viewed from multiple perspectives called *dimensions*. For example, sales for a company could be viewed in the dimensions of product model, geography, time, or salesperson, or viewed as a combination of dimensions, such as sales during a specified time period by a particular product model in the southwest United States. The dimensions are predefined, based on what are viewed to be meaningful for that particular database, and the summarized data values are automatically calculated. One of the most common types of software used in conjunction with a multi-dimensional database is *Online Analytical Processing* (*OLAP*).

### NoSQL Databases

Object-oriented and multidimensional databases are two examples of *NoSQL* (*Not Only SQL*) *databases*. The term *NoSQL* refers to a wide variety of different database technologies that were developed in order to overcome some of the limitations of relational databases. For example, the volume of data generated by today's applications and the frequency with which this data is accessed can create performance and processing issues with relational databases. NoSQL databases are organized differently than relational databases are organized and so usually they do not use tables and SQL. NoSQL databases are increasingly being used for big data and IoT applications, as well as for cloud databases, discussed next.

## CLOUD DATABASES

**TIP**

Two APIs commonly used to connect applications written in programming languages (such as Java and C++) and databases include *JDBC (Java Database Connectivity)* and *ODBC (Open Database Connectivity)*.

Databases are extremely common on the Web. Virtually all companies that offer product information, online ordering, research resources, or similar activities via a Web site use a database in conjunction with that site. For instance, one of the largest **cloud databases** belongs to Amazon.com, which stores data about its customers and their orders, products for sale, and customer reviews of products. In addition, it stores the actual text of many books so they can be searched and viewed online. Cloud databases are also increasingly used to store user-generated content (that individuals upload to be shared with others), such as content uploaded to Flickr, YouTube, Facebook, Pinterest, and other social media. A few examples of cloud databases are discussed next, followed by a look at how cloud databases typically work. For a closer look at cloud databases and how you may be able to create one, see the Technology and You box.

### Examples of Cloud Databases in Use

Cloud databases today are used for a variety of purposes. One purpose is information retrieval—the Web is, in essence, a huge storehouse of data waiting to be retrieved. Data

---

>**Multidimensional database (MDDB).** A type of database designed to be used with data warehousing. >**Cloud database.** A database, typically hosted on a cloud database provider's servers, that is accessible to users via the Web.

## TECHNOLOGY AND YOU

### Cloud Databases

With individuals and businesses embracing cloud computing today, it should be no surprise that cloud databases have emerged. The use of cloud databases is growing rapidly; in fact, one recent study estimated that the global cloud database market will exceed $14 billion by 2019.

Cloud databases are typically built using the infrastructure of a cloud provider (such as *Microsoft Azure*, *Amazon Web Services databases*, or *Google Cloud SQL*). Also known as *Database-as-a-Service* (*DBaaS*), cloud databases enable businesses to create an easily scalable database with less in-house hardware and maintenance requirements, and to only pay for the storage and traffic they use. Cloud databases can also be set up for mobile access when appropriate. However, businesses utilizing databases hosted in the cloud need to ensure that those databases are adequately protected against security and privacy breaches, as well as have a recovery plan in case of a disaster or the bankruptcy of the cloud provider.

For individuals, the most recent versions of Microsoft Access include the ability to make custom *Access web apps* (see the accompanying illustration)—databases that you build in Access that are stored in the cloud (on a *Sharepoint site*), shared with others, and accessed via a Web browser.

**With Microsoft Access, you can create custom cloud databases.**

to be accessed and displayed via a Web page is often stored in a database (hosted either on site or in the cloud), and Web site visitors can request and view information upon demand. Search sites are perhaps the most obvious cloud database application, retrieving and displaying links to Web pages based on the search term supplied by the user. Another common use of cloud databases is to support and facilitate e-commerce, such as to display product information, pricing, customer information, shopping cart content, order information, and more upon demand. Other information commonly retrieved and displayed from cloud databases include product information, press releases, and other documents retrieved from company Web sites; ZIP codes, driving directions, maps, and more retrieved from reference sites (see the Switchboard Web site in Figure 12-22); and photos and videos retrieved from photo and video sharing sites.

Cloud databases allow Web pages to be *dynamic Web pages*; that is, Web pages in which the appearance or content of the pages changes based on the user's input or stated preferences instead of just displaying *static* information via the Web pages included on the site. In addition to being used to supply data on demand (such as via a Web site search), cloud databases also allow Web sites to display personalized content for each visitor, such as to create a personalized page that displays information based on a user's past activities, as is the case with the Amazon.com Web page shown in Figure 12-22.

SYS

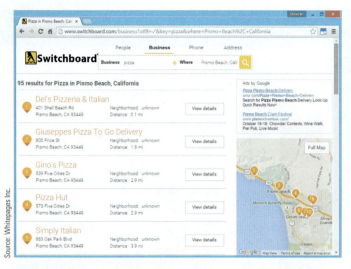

Source: Whitepages Inc.

Source: Amazon.com, Inc.

**REFERENCE SITE**
This site stores address information for individuals and businesses in the United States. After the user enters a name or category and a location (in this case, pizza in Pismo Beach, California), the matching information is retrieved from the database.

**PERSONALIZED SITE**
This site retrieves information from its database to create personalized pages for signed-in viewers, such as recently viewed products and recommendations based on viewed and purchased products.

**FIGURE 12-22**
Many Web pages are used in conjunction with a cloud database.

## How Cloud Databases Work

The request to retrieve information from or store data in a cloud database is typically initiated by the Web site visitor. Filling out a Web page form and selecting an option from a menu displayed on a Web page are common ways cloud database requests are made. The request is received by the Web server, which then converts the request into a database query and passes it on to the database server with the help of middleware, discussed in more detail next. The database server retrieves the appropriate information and returns it to the Web server (again, via middleware); that information is then displayed on the visitor's screen in the form of a Web page. This process is illustrated using the L.L. Bean Web site and search feature in Figure 12-23.

### Middleware

Software that connects two otherwise separate applications (such as a Web server and a DBMS in order to tie a database to a Web site) is referred to as **middleware**. Middleware for cloud database applications is commonly written as *scripts*—short sections of code written in a programming or scripting language that are executed by another program. JavaScript and VBScript (discussed in Chapter 11) are two scripting languages often used in conjunction with cloud databases, such as to write Active Server Pages (ASPs). Other languages commonly used to connect databases to Web sites are Java, C, and Perl (all discussed in Chapter 11 and often used to write CGI scripts), and PHP. (ASPs, CGI scripts, and PHP are discussed next). As an alternative to writing scripts from scratch, many Web site authoring programs include capabilities that allow the Web developer to select the appropriate menu options and enter the needed information while a Web site is being created in order to automatically generate the scripts required to connect dynamic Web pages to a database. This capability allows even novice Web developers to include input forms and search capabilities easily on their sites, as well as connect the site and a database, without having to write any scripts directly.

> **Middleware.** Software used to connect two otherwise separate applications, such as a Web server and a database management system.

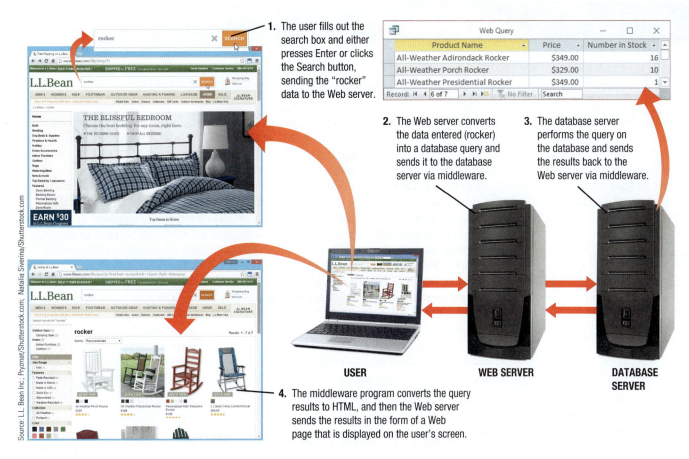

1. The user fills out the search box and either presses Enter or clicks the Search button, sending the "rocker" data to the Web server.

2. The Web server converts the data entered (rocker) into a database query and sends it to the database server via middleware.

3. The database server performs the query on the database and sends the results back to the Web server via middleware.

4. The middleware program converts the query results to HTML, and then the Web server sends the results in the form of a Web page that is displayed on the user's screen.

**USER**    **WEB SERVER**    **DATABASE SERVER**

**FIGURE 12-23**
A cloud database in action.

## CGI Scripts

A *CGI* (*common gateway interface*) *script* is a set of instructions written in a programming language (such as C, Perl, Java, or Visual Basic) and designed to accept data from and return data to a Web page visitor. CGI scripts reside on and are executed by the Web server, and they handle tasks, such as processing input forms and information requests. On very busy sites, CGI scripts can slow down server response time significantly because they process each request individually.

## Active Server Pages (ASPs)

*Active Server Pages* (*ASPs*) are dynamic Web pages that have the extension *.asp*. ASPs work similarly to dynamic Web pages utilizing CGI scripts but the code to tie the database to the Web site is typically written in JavaScript or VBScript.

## PHP Scripts

As discussed in Chapter 11, *PHP* (*PHP: Hypertext Preprocessor*) is a scripting language that is increasingly being used to create dynamic Web pages. It uses code similar to Perl or C++ that is inserted into the HTML code of a Web page using special PHP tags. PHP scripts reside on and are executed by the server. They are typically used to perform tasks similar to CGI scripts and ASPs but they have the advantage of high compatibility with many types of databases.

SYS

# SUMMARY

## WHAT IS A DATABASE?

A **database** is a collection of related data that is stored and organized in a manner that allows information to be retrieved as needed. Most databases consist of one or more **tables**; each table contains a collection of related **records** (**rows**), each of which, in turn, is a collection of related **fields** (**columns**).

A **database management system** (**DBMS**) is a software program used to create database applications—data can be stored in and information can be retrieved from more than one table at a time. A relational database is the most common type of computerized database. This type of database relates data in various database tables by using a **primary key**—a field in a table that contains unique data that is unlikely to change and that is used to uniquely identify each record in that table.

The individuals involved with a DBMS include *database designers*, *database developers*, *database programmers*, *database administrators*, and *users*. Over the years, databases have evolved from *flat files* to collections of tables and objects that support interrelated multimedia content with a minimum of data redundancy.

A DBMS offers several advantages over file management systems. Among these advantages are faster response times, lower operating costs, lower data storage requirements, improved data integrity, and better data management. The biggest potential disadvantage is a greater vulnerability to failure.

## DATA CONCEPTS AND CHARACTERISTICS

Data in a database has a definite hierarchy. Data is entered as characters into fields in the database. Related fields form records, related records form tables, and a group of related tables forms the database.

One task involved with setting up a database is **data definition**—the process of describing data to be entered into a DBMS. The data definitions are used to create a *table structure* for each table. The table structure contains a description of the data to be entered into the table (field name, data type, and other properties). The **data dictionary** contains information (called **metadata**) about all data in the database application. Different types of databases may relate their **entities** differently. Common types of entity relationships include *one-to-one* (*1:1*), *one-to-many* (*O:M*), and *many-to-many* (*M:M*). A characteristic of an entity is called an **attribute**. Entities typically become database tables; attributes typically become table fields.

Because data is so vital to an organization, **data integrity**, **data validation**, and **data security** must be maintained to ensure the quality of information retrieved from the database and the safety of the database. Good data validation techniques (such as specifying an allowable range of values or a mandatory format) enforced on a *per transaction* basis and coupled with data *locking* when data is being modified can help ensure data integrity and data validation. Good access control methods can help increase data security. Good backup procedures are essential. **Data privacy** is a growing concern as data breaches become more widespread and as businesses need to comply with regulations related to securing and protecting the data they store in their databases.

Databases typically use **indexes** to more easily locate data when it is requested. In conjunction with or as an alternative to **indexed organization**, **direct organization** can be used. Direct organization uses hashing to provide for rapid direct access. Both indexed and direct organization can be used for *real-time* transaction processing.

## DATABASE CLASSIFICATIONS

Database systems can be classified as **single-user** or **multiuser database systems**, depending on how many users need to access the database. **Client-server database systems** are accessed via a network by client computers at the *front end*; the database resides on server computers at the *back end*. In an *n-tier database system*, at least one piece of middleware exists between the client and the server.

Many database systems are set up as **distributed database systems**. Instead of a single central database located on a central computer (as in a **centralized database system**), the database is divided among several smaller computers or servers that are connected and accessed via a network. **In-memory databases** (**IMDBs**), also called *main memory databases* (*MMDBs*), hold all data in the main memory of the computer.

**Chapter Objective 4:**
Identify some basic database classifications and discuss their differences.

## DATABASE MODELS

Database models have evolved over time. Traditionally, database systems have conformed to one of three common types: hierarchical, network, and relational, although only the relational model is widely used today. A *hierarchical database management system* stores data in the form of a tree, in which the relationship between data elements is usually one-to-many. In a *network database management system*, the relationship between data elements is typically either one-to-many or many-to-many. The **relational database management system** (**RDBMS**) stores data in tables related by primary keys and is the most widely used database model today. The growing interest in other data types and the need to combine them into multimedia formats for applications have given rise to the **object-oriented database management system** (**OODBMS**). These databases use storable entities called *objects*. An object contains both data and relevant code; data can be virtually any type, such as a video clip, photograph, text, or music. A **hybrid XML/relational database** can store both XML data and relational data. Applications such as data warehousing have led to another type of data model—the **multidimensional database** (**MDDB**), which allows data to be viewed using multiple dimensions.

To create a relational database, the tables are designed based on the purpose of the database, the fields that need to be included, each field's properties, and the relationships between the tables included in the database. The table structure is then evaluated and modified as needed to minimize redundancy—a process called **normalization**. Next, the structure of each table is created and data is entered into the database. Both the table structure and the data contained in a table can be modified as needed. Table data can be viewed and modified using a **form** for a more formal appearance. Information is usually retrieved using **queries** (to retrieve specific information from a database that matches specified criteria) and **reports**. Queries most often use **structured query language** (**SQL**). Once a database has been designed and created, regular maintenance activities are needed.

**Chapter Objective 5:**
List the most common database models and discuss how they are used today.

**Chapter Objective 6:**
Understand how a relational database is designed, created, used, and maintained.

## CLOUD DATABASES

**Cloud databases** are plentiful on the Web. When information is retrieved via an input form or other interactive element on a Web page, a database is used. In addition to being used for information retrieval, databases are also used for a variety of e-commerce and *dynamic* Web page activities.

When a request for information is transferred from a Web page to a database, it is converted—using **middleware** software—to a request the database can process. The retrieved information is then passed back to the Web server and displayed in the form of a Web page; dynamic Web pages may be *Active Server Pages (ASPs)*. Middleware for cloud database application is commonly written as *scripts*, such as *CGI* or *PHP* scripts.

**Chapter Objective 7:**
Describe some ways databases are used on the Web.

# REVIEW ACTIVITIES

## KEY TERM MATCHING

a. database

b. data dictionary

c. data validation

d. index

e. middleware

f. primary key

g. query

h. record

i. relational database management system (RDBMS)

j. table

**Instructions**: Match each key term on the left with the definition on the right that best describes it.

1. _____ A collection of related data that is stored in a manner enabling information to be retrieved as needed.

2. _____ A collection of related fields in a database. Also called a row.

3. _____ A request to see information from a database that matches specific criteria.

4. _____ A small table containing a primary key and the location of the record belonging to that key; used to locate records in a database.

5. _____ A specific field in a database table that uniquely identifies the records in that table.

6. _____ A type of database system in which data is stored in tables related by common fields; the most widely used database model today.

7. _____ In a relational database, a collection of related records (rows).

8. _____ Software used to connect two otherwise separate applications, such as a Web server and a database management system.

9. _____ The process of ensuring that data entered into a database matches the data definition.

10. _____ The repository of all data definitions in a database.

## SELF-QUIZ

1. Data definition

2. Data integrity

3. Data security

**Instructions**: Circle **T** if the statement is true, **F** if the statement is false, or write the best answer in the space provided. **Answers for the self-quiz are located in the References and Resources Guide at the end of the book**.

1. T  F  In a relational database, more than one table can be included in a database.

2. T  F  Normalization is used to minimize data redundancy.

3. T  F  Using usernames and passwords is a data validation technique.

4. T  F  A database that stores all data in memory instead of on a hard drive is called a cloud database.

5. T  F  Dynamic Web pages commonly use databases.

6. In a student information database, *Name* would be considered a(n) _____ in the table, while all of Jennifer Mitchell's information would be a(n) _____.

7. Data _____ refers to the accuracy of data.

8. When _____ organization is used, a hashing procedure determines where data is stored.

9. The terms *front end* and *back end* refer to _____ database systems.

10. Match each term with its example, and write the corresponding number in the blank to the left of the example.

    a. _____ When the database does not allow a user to enter a letter in a phone number field.

    b. _____ Requiring users to log on to a database system via a fingerprint reader.

    c. _____ Assigning a field the property of "required."

1. Of the data types Text, Number, or Yes/No, which would be the most appropriate for a phone number field that needs to store data in the format (123)555-7890? Explain your answer.

2. Of the following fields, which would be the most appropriate for the primary key in a customer information table? Explain your answer.

   **a.** Customer Name   **b.** Customer Number   **c.** Phone Number   **d.** Customer Address

3. Refer to the two relational database tables below and answer the following questions:

   **a.** Which employees work in the Accounting department and make at least $60,000 per year?

   **b.** Which employees have Hurt as their manager?

   **c.** In which of the preceding questions did you have to relate data in both tables to get an answer? Through what field(s) did you relate the tables?

**EMPLOYEE TABLE**

| NAME | LOCATION | DEPARTMENT | SALARY |
|------|----------|------------|--------|
| Doney | Phoenix | Accounting | $58,000 |
| James | San Diego | Sales | $44,000 |
| Giles | San Diego | Accounting | $62,000 |
| Smith | Miami | Accounting | $73,000 |

**OFFICE TABLE**

| LOCATION | MANAGER |
|----------|---------|
| San Diego | Hurt |
| Cleveland | Holmes |
| Miami | Jonas |
| Phoenix | Alexis |

4. Suppose that you need to create a two-table database to record information for a DVD rental kiosk. The following information needs to be recorded:

   ➤ For all movies: Movie number, title, category, rental rate, and whether or not it is available for rent; for all rented movies, the customer who rented the movie and the due date will also need to be recorded

   ➤ For all customers: Customer number, name, address, city, state, ZIP code, and phone number

   Create a preliminary design (use Figure 12-14 for reference, if needed) for a possible two-table database for this scenario (Movie table and Customer table), locating the fields in the most appropriate tables and having a minimum of redundancy.

5. For Exercise 4, is there a field in common in both tables that is appropriate to use as a primary key to relate the two tables? If so, which field? If not, redo Exercise 4 to include an appropriate primary key.

1. It is becoming increasingly common for biometric devices to be used to grant or deny access to facilities, as well as to identify consumers for financial transactions. In order to facilitate this, some data about each participant's biometric features must be stored in a database. How do you feel about your biometric characteristics being stored in a database? Does it depend on whether the system belongs to your bank, employer, school, or the government? Because biometric features cannot be reset, are you at risk using a biometric ID system? Why or why not?

2. There are numerous databases that contain personal, but public, information about individuals. Today much of this data is available online. How do you feel about your personal information being contained in databases that other individuals can access or that might be breached via the Internet? Do you mind that anyone with an Internet connection might be able to find out how much you paid for your house, if you are married, where you live, and other personal information?

# PROJECTS

**HOT TOPICS**

1. **National Databases** There are a number of databases—such as the FBI's *Next Generation Identification* (*NGI*) database (which was discussed in the Trend box), the military's *Biometrics Automated Toolset* (*BAT*) database, and the Homeland Security Department's *Automated Biometric Identification System* (*IDENT*) database—in use today for national security purposes. Other national databases include those used by the Internal Revenue Service and the Social Security Administration, as well as a new national network that utilizes databases is the one associated with the state Health Insurance Marketplaces.

   For this project, select one national database (either one of the ones listed in the previous paragraph or an alternate database). Determine the purpose of the database, who has access to it, and if it has proven to be useful. Have there been any recent security breaches or other privacy concerns with your selected database? Has there been any movement toward a national database for citizen identification or other new national database containing information about citizens? At the conclusion of your research, prepare a one-page summary of your findings and opinions and submit it to your instructor.

**SHORT ANSWER/ RESEARCH**

2. **Cloud Databases** As discussed in the chapter, many Web pages today utilize databases to display information requested by visitors, for customized Web pages, and other dynamic applications.

   For this project, visit one Web site that utilizes a database such as Switchboard (www.switchboard.com), the Internet Movie Database Web site (imdb.com), Google Maps (maps.google.com), or Amazon.com (www.amazon.com), and request some information from the site in order to utilize its database. Were you satisfied with the results? Did the database return the correct results in a timely manner? Do you have any suggestions to improve the user interface, such as different directions, additional options, and so forth? At the conclusion of this project, submit a one-page summary of your experience and your recommendations to your instructor.

**HANDS ON**

3. **Designing a Database** While designing a database system for a large enterprise is a highly complex task, designing a small relational database can be a fairly straightforward process.

   For this project, design a relational database to contain data about the students, instructors, and class offerings at your school. The database should consist of three tables (one each for students, classes, and instructors), and each table should have at least four fields. Select an appropriate primary key for each table and determine which of the tables will be related. On paper, design one input screen, one query screen, and one report that might be used with this system; annotate each design with the table and field names for each piece of information to be included. Did any of your three designs utilize data from more than one table? If so, make sure that it is possible to do that, based on your table design and stated relationships. Be sure to include at least one sample record for each table in your design documentation. At the conclusion of this project, submit the completed database design to your instructor.

4. **Multimedia Uploads** There are many Web sites designed to allow individuals to upload photos, videos, and other multimedia content and then visitors can search the site to locate the content they want to view. In addition, multimedia content is often added to pages located on Facebook and other social media. While people certainly have the right to share photos and videos of themselves online if they want to, many individuals upload multimedia content that also includes their friends or other individuals. Often, photos and videos are taken at social gatherings and other situations where the person being photographed or filmed may not be portrayed at their best. Because there are potential ramifications for any compromising content located online (for instance, many schools monitor social media for inappropriate behavior and many employers check Facebook profiles of job applicants), should individuals get permission for everyone in a photo or video before posting it online? Why or why not? What if the content caused the individual to be reprimanded at school or work, or cost the individual a scholarship or job? Would that change your opinion? How would you feel if you ran across a photo or video of yourself online that you did not upload or give permission to be shared online?

For this project, form an opinion about the ethical ramifications of uploading photos or videos containing others without their permission and be prepared to discuss your position (in class, via an online forum, or via a class blog, depending on your instructor's directions). You may also be asked to write a short paper expressing your opinion.

**ETHICS IN ACTION**

5. **Certifications** There are certification exams available for database skills, such as the certifications offered by Oracle and ICCP (Institute for the Certification of Computing Professionals).

For this project, select two database certification programs and research them. Find out who offers them, how long it takes to complete them, how much the programs and exams cost, and how obtaining that certification can benefit you. Try to find job openings that mention one of your selected database certifications. What positions did you find, and what is the starting salary? Do the jobs require experience as well? A college degree? Would you be interested in taking one of these certification programs? Share your findings with the class in the form of a short presentation. The presentation should not exceed 10 minutes and should make use of one or more presentation aids, such as a whiteboard, handouts, or a computer-based slide presentation (your instructor may provide additional requirements). You may also be asked to submit a summary of the presentation to your instructor.

**PRESENTATION/ DEMONSTRATION**

**SYS**

6. **Is Big Data Getting Too Big?** Big data collection today by businesses and the government can include viewed Web pages, browsing habits, sensor signals, smartphone location trails, purchasing habits, surveillance photos, phone call and e-mail metadata, and more—and it is being used with analytic software to make sense of it all. While proponents embrace this new trend as allowing businesses, the government, and other organizations to make smarter decisions, there are also concerns about infringements on personal privacy. According to Craig Mundie, a former senior adviser at Microsoft, "There's no bad data, only bad uses of data." Do you agree? Is it the use, rather than the collection, of data that should be our prominent concern? Or is the issue whether or not the data should be collected in the first place? Do you have concerns about the collection of big data today? What about the recent revelations about the data the National Security Agency (NSA) has been collecting and the growing use of healthcare databases? Once personal data has been collected and stored, is it possible for it to be secured adequately? Are you comfortable with data about yourself being stored in a database? Should the collection of data be regulated more stringently? Why or why not?

Pick a side on this issue, form an opinion and gather supporting evidence, and be prepared to discuss and defend your position in a classroom debate or in a one- to two-page paper, depending on your instructor's directions.

**BALANCING ACT**

# expert insight on...

# Systems

Stuart Feldman is a former President of ACM and was recently a Vice President of Engineering at Google. He is a member of the Board of Directors of the AACSB (Association to Advance Collegiate Schools of Business), a Fellow of the IEEE, a Fellow of the ACM, and serves on a number of government advisory committees. He is a recipient of the 2003 ACM Software System Award for creating a seminal piece of software engineering known as Make, a tool for maintaining computer software. Stuart has a Ph.D. in Mathematics from MIT.

## A Conversation with STUART FELDMAN

### Former President of ACM and Vice President, Engineering, Google

*"The types of data to be managed are also shifting—most is now visual, audio, or executable."*

### My Background . . .

I am one of the original computer brats—I learned to program on a vacuum tube machine in the early 1960s as a kid at a summer course. I was enthralled by computer programming, and the ability to create programs that did new and surprising things.

Throughout my computer career, I've worked as a computer science researcher at Bell Labs, as a research manager and software architect at Bellcore, and as Vice President for Computer Science at IBM Research. I most recently was a Vice President at Google (and responsible for engineering activities at Google's offices in the eastern parts of the Americas and in Asia, as well as some specific products). I was also President of ACM (Association for Computing Machinery)—the largest computing society in the world. Overall, my career has been spent in research and engineering at very high-tech companies working on the cutting edge of computing. It's fun and exciting.

### It's Important to Know . . .

**The world of data has shifted radically.** I can remember when a megabyte was a lot of information. Today, tens of gigabytes fit on a thumb drive, a few terabytes fit on an inexpensive disk, large companies manage petabytes—and exabytes are coming soon. The types of data to be managed are also shifting—most is now visual, audio, or executable. We access data and information not only through desktop computers but also through portable devices—laptops, phones, and tablets.

**Programming languages last a long time.** While most programmers write in dynamic languages (such as Perl, Python, and JavaScript) today, COBOL and FORTRAN programs are still being written and variants of C are still being born. And even more people do programming without thinking about it (such as creating word processing macros, spreadsheet formulas, and fancy Web pages). We will almost certainly see this continue—a hard core of experts supporting basic systems and tools, and millions (soon billions) of people doing occasional programming and customization.

**The impact of systems on society is tremendous.** System capabilities have made enormous increases in efficiency possible, and have also opened up new types of business and social activities. Think about how banking has changed in the last decade, and about how you look up information and find people. Also, think about how personal communication and expectations have shifted from sending letters with a stamp, to sending e-mail, to staying in touch with others on a continual basis via texting, blogging, and social networks. Perhaps our attention span has shrunk, but our ability to reach out has increased. Information systems support globalization and rapid business change—sharing of information, shifting of jobs, and the creation of new jobs and whole new types of careers.

### How I Use this Technology . . .

I spend a lot of time writing papers and presentations, so I use Google Docs and Microsoft Office applications—both complex systems that maintain data and perform reliably—to create documents and collaborate with others. I keep almost all of my digital information in the cloud and I carry a smartphone or tablet everywhere to maintain contact with information and communications. I use secure, integrated financial systems when I perform online financial transactions and I use my favorite system (the World Wide Web) many times a day for research, communications, personal interactions, shopping, and amusement.

Courtesy ACM; Google Inc.

## What the Future Holds . . .

The cost of computing, measured in cost of instructions executed or information stored or transmitted, will continue to drop. In addition, the value of information and knowledge that is encapsulated in computer programs and online services will increase—once something is in code, it can be used and replicated at low incremental cost. This will continue to drive our digitization and automation of activities.

There will also be the increasing ability to do massive amounts of computing for enormous numbers of users and to apply computing resources to problems that were too expensive to address just a few years ago. This will be facilitated by the increased use of integration, as well as by dynamic languages and the increased use of Web standards.

There will be new service computing models, ranging from enterprise integration to user-based mashups to entirely new service industries like Google search tools and remote medical advice. Mobile apps have become a great way to connect information and enhance interactions, and they are a new source of revenue for developers. For program development, we'll see increasing agility—shifting from waterfall and rigid development methods to more exploratory, prototype-based methods and fast trials and iterations. Verification and testing will continue to be essential—lives and jobs frequently depend on systems today.

Perhaps the biggest shifts will come from our increasing dependence on information and access, the risks when things go wrong, and the possibilities of new applications that can improve our lives. For instance, as information arrives and can be examined more easily, we can do a better job of managing our health, our activities, and our personal interactions.

> *"...once something is in code, it can be used and replicated at low incremental cost."*

## My Advice to Students . . .

IT jobs, computer applications, programming languages, approaches to system development, and business needs are always changing. The best preparation for a long and successful career is to understand the fundamentals of computing deeply, and be able to apply them to new situations. You need to become expert in some area—such as a programming language, a methodology, or an environment—but you also must always be prepared to learn new technologies and gain new expertise, as well as to learn what people want to do with computers.

---

### Discussion Question

Stuart Feldman points out how our expectations for the systems we use today have shifted—for example, we demand faster communications and information retrieval. What are your expectations when you send an e-mail message or post a photo or video on a social network? Do you expect an immediate response? Are you disappointed if you don't get immediate feedback? How does instant access to communications, news, personal status, and other timely information affect our society today? Be prepared to discuss your position (in class, via an online class forum, or via a class blog, depending on your instructor's directions). You may also be asked to write a short paper expressing your opinion.

---

> **For access to Google search tools and applications, visit www.google.com. There are some excellent papers available at research.google.com. For more information about ACM or to access the ACM Digital Library, visit www.acm.org.**

# module

# Technology and Society

No study of technology is complete without a look at the growing impact of computers and related technologies on society and our daily lives. As the use of computing devices continues to become increasingly integrated into our lives at school, on the job, at home, and on the go, the associated risks increase. Our networked society also creates new ethical, access, and environmental issues; impacts our physical and mental health; and creates new intellectual property rights issues, such as how intellectual property is used and distributed via the Internet and how it can be protected.

Security risks related to computers, networks, and the Internet were discussed in Chapter 9. Chapter 13 looks at some additional societal issues, including those related to intellectual property rights, ethics, health, access, and the environment.

Peopleimages/iStockphoto

*". . .moderation and balance with respect to technology are essential."*

For more comments from Guest Expert **Jim Griffith** of eBay, see the **Expert Insight on . . . Technology and Society** feature at the end of the module.

# chapter 13

# Intellectual Property Rights, Ethics, Health, Access, and the Environment

**After completing this chapter, you will be able to do the following:**

1. Understand the different types of intellectual property rights and how they relate to computer use.

2. Explain what is meant by the term *ethics* and provide several examples of unethical behavior in computer-related matters.

3. Describe some possible physical and emotional health risks associated with the use of computers.

4. Discuss the impact that factors such as nationality, income, race, education, and physical disabilities may have on computer access and use.

5. Suggest some ways computer users can practice green computing and properly dispose of obsolete computer equipment.

6. Discuss the current status of legislation related to intellectual property rights, ethics, access, and the environment in relation to computers.

# OVERVIEW

**W**hile computers and related technology add convenience and enjoyment to our daily lives, they also can make it easier to perform some types of illegal or unethical acts, can cause serious health and emotional problems, and can have a negative impact on the environment. In addition, although computer use is becoming almost mandatory in our society, many believe that access to technology is not equally available to all individuals. This chapter continues where Chapter 9 left off by exploring computer-related societal issues that go beyond security and privacy.

The chapter begins with a look at a legal issue that all computer users should be aware of—intellectual property rights. The specific types of intellectual property rights are discussed, along with examples of the types of property that each right protects. Next is a discussion of ethics, including what they are and a variety of ethical issues surrounding computer use by individuals and businesses. Topics include the ethical use of copyrighted material, ethical uses of resources and information, unethical use of digital manipulation, and ethical business practices and decision making. The chapter continues with a look at health-oriented concerns, including the impact computers may have on a user's physical and emotional health, as well as strategies individuals can use to lessen those risks. Next, we turn to the issue of equal access, including a discussion of the digital divide and how other factors—such as gender, age, and physical disabilities—may affect computer access and use. We then look at the potential impact of computers on our environment and some ways of lessening that impact. The chapter closes with a look at legislation related to the issues discussed in this chapter. ■

# INTELLECTUAL PROPERTY RIGHTS

**Intellectual property rights** are the legal rights to which the creators of *intellectual property*—original creative works—are entitled. Intellectual property rights indicate who has the right to use, perform, or display a creative work and what can legally be done with that work; how long the creator retains rights to the property; and other related restrictions. Examples of intellectual property include music and movies; paintings, computer graphics, and other works of art; poetry, books, and other types of written works; symbols, names, and designs used in conjunction with a business; architectural drawings; and inventions. The three main types of intellectual property rights are copyrights, trademarks, and patents. Copyrights, trademarks, and patents are issued by individual countries; U.S. intellectual property rights are discussed in more detail next.

SOC

> **Intellectual property rights.** The legal rights to which creators of original creative works (such as artistic or literary works, inventions, corporate logos, and more) are entitled.

**BOOK COPYRIGHT NOTICES**

©2015 San Diego Zoo Global

**WEB SITE COPYRIGHT NOTICES**

 **FIGURE 13-1**

**Copyright statements.** Are often included on books, Web sites, and other original copyrighted works.

*Source: San Diego Zoo Global*

✓ **TIP**

The first copyright termination victor was Victor Willis, the lead singer of the Village People, who, in 2013, was granted control of his share of the copyright to *YMCA* and other songs he wrote in the late 1970s.

## Copyrights

A **copyright** is a form of protection available to the creator of an original artistic, musical, or literary work, such as a book, movie, software program, song, or painting. It gives the copyright holder the exclusive right to publish, reproduce, distribute, perform, or display the work. The *1976 Copyright Act* extends copyright protection to nonpublished works, so, immediately after creating a work in some type of material form (such as on paper, film, videotape, or a digital storage medium), the creator automatically owns the copyright of that work. Consequently, the creator is entitled to copyright protection of that work and has the right to make a statement, such as "Copyright © 2016 John Smith. All rights reserved." Although works created in the United States after March 1, 1989, are not required to display a copyright notice in order to retain their copyright protection, displaying a copyright statement on a published work (see Figure 13-1) reminds others that the work is protected by copyright law and that any use must comply with copyright law. Only the creator of a work (or his or her employer if the work is created as a *work for hire*; that is, within the scope of employment) can rightfully claim copyright. Copyrights can be registered with the *U. S. Copyright Office*. Although registration is not required for copyright protection, it does offer an advantage if the need to prove ownership of a copyright ever arises, such as during a copyright-infringement lawsuit. Most countries offer some copyright protection to works registered in other countries.

Anyone wanting to use copyrighted materials must first obtain permission from the copyright holder and pay any required fee. One exception is the legal concept of *fair use*, which permits limited duplication and use of a portion of copyrighted material for specific purposes, such as criticism, commentary, news reporting, teaching, and research. For example, a teacher may legally read a copyrighted poem for discussion in a poetry class, and a news crew may videotape a small portion of a song at a concert to include in a news report of that concert. Copyrights apply to both published and unpublished works and remain in effect until 70 years after the creator's death. Copyrights for works registered either by an organization or as anonymous works last 95 years from the date of publication or 120 years from the date of creation, whichever is shorter. One recent issue is the *termination rights* granted to musicians and songwriters in the *1976 Copyright Act*—if they originally gave music rights to their publisher, they can request those rights back after 35 years (because the law went into effect in 1978, the first set of rights became eligiable for termination in 2013).

It is important to realize that purchasing a copyrighted item (such as a book, painting, or movie) does not change the copyright protection afforded to the creator of that item. Although you have purchased the right to use the item, you cannot legally duplicate it or portray it as your own creation. Some of the most widely publicized copyright-infringement issues today center around individuals illegally distributing copyright-protected content (particularly music, movies, and e-books) via the Internet, as discussed later in this chapter.

To protect their rights, some creators of digital content (such as art, music, photographs, and movies) use **digital watermarks**—a subtle alteration of digital content that is usually not noticeable when the work is viewed or played but that identifies the copyright holder. For instance, the digital watermark for an image might consist of slight changes to the brightness of a specific pattern of pixels that are imperceptible to people but are easily read by software. Digital watermarks can also be made visible, if desired, such as to add the name of a company or Web site URL to a photo being posted online, or to inform individuals that the photo is copyrighted and should not be used elsewhere.

> **Copyright.** The legal right to sell, publish, or distribute an original artistic or literary work; it is held by the creator of a work as soon as it exists in physical form. > **Digital watermark.** A subtle alteration of digital content (typically added and viewed with software) that is usually not noticeable when the work is viewed or played but that identifies the copyright holder.

Digital watermarks can be added to images, music, video, TV shows, e-books, and other digital content found online or distributed in digital form to identify their copyright holders, their authorized distributors, and other important information. Digital watermarks are typically added with software and, as shown in Figure 13-2, are usually invisible until they are read with appropriate software (such as Adobe Photoshop or a proprietary reader). The purpose of digital watermarking is to give digital content a unique identity that remains intact even if the work is copied, edited, compressed, or otherwise manipulated. For instance, movies sent to movie theaters typically include a digital watermark that can be used to trace a pirated movie back to the theater where the pirated movie was created in order to help authorities locate and prosecute the criminal. Some digital watermark services also offer search services that continually scan the Web to locate digitally watermarked images and notify the copyright holder when those images are found. Because of the vast amount of copyrighted content distributed via the Internet today, the market for digital watermarking technology is growing rapidly. For a look at a new application for digital watermarking—linking rich media to published content—see the Trend box.

The invisible watermark is embedded into the photo.

The information contained in the watermark can be viewed using an image editing program.

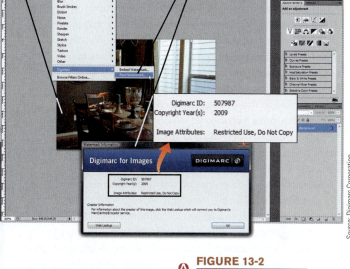

Source: Digimarc Corporation

**FIGURE 13-2**
Digital watermarks.

Another rights-protection tool used with digital content is **digital rights management (DRM) software**. DRM software is used to control the use of a work. For instance, DRM software used in conjunction with business documents (called *enterprise rights management*) can protect a sensitive business document by controlling usage of that document, such as by limiting who can view, print, or copy it. DRM software used with digital content (such as movies, e-books, and music) downloaded or streamed via the Internet can control whether or not a downloaded file can be copied to another device, as well as make a video-on-demand movie or a rented e-book unviewable after the rental period expires.

## Trademarks

A **trademark** is a word, phrase, symbol, or design (or a combination of words, phrases, symbols, or designs) that identifies and distinguishes one product or service from another. A trademark used to identify a service is also called a *service mark*. Trademarks that are claimed but not registered with the *U.S. Patent and Trademark Office* (*USPTO*) can use the mark ™; nonregistered service marks can use the symbol ℠. The symbol ® is reserved for registered trademarks and service marks. Trademarks for products usually appear on the product packaging with the appropriate trademark symbol; service marks are typically used in the advertising of a service because there is no product on which the mark can be printed. Trademarked words and phrases—such as iPhone®, Chicken McNuggets®, Google Earth™, and FedEx 1Day℠—are widely used today. Trademarked logos (see Figure 13-3) are also common. Trademarks last 10 years, but they can be renewed as many times as desired, as long as they are being used in commerce.

In addition to protecting the actual trademarked words, phrases, or logos, trademark law also protects domain names that match a company's trademark, such as Amazon.com and Lego.com. There have been a number of claims of

**FIGURE 13-3**
Examples of trademarked logos.

Source: McDonald's Corporation; SONIC; eBay Inc.; Microsoft Corporation

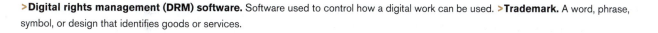

> **Digital rights management (DRM) software.** Software used to control how a digital work can be used. > **Trademark.** A word, phrase, symbol, or design that identifies goods or services.

# TREND

## New Applications for Digital Watermarking

While digital watermarks are still used to identify and help protect digital content from misuse, new applications for this technology are emerging. One such technology is *Digimarc Discover*, which enables your smartphone or tablet to recognize media (such as newspapers, magazines, product packaging, television shows, and music) in your immediate surroundings to provide you with online content linked to that media, such as downloading a coupon for a product shown in a magazine ad, viewing a video related to a magazine article, displaying pricing and product information corresponding to a product's packaging, and viewing band information for the song currently being played over a restaurant's sound system.

Available as a mobile app for smartphones and other mobile devices, Digimarc Discover uses your smartphone's camera and microphone to "look and listen" to surrounding media. The app recognizes the digital watermarks embedded in the media (such as in the textbook shown in the accompanying illustration), and then the appropriate options for the available online content and services are displayed on the phone (such as a virtual tour of the Colosseum, historical photos and other information, or prices for upcoming flights to Rome).

Applications such as Digimarc Discover that use digital watermarks enable publishers, advertising agencies, and other companies to make a variety of rich media available to customers without having to give up valuable space in print publications or product packaging (as is required with a QR code or other code that needs to be displayed on the printed media in order to be functional).

Source: Digimarc Corporation

---

online trademark infringement in recent years, particularly those involving domain names that contain, or are similar to, a trademark. For instance, several celebrities—such as Madonna and Tracy Morgan—have fought to be given the exclusive right to use what they consider their rightful domain names (Madonna.com and TracyMorgan.com, respectively). Other examples include Twitter's complaint against an organization using the domain name *twitter.org*, RadioShack's objection to a private individual using *shack.com* for the Web site of his design business, and Microsoft being accused by British Sky Broadcasting Group of trademark infringement with its SkyDrive service.

While businesses and individuals can file lawsuits to recover a disputed domain name, a faster and less-expensive option is to file a complaint with a dispute resolution provider, such as the *World Intellectual Property Organization* (*WIPO*). WIPO is a specialized agency of the United Nations and attempts to resolve international commercial disputes about intellectual property between private parties. This includes domain name disputes; in fact, WIPO has resolved more than 30,000 domain name dispute cases since it was formed. Complainants pay a filing fee to start the resolution process, and then WIPO has the power to award the disputed domain name to the most appropriate party. If the domain name was acquired with the intent to profit from the goodwill of a trademark belonging to someone else (such as by generating revenue from Web site visitors intending to go to the trademark holder's Web site or by trying to sell the domain name to the trademark holder at an inflated price) or to otherwise abuse a trademark, the act of acquiring that domain name is deemed to be **cybersquatting** and the

---

> **Cybersquatting.** The act of registering a domain name with the intent to profit from the goodwill of a trademark belonging to someone else.

trademark holder generally prevails. If the current domain name holder has a legitimate reason for using that name and does not appear to be a cybersquatter, however, WIPO may allow the holder to continue to use that domain name. For instance, WIPO ruled that TracyMorgan.com and twitter.org were confusingly similar to the actor's name and the trademark owned by Twitter, respectively, and that neither owner of the disputed domain names had a legitimate interest in their respective domain name, so WIPO transferred the disputed domain names to Tracy Morgan and Twitter, respectively. However, the owner of the design business (whose last name is Shackleton and whose nickname is "Shack") was allowed to keep the shack.com domain name because it was ruled that he had a legitimate interest in that name. The *Anticybersquatting Consumer Protection Act*, which was signed into law in 1999, makes cybersquatting illegal and it allows for penalties up to $100,000 for each willful registration of a domain name that infringes on a trademark.

Many recent cybersquatting cases are because of *typosquatting*—the act of registering a domain name that is similar to a trademark or domain name but that is slightly misspelled in hopes that individuals will accidentally arrive at the fraudulent site when trying to type the URL of the legitimate site. These fraudulent sites often contain pay-per-click advertising used to generate revenue for the typosquatter; they can also be phishing sites that use spoofed Web pages to try to obtain sensitive information from visitors (as discussed in Chapter 9), or they can redirect visitors to sites for competing products or services. To prevent typosquatting and to protect their brands and other trademarks, many companies register variations of their domain names proactively. For instance, Verizon has registered more than 10,000 domain names related to its three most visible brands (Verizon, VZ, and Fios). If a cybersquatter is causing enough damage to warrant it, companies can file a lawsuit against the cybersquatter. For instance, Verizon once sued a company for unlawfully registering 663 domain names that were either identical or confusingly similar to Verizon trademarks. In late 2008, Verizon was awarded more than $33 million in that case, which is still the largest cybersquatting judgment to date. Another form of cybersquatting involves individuals not affiliated with a company opening social media accounts using the company's brand names or variations of its brand names—typically either to use the account to sell pirated goods posing as the legitimate company, or in hopes the company will pay them to relinquish control of the accounts.

## Patents

Unlike copyrights (which protect artistic and literary works) and trademarks (which protect a company's logo and brand names), a **patent** protects inventions by granting exclusive rights of an invention to its inventor for a period of 20 years. A patented invention is typically a unique product, but it can also be a process or procedure that provides a new way of doing something or that offers a new technical solution to a problem. Like trademarks, U.S. patents are issued by the U.S. Patent and Trademark Office (USPTO). A recent patent issued to Apple for a new hotspot device is shown in Figure 13-4.

The number of patent applications, particularly those related to computer and Internet products, has skyrocketed in

**V FIGURE 13-4**
**Patents.** The patent shown here is for a new hotspot device.

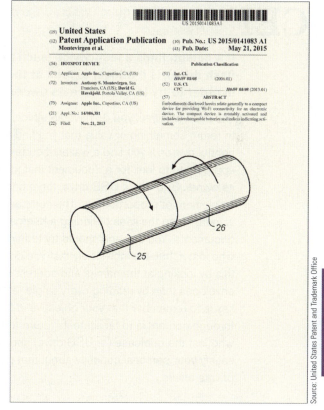

Source: United States Patent and Trademark Office

---

> **Patent.** A form of protection for an invention that can be granted by the government; gives exclusive rights of an invention to its inventor for 20 years.

recent years. In the United States, patents have also been granted for Internet business methods and models, such as Priceline.com's name-your-own-price business model and Amazon.com's one-click purchase procedure. One controversial patent granted to Google in 2013 is for "pay-for-gaze" advertising—a business model for charging advertisers according to the number of views an ad receives via a "head mounted gaze tracking device" (speculated to be Google Glass). When a product or business model is patented, no other organization can duplicate it without paying a royalty to the patent holder or risking prolonged patent litigation. Patent issues sometimes interfere with a company's new products or services and tech companies are regularly sued for patent infringement. For instance, Apple has been sued in several patent infringement lawsuits related to its iPhone, Microsoft has claimed that Linux infringed on many of its patents, and Marvell Technology was recently ordered to pay $1.17 billion for infringing on disk drive patents held by Carnegie Mellon University.

Patents can be difficult, expensive, and time consuming to obtain. However, companies routinely seek patents for new inventions (IBM was awarded 7,481 patents in 2014 and has been the patent leader for more than 20 years). Patents can also be very lucrative; consequently, businesses have been acquired, at least in part, for their patents, and patents are sometimes purchased outright. For example, Microsoft recently agreed to pay AOL $1 billion for 800 undisclosed technology patents.

## ASK THE EXPERT

Courtesy Computer Ethics Institute

**CEI** **Dr. Ramon C. Barquin,** President, Computer Ethics Institute

**If a person finds a lost device (such as a USB flash drive), is it ethical to look at the contents in order to try to determine its owner?**

The answer is yes, you do have an ethical obligation to return something of value that you find to its rightful owner. If you find a wallet, it certainly is appropriate to look for a document that identifies its owner. But, with a USB drive, there has to be an element of proportionality. The comparison here is more along the lines of finding a briefcase full of documents. You can and should try to find the person who lost it, but it is more likely that you could do this by looking at the names and addresses on the envelopes than by reading every single letter. The key is to remember that your objective in browsing through content is to facilitate its return to the person who lost the briefcase (or USB drive) and not to satisfy your personal curiosity about that person's private affairs.

## ETHICS

The term **ethics** refers to standards of moral conduct. For example, telling the truth is a matter of ethics. An unethical act is not always illegal (although it might be), but an illegal act is usually viewed as unethical by most people. For example, purposely lying to a friend is unethical but usually not illegal, while perjuring oneself in a courtroom as a witness is both illegal and unethical. Whether or not criminal behavior is involved, ethics guide our behavior and play an integral role in our lives.

Much more ambiguous than the law, ethical beliefs can vary widely from one individual to another. Ethical beliefs may also vary based on one's religion, country, race, or culture. In addition, different ethical standards can apply to different areas of one's life. For example, *personal ethics* guide an individual's personal behavior and *business ethics* guide an individual's workplace behavior. **Computer ethics** relate to an individual's computer use and are significant today because the proliferation of computers and other technology in the home and workplace provides more opportunities for unethical acts than in the past. The Internet also makes it easy to distribute information that many individuals would view as unethical

---

> **Ethics.** Overall standards of moral conduct.  > **Computer ethics.** Standards of moral conduct as they relate to computer use.

## TECHNOLOGY AND YOU

### Virtual Currency—Real or Not?

While *Second Life*, *World of Warcraft*, and other virtual worlds only exist in cyberspace, there is nothing virtual about the money being made. For instance, Ailin Graef became the first virtual world millionaire when her Second Life assets (measured in *Linden dollars*) topped $1 million in U.S. dollars.

While some types of a *virtual currency* (a digital representation of value) like Linden dollars and *World of Warcraft gold* are designed to be used in a virtual world, others are designed to be used in the real world (the IRS defines virtual currency that acts as a substitute for real currency as *convertible virtual currency*). For instance, digital gift cards like *Facebook Game Cards* and *Nintendo Points* can be used to purchase games and apps on Facebook or for Nintendo devices, respectively, and *Amazon Coins* can be used to purchase apps, games, and in-app items. And one of the most prominent convertible virtual currencies, *Bitcoins*, can be used to make purchases in numerous online games and at some online retailers (see the accompanying illustration).

One issue surrounding the growing use of virtual currency is whether or not it is a real currency and, as such, is subject to existing laws. However, a federal judge may have ended the controversy in 2013 with an opinion issued in a fraud case related to a Bitcoin-based Ponzi scheme worth millions of dollars. The defendant challenged the fraud charges on the basis that Bitcoins do not meet the definition of currency—the judge disagreed and ruled that Bitcoin is a currency or form of money, in the same way that gold and silver are commodities that are recognized as money. Today, some states are regulating the sale of virtual currency by requiring a license (such as New York's *BitLicense*) for all companies that offer virtual currency services to customers.

Another issue is the taxability of virtual profits. When virtual goods are cashed out for actual cash, it's clear that the profits should be reported as taxable income. But what about taxing virtual profits that never leave the virtual world? This issue is complicated by the fact that goods or services obtained through barter or as prizes are taxable in the United States under current law, and the fact that virtual transactions have real-world value. Some countries have already made that decision, such as Australia, which has implemented taxes on virtual income, and South Korea, which has a *value-added tax* (*VAT*) on individuals with virtual income over a certain amount. In the United States, the IRS recently ruled that virtual currency is treated as property for U.S. federal tax purposes. Specifically, wages and other payments made to service providers using virtual currency are subject to income tax, and gains or loss from the sale of virtual currency depend on whether or not the currency is a capital asset.

Source: Bitcoin Project; Amazon.com

**Virtual currencies are most often used online.**

(such as computer viruses and spyware), as well as to distribute copies of software, movies, music, and other digital content in an illegal and, therefore, unethical manner.

Whether at home, at work, or at school, individuals encounter ethical issues every day. For example, you may need to make ethical decisions such as whether or not to accept a relative's offer of a free copy of a downloaded song or movie, whether or not to have a friend help you take an online exam, whether or not to upload a photo of your friend to Facebook without asking permission, whether or not to post a rumor on a campus gossip site, or whether or not to report as taxable income the virtual money you make online, as discussed in the Technology and You box.

As an employee, you may need to decide whether or not to print your child's birthday party invitations on the office color printer, whether or not to correct your boss if he or she gives you credit for another employee's idea, or whether or not to sneak a look at information that technically you have access to but have no legitimate reason to view. IT employees, in particular, often face this latter ethical dilemma because they typically have both access and the technical ability to retrieve a wide variety of personal and professional information about other employees, such as their salary information, Web-surfing history, and e-mail.

**TIP**

Social media has introduced new ethical dilemmas, such as whether or not businesses have the right to reprimand employees over social media activity and whether or not schools have the right to limit the communications teachers have with students via social media.

Businesses also deal with a variety of ethical issues in the course of normal business activities—from determining how many computers on which a particular software program should be installed; to identifying how customer information should be obtained, used, and shared; to deciding business practices. **Business ethics** are the standards of conduct that guide a business's policies, decisions, and actions.

## Ethical Use of Copyrighted Material

Both businesses and individuals should be very careful when copying, sharing, or otherwise using copyrighted material to ensure that the material is used in both a legal and an ethical manner. Common types of copyrighted material encountered on a regular basis include books, Web-based articles, music, e-books, movies, and software; these topics are covered next.

### Books and Web-Based Articles

**TIP**

For a review of how to cite online material properly, refer to Figure 8-16 in Chapter 8.

Copyright law protects print-based books, newspaper articles, e-books, Web-based articles, and all other types of literary material. Consequently, these materials cannot be reproduced, presented as one's own original material, or otherwise used in an unauthorized manner. Students, researchers, authors, and other writers need to be especially careful when using literary material as a resource for papers, articles, books, and so forth, to ensure the material is used appropriately and is properly credited to the original author. To present someone else's work as your own is **plagiarism**, which is both a violation of copyright law and an unethical act. It can also get you fired, as some reporters have found out the hard way after faking quotes or plagiarizing content from other newspapers. Some examples of acts that would normally be considered plagiarism or not considered plagiarism are shown in Figure 13-5.

With the widespread availability of online articles and fee-based online term paper services, some students might be tempted to create their papers by copying and pasting excerpts of online content into their documents to pass off as their original work. But these students should realize that this is plagiarism, and instructors can usually tell when a paper is created in this manner. There are also online resources instructors can use to test the originality of student papers; the results of one such test are shown in Figure 13-6. Most colleges and universities have strict consequences for plagiarism, such as automatically failing the assignment or course, or being expelled from the institution. As Internet-based plagiarism continues to expand to younger and younger students, many middle schools and high schools are developing strict plagiarism policies as well.

**FIGURE 13-5**

Examples of what is and what is not normally considered plagiarism.

| PLAGIARISM | NOT PLAGIARISM |
| --- | --- |
| A student including a few sentences or a few paragraphs written by another author in his essay without crediting the original author. | A student including a few sentences or a few paragraphs written by another author in his essay, either indenting the quotation or placing it inside quotation marks, and crediting the original author with a citation in the text or with a footnote or endnote. |
| A newspaper reporter changing a few words in a sentence or paragraph written by another author and including the revised text in an article without crediting the original author. | A newspaper reporter paraphrasing a few sentences or paragraphs written by another author without changing the meaning of the text, including the paraphrased text in an article, and crediting the original author with a proper citation. |
| A student copying and pasting information from various online documents to create her research paper without crediting the original authors. | A student copying and pasting information from various online documents and using those quotes in her research paper either indented or enclosed in quotation marks with the proper citations for each author. |
| A teacher sharing a poem with a class, leading the class to believe the poem was his original work. | A teacher sharing a poem with a class, clearly identifying the poet. |

> **Business ethics.** Standards of moral conduct that guide a business's policies, decisions, and actions. > **Plagiarism.** Presenting someone else's work as your own.

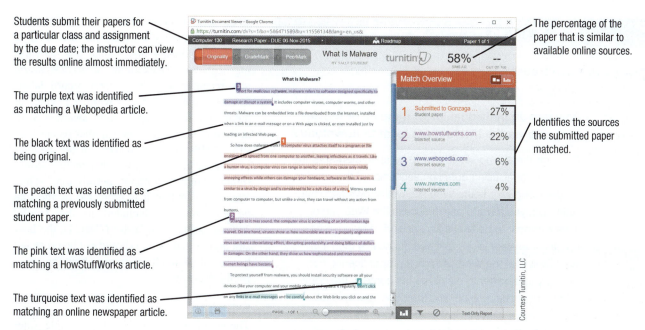

Students submit their papers for a particular class and assignment by the due date; the instructor can view the results online almost immediately.

The purple text was identified as matching a Webopedia article.

The black text was identified as being original.

The peach text was identified as matching a previously submitted student paper.

The pink text was identified as matching a HowStuffWorks article.

The turquoise text was identified as matching an online newspaper article.

The percentage of the paper that is similar to available online sources.

Identifies the sources the submitted paper matched.

Courtesy Turnitin, LLC

## Music

There have been many issues regarding the legal and ethical use of music over the past few years. The controversy started with the emergence and widespread use of *Napster* (the first peer-to-peer (P2P) music sharing site that facilitated the exchange of music files from one Napster user's computer to another). Many exchanges via the original Napster service violated copyright law and a flood of lawsuits from the music industry eventually shut down Napster and other P2P sites that were being used to exchange copyright-protected content illegally. Additional issues arose with the introduction of recordable and rewritable CD and DVD drives, portable digital media players, smartphones, and other devices that can be used to duplicate digital music. Some issues regarding the legal and ethical use of digital music have been resolved over the years. For instance, downloading a music file from a P2P site without compensating the artist and record label is a violation of copyright law and an unethical act; so is transferring legally obtained songs to a storage medium to sell or give to others. Today's wide availability of music stores and other onlines sources for legal music downloads and streaming (such as Pandora, iHeartRadio, and *Spotify* shown in Figure 13-7) give individuals a legal alternative for obtaining digital music quickly and easily. However, illegal music exchanges are still taking place and law enforcement agencies, as well as the Recording Industry Association of America (RIAA), are pursuing individuals and download sites that violate music copyrights. At the present time, a group of RIAA music labels are suing the *MP3Skull* piracy site for $22 million in damages, a permanent injunction that prevents domain name registrars from working with the site, and the rights to its domain names.

Once an MP3 file or audio CD has been obtained legally, however, most experts agree that it falls within the fair use concept for an individual to transfer those songs to a CD, computer, portable digital media player, or smartphone, as long as it is for personal, noncommercial use and does not violate a user agreement. In the past, songs downloaded from some online music stores included DRM controls, which prevented the songs from being copied to other devices. While this helped prevent the illegal copying of downloaded songs from one user to another, it also prevented users from transferring legally downloaded music from one of their devices to another. In response to user protests, many music stores today offer their songs in the universal (and DRM-free) MP3 format so they can be played on a wide range of devices.

One long-standing controversy related to digital music is the issue of royalties. While conventional radio stations pay licensing fees to air music, they have been battling record companies for years over whether or not the broadcasters should pay a royalty each time a song is aired—especially for songs recorded before 1972, which is

**FIGURE 13-6**
**Results of an online originality test.**

**FIGURE 13-7**
**Music apps.** Allow you to legally listen to music on demand on your devices.

Source: Spotify AB

SOC

## ASK THE EXPERT

Rhapsody  **Dave Hauser,** Senior Counsel, Business & Legal Affairs, Rhapsody International Inc.

**How can an individual know if music or movies available via the Internet are legal to download?**

Although there is no single way to be absolutely sure the content is legal, using common sense about the source will go a long way. Is the Web site well known and reputable? Did you have to pay to access the Web site or does it appear to be financially supported by advertising? If the answer is yes to these questions, then it is more likely that the Web site has a proper license from the copyright owner to distribute the content, the copyright owner is being paid, and the download is legal. If, on the other hand, the Web site appears to be "too good to be true," with no fees or advertisements, no terms of use, or is a disreputable or an unknown source, there is a strong likelihood that the Web site is not properly authorized to distribute the content. If so, don't use it because both you and the Web site could be held liable for copyright infringement with statutory damages of up to $150,000 per infringement.

when federal copyright law began to protect recordings (songs recorded before 1972 are protected only under state law, to varying degrees). For example, *Sirius XM Radio* was recently sued by several record labels for using pre-1972 songs without paying for them—the record labels were awarded $210 million in back royalties. Another recent lawsuit (against *Vimeo*) focuses on the liability of content hosts for posts that include copyrighted content without permission. While Vimeo argues that it is protected by the *safe harbor provision* included in the *Digital Millennium Copyright Act (DMCA)*, the lawsuit argues that Vimeo should not be protected because it should have known about the copyright infringement.

### E-Books

The popularity of e-books (for example, sales for e-books at Amazon.com have surpassed print books for several years) has resulted in legal and ethical issues similar to those found in the digital music industry, as well as a rapid increase in piracy. In fact, some e-books have been shared or downloaded illegally more than 100,000 times within the first few days of an e-book release.

### Movies

Since 1984, when Disney and Universal sued Sony to stop production of the *Betamax* (the first personal VCR), concern about movie piracy has increased dramatically. The lawsuit was eventually decided in Sony's favor—the Supreme Court upheld the consumers' rights to record shows for convenience (called *time shifting*), as long as it was for personal use. As a result of this decision, VCR use became commonplace. Interestingly, in direct contrast to the views held by the entertainment industry in 1984, videos have been credited with boosting Hollywood's revenues tremendously over the years. Nevertheless, the entertainment industry continues to be concerned about the ability of consumers to make copies of movies—especially today, because digital content can be duplicated an unlimited number of times without losing quality. The Motion Picture Association of America (MPAA) estimates that more than 700 million movies and TV shows were shared illegally via P2P sites in the United States in one year alone.

**FIGURE 13-8**

**Netflix.** Allows you to legally stream movies and TV shows to your TV, computer, or mobile device.

There are many online services that can be used to download or stream movies, TV shows, and other video content (one example is shown in Figure 13-8). To prevent individuals from making unauthorized copies of feature films purchased on DVDs or downloaded via the Internet, many of these items contain copy protection or some other form of DRM. Movie pirates, however, can often circumvent copy protection with software and other tools in order to duplicate the movies and create illegal copies. Pirated copies of movies are also often created today by videotaping them with a camcorder during a prerelease screening or on the opening day of a movie. This practice has resulted in a vast number of movies becoming illegally available on DVDs and via the Internet at about the same time they arrive in theaters. As a result, Congress passed the *Family Entertainment and*

*Copyright Act of 2005*, which makes transmitting or recording a movie during a performance at a U.S. movie theater illegal. To help identify and prosecute a "cammer," most movie studios now embed invisible digital watermarks in each print released to a theater. The information contained in these watermarks can be used to identify the location where the movie was recorded once a bootleg copy of a movie is discovered.

The access to both authorized and unauthorized copies of movies via the Internet, as well as the widespread use of DVRs and DVD players today, create new legal and ethical dilemmas for individuals. If one individual records a television show and then shares it with a friend via the Internet or a DVD disc, does that go beyond the concept of fair use? What if you download a video-on-demand movie and then share it with a friend? Is that any different, legally or ethically, from sharing a movie rented from a brick-and-mortar video store with a friend before you return it? What about the placeshifting products on the market, such as the Slingbox discussed in Chapter 7? If you use such a product to transfer a movie or TV show obtained through your cable or satellite TV connection to another location, are you rebroadcasting that content or simply placeshifting it?

While the answers to these questions have yet to be unequivocally decided, distributing bootleg copies of movies via the Internet is both illegal and unethical. There have been many local, state, and federal operations in the United States and other countries in recent years focused on targeting online piracy of copyrighted software, movies, music, and games and the MPAA regularly pursues civil litigation against movie pirates. Other strategies include increasing the availability of legal content online, continuing to develop technologies that prevent the duplication of digital content, working with online advertising networks and online payment companies to discourage them from placing ads or facilitating payments on pirate sites, and adding technologies (such as *Digital Copy*) that enable consumers to watch purchased video content on more than one personal device.

## Software

*Software piracy* is the unauthorized copying of a computer program; it is illegal in the United States and many other—but not all—countries. Software piracy can take many forms, including individuals making illegal copies of programs to give to friends, businesses installing software on more computers than permitted in the program's end-user license agreement (EULA), computer retailers installing unlicensed copies of software on computers sold to consumers, and large-scale operations in which the software and its packaging are illegally duplicated and then sold as supposedly legitimate products. Pirated software is commonly offered for sale at online auctions; it can also be downloaded from some Web sites and P2P file sharing services.

Software piracy affects both individuals and businesses. For instance, some software companies charge higher prices and have less money available for research and development because of the losses from software pirates, which ultimately hurts law-abiding consumers. In addition, individuals and businesses risk infection from malware included with pirated software. In fact, a recent study by research firm IDC estimates that the total annual cost to businesses of dealing with malware from pirated software exceeds $490 billion.

To counteract piracy performed because of time or convenience issues, many software companies offer consumers the option of downloading software and, therefore, giving them a legal option for obtaining software that is as fast and convenient as downloading a pirated version. Another antipiracy tool is requiring a unique activation code (also called a *registration code*, an *activation key*, or a *product key*) before the software can be installed, before certain key features of a program are unlocked, or after a trial period has expired (see the WinZip screen in Figure 13-9). Typically, the activation code is included in the product packaging (for software purchased on CD or DVD) or it is displayed on the screen or is sent

**FIGURE 13-9**
**Activation codes.**

The activation code supplied after purchasing the software needs to be entered here before the program can be used.

Source: WinZip Computing

# INSIDE THE INDUSTRY

## Digital Counterfeiting

The availability of high-quality, full-color imaging products (such as scanners, color printers, and color copiers) has made *digital counterfeiting*—creating counterfeit copies of physical items (such as currency and other printed resources) using computers and other types of digital equipment—easier and less costly than in the recent past. The U.S. Secret Service estimates that more than 60% of all counterfeit money today is produced digitally—up from 1% in 1996. With digital counterfeiting, the bill (or other item to be counterfeited) is either color copied or it is scanned into a computer and then printed. In addition to counterfeiting currency, other items that are digitally counterfeited include fake business checks, credit cards, printed collectibles (such as baseball cards or celebrity autographs), and fake identification papers (such as corporate IDs, driver's licenses, passports, and visas)—see the accompanying photo. Counterfeiting is illegal in the United States and is taken very seriously. For creating or knowingly circulating counterfeit currency, for instance, offenders can face up to 15 years in prison for each offense.

To prevent the counterfeiting of U.S. currency, the Treasury Department releases new currency designs every 7 to 10 years. These new designs contain features such as *microprinting*, *watermarks*, a *security thread*, a *security ribbon, color-shifting ink,* and *raised printing* that make the new currency much more difficult to duplicate than older currency. Because the watermarks, security thread, and security ribbon are embedded in the paper, and because the paper used with real U.S. bills cannot legally be made by paper mills for any other purpose, counterfeiters are unable to duplicate these security features when creating counterfeit bills. In addition, hardware and software companies that have adopted the *counterfeit deterrence system* (*CDS*) developed by the *Central Bank Counterfeit Deterrence Group* (*CBCDG*) help to deter the use of digital counterfeiting. For instance, Adobe Photoshop does not allow images of U.S. currency to be edited and many color copiers print invisible codes on copied documents, making counterfeit items copied on those machines traceable.

Measures for preventing the counterfeiting of other types of documents—such as checks and identification cards—include using RFID tags, digital watermarks, and other difficult-to-reproduce content. For example, new *smart labels* (see one example in the accompanying illustration) that can be attached to paper-based documents, as well as to product labels and packaging for other physical products that are frequently counterfeited, can be used to verify that a document or product is genuine.

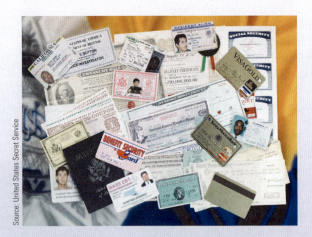
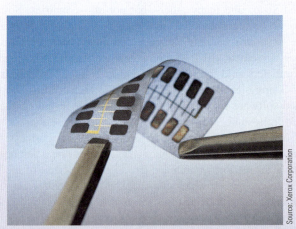

**Digitally counterfeited documents (left); smart labels (right).**

to the user via e-mail once payment is made (for downloaded software). A related tool is checking the validity of a software installation before upgrades or other resources related to the program can be accessed. The goal of these techniques is to make pirated software unusable enough so that individuals will buy the licensed software.

Other antipiracy techniques used by software companies include watching online auction sites and requesting the removal of suspicious items, as well as buying pirated copies of software via Web sites and then filing lawsuits against the sellers. For a look at another way items are duplicated and distributed as genuine—digital counterfeiting—see the Inside the Industry box.

## Ethical Use of Resources and Information

A variety of resources (such as school computers, company computers, and equipment) and types of information (such as customer or employee information) can be used in an unethical manner. For example, some employees use company computers for personal use, some students perform dishonest acts while completing assignments or taking exams, and some job applicants provide erroneous or misleading information during the application or interview process.

### Ethical Use of School or Company Resources

What is considered proper and ethical use of school or company resources may vary from school to school or company to company. To explain what is allowed, many schools and businesses have policies that specify which activities are allowed and which are forbidden. Often, these policies are available as a written **code of conduct** that is included in a student or employee handbook. They are also often available online via an organization's intranet or Web site (a code of conduct was shown in Figure 9-6 in Chapter 9). Policies can vary; for example, one school may allow the use of school computers to download software and another school may not, and one business may allow limited use of the office photocopier or printer for personal use while another may forbid it. As a result, all students and employees should find out what is considered ethical use of resources at their school or place of business, including what types of computer and Internet activities are considered acceptable, and what personal use (if any) of resources, such as computers, printers, photocopiers, telephones, and fax machines, is allowed. To enforce its policies, businesses may use employee monitoring, which was discussed in Chapter 9.

Another code widely used by various industries and organizations is a **code of ethics**. Codes of ethics (see the IEEE code of ethics in Figure 13-10) summarize the moral guidelines adopted by a professional society or other organization. They typically address such issues as honesty, integrity, proper use of intellectual property, confidentiality, and accountability. So, while codes of conduct usually address specific activities that can and cannot be performed, codes of ethics cover broader ethical standards of conduct.

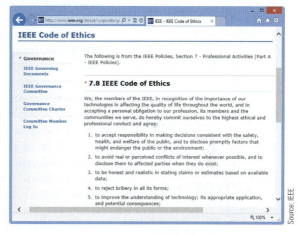

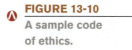

**Source: IEEE**

Although employees are typically forbidden from revealing confidential or proprietary information to outsiders, a dilemma exists when that information is related to an illegal, an unethical, or a dangerous activity involving the business. Employees who reveal wrongdoing within an organization to the public or to authorities are referred to as *whistle-blowers*. These individuals have varying degrees of protection from retaliation (such as being fired) for whistle-blowing. The type and extent of protection depends on the kind of wrongdoing and the organization involved, as well as the state in which the company and employee are located. The *Sarbanes-Oxley Act* (also called the *Corporate Responsibility Act* and signed into law in mid-2002) provides federal protection for whistle-blowers who report alleged violations of Securities and Exchange Commission rules or any federal law relating to shareholder fraud.

**FIGURE 13-10**
A sample code of ethics.

### Ethical Use of Employee and Customer Information

While a business may be legally bound by such restrictions as employee confidentiality laws, union contracts, and its customer privacy policy, there are gray areas inside which ethical decisions need to be made. For example, should an ISP comply with a request from a government for customer e-mail records or the identity of a customer matching an IP address? Should a company use marketing data that was mined from individuals' social networking

> **Code of conduct.** A policy, often for a school or business, that specifies allowable use of resources, such as computers and other equipment.
> **Code of ethics.** A policy, often for an organization or industry, that specifies overall moral guidelines adopted by that organization or industry.

sites? Or should a business share or sell customer information, even if it is legal to do so? This latter decision is one that many businesses have struggled with, especially in challenging economic times when a quick source of revenue gained from selling customer data is tempting. Although some businesses have succumbed to this temptation and have sold their customer lists, others believe that any short-term gains achieved through ethically questionable acts will adversely affect customer loyalty and will ultimately hurt the business in the long run. An emerging issue is who owns an employee's work-related social media accounts. There have been several lawsuits surrounding this issue, such as an employee who took company Twitter followers with him to a new company and an employee who discovered that her employer was posting tweets from her account when she was in the hospital. It is expected that soon social media laws will be developed to resolve these types of issues.

To prepare future employees for these types of decisions, most business schools incorporate business ethics into their curriculum. For example, the *Giving Voice to Values* (*GVV*) business school curriculum, created by the Aspen Institute and Yale School of Management and being piloted at over 50 institutions, focuses on ethical implementation of values-based leadership.

## Cheating and Falsifying Information

Just as the Internet makes it easier for individuals to plagiarize documents, the use of computers, mobile devices, and the Internet also makes it easier for individuals to cheat on assignments or exams, or to perform other similar unethical acts.

Unfortunately, cheating at all levels is rampant today. Recently, for instance, 78 cadets at the Air Force Academy were accused of cheating on an online calculus test, about 70 students at Harvard University were required to withdraw from school for one year after nearly half of the students in a class were suspected of cheating on a take-home final exam, and three San Diego elementary schools lost their standardized API scores for two years after teachers were accused of various forms of cheating during the state tests. Acts of cheating commonly performed today include creating a paper from material plagiarized from Web sites, storing notes on a smartphone to view during a test, texting answers to another student during a test, or taking photos of exam questions to pass on to a student taking the test at a later time. In addition to technology making it easier to cheat, it also may make it feel less like cheating. During one recent study of middle and high school students, for instance, about 25% of the students didn't think storing notes on a smartphone or texting during an exam constituted cheating.

Traditionally, it was typically weaker students who cheated to prevent failing a course or an exam. Today, however, studies have shown that honor students and others with higher GPAs are more likely to cheat, possibly due to the increased competition and pressure to succeed—according to Donald McCabe of Rutgers University, "Students have told me over the years they have to get the job done, and they don't care how." But whether they realize it or not, students who choose to cheat are cheating themselves of an education. They are also being unfair to honest students by possibly altering the grading curve. Widespread cheating can also have a negative impact on society, such as when underprepared employees enter the workforce.

**FIGURE 13-11**

**Academic honor codes.** Students at Smeal College of Business sign the honor code during the first week of classes.

To explain to students what behavior is expected of them, many schools are developing *academic honor codes*. Research has shown that having an academic honor code effectively reduces cheating. For example, one McCabe study found that cheating on tests on campuses with honor codes is typically one-third to one-half less than on campuses that do not have honor codes, and the level of cheating on written assignments is one-quarter to one-third lower. To bring attention to their honor codes, some schools encourage incoming students to sign their honor codes upon admission. For instance, all Penn State Smeal College of Business students are invited to sign the school's honor code publicly (see Figure 13-11) at the beginning of each semester. Regardless of whether or not students choose to sign the honor code, they are required to abide by it.

Like academic cheating, lying on a job application or résumé is more common than most of us may think it is. The practice of providing false

Source: Matthew Ross of the Smeal College of Business

information in an attempt to look more qualified for a job, sometimes referred to as *résumé padding*, is both dishonest and unethical. It is also widespread. In a recent study by employment screening service HireRight, 69% of the companies surveyed reported catching a job candidate lying on his or her résumé. In addition to being unethical, providing false information to a potential employer can have serious consequences—many companies have a policy that lists termination as the appropriate action for employees who were hired based on falsified résumés or applications. Being blacklisted from an industry or being sued for breach of contract are also possibilities. Résumé writers should remember that background checks are easily available online, which means credentials are easy to check and verify. Even if individuals believe they will not be caught, applicants should not embellish their résumés or job applications to any extent because it is an unethical thing to do. Another recent ethical issue surrounding IT employees is cheating on IT certification exams. Copies of certification questions and entire certification exams are available for purchase online, and some Web sites offer the services of "gunmen" (usually located in Asia) who will take certification tests for individuals for a fee. In response, companies that offer IT certifications are looking at the security of their testing processes to try to put a stop to this new type of cheating.

There are personal situations that may tempt some individuals to provide inaccurate information, such as when writing online dating profiles, participating in chat rooms, or in other situations when individuals may wish to appear to be someone different from who they really are. There are differing opinions about how ethical these actions are—some individuals believe that it is a person's right to portray himself or herself in any way desired; others feel that any type of dishonesty is unethical.

## Online Hoaxes and Digital Manipulation

Most people realize that information in print media can, at times, be misleading and that photos can be manipulated. Information found on the Internet may also be inaccurate, misleading, or biased. Some of this type of information is published on Web pages; other information is passed on via e-mail. Two types of computer-oriented misinformation include online hoaxes and digital manipulation.

### Online Hoaxes

An **online hoax** is an inaccurate statement or story—such as the "fact" that flesh-eating bacteria have been found in banana shipments or that Applebee's will send you a gift certificate for forwarding an e-mail—spread via the Internet. These hoaxes are sometimes published on Web pages, but they are more commonly spread via e-mail or social media. Common online hoax subjects include nonexistent computer viruses, serious health risks, impending terrorist attacks, chain letters, and free prizes or giveaways. Inaccurate information posted online just to be misleading can also be considered an online hoax. E-mail hoaxes are written with the purpose of being circulated to as many people as possible. Some are started as experiments to see how fast and how far information can travel via the Internet; others originate from a joke or the desire to frighten people. Similar to spam, e-mail hoaxes can be annoying, waste people's time, bog down e-mail systems, and clog users' Inboxes. Because online hoaxes are so common, it is a good idea to double-check any warning you receive by e-mail or read on a Web site before passing that warning on to another person, regardless of how realistic or frightening the information appears to be (sites like the one shown in Figure 13-12 can help you research potential hoaxes).

**FIGURE 13-12**

**Hoax-Slayer.** This is one site that can be used to research possible online hoaxes.

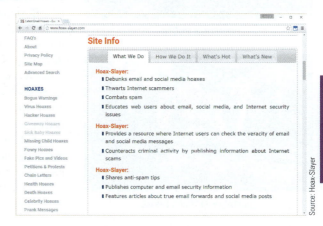

Source: Hoax-Slayer

SOC

---

>**Online hoax.** An inaccurate statement or story spread through the use of computers.

## Digital Manipulation

Computers make it very easy to copy or modify text, images, photographs, music, and other digital content. In addition to being a copyright concern, **digital manipulation** (digitally altering digital content) can be used to misquote individuals, repeat comments out of context, retouch photographs—even create false or misleading photographs—and so is an ethical concern, as well. While there are some beneficial, ethical, noncontroversial applications of digital manipulation (such as aging photos of missing children to show what they may look like at the present time, or altering photos of wanted criminals or suspects to show possible alternate appearances for law enforcement purposes), the matter of altering photos for publication purposes is the subject of debate. Some publications and photographers see no harm in altering photographs to remove an offending item (such as a telephone pole behind someone's head), to remove red-eye or otherwise make someone look a little more attractive, to illustrate a point, or to increase circulation; others view any change in content as unethical and a great disservice to both the public and our history. For example, fifty years from now, will anyone know that a staged or altered photograph of a historical event was not an actual depiction of the event?

Although manipulation of photographs has occurred for quite some time in tabloids and other publications not known as being reputable news sources, there have been several incidents of more reputable news publications using digitally altered photographs in recent years. Many of these became known because the unaltered photograph was used in another publication at about the same time. One of the most widely publicized cases occurred in 1994, just following the arrest of O. J. Simpson. While *Newsweek* ran Simpson's mug shot unaltered, *TIME* magazine darkened the photograph, creating a more sinister look and making Simpson's skin color appear darker than it actually is. This photo drew harsh criticism from Simpson supporters who felt the photograph made him appear guilty, the African-American community who viewed the alteration as an act of racial insensitivity, and news photographers who felt that the action damaged the credibility not only of that particular magazine but also of all journalists.

A more recent example is the case of a one-time Pulitzer Prize finalist who resigned from a Toledo, Ohio, newspaper after it was discovered that he had submitted for publication nearly 80 doctored photos in just the 14 weeks prior to his resignation, including one sports photo of a basketball game with a digitally added basketball placed in midair. Other recent instances of digitally manipulated images being printed in news media include a photo of an Iranian missile test that appeared in many newspapers but that contained a digitally added missile to replace one that did not fire during the test; a photo of a Boston Marathon bombing victim that appeared in the New York *Daily News* but that was edited to make the victim's injuries appear less severe than they were; and an altered photo of Michelle Obama at the Academy Awards—instead of showing the real sleeveless, scoop neck gown she wore, Iran's Fars News Agency added sleeves and a higher neckline to the photo that is posted on its Web site (see Figure 13-13).

Perhaps the most disturbing thing about known alterations such as these is that some may never have been noticed and, consequently, may have been accepted as true representations. Adding to the problem of unethical digital manipulation is that, unlike film cameras, digital cameras don't have photo negatives that could be used to show what photographs actually looked like at the time they were taken. Although some publications allow the use of "photo illustrations," others have strict rules about digital manipulation—especially for

**FIGURE 13-13**

**Digital manipulation.** The digitally manipulated photo (bottom) added sleeves and a higher neckline to the real photo (top) of Michelle Obama.

**ORIGINAL PHOTO**

**DIGITALLY ALTERED PHOTO**

Chris Pizzello/Invision/AP

> **Digital manipulation.** The alteration of digital content, usually text or photographs.

news photojournalists. For example, 20% of the photos in the final round of the 2015 World Press Photo competition were disqualified due to excessive digital manipulation.

## Ethical Business Practices and Decision Making

Most businesses must make a variety of ethics-related business decisions, such as whether or not to sell a product or service that some may find offensive or objectionable, whether or not to utilize services that mine social networking sites for personal data for marketing purposes, whether or not to install video cameras in the workplace for monitoring purposes, and whether or not to perform controversial research. In addition, corporate integrity, as it relates to accounting practices and proper disclosure, is a business ethics topic that has come to the forefront recently.

### Fraudulent Reporting and Other Scandalous Activities

Following the large number of corporate scandals occurring in the past decade or so, business ethics have moved into the public eye. The scandals, such as the ones surrounding executives at Enron, Tyco International, and WorldCom, involved lies, fraud, deception, and other illegal and unethical behavior. This behavior forced both Enron and WorldCom into bankruptcy proceedings. When asked to comment on the scandals, then 3Com Chief Executive Officer Bruce Claflin said on CNBC, "I would argue we do not have an accounting problem—we have an ethics problem."

In reaction to the scandals, Congress passed the *Sarbanes-Oxley Act of 2002*. This law includes provisions to improve the quality of financial reporting, independent audits, and accounting services for public companies; to increase penalties for corporate wrongdoing; to protect the objectivity and independence of securities analysts; and to require CEOs and CFOs to vouch personally for the truth and fairness of their company's disclosures. Businesses need to keep current laws in mind, as well as the businesses' ethical standards, when preparing financial reports, press releases, and other important documents that represent a company's position.

### Ethically Questionable Business Decisions

One ethical issue a business may run into is whether or not to implement a business process or decision that is ethically questionable. For example, Marriott was recently fined by the FCC for blocking Internet access from attendees at a conference in order to force them to purchase Internet access from the hotel, Uber has been accused of having employees schedule and then cancel rides via competing firms to decrease the competitor's availability, and Google is under investigation in the European Union for distorting search results to drive shoppers to the Google shopping service. Other ethically questionable business decisions relate to customer privacy. For example, several plastic surgeons have been sued recently for posting pre-op and post-op photos of patients on their Web sites; in one current case, the photos were posted even though the patient signed a statement that she did not give consent to use her photos for promotional purposes.

### Ethically Questionable Products or Services

Another ethical issue a business may run into is whether or not to sell products or services that some people find objectionable. For example, the eBay Web site states that it prohibits the sale of some controversial or sensitive items, in addition to illegal items. For instance, it will not allow live or mounted animals, ivory, weapons, military items, mailing lists, and potentially offensive material including ethnically offensive material and Nazi memorabilia, even though sellers may legally be able to sell such items elsewhere.

Another ethical decision for businesses that allow individuals to upload content to their Web sites (such as social networking sites, wikis, classified ad sites, forums, and photo or video sharing sites) is how (if at all) they should monitor the content posted on their sites. For instance, YouTube relies on the user community to flag videos that

**TIP**

The widespread use of social media has also led to a new ethics dilemma in the medical field—whether or not to use social networking sites to evaluate patient behaviors that affect treatment, such as the recent incident of a liver transplant team finding a photo that a transplant candidate had posted on his Twitter feed that showed him drinking, which contradicted his claims of sobriety.

**SOC**

might be inappropriate for some viewers (such as the Saddam Hussein execution video posted on YouTube shortly after that execution took place); flagged videos are reviewed by YouTube staff and removed if they violate YouTube guidelines. In another example, Craigslist has been under fire for years for numerous crimes (including rape, murder, prostitution, and attempted baby-selling) that have occurred via ads posted on its site and, recently, police investigators announced that they believe Facebook pages are being used by terrorists to recruit young people in Indonesia. In response, Craigslist has eliminated its adult services category and Facebook says it removes any reported content that promotes terrorism or contains direct statements of hate and disables the account.

Companies that do business in more than one country also have global considerations to address. For instance, a Brazilian court once ordered YouTube to shut down access to a racy video clip of a Brazilian celebrity and her boyfriend on the beach, even though YouTube is a U.S. company. Cultural issues such as these are discussed in more detail shortly.

Another decision is the need for age verification. To protect children from predators, many states are pushing social networking sites, such as Facebook, to implement age-verification systems. At the present time, the minimum age to open an account on many social networking sites (including Facebook, Kik, and Snapchat) is 13 but the age isn't verified (Facebook, for instance, just requires the individual creating the account to enter an appropriate birth date). Age-verification procedures also benefit the adults who use these sites so they know they are acting appropriately with other members. Businesses that offer products or services that are inappropriate for children (such as alcohol, tobacco, adult movies and video games, pornography, online gambling, and even movie previews) also need to make decisions regarding access; for example, the types of safeguards they need to provide in order to ensure children do not have access to these products and services. They also need to determine if the company is required legally, or just ethically, to provide these safeguards. This is especially significant for businesses with an e-commerce presence. In a conventional store, individuals can be asked to show an ID to prove they are of the required age before they are allowed to buy tobacco products, alcohol, pornographic materials, and other products that cannot legally be sold to minors. But, during an online transaction, it is much more difficult to verify that a buyer is the required age.

To comply with state and federal laws, as well as to protect themselves from potential litigation, Web sites selling or providing adult products and services should implement adequate age-verification procedures. Some sites require visitors to click a statement declaring they are the required age or to enter a valid credit card number before accessing or purchasing adult-only content or products. However, these precautions can be bypassed easily by underage visitors. Other sites require proof of age at delivery, which is a safer precaution for physical goods purchased online and is required by law in some states for certain types of shipments. Even safer is using an *online age- and identity-verification service*, such as *Veratad* (which verifies individuals based on comparing submitted personal information with public records from trusted sources) or *Jumio* (which verifies individuals by capturing and validating an official document such as a driver's license or passport—see Figure 13-14).

The decisions about which products or services to offer online and offline are important—and sometimes difficult—ethical decisions for businesses to make. Typically, these decisions are based on the company's overall corporate mission and desired public image. Consequently, some businesses may choose not to sell adult-only content at all. Others may decide to sell it via the Internet only in conjunction with a third-party age- and identity-verification service, or to sell those products or services online but require an adult to sign for the items when they are delivered. Still other businesses may feel that a warning statement or similar precaution on their Web sites is all that is needed, and that it is the parents' responsibility to make sure their children do not purchase illegal or inappropriate items or view adult-only content via the Internet.

**FIGURE 13-14**

**Online age- and identity-verification services.** This service uses a smartphone app that scans a customer's official document to verify he or she is the required age for a transaction.

Source: Jumio, Inc.

## Workplace Monitoring

As discussed in Chapter 9, the majority of businesses in the United States today monitor employees to some extent. Although businesses have the right and responsibility to ensure that employees are productive and that company resources are not being abused, many believe that businesses also have an ethical responsibility to inform employees of any monitoring that takes place. This is especially true in countries other than the United States, such as in the European Union where companies are much more limited in what types of monitoring they can do legally without notifying employees. One related issue that is occurring during the hiring process is social media scrutiny. While it is not unusual or viewed as unethical for a company to view the public information an applicant posts online, some hiring managers are asking applicants to log on to their social media accounts during interviews in order for the manager to review the content, and some require applicants and employees to be Facebook friends with their human resources liasons—which is considered by many to cross the ethical line.

## Cultural Considerations

With today's global economy, businesses also need to be sensitive to the ethical differences that may exist among different businesses located in the same country, as well as among businesses located in different countries. Ethics are fundamentally based on values, so when beliefs, laws, customs, and traditions vary among businesses, the ethics associated with those businesses will likely differ as well.

Ethical decisions need to be made whenever a business practice or product is legal or socially acceptable in one country but not in another. For instance, an individual may be able to purchase a bootleg copy of a software program, music CD, or movie in person or online from vendors in countries (such as China or Thailand, shown in Figure 13-15) where copies of these types of items are legal or where copyright law is not strongly enforced. This raises the question of ethical responsibility. Is it the individual's responsibility not to make these types of unethical purchases, even if technology makes it possible? What legal and ethical responsibility do online auction sites and other businesses that may unknowingly facilitate illegal transactions have to ensure that customers do not have access to products or services that are illegal in their customers' locations?

In addition to legal issues, organizations conducting business in other countries should also take into consideration the ethical standards prevalent in the countries with which they do business. Factors such as gender roles, religious beliefs, and cultural customs should be considered and respected when corresponding, negotiating, and otherwise interacting with businesses located in other countries. For example, some cultures may require a handshake or other ritual that is impossible to carry out online in order to close a deal. In this case, while the terms of the deal may be carried out online, the deal itself would need to be closed in person. Businesses should also be careful not to offend individuals from other countries or other cultures that they do business with. Some straightforward questions acceptable in the United States—such as a request to verify certain numbers or double-check a source—may be viewed as an insult in some cultures. And in some countries, you can be arrested for some types of social media posts, such as the teacher who is currently serving 11 years in prison in Kuwait for posting an insulting tweet about the country's ruler.

To prepare students properly to succeed in our global economy, some business schools include diversity and cross-cultural training in their curriculum. Similarly, some international organizations arrange for their employees to have such training prior to traveling out of the country.

iStockphoto.com/tbradford

**FIGURE 13-15**

**Cultural considerations.** In some countries, bootleg copies of music CDs and movie DVDs are sold openly.

**CAUTION  CAUTION  CAUTION  CAUTION  CAUTION  CAUTION  CAUT**

When purchasing goods from another country, it is important to realize that the laws regarding the sale of products, as well as the laws regarding the privacy of personal information supplied to a vendor during a transaction, vary from one country to another. Avoid purchasing questionable goods online and avoid providing personal information to any Web site in a country that may have lax privacy laws—as a minimum, be sure to read the privacy statements for any Web site carefully before you provide them with any personal information you do not want to be shared with others.

## COMPUTERS AND HEALTH

Despite their many benefits, computers can pose a threat to a user's physical and mental well-being. Repetitive stress injuries and other injuries related to the workplace environment are estimated to account for one-third of all serious workplace injuries and cost employees, employers, and insurance companies in lost wages, healthcare expenses, legal costs, and workers' compensation claims. Other physical dangers (such as heat burns and hearing loss) can be associated with computers and related technology, and there are some concerns about the long-term effect of using computers and other related devices. Stress, burnout, computer/Internet addiction, and other emotional health problems are more difficult to quantify, although many experts believe computer-related emotional health problems are on the rise. While researchers are continuing to investigate the physical and emotional risks of computer use and while researchers are working to develop strategies for minimizing those risks, all computer users should be aware of the possible effects of computers on their health, and what they can do today to stay healthy.

### Physical Health

Common physical conditions caused by computer use include eyestrain, blurred vision, fatigue, headaches, backaches, and wrist and finger pain. Some conditions are classified as **repetitive stress injuries** (**RSIs**), in which hand, wrist, shoulder, or neck pain is caused by performing the same physical movements over and over again. For instance, extensive keyboard and mouse use has been associated with RSIs, although RSIs can be caused by non-computer-related activities, as well. One RSI related to the repetitive movements made when using a keyboard is **carpal tunnel syndrome** (**CTS**)—a painful and crippling condition affecting the hands and wrists. CTS occurs when the nerve in the *carpal tunnel* located on the underside of the wrist is compressed. An RSI associated with typing on the tiny keyboards commonly found on smartphones and other mobile devices is **De Quervain's tendonitis**—a painful condition affecting the tendons on the thumb side of the wrists. Another physical condition is *computer vision syndrome* (*CVS*)—a collection of eye and vision problems associated with computer and mobile device use. The most common symptoms are eyestrain or eye fatigue, dry eyes, burning eyes, light sensitivity, blurred vision, headaches, and pain in the shoulders, neck, or back. Eyestrain and CVS are growing more common as individuals are increasingly reading content on the small displays commonly built into smartphones and other mobile devices. Other conditions related to mobile device use include *gorilla arm* (a term coined by Apple's Steve Jobs to refer to the arm fatigue associated with the prolonged vertical use of a touch screen) and *iPad shoulder* (a term used to refer to the shoulder and neck injuries that people who look down at a tablet in their laps are at risk for).

> **TIP**
>
> A recent study found that 20–30% of viruses on a glass surface like a smartphone screen will transfer to your fingertips—to be safe, don't touch your mouth or eyes while using your phone, unless you wash your hands first.

> **TIP**
>
> To avoid gorilla arm, use an external keyboard if you need to do much typing while your touch screen computer or tablet is in a stand.

>**Repetitive stress injury (RSI).** A type of injury, such as carpal tunnel syndrome, that is caused by performing the same physical movements over and over again. >**Carpal tunnel syndrome (CTS).** A painful and crippling condition affecting the hands and wrists that can be caused by computer use. >**De Quervain's tendonitis.** A painful condition affecting the tendons on the thumb side of the wrist.

Some recent physical health concerns center around the heat from devices commonly held in the hands or lap. For instance, studies have indicated that the temperature on the underside of a notebook computer can exceed 139° Fahrenheit and an iPad can reach 116° Fahrenheit when performing CPU-intensive tasks. *Laptop desks* or notebook cooling stands (such as the one shown in Figure 2-14 in Chapter 2) can help protect your lap when it must be used as your work surface.

Another growing physical health concern is noise-induced hearing loss, mainly due to playing music on mobile devices with the volume turned up high and to the earbud headsets typically used with these devices that deliver sound directly into the ear. In addition, people often listen to the music stored on these devices while they are on the go; as a result, they may increase the volume in an attempt to drown out outside noise, further posing a risk to their hearing. To protect against hearing loss, experts suggest a 60/60 rule, which means using earbuds for only about 60 minutes per day with the volume less than 60% of the device's maximum volume. For extended use, *noise reduction headphones* that help block out external noise to allow listeners to hear music better at lower volumes can help, as can using over-the-ear-headphones instead of earbuds and using an external speaker whenever possible.

Another danger is text messaging while driving. There have been many cases of texting-related car accidents, including many fatalities, and it is estimated that at least 25% of all auto collisions involve mobile phones. According to an AT&T study, 70% of people engage in smartphone activities (including texting, e-mailing, and social networking activities) while driving. Currently, 46 states in the United States have laws against texting while driving and 14 have laws against using a handheld phone while driving. Many states also have stricter laws for specific categories of drivers; for instance, 38 states ban mobile phone use by novice drivers and 20 states prohibit it by school bus drivers. While some feel these laws are a step in the right direction, studies have found that even using a mobile phone with a hands-free device still distracts drivers. One possible solution is using a service or an app (see Figure 13-16) that disables the driver's phone when the car is in motion. These services and apps are most commonly used by parents to protect their children and by employers to protect their employees as well as reduce their liability in case of an accident. Typically, the service or app responds to all incoming calls and texts to state that the owner is driving; for safety reasons, virtually all services and apps permit outgoing 911 calls. In addition, the U.S. Department of Transportation is requesting that automakers incorporate features in new cars to reduce driver smartphone use, such as disabling smartphones that are paired with the car when the car is in motion or including a proximity sensor that sets off an alarm (similar to a seatbelt reminder) whenever the driver uses a phone.

An additional health concern is the possible risks due to the radiation emitted from wireless devices, such as smartphones, Wi-Fi and Bluetooth devices, wireless peripherals, and so forth. Mobile phones, in particular, have been studied for years because of their close proximity to the user's head. The results of the studies have been conflicting, with many experts believing that the possible health risks (such as cancer and brain tumors) due to wireless technology have been exaggerated, and others believing the risks are very real. According to the FDA, the majority of studies have not found an association between cell phone use and any health problems. However, until more conclusive research results are available, some health officials recommend keeping the device away from your head as much as possible, such as by using the speakerphone mode or a Bluetooth headset, or by texting instead of talking. In addition, parents may want to limit the amount of time their children spend on a smartphone.

Courtesy Cellcontrol

**FIGURE 13-16**

**Safe driving apps.** Restrict mobile phone use when the car is in motion.

## What Is Ergonomics?

**Ergonomics** is the science of fitting a work environment to the people who work there. It typically focuses on making products and workspaces more comfortable and safe to use. With respect to computer use, it involves designing a safe and effective workspace, which includes properly adjusting furniture and hardware and using *ergonomic hardware* when needed. A proper work environment—used in conjunction with good user habits and procedures—can prevent many physical problems caused by computer use. A proper work environment is important for anyone who works on a computer or mobile device, including employees using a computer, tablet, or smartphone on the job, individuals using one of these devices at home, and children doing computer activities or texting while at home or at school.

## Workspace Design

The design of a safe and an effective computer workspace—whether it is located at work, home, or school—includes the placement and adjustment of all the furniture and equipment involved, such as the user's desk, chair, computing device, and peripheral devices such as a keyboard and monitor. Workspace lighting or glare from the sun also needs to be taken into consideration. Proper workspace design can result in fewer injuries, headaches, and general aches and pains for computer users. Businesses can reap economic benefits from proper workspace design, such as fewer absences taken by employees, higher productivity, and lower insurance costs. For example, when one government department in New Jersey installed ergonomically correct workstations in its offices, computer-related health complaints fell by 40% and doctor visits dropped by 25% in less than one year.

Proper placement and adjustment of furniture is a good place to start when evaluating a workspace from an ergonomic perspective (see Figure 13-17). The desk should be placed where the sun and other sources of light cannot shine directly onto the screen or into the user's eyes. The monitor should be placed directly in front of the user about an arm's length away, the top of the screen should be no more than 3 inches above the user's eyes once the user's chair is adjusted, and a *document holder* should be used for individuals who refer to written documents frequently while working on their computers in order to minimize the movement of looking between a document and the monitor. The desk chair should be adjusted so that the keyboard is at, or slightly below, the height at which the user's forearms are horizontal to the floor (there are also special *ergonomic chairs* that can be used, when desired).

**FIGURE 13-17**

**Workspace design.** Shown here are some guidelines for designing an ergonomic workspace.

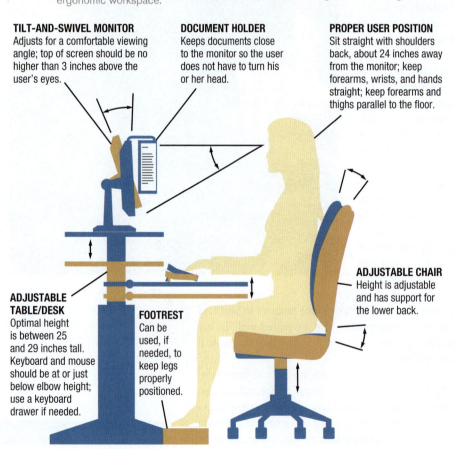

**TILT-AND-SWIVEL MONITOR**
Adjusts for a comfortable viewing angle; top of screen should be no higher than 3 inches above the user's eyes.

**DOCUMENT HOLDER**
Keeps documents close to the monitor so the user does not have to turn his or her head.

**PROPER USER POSITION**
Sit straight with shoulders back, about 24 inches away from the monitor; keep forearms, wrists, and hands straight; keep forearms and thighs parallel to the floor.

**ADJUSTABLE TABLE/DESK**
Optimal height is between 25 and 29 inches tall. Keyboard and mouse should be at or just below elbow height; use a keyboard drawer if needed.

**FOOTREST**
Can be used, if needed, to keep legs properly positioned.

**ADJUSTABLE CHAIR**
Height is adjustable and has support for the lower back.

> **Ergonomics.** The science of fitting a work environment to the people who work there.

A footrest should be used, if needed, to keep the user's feet flat on the floor once the chair height has been set. The monitor settings should be adjusted to make the screen brightness match the brightness of the room and to have a high amount of contrast; the screen should also be periodically wiped clean of dust. An emerging trend is workspaces that allow the user to stand while working. Some *standing desks* (such as the one shown in Figure 13-18) are referred to as *sit/stand desks* because they are adjustable in order to enable the user to alternate between sitting and standing.

While the workspace design principles just discussed and illustrated in Figure 13-17 apply to users of desktop computers, portable computers, and mobile devices, an ergonomic workspace is more difficult to obtain when using a portable computer or mobile device. To create a safer and more comfortable work environment, users of these devices should work at a desk and attach and use a separate keyboard and mouse whenever possible, both at home and while traveling (*travel mice* and *travel keyboards*, which are smaller and lighter than conventional models, can make this easier). The device should also be elevated whenever possible to create a better viewing angle. To help with this and with connecting peripheral devices, docking stations as well as notebook and tablet stands can be used.

While a keyboard, mouse, monitor, and printer can be connected to a portable computer directly, a **docking station** is designed to connect a portable computer to peripheral devices more easily—the computer connects to the docking station, and then the devices connected to the ports on the docking station can be used with that computer. Docking stations are often used in homes and offices when a portable computer is used as a primary computer—typically, the peripheral devices remain connected to the docking station and the computer is just connected and disconnected as needed. For example, the docking station shown in Figure 13-19 has a DVI port and an HDMI port to connect additional monitors, an Ethernet port to connect to a wired network, and a USB port to connect USB devices (such as a keyboard, mouse, or external storage device). A **notebook stand** or **tablet stand** (also shown in Figure 13-19) is designed primarily to elevate a notebook computer or tablet to the proper height for easier viewing. If the notebook or tablet stand has built-in USB ports, USB peripheral devices can be connected to the stand; if not, any peripheral devices (such as a keyboard and mouse) to be used with the device while it is inserted into the stand need to be connected directly to the device (typically via a USB or Bluetooth connection). In addition to helping with screen placement and connectivity, notebook and tablet stands also allow air to circulate around the bottom of the device. For additional cooling, some notebook stands have a built-in cooling fan that is powered

Source: Ergotron Inc.

▲ **FIGURE 13-18**
**Standing desks.**

**TIP**

You can also use a USB hub as a docking station if your device has a USB port—just keep your USB devices connected to the USB hub and connect the hub to your device when you are at home.

▼ **FIGURE 13-19**
**Docking stations and device stands.**

Source: Kensington Computer Products Group

**DOCKING STATIONS**

Source: Otter Products, LLC

**TABLET STANDS**

Source: Bluelounge

**SMARTPHONE DOCKS**

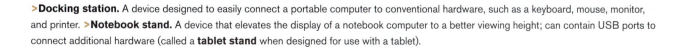

>**Docking station.** A device designed to easily connect a portable computer to conventional hardware, such as a keyboard, mouse, monitor, and printer. >**Notebook stand.** A device that elevates the display of a notebook computer to a better viewing height; can contain USB ports to connect additional hardware (called a **tablet stand** when designed for use with a tablet).

**FIGURE 13-20**

Ergonomic tips for portable computer and tablet users.

**FIGURE 13-21**

Ergonomic hardware.

(via a USB port) by the computer. Docks are also available for smartphones (refer again to Figure 13-19) to connect the smartphone to an external monitor, to a keyboard or mouse, or to an external storage device. Some additional ergonomic tips for users of portable computers and tablets are included in Figure 13-20. Some of these tips apply to smartphones as well; additional smartphone tips include limiting the duration of use, reducing keystrokes by using text shortcuts and voice input, avoiding looking down at the device excessively, using the speakerphone feature or a Bluetooth headset, and switching hands periodically.

## Ergonomic Hardware

In addition to the workspace devices (adjustable chairs and tables, footrests, docking stations, device stands, laptop desks, and so on) already discussed, **ergonomic hardware** can be used to help users avoid physical problems due to extensive computer use or to help alleviate the discomfort associated with an already existing condition. Some of the most common types of ergonomic hardware are shown in Figure 13-21 and discussed next.

➤ *Ergonomic keyboards* (see Figure 13-21) use a shape and key arrangement designed to lessen the strain on the hands and wrists.

➤ *Keyboard folios* (such as the one shown in Figure 13-21) add a keyboard to a tablet so the keyboard can be used for data input.

➤ *Trackballs* are essentially upside-down mice and *ergonomic mice* use a more ergonomically correct design; both can be more comfortable to use than a conventional mouse. A trackball was shown in Figure 4-9 in Chapter 4; the ergonomic mouse shown in Figure 13-21 is a *vertical mouse*, designed to be used in a vertical position.

➤ *Tablet arms* connect to a desk or to a monitor and hold a tablet at the proper height for comfortable viewing.

**DESKTOP ERGONOMIC KEYBOARDS**

**KEYBOARD FOLIOS**

**ERGONOMIC MICE**

**TABLET ARMS**

**KEYBOARD DRAWERS/TRAYS**

**COMPUTER GLOVES**

Source: Kinesis Corporation; Microsoft Corporation; Ergotron, Inc.; Brown Medical Industries, Inc.

>**Ergonomic hardware.** Hardware, typically an input or output device, that is designed to be more ergonomically correct than its nonergonomic counterpart.

➤ *Document holders* can be used to keep documents close to the monitor, enabling the user to see both the document and the monitor without turning his or her head.

➤ *Antiglare screens*—also called *privacy filters*—cover the display screen and can be used to lessen glare and resulting eyestrain. Many antiglare screens double as privacy screens, preventing others sitting next to you (such as on an airplane) from reading what is displayed on your display screen.

➤ *Keyboard drawers/trays* lower the keyboard so it is beneath the desk or table top, enabling the user to keep his or her forearms parallel to the floor more easily.

➤ *Computer gloves* support the wrists and thumbs while allowing the full use of the hands. They are designed to prevent and relieve wrist pain, including carpal tunnel syndrome, tendonitis, and other RSIs.

## Good User Habits and Precautions

In addition to establishing an ergonomic workspace, computer users can follow a number of preventive measures while working on their computers or mobile devices (see Figure 13-22) to help avoid physical problems. Finger and wrist exercises, as well as frequent breaks in typing, are good precautions for helping to prevent repetitive hand and finger stress injuries. Using good posture and periodically taking a break to relax or stretch the body can help reduce or prevent back and neck strain. Rotating tasks—such as alternating between computer work, phone work, and paperwork every 15 minutes or so—is also a good idea. For locations where some glare from a nearby window is unavoidable at certain times of the day, closing the curtains or blinds can help to prevent eyestrain. All device users should refocus their eyes on an object in the distance for a minute or so, on a regular basis, and smartphone and mobile device users should increase font size and light level when viewing text on a small display screen. Eyeglass wearers should discuss any eye fatigue or blurriness during computer use with their eye doctors—sometimes a different lens prescription or special *computer glasses* can be used to reduce eyestrain while working on a computer. Computer glasses are optimized for viewing in the intermediate zone of vision where a computer monitor usually falls; that is, closer than glasses designed for driving and farther away than glasses designed for reading.

**FIGURE 13-22**

Good user habits. These preventative measures can help avoid discomfort while working on a computer or mobile device.

| CONDITION | PREVENTION |
|---|---|
| Wrist/arm/ hand soreness and injury | ➤ Use a light touch on a keyboard and touch screen.<br>➤ Rest and gently stretch your fingers and arms every 15 minutes or so.<br>➤ Keep your wrists and arms relaxed and parallel to the floor when using a keyboard.<br>➤ When using a touch screen for extended periods of time, place the device more horizontally than vertically.<br>➤ When using a device with a small keyboard, type short messages, take frequent breaks, and use a separate keyboard whenever possible.<br>➤ Use an ergonomic keyboard, ergonomic mouse, computer gloves, and other ergonomic devices if you begin to notice wrist or hand soreness. |
| Eyestrain | ➤ Cover windows or adjust lighting to eliminate glare.<br>➤ Rest your eyes every 15 minutes or so by focusing on an object in the distance (at least 20 feet away) for one minute and then closing your eyes for an additional minute.<br>➤ Make sure your display's brightness and contrast settings are at an appropriate level and the display is placed at an appropriate distance from your eyes.<br>➤ Use a larger text size or lower screen resolution, if needed. |
| Sore or stiff neck | ➤ Use good posture; never hunch over a keyboard or device.<br>➤ Place your display and any documents you need to refer to while using your device directly in front of you.<br>➤ Adjust your display to a comfortable viewing angle with the top of the screen no higher than 3 inches above your eyes.<br>➤ Use a headset or the phone's speakerphone function if you spend a significant amount of time on the phone; never prop a phone between your face and shoulders. |
| Backache; general fatigue | ➤ Use good posture and adjust your chair to support your lower back; use an ergonomic chair, if needed.<br>➤ Use a footrest, if needed, to keep your feet flat on the floor.<br>➤ Walk around or stretch briefly at least once every hour.<br>➤ Alternate activities frequently.<br>➤ When traveling, carry only essential, lightweight devices. |
| Ringing in the ears; hearing loss | ➤ Turn down the volume when using headphones (you should be able to hear other people's voices).<br>➤ Wear over-the-ear-headphones instead of earbuds.<br>➤ Limit the amount of time you use headphones or earbuds.<br>➤ Use external speakers instead of headphones when possible. |
| Leg discomfort or burns | ➤ Use a laptop desk, cooling stand, or other barrier between a portable computer and your legs when using a computer on your lap. |

**SOC**

## Emotional Health

The extensive use of computers and mobile devices in the home and office in recent years has raised new concerns about emotional health. Factors such as financial worries, feelings of being overworked, being unable to relax, and information overload often produce emotional stress. Decades of research have linked stress to a variety of health concerns, such as heart attacks, stroke, diabetes, and weakened immune systems. Workers who report feeling stressed incur more healthcare costs—according to the American Institute of Stress, stress costs U.S. employers more than $300 billion each year in healthcare, missed work, and stress-reduction services provided to employees.

For many individuals, computer use or computer-related events are the cause of, or at least partially contribute to, the stress that they experience. Another emotional health concern related to computer use is addiction to the Internet or another technology.

## Stress of Ever-Changing Technology

When computers were first introduced into the workplace, workers needed to learn the appropriate computer skills if their jobs required computer use. Airline agents, for example, had to learn to use computer databases. Secretaries and other office employees needed to learn to use word processing and other office-related software, and customer service representatives needed to learn how to use e-mail. Today, many people entering the workforce are aware of the technology skills they will need to perform the tasks associated with their chosen professions. However, as computers and mobile devices have become continually more integrated into our society, jobs that did not require the use of a computer or a mobile device in the recent past frequently require it today, and individuals are increasingly required to use a computing device in day-to-day activities (see Figure 13-23). They may also be required to use a smartphone while on the go to keep in touch with the office and clients. And, at the rapid pace that technology keeps changing, many workers must regularly learn new skills to keep up to date. For example, they may need to upgrade to a new version of a software program, learn how to use a new software program, or learn how to use a new smartphone feature or app. Although some find this exciting, the ongoing battle to stay current with changing technology creates stress for many individuals.

**▼ FIGURE 13-23**

**Ever-growing computer use.** Many jobs and tasks that did not require computer use in the past require it today.

**POLICE OFFICERS**

iStockphoto.com/jacomstephens

**AIRPLANE MECHANICS**

Courtesy of Dell Inc.

**RESTAURANT SERVERS**

Source: DE SANTOS

**FIELD WORKERS**

Courtesy WI

## Impact of Our 24/7 Society

One benefit of our communications-oriented society is that one never has to be out of touch. With the use of smartphones, tablets, and portable computers, as well as the ability to access e-mail and company networks from virtually anywhere, individuals can be available around the clock, if needed. Although the ability to be in touch constantly is an advantage for some people under certain conditions, it can also be a source of stress. For example, employees who feel that they are "on call" 24/7 and cannot ever get away from work may find it difficult to relax during their downtime (see Figure 13-24). In fact, 41% of the respondents in a recent study said they feel guilty or stressed about taking time off from work. Others (nearly half of employees, according to a recent study) are expected by their companies to be available to do some work while on vacation. In either case, individuals may feel like they are always "on the job" with no time to recharge, which can affect their personal lives, emotional health, and overall well-being. Finding a balance between work time and personal time is important for good emotional health. There is also concern about the increasing use of smartphones, tablets, and other devices with bright screens in bed. In addition to being a distraction (particularly for children and teenagers), studies indicate the light from these devices can disrupt sleep.

## Information Overload

Although the amount of information available through the Internet is a great asset, it can also be overwhelming at times. When you combine Internet information with TV and radio news broadcasts; newspaper, journal, and magazine articles; and phone calls, voice mail messages, text messages, and faxes, some Americans are practically drowning in information. The amount of e-mail received each day by some individuals and organizations is almost unfathomable. For example, the U.S. Senate receives millions of e-mail messages each day, and one study found that workers in small- to medium-sized businesses in the United States spend half of their workday dealing with e-mail messages. Several strategies can be used to avoid becoming completely overwhelmed by information overload.

For efficiently extracting the information you need from the vast amount of information available over the Internet, good search techniques are essential. Perhaps the most important thing to keep in mind when dealing with information overload is that you cannot possibly read everything ever written on a particular subject. At some point in time when performing Internet research, the value of additional information decreases and, eventually, it is not worth your time to continue the search. Knowing when to quit a search or when to try another research approach is an important skill in avoiding information overload.

Efficiently managing your incoming e-mail is another way to avoid information overload. Tools for managing e-mail can help alleviate the stress of an overflowing Inbox, as well as cut down the amount of time you spend dealing with your online correspondence. As discussed in Chapter 9, e-mail filters can be used to route messages automatically into specific folders (such as suspected spam into a Spam folder) based on criteria you set. When you go through your Inbox, first delete any messages that you don't need to read (such as advertisements that didn't get sent to your Spam folder) and then you can concentrate on the messages remaining in your Inbox. If you need to follow up on a message at a later time, flag it so you don't have to worry about forgetting to follow up at the appropriate time. Many e-mail programs, such as Microsoft Outlook, allow you to flag messages, as well as to add a reminder alarm so you will be reminded automatically when it is time to respond. Gmail allows you to flag messages with stars, as well as to add e-mail messages to your *Tasks list*, as shown in Figure 13-25. Because it can take up to 25 minutes after an interruption to concentrate fully again on a task, productivity training companies advise treating e-mail like physical mail and opening it only a limited number of times per day. To help avoid the temptation of checking e-mail more frequently, close your e-mail program,

**FIGURE 13-24**

**Our 24/7 society.** With smartphones, tablets, and portable computers, many individuals are available 24/7.

**TIP**

For a review of how to perform efficient and effective Internet searches, refer again to Chapter 8.

**FIGURE 13-25**

**Gmail stars and the Tasks list can help you organize your Inbox.**

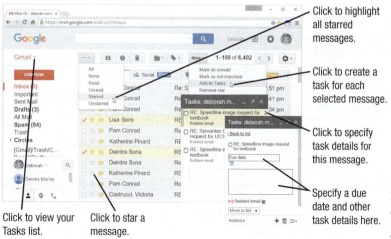

Click to highlight all starred messages.

Click to create a task for each selected message.

Click to specify task details for this message.

Specify a due date and other task details here.

Click to view your Tasks list.

Click to star a message.

Source: Google Inc.

turn off your new e-mail alert notifier, or mute your speakers so you do not hear new messages arrive. You may also wish to turn off notifications of texts and social media updates on your smartphone and just check it periodically for updates.

## Burnout

Our heavy use of computers, combined with information overload and 24/7 accessibility via technology, can lead to **burnout**—a state of fatigue or frustration brought about by overwork. Burnout is often born from good intentions—when, for example, hardworking people try to reach goals that, for one reason or another, become unrealistic. Early signs of burnout include a feeling of emotional and physical exhaustion, no longer caring about a project that used to be interesting or exciting, irritability, feelings of resentment about the amount of work that needs to be done, and feeling pulled in many directions at once.

When you begin to notice the symptoms of burnout, experts recommend reevaluating your schedule, priorities, and lifestyle. Sometimes, just admitting that you are feeling overwhelmed is a good start to solving the problem. Taking a break or getting away for a day can help put the situation in perspective. Saying no to additional commitments and making sure that you eat properly, exercise regularly, and otherwise take good care of yourself are also important strategies for coping with and alleviating both stress and burnout.

## Internet and Technology Addiction

When an individual's use of the Internet interferes with normal living and causes severe stress to family and other loved ones, it is referred to as **Internet addiction** (also called *Internet dependency, Internet use disorder, Internet compulsivity, cyberaddiction, Internet gaming addiction,* and *technology addiction,* depending on the technology being used). Addictive behavior can include compulsive use of the Internet, a preoccupation with being online, lying about or hiding Internet activities, and an inability to control the behavior. According to Dr. Kimberly Young, an expert on Internet addiction and the director of the Center for Internet Addiction Recovery in Pennsylvania, Internet addiction is a compulsive behavior that completely dominates the addict's life (see Figure 13-26 for Dr. Young's list of Internet addiction symptoms). Studies suggest that 15% of U.S. children and young adults show symptoms of Internet addiction and more than 7% of the overall population in Asia is addicted to the Internet. Internet addiction is considered a serious disorder and is being considered for inclusion as a new diagnosis in the upcoming revision of the *Diagnostic and Statistical Manual of Mental Disorders* (*DSM-V*).

Originally, Internet addiction sufferers were stereotyped as younger, introverted, socially awkward, computer-oriented males. However, with the increased access to computers and the Internet today, this stereotype is no longer accurate. Internet addiction can affect anyone of any age, race, or social class and can take a variety of forms. Some individuals become addicted to e-mailing or text messaging. Others become compulsive online shoppers or online gamblers, or become addicted to social media activities. Still others are addicted to cybersex, cyberporn, or online gaming, or struggle with real-world relationships because of online relationships. Currently,

**FIGURE 13-26**

**Questions to help identify Internet addiction.** You may be addicted to the Internet if you answer "yes" to at least five of these questions.

**SIGNS OF INTERNET ADDICTION**

Do you feel preoccupied with the Internet (think about the previous online activity or anticipate the next online session)?

Do you feel the need to use the Internet with increasing amounts of time in order to achieve satisfaction?

Have you repeatedly made unsuccessful efforts to control, cut back, or stop Internet use?

Do you feel restless, moody, depressed, or irritable when attempting to cut down or stop Internet use?

Do you stay online longer than originally intended?

Have you jeopardized or risked the loss of a significant relationship, job, educational, or career opportunity because of the Internet?

Have you lied to family members, a therapist, or others to conceal the extent of involvement with the Internet?

Do you use the Internet as a way of escaping from problems or of relieving a dysphoric mood (e.g., feelings of helplessness, guilt, anxiety, depression)?

Courtesy of Dr. Kimberly Young, Director of the Center for Internet Addiction Recovery

---

>**Burnout.** A state of fatigue or frustration usually brought on by overwork. >**Internet addiction.** The problem of overusing, or being unable to stop using, the Internet.

*Internet sex addiction* to chat rooms and online pornography are two of the most common forms of Internet addiction.

Like other addictions, addiction to using a computer, the Internet, texting, or other technology may have significant consequences, such as relationship problems, job loss, academic failure, health problems, financial consequences, loss of custody of children, and even suicide. There is also growing concern about the impact of constant use of technology among teenagers. In addition to texting and posting to Facebook, many teens are taking these devices to bed with them, raising concerns about sleep deprivation and its consequences, such as concentration problems, anxiety and depression, and unsafe driving. Internet addiction is also increasingly being tied to crime and even death in countries (such as China and South Korea) that have high levels of broadband Internet access. For instance, Internet addiction is blamed for much of the juvenile crime in China, a number of suicides, and several deaths from exhaustion by players unable to tear themselves away from marathon gaming sessions.

Internet addiction is viewed as a growing problem worldwide. Both China and South Korea have implemented military-style boot camps to treat young people identified as having Internet addiction—China alone has more than 250 camps set up across the country. In the United States, there are a number of inpatient treatment centers that treat Internet addiction, such as the reSTART program in the state of Washington and the Internet Addiction Recovery and Treatment Program at the Bradford Regional Medical Center in Pennsylvania—the first hospital-based Internet addiction treatment and recovery program in the United States.

Many experts believe that while Internet addiction is a growing problem, it can be treated, similar to other addictions, with therapy, support groups, and medication. Research to investigate its impact, risk factors, and treatment possibilities, as well as investigate treatment differences among the various types of technology abuse, is ongoing. New studies are also looking at the overall impact of technology and how its overuse or abuse may also impact people's lives in order to identify other potential problems and possible solutions.

## ACCESS TO TECHNOLOGY

For many, a major concern about the increased integration of computers and technology into our society is whether or not technology is accessible to all individuals. Some believe there is a distinct line dividing those who have access and those who do not. Factors such as age, gender, race, income, education, and physical abilities can all impact one's access to technology and how one uses it.

### The Digital Divide

The term **digital divide** refers to the gap between those who have access to information and communications technology and those who do not—often referred to as the "haves" and "have nots." Typically, the digital divide is thought to be based on physical access to computers, the Internet, and related technology. Some individuals, however, believe that the definition of the digital divide goes deeper than just access. For example, they classify those individuals who have physical access to technology but who do not understand how to use it or are discouraged from using it in the "have not" category. Groups and individuals trying to eliminate the digital divide are working toward providing real access to technology (including access to up-to-date hardware, software, Internet, and training) so that it can be used to improve people's lives. In addition to access to computers and the Internet, digital divides related to other technologies may exist as well. For instance, one recent

**TIP**

To fight Internet addiction, China also bans minors from Internet cafés and Taiwan fines parents who allow children under two years of age to use electronic devices or who allow older children to spend excessive time using electronic devices.

**TIP**

Many people today—regardless of income level—view having a mobile phone as a necessity, not a luxury.

>**Digital divide.** The gap between those who have access to technology and those who do not.

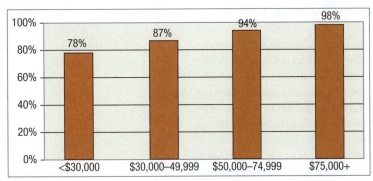

INCOME

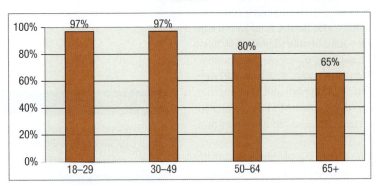

AGE

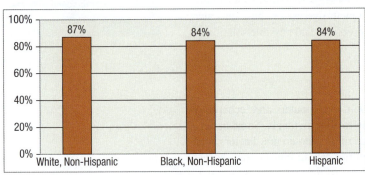

RACE

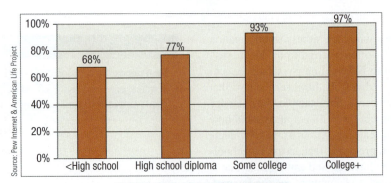

HIGHEST LEVEL OF EDUCATION OBTAINED

Source: Pew Internet & American Life Project

⚠ **FIGURE 13-27**

**Key U.S. Internet use statistics.** Shows the percentage of individuals in each category who use the Internet.

study revealed a digital divide in electronic health records (EHRs) at hospitals in the United States. The study found that hospitals that primarily serve low-income patients are less likely to have adopted EHRs and other safety-related technologies (such as clinical decision supports, electronic medication lists, and computerized discharge summaries) than hospitals with more affluent patients.

The digital divide can refer to the differences between individuals within a particular country, as well as to the differences between countries. Within a country, use of computers and related technology can vary based on factors such as age, race, education, and income.

### The U.S. Digital Divide

Although there is disagreement among experts about the current status of the digital divide within the United States, there is an indication that it is continuing to shrink. While the digital divide involves more than just Internet use—it involves the use of any type of technology necessary to succeed in our society—the growing amount of Internet use is an encouraging sign. As discussed in Chapter 8, more than 87% of the U.S. adult population are Internet users, using the Internet at work, home, school, or another location. Free Internet access at libraries, school, and other public locations, as well as the availability of low-cost computers and low-cost or free Internet access in many areas today, has helped Internet use begin to approach the popularity and widespread use of telephones and TVs, and has helped it become more feasible for low-income families today than in the past. In general, however, according to recent reports by the Pew Internet & American Life Project, individuals with a higher level of income or a higher level of education are more likely to go online, and younger individuals are more likely to be online than older Americans. Some overall demographic data about Internet use in the United States is shown in Figure 13-27. Similar trends occur with digital divide statistics for other technologies. For example, 96% of Americans with an annual income between $75,000 and $100,000 own a mobile phone and 81% own a smartphone (compared with 87% and 52%, respectively, of individuals earning less than $30,000), and 98% of Americans aged 18 to 29 own a mobile phone and 86% own a smartphone (compared with 76% and 30%, respectively, of individuals 65 or older).

Because the United States is such a technologically advanced society, reducing—and trying to eliminate—the digital divide is extremely important to ensure that all citizens have an equal chance to be successful in this country. Although there has been lots of progress in that direction, more work still remains. For instance, the Navajo Nation (a sovereign tribal nation with more than 250,000 citizens living across 27,000 square miles in New Mexico, Arizona, and Utah) has lagged significantly behind the rest of the United States in terms of technology. Many schools lack computers and Internet access, many residents have to drive seven or eight miles over roads impassable during rain or snow storms to reach the nearest telephone, and even some government entities within the Navajo Nation have dial-up or no Internet access. However, this is slowly changing as a result of the *Internet to the Hogan* project—a project designed to end the digital divide in the Navajo Nation. It will first provide Internet to tribal colleges and other central locations, which will be extended to community-based chapter houses, and then to schools, medical clinics, hospitals, firehouses, and homes.

Many individuals view technology as essential for all Americans today. For instance, students need access to devices and Internet resources to stay informed and be prepared for further education and careers. As already discussed, most jobs in the United States require some sort of computer or Internet use. And the Internet is becoming an increasingly important resource for older Americans, particularly for forming decisions about health and healthcare options. However, it is important to realize that not all individuals want to use computers or go online. Just as some people choose not to have televisions, mobile phones, or other technologies, some people—rich or poor—choose not to have a computer or go online. Sometimes this is a religious decision; at other times, it is simply a lifestyle choice.

## The Global Digital Divide

While the digital divide within a country is about some individuals within that country having access to technology and others not having the same access, the global digital divide is about some countries having access to technology and others not having the same level of access. It is becoming increasingly important for all countries to have access to information and communications technology in order to be able to compete successfully in our global economy. The global digital divide is perhaps more dramatic than the U.S. digital divide. According to InternetWorldStats.com, more than 3.2 billion people globally are online—only about 45% of the world's population. With nearly 88% of its population online, North America is the leading world region in Internet users; with only 27% of its population online, Africa has one of the lowest percentages of Internet users.

For some, it is difficult to imagine how computers and the Internet would benefit the world's hungry or the 1.3 billion people in the world without access to reliable electricity. Others view technology as a means to bridge the global digital divide. For instance, smartphones and computers with solar-rechargeable batteries can be used in developing countries for education and telemedicine. A variety of wireless Internet projects that are designed to bring wireless Internet to remote areas of the world are also helping to bridge the gap. These projects provide Internet access to rural schools and homes, as well as provide services (such as telemedicine) to remote villages that would not otherwise have those services available.

For personal computer use, new products are emerging that could help lessen the global digital divide. Perhaps the most widely known project in this area is the *One Laptop Per Child* (*OLPC*) project. The goal of OLPC is to ensure that every child in the world has access to a rugged, low-cost, low-power connected laptop (see Figure 13-28) in order to provide them with access to new channels of learning, sharing, and self-expression. The current model of the *XO laptop* developed by OLPC is the *XO-4 Touch*.

**FIGURE 13-28**
The OLPC XO laptop.

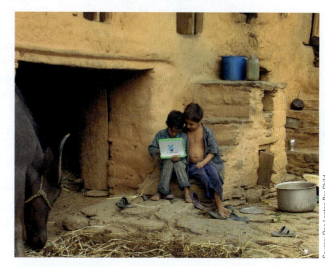

Source: One Laptop Per Child

SOC

Source: One Laptop Per Child

**FIGURE 13-29**

The low-cost XO tablet.

The XO laptop is made of thick plastic for durability with a display that can be viewed in direct sunlight and the rubber keyboard is sealed to keep out dirt and water. The XO is very energy-efficient, and it can be charged via an electrical outlet, as well as from a car battery, foot pedal, or pull string. It is Linux-based and includes a Wi-Fi adapter, flash memory slot, built-in video camera, microphone, touchpad, 7.5-inch touch screen, accelerometer, keyboard, and USB ports; has 1 or 2 GB of RAM; and uses 4 or 8 GB of flash memory for storage. More than 2.4 million children and teachers worldwide have been provided with an XO laptop. According to OLPC, making it possible for students in developing countries to have a laptop will greatly impact their education, as well as society as a whole. They believe that by empowering children to educate themselves, a new generation will ultimately be better prepared to tackle the other serious problems (poverty, malnutrition, disease) facing their societies. A low-cost Android tablet version—the *XO Tablet* shown in Figure 13-29—recently became available; it is being distributed to schools serving underprivileged children in the United States and is also available to the general public.

## Assistive Technology

Research has found that people with disabilities tend to use computers and the Internet at rates below the average for a given population. Part of the reason may be that some physical conditions—such as visual impairment or limited dexterity—make it difficult to use a conventional computer system. That is where **assistive technology**—hardware and software specially designed for use by individuals with physical disabilities—fits in. While assistive technology is not currently available to help with all types of computer content (such as streaming video and other multimedia content, which is increasingly found on Web pages), there has been much improvement in assistive technology in recent years. In addition, researchers are continuing to develop additional types of assistive technology, such as *multimedia accessibility tools* to help individuals with visual impairments better control and experience Web-based multimedia. This growth in assistive technology is due in part to demands by disabled individuals and disability organizations for equal access to computers and Web content, as well as the *Americans with Disabilities Act* (*ADA*). The *ADA* requires companies with 15 or more employees to make reasonable accommodations for known physical or mental limitations of otherwise qualified individuals, unless doing so results in undue hardship for the company.

To help provide individuals with physical disabilities equal access to technology, assistive input and output devices—such as Braille keyboards, specialized pointing devices, large monitors, and screen readers—are available for personal computers, as well as some smartphones and other mobile devices. In addition, there are apps and devices designed to assist people with disabilities with day-to-day tasks. For example, mobile apps can identify the price and name of a product, as well as read label information out loud, once a product label is scanned with a smartphone camera; talking GPS devices can guide blind or low-vision individuals; and *augmentative and alternative communication* (*AAC*) tablets (such as the one shown in Figure 13-30), or a conventional tablet with an AAC app, can help people who are unable to use verbal speech to communicate with others.

**FIGURE 13-30**

AAC systems help individuals with speech disabilities communicate with others.

Source: Tobii AB

> **Assistive technology.** Hardware and software specifically designed for use by individuals with physical disabilities.

**BRAILLE KEYBOARDS**
The keys on this keyboard contain Braille overlays.

**ONE-HANDED KEYBOARDS**
Each key on this half keyboard contains two letters (one set for the keys normally on the right half of the keyboard and one set for the left half) so all keys can be reached with one hand.

**EYE TRACKING SYSTEMS**
Cameras track the user's eye movements, which are used to select icons and other objects on the screen.

## Assistive Input Systems

*Assistive input devices* allow for input in a nontraditional manner (see Figure 13-31). For example, *Braille keyboards*, large-print keyboards, or conventional keyboards with Braille or large-print key overlays are available for visually impaired computer users. *Keyguards*—metal or plastic plates that fit over conventional keyboards—enable users with limited hand mobility to press the keys on a keyboard (using his or her fingers or a special device). *One-handed keyboards* are designed to be used with only one hand, and speech recognition systems allow data and commands to be input hands-free, as discussed in Chapter 4. *Switches*—hardware devices that can be activated with hand, foot, finger, or face movement, or with sips and puffs of air—can also be used to input data and commands. Some conventional input devices can also be used for assistive purposes, such as scanners, which—if they have optical character recognition (OCR) capabilities—can input printed documents as text that can be enlarged on the screen or read aloud.

Assistive pointing devices can be used to move and select items with an on-screen pointer; they can also be used to enter text-based data when used in conjunction with an on-screen keyboard. Examples include *foot-controlled mice*, *head pointing systems* that control the on-screen pointer using head movement, and *eye tracking systems* that allow users to select items on screen using only their gaze. For example, the eye tracking system shown in Figure 13-31 connects to nearly any Windows device and translates eye gazes to Windows touch commands.

## Assistive Output Systems

Some examples of *assistive output devices* that can be used by blind and other visually impaired individuals are shown in Figure 13-32. A *screen reader* is a software program that reads aloud all text information available via the computer screen, such as

**FIGURE 13-31**
Assistive input devices.

**TIP**

Assistive hardware is also used by the general population, such as voice input systems for voice commands and input, as well as head pointing systems for gaming and virtual reality (VR) applications.

**FIGURE 13-32**
Assistive output devices.

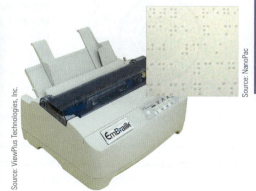

**SCREEN READER SOFTWARE**

**BRAILLE DISPLAYS**

**BRAILLE PRINTERS**

instructions, menu options, documents, and Web pages. *Braille displays* are devices that can be attached to conventional computers or mobile devices and that continuously convert screen output into Braille form. *Braille printers* (also called *Braille embossers*) print embossed output in Braille format on paper instead of, or in addition to, conventional ink output.

Some operating systems also include accessibility features. For instance, recent versions of Windows and OS X include a screen reader, on-screen keyboard, speech recognition capabilities, and settings that can be used to magnify the screen, change text size and color, convert audio cues into written text, and otherwise make the computer more accessible.

# ENVIRONMENTAL CONCERNS

The increasing use of computers in our society has created a variety of environmental concerns. The amount of energy used to power personal computers, servers, and computer components, as well as the heat generated by computing equipment, is one concern. Another is our extensive use of paper, DVDs, toner cartridges, and other disposables, and how much of it ends up as trash in landfills. The hazardous materials contained in computer equipment or generated by the production of computers and related technology, as well as the disposal of used computing products, are additional concerns. With an increasing amount of attention being focused on energy usage and carbon emissions, businesses and individuals are paying more attention to energy costs and their *carbon footprint* (the amount of carbon dioxide produced to support activities), as well as the carbon footprints of their suppliers and business partners.

**FIGURE 13-33**
Eco-labels.

UNITED STATES

EUROPEAN UNION

KOREA

BRAZIL

AUSTRALIA

Source: U.S. Environmental Protection Agency; ENERGY STAR program; European Commission; Korea Environmental Labeling Association (KELA); ABNT - ASSOCIAÇÃO BRASILEIRA DE NORMAS TÉCNICAS; Good Environmental Choice Australia

## Green Computing

The term **green computing** refers to the use of computers in an environmentally friendly manner. Minimizing the use of natural resources, such as energy and paper, is one aspect of green computing. In 1992, the U.S. Environmental Protection Agency (EPA) introduced **ENERGY STAR** as a voluntary labeling program designed to identify and promote energy-efficient products to reduce greenhouse gas emissions. Computers and monitors were among the first labeled products; an ENERGY STAR-qualified computer will use between 30% and 75% less energy, depending on how it is used. Today, the ENERGY STAR label (see Figure 13-33) appears on computing devices, office equipment, residential heating and cooling equipment, major appliances, lighting, home electronics, and more. **Eco-labels**—environmental performance certifications—are also used in other countries; Figure 13-33 shows some examples.

## Energy Consumption and Conservation

With the high cost of electricity today, power consumption and heat generation by computers are key concerns for businesses today. Today's faster and more powerful computers tend to use more energy and run hotter than computers from just a few years ago, which leads to greater cooling costs. Servers, in particular, are power hungry, using about 60% of their maximum power while idle. Consequently, consolidating servers (such as by the use of virtualization) is a common energy-saving tactic used by businesses today (for example, AOL recently decommissioned nearly 10,000 servers and saved about $5 million total, with $1.65 million of the savings attributed to energy savings). Other strategies include powering down computers when they are not in use, using desktop

> **Green computing.** The use of computers in an environmentally friendly manner. > **ENERGY STAR.** A program developed by the Environmental Protection Agency (EPA) to encourage the development and use of energy-saving devices. > **Eco-label.** A certification, usually by a government agency, that identifies a device as meeting minimal environmental performance specifications.

virtualization, and utilizing cloud computing. Green computing can have tremendous financial benefits. In fact, a recent report from the Natural Resources Defense Council (NRDC) estimates that a 40% reduction in energy consumption by U.S. data centers (which is only about one-half of what is technically possible) would save U.S. businesses $3.8 billion annually.

In response to the growing emphasis on green computing today, hardware manufacturers are working to develop more energy-efficient personal computers, servers, microprocessors, storage systems, displays, power supplies, motherboards, and other computer components. Some energy-saving features found on computer hardware today include devices (such as computers and printers) that can go into very low-power sleep mode when not in use, low-power-consumptive chips and boards, high-efficiency power supplies, energy-efficient flat-panel displays, liquid cooling systems, and CPUs that power up and down on demand. The energy savings by using more energy-efficient hardware can be significant. For instance, moving to an LED flat-panel display instead of a conventional LCD display saves around 12% in energy consumption.

While ENERGY STAR-qualified computers deliver substantial energy savings over conventional computers, computers can still draw quite a bit of power when they are in stand-by and sleep modes—particularly with a screen saver enabled. Because of this, it is important for businesses, schools, and individuals to power down computers manually or automatically (using software or power-saving settings) when they are not in use to save power. Mobile phone manufacturers are also working to reduce the environmental impact of their products, such as displaying reminders on the phones to unplug them from their chargers when they are fully charged because chargers can draw up to five watts per hour even if nothing is plugged into them. Other devices that draw power when they are turned off (sometimes called *energy vampires*) include computers, home electronics, and home appliances. In fact, it is estimated that energy vampires add about 10% or more to U.S. household monthly energy bills. To determine how much power a device is using, you can use a special device like the *Kill a Watt* shown in Figure 13-34. This device displays the amount of power (in kilowatts or dollar value) any device plugged into it is currently using. To save on vampire power costs, unplug your devices when you are not using them (you can connect your electronic devices to a power strip and just switch off the power at the power strip to make this process easier). However, don't cut the power to any device (such as a wireless router, DVR, or cable box) that will need to be active to perform a needed function. *Smart power strips* that turn off outlets on the strip when it senses those devices aren't being used and *smart charging stations* that recharge USB devices and shut off when the devices are fully charged are other power-saving alternatives.

*Source: P3 International Corporation*

**FIGURE 13-34**

**Energy usage monitors.** This monitor displays in real time the amount of electricity (in kilowatt-hours or approximate cost) a connected device is using.

## Alternate Power

In addition to more energy-efficient hardware, other possibilities for greener computing are being developed, such as alternate power sources for computers and mobile devices. For instance, *solar power* is a growing alternative for powering electronic devices, including portable computers and smartphones. With solar power, *solar panels* convert sunlight into direct current (DC) electricity, which is then stored in an external battery or directly in the battery of a connected device.

Although it has been expensive to implement in the past, improvements in solar technology are making its use more feasible for a greater number of individuals. Today's solar panels are typically *thin-film solar panels*, which are created by printing nanoparticles onto rolls of thin, flexible panels. Thin-film panels use a much thinner level of *photovoltaic (PV) materials* (which converts visible light into direct current or DC) and are a fraction of the cost of earlier generations. While *photovoltaic cells (PV cells)* used in solar panels traditionally use silicon, other materials are being developed for use in PV cells. To encourage this development, Harvard University recently released a list of 20,000 organic compounds that may be viable replacements for silicon. As the flexibility of solar manufacturing increases and the price decreases, solar panels are becoming available for an

**SOC**

**SOLAR COMPUTER AND TABLET BAGS**

**SOLAR BACKPACKS**

**HAND-POWERED CHARGERS**

 **FIGURE 13-35**

**Alternate power.**
Solar and hand power
can be used to power
smartphones, GPS
devices, portable
computers, and other
devices.

increasing number of applications. For instance, solar charging capabilities are being built into a variety of mobile accessories, such as computer bags, tablet cases, and backpacks (see Figure 13-35). As also shown in this figure, hand-powered chargers can also be used to power portable computers, smartphones, and other mobile devices. While currently these devices are most often used wherever dependable electricity is not available, such as in developing countries and while outdoors, *transparent solar panels* are in the research stage and are expected to eventually be built into the screens of smartphones, tablets, and other devices to charge those devices on a continual basis—they may even be built into car sunroofs and the windows of buildings. For a look at other options for powering your devices while you are on the go, see the How It Works box.

Solar power can be also used to power more permanent computer setups. For instance, some Web hosting companies in the United States (such as AISO.net) are now 100% solar powered and the solar panels that cover most of the rooftops at Google's Mountain View, California, headquarters power 30% of the energy needs for that complex. Solar power plants are also being implemented (for example, Apple is building a solar farm in China to offset energy used by its offices and retail stores in order to continue working toward its goal of all global operations using 100% renewable energy), and some experts predict that many buildings in the future will be *solar buildings* with solar cells integrated into the rooftop, walls, and windows of the building to generate electricity.

## Green Components

In addition to being more energy-efficient, computers today are being built to run quieter and cooler, and they are using more recyclable hardware and packaging. Many computer manufacturers are also reducing the amount of toxic chemicals being used in personal computers. For instance, Dell bans the use of some hazardous chemicals, such as cadmium and mercury; has reduced the amount of lead used in several desktop computers; and meets the European Union requirement of being completely lead-free for all electronics shipped to the EU. Some smartphones are also going green, being made out of recycled plastics, including solar panels to charge the phone's battery, and including a pedometer and other apps to calculate the volume of $CO_2$ emissions you have avoided by not driving.

## Recycling and Disposal of Computing Equipment

Another environmental concern is the amount of trash—and sometimes toxic trash—generated by computer use. One concern is paper waste. Despite the increase in the use of electronic forms, electronic signatures, e-books, online newspapers and magazines, and online banking, it appears that the so-called *paperless office* that many visionaries predicted has not yet arrived. Instead, research indicates that global paper use is still increasing, and at least 40% of all wood harvested in the world today ends up as paper. North Americans alone consume more than 500 pounds of paper per person per year. One possible solution for the future (e-paper) was discussed in Chapter 4. There are also utilities, such as *PrintWhatYouLike.com* and *GreenPrint*, designed to reduce paper consumption. These utilities eliminate images, blank pages, and other non-critical content located on documents and/or Web pages in order to print just the necessary content on the least number of pages possible.

In addition to paper-based trash, computing refuse includes used toner cartridges, obsolete or broken computers and peripherals, and discarded CDs, DVDs, and other storage media. Mobile phones that are discarded when individuals upgrade their phones or switch providers—as well as new disposable consumer products, such as disposable digital cameras—also add to the alarming growth of **e-waste** (also called *e-trash*) generated today.

>**E-waste.** Electronic waste or trash, such as discarded computer components; also called e-trash.

## HOW IT WORKS

### Power to Go

Tired of your smartphone, laptop, smart watch, or fitness band battery running out of power at inopportune times? Well, there are several new *portable power devices* available to let you bring additional power with you. Some devices, typically the size of a USB flash drive or a smartphone (depending on their capacity), consist of a power pack with built-in connectors (typically a USB port) to connect your various devices (see one example of a power pack in the accompanying illustration). Most of these power packs can be recharged via a USB cable and portable computer; some also can be plugged into a wall outlet for faster recharging. An option geared toward commuters is the *PowerCup power inverter* that is shaped like a large portable coffee container so it fits nicely in a car cup holder. The PowerCup connects to the car via the car's 12-volt power outlet and can power up to two regular devices (such as a laptop or DVD player) using standard AC plugs, as well as one USB-powered device (such as a smartphone).

One unique option (shown in the accompanying photo) is the *Jaq* device, which uses *fuel cell* technology to create energy from water and salt (fuel cells produce electricity using a chemical reaction). This pocket-sized device connects to any mobile device with a USB connection (such as a smartphone, digital media player, or tablet) to provide nearly instant power to the device (the charger uses single-use *PowerCards* containing salt and water—one card charges approximately one smartphone).

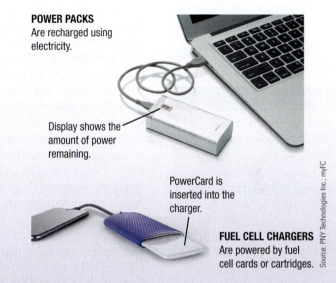

**POWER PACKS**
Are recharged using electricity.

Display shows the amount of power remaining.

PowerCard is inserted into the charger.

**FUEL CELL CHARGERS**
Are powered by fuel cell cards or cartridges.

Source: PNY Technologies Inc.; myFC

Compounding the problem of the amount of e-waste generated today is the fact that computers, smartphones, and related hardware contain a variety of toxic and hazardous materials. For instance, a single desktop computer may contain up to 700 different chemical elements and compounds, many of which (such as arsenic, lead, mercury, and cadmium) are hazardous and expensive to dispose of properly.

A global concern regarding e-waste is where it all eventually ends up. Much of it ends up in municipal landfills that are not designed for toxic waste. And, even worse, the majority of all computer equipment sent to recyclers in developed countries (at least 80%, according to most estimates) ends up being exported to developing countries (such as China, India, and Nigeria) with more lax environmental standards, legislation, or enforcement than in the United States. Much of the e-waste exported to these countries is simply dumped into fields or processed with rudimentary and dangerous technologies that release toxins into the air and water. Despite the potential danger of these components, rural villagers are often employed to try to repair equipment or reclaim metals or plastic (see Figure 13-36)—hardware that cannot be repaired or reclaimed is often burned or treated with acid baths to try to recover precious metals but such processes release very dangerous pollutants. Activists believe unchecked exportation by the United States and other countries—such as England, Japan, Australia, and Canada—has been going on for at least 10 years. The primary reason for exporting e-waste is cost—proper disposal of a computer in the United States costs between $5 and $10, compared with $1 or less in third-world countries. Another reason is that U.S. states are increasingly banning dangerous computing equipment—such as CRT monitors—from landfills.

**FIGURE 13-36**
**E-waste.** E-waste is often exported to developing countries.

Source: Basal Action Network

SOC

While it is difficult—or, perhaps, impossible—to reverse the damage that has already occurred from e-waste, many organizations are working to develop ways to protect people and the environment from future contamination. For instance, the *Basal Action Network* has worked with industry leaders to create the *e-Stewards Standard* certification program designed to help individuals and organizations locate responsible electronics recyclers, and *Clean Production Action* and *Greenpeace* have created programs to push hardware manufacturers to stop using toxic chemicals in their products. Some countries have environmental regulations (such as Europe's regulations that require manufacturers to avoid use of toxic substances and that forbid exporting hazardous wastes to developing countries). In Europe, Japan, and increasingly in some U.S. states, laws are based on the policy of *extended producer responsibility* (*EPR*), where manufacturers are responsible for the entire life cycle of their products and packaging, including recycling. In response, computer manufacturers are beginning to produce more environmentally friendly components, such as system units made from recyclable plastic, nontoxic flame-retardant coatings, and lead-free solder on the motherboard.

Even though recycling computer equipment is often difficult because of toxic materials and poor product designs, proper recycling is essential to avoid pollution and health hazards. Some recycling centers will accept computer equipment, but many charge a fee for this service. Many computer manufacturers have voluntary take-back programs that will accept obsolete or broken computer equipment from consumers at a minimal cost. Expired toner cartridges and ink cartridges can sometimes be returned to the manufacturer (using the supplied shipping label included with some cartridges) or exchanged when ordering new cartridges; the cartridges are then *recharged* (refilled) and resold. Cartridges that cannot be refilled can be sent to a recycling facility. In addition to helping to reduce e-waste in landfills, using recharged printer cartridges saves the consumer money because they are less expensive than new cartridges. Other computer components—such as CDs, DVDs, USB flash drives, and hard drives—can also be recycled through some organizations, such as *GreenDisk*. GreenDisk accepts shipments of all types of storage media (plus printer cartridges, mobile phones, mice, notebook computers, chargers, and more) for a modest charge (such as $9.95 for 25 pounds of items if you ship them yourself); it reuses salvageable items and recycles the rest. There are also a number of recycling programs specifically designed for discarded mobile phones. These programs typically refurbish and sell the phones; many organizations donate a portion of the proceeds to nonprofit organizations.

In lieu of recycling, older equipment that is still functioning can be used for alternate purposes (such as for a child's computer, a personal Web server, or a DVR), or it can be donated to schools and nonprofit groups. Some organizations accept and repair donated equipment and then distribute it to disadvantaged groups or other individuals in need of the hardware. In the United States, for instance, *Operation Homelink* refurbishes donated computers and sends them free of charge to families of U.S. military personnel deployed overseas, who then use the computers to communicate with the soldiers via e-mail, social media, and video calls (see Figure 13-37).

For security and privacy purposes, data stored on all computing equipment should be completely removed before disposing of that equipment so that someone else cannot recover the data stored on that device. As discussed in Chapter 9, hard drives should be wiped clean (not just erased) using special software that overwrites the data on the drive several times to ensure it is completely destroyed; storage media that cannot be wiped (such as rewritable DVDs) or that contain very sensitive data (such as business hard drives being discarded) should be shredded. The shredded media is then typically recycled.

▽ **FIGURE 13-37**

**Operation Homelink.** The family of this soldier about to be deployed will use this refurbished laptop to communicate with him while he is overseas.

Source: Operation Homelink

Consumers and companies alike are increasingly recognizing the need for green computing, including end-of-life reuse and recycling. Support for nationwide legislation is growing, and manufacturers are seeing the economic and social advantages of producing more easily recyclable and less toxic hardware. So, even though computer manufacturing and recycling have a long way to go before computing equipment stops being an environmental and health hazard, it is encouraging that the trend is moving toward creating a safer and less-wasteful environment.

## RELATED LEGISLATION

There have been several new laws over the past decade or so attempting to revise intellectual property laws to reflect digital content and the Internet. For instance, the *Family Entertainment and Copyright Act of 2005* makes it illegal to transmit or record a movie being shown at a movie theater; the *U.S. Anticybersquatting Consumer Protection Act of 1999* makes domain name cybersquatting illegal; and the *Digital Millennium Copyright Act* (*DMCA*) makes it illegal to circumvent antipiracy measures built into digital media and devices. Other laws, such as ones to increase the penalties for illegally sharing music and movies via the Internet, are proposed on a regular basis.

# ASK THE EXPERT

**David Beschen,** President, GreenDisk Inc.

*Courtesy GreenDisk, Inc.*

### How large of a problem is e-waste today and what can we do about it?

According to a recent EPA report, over 5 million tons of e-waste were in storage in the United States and another 2.5 million tons were prepped for end-of-life but only 25% of those devices were recycled. Many of these devices contained some of the worst toxins on earth, as well as things we do not want "recycled," such as private information belonging to the individuals and businesses that used the devices.

Properly recycling e-waste is important to the environment, our health, and our privacy. It keeps our electronic waste out of landfills (and our garages). However, in our experience at GreenDisk, people simply do not know what to do with their obsolete technology and they have no sense of urgency to do anything with it. And, unfortunately, current e-waste solutions are neither easy to use nor well promoted. Consequently, we need to keep inventing products that use recycled materials, keep implementing incentives to promote recycling among both the producers and the end users, and keep our old technology heading into recycle bins (and, even better, into our new stuff).

Legislation regarding ethics has been more difficult to pass—or to keep as law once it has passed. For example, as discussed in Chapter 8, the *Communications Decency Act* that was signed into law in 1996 and made it a criminal offense to distribute patently indecent or offensive material online was eventually declared unconstitutional on the basis of free speech. The courts so far have had difficulty defining what is "patently offensive" and "indecent," as well as finding a fair balance between protection and censorship. Consequently, very few ethically oriented laws have been passed in recent years. Two of the most significant recent legislation regarding accessibility are *The Individuals with Disabilities Education Act of 1997*, which requires schools in all states to ensure a free public education for all students with disabilities (including the use of any necessary assistive technology) and the 1998 amendment to *Section 508* of the *Rehabilitation Act,* which requires federal agencies to make their electronic and information technology accessible to people with disabilities. This latter act applies to all federal Web sites, as well, creating a trend of Web sites that are *Section 508 compliant*. While there are currently no federal computer recycling laws in the United States, federal agencies are required to purchase energy-efficient electronic products. In addition, some federal laws (such as the *Sarbanes-Oxley Act* and *HIPAA*) have established privacy and data protection standards for companies disposing of computer hardware that contained specific types of data and some states have implemented laws related to electronic waste.

# SUMMARY

## INTELLECTUAL PROPERTY RIGHTS

**Chapter Objective 1:**
Understand the different types of intellectual property rights and how they relate to computer use.

**Intellectual property rights** specify how *intellectual property*, such as original music compositions, drawings, essays, software programs, symbols, and designs, may be lawfully used. **Copyrights** protect the creators of original artistic or literary works and are granted automatically once a work exists in a physical medium. A copyright can be registered, which provides additional protection should infringement occur. The copyright symbol © can be used to remind others that content is copyrighted; **digital watermarks** can be incorporated into digital content so that the copyright information can be viewed, even if the work is altered. **Digital rights management** (**DRM**) **software** can be used to protect the rights of creators and to manage digital content, such as art, music, photographs, and movies. **Trademarks** are words, phrases, symbols, or designs that identify an organization's goods or services and can be either claimed (and use the symbol ™ or ℠) or registered (and use the symbol ®). Registering a domain name with the intent to profit from someone else's trademark is called **cybersquatting**. **Patents** grant an exclusive right to an invention for 20 years. In addition to products, processes and procedures may be patented as well.

## ETHICS

**Chapter Objective 2:**
Explain what is meant by the term *ethics* and provide several examples of unethical behavior in computer-related matters.

**Ethics** are standards of moral conduct. *Personal ethics* guide one's personal life, **business ethics** provide the standards of conduct guiding business decisions, and **computer ethics** provide the standards of conduct with respect to computers and computer use. Computer ethics have taken on more significance in recent years because the increased use of computers in the home, in the workplace, and at school provides more opportunities for unethical behavior than in the past.

Today one of the most important ethical concerns regarding computers is using someone else's property in an improper way. Books, music, movies, and other types of intellectual property are protected by copyright law, but they are still often used in an illegal or unethical manner. Presenting someone else's work as your own is referred to as **plagiarism**, which is illegal and unethical. It is becoming increasingly common for businesses and schools to establish **codes of conduct** to address what behavior is considered ethical and unethical at that particular organization. Some organizations and industries publish **codes of ethics** listing overall standards of conduct, such as honesty, fairness, confidentiality, and more.

An **online hoax** is an inaccurate statement or story spread through the use of computers, often by e-mail. It is a good idea to make sure questionable information is not an online hoax before passing the information on to others. **Digital manipulation** is the use of computers to modify something in digital form, usually text or a photograph. Ethics are highly intertwined with determining business practices and making business decisions. Decisions, such as which financial information to publicize, which products or services to provide, which safeguards (if any) to establish with products or services that are illegal for minors or objectionable to some individuals, and what types of workplace monitoring to use, all require ethical consideration.

Because ethics are fundamentally based on values, different types of businesses may have different ethics. Ethics and moral standards may vary from country to country and from culture to culture. In addition to legal considerations, businesses with global connections should consider the prevailing ethical standards of all countries involved when making business decisions.

## COMPUTERS AND HEALTH

Since the entry of computers into the workplace and their increased use in our society, they have been blamed for a variety of physical ailments. **Carpal tunnel syndrome** (**CTS**), **De Quervain's tendonitis**, and other types of **repetitive stress injuries** (**RSIs**) are common physical ailments related to computer use; *computer vision syndrome* (*CVS*), eyestrain, fatigue, backaches, and headaches are additional possible physical risks.

**Ergonomics** is the science of how to make a computer workspace, hardware, and environment fit the individual using it. Using an ergonomically correct workspace and **ergonomic hardware** can help avoid or lessen the pain associated with some RSIs. In addition, all users should use good posture, take rest breaks, alternate tasks, and take other common-sense precautions. For portable computers, **docking stations**, **notebook stands**, and **tablet stands** can be used to create more ergonomically correct workspaces.

The *stress* of keeping up with ever-changing technology, layoffs, always being in touch, fear of being out of touch, information overload, **burnout**, and **Internet addiction** are all possible emotional problems related to computer use.

**Chapter Objective 3:**
Describe some possible physical and emotional health risks associated with the use of computers.

## ACCESS TO TECHNOLOGY

The **digital divide** refers to the gap between those who have access to computers and communications technology and those who do not. There can be a digital divide within a country or between countries. Globally, the digital divide separates countries with access to technology from those without access to technology.

Research suggests that people with disabilities tend to use computers and the Internet at rates lower than the average population. Part of the reason may be because some types of conventional hardware—such as keyboards and monitors—are difficult to use with some types of physical conditions. **Assistive technology** includes hardware and software that makes conventional computer systems easier for users with disabilities to use.

**Chapter Objective 4:**
Discuss the impact that factors such as nationality, income, race, education, and physical disabilities may have on computer access and use.

## ENVIRONMENTAL CONCERNS

**Green computing** refers to using computers in an environmentally friendly manner. It can include using environmentally friendly hardware (such as devices approved by an **eco-label** system like the **ENERGY STAR** certification used in the United States), as well as using procedures (such as consolidating servers and using power management features to place devices into standby or sleep mode when not in use) to reduce energy consumption. Environmentally friendly computers are starting to come on the market, and alternate-powered hardware is beginning to become available.

In addition to practicing green computing when buying and using computer equipment, discarded equipment should be reused whenever possible. Computer equipment that is still functioning may be able to be donated and refurbished for additional use, and toner and ink cartridges can often be refilled and reused. Hardware that cannot be reused should be recycled if possible, or properly disposed of if not recyclable so that it does not end up as hazardous **e-waste** in landfills. Storage media containing personal or sensitive data should be disposed of properly, such as wiped or shredded before being reused or recycled.

**Chapter Objective 5:**
Suggest some ways computer users can practice green computing and properly dispose of obsolete computer equipment.

## RELATED LEGISLATION

There are numerous laws in place to protect intellectual property. Because moral and ethical standards are more difficult to agree on, ethical legislation is slower in coming. However, some laws have been implemented. The most significant legislation regarding accessibility is the 1998 amendment to the *Rehabilitation Act* requiring federal agencies to make their electronic and information technology accessible to people with disabilities. In the United States, some federal regulations and state laws impact the disposal of computer hardware.

**Chapter Objective 6:**
Discuss the current status of legislation related to intellectual property rights, ethics, access, and the environment in relation to computers.

# REVIEW ACTIVITIES

## KEY TERM MATCHING

**a.** assistive technology

**b.** computer ethics

**c.** copyright

**d.** digital divide

**e.** ergonomic hardware

**f.** intellectual property rights

**g.** Internet addiction

**h.** patent

**i.** plagiarism

**j.** trademark

**Instructions:** Match each key term on the left with the definition on the right that best describes it.

1. _____ A form of protection for an invention that can be granted by the government; gives exclusive rights of an invention to its inventor for 20 years.

2. _____ A word, phrase, symbol, or design that identifies goods or services.

3. _____ Hardware and software specifically designed for use by individuals with physical disabilities.

4. _____ Hardware, typically an input or output device, that is designed to be more ergonomically correct than its nonergonomic counterpart.

5. _____ Presenting someone else's work as your own.

6. _____ Standards of moral conduct as they relate to computer use.

7. _____ The gap between those who have access to technology and those who do not.

8. _____ The legal right to sell, publish, or distribute an original artistic or literary work; it is held by the creator of a work as soon as it exists in physical form.

9. _____ The problem of overusing, or being unable to stop using, the Internet.

10. _____ The rights to which creators of original creative works (such as artistic or literary works, inventions, corporate logos, and more) are entitled.

## SELF-QUIZ

**Instructions:** Circle **T** if the statement is true, **F** if the statement is false, or write the best answer in the space provided. **Answers for the self-quiz are located in the References and Resources Guide at the end of the book.**

1. **T F** All unethical acts are illegal.

2. **T F** Changing the background behind a television newscaster to make it appear that he or she is reporting on location instead of from inside the television studio would be an example of digital manipulation.

3. **T F** Carpal tunnel syndrome can be caused by using a computer keyboard.

4. **T F** As computer use has become more common, the potential for stress related to computer use has decreased.

5. **T F** Assistive technology is hardware and software designed to help all beginning computer users learn how to use a computer.

6. A software program would be protected by _____ law, while a corporate logo would be protected by _____ law.

7. Turning in a copy of a poem you found on a Web site as your original composition for a poetry class assignment is an example of _____.

8. Registering the domain name microsft.com to profit from it would be an act of _____.

9. The _____ can be used to describe discrepancies in access to technology by individuals within a country, as well as to compare access from country to country.

10. Match each term to its description or example, and write the corresponding number in the blank to the left of each description or example.

a. _____ What the symbol © stands for.

b. _____ Can vary from another's depending on his or her values, culture, and so forth.

c. _____ A warning about a nonexistent virus spread via e-mail.

d. _____ A subtle alteration of digital content that identifies the copyright holder.

1. Online hoax
2. Copyright
3. Digital watermark
4. Ethics

---

1. For each of the following situations, write the appropriate letter—E (ethical) or U (unethical)—in the blank to the right of the situation to indicate how most individuals would view the act.

**Situation**

a. A teenager rips a new CD she just bought and e-mails the MP3 files to all her friends.

b. A photographer combines two of his photographs to create a new composite artistic piece.

c. A physician incorporates another doctor's research into her journal article submission, including the researcher's name and article in her submission.

**Type of Situation**

_____

_____

_____

2. Match each term with its related example, and write the corresponding number in the blank to the left of each example.

a. _____ Assistive hardware

b. _____ Server consolidation

c. _____ Docking stations

d. _____ E-mail filters, stars, and flags

1. Green computing
2. Ergonomics
3. Information overload
4. Digital divide

3. Assume that you have created a Web site to display your favorite original photographs. Is the site and/or your photographs protected by copyright law? Why or why not?

4. List three possible negative physical effects that can result from computer use and describe one way to lessen each effect.

5. List three possible negative effects on the environment that can result from computer use and describe one way to lessen each effect.

---

1. There are research services available online that can be used by students preparing term papers. Is the use of these services ethical? Is the use of programs to detect plagiarism by instructors ethical? How can the problem of plagiarism and other forms of cheating at schools today be resolved? Whose responsibility is it to ensure students do not cheat themselves out of a proper education?

2. While the Web contains a vast amount of extremely useful information, some content can be harmful. Think about suicide Web sites that explain in detail how to kill oneself, Web sites that broadcast the beheadings by terrorists, and Web sites that explain how to build bombs. If a Web site instructs visitors how to perform an illegal act, should the site's creators be criminally liable if a visitor carries out those instructions? Who, if anyone, is responsible for preventing potentially harmful information from being shared via the Web? Is there any Internet content that you believe a government has the right or obligation to censor? If so, what? Where should the line between freedom of speech and national or personal safety be drawn?

SOC

# PROJECTS

1. **Portable Power** As discussed in the chapter How It Works box, there are a number of portable power devices that you can carry with you to power your devices while you are on the go.

   For this project, select one portable power device and research it. How does it charge, how long does it take to fully charge, and how much power does it provide once it is fully charged? What types of devices can it be used with and how does it connect to them? How large is it and how much does it weigh? How much does it cost? Would you have used this product anytime in the past month if you had access to it? Do you find this product useful? Why or why not? At the end of your research, prepare a one-page summary of your findings and opinions and submit it to your instructor.

2. **Copyright Registration** Think of an original creation (paper, poem, photograph, or song) to which you believe you are entitled copyright protection and assume that you would like to register a copyright for your creation.

   For this project, research how you would obtain a copyright for your chosen creation. Visit the U.S. Copyright Office Web site (search for it using a search site) and determine the necessary procedure for registration, the required paperwork, and the necessary fee. Use the information located on the site to make sure your creation is entitled to copyright protection, then find the appropriate online registration form (if one is available online). If possible, open and print just one page of the form. From the site, also determine what notice you will receive once your copyright claim has been recorded and how long it will take to receive it. Prepare a short summary of your findings to submit to your instructor, stapled to the single page of the appropriate application if you were able to print it.

3. **Ergonomic Workspaces** Some aspects of an ergonomic workspace, such as a comfortable chair and nonglaring light, may feel good right from the beginning. Others, such as using an ergonomic keyboard or wrist rest, may take a little getting used to.

   For this project, find at least one local store that has some type of ergonomic equipment—such as adjustable office chairs, desks with keyboard drawers, standing desks, ergonomic keyboards, or notebook stands—on display that you can try out. Test each piece, adjusting it as needed, and evaluate how comfortable it seems. Next, evaluate your usual computer workspace. Are there any adjustments you should make or any new equipment you would need to acquire to make your workspace setup more comfortable? Make a note of any changes you could make for free, as well as a list of items you would need to purchase and the estimated cost. Prepare a short summary of your findings to submit to your instructor. If you made any adjustments to your regular workspace during this project, be sure to include a comment regarding whether or not you think it increased your comfort.

4. **Toxic Devices** As discussed in the chapter, computers, mobile devices, and other hardware can contain a variety of toxic and hazardous materials. Is it ethical for manufacturers to continue to use hazardous materials in their products? What if a restriction on these compounds severely limited the types of electronic equipment that could be manufactured or significantly increased the price? Is it ethical for consumers to buy products that are made of hazardous materials or are not recyclable? What efforts should be made to recycle e-waste in the United States and who is ethically responsible for the cost—the manufacturers, the consumers, or the government? Should the government require the recycling of e-waste? Should it ban the exportation of e-waste?

    For this project, form an opinion about the ethical ramifications of toxic devices and e-waste and be prepared to discuss your position (in class, via an online class forum, or via a class blog, depending on your instructor's directions). You may also be asked to write a short paper expressing your opinion.

**ETHICS IN ACTION**

5. **Recycle or Trash?** As mentioned in the chapter, a great deal of obsolete computing equipment eventually ends up in a landfill, even though there may be alternative actions that could be taken instead.

    For this project, research what options would be available to discard the following: (1) a 10-year-old computer that is no longer functioning, (2) a 4-year-old computer that still works but is too slow for your needs, and (3) a used-up toner cartridge for a laser printer. Check with your local schools and charitable organizations to see if they would accept any of these items. Check with at least one computer manufacturer and one recycling company to see if they would accept the computers, and, if so, what the procedure and cost would be. Check with at least one vendor selling recharged toner cartridges to see if it buys old cartridges or requires a trade-in with an order. Share your findings with the class in the form of a short presentation. Be sure to include any costs associated with the disposal options you found, as well as your recommendation for each disposal situation. The presentation should not exceed 10 minutes and should make use of one or more presentation aids, such as a whiteboard, handouts, or a computer-based slide presentation (your instructor may provide additional requirements). You may also be asked to submit a summary of the presentation to your instructor.

**PRESENTATION/ DEMONSTRATION**

6. **Is It Ethical to Post Compromising Photos or Videos of Others?** Posting photos and videos on Facebook, YouTube, and other social media is an everyday activity for many individuals. When you post a photo of just yourself or of others who are aware that the content is going online, it isn't controversial. But what if the photo or video is less than flattering or shows the individual in a compromising position? Is it OK to post the content without asking the individual first? What if you post it but don't tag the individual so he or she isn't identified—does that make a difference? What if you don't tag the person but someone else does—is it your fault for posting the content originally? What if the individual knows you are posting it but then regrets it later—should you remove the item? What if a photo or video you post causes someone else a problem (such as an angry parent or a partner, or a lost job opportunity)? Is it ever ethical to post potentially compromising photos or videos of others online? Why or why not?

    Pick a side on this issue, form an opinion and gather supporting evidence, and be prepared to discuss and defend your position in a classroom debate or in a one- to two-page paper, depending on your instructor's directions.

**BALANCING ACT**

SOC

# Technology and Society

*Courtesy eBay. The eBay logo is a trademark of eBay Inc.*

**Jim Griffith, aka "Griff,"
is the Dean of eBay
Education, a roving
eBay ambassador, an
eBay spokesperson,
the host of eBay Radio,
and the author of *The
Official eBay Bible*.
An enthusiastic eBay
buyer and seller since
1996, Griff spends
nearly all his waking
hours teaching others
how to use eBay
effectively, safely,
and profitably, and
spreading the word
about eBay across
print, radio, and TV.
Griff has worked for
eBay for 20 years.**

## A Conversation with JIM GRIFFITH
### Dean of eBay Education, eBay

> *"The important point to keep in mind is that intellectual property is as protected as physical personal property."*

### My Background . . .

Although I have many roles at eBay, my most public role—Dean of eBay Education—is unique, slightly unorthodox, and best understood in the context of my history with the company. I was originally a user on eBay in the very early days (1996) and spent a lot of time assisting other buyers and sellers on eBay's one chat board. My posts came to the attention of eBay founder Pierre Omidyar who offered me a job as eBay's first customer support rep. I continued to be an active member of the eBay community along with my new duties at the time, which included assisting and teaching buyers, sellers, and eBay employees how to use eBay. Over time, I also became an eBay spokesperson, lead instructor of our eBay University program, author of *The Official eBay Bible* (now in its third edition), and host of eBay Radio.

In addition to the obvious knowledge of the eBay Web site, our policies, and the basics of business, the skills that proved to be most critical during my twenty-year tenure at eBay (and I should say I am still refining them) would be diplomacy, empathy, civility, and a strong sense of self-deprecating humor.

### It's Important to Know . . .

**Intellectual property rights are easily misunderstood.** While most governments provide the legal framework necessary to protect the intellectual property rights of owners, for many people, these rights are not so apparent. The important point to keep in mind is that intellectual property is as protected as physical personal property. Just as you would not want your personal property stolen, misused, or used without your permission, the same holds true for intangible property like copyrights and trademarks. Unauthorized use of another's intellectual property is theft.

**In business, as in life overall, it is critical to adopt a code of ethics that guides your business practices and decisions.** A sound code of ethics involves keeping abreast of the laws and regulations that govern business transactions and interactions both between employees and between companies. A good rule of thumb when it comes to compliance with a code of ethics is to make sure you can always answer "Yes" to the question, "Is this the right thing to do?"

**Responding to environmental concerns is no longer optional.** A successful company today must consider both the civic and financial costs of recycling and repurposing its output so as to have the smallest impact on the environment as possible. All companies must work to lower energy consumption, create products that can be recycled or reused, and decrease the company's carbon footprint.

### How I Use this Technology . . .

Besides working for eBay, I am an avid consumer and seller online. I make at least one online purchase a day (like many eBay shoppers, usually via my smartphone) and I always have a selection of items up for sale on eBay. My e-commerce activities, along with my job of instructing and assisting buyers and sellers to navigate and utilize eBay and PayPal, requires an extensive working knowledge of and familiarity with these Web sites, as well as eBay policies regarding intellectual property rights and ethical behavior.

## What the Future Holds . . .

Over the past few years, we've seen the downsizing of technology (cell phones are now more powerful than a desktop computer from 10 years ago!), as well as unforeseen innovations like the so-called "sharing economy" (such as Uber and Airbnb). As industries no longer meet the needs of customers, they will evolve. For example, the cable TV industry is rapidly changing in response to customers having access to a wide variety of online digital content delivered on demand to their devices and an increasing number of customers choosing to "cut the cord" to traditional cable TV service. Because the digital universe has changed drastically since the *Digital Millennium Copyright Act* was enacted in 1998, expect to see legislative attempts to refine and update copyright law.

As individuals continue to obtain and use an increasing number of digital devices for a growing number of tasks, the importance of moderation and balance with respect to technology will increase. For those that work with computers every day, the tendency toward burnout is high and one of the biggest contributors to burnout is a skewed work/life balance. It is also important to make sure that using a computer or other device doesn't cause physical harm—setting up an ergonomically-sound work environment, as well as safe work habits, can help.

Climate change is probably the single biggest driver of change in the world today and in the future. Switching to renewable energy, purchasing green business supplies, and limiting waste can help reduce our negative impact on the environment. In addition to employing these as standard business practices, eBay also helps the environment by extending the usefulness of objects beyond their assumed life cycle.

> " *All companies must work to lower energy consumption . . . and decrease the company's carbon footprint.* "

## My Advice to Students . . .

One of the biggest threats associated with computers and the Internet is our growing reliance on them to do our thinking for us without questioning or validating the results. While the Internet is the world's biggest research resource, you need to validate what you read online before considering it true.

In addition, moderation and balance with respect to technology are essential. For both mental and physical health, divide up your workday so that you are actively spending time away from computers and other devices. Take a walk. Ride a bike. Visit with friends (but keep your cell phone at home or in your pocket!).

## Discussion Question

Jim Griffith believes that it is the responsibility of all companies to respond to environmental concerns, such as creating products that can be recycled or reused. Think of a product you recently purchased. Did the product packaging suggest ways to recycle or reuse the product past its normal life? If so, did that factor into your decision to buy the product? Should companies be prohibited from selling products that cannot be recycled or repurposed in some manner? Why or why not? Be prepared to discuss your position (in class, via an online class forum, or via a class blog, depending on your instructor's directions). You may also be asked to write a short paper expressing your opinion.

>**For more information on eBay, visit www.ebay.com. For more information about effective, safe, and successful buying or selling on eBay, refer to** *The Official eBay Bible* **by Jim "Griff" Griffith.**

# REFERENCES AND RESOURCES
## *GUIDE*

## INTRODUCTION

When working on a computer or taking a computer course, you often need to look up information related to computers, smartphones, and other devices. For instance, you may need to find out when the IBM PC was first invented, you may want tips about what to consider when buying a new device, or you may want to find out more about how numbering systems work. To help you with the tasks just mentioned and more, this References and Resources Guide brings together in one convenient location a collection of technology-related references and resources.

## OUTLINE

# COMPUTER HISTORY TIMELINE

The earliest recorded calculating device, the abacus, is believed to have been invented by the Babylonians sometime between 500 B.C. and 100 B.C. It and similar types of counting boards were used solely for counting.

## 500 B.C.

Blaise Pascal invented the first mechanical calculator, called the Pascaline Arithmetic Machine. It had the capacity for eight digits and could add and subtract.

## 1642

Dr. John V. Atanasoff and Clifford Berry designed and built ABC (for Atanasoff-Berry Computer), the world's first electronic, digital computer.

## 1937

**Precomputers and Early Computers**

## 1621

## 1804

French silk weaver Joseph-Marie Jacquard built a loom that read holes punched on a series of small sheets of hardwood to control the weave of the pattern. This automated machine introduced the use of punch cards and showed that they could be used to convey a series of instructions.

## 1944

The Mark I, considered to be the first digital computer, was introduced by IBM. It was developed in cooperation with Harvard University, was more than 50 feet long, weighed almost five tons, and used electromechanical relays to solve addition problems in less than a second; multiplication and division took about 6 and 12 seconds, respectively.

The slide rule, a precursor to the electronic calculator, was invented. Used primarily to perform multiplication, division, square roots, and the calculation of logarithms, its widespread use continued until the 1970s.

Source: 500, 1642, 1804, 1944: IBM Corporate Archives; 1621: Mark Konshak, Curator, sliderulemuseum.com; 1937: Iowa State University

## Precomputers and Early Computers (before approximately 1946)

Most precomputers and early computers were mechanical machines that worked with gears and levers. Electromechanical devices (using both electricity and gears and levers) were developed toward the end of this era.

## First Generation (approximately 1946–1957)

Powered by vacuum tubes, these computers were faster than electromechanical machines, but they were large and bulky, generated excessive heat, and had to be physically wired and reset to run programs. Input was primarily on punch cards; output was on punch cards or paper. Machine and assembly languages were used to program these computers.

The UNIVAC 1, the first computer to be mass produced for general use, was introduced by Remington Rand. In 1952, it was used to analyze votes in the U.S. presidential election and correctly predicted that Dwight D. Eisenhower would be the victor only 45 minutes after the polls closed, though the results were not aired immediately because they weren't trusted.

The COBOL programming language was developed by a committee headed by Dr. Grace Hopper.

The first floppy disk (8 inches in diameter) was introduced.

UNIX was developed at AT&T's Bell Laboratories; Advanced Micro Devices (AMD) was formed; and ARPANET (the predecessor of today's Internet) was established.

IBM unbundled some of its hardware and software and began selling them separately, allowing other software companies to emerge.

## 1951          1960          1967          1969

---

**First Generation**          **Second Generation**   **Third Generation**

---

## 1947          1957          1964          1968

The FORTRAN programming language was introduced.

Robert Noyce and Gordon Moore founded the Intel Corporation.

John Bardeen, Walter Brattain, and William Shockley invented the transistor, which had the same capabilities as a vacuum tube but was faster, broke less often, used less power, and created less heat. They won a Nobel Prize for their invention in 1956 and computers began to be built with transistors shortly afterwards.

The first mouse was invented by Doug Engelbart.

The IBM System/360 computer was introduced. Unlike previous computers, System/360 contained a full line of compatible computers, making upgrading easier.

Source: 1951: U.S. Census Bureau; 1960: U.S. Navy; 1964a: SRI International; 1964b; 1969: IBM Corporate Archives

## Second Generation (approximately 1958–1963)

Second-generation computers used transistors instead of vacuum tubes. They allowed the computer to be physically smaller, more powerful, more reliable, and faster than before. Input was primarily on punch cards and magnetic tape; output was on punch cards and paper; and magnetic tape and disks were used for storage. High-level programming languages were used with these computers.

## Third Generation (approximately 1964–1970)

The third generation of computers evolved when integrated circuits (IC)—computer chips—began being used instead of conventional transistors. Computers became even smaller and more reliable. Keyboards and monitors were introduced for input and output; magnetic disks were used for storage. The emergence of the operating system meant that operators no longer had to manually reset relays and wiring.

**REF**

The first microprocessor, the Intel 4004, was designed by Ted Hoff. The single processor contained 2,250 transistors and could execute 60,000 operations per second.

Bill Gates and Paul Allen wrote a version of BASIC for the Altair, the first computer programming language designed for a personal computer. Bill Gates dropped out of Harvard to form Microsoft with Paul Allen.

Software Arts' Visi-Calc, the first electronic spreadsheet and business program for personal computers, was released. This program is seen as one of the reasons personal computers first became widely accepted in the business world.

IBM introduced the IBM PC. This DOS-based PC used a 4.77 MHz 8088 CPU with 64 KB of RAM and quickly became the standard for business personal computers.

# 1971  1975  1979  1981

## Fourth Generation

# 1972  1976  1980  1982

The C programming language was developed by Dennis Ritchie at Bell Labs.

Seymour Cray, called the "father of supercomputing," founded Cray Research, which would go on to build some of the fastest computers in the world.

Sony Electronics introduced the 3.5-inch floppy disk and drive.

Seagate Technology announced the first Winchester 5.25-inch hard disk drive, revolutionizing computer storage.

Steve Wozniak and Steve Jobs founded Apple computer and released the Apple I (a single-board computer), followed by the Apple II (a complete personal computer that became an instant success in 1977). They originally ran the company out of Jobs' parents' garage.

Intel introduced the 80286 CPU.

IBM chose Microsoft to develop the operating system for its upcoming personal computer. That operating system was PC-DOS.

*TIME* magazine named the computer its "Machine of the Year" for 1982, emphasizing the importance of the computer in our society.

Source: 1971, 1982: Intel Corporation; 1972: Photograph courtesy of the Charles Babbage Institute; 1975: Microsoft Archives; 1979: Dan Bricklin, www.jimraycroft.com; 1981, 1982: IBM Corporate Archives

## Fourth Generation (approximately 1971–present)

The fourth generation of computers began with large-scale integration (LSI), which resulted in chips that could contain thousands of transistors. Very large-scale integration (VLSI) resulted in the microprocessor and the resulting microcomputers. The keyboard and mouse are predominant input devices, though many other types of input devices are now available; monitors and printers provide output; and storage is obtained with magnetic disks, optical discs, and memory chips.

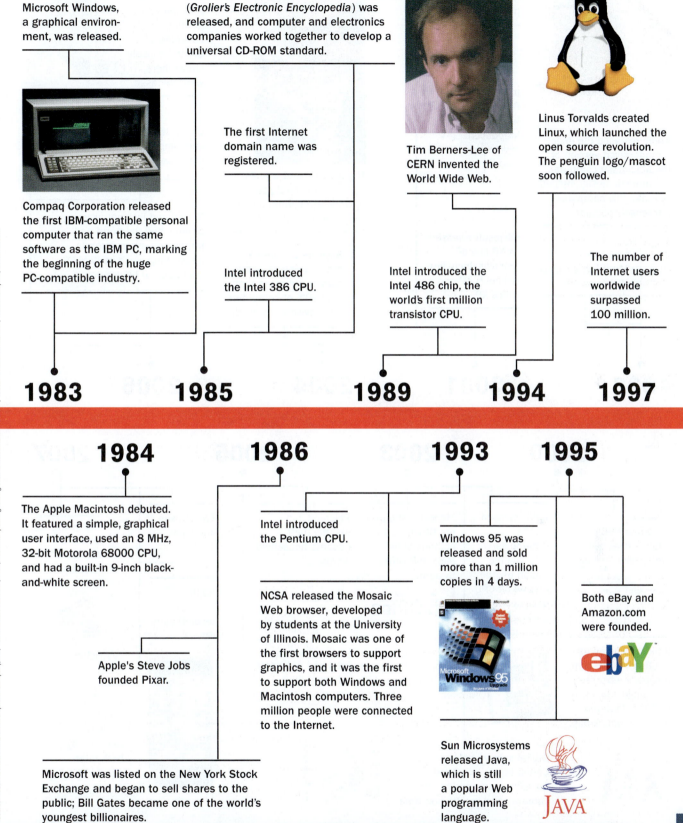

The first version of Microsoft Windows, a graphical environment, was released.

The first general-interest CD-ROM product (*Grolier's Electronic Encyclopedia*) was released, and computer and electronics companies worked together to develop a universal CD-ROM standard.

Linus Torvalds created Linux, which launched the open source revolution. The penguin logo/mascot soon followed.

Compaq Corporation released the first IBM-compatible personal computer that ran the same software as the IBM PC, marking the beginning of the huge PC-compatible industry.

The first Internet domain name was registered.

Tim Berners-Lee of CERN invented the World Wide Web.

The number of Internet users worldwide surpassed 100 million.

Intel introduced the Intel 386 CPU.

Intel introduced the Intel 486 chip, the world's first million transistor CPU.

## 1983    1985    1989    1994    1997

## 1984    1986    1993    1995

The Apple Macintosh debuted. It featured a simple, graphical user interface, used an 8 MHz, 32-bit Motorola 68000 CPU, and had a built-in 9-inch black-and-white screen.

Intel introduced the Pentium CPU.

Windows 95 was released and sold more than 1 million copies in 4 days.

Both eBay and Amazon.com were founded.

NCSA released the Mosaic Web browser, developed by students at the University of Illinois. Mosaic was one of the first browsers to support graphics, and it was the first to support both Windows and Macintosh computers. Three million people were connected to the Internet.

Apple's Steve Jobs founded Pixar.

Microsoft was listed on the New York Stock Exchange and began to sell shares to the public; Bill Gates became one of the world's youngest billionaires.

Sun Microsystems released Java, which is still a popular Web programming language.

Source: 1983: Hewlett-Packard Development Company, L.P.; 1989: Fabian Bachrach; W3C; 1994: Larry Ewing lewing@isc.tamu.edu and The GIMP; 1995a: Microsoft Museum; 1995b: eBay Inc; 1995c: Oracle

Apple introduced the iPod personal music player.

Intel's first 64-bit CPU, the Itanium, was introduced.

Apple released the iMac, a modernized version of the Macintosh computer. Its futuristic design helped to make this computer immensely popular.

Microsoft shipped Windows 98.

Microsoft released its XP line of products, including Windows XP and Office XP.

The Internet and wireless networks enabled people to work and communicate with others while on the go.

Spyware became a major problem; some studies indicated that over 80% of computers had spyware installed.

New Internet-enabled gaming consoles, like the Wii console shown here, were released.

Use of the Internet for online shopping and entertainment continued to grow.

Broadband Internet access approached the norm and improvements to wireless networking (such as WiMAX) continued to be developed.

# 1998    2001    2004    2006

# 2000    2003    2005    2007

The first USB flash drives were released.

AMD released the 64-bit Opteron server CPU and the Athlon 64, the first 64-bit CPU designed for desktop computer use.

Microsoft shipped the Office 2003 editions of its Microsoft Office System.

**Microsoft Office**

Phishing and identity theft became household words.

Twitter was launched.

Apple released the revolutionary iPhone.

Microsoft released Windows Vista and Office 2007.

**Windows Vista**

Intel introduced its Pentium 4 CPU chip. A popular advertising campaign, launched in 2001, featured the Blue Man Group.

Digital camera sales in the United States exceeded 14 million, surpassing film camera sales for the first time.

Intel and AMD both released their first dual-core CPUs.

Quad-core CPUs were released by both Intel and AMD.

Source: 2000a: Kingston Technology Corporation; 2000b: Intel Corporation; 2001: Apple, Inc.; 2003a: © 2003, 2005, 2006, 2007 Advanced Micro Devices, Inc.; 2003b, 2004: Microsoft Corporation; 2003c: iStockphoto.com/kingvald; 2006: iStockphoto.com/sara_winter; 2007a: Belkin International, Inc.; 2007b: Microsoft Corporation

Netbooks were introduced.

Google introduced the Chrome Web browser.

Use of social networking sites exploded; Facebook announced it had more than 100 million users.

## 2008

Microsoft released Office 2010, which included cloud versions for the first time.

Microsoft introduced Kinect, the first voice and movement controller.

Apple released the iPad, which started a tablet trend.

## 2010

Social media took off; Facebook hit 1 billion active users.

Microsoft released Windows 8, Office and Office 365.

The availability and use of Android phones and tablets soared.

## 2012

Apple released the iPhone 6, which included Apple Pay and the Touch ID fingerprint reader.

The first octocore smartphones became available.

Fitness bands, such as the Fitbit, became mainstream.

## 2014

**Fifth Generation**

## 2009

Geobrowsing applications became more prominent; 4G phones became available.

Notebooks outsold desktops.

Cloud computing entered the mainstream for both individuals and businesses.

Microsoft released Windows 7.

## 2011

Supercomputer Watson beat human players in *Jeopardy!*.

Amazon sold more e-books than print books and released Kindle Fire, the first color e-book reader.

## 2013

Google Glass became available.

HTML5 took off and started to change the way Web pages were developed.

Touch computing became common with a variety of devices, including desktop PCs.

Apple released the Apple Watch.

More than two-thirds of all U.S. adults owned a smartphone.

## 2015

Microsoft released Windows 10 and Office 2016.

Windows
Office

Approximately 4 million consumer drones were sold; the U.S. government initiated mandatory drone registration.

## Fifth Generation (now and the future)

The fifth generation of computers is in its infancy stage. Today, fifth-generation computers tend to be based on artificial intelligence and include voice and touch input. In the future, they are expected to be constructed differently, such as in the form of optical computers, tiny computers that utilize nanotechnology, and as general-purpose computers built into desks, home appliances, and other everyday devices.

**REF**

Source: 2008a: Courtesy of Dell Inc.; 2008b: Google Inc.; 2009a: T-Mobile USA, Inc.; 2009b: Google Inc.; 2009c: Microsoft Corporation; 2010: iStockphoto.com/Jill Fromer; 2011: IBM Corporation; 2012a: Facebook; 2012b: Samsung; 2013a: Google Inc.; 2013b: Courtesy of Dell Inc.; 2014a: Apple, Inc.; 2014b: Fitbit Inc.; 2015a: Apple, Inc.; 2015b: Microsoft Corporation; 2015c: Airwave

# GUIDE TO BUYING A PC

**B**efore buying a new computer or other computing device, it is important to give some thought to what your needs are, including what software you want to run, any other devices with which you need to be compatible, how you might want to connect to the Internet, and how much portability is needed. This section of the References and Resources Guide explores topics related to buying a new personal computing device. ∎

## Analyzing Needs

When referring to a computing device, a need refers to a functional requirement that the device must be able to meet. For example, at a retail store, a computer system would need to be able to enter barcodes automatically from items being purchased, compute the appropriate sales tax, keep track of product inventories, and print receipts and needed reports. Portability is another example of a possible need. For example, if you need to take your device with you as you travel or work out of the office, you will need a portable computer or a tablet instead of a desktop computer.

Selecting a device for home or business use must begin with the all-important question "What do I want the device to do?" Once you have determined what tasks it will be used for and the amount of portability that is needed, you can choose among the software and hardware alternatives available. Making a list of your needs in the areas discussed in the next few sections can help you get a picture of what type of system you are shopping for. If you are not really sure what you want a system to do, you should think twice about buying one—you can easily make expensive mistakes if you are uncertain about what you want a system to do. Some common decision categories are discussed next; Figure R-1 provides a list of questions that can help you define the type of device that will meet your needs.

**▼ FIGURE R-1**

Questions to consider when getting ready to buy a computing device.

### POSSIBLE QUESTIONS

What tasks will I be using the device for (writing papers, accessing the Internet, watching TV, making phone and video calls, composing music, playing games, etc.)?

Do I have an operating system preference? Are there any other devices I need my documents and storage media to be compatible with?

How fast do I need the system to be?

Do I need portability? If so, do I need a powerful desktop replacement notebook or will a less-powerful notebook or a tablet suffice?

What size screen do I need? Do I need to be able to connect to a second monitor or an HDTV set? If so, do I need wireless connectivity?

What removable storage media will I need to use (such as DVDs, flash memory cards, or USB flash drives)?

What types of Internet access will I be using (such as DSL, cable, satellite, or mobile wireless)?

What types of networks will I need to connect to (wired, Wi-Fi, cellular)? What type of network adapter is needed to connect to those networks? Is that adapter commonly built into the devices I am considering?

What additional hardware do I need (scanner, printer, wireless router, digital camera, notebook stand, or tablet stand, for example)?

What brand(s) do I prefer? When do I need the device?

Do I want to pay extra for a better warranty (such as a longer time period, more comprehensive coverage, or on-site service)?

## Application Software Decisions

Determining what functions you want the system to perform will also help you decide which software is needed. Most users start with an application suite containing a word processor, spreadsheet, and other programs—either installed or cloud software. In addition, specialty programs or apps, such as tax preparation, drawing, home publishing, reference software, games, and more, may be needed or desired.

Not all software is available for all operating systems. Consequently, if a specific piece of software is needed, that choice may determine which operating system you need to use. In addition, your operating system and application software decisions may already be made for you if your documents need to be compatible with those of another computer (such as other office computers or between a home and an office computer).

## Platforms and Configuration Options

If your operating system has already been determined, that is a good start in deciding the overall platform you will be looking for—most users will choose between the PC-compatible and Apple platforms. PC-compatible computers usually run either Windows or Linux; Apple computers almost always use OS X. Mobile devices typically run either Android or iOS.

Configuration decisions initially involve determining the size of the device desired (see Figure R-2). For nonportable systems, you have the choice between tower, desktop, or all-in-one configurations; in addition, the monitor size needs to be determined. Fully functioning personal computers can be notebook or tablet computers. For tablet computers, you need to decide if you will require keyboard use on a regular basis; if so, a hybrid notebook-tablet computer would be the best choice. If a powerful fully functioning computer is not required, you may decide to go with an even more portable option, such as a netbook or tablet.

You should also consider any other specifications that are important to you, such as the size and type of internal storage (hard drive or flash memory media, for instance), types of other storage devices needed, amount of memory required, and so forth. As discussed in the next section, these decisions often require reconciling the features you want with the amount of money you are willing to spend.

## Power vs. Budget Requirements

As part of the needs analysis, you should look closely at your need for a powerful system versus your budgetary constraints. Most users do not need a state-of-the-art system. Those who do should expect to pay more than the average user. A device that was top of the line six months or a year ago is usually reasonably priced and more than adequate for most users' needs. Individuals who want a device only for basic tasks, such as using the Internet and word processing, can likely get by with an inexpensive device designed for home use.

When determining your requirements, be sure to identify the features and functions that are absolutely essential for your primary computing tasks (such as a large hard drive and lots of memory for multimedia applications, a fast video card for gaming, a fast Internet connection, the ability to easily connect to a large external monitor, and so forth). After you have the minimum configuration determined, you can add optional or desirable components, as your budget allows.

## Listing Alternatives

After you consider your needs and the questions mentioned in Figure R-1, you should have a pretty good idea of the hardware and software you will need. You will also know what purchasing options are available to you, depending on your time frame (while some retail stores have systems that can be purchased and brought home the same day, special orders or some systems purchased online will take longer). The next step is to get enough information from possible vendors to compare and contrast a few alternative systems that satisfy your stated needs. Most often, these vendors are local stores (such as computer stores, warehouse clubs, and electronic stores) and/or online stores (such as manufacturer Web sites and online retailers). To compare prices and specifications for possible systems, find at least three systems that meet or exceed your needs by looking through newspaper advertisements, configuring systems online, or calling or visiting local stores. A comparison sheet listing your criteria and the systems you are considering, such as the one in Figure R-3, can help you summarize your options. Although it is sometimes very difficult to compare the prices of systems since they typically have somewhat different configurations and some components (such as CPUs) are difficult to compare, you can assign an approximate dollar value to each extra feature a system has (such as $50 for an included printer or a larger hard drive). Be sure to also include any sales tax and shipping charges when you compare the prices of each total system.

**DESKTOPS**

**NOTEBOOKS**

**HYBRID NOTEBOOK-TABLETS**

**FIGURE R-2**
Configuration options.

| COMPONENT | EXAMPLE OF DESIRED SPECIFICATIONS | SYSTEM #1 VENDOR: | SYSTEM #2 VENDOR: | SYSTEM #3 VENDOR: |
|---|---|---|---|---|
| Type of device | Notebook computer | | | |
| Operating system | Windows 10 | | | |
| Manufacturer | HP, Acer, Toshiba, or Dell | | | |
| CPU | Intel quad core | | | |
| RAM | 16 GB or higher | | | |
| Hard drive | 2 TB or higher SSHD | | | |
| Removable storage | Flash memory card reader | | | |
| Optical drive | Blu-ray Disc drive | | | |
| Monitor | Widescreen 17"; touch screen | | | |
| Video card and video RAM | Prefer dedicated video card with 2 GB video RAM minimum | | | |
| Camera/microphone | HD webcam and integrated microphone | | | |
| Keyboard/mouse | Bluetooth keyboard and mouse | | | |
| Sound card/speakers | No preference | | | |
| Modem | None | | | |
| Networking | Wi-Fi (802.11ac); Bluetooth; Ethernet | | | |
| Printer | Laser if get a good package deal | | | |
| Included software | Microsoft Office 365 University | | | |
| Warranty | 3 years min. | | | |
| Other features | 2 USB 3.0 ports minimum | | | |
| Price | | | | |
| Tax | | | | |
| Shipping | | | | |
| TOTAL COST | | | | |

**A FIGURE R-3**

**Comparing computing alternatives.** A checklist such as this one can help to organize your desired criteria and evaluate possible systems.

If your budget is limited, you will have to balance the system you need with extra features you may want. But do not skimp on memory or hard drive space because sufficient memory can help your programs to run faster and with fewer problems, and hard drive space is consumed quickly. Upgrading the memory, CPU, or hard drive at the time of purchase is often significantly cheaper than trying to upgrade those features later. A good rule of thumb is to try to buy a little higher system than you think you need. On the other hand, do not buy a top-of-the-line system unless you fall into the power user category and really need it. Generally, the second or third system down from the top of the line is a very good system for a much more reasonable price. Some guidelines for minimum requirements for a new computer for most home users are as follows:

- ➤ A relatively fast multi-core CPU.
- ➤ 8 GB of RAM for desktop and notebook users.
- ➤ 1 TB or more hard drive space.
- ➤ Recordable or rewritable DVD or Blu-ray Disc drive.
- ➤ Network adapter or modem for the desired type(s) of Internet access.
- ➤ Sound card and speakers; built-in webcam and microphone.
- ➤ At least 2 USB ports.
- ➤ A built-in flash memory media reader.

# A LOOK AT NUMBERING SYSTEMS

**A**s discussed in Chapter 2 of this text, a numbering system is a way of representing numbers. People generally use the *decimal numbering system* explained in Chapter 2 and reviewed next; computers process data using the *binary numbering system*. Another numbering system related to computer use is the *hexadecimal numbering system*, which can be used to represent long strings of binary numbers in a manner more understandable to people than the binary numbering system. Following a discussion of these three numbering systems, we take a look at conversions between numbering systems and principles of computer arithmetic, and then close with a look at how to perform conversions using a scientific calculator. ■

## The Decimal and Binary Numbering System

The *decimal (base 10)* numbering system uses 10 symbols—the digits 0, 1, 2, 3, 4, 5, 6, 7, 8, and 9—to represent all possible numbers and is the numbering system people use most often. The *binary (base 2)* numbering system is used extensively by computers to represent numbers and other characters. This system uses only two digits—0 and 1. As illustrated in Figure 2-3 in Chapter 2, the place values (columns) in the binary numbering system are different from those used in the decimal system.

 **FIGURE R-4**

Hexadecimal characters and their decimal and binary equivalents.

## The Hexadecimal Numbering System

Computers often output diagnostic and memory-management messages and identify network adapters and other hardware in *hexadecimal (hex)* notation. Hexadecimal notation is a shorthand method for representing the binary digits stored in a computer. Because large binary numbers—for example, 1101010001001110—can easily be misread by people, hexadecimal notation groups binary digits into units of four, which, in turn, are represented by other symbols.

The hexadecimal numbering system is also called the *base 16 numbering system* because it uses 16 different symbols. Since there are only 10 possible numeric digits, hexadecimal uses letters instead of numbers for the additional 6 symbols. The 16 hexadecimal symbols and their decimal and binary counterparts are shown in Figure R-4.

The hexadecimal numbering system has a special relationship to the 8-bit bytes of ASCII and EBCDIC that makes it ideal for displaying addresses and other data quickly. As you can see in Figure R-4, each hex character has a 4-bit binary counterpart, so any combination of 8 bits can be represented by exactly two hexadecimal characters. For example, the letter N (represented in ASCII by 01001110) has a hex representation of *4E* (see the Binary Equivalent column for the hexadecimal characters *4* and *E* in Figure R-4).

| HEXADECIMAL CHARACTER | DECIMAL EQUIVALENT | BINARY EQUIVALENT |
|---|---|---|
| 0 | 0 | 0000 |
| 1 | 1 | 0001 |
| 2 | 2 | 0010 |
| 3 | 3 | 0011 |
| 4 | 4 | 0100 |
| 5 | 5 | 0101 |
| 6 | 6 | 0110 |
| 7 | 7 | 0111 |
| 8 | 8 | 1000 |
| 9 | 9 | 1001 |
| A | 10 | 1010 |
| B | 11 | 1011 |
| C | 12 | 1100 |
| D | 13 | 1101 |
| E | 14 | 1110 |
| F | 15 | 1111 |

## Converting Between Numbering Systems

In Figure 2-3 in Chapter 2, we illustrated how to convert from binary to decimal. Three other types of conversions computer professionals sometimes need to make are discussed next.

### Hexadecimal to Decimal

As shown in Figure R-5, the process for converting a hexadecimal number to its decimal equivalent is similar to converting a binary number to its decimal equivalent, except the base number is 16 instead of 2. To determine the decimal equivalent of a hexadecimal number (such as 4F6A, as shown in Figure R-5), multiply the decimal equivalent of each individual hex character (determined by using the table in Figure R-4) by the appropriate power of 16 and then add the results to obtain the decimal equivalent of that hex number.

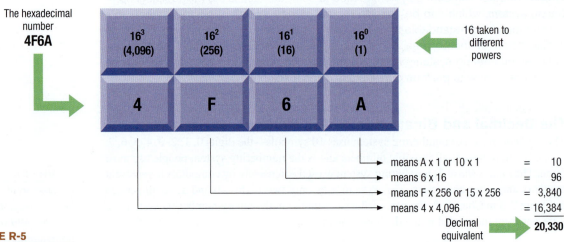

**FIGURE R-5**

**The hexadecimal (base 16) numbering system.** Each digit in a hexadecimal number represents 16 taken to a different power.

### Hexadecimal to Binary and Binary to Hexadecimal

To convert from hexadecimal to binary, we convert each hexadecimal digit separately to 4 binary digits (using the table in Figure R-4). For example, to convert F6A9 to binary, we get

| F | 6 | A | 9 |
|------|------|------|------|
| 1111 | 0110 | 1010 | 1001 |

or 1111011010101001 in binary representation. To convert from binary to hexadecimal, we go through the reverse process. If the number of digits in the binary number is not divisible by 4, we add leading zeros to the binary number to force an even division. For example, to convert the binary number 1101101010011 to hexadecimal, we get

| 0001 | 1011 | 0101 | 0011 |
|------|------|------|------|
| 1 | B | 5 | 3 |

or 1B53 in hexadecimal representation. Note that three leading zeros were added to change the initial 1 to 0001 before making the conversion.

### Decimal to Binary and Decimal to Hexadecimal

To convert from decimal to either binary or hexadecimal, we can use the *remainder method*. To use the remainder method, the decimal number is divided by 2 (to convert to a binary number) or 16 (to convert to a hexadecimal number). The *remainder* of the division operation is recorded and the division process is repeated using the *quotient* as the next dividend, until the quotient becomes 0. At that point, the collective remainders (written backwards) represent the equivalent binary or hexadecimal number (see Figure R-6).

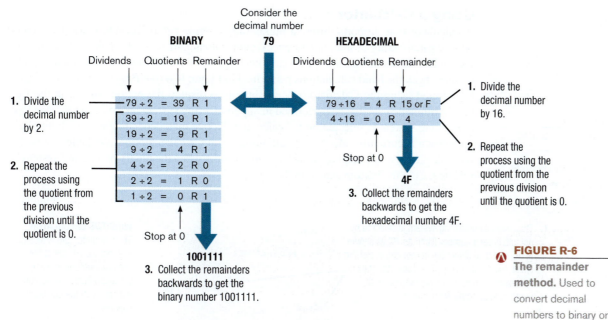

Consider the decimal number 79

**BINARY**

Dividends Quotients Remainder

1. Divide the decimal number by 2.

| 79 ÷ 2 | = 39 | R 1 |
| 39 ÷ 2 | = 19 | R 1 |
| 19 ÷ 2 | = 9 | R 1 |
| 9 ÷ 2 | = 4 | R 1 |
| 4 ÷ 2 | = 2 | R 0 |
| 2 ÷ 2 | = 1 | R 0 |
| 1 ÷ 2 | = 0 | R 1 |

2. Repeat the process using the quotient from the previous division until the quotient is 0.

Stop at 0

**1001111**

3. Collect the remainders backwards to get the binary number 1001111.

**HEXADECIMAL**

Dividends Quotients Remainder

| 79 ÷ 16 | = 4 | R 15 or F |
| 4 ÷ 16 | = 0 | R 4 |

Stop at 0

**4F**

3. Collect the remainders backwards to get the hexadecimal number 4F.

1. Divide the decimal number by 16.

2. Repeat the process using the quotient from the previous division until the quotient is 0.

**FIGURE R-6**
**The remainder method.** Used to convert decimal numbers to binary or hex format.

A table summarizing all the numbering system conversion procedures covered in this text is provided in Figure R-7.

**FIGURE R-7**
**Summary of conversions.**

| FROM BASE | TO BASE | | |
|---|---|---|---|
| | **2** | **10** | **16** |
| **2** | | Starting at the rightmost digit, multiply binary digits by $2^0$, $2^1$, $2^2$, etc., respectively, and then add products. | Starting at the rightmost digit, convert each group of four binary digits to a hex digit. |
| **10** | Divide repeatedly by 2 using each quotient as the next dividend until the quotient becomes 0, and then collect the remainders in reverse order. | | Divide repeatedly by 16 using each quotient as the next dividend until the quotient becomes 0, and then collect the remainders in reverse order. |
| **16** | Convert each hex digit to four binary digits. | Starting at the rightmost digit, multiply hex digits by $16^0$, $16^1$, $16^2$, etc., respectively, and then add products. | |

## Computer Arithmetic

To most people, decimal arithmetic is second nature. Addition and subtraction of binary and hexadecimal numbers is not much different from the process used with decimal numbers—just the number of symbols used in each system varies. For instance, the digits in each column are added or subtracted and you carry to and borrow from the column to the left as needed as you move from right to left. Instead of carrying or borrowing powers of 10, however—as you would in the decimal system—you carry or borrow powers of 2 (binary) or 16 (hexadecimal).

Figure R-8 provides an example of addition and subtraction with decimal, binary, and hexadecimal numbers.

**FIGURE R-8**
**Adding and subtracting with the decimal, binary, and hexadecimal numbering systems.**

| | DECIMAL | BINARY | HEXADECIMAL |
|---|---|---|---|
| | 1 | 1 1 1 | 1 |
| | 144 | 100101 | 8E |
| | + 27 | + 10011 | + 2F |
| **Addition** | 171 | 111000 | BD |
| | 3 | 0 0 | 7 1 |
| | 144 | 100101 | 8E |
| | - 27 | - 10011 | - 2F |
| **Subtraction** | 117 | 10010 | 5F |

**REF**

## Using a Calculator

A calculator that supports different numbering systems can be used to convert numbers between numbering systems or to check conversions performed by hand. For example, Figure R-9 shows how to use the Programmer option of the Windows 10 Calculator app to double-check the hand calculations performed in Figure R-6 (the *Programmer* option must be selected using the Calculator's Menu button to display the options shown in the figure). Arithmetic can also be performed in any numbering system on a calculator, once that numbering system is selected on the calculator. Notice that, depending on which numbering system is currently selected, not all numbers on the calculator are available—only the possible numbers are displayed, such as only 0 and 1 when the binary numbering system is selected, as in the bottom screen in the figure.

**FIGURE R-9**

Using a calculator to convert between numbering systems and perform arithmetic.

1. The decimal numbering system is selected by default; enter a number (such as 79, as shown here), and then select the numbering system to which the number should be converted (hex in this example, though preview values of all numbering systems are displayed).

The decimal numbering system is currently selected.

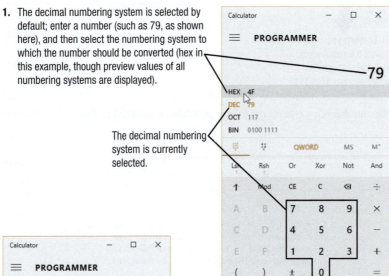

**WINDOWS CALCULATOR**
The Calculator app is included in Windows 10; select the *Programmer* option using the Menu button in the upper left corner of the Calculator window.

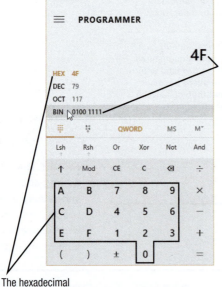

2. The number is now displayed in hex notation and only the 16 symbols used in the hexidecimal numbering system are available. To convert the number to binary, select that numbering system.

The hexadecimal numbering system is currently selected.

**NUMBERING SYSTEMS**
Numbers and operators can be used to perform arithmetic using any of the four numbering systems. Note that not all numbers on the calculator are available—only the ones appropriate for the selected numbering system.

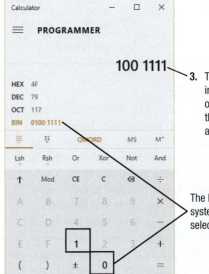

3. The number is now displayed in binary representation and only the two symbols used in the binary numbering system are available.

The binary numbering system is currently selected.

# CODING CHARTS

As discussed in Chapter 2 of this text, coding systems for text-based data include ASCII, EBCDIC, and Unicode. ∎

**▼ FIGURE R-10**
ASCII and EBCDIC binary codes for typical keyboard symbols.

## ASCII and EBCDIC

Figure R-10 provides a chart listing the 8-digit ASCII and EBCDIC representations (in binary) for most of the symbols found on a typical keyboard.

| SYMBOL | ASCII | EBCDIC | SYMBOL | ASCII | EBCDIC | SYMBOL | ASCII | EBCDIC |
|---|---|---|---|---|---|---|---|---|
| A | 0100 0001 | 1100 0001 | e | 0110 0101 | 1000 0101 | 8 | 0011 1000 | 1111 1000 |
| B | 0100 0010 | 1100 0010 | f | 0110 0110 | 1000 0110 | 9 | 0011 1001 | 1111 1001 |
| C | 0100 0011 | 1100 0011 | g | 0110 0111 | 1000 0111 | ( | 0010 1000 | 0100 1101 |
| D | 0100 0100 | 1100 0100 | h | 0110 1000 | 1000 1000 | ) | 0010 1001 | 0101 1101 |
| E | 0100 0101 | 1100 0101 | i | 0110 1001 | 1000 1001 | / | 0010 1111 | 0110 0001 |
| F | 0100 0110 | 1100 0110 | j | 0110 1010 | 1001 0001 | - | 0010 1101 | 0110 0000 |
| G | 0100 0111 | 1100 0111 | k | 0110 1011 | 1001 0010 | * | 0010 1010 | 0101 1100 |
| H | 0100 1000 | 1100 1000 | l | 0110 1100 | 1001 0011 | + | 0010 1011 | 0100 1110 |
| I | 0100 1001 | 1100 1001 | m | 0110 1101 | 1001 0100 | , | 0010 1100 | 0110 1011 |
| J | 0100 1010 | 1101 0001 | n | 0110 1110 | 1001 0101 | . | 0010 1110 | 0100 1011 |
| K | 0100 1011 | 1101 0010 | o | 0110 1111 | 1001 0110 | : | 0011 1010 | 0111 1010 |
| L | 0100 1100 | 1101 0011 | p | 0111 0000 | 1001 0111 | ; | 0011 1011 | 0101 1110 |
| M | 0100 1101 | 1101 0100 | q | 0111 0001 | 1001 1000 | & | 0010 0110 | 0101 0000 |
| N | 0100 1110 | 1101 0101 | r | 0111 0010 | 1001 1001 | \ | 0101 1100 | 1110 0000 |
| O | 0100 1111 | 1101 0110 | s | 0111 0011 | 1010 0010 | $ | 0010 0100 | 0101 1011 |
| P | 0101 0000 | 1101 0111 | t | 0111 0100 | 1010 0011 | % | 0010 0101 | 0110 1100 |
| Q | 0101 0001 | 1101 1000 | u | 0111 0101 | 1010 0100 | = | 0011 1101 | 0111 1110 |
| R | 0101 0010 | 1101 1001 | v | 0111 0110 | 1010 0101 | > | 0011 1110 | 0110 1110 |
| S | 0101 0011 | 1110 0010 | w | 0111 0111 | 1010 0110 | < | 0011 1100 | 0100 1100 |
| T | 0101 0100 | 1110 0011 | x | 0111 1000 | 1010 0111 | ! | 0010 0001 | 0101 1010 |
| U | 0101 0101 | 1110 0100 | y | 0111 1001 | 1010 1000 | \| | 0111 1100 | 0110 1010 |
| V | 0101 0110 | 1110 0101 | z | 0111 1010 | 1010 1001 | ? | 0011 1111 | 0110 1111 |
| W | 0101 0111 | 1110 0110 | 0 | 0011 0000 | 1111 0000 | @ | 0100 0000 | 0111 1100 |
| X | 0101 1000 | 1110 0111 | 1 | 0011 0001 | 1111 0001 | _ | 0101 1111 | 0110 1101 |
| Y | 0101 1001 | 1110 1000 | 2 | 0011 0010 | 1111 0010 | ' | 0110 0000 | 1011 1001 |
| Z | 0101 1010 | 1110 1001 | 3 | 0011 0011 | 1111 0011 | { | 0111 1011 | 1100 0000 |
| a | 0110 0001 | 1000 0001 | 4 | 0011 0100 | 1111 0100 | } | 0111 1101 | 1101 0000 |
| b | 0110 0010 | 1000 0010 | 5 | 0011 0101 | 1111 0101 | ~ | 0111 1110 | 1010 0001 |
| c | 0110 0011 | 1000 0011 | 6 | 0011 0110 | 1111 0110 | [ | 0101 1011 | 0100 1010 |
| d | 0110 0100 | 1000 0100 | 7 | 0011 0111 | 1111 0111 | ] | 0101 1101 | 0101 1010 |

**REF**

| | | | | | | | | |
|---|---|---|---|---|---|---|---|---|
| A 0041 | N 004E | a 0061 | n 006E | o 0030 | ( 007B | * 002A | ■ 25A0 | অ 0985 |
| B 0042 | O 004F | b 0062 | o 006F | 1 0031 | \| 007C | + 002B | □ 25A1 | গ 0997 |
| C 0043 | P 0050 | c 0063 | p 0070 | 2 0032 | } 007D | , 002C | ▲ 25B2 | ে 09C7 |
| D 0044 | Q 0051 | d 0064 | q 0071 | 3 0033 | ~ 007E | - 002D | ℅ 2105 | ৶ 09F6 |
| E 0045 | R 0052 | e 0065 | r 0072 | 4 0034 | ! 0021 | . 002E | ℞ 211E | چ 0685 |
| F 0046 | S 0053 | f 0066 | s 0073 | 5 0035 | " 0022 | / 002F | ⅓ 2153 | ڴ 06B4 |
| G 0047 | T 0054 | g 0067 | t 0074 | 6 0036 | # 0023 | £ 20A4 | ⅔ 2154 | ڪ 06AA |
| H 0048 | U 0055 | h 0068 | u 0075 | 7 0037 | $ 0024 | Σ 2211 | ♛ 2655 | α 03B1 |
| I 0049 | V 0056 | i 0069 | v 0076 | 8 0038 | % 0025 | ∅ 2205 | ☂ 2602 | β 03B2 |
| J 004A | W 0057 | j 006A | w 0077 | 9 0039 | & 0026 | √ 221A | ❐ 2750 | Δ 0394 |
| K 004B | X 0058 | k 006B | x 0078 | [ 005B | ' 0027 | ∞ 221E | ❂ 2742 | φ 03A6 |
| L 004C | Y 0059 | l 006C | y 0079 | \ 005C | ( 0028 | ≤ 2264 | ➲ 27B2 | Ω 03A9 |
| M 004D | Z 005A | m 006D | z 007A | ] 005D | ) 0029 | ≥ 2265 | ♥ 2665 | Ÿ 03AB |

**FIGURE R-11**
Selected Unicode codes.

**FIGURE R-12**
Using Unicode.

# Unicode

Because consistent worldwide representation of symbols is increasingly needed today, use of Unicode is growing rapidly. Unicode can be used to represent every written language, as well as a variety of other symbols. Unicode codes are typically listed in hexadecimal notation—a sampling of Unicode is shown in Figure R-11.

The capability to display characters and other symbols using Unicode coding is incorporated into many programs. For instance, when the Symbol dialog box is opened using the Insert tab in Microsoft Word, the Unicode representation (as well as the corresponding ASCII code in either decimal or hexadecimal representation) can be viewed (see Figure R-12). Some programs allow you to enter a Unicode symbol using its Unicode hexadecimal value. For instance, in Microsoft Office programs you can use the [Alt]+[X] command when the insertion point is just to the right of a Unicode hex value to convert that hex value into the corresponding symbol. For example, the keystrokes

2264[Alt]+[X]

result in the symbol corresponding to the Unicode code 2264 (the less than or equal sign ≤) being inserted into the document; entering 03A3 and then pressing [Alt]+[X] inserts the symbol shown in the Word 2016 screen in Figure R-12.

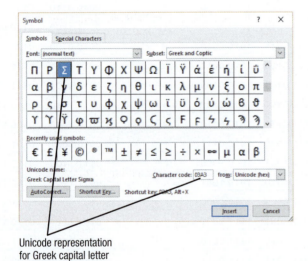

**UNICODE REPRESENTATION**
The Symbol dialog box shown here lists the Unicode representation of each symbol as it is selected. If preferred, the ASCII representation can be displayed.

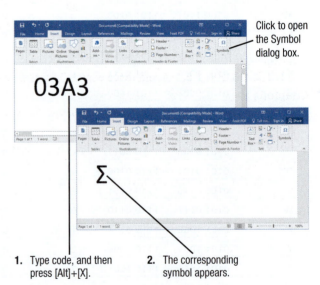

1. Type code, and then press [Alt]+[X].
2. The corresponding symbol appears.

**INSERTING SYMBOLS USING UNICODE**
In Microsoft Office programs, typing the hexadecimal Unicode code for a symbol and then pressing [Alt]+[X] displays the corresponding symbol.

# ANSWERS TO SELF-QUIZ

**Chapter 1**

1. T 2. F 3. F 4. T 5. F 6. Input 7. hybrid notebook-tablet, convertible tablet, or 2-in-1 computer 8. Virtualization 9. hyperlink 10. a. 4 b. 2 c. 1 d. 3

**Chapter 2**

1. T 2. F 3. T 4. T 5. F 6. terascale computing 7. quad-core 8. port 9. multiprocessing 10. a. 6 b. 2 c. 4 d. 9 e. 7 f. 1 g. 8 h. 5 i. 3

**Chapter 3**

1. F 2. T 3. F 4. T 5. F 6. C 7. volatile 8. optical 9. smart card 10. flash memory

**Chapter 4**

1. F 2. T 3. T 4. T 5. F 6. handwriting recognition 7. scanner, optical scanner, flatbed scanner, or portable scanner 8. pixel 9. flat-panel, LED, or LCD; cathode-ray tube or CRT 10. a. 2 b. 5 c. 1 d. 4 e. 3

**Chapter 5**

1. T 2. F 3. T 4. F 5. F 6. Linux 7. iOS 8. file compression 9. back up 10. a. 2 b. 3 c. 1

**Chapter 6**

1. T 2. T 3. F 4. F 5. F 6. open source 7. insertion point or cursor 8. cloud software, Web-based software, Software as a Service (SaaS), or cloudware 9. table 10. a. 2 b. 4 c. 1 d. 3

**Chapter 7**

1. F 2. T 3. F 4. T 5. F 6. bus 7. dual-mode 8. personal area network or PAN 9. virtual private network or VPN 10. a. 3 b. 4 c. 1 d. 5 e. 2

**Chapter 8**

1. F 2. F 3. T 4. T 5. F 6. Digital Subscriber Line or DSL 7. keyword; directory 8. e-commerce 9. online auction 10. a. 2 b. 4 c. 1 d. 3

**Chapter 9**

1. F 2. T 3. F 4. T 5. F 6. war driving 7. Biometric 8. disaster recovery or business continuity 9. digital signature 10. a. 3 b. 4 c. 1 d. 2

**Chapter 10**

1. T 2. F 3. F 4. T 5. F 6. inference engine 7. systems analyst 8. tangible 9. prototype 10. a. 2 b. 3 c. 1

**Chapter 11**

1. F 2. T 3. T 4. F 5. F 6. variable 7. interpreter 8. logic 9. agile 10. a. 3 b. 2 c. 5 d. 4 e. 1

**Chapter 12**

1. T 2. T 3. F 4. F 5. T 6. field or column; record or row 7. integrity 8. direct 9. client-server 10. a. 2 b. 3 c. 1

**Chapter 13**

1. F 2. T 3. T 4. F 5. F 6. copyright; trademark 7. plagiarism 8. cybersquatting or typosquatting 9. digital divide 10. a. 2 b. 4 c. 1 d. 3

# INDEX